# Basic Processes of
# Learning, Cognition,
# and Motivation

# Basic Processes of Learning, Cognition, and Motivation

## STEPHEN M. CORMIER
### The George Washington University

**LEA** LAWRENCE ERLBAUM ASSOCIATES, PUBLISHERS
1986   Hillsdale, New Jersey                              London

The author is currently at the
U.S. Army Research Institute,
Alexandria, VA 22333.

Lawrence Erlbaum Associates, Inc., Publishers
365 Broadway
Hillsdale, New Jersey 07642

**Library of Congress Cataloging-in-Publication Data**

Cormier, Stephen M.
   Basic processes of learning, cognition, and
motivation.

   Bibliography: p.
   Includes indexes.
   1. Human information processing.  2. Learning,
Psychology of.  3. Motivation (Psychology)
4. Cognition.  5. Mammals--Behavior.  6. Neuro-
psychology.  I. Title.
BF455.C683   1986        156'.3              86-1306
ISBN 0-89859-689-0

*51, 488*

Printed in the United States of America
10  9  8  7  6  5  4  3  2  1

# Table of Contents

**v**

# Preface

The main objective of this book is to provide a hard-headed theoretical integration of several different major areas of research on learning, cognition, and motivation in humans and other mammals. By hard-headed, I simply mean that the concepts were generated from empirical data and are testable. Since an integrative theory must of necessity integrate apparent diversity, such an approach involves the identification and description of the most fundamental factors (structural processes) underlying the observed capacities of humans and animals in the domain of learning and motivation.

Several major tenets have guided my efforts. First, I feel that there is safety in numbers. I have not relied on the results from an individual study unless there are multiple confirmations of its basic findings. Essentially, I have followed the logic of meta-analysis in formulating the present concepts. When the signal to noise ratio is low and your measurement techniques have uncertain reliability, the results of many studies considered together are likely to be more illuminating and conclusive than any single study, no matter how well conducted.

Second, I have always tried to consider behavioral data in the light of what is known at the neurological level and vice versa. In my view, a hypothesized structural process should always be neurologically plausible as well as providing an explanation of behavioral or memorial phenomena. One advantage of this requirement is to limit the number of possible alternatives to the hypothesized process. In addition, congruence between neurological and behavioral data decreases the odds that some experimental artifact is being reified as a psychological process.

Third, I believe that the best criterion for the worth of a new formulation is the degree to which it increases our ability to predict behavioral or memorial performance. In the present context, I have tried to analyze the compatibility of the proposed processes with research findings published after the constructs were formulated. Since these newer findings could not have been implicitly or explicitly taken into consideration by me during the construction of the theory, they provided at least a limited test of the predictive utility of the constructs. Enough of the basic ideas were supported in this way (in my subjective judgment) to encourage me into thinking that I at least was on the right track in some important respects.

Apart from a new theoretical formulation, this book has the desirable feature of providing a convenient source for a wide variety of empirical research on important aspects of learning, cognition, and motivation. There are extensive citations from both human and animal studies dealing with memory, motivation, cognitive development, perception, conditioning, habituation, intelligence, verbal learning, etc. In addition, a wide variety of methodological approaches are employed in these studies ranging from the analysis of evoked brain potentials, the effects of neural lesions, and chemical or electric brain stimulation to verbal learning and memory, instrumental and classical conditioning, and cognitive reasoning. Thus, a reader should be able to get a sense of the current state of research in these areas. In this regard, I should note that I have tried to discuss these issues at the level of the first or second year graduate student in experimental psychology because readers are unlikely to be expert in all of them.

The book has had an extensive period of development since its inception in 1976. (An earlier version of Chapter 11 was published by the Psychonomic Society in 1981 in their journal Physiological Psychology.) A rough draft of the book was written between 1976 and 1979. Because of my full time job, succeeding revisions had to be undertaken on evenings and weekends. In this connection, it should be noted that this book is not an official document of the Army Research Institute nor does it necessarily reflect its views. I would like to thank Dr. Warren Simmons and Prof. Philip Dunham, for their valuable comments on the manuscript. I would also like to thank Jonathan T. McMullen, whose typing skill and ability to decipher my hieroglyphics were truly remarkable, the George Washington University Medical Graphic Arts Department for the illustrations, and my father Gerard Cormier for many hours spent with the references and other editorial assistance. I take the blame for the faults that remain.

Sept. 15, 1985
Arlington, VA
Stephen M. Cormier

# Section I

## The Theoretical Argument

# Chapter 1

## The Theoretical Approach

This introduction is proof that psychology has come full circle, since in it I will try to justify the usefulness of an integrative theory of learning and motivation. A generation ago, Skinner (1950) was advancing the then radical idea that empirical research was sufficient for a science of psychology, independently of formal theories. In particular, the large scale theories of learning and motivation by such psychologists as Hull and Tolman, which were dominant at the time, were criticized by Skinner as leading to increasingly sterile research. Their reliance on unobservable variables led to forced explanations of data and theoretical hairsplitting according to this view. An explanation of an observed behavior in terms of processes occurring at a different level of description was deemed inadmissible.

Perhaps one of the most penetrating of Skinner's criticisms of these theories was that they were essentially built on quicksand, i.e., an insufficient base of empirical data. Looked at retrospectively, it is amazing how few studies were used (or available) in the construction of the basic theoretical assumptions made by the major theorists of the time. The reliance of major constructs on just a few studies was perhaps a reflection of the influence of the physical sciences on the theoretical constructions of psychology (e.g., Hull, 1943, Lewin, 1938). It is true that major theoretical insights have been made in such fields as physics on the basis of a few well-controlled studies. However, it wasn't fully appreciated that the ability to control the variability and reactivity of the experimental materials is much greater in the physical sciences than in biosocial sciences such as psychology.

3

This lack of an adequate experimental base resulted in the quick disproof of many of the theoretical constructs put forth. Initially, the theories were modified and stretched in order to accommodate the new research findings. Soon, however, this process reached a breaking point and the theories were abandoned, at least in their totality. Individual principles and ideas derived from Hull's theory have had a longer life, but they are no longer necessarily connected to the theoretical framework from which they emerged.

The dissolution of the major theories of the 1930s and 1940s led to a theoretical approach known as the minitheory. Since the broad theories had been found wanting, psychologists lowered their sights, foreswore theories of broad scope, and attempted to discover the principles operating in a limited class of psychological phenomena. Thus, for example, instead of a theory of learning there might be a minitheory on the partial reinforcement effect. The principles used to explain such a phenomenon had no necessary relationship with those postulated for other psychological phenomena. Often, no attempt was made even to maintain a consistent terminology across these minitheories.

Although one would think that it would be easier to develop a successful theory for a small area than for a broad one, the actual results have not been so clear. Very few of the minitheories developed in the past 25 years have had their basic assumptions stand up against new research data. The relative failure of the minitheory approach, I believe, is again the result of not sufficiently considering the difference between the physical sciences and psychology. Almost all molar behavior is dependent on a complex set of variables; once these kinds of behaviors are made the main focus of study, there is no way to avoid dealing with a number of psychological variables operating at the same time. What I am arguing is that restricting theoretical development to small areas can be illusory if even these areas contain a large number of ostensible variables which can affect the expression of behavior. When a particular phenomenon is based on several fundamental variables, it may actually be more difficult to obtain the necessary variability in these factors to identify them when studying a limited domain. This can be a severe problem in any attempt to extend the theoretical approach to related but distinct areas where the interactions may differ. The main point is that although the minitheory was developed in order to gain greater accuracy in prediction, it is unlikely to do so without a clear understanding of which factors are relevant and which are irrelevant beforehand.

Another possible problem with the minitheory approach is the danger of insularity. Once basic assumptions become embedded in an area, they can be difficult to dislodge without a fresh perspective. To the extent that one is asking the same questions over

4

and over, a different approach to the problem is less likely to present itself. In my opinion, the development of minitheories has led to a theoretical picture which is fragmented into dozens of tiny fields. While specialization can be useful for experimental analysis, it still would be highly desirable to have some body of knowledge or set of factors which was shared by all fields of psychology.

More recently, there has been an increase in the number of theoretical articles advancing a general viewpoint or way of looking at various phenomena (e.g., Bolles, 1972a; Craik & Lockhart, 1972). These types of articles present a more general approach than the minitheory but are much less ambitious and detailed than the formal theories of the past. Although these positions can sometimes suffer from vagueness or lack of testability, a rethinking of basic assumptions was probably a necessity for one very good reason. Experimental psychology has had a disturbing problem in finding satisfactory explanations for the most basic phenomena, even on issues that have been a focal point of research for half a century. Some obvious examples are the distinction between classical and instrumental conditioning, retroactive and proactive interference in human learning, the partial reinforcement effect, and the existence of general or specific cognitive aptitudes.

Given the failure of previous integrative theories to explain the basic issues of learning and motivation, why should another attempt be made? The best answer I can provide is that the fundamental reason for the earlier failures is no longer the limiting condition it once was. While Skinner may have been correct in pointing to the paucity of experimental data which could be used for theory construction in the 1930s and 1940s, anyone going through the experimental literature of even the past 5 years could easily be convinced that we suffer more from an excess than a lack of data. Another reason is that the lack of fundamental principles in experimental psychology makes it difficult to link studies into logical groupings or determine whether different studies are manipulating the same variables in their procedures.

One other deficiency of the earlier theories was a failure to systematically compare and analyze data from different specializations. When interpreting data from one particular area, little attention was paid by theorists as to whether data from other areas supported that particular interpretation or not. This practice was in sharp contrast to the speed with which findings in one area were applied to other areas, e.g., Pavlovian conditioning used as the basis for human learning or "superstitious" responding in pigeons and in humans. Of course, in part, the lack of an adequate data base inhibited systematic comparisons across levels of descriptions. At the present time, however, much work has been done in all the major areas of experimental psychology. This research is

5

methodologically more sophisticated and has a better record with regard to replication than earlier research.

The method of constructing the present theory was based on an idea derived from Campbell and Fiske's (1959) discussion of construct validity. Although the article concerns the identification of constructs through various aptitude and achievement tests, I think that the principles have a more general applicability. Constructs identified by experiments are no less subject to validation issues than those identified through tests. Since the main objective of the present theory is the identification of basic variables or constructs involved in learning and motivation, any way of improving the accuracy and validity of constructs is to be sought.

Campbell and Fiske make a number of points that bear on the identification of constructs. In identifying and validating a construct, they note that validation is typically convergent; that is, a construct is confirmed by independent measurement procedures. However, discriminant validation is needed as well since we must be able to distinguish a particular construct from other constructs. Each test or task used for measurement is a trait-method unit, a union of a particular trait content with measurement procedures not specific to that content. It is important to note that there is no reason why a trait in this context need only refer to particular aptitudes (e.g., verbal, quantitative). We can just as easily substitute the particular capabilities or processes of an organism, whether animal or human.

With regard to the trait-method unit, in order to estimate the relative contributions of trait and method variance in a given situation more than one trait as well as more than one method must be employed in the validation process. Those aspects of behavior produced by procedural factors cannot be separated from the properties of the trait or behavioral factor which is being studied unless several different procedures are used to study the trait. Any procedurally based behaviors will change when the procedures change. However, since the behavioral trait is inherent in the organism, it will remain the same. The more different procedures are used, the more clearly the unchanging behavioral trait can be defined.

The theory presented here is really an attempt to apply a construct validation approach to the experimental literature of psychology. Although it is impossible to use the particular correlation approach devised by Campbell and Fiske for the identification of human aptitudes in the present case, it is still possible to apply their system in a more general way to achieve the same objectives. The basic idea was to go through the experimental literature and try to identify those variables or constructs which seemed to have the widest applicability in terms of integrating findings in diverse fields of psychology. The more independent evidence bearing on a particular psychological construct, the more confidence we can place in its existence and in its importance. Additionally, the construct should be able to explain data that cannot be handled just as parsimoniously by other existing constructs or variables. The intent is to be able to identify a number of basic constructs which seem to be of fundamental importance in the behavior of organisms in the sense that they express themselves in a wide variety of situations. This is not to say that these factors will be the sole determinants of behavioral phenomena, but simply that these are variables which will exert some effect consistently in a wide variety of situations.

At this stage, an identification of qualitative variables is probably as much as can be hoped for. Quantitative research depends on the prior identification of the relevant variables. I believe that much psychological research has been plagued by an inability to separate major from minor variables. Equality may be a desirable goal in other areas, but it is extremely detrimental when applied to theoretical variables. The situation can be compared to a physicist announcing that the presence or absence of air conditioning was a factor to be considered in the cooling rate of a black body, without understanding that the air conditioner was simply manipulating the more fundamental variable of temperature. It is hard to know how many psychological experiments are finding differences in behavior by manipulation of the psychological equivalent of the air conditioner.

It is worth pursuing this example in a little more detail. We will provide more concreteness by supposing that the physicist is being asked to determine the rate of cooling of a cup of coffee on a kitchen table. In such circumstances, a variety of factors can influence the rate at which the coffee cools, e.g., the time of day, the season, the altitude, the size of the cup, whether the window is open, whether air conditioning is on, etc. In fact, there are practically an infinite number of such factors that we could manipulate which would significantly affect the cooling rate of the coffee.

However, the physicist would know that all of these variables are influencing the cooling rate only because they are inducing variations in the fundamental factors of temperature and pressure. There are innumerable ways of producing changes in temperature and pressure, but this fact is of marginal theoretical importance. The point is that the physicist has an understanding of what factors are primary processes and which factors are procedural means of inducing variations in these primary processes.

Thus, when a physicist examines physical phenomena, he/she is able to bring to bear well-defined fundamental concepts such as energy, mass, momentum, electrical charge to the analysis of any given problem. When we turn to the situation in psychology,

7

what analogous fundamental factors would a psychologist employ in the analysis of psychological phenomena? Concepts such as reinforcement, attention, and motivation are vague terms with multiple meanings or circular definitions which are variously interpreted by different psychologists. In addition, many psychological concepts are simply terms for the procedures employed by the psychologist e.g., conditioning, retroactive interference, recognition. What is needed are concepts which can be defined with at least qualitative precision and which can be shown to be fundamental to the expression of memorial and behavioral phenomena.

A few comments on the organization and content of the book are in order at this point. The next chapter is a discursive outline of the basic principles which comprise match-mismatch theory. In a sense the rest of the book is simply a justification and explanation of the reasons these principles were formulated and/or adopted as fundamental in the expression of vertebrate behavior, in particular mammalian behavior. A more rigorous presentation of the theory is in the Appendix.

The second section, containing Chapters 3, 4, and 5, focuses on the most general processes assumed to underlie learning and motivation. Stimulus analyzing processes comprising an information processing mechanism (IPM) are assumed to interact with response and motivational variables. Each factor is discussed individually and an initial justification for its fundamental importance to behavior is provided by examination of relevant empirical evidence. Since these factors will be encountered repeatedly throughout the book, it was not necessary to provide all of the evidence which supports their existence and theoretical description within the confines of this chapter. The remaining chapters examine the effect of these variables in particular situations and introduce a few additional factors with more specific applicability.

The third section presents the behavioral and neurological data which support the theoretical assumptions concerning the behavioral analysis division of the IPM. This division of the IPM is assumed to govern the expression of affective responses, reinforced learning and habituation through the operation of two separate but interacting components: the reinforcer system and the habituative system.

In Chapter 6, the operating principles of the reinforcer and habituative systems are presented. The way in which the fundamental factors of Section II exert their effect in these two systems on the expression of behaviors to reinforcing stimuli and the habituation of responses to neutral stimuli are analyzed.

Chapter 7 examines the effect of the proposed factors as they relate to the phenomenon of habituation, or the waning of response to repeated presentations of a stimulus. A detailed examination of the way in which organisms manifest habituation is presented and the empirical findings are analyzed in the context of the proposed theoretical principles which most directly exert their effect on such phenomena.

Chapters 8, 9, and 10, concern particular phenomena which form important aspects of behavior found in classical and instrumental learning. The nature of conditioned reinforcers, possessing either excitatory or inhibitory qualities, are discussed in Chapter 8. In Chapter 9, stimulus selection or the differential control of particular elements of the stimulus field over behavior is analyzed. Chapter 10 concerns animal and human behavior on operant schedules of reinforcement.

The eleventh chapter provides a detailed look at some of the neurological foundations of the behavioral analysis division of the IPM in the context of a theory of limbic system function. By virtue of its medial position between higher and lower brain regions, the limbic system provides an excellent means of relating not only data from different descriptive levels but also data dealing with behaviors of varying complexity.

Section IV examines in more detail the properties of the sensory-perceptual division of the IPM as they relate to learning and memory. The human learning literature is heavily represented here. In Chapter 12, the basic memory processes of the IPM are presented and discussed. The objective is to show how the interaction of a few basic stimulus analyzing processes can provide a framework for understanding memory phenomena. Chapter 13 examines these concepts in light of the extensive research on encoding and retrieval phenomena. In Chapter 14, data concerning the functional organization of memories are presented and discussed.

In Section V, the relation between the basic processes presented in previous sections and intellectual or cognitive capacity is discussed. Chapter 15 discusses the effect of developmental changes in basic processes of the IPM on cognition and memory. Chapters 16 and 17 discuss the way in which these basic factors form part of the substrate of general intelligence and specific aptitudes respectively.

The documentation for the various principles is as complete as I could reasonably make it without being redundant or verbose. It should be noted that the proposed factors are consistent with much more evidence than is cited here. No individual study mentioned in this book is crucial as the basis for any of these factors, and in fact it could be said that all of the references used here could be replaced by another set which would also provide firm support for the theory. I have tried to clearly separate statements that I regard as based on solid evidence from those that are more speculative. The latter I have tried to keep to a minimum, but probably with only mixed success. However, I think that the reader will be able to distinguish the two without undue difficulty.

One final comment: since such a wide variety of experimental research is discussed in the course of the book, I was unable to assume that readers would have equal familiarity with the nature of all of these different areas. To make the book more comprehensible, I have tried to include enough information in the discussions of studies to make it possible for readers who have only modest knowledge of a non-specialty area to at least follow the line of argument.

# Chapter 2
## Outline of the Theory

Although it is essential for readers to have an understanding of the overall theory in order to be able to place each book section in its proper context, a rigorous presentation of the theoretical principles at this point would not be particularly meaningful. Therefore, this chapter presents the major theoretical points to be addressed in the rest of the book in a more discursive format to aid general comprehension of the theory. A more rigorous presentation of the theory is contained in the Appendix.

### THEORETICAL SYNOPSIS

The mammalian brain can be conceptualized as the control mechanism for three functions: life maintenance, information processing, and motoric output. Life maintenance structures are mainly contained within the brain stem and are essential to vegetative functions which maintain homeostasis in the broadest sense. Motoric output structures are present both subcortically and cortically and control the skeletal movements. The information processing mechanism (IPM) is composed of subcortical and cortical structures which are devoted to information processing and analysis. The present theory describes (some of) the structural characteristics of the IPM in terms of its intrinsic functions and its effect on the coordination of life maintenance and motoric output functions.

The interactions of eight major factors are assumed to provide much of the form and direction of mammalian (and human) behavior.

Three of these factors involve stimulus analysis: unrestricted memory formation, which provides the basis for precision encoding of the stimulus field; analogical encoding, in which the form of the internal representation or memory of an event reflects the perceptual-analytic operations performed on it by the relevant sensory systems; and match-mismatch retrieval, in which the attributes of a processed event are compared with the attributes of internal representations already in permanent memory. A match between attributes forms the basis of the retrieval of memories from permanent memory (recognition or recall).

Three more of these eight factors relate to three functionally distinct response classes. The orienting response occurs to unanticipated events in the environment, and its function is to facilitate the processing of information through the IPM. Species-specific behaviors are responses with a strong genetic component for their organization. Their performance tends to inhibit the processing of information through the IPM. Voluntary responses comprise all learned responses as well as a small class of unlearned motoric behaviors (e.g., locomotion) which are not terminal components of species-specific behavioral sequences. These responses are neutral with respect to information processing functions.

The last two general factors involve motivational processes. Mood states are relatively sustained behavioral states produced by the effects of a neurochemical on specific brain areas combined with the neural processing of particular unconditioned stimuli (or associated cues). The mood state provides the support for an integrated sequence of species-specific behaviors to occur over time. Opponent processes refer to the reciprocal interactions of different mood states. The evocation of one mood state "A" leads to delayed evocation of a different mood state "B" which opposes or complements the organismic effects of "A" in characteristic ways (e.g., arousal vs. depression, hunger vs. thirst, etc.).

These eight factors operate within the context of the mammalian brain and its structural components. Much of the book is concerned with the elucidation and analysis of the structural and functional properties of the IPM and its interaction with response and motivational factors.

The IPM is composed of two main divisions: the sensory-perceptual division and the behavioral analysis division. The sensory-perceptual division is in turn composed of the five sensory systems, from sensory receptors to cortical analysis and association regions. This division analyzes sensory information and performs cognitive manipulations of internal representations stored within its confines.

The behavioral analysis division is composed of two distinct but interacting systems: the reinforcer system and the habituative system, both of which are located within the confines of the

12

frontal-reticular system in the mammalian brain. The behavioral analysis division as a whole is responsible for the association of stimulus events with organismic responses. Through its control over the OR, it can exert a feedback effect on sensory processing. The reinforcer system processes salient stimuli such as unconditioned reinforcers and stimuli (cues) in close proximity to the occurrence of reinforcers. It exerts an inhibitory influence on the habituative system. This latter system processes nonsalient stimuli and generally habituates organismic responses to them. However, in appropriate circumstances, this stimulus information can be protected from habituation if it possesses some correlation

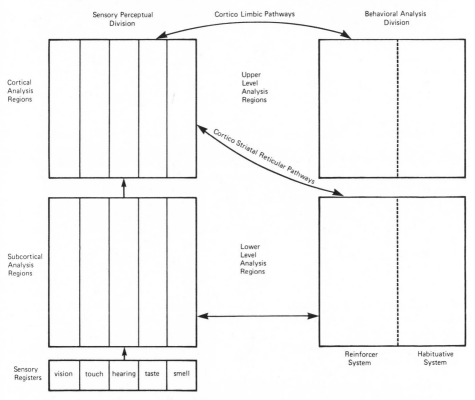

**Fig. 2-1 . The Information Processing Mechanism .** The large-scale structural components of the IPM are depicted. The sensory-perceptual division is comprised of the five sensory systems from sensory registers to high level sensory cortex. The behavioral analysis division is comprised of the reinforcer and habituative systems. Information is transmitted between the sensory-perceptual division and the behavioral analysis division at both cortical and sub-cortical levels.

with the occurrence of motivationally significant events. However, cues processed through the habituative system do not have the affective attributes of cues processed through the reinforcer system.

OUTLINE OF THE THEORY

## Structure of the IPM

The IPM has two major divisions:  the sensory-perceptual division, which performs modality-specific (perceptual) processing, and the behavioral analysis division, which fosters associations between sensory information and motivational and motoric responses (cf. Fig. 2-1).  Different neural structures subserve these two divisions.  Loosely, the sensory-perceptual division is composed of the subcortical and cortical regions of the five sensory systems while the behavioral analysis division is composed of structures in the frontal-reticular system (cf. Chapters 11, 12, 15, 16, 17).

## The Sensory Perceptual Division

Encoding Processes.  The sensory-perceptual division of the IPM analyzes sensory information through its five sensory systems (cf. Fig. 2-2).  This information is transduced in the sensory registers which are the sites of initial sensory analysis.  Only a portion of the information content in the sensory registers is relayed to the subcortical and cortical analysis regions.  All information that passes through the sensory registers will be retained in permanent form in the IPM  (cf. precision encoding: Chapter 3; unrestricted memory formation:  Chapter 12).

Once a stimulus passes through the sensory registers, it can be in one of two states:  active (working) memory or inactive (secondary) memory.  Working memory consists only of those items that are in a current state of activation, i.e., which do not need to be retrieved to be available to the organism.  Inactive or secondary memory consists of all other (permanent) memorial representations in the nervous system (cf. the distinction between working memory and short-term memory:  Chapters 12, 15).

The nature of the perceptual operations that are performed on the processed information determines to a large extent its memorial characteristics.  The memorial representations of processed information are retained in the neural areas performing the particular perceptual-analytic operations.

Implication:  Precision encoding of stimulus events and context occurs in an analogical form determined by the particular

14

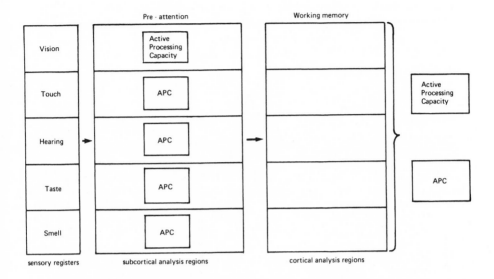

**Fig. 2-2 . The Sensory-Perceptual Division .** At lower processing levels, information can be processed in parallel in the five sensory systems. At higher levels, however, active processing activity is reduced so that only a few distinct stimulus events can be processed simultaneously.

modalities and perceptual operations performed on the processed information (cf. analogical encoding: Chapter 3).

Implication: Multiple overlapping but non-identical representations of a stimulus will be formed in all of the different neural structures of the IPM which are involved in its analysis. This process reduces the loss of memories from neuronal damage (cf. Chapters 12, 17).

Implication: Differences in the character and efficiency of these perceptual-analytic operations form the basis of species and individual differences for specific cognitive aptitudes (cf. Chapter 17).

Retrieval Processes. All information is retrieved from secondary memory through the action of the match-mismatch retrieval process, in which processed stimuli are compared with memorial representations. Retrieval can occur when the processed stimuli,

15

acting as retrieval cues, have attributes which overlap (match) the attributes of particular inactive representations at some criterion level. The nature of the perceptual capacities of particular sensory systems will determine the way in which the match-mismatch processes controls the comparison of representations (e.g., parallel or sequential processing).

Implication: Retrieval of a particular memory can be affected by any contingent factor such as differentiation, association, or context which alters the probability of overlap between the attributes of a retrieval cue with that memory (cf. match-mismatch process: Chapter 3; retrieval phenomena: Chapter 13).

Implication: The processing of a stimulus can initiate the retrieval of a related memorial representation so that both items are in an active state concurrently (cf. study-phase retrieval: Chapters 12,14).

Interaction: The interaction of study-phase retrieval with unrestricted memory formation of information in active memory permits the structuring of memory. While one stimulus is being processed, related memories can be retrieved and, thus, placed in conjunction with the processed stimulus in active memory. Since all information in active memory is retained in permanent form, the continuous operation of this process results in the establishment of organized sets of overlapping traces (cf. Chapters 12, 14).

Implication: Stimulus abstraction can occur through the repeated study phase retrieval of the encodings of previous presentations of the stimulus. The common features of the juxtaposed traces will increasingly predominate in the new conjoint trace formed each time, through the loss of idiosyncratic elements due to mutual interference. The removal of idiosyncratic elements aids accessibility because of a reduction in the amount and complexity of the retrieval cue attributes needed to match the trace (cf. priming/inhibition: Chapter 12; stimulus abstraction: Chapter 14).

Motivational and Motoric Response Classes

The IPM interacts with three functional response classes: the orienting response (OR), species-specific responses, and voluntary responses. Each of these response classes is composed of responses which possess both motoric and visceral components. The response classes can be differentiated by their effect on the stimulus analysis capacities of the IPM.

The OR is a centrally integrated response which occurs as the result of a mismatch between an internal representation in working memory and the stimulus environment. Its occurrence facilitates the processing of information through the sensory-perceptual division. Early components of the OR are modality specific while later components are modality nonspecific.

The OR is prerequisite to the occurrence of changes in the associative relationship between particular stimuli and responses. The strength of the OR is inversely related to the probability of an event in a given situation--the less probable the event, the stronger the OR (cf. the OR: Chapter 4; stimulus selection: Chapter 9). Species-specific responses are genetically organized responses common to all members of a species (or at least to same-sex conspecifics. Their performance results in a decreased capacity for stimulus analysis, because they inhibit OR occurrence. Their form and occurrence are dependent on two fundamental motivational processes: mood states and opponent processes (cf. Chapter 4).

A mood state is the product of the effects of a neurotransmitter on specific brain areas combined with the neural processing of particular reinforcing stimuli. It is a relatively sustained response which provides the support for an integrated series of species-specific behaviors to occur. Only reinforcing stimuli can induce a mood state (cf. Chapter 5).

A reinforcer initiates a primary mood state "A" which is correlated with the magnitude of the reinforcer. The initiation of the primary state induces the emergence of an opponent mood state "B" whose affective goal is opposite to the "A" state and whose strength is directly related to that of the primary state. The opponent state occurs when the probability of reinforcer occurrence for the primary state becomes low (cf. Chapter 5).

> Implication: The initiation of one mood state sets up the physiological and neurological sequence of events which results in the induction of reciprocal mood states. The opponent state serves to disengage the organism from the influence of an "A" state (e.g., food seeking) when the probability of goal attainment is low (cf. adjunctive behaviors, pausing: Chapter 10).

Voluntary responses are not dependent for their occurrence on the induction of a particular mood state since they have no necessary relationship with particular reinforcing stimuli. This response class is composed of all learned responses as well as a small class of relatively unlearned motoric behaviors such as locomotion which are not terminal components of species-specific behavioral

17

sequences. These responses are neutral in their effect on stimulus analysis.

Rule-Based Behavior

Human behavior is the result of match-mismatch (non-rule-based) structural processes interacting with rule-based behavior. The latter behaviors are founded on non-rule-based processes but are not adequately described by them. However, match-mismatch processes do exert a profound effect on the form and characteristics of rule-based behavior (cf. Chapters 3, 10, 12, and 13).

Match-mismatch processes can be indirectly modified by rule-based behavior to the extent that verbal-symbolic mediation provides an alternative means of producing the essential conditions for the operation of a particular structural process (cf. human behavior and reinforcement: Chapter 10).

Implication: In humans, there is a great increase in the freedom with which exteroceptive stimuli become inducers of particular mood states and in the kind of responses that become associated with those mood states (cf. Chapter 4; the amygdala and behavior: Chapter 11).

Implication: To the extent that verbal-symbolic rules or strategies are utilized, more idiosyncratic responses and response biases should be observed. Conversely, the more they are minimized, the more clearly that behavior should reflect match-mismatch processes (cf. Chapter 3; mnemonic strategies: Chapter 13).

The Behavioral Analysis Division

The behavioral analysis division of the IPM receives copies of internal representations processed through the sensory-perceptual division. Its function is to foster the connection of motivationally significant stimuli with appropriate organismic responses while inhibiting organismic responses to stimuli with declining or nil motivational significance (cf. Fig. 2-3).

The behavioral analysis division is composed of two independent but interacting components: the reinforcer system and the habituative system. These systems control OR occurrences to exteroceptive stimuli but are not involved in perceptual analysis per se. However, since the OR is prerequisite to associative processing, the reinforcer and habituative systems play an important role in determining which elements of the stimulus field will be most directly attended to by the organism (cf. Chapters 6, 9).

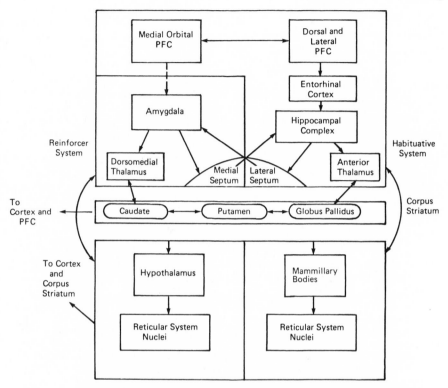

**Fig. 2-3. The Behavioral Analysis Division .** This division is composed of structures in the frontal-reticular system. As with the sensory-perceptual division, lower processing levels can function semi-independently of higher processing levels. The striatal complex provides an alternate connection between the cortex and lower level structures which bypasses the upper level structures in this division.

## The Reinforcer System

The reinforcer system processes reinforcing stimuli and controls the induction of appropriate mood states which subserve species-specific behaviors. Its activation tends to inhibit the processing functions of the habituative system. As reinforcing stimuli are processed through the reinforcer system, a mood state is induced which makes the appropriate species-specific behaviors more probable. In mammals, the connections between the mood state and a particular unconditioned reinforcer as well as between the mood state and particular species-specific responses are open to environmental influence early in life to a limited degree.

The activation of the reinforcer system by a reinforcing stimulus results in the registration of the contents of working memory with respect to the stimuli and responses that are in association with the reinforcer. Stimuli in working memory at the time of reinforcer occurrence can become part of the total stimulus complex. This complex includes the affective responses occurring to the reinforcer. The reinforcer system increases the associative value of these different stimuli by imparting common affective attributes to their respective representations (cf. Chapters 6, 11).

Implication: Redintegrative cues for the reinforcer representation assume the psychological (affective) properties of the reinforcer through their activation of the reinforcer representation (cf. Chapter 8).

Implication: Since the reinforcer induces a primary mood state, an opponent state will appear when the reinforcer probability declines. In the same way that stimuli in working memory at the time of reinforcer occurrence become redintegrative cues for the cue-reinforcer complex, stimuli processed during the activation of the opponent state become redintegrative cues for that state, i.e., assume its psychological properties and function as conditioned inhibitors. Because of this shift in the nature of the mood state, stimuli must be in working memory during reinforcer occurrence in order to acquire and maintain its affective properties (cf. Chapter 5; conditioned inhibition: Chapter 8).

The amygdala is an important high level structure of the reinforcer system. It augments the neural and endocrine response to the occurrence of a reinforcing stimulus, thereby aiding the induction of an appropriate mood state. It influences certain homeostatic functions, but only in modulatory fashion through its processing of motivationally significant stimuli (cf. Chapter 11).

The Habituative System

The habituative system processes and habituates any stimulus which is not an unconditioned reinforcer at the time of its presentation nor which is in temporal proximity to an unconditioned reinforcer. This system is more sensitive to stimulus changes in the environment than the reinforcer system and, through its partial control over the OR, can direct attention to nonsalient stimuli (cf. the habituative system: Chapter 6; Chapter 7).

Lower level structures of the habituative system, lying below the level of the hippocampus, are principally involved in the habituation of stimuli controlling species-specific responses as well as stimuli with low representational complexity (cf. Chapter 7; the human amnesic syndromes: Chapter 15).

In lower order habituation, dishabituation occurs as the result of a sensitization state induced by a stimulus other than the habituated stimulus. The dishabituating stimulus must increase arousal levels so as to facilitate all related responses above their normal level.

Upper level structures of the habituative system, from the hippocampus to the prefrontal cortex, are involved with the processing of nonsalient stimulus information and habituation of the OR to stimuli with relatively high representational complexity. In this case, dishabituation occurs as the result of a mismatch between the internal representation and the stimulus processed through the habituative system. It is a stimulus specific loss of habituation which does not affect response levels to other stimuli (cf. Chapter 7; the human amnesic syndromes: Chapter 15).

Because of their capacity to activate the OR and subsequently process nonsalient stimulus information, the upper level structures of the habituative system process cues for reinforcement which are not temporally proximate to reinforcer occurrence (secondary cues). The habituation of these secondary cues is prevented, however, by the subsequent occurrence of the reinforcing (primary) cues processed through the reinforcer system.

Secondary cues cannot acquire conditioned reinforcing properties because they are processed through the habituative system. Only stimuli processed through the reinforcer system can acquire reinforcing properties (cf. the habituative system: Chapter 6; secondary cues: Chapter 8; partial reinforcement schedules: Chapters 9 and 10; hippocampal function: Chapter 11).

Implication: The habituative system will operate in the habituation paradigm and also in three other circumstances: during extinction, during non-reinforced trials in partial reinforcement, and when there is a temporal interval that exceeds the limits of reinforcer system processing, i.e., when the lack of reinforcer proximity frees the habituative system from inhibition by the reinforcer system (cf. Chapters 6, 8, and 11).

Implication: Since secondary cues are not (conditioned) reinforcers, they cannot gain direct control over species-specific responses. They can only control voluntary responses (cf. Chapters 6, 8, and 11).

Interaction: The capacity for nonsalient stimulus processing interacts with the structural processes of the OR and study-phase retrieval to provide the substrate for general intelligence or the g aptitude (cf. Chapter 16).

21

The hippocampus is an important high level structure of the habituative system which controls the processing of novel or nonsalient stimuli which are not reinforcing. It habituates these stimuli unless its habituative function is inhibited by the activation of the reinforcer system.

The hippocampal theta waves occurring during various activities in different species, most typically with voluntary movements, are a reflection of a general capability of cue processing through this system. It is a nonspecific state in which the theta waves indicate processing capability, not necessarily actual processing of changes in the associative strength of stimuli (cf. voluntary responses: Chapter 4; the theta wave: Chapter 11).

The septum is a coordinating structure between the reinforcer and habituative systems. It is composed of two functionally distinct regions, the medial septum and the lateral septum. The medial septum transmits information from the reinforcer system to the hippocampus while the lateral septum receives information from the hippocampus (cf. Chapter 11).

The lateral septum decreases the motivational properties of sensory information to avoid having the organism respond too powerfully to their positive or negative qualities.

Implication: It has a reciprocal relationship with the action of the amygdala in controlling organismic responsiveness to motivationally significant stimuli (cf. Chapter 11).

Implication: It decreases the conditioned reinforcing properties of primary cues associated with reinforcement (cf. Chapter 11).

The medial septum controls processing through the hippocampus and habituative system by means of its pacemaker cells for the theta wave. It controls the degree of hippocampal activation through this process.

Habituative system structures above the level of the hippocampus, such as the entorhinal cortex and prefrontal cortex, are involved in the maintenance of attention to nonsalient stimuli and the associative processing of these cues. They do not have a direct habituative function (cf. Chapter 16).

22

# Section II
## The Information Processing Mechanism: General Processes

In this section, some of the fundamental processes of the information processing mechanism are described and analyzed. The processes selected for discussion are those which would seem to have the most general effects on learning and motivational capacities in humans and other mammals.

Learning and motivation are viewed as the result of an interaction between an information processing mechanism and the particular characteristics of an organism's nervous system. The IPM is assumed to be general across mammalian species in much the same way that the action of the neuron is general across species (although some properties are common to all vertebrate species). That is, the principles of operation of the IPM are assumed to be much the same in whatever mammalian organism we examine. Naturally, as we move up the phylogenetic scale, a few additional capacities will be found. Many of these additional higher order capacities are capable of formulation within the terms of match-mismatch theory. Human beings are a partial exception to this, in that verbal-symbolic behavior in its rule-based aspect (i.e., the application of rules to guide behavior) is not assumed to be adequately described within this framework. However, it is maintained that all rule-based behavior must be founded on non-rule-based (match-mismatch) processes which exert a profound effect on their acquisition and use.

The characteristics of an organism's nervous system (e.g., sensory systems, species specific responses, homeostatic mechanisms) are more idiosyncratic than the IPM, but we can assume a great deal of generality within a species and a limited amount across similar species. Essentially, the nervous system of a given species, through evolutionary adaptation, utilizes the IPM to meet its particular requirements; it gives the mechanism a unique coloring, so to speak. In so doing, it restricts the potential functioning of the mechanism in some situations and enhances it in others. The advantage of this to the organism is that in a particular situation, it only has to examine a limited number of possible correlations between events, those correlations examined being determined by the characteristics of its nervous system. The disadvantage, of course, is that a situation may involve correlations not taken into account.

The IPM developed in the present theory takes as its point of departure Sokolov's (1963, 1969) two-stage model which was formulated to explain the habituation and dishabituation of the orienting response (OR) to novel stimuli. Sokolov, in studying the OR of humans to novel stimuli, noticed that, although the OR could become habituated by repeatedly presenting a neutral stimulus, almost any noticeable change in the stimulus would produce dishabituation of the OR. For example, increases or decreases in stimulus intensity or duration produced dishabituation of an OR to a stimulus; even the omission of a presentation of a repeating stimulus caused the OR to reappear (cf. Fredrikson et al, 1984; Koepke & Pribram, 1967; Peeke & Veno, 1973; Wagner, 1978).

Up until these demonstrations, habituation had commonly been viewed as a single-stage process in which appropriate neurons became refractory to further stimulation by the same stimulus. This explanation is inadequate in showing how a particular sequence of three tones can be habituated, but when the same three tones are presented in a different order they can again evoke the OR. It is especially inadequate as an explanation of how a reduction in the intensity of a habituated stimulus or its complete omission could cause dishabituation. Sokolov argued that these results necessitated the hypothesis that the habituated stimulus was somehow represented precisely in the nervous system. This stimulus representation could then be compared with the external stimulus to see if they were the same.

In Sokolov's two-stage model, the first stage represents a system devoted to stimulus analysis, through which relevant information such as intensity, duration, spatial and temporal patterning, and quality are encoded and stored. This system in turn controls a response system devoted to production of the OR. During habituation, a stimulus model or representation is assumed to be formed in the brain due to the presentation of an exteroceptive stimulus. This neural model is compared with external stimuli and if the two match on relevant dimensions, the organism does not make an OR to the stimulus. A mismatch, on the other hand, produces dishabituation of the OR (O'Connor, 1966).

24

Thus, Sokolov, in developing a two-stage model, was forced to assume a sophisticated system of stimulus encoding, storage, and comparison in what had formerly been considered a primitive form of learning because of its existence in simple organisms and even in the spinal cord (Thompson, 1967). (Of course, the possibility exists that there are simple and complex forms of habituation. This point is examined in the next section.) It will be noticed that Sokolov's theory bears some relation to template theories of perception, with their attendant difficulties in handling stimulus variability. However, the representation of the encoded stimulus should not be viewed simplistically. Sokolov (1969) himself notes that the stimulus model is not to be considered as static or fixed, but rather as dynamic and sensitive to the most recent characteristics of the stimulus.

This description is not sufficient, however, and it should be clear that the nature of the stimulus representation is a very profound and difficult question. Discussions of different aspects of this problem will be found in this and later sections.

At this point, we are confronted with the fact that organisms appear able to detect small changes in habituated stimuli even when these changes involve removal of stimulus components. What makes these findings so interesting is that the organism is sensitive to changes in stimuli which are not being attended to. This would seem to imply that the processing capabilities involved in these situations need not be under active control by the organism.

In addition, these findings suggest that a specific stimulus memory of some kind is stored which can then be compared with environmental stimuli. It is hard to conceive how an organism could be sensitive to the kind of stimulus parameters that are known to have an effect without this kind of memory capacity. This is as much as we need to borrow from Sokolov's theory in order to begin to discuss the basic stimulus analyzing and response properties of the IPM.

# Chapter 3
## Stimulus Analyzing Processes

The present theory makes the following initial assumption: an information processing mechanism is hypothesized to provide the basis for the non-rule-based learning capacities exhibited by mammals and to a lesser degree other vertebrates. Its interaction with organismic motivational characteristics affects the way in which its behavioral capacities are expressed. An organism, when exposed to a novel stimulus, encodes a precise representation of that stimulus in the central nervous system. In addition, details of the context in which the stimulus occurs are also encoded; these can include background stimuli, the internal state of the organism and the responses occurring concurrently with the stimulus. This memorial representation is then used as the basis for stimulus recognition and as the basis for appropriate responding in many different learning situations.

Let's see how far this line of thought can take us. The first requirement is to delve into the specific capacities that the IPM is hypothesized to possess, concentrating first on its stimulus analyzing properties. There are three issues that I think need to be handled at the outset. First, it needs to be shown that organisms can precisely encode different parameters of stimuli in a variety of learning paradigms. Second, given that the encoding capacities of the IPM have to operate in a wide variety of situations and across different species, it would be useful to demonstrate that such encoding could take place with a minimum of attention or effort on the part of the organism. In my opinion, some form of analogical encoding would be more compatible with such restrictions than other forms of stimulus processing because it would seem to place fewer demands on the IPM with respect to recoding of the stimulus. This issue will be closely examined. Third, it would seem necessary to show that a match-mismatch process of stimulus comparison using a memorial representation is an integral part of learning and motivated behavior.

## PRECISION ENCODING OF THE STIMULUS FIELD

### Precision Encoding in Animals

The demonstration that organisms precisely encoded stimuli which were habituated was a surprising finding simply because habituation had been viewed as a primitive form of learning. The notion that organisms can precisely encode stimuli when engaged in learning for reinforcement or in more cognitive tasks is less controversial. It is interesting that evidence of precise encoding is implicit in many areas of learning, but the phenomenon has rarely been studied for its own sake (cf. Vaughan & Greene, 1984).

One discrimination paradigm which has provided evidence for the formation of stimulus representations in animals has been the delayed matching-to-sample (DMTS) procedure. From a set of comparison stimuli, subjects select the stimulus which is identical to a prior sample stimulus on one or more dimensions. The delay interval occurs between presentation of the sample and the comparison set. Thus, the organism must have a memorial representation of the sample in order to solve the problem (cf. Carter & Werner, 1978; Cook, 1980). Successful performance has been found in a variety of organisms, including pigeons (Riley & Roitblat, 1978) and monkeys (Medin, 1977).

The memorial nature of the controlling stimuli is supported by findings that interventions which would be expected to disrupt memory for the sample stimulus in fact decrease performance on the DMTS task, e.g., delay (Roberts & Grant, 1974), interference by an intervening stimulus (Zentall & Hogan, 1977), or contextual change (Transberg & Rilling, 1980). It should be noted that not all stimuli or stimulus attributes are learned or retained equally well (Carter & Werner, 1978). For example, matching performance with geometric forms is generally lower than with color or line orientations for pigeons and monkeys (Devine et al., 1977). The particular encoding capacities of organisms will clearly reflect species-specific differences. However, this does not mean that within this general constraint, mammalian species cannot precisely encode their stimulus environment.

There have been a number of instrumental conditioning and discrimination studies which indicate that the qualitative and

27

quantitative characteristics of the reinforcer are being encoded by the organism (Brodigan & Peterson, 1976; Capaldi et al., 1976; DeLong & Wasserman, 1981; Tinklepaugh, 1928; Trapold & Overmier, 1972). For example, in the Capaldi et al. study, rats were trained on a discrete trial barpressing task for one or five food pellets. If an independently trained CS was presented during the discrete trial task, performance was facilitated if the CS had been associated with the same reward magnitude that the rat was now receiving. Performance was retarded if the CS signaled a different reward magnitude than was currently being received, even if the CS had been associated with a larger reward. This result indicates that rats are able to encode differences in reward magnitudes for the same reinforcer. The Tincklepaugh study demonstrated that monkeys could remember qualitative differences in reinforcers in a delayed choice procedure; they exhibited searching behavior when a less favored reward was substituted for a favored reward. Edwards et al. (1982) have further shown that overt behaviors do not necessarily mediate the performance for different expected reinforcers (cf. Medin, 1977; Gaffan, 1979).

Several studies by Rescorla and his associates indicate that the representation of the US (reinforcer) is not a static entity but is sensitive to changes in the exteroceptive stimulus, as was seen in the habituation studies. Rescorla (1973a) trained rats in a Pavlovian fear conditioning procedure in which a neutral stimulus was paired with an aversive US, in this case, a loud noise. The noise US was then presented by itself outside of the conditioning procedure until it was somewhat habituated. When the CS which had been paired with the US was tested, it was found to have diminished strength even though it had not been partially habituated with the US. Thus, modifications of the representation of the US can be shown not only to be possible, but also to exert an effect on related memorial representations. Similar results were found using appetitive reinforcers (Holland & Rescorla, 1975). Conversely, the CS can evoke representations or memory of the US which can substitute for the actual US in the formation of new associations (Holland, 1981).

Animals have been shown to be highly sensitive to contextual or background stimuli present during a learning task. The sensitivity to such contextual stimuli is revealed by the effect that changes in such stimuli have on responding (e.g., Hickis et al., 1977; Welker et al., 1974). In the Welker et al. study, pigeons were trained to peck an unlighted key for food. Concurrently, a houselight and a 1000 Hz tone were present, but non-contingently related to reward. Following this training, the pigeons were taught a discrimination in which pecking the key with a green light was rewarded (S+) while pecking the key with a white light was not (S-). If the contextual stimuli (i.e., the tone and houselight) were absent during this discrimination training there was a large decrement in responding. When the contextual stimuli accompanied the green light, discrimination was enhanced. On the other hand, when they accompanied the white light, discrimination was reduced. Thus, the encoding of the stimulus environment by pigeons can include background stimuli, even when they have no contingent relationship to reinforcement, and these contextual representations have a substantial effect on learned behavior.

Animals have been shown to be sensitive to other types of contextual stimuli. Chiszar and Spear (1969) found decrements in T maze performance of rats upon changing from one apparatus to another even though the procedure remained the same. McAllister and McAllister (1967) demonstrated that apparatus cues were extremely important in the maintenance of avoidance conditioning. Holloway and Wansley (1973) showed that retention of a passive avoidance response was best when testing was given at the same time of day as the original training compared to testing at times different from training.

Precision Encoding in Humans

Humans seem to have a similar ability to precisely encode their stimulus environment. Kintsch & Bates (1977) studied recognition memory for statements given in a lecture. These fell into three types: topic statements, details, and extraneous remarks such as jokes and announcements. Even with a 2 day delay there was verbatim memory for all three types. Hayes-Roth and Hayes-Roth (1977) and Hasher and Griffin (1978) both have shown that lexical or verbatim information is present in memory even when subjects are concentrating on the meaning of verbal passages.

The memory for verbatim information seems to occur at a very basic processing level. Anderson and Paulson (1977), in studying the representation of verbatim information in human memory, found that these memories can be interfered with by the interpolation of meaningless strings of similar words. This indicates that the encoding of verbatim information is similar to the way meaningless strings of words are encoded. Memory for meaning is not affected by such interpolated material, however. Kolers and Ostry (1974) showed that recognition memory for the typography in which sentences were presented was significantly better than chance 32 days after the initial reading. Hintzman et al. (1972) showed that subjects could retrieve information about the modality in which verbal material was presented (i.e., visual or auditory).

Memory for material presented a number of times seems to include information directly related to frequency. Hasher and Chromiak (1977) studied memory for frequency in four age groups from second grade to college. Second graders were as likely to process frequency differences as the college students, with or without specific instructions to that effect. Salthouse (1977), in examining perceptual formation with dot patterns, found evidence for multiple specific representations in early stages of experience with the stimuli before their replacement by a more generic representation later on.

As with animals, human encoding seems to be very sensitive to context effects (cf. Tulving, 1976). For example, Light and Schurr (1973) and Jacoby and Hendricks (1973) have shown that recognition is highest when the order in which words are tested most closely approximates their study order. Tulving (1974) has shown the recognition of words presented in pairs declines when the words are presented by themselves.

Memory for an expected but omitted stimulus is also found in human learning. Badia and Defran (1970) set up a variation of the stimulus omission paradigm in order to approximate a classical conditioning paradigm. Human subjects were presented with a (CS) tone which reliably preceded a (US) light. Omission of the light caused an OR to reappear even when the light was fully habituated. This finding is interesting because changes in the presentation of the CS-US pair in a true classical conditioning experiment often result in disruptions in the conditioned response (CR) and unconditioned response (UR) (e.g., Pavlov, 1927). As Badia and Defran note, this is very probably due to the reoccurrence of the OR to the stimulus changes.

Time Estimation

One interesting finding that was noted in the habituation studies was the apparent ability to precisely encode temporal and sequential relationships. Recent research has confirmed this time estimation capacity of organisms in a variety of situations (cf. Church, 1978; Gibbon, 1977; Killeen, 1975; Roberts & Smythe, 1979; Weisman et al., 1980).

Stubbs (1968), in one of the first such studies, trained pigeons to discriminate the duration of a stimulus through a choice procedure. One response was reinforced after presentation of a stimulus duration below a certain criterion while another response was reinforced after a stimulus duration above a certain criterion. Stubbs found that a pigeon's accuracy in identifying stimulus duration followed a logarithmic function, in which equal logarithmic difference from the cutoff on the long or short duration side yielded equal accuracy of duration discrimination. This study and others have provided strong evidence that the estimation of time by an organism follows a general form of Weber's Law of stimulus discrimination (cf. Church & Deluty, 1977; Gibbon, 1977; Stubbs, 1976). This is an important finding since it firmly ties in duration with other types of stimulus characteristics as all following the same

30

basic psychophysical laws. Thus it seems that organisms analyze and process duration in ways similar to those used with stimulus dimensions such as intensity.

Explanations of time estimation through the use of covert or overt mediating responses have generally not been supported by the studies of temporal discrimination on fixed interval (FI) reinforcement schedules. For example, Dews (1962, 1970) has shown that interrupting a series of responses, using a timeout procedure involving S+ withdrawal, did not seem to affect the temporal discrimination of successive segments of a fixed interval. In addition, animals have been shown to be very sensitive in their responding to the proportion of the interval that has elapsed (LaBarbera & Church, 1974; Libby & Church, 1974).

This representative sampling of studies provides a good basis for extending the processing capabilities found in the habituation studies to many other behavioral situations. Indeed, it would be highly surprising if organisms could precisely encode stimuli to which they were habituating and be unable to do the same with stimuli which were reinforcing or cues to reinforcement, or in the case of humans, verbal information. The diversity and range of species which exhibit these processing capabilities as well as the variety of learning situations in which they are displayed adds confidence to the hypothesis that we are seeing a fundamental property of the nervous system with regard to learning. Thus, it seems possible to extend Sokolov's hypothesis of detailed encoding of novel stimuli in habituation to many other learning situations as proposed in the current theory. As one of the properties of the IPM, this encoding capacity raises the question of what form the internal representation takes. This is far too complex a question to answer all at once and even the entire theory can do no more than suggest some partial answers. However, at this point, we can examine one specific point, namely, the degree to which analogical properties govern the relationship between the external stimulus and the internal representation.

## ANALOGICAL REPRESENTATIONS

Theories concerning the form of memorial representations have ranged from hypotheses of templates to abstract propositions (cf. Anderson & Bower, 1973; Neisser, 1967). The most recent discussions have centered around two possibilities: an analogical representation which is isomorphic to the stimulus in some important (perceptual) dimensions (Hayes-Roth, 1979; Shepard & Chipman, 1970) or an abstract propositional code or descriptive symbol structure which, while it may contain the same information as an analogical representation, does not have an isomorphic relationship to the external stimulus (Anderson, 1978; Pylyshyn, 1973).

One way to conceptualize the distinction between abstract propositions and analogical representations is to consider a graphic representation of an object on a computer screen. The computer graphic retains some (but far from all) of the perceptual qualities of the original object in analogical form. However, the computer graphic also exists in a computer program which specifies in propositional form the details of the graphic.

It should be noted that Anderson (1978) essentially argues that the issue is not resolvable experimentally, since any data supporting an analogical theory could be explained using appropriate propositional assumptions as well. There has been a certain amount of controversy about this contention (e.g., Hayes-Roth, 1979; Pylyshyn, 1979). While I am able to appreciate the logical basis of Anderson's arguments, I'm not convinced that this possibility represents a real problem in the practical sense. It is always possible to construct alternative theories on even the most solidly based evidence; in these cases, testability, plausibility, and parsimony are used as the basis for deciding between different hypotheses. I will proceed on that assumption in the present case.

There can be little doubt that decisions about the form of the internal representation are difficult to make because of the indirect nature of the evidence. The theoretical methods used in match-mismatch theory can build a plausible case by showing that data at different descriptive levels using different methods all support similar conclusions. I find that the analogical position fits in better with some of the general characteristics of stimulus analysis by organisms, at least for those stimuli which fall within the domain of the current theory. However, this does not rule out the existence of propositional encodings per se.

First of all, as we have seen, animals not particularly high on the phylogenetic scale possess a well-developed capacity to precisely encode their stimulus environment. Taken together with the evidence from the habituation studies, we are confronted with the fact that organisms can engage in extensive stimulus analysis even when their overt attentional or processing capabilities are relatively limited. While not directly implying analogical encoding, these data are more difficult to reconcile with an abstract, propositional encoding. A propositional encoding presumably requires a more extensive recoding of the stimulus in contrast to an analogical encoding which can make more direct use of the information derived through perceptual analysis in the sensory systems. Second, it would seem useful for organisms to retain as much stimulus-specific information as possible. The more recoding performed on a processed stimulus, the more likely that information will be lost. Third, it is conceptually difficult to see how the information from certain sensory systems can be converted into abstract, propositional forms. In particular, gustatory or olfactory information would seem to be refractory to other forms of coding (cf. Engen & Ross, 1973; Lawless & Engen, 1977). While it is remotely possible that humans could recode such stimuli or at least verbally label them, this seems implausible with animals. Leaving aside these general considerations, let's examine some of the specific data which support the existence of analogical encoding.

Perceptual Imagery

Some of the most compelling data in support of analogical representations are studies involving the mental rotation of objects or shapes (Cooper, 1975; Paivio, 1978; Shepard & Podgorny, 1978). In the Cooper study, subjects were presented with random angular shapes. The shapes were then rotated or reversed in the plane of the picture and shown again to the subjects who had to determine whether the rotated form was standard (non-reversed but different orientation) or reflected (reversed and different orientation). The average time that subjects took to make this determination was a linear function of the angular difference between the original form and its rotated version. That is, the more the shape's new orientation deviated from the target orientation, the longer it took the subject to identify it as standard or reflected. This result provides a strong indication that the subjects were mentally rotating the variant back to the orientation of the target and then mentally comparing the two (cf. Shepard, 1984).

When subjects were told ahead of time of the identity and orientation of the variant form to be presented and then asked whether the variant and original shapes were the same, the reaction time (RT) for making a determination was constant. However, the time that subjects took to prepare for the form's presentation again increased linearly with the angular deviation from the original.

Paivio (1978) showed that determining the relative size of the angles for the hour and minute hands on two clocks was a direct function of the size of the angular difference. The clock times were presented in digital form and required the subject to make the necessary transformations mentally. It is difficult to see how manipulation of non-analogical propositions could display these characteristics.

There have been quite a few other studies dealing with various aspects of visual images, although I think that they are less compelling in and of themselves than the mental rotation studies. Segal and Fusella (1970) compared sensitivity for visual and auditory stimuli in a simple detection task performed concurrently with an imaging task, in which the subject had to generate mental pictures and sounds. The detection of stimuli was hampered by

33

simultaneous imaging, particularly when the modality of the image corresponded to that of the external stimulus. Davidson and Schwartz (1977) performed a somewhat similar experiment but measured EEG activity in brain areas relevant to the modalities being tested (e.g., visual-occipital cortex, kinesthetic-sensorimotor cortex). Subjects were asked to image a flashing light, a tapping sensation on the right forearm or both together. The visual imagery generated by the subject elicited greater occipital activity than did kinesthetic imagery which, conversely, elicited greater sensorimotor activity. Imaging of both together produced occipital activity roughly in between the other two conditions. Since imagery in particular modalities seems to elicit specific changes in EEG activity in corresponding sensory regions, an analogical form of imagery is suggested over an abstract, propositional code.

Shiffrin (1973) and Tversky (1969) have shown that memory for pictures has different characteristics than verbal material, even when the verbal material is simply a label or description of the pictures. In the former study, for example, primacy and recency effects were seen for verbal but not for pictorial materials, which Shiffrin believed due to the absence of rehearsal for picture encodings. Lawless and Engen (1977) found that rehearsal did not affect odor recognition, unlike verbal materials. It seems possible that such information is inherently difficult to rehearse. If an abstract, propositional code were being uniformly employed, these differences would not be likely.

Another relevant phenomenon is configural learning or conditioning, in which a compound stimulus is processed as something more than the sum of its elements. Even under conditions which should increase the likelihood of propositional encoding, Anderson and Paulson (1978) found evidence for such configural (perceptual) effects. Of course, configural effects are well known in various areas of learning (cf. Razran, 1965). Configural learning is not particularly easy to explain using propositions as the basis for encoding because of the complexity of the configural stimulus. Take, for example, a number of musical instruments playing a chord; the sound characteristics are obviously dependent on the interaction of the individual instruments. The overtone pattern of one instrument can reinforce or cancel overtones in other instruments, thus affecting the sound quality. To encode this sound pattern without being able to preserve in some isomorphic form the stimulus characteristics and interrelationships would seem to be extremely difficult.

Neurological Data

As Anderson (1978, 1979) has noted, neurological data offer the most promising approach to deciding between alternative theories of internal stimulus representations. There are essentially two different methodologies that have been used in the neurological studies to be presented, namely, electrophysiological recording of neurons and brain waves, and the behavioral testing of animals and humans with particular neurological deficits.

Interesting evidence has been obtained from unit recordings of neurons in animals exposed to unusual visual environments while young. Blakemore and Cooper (1970) raised kittens in restricted visual environments in which either horizontal or vertical lines were present but not both. These kittens were later examined for neuronal response in the visual system. Although binocularity was not affected, the orientation sensitivities of the neurons were completely abnormal. No neurons were found that had optimal sensitivities to orientations within 20% of the non-presented orientation. That is, animals exposed to vertical, but not horizontal, lines showed no neurons optimally sensitive to horizontal lines. There were many vertically sensitive neurons, however. The opposite was true for kittens exposed to horizontal but not vertical lines. Importantly, passive degeneration of underused visual cortex was not found, arguing against a selective loss of neurons in the non-exposed orientation.

Hirsch and Spinelli (1970) raised kittens from birth with goggles over their eyes, one eye viewing horizontal lines and the other viewing vertical lines painted on the opaque lens. Recording from neurons in the visual cortex, the authors found that the receptive fields were either vertically or horizontally sensitive; no oblique fields were found. Just as crucially, the neurons with horizontal sensitivity were activated only by stimuli presented to the eye originally exposed to horizontal lines. The same pattern held true for the vertically sensitive units and the eye exposed to vertical lines. Unlike the Blakemore and Cooper study, binocularity was lost for these units (cf. Pettigrew & Freeman, 1973). Freeman and Thibo (1973) found a somewhat similar effect in some humans who suffer from ocular astigmatism. These individuals display different resolving powers for vertical and horizontal orientations. Decreased evoked potential responses were correlated with reduced resolution capacity for a particular orientation.

Leventhal and Hirsch (1975) clarified the roles of environment and genetic inheritance in the specificity of visual cortical neurons. Using a procedure similar to Hirsch and Spinelli, they exposed each eye to diagonals slanted in different directions. Later testing showed that some units responded preferentially to diagonal lines while others responded best to vertical or horizontal lines. This result indicates a certain prepotency to horizontal and vertical orientations in visual neurons since the kittens were not exposed to these orientations. However, only those kittens

35

exposed to diagonal lines had neurons which responded preferentially to diagonal lines.

These findings suggest a number of things relevant to our discussion of analogical encoding. First of all, some neurons are capable of modeling the specific characteristics of exteroceptive stimuli. Some basic types of stimuli seem to be prepotent since internal representations of them can be formed as long as they are not specifically interfered with. However, more complex or unusual stimuli have to be actually exposed to the organism before internal representations of them can be formed. Second, since this modeling is occurring in a perceptual system, it seems unlikely that abstract codes are being established for these kinds of stimuli. The development of the internal representations has an effect on the later perceptual capacities of the organism. The specificity of the modeling of exteroceptive stimuli argues against a simple explanation in terms of perceptual system development independent of memorial effects, however. Third, this neuronal modeling takes place with minimal active processing on the part of the organism. This statement can be made rather confidently since these effects have been demonstrated in animals anesthetized during stimulus presentation.

With respect to the question of processing effort involved in analogical versus propositional encoding, Milner (1968) conducted an interesting comparison of patients having right temporal lobe damage with patients with damage to other brain areas such as the frontal, parietal, or left temporal regions. The task used was the recognition of faces from photographs in the presence of distractors. The first experiment employed an irrelevant visual task between the presentation of the faces and the recognition test while the second experiment had an equivalent delay but no visual filler task between presentation and test. On these tasks, the right temporal patients showed severe impairment compared with the other groups. In the third experiment, no delay was present between presentation and test and interestingly, no significant differences were observed between the right temporal group and the others. This result was due not to improvement by the right temporal group but to a decrement in the other groups who were apparently using the delay in order to recode the visual information. Although the deficit was quite clear with faces, structurally simple stimuli such as hues or flashing lights failed to show the effect. Thus, humans may well be able to recode non-verbal stimuli into some verbal or abstract symbolic form, but only with more processing effort. The lack of a deficit for simple stimuli, which presumably are easily processed, bears out this interpretation.

The potential ability of humans to recode stimuli of course makes analysis of encoding differences more difficult, since a stimulus processed in one form may be converted to another by the subject. The best known finding concerning this phenomenon is probably the phonological recoding of visually presented verbal material (cf. Crowder, 1976; Seymour, 1979). Thus, we cannot conclude that, simply because a propositional encoding of a non-verbal stimulus exists, an analogical encoding of the same stimulus does not.

## Theoretical Considerations

As with any sustained controversy, it is clear that both sides possess some cogent arguments in support of their basic hypotheses. For example, it has not been demonstrated that differences in memory result from hypothesized analogical encoding. In fact, a certain amount of evidence suggests that the content of a memory per se does not play a large or consistent role in retention of the item (cf. Postman & Burns, 1973; Spear, 1978). The same kind of factors that improve retention for verbal material have a similar effect on non-verbal material (cf. Richardson, 1978) raising the question of whether both are stored in the same kind of representation.

Pylyshyn (1973, 1979) has also stressed that whatever form the internal representation is assumed to take, it still represents a highly processed entity in no way similar to the actual stimulus. The relationship between the internal representation and the external stimulus cannot be the same as that between a physical model or analog and the physical stimulus (e.g., a locomotive and a scale model). The stimulus object has many properties which cannot be derived from the internal representation. A visual image of a locomotive would not include its weight, for example. In addition, transformations can be performed on the internal representation which would be impossible on the stimulus object. For example, as Pylyshyn notes, it does not seem to take any more time to scan an internal representation of a large as compared to a small object.

There are several points to consider with respect to the above arguments. First, there can be little doubt that internal representations, whether or not they are analogical, are not related in a simple or completely direct way to the external stimulus. However, this is not an overwhelming argument against analogical encoding or in favor of propositional encoding. Shepard and Chipman (1970) note that parallelism can exist in the relations between different internal representations and the corresponding external objects without any structural resemblance existing between the two.

It is apparent that only information which can be encoded through a particular sensory modality can be involved in an analogical encoding of a stimulus presented in that modality. I can't directly perceive the weight of an object through my eyes, for

37

example. The limitations of the IPM with respect to the amount of information that can be processed simultaneously about a stimulus also represents a limiting factor. However, this doesn't negate the possibility that specific properties are represented in an analogical form. The important test would seem to be whether some relevant and important properties of the stimulus object are represented analogically in the internal representation.

In the current theory, it is the nature of the perceptual operations that are performed in a particular modality which indicate the possible modeling properties that an internal representation can possess. In this view, the perceptual capacities of the organism define the analogical properties of memorial representations in a particular species. This leads us to the second point in favor of analogical encodings--they reduce the processing effort required for the formation of internal representations. This point would especially be useful in stimulus recognition where context and other subtle distinctions can play a large role in successful retrieval (cf. Underwood, 1983). We must keep in mind that the memory capabilities of animals cannot be explained with cognitive processes that are suitable only with regard to verbal-symbolic materials in humans.

In addition, precise encoding can take place without much attention or apparent processing effort on the part of the organism; as we saw in the neurological studies, internal representations of visual stimuli could be formed even while the animal was anesthetized. On the behavioral side, detailed encoding of contextual stimuli and of habituated stimuli also suggest that at least with non-verbal stimuli, the processing involved can take place in at least semi-automatic fashion. This seems hard to reconcile with a propositional or completely abstract encoding process.

Thus, analogical encoding would seem to be an important process, taken together with other capacities, in allowing a sophisticated analysis and representation of the stimulus environment without the necessity of imputing all of the cognitive skills of humans to animals. The generality of the solution is an important point in its favor. While it is clear that humans could possibly encode any stimulus using a verbal or abstract propositional form, the same cannot be said for organisms not possessing an advanced symbolic capacity.

One other point that should be considered with respect to arguments for propositional encoding is the empirical domain which is being cited. Most of the evidence used by proponents such as Anderson and Pylyshyn comes from more cognitive tasks, using humans as subjects. There can be little doubt that humans in these situations are quite capable of sophisticated propositional or other symbolic encodings, even of stimuli that could be encoded analogically. For example, Holyoak (1977) showed that subjects, when asked to choose the larger of two objects from memory, could compare the size of objects with or without the use of visual imagery. However, the fact that subjects can encode some stimulus in propositional form is essentially irrelevant to whether analogical encoding is employed by organisms.

The objections of Pylyshyn, in particular, I believe to be somewhat dependent on the particular tasks that are examined by him. The major brunt of criticism is borne by studies of visual imagery which tap, not the encoded representation of a stimulus, but rather the ability of a subject to generate a representation from information (whether propositional or analogical) in long-term or inactive memory. It seems intuitively unlikely that a person can generate a visual image or other type of representation which contains all the information retained about the item if only because of the well-known processing limitations of working memory (e.g., Schneider & Shiffrin, 1977). Working memory contains activated representations which do not need to be retrieved to be available to the organism (cf. Chapter 12). For example, it is difficult to mentally generate even two instruments playing at the same time in a musical piece, yet very subtle differences between two performances of the music can be easily discerned. A similar point could be made with complex visual stimuli which can be encoded in detailed form but which cannot be generated by the subject in all their complexity. Thus, the objections concerning the lack of analogical relations between all the parameters of the external stimulus and the internal representation lose some of their force when directed at studies requiring the generation of representations in working memory as opposed to the recognition of stimuli.

The fact that children often use learning strategies that approximate those seen in animals while those exhibited by adults are quite different provides a clue that the development of linguistic and symbolic abilities (i.e., verbal mediation) changes the way that information processing takes place (cf. Bisanz & Resnick, 1978; Kendler & Kendler, 1968; Lubow et al., 1975). This would suggest that the use of propositional encodings should be limited in young children and should increase as they grow older. My own view, therefore, is that analogical encoding is used extensively and perhaps totally in the information processing systems of animals and that both analogical and propositional encoding are exhibited in humans. A direct relationship between symbolic and verbal capacity and the use of propositional encoding is a distinct possibility that should be investigated.

Whatever the final resolution of this problem, I would like to re-emphasize the importance of considering the full range of evidence relevant to the question, in judging the adequacy of hypotheses about the form of the internal representation. I believe that this provides the best route to distinguish between rival hypotheses with good empirical backing. With these kinds of disputes, I suspect that this process will show the domains within which each principle rules rather than proving or disproving one or the other. I think that this will be the case in the present dispute.

## MATCH-MISMATCH PROCESSES

### Definitions

Once an internal representation has been formed, its usefulness will be determined by the extent to which it can be and is used. By this, we generally mean that the stimulus or event must occur again and on these occasions it must be recognized as such by the organism. This recognition process would seem to necessitate some way of comparing the exteroceptive stimulus (or more precisely its processed equivalent) with the internal representations available to the organism.

This comparison or match-mismatch process should not be seen as a unitary function, but rather as a rubric for a collection of integrated activities, all of which are involved in stimulus recognition and its behavioral expression. This creates a problem in that research into this question tends to be widely scattered and can be difficult to interrelate. Another problem is that because some kind of comparison process seems such an intuitive part of recognition and retrieval of memorial representations, it tends to be taken for granted rather than being subjected to intensive and explicit investigation.

Nevertheless, it should be noted that these operations are among the most vital and uniformly important that an organism can perform, at least if it is to function at more than a reflexive level. The organism has to be able to correctly interpret environmental stimuli in virtually continuous fashion to survive, and to do so, its internal representations must be effectively compared with stimuli as they are processed.

Since the comparison or match-mismatch process is subject to a number of different definitions and conceptual interpretations, it is advisable to clarify what phenomena are at issue. In its simplest procedural form, the match-mismatch process would involve a yes-no judgment of identity between a stimulus and an internal representation. The basic simplicity of the yes-no comparison lies in the fact that a difference can be detected without the necessity of (perceptually) defining what that difference is. Clearly such a comparison could be consistent even with neuronal systems with limited information processing capabilities, although subtle stimulus differences would necessarily be beyond their resolution capacity. Increases in the sophistication of an identity comparison process would be based on an increase in the number of dimensions on which differences could be detected.

Another form which a match-mismatch comparison could take would be equivalent to a contextual recognition or recall decision. In this situation the organism must be able to differentiate between different occurrences of the same stimulus. Contextual recognition (recall) is necessarily an associative process since it is the presence of other stimuli occurring with the target stimulus which permit the organism to make the necessary comparisons. The context is a stimulus associated with the target stimulus, in other words. On the other hand, yes-no recognition can be either associative or non-associative.

A third way in which a match-mismatch process could be performed would be the matching of a stimulus with a generated representation constructed by the subject or previously retrieved into working memory from inactive memory. The prior retrieval of the internal representation could be due either to the occurrence of predictive cues associated with the stimulus occurrences, or in the case of humans, to verbal symbolic mediation.

The match-mismatch process can also be classified according to the behavioral outcome of the comparison. For example, in the habituation paradigm, a match between the stimulus and representation maintains habituation and a mismatch leads to dishabituation. In a conditioning paradigm, however, a match would maintain whatever response had been learned to the stimulus while a mismatch would lead to no response or the occurrence of behaviors other than the learned response.

The question that confronts us is whether these procedural or outcome distinctions involve different match-mismatch processes or whether they involve differences in other factors while the same match-mismatch process is used throughout. The investigation of the comparison process is complicated by the fact that it is easier to study the criteria by which a match-mismatch decision is made than it is to study the way in which the comparison of stimulus and representation is accomplished. For example, by changing the intensity of a previously habituated stimulus we can parametrically determine the relationship between such changes and the degree of dishabituation. By this means, we can infer the organismic criteria involved in a match-mismatch decision on this dimension. However, this does not directly help us understand how the stimulus and representation are actually compared with each other in order to arrive at a decision of sameness or difference.

There are two separate issues that are involved in an analysis of the comparison process (see Figure 3-1). First, how does the brain determine which representations to compare with a presented

41

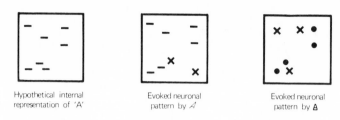

Hypothetical internal
representation of 'A'

Evoked neuronal
pattern by 𝒜

Evoked neuronal
pattern by **Δ**

B    Conjunctive Equivalence

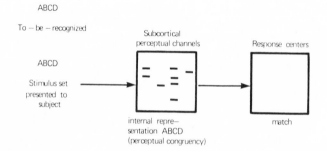

ABCD

To – be – recognized

ABCD

Stimulus set
presented to
subject

Subcortical
perceptual channels

Response centers

internal repre—
sentation ABCD
(perceptual congruency)

match

Disjunctive Equivalence

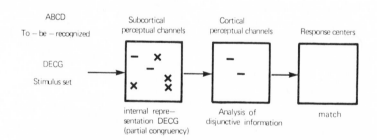

ABCD

To – be – recognized

DECG

Stimulus set

Subcortical
perceptual channels

Cortical
perceptual channels

Response centers

internal repre—
sentation DECG
(partial congruency)

Analysis of
disjunctive information

match

**Fig. 3-1 . Match-Mismatch Retrieval .**   A) Each internal representation has a characteristic neuronal pattern evoked during its processing or retrieval. Recognition occurs
when the neuronal pattern is re-evoked.  Discrepant elements or features which do not
inhibit the activation of the neuronal pattern do not affect recognition, but when discrepant features evoke a different  existing pattern recognition failure can occur.
B)  The comparison process can occur at different processing stages as a function of
stimulus or task complexity (cf. memorial processes, automatization: Chapter 12).

stimulus? Second, how does the brain relate the attributes of the stimulus with those of the representation or set of representations that have been selected for comparison?

Influence of Encoding Processes

With respect to the first issue, the encoding and retrieval processes of the IPM must play a critical role. The way in which the stimulus has been encoded on previous occurrences will clearly play a major role in determining the decision process with respect to the latest occurrence of the stimulus. Presumably, if the presented stimulus is processed (encoded) with attributes similar to those contained in the internal representation, then the probability of a match is increased.

Although perception per se is outside the scope of the theory, it will be useful to consider some of the evidence relevant to this topic. The basis for stimulus recognition (e.g., recognizing the letter "A" across occurrences) has long been a contentious topic (e.g., Bowhuis, 1978; Dodwell, 1970; Neisser, 1967). One of the difficulties is that a stimulus often occurs in a slightly different form from occurrence to occurrence. How does the IPM recognize the variants as the same stimulus that has occurred previously? In the case of certain stimuli such as words, the context in which they occur helps restrict the number of possibilities, but this cannot be a general solution.

Most theories of stimulus recognition processes have centered on visual stimuli and generally fall into either featural or holistic types of explanations. Featural theories assume that stimuli or events are composed of a number of individual properties which together specify a unique object (cf. Gibson, 1969; Keryen & Baggen, 1981; Tversky, 1977). In this approach we could assume that the features or attributes of a stimulus event would be compared to the features present in the internal representation. In the event of featural matches in excess of a certain criterion, a recognition of the stimulus would occur.

Since the number of features comprising a stimulus is possibly quite large, it makes sense to arrive at a recognition decision without having to compare all of the features. One way would be to look for distinctive features which are unique or restricted to a small set of items which include the target stimulus. For example, if we see a dot above a letter we know it must be "i" or "j."

The use of distinctive features in the comparison process is supported by a variety of behavioral and neurological evidence. The use of distinctive features in the process of recognition has been supported with graphemes (Gibson, 1969; Neisser & Lazar, 1964), phonemes (Liberman, 1982), and visual shapes (Julesz, 1967). Pritchard et al. (1960) showed that stabilized images on the retina

43

tended to fragment and disappear. The important point is that the fragmentation occurred in a systematic way, with discrete features such as angles and lines disappearing as a unit. In addition there is evidence that visual fixations tend to cluster around specific distinctive features, even in infants (Kessen et al., 1972). It seems logical to assume that featural analysis would be particularly useful with complex stimuli which would be difficult to encode in their entirety (Gibson, 1969).

In addition, featural matches between similar features may be subject to inhibition by incompatible elements. To return to our example of the letter A, critical features are the two vertical lines forming a vertex and a horizontal line which spans the gap between them. Recognition of the letter A is undoubtedly dependent not only on the presence of these two features but also on the non-presence of additional features which do not conform with them. Thus, we can recognize variants such as , A , or $A$ as A letter A's but cannot with A, N , or A.

It is important to note that featural analysis does not necessarily mean that the recognition of every stimulus is typically accomplished by the isolated matching of particular features. Reed and Johnson (1975) and McClelland (1978) have shown that configural effects exist in the perception of simple stimuli such as line segments. Williams and Weisstein (1978) showed that line segments were identified more accurately when they were part of coherent, three-dimensional figures than they were in less coherent, two-dimensional figures. Harvey and Gervais (1981), in analyzing the relationship between the Fourier spectra of visual textures with their perceptual appearance, concluded that the visual internal representation was based on spatial frequency analysis (sinusoidal variations in luminance across a surface) rather than on feature extraction (cf. Cooper, 1980).

This pattern of results indicates that the perceptual processes involved in the encoding can play an important role in determining the kinds of representations in inactive memory which can be matched by a processed stimulus. Stimuli encoded in analytic fashion as a collection of features have some probability of a match with internal representations which contain some or all of those features. Conversely, stimuli encoded holistically have less probability of matching such featural encodings (cf. encoding and retrieval processes: Chapters 12, 13).

The Comparison Process

We turn now to the second issue, which involves the way in which representations and stimuli are compared with each other. Because of the methodological difficulties in investigating this process, much of the relevant work has been conducted with humans

44

using the Sternberg (1966) symbol classification task. In that experiment, subjects were given a short set of symbols which were committed to memory. The subjects were then presented with a stimulus probe which they had to classify as a member or non-member of the set that they had been given, with reaction time (RT) as the measure. The time it takes to respond can be logically divided into encoding, comparison, retrieval, and output operations. By selecting variables which should only have an effect on one of the operations, some determinations about their existence and character-istics can be made on the basis of the observed results. Evidence supporting the existence of a comparison process which is distinct from encoding and retrieval operations has been found (Sternberg, 1969).

The available research indicates that the time taken to recog-nize a stimulus under these conditions is a direct function of the memory set size, stimulus set size, and the similarity between stimulus targets and distractor items (cf. McIntyre et al., 1970; Schneider & Shiffrin, 1977; Teichner & Krebs, 1974). Blough (1984) has been able to extend some of these findings to pigeons using a visual search task. RT increased as memory set size increased from one to four items and as target-distractor similarity increased. Increasing the amount of practice reduced the effect of memory set size on RTs, a finding which has been repeatedly shown with humans.

As Seymour (1979) notes, the time required for a match-mismatch decision should be dependent on the rate at which information is being transmitted to the components responsible for comparison and on the threshold value for a judgment of same or different. Thus, manipulations which affect either of these factors, such as those mentioned above, should affect the comparison process directly.

In this connection, a long-standing controversy has existed over the question of serial versus parallel processing of items in the comparison process. Sternberg (1969) has suggested on the basis of his results that the method of comparison is serial and exhaustive. The stimulus would be compared sequentially with all the representations in the memory set and only then a decision made on which comparison involved a match.

This hypothesis was based on the finding that the RT's for both "same" and "different" response increased as a linear function of the size of the memory set, which would indicate that subjects do not terminate the comparison process when they attain a match. However, results supporting the serial exhaustive model seem to be confined to particular conditions (e.g., fixed memory set) but the use of other stimuli can result in logarithmic functions not consonant with the model (cf. Briggs, 1974).

Alternative theories concerning the method of comparison have centered on serial, self-terminating models or parallel processing models with limited capacity, which can be difficult to distinguish in terms of their predictions (Corcoran, 1971; Taylor, 1976). For example, Nickerson and Pew (1973) provided evidence supporting the idea that features are compared sequentially, but items are compared in parallel. Conjunctive equivalences in which two arrays are identical at all positions (e.g., ABCD, ABCD) were recognized faster than were disjunctive equivalences which contain only partial identity (e.g., ABCD, EFCG).

Actually the finding that decisions of identity are faster than decisions of partial equivalence has been demonstrated in divergent tasks. Posner and Keele (1967) showed that when subjects compare stimuli (e.g., the letter "A") the RT in deciding two items are physically identical is faster than deciding they have the same name or meaning. Thus, if subjects are asked to respond when two letter A's are given, they can respond faster when they are both uppercase (AA) than when one is uppercase and the other lowercase (Aa). These data have been confirmed with a variety of stimulus materials and procedures (cf. Nickerson, 1978). It has been argued that same and different judgments may reflect different subprocesses and in fact, a number of variables have differing effects on same versus different judgments, e.g., familiarity, stimulus probability (Egeth & Blecker, 1971; Thomas, 1974). One possibility is that judgments of identity are capable of being performed at earlier stages of processing and thus require fewer operations prior to comparison; another is that identity decisions can make use of a holistic (parallel) comparison process while differences require sequential processing (cf. Hughes et al., 1984).

If, as was contended in previous sections, the nature of the perceptual operations performed on the stimulus during processing plays an important role in determining the characteristics of the internal representation, it seems equally logical that such a process would also be implicated in recognition. It would seem that in order for a match to occur, an exteroceptive stimulus needs to be analyzed in approximately the same way as previous occurrences that served as the basis for the internal representation. Thus, if the visual system has several ways of processing stimuli, then we should find a similar parallel in the recognition process at the behavioral level (cf. Handel et al., 1980).

The same logic can be applied to all of the perceptual systems. The bases for a match between stimulus and internal representation will depend in part on the ways in which the stimuli are characteristically analyzed in that particular modality. Modalities other than vision may reveal differences in the nature of the perceptual analysis and therefore in the way in which the match-mismatch function is accomplished (cf. stimulus association: Chapters 12, 14; specific aptitudes: Chapter 17).

Whether the differences in the rate at which information is assembled or accumulated also reflect themselves in a multiplicity of ways in which the match-mismatch decision is actually reached (i.e., Seymour's second point) is unclear. In fact the whole question of response bias, whether in setting threshold levels for response or altering the qualitative basis for a decision, has usually been treated as a given rather than analytically examined.

More generally, there is a real paucity in the number of procedures used to directly examine the match-mismatch process. Much of what data exist have been generated in a few kinds of tasks employing human subjects. These data have to be cautiously interpreted with respect to the delineation of structural processes because of the flexible processing strategies that are available to humans. There is considerable evidence to suggest that some of the observed results are due to voluntary strategies on the part of the subjects rather than the straightforward operation of a basic match-mismatch process. This possibility, of course, would make it difficult to assert that a match-mismatch process possesses the particular properties displayed in these symbol classification tasks across mammalian species. For example, in four-letter arrays, the RT for "different" decisions increases as the position of the discrepant symbol moves from left to right across the array (Henderson & Henderson, 1975). It is hard to imagine that this can be the result of a basic property of the match-mismatch process.

The value of these kinds of studies in the elucidation of the characteristics of the match-mismatch process would be greatly enhanced by independent evidence which could provide convergence on particular findings. Evidence from animal studies would be particularly useful in teasing apart the structural properties from the voluntary. However, it must be admitted that the investigation of the match-mismatch process is difficult enough with humans, but with animals the problems are greatly magnified.

The neurological data are also scanty except with respect to brain wave measures which are discussed in the sections on the OR and habituation. At the level of the individual neuron, it is known that neurons exist which have the properties of comparators. These neurons fire when there is a difference between the presented stimulus and the "expected" stimulus. There is some correlation between such activity and behavioral measures such as dishabituation for certain neuron populations (e.g., hippocampus), although the behavioral consequence of comparator neurons in the sensory areas is less clear (Thatcher & John, 1977; Vinogradova, 1975).

# Chapter 4

# Response Processes

Having discussed some of the most general stimulus-analyzing properties of the IPM, we will now turn to a discussion of some general response factors. As we saw previously, Sokolov's model involved a stimulus analyzing stage which in turn controlled a separate response stage. One of the basic tenets of match-mismatch theory is that while it certainly makes sense to divide neural functions in terms of this distinction, it is not appropriate to conclude that a strictly sequential system is in operation. Instead, the performance of different types of responses have differing, direct effects on stimulus analysis. It is argued that these response effects on the stimulus analyzing capacities of the IPM provide an excellent means of making functional distinctions between response classes.

Neurologically speaking, it can be shown that brain regions responsible for internal response (e.g., visceral, homeostatic, hormonal) can be quite distinct from regions which control motoric function. However, it is argued that a distinction based on this finding is misleading when applied to the analysis of behavior. There have been a number of previous attempts to define different response classes, perhaps most notably by Rescorla and Solomon (1967). They suggested that autonomic versus skeletal responses might provide the basis for the distinction between classical and instrumental conditioning. Classical conditioning would apply to autonomic responses while instrumental conditioning would affect skeletal responses. This distinction had been suggested by a number of other researchers as well, including Skinner (1938).

48

Although consistent with much research up to that time, this distinction became less tenable with the development of several new areas of investigation, most particularly autoshaping and ethological approaches to learning and behavior. It became apparent that both autonomic and skeletal responses were very much intertwined and that there was no neat distinction between autonomic and skeletal responses in relation to the type of conditioning possible with each (cf. Hearst, 1975; Jenkins, 1977).

As stated in Chapter 2, the present theory assumes that there are three functional response classes that exist in all mammals: (a) species-specific responses, (b) voluntary responses, and (c) the OR. Each of these response classes is composed of responses which involve both motoric and visceral components. Although there is some basis for assuming that the relative mix or interaction of motoric and hormonal/visceral components may tend to differ across response class, this cannot serve as the justification for the assignment of functional distinctions. We now examine some of the characteristics of these response classes and their constituent responses.

## THE ORIENTING RESPONSE

The orienting response to novel stimuli is a centrally integrated response which involves the entire organism. Electrophysiological events, overt skeletal movements, and various homeostatic or biochemical changes are known to be associated with its occurrence (cf. Graham, 1973; Ohman, 1979; Sokolov, 1969). One of the most consistent overt behaviors correlated with the OR is pausing; that is, the interruption of the ongoing activities of the organism in a brief cessation of movement. In many cases, orienting of sensory receptors such as eyes and ears takes place as the organism attempts to identify the stimulus. In general, these two behaviors, pausing and orientation to the stimulus, occur sequentially to a novel stimulus (Bykov, 1965).

As Barry (1979, 1982) has noted, the response components of the OR can be fractionated to some extent, given different stimulus conditions. Such response measures as heart rate (HR), galvanic skin response (GSR), cephalic pulse amplitude and pupillary dilation do not necessarily show a consistent relationship with each other. There are two points to consider. First, it should be remembered that basic visceral functions are almost always going to be under the simultaneous influence of a number of internal factors since they are vital to the moment-to-moment functioning of the organism. Second, the concept of the OR has been applied to such a variety of situations that there is serious doubt as to whether the same functional response is really involved (cf. Naatanen, 1979). In the present theory we apply the term <u>orienting response</u> only to the response which occurs as a result of mismatches between internal representations and the stimulus environment and which functions to facilitate the processing of information (cf. Sokolov, 1975).

From the present theoretical standpoint, the fundamental importance of the OR is attested to by two facts. First of all, it can be demonstrated in all mammals, including humans. This confirms the potential generalizability of the phenomenon as a basic response type. Second, the OR seems to be one of the most important foundations of learning capacity in animals and humans, a subject we will consider now.

## The OR and Learning

As we saw in the habituation studies, an OR is evoked when some aspect of the habituated stimulus context changes. This evocation of the OR is not limited to the habituation paradigm by any means; in a reinforcement situation the OR will occur to changes in the nature of reinforcement (e.g., Biferno & Dawson, 1977; Pearce & Kaye, 1984). As O'Connor (1966) has noted, in a conditioning experiment, each change in the conditions of stimulation evokes an active process of attention embodied by the OR to fulfill twin goals: maximize information processing capacities to analyze the new situation, and delay action until the appropriate course is clear. These goals presumably reflect themselves in the overt pausing and orienting exhibited in conjunction with internal measures of the OR.

The occurrence of the OR is important to stimulus processing in all conditioning situations which involve changes in the patterns of reinforcement. Russian psychologists were among the first to investigate the role of the OR in later stages of conditioning. For example, Dolin et al. (1965) showed that errors on discrimination performance by dogs could be corrected by re-evoking the OR, which promoted the refinement of the discrimination learning. Waters et al. (1977) have shown that habituation to stimuli that were later used as distractors improved task performance of human subjects with regard to mathematical problems by reducing ORs to these irrelevant stimuli. In addition, the cessation of reinforcement in extinction has also been found to evoke the OR (Vinogradova, 1975, 1978; Crowne & Radcliffe, 1975). Thus, this research leads to the conclusion that in animals and humans, the OR is present in all phases of learning situations in which changes in stimulus and reinforcement presentation are occurring.

Both Russian and American psychologists have found it to be exceedingly difficult to condition a stimulus paired with reinforcement if the stimulus has been repeated enough previously so that the OR to it has become habituated (cf. Lubow, 1973; Paramonova, 1965). When such a stimulus was used, successful conditioning was reported only when the stimulus once again began to evoke the OR. Conversely, a completely novel stimulus was also not optimal for use as a CS. The best stimulus for such a purpose was one which had been presented enough times so that the OR was somewhat diminished in strength, but not completely absent.

Lubow reported that nonreinforced preexposure of a stimulus later used as a CS resulted in a decrement or latent inhibition in the acquisition phase of a classically conditioned defensive response. The observed decrement was found to be a function of the frequency of preexposures. In addition, the size of the decrement remained constant over four days of acquisition. Reiss and Wagner (1972) showed that the decrement due to the preexposure is not the result of a conditioned inhibition effect. In other words, the preexposed CS did not exhibit active response inhibiting properties, but rather seemed to go unnoticed by the organism. Halgren (1974) showed also that the CS had not acquired specific associative control over some competing behavior during the pre-exposure phase.

Thus, the elicitation of an OR by a stimulus seems essential for conditioning of it to take place; however, once a stimulus asymptotically controls a response, the OR habituates. This is an important point since it distinguishes the OR from the other two proposed response classes. Both species-specific responses and instrumental, voluntary or cognitive responses are maintainable behavior. However, the OR is a sporadic behavior that is dependent on some form of novelty being present in the stimulus environment. Obviously, repetition of a novel event decreases its novelty, so steady state orienting responses are highly improbable. This lack of OR maintainability is confirmed by the difficulty of using the OR as a conditioned response. Conversely, the other two proposed response classes are not dependent on the OR for their maintenance. Thus, there is a clear dissociation between the OR and the other two response classes.

Electrophysiological Data

Recent research on the human OR has concentrated on the electrophysiological events that coincide with the more overt behavioral responses, in particular the P300 complex. This is an event-related potential consisting of a negative wave 200 msec after the event, then a positive wave 300 msec after the event, followed by slow waves. Investigation of this wave complex has cast new light on orienting responses and has revealed possible differences between human and animal behavior in this respect (cf. Simson et al., 1976). It is particularly useful because it may be a measure of the timing of stimulus evaluation processes unconfounded by response factors (Magliero et al., 1984).

As Duncan-Johnson and Donchin (1977) note, two factors have been well-documented as determinants of the P300 wave elicited by task relevant stimuli: the a priori probability of the stimuli and the sequence of immediately preceding stimuli. In their experiment, they presented random sequences of high and low tones at nine different probability levels ranging from .10 to .90. The lower the probability the greater the amplitude of the P300 complex. In addition, repetition of a tone diminished the magnitude of the event-related potential, regardless of its a priori probability. In other words, the more unexpected or the less frequent the event, the greater the magnitude of the P300 wave (Fitzerald & Picton, 1981).

In addition, the same physical stimulus can yield different P300 complexes and different stimuli which are equally unexpected can evoke the same P300 complex. As Schwartz (1976) notes, there is no convincing evidence that these evoked potentials reflect the actual physical parameters of the stimulus; instead they would seem to be indications of detection of potentially important stimulus information in the environment. In support of this notion, the largest P300 amplitudes are produced by stimulus changes requiring a response (Kaufman et al., 1982). In this view, these evoked potentials represent a general attentional operation or process rather than the specific content of the stimulus. Earlier components of the evoked potential such as the N200 wave are modality specific, however (McCallum et al., 1983; Picton et al., 1978). It may well be that earlier components reflect an involuntary OR while later components such as the P300 are more indicative of voluntary attention (cf. Naatenen et al., 1982).

The importance of expectancy in the occurrence and magnitude of evoked potentials has been demonstrated in a number of experiments with human subjects. Porjesz and Begleiter (1975) studied the effect of self-generated expectancy on the visual evoked potential to physically identical stimuli. The subject chose to see either a bright or dim flash of light; however, a visual stimulus of medium intensity was actually presented. The evoked potential resembled the response seen with the visual stimulus that was expected to be presented, either bright or dim. Thus, the same physical stimulus could evoke significantly different evoked potentials, suggesting that the expectancy of a particular stimulus can be as important to the form of the P300 response as the actual physical parameters of the presented stimulus.

Johnson and Donchin (1982) showed that the P300 amplitude for low probability stimulus sequences was influenced by the degree of knowledge that the subject possessed about event probabilities. To the extent that actual stimulus occurrences were more and more incongruent with expected probabilities, P300 amplitude increased, presumably because of more thorough processing.

Ruchkin et al. (1975) investigated a point with relevance to previous findings of the effects of stimulus omission on OR dishabituation. The P300 wave to the occurrence or non-occurrence of an auditory stimulus was analyzed. It was found that the parameters of the P300 wave were affected similarly by presentation or omission of a stimulus with a certain a priori probability. Greater wave magnitudes were found with less frequent events, whether they involved stimulus presentation or omission while smaller magnitudes were found with more frequent events. Thus, a P300 wave emitted to the non-occurrence of an expected stimulus seems to display the same properties as one evoked by an actual presented stimulus. In fact, the stimulus omission effect is apparently easier to detect using EEG measures than it is behaviorally (Siddle et al., 1983). Interestingly, Hillyard (1971) demonstrated that a P300 wave does not occur when a subject correctly decides that a stimulus has not occurred on a signal detection task nor when he incorrectly thinks that a stimulus has occurred.

These points are important in a number of ways to the present theory. First of all, the P300 wave, itself, would not seem to be the site where actual match-mismatch processes are occurring as some have suggested (cf. Ford & Hillyard, 1981) since the physical parameters of the stimulus do not seem sufficiently important to the waves' elaboration. Instead, it seems to be the consequence of a mismatch between the internal representation and the environment, functioning to enhance the stimulus processing of the individual. However, early components of the P300 complex may be sensitive to stimulus characteristics. Second, the dissociation of the OR from other response classes requires a convincing separation of at least some of its properties from those found in other responses. The detection of stimulus changes or disconfirmed hypotheses seems, in the OR, to be quite removed from the necessary stimulus analysis that would support actual response selection. As we saw previously, the OR tends to fade out as conditioning or learning takes place. This behavioral finding would seem to be consonant with the electrophysiological findings that have been cited here. Obviously there have to be close connections with the OR and higher levels of information processing (cf. McCarthy & Donchin, 1976); however, there would seem to be definite distinctions in the domain handled by each.

The research discussed in this section should have provided initial justification for viewing the OR as an identifiable response with discrete properties which distinguish it from other responses and which provide some basis for viewing it as fundamentally separate from other general types of responses. On the convergent side, research from a number of descriptive levels offers a strikingly similar picture of the properties of the OR. On the discriminative side, clear separations of function and temporal coincidence between the OR and other response types indicate that a real distinction may exist between them.

## SPECIES-SPECIFIC RESPONSES

The next response class that we examine is species-specific responses. Although taken literally this is not a very meaningful label, it is a common term for responses that are viewed as having some significant instinctive component. Generally, these are behaviors which are controlled by stimuli associated with feeding, hunting, flight, social behaviors, etc.

Many descriptions of species-specific behaviors can, of course, be found in the ethological literature (e.g., Dewsbury, et al., 1982; Hinde, 1970; Klopfer, 1973). Some of these behaviors have become quite well-known including the aggressive response of the stickleback, the honey-bee's flight, and the egg-retrieving response of the grey-lag goose. Rather than restating an extensive literature well-covered elsewhere, I want to focus on those points that are crucial to the argument at hand; in particular, those properties of the species-specific responses which allow a distinction to be made between them and the other two proposed response classes.

### Behavioral Characteristics

There are a number of characteristics that can aid in distinguishing this response class from what are typically called voluntary or instrumental responses. The two central behavioral factors are probably the ubiquity of a response to particular stimuli within a species and the degree to which specific environmental experience is required for the development or acquisition of the response. Although these two dimensions are interrelated, it is easier to take them in sequence.

The importance of ubiquity in determining species-specific responses lies not only in the suggestion of a genetic basis for the particular response but also in the demonstration of its occurrence in a wide variety of environmental situations. In other words, environmental invariance is less likely as the proximate cause of a behavior that occurs in widely scattered members of a species that do not come in contact with each other. This does not preclude the possibility that there is some specific stimulus acting as a releaser; however, the existence of such a releaser is further indication of the species-specific nature of a response (cf. Fagan, 1971).

54

The male stickleback fish has a characteristic aggressive response to the intrusion of another male into his territory. The response occurs in all normal males of the species. Research has shown that the stimulus triggering the aggressive response is invariably the red spot on the belly of the intruding male, a marking which is typical of the male stickleback. The invariance of this eliciting stimulus cannot be explained as an environmental invariance which causes a particular response on the part of the fish, since the male intruder obviously has many other characteristics that are as stable as the red spot. Thus, if the intrusion of a male created a situation where fighting occurred, any conditioning or learning should be associated to different stimuli of the intruder by different males. There is no logical reason why males would respond to only one characteristic in particular and ignore all the rest if the aggressive response was learned in some way by the male. However, the red spot is the key stimulus which evokes the response in all males. This is a relatively clear and noncontroversial example, of course, but the principle can be extended to areas that are less clear-cut.

In general, we are looking for situations where all of the members of a species respond in a particular way to a triggering stimulus which is only one of a number of stimuli present in the evoking situation. Examples of such behaviors can be found in species ranging from insects, fish, and amphibians up to human beings. In the human infant, for example, at the age of two months, smiles can be elicited by a person bending close to the infant while facing it. The same response can also be elicited by a mask with just two dark circles where the eyes should be. If the eyes are missing, then the stimulus is inadequate in triggering the smiles regardless of the representational accuracy in other respects (Spitz & Cobliner, 1965).

The pecking responses of birds, such as pigeons and chickens, provide another example of species-specific responses controlled by particular "releasers." Hunt and Smith (1967) showed that the pecking responses of naive chicks were directed at small objects which contrasted with the background, particularly when they were shiny and of high contrast. In other words, species-specific pecking occurred to objects possessing the visual characteristics of food or water droplets. On the other hand, these same chicks would not make pecking responses when they were standing in pools of water. Thus, water in a form which displayed certain specific visual features elicited pecking; in the absence of such features, water did not elicit pecking (cf. Kovach, 1983).

As with the stickleback, this species-specific behavior is triggered by specific stimuli which are only a part of the total complex of cues occurring in the situation. Nevertheless, all normal members of the species (or at least all members of a

55

particular sex) respond to the same subset of cues in a predictable manner without any special discriminative training. This is a powerful indication of a genetically organized response.

The other behavioral factor in identification of species-specific response patterns is the role that environmental experience plays in the development or maintenance of the response. Many responses classified as innate will show disruption or deterioration if the organism is given abnormal environmental experience in infancy (cf. McDonald, 1983; Riesen, 1961; Scott, et al., 1974). The criterion in this situation would probably be the extent of specific experience necessary for the response pattern to be exhibited or maintained. There are three lines of experimental evidence which can be brought to bear on this point. The first involves the exposure of a naive organism to the specific cues which elicit the species-specific response in normal organisms of the same species. The successful performance of the response in this situation would indicate a significant innate component to the response. The second line of evidence centers on response patterns that need minimal amounts of practice for successful performance in comparison to arbitrary responses of equivalent difficulty. The third line of evidence concerns responses which are difficult to control using a reinforcer other than the specific one which elicits the response pattern under naturalistic conditions. These three areas of research will be taken in turn.

One example concerning the first point is the lordosis response of the female rat to specific sensory information imparted by the male such as his forepaws on her flanks (Bermant & Sachs, 1973). The important point is that the response is correctly executed in naive as well as experienced females when the appropriate stimulus and internal (hormonal) conditions are present. Similarly, naive nonpregnant female rats can exhibit appropriate maternal behavior to novel pups after they have been pretreated with estrogen although they do not respond maternally as quickly as do parturient females with their own pups (Mayer & Rosenblatt, 1980).

Mallard ducklings exhibit instinctive differential responding to various vocalizations from the mother (Miller, 1980). The ducklings will inhibit their own vocalizations and engage in freezing behavior when the reconnaissance (alarm) call is performed by the hen. On the other hand, the assembly call excites the ducklings' vocalizations. The specificity of this response has also been demonstrated prenatally in Peking duck embryos as measured by the rate of a bill-clapping response (Gottlieb, 1979).

An example of a response requiring minimal practice for its successful and complete execution is the suckling response of rat pups. Stoloff et al. (1980) showed that nipple attachment behavior was disrupted by isolating the pups on the third through the fifth day postnatally. However, nipple attachment was maintained when

56

the isolation-reared pups were given 6 to 12 opportunities to search for, locate, and attach to the nipples of an anesthetized mother on days 3 and 4.

Another example concerning the second point is the one-way and freezing avoidance responses of the rat. Rats very rapidly learn to run to a safe compartment or freeze in order to avoid or escape aversive stimulation in comparison to their rate of acquisition of other types of avoidance responses (e.g., Bolles, 1970). As Blanchard and Blanchard (1971) have shown, presentation of an unconditioned aversive stimulus such as the sight of a cat will elicit freezing in rats unable to escape and fleeing when escape is possible.

With respect to the third line of evidence, a variety of studies have found that some response patterns are constrained in their conditionability to different reinforcers (cf. Domjan, 1983). For example, Annable and Wearden (1979) demonstrated that food reinforcement for paw washing was effective in increasing its rate of response; however, the same was not true when face washing was food reinforced. Instead, the (nonreinforced) paw washing response showed rate increases (cf. Shettleworth, 1975).

It should be emphasized that these three lines of evidence each provide converging rather than definitive evidence on the species-specific nature of a particular response or response pattern. The appearance of a response constraint to a particular stimulus in the naive organisms of a species is indicative of at least some level of genetic organization of the response. The amount of experience necessary for maintenance and complete elaboration of the response as well as its degree of conditionability by arbitrary reinforcers provides information about the boundary conditions of such genetic organization.

Neurological Characteristics

Species-specific behaviors can also be defined in terms of their neurological characteristics. Species-specific behaviors can be elicited in fully integrated form by chemical or electrical stimulation of appropriate subcortical areas in naive organisms (e.g., Hess, 1957). Obviously, voluntary behaviors which must be learned will not be exhibited in this fashion. For example, cats show a typical response pattern of stalking and then silently biting the neck of prey such as a rat when such a stimulus is present in the environment. Roberts and Bergquist (1968), by stimulating the appropriate location in the hypothalamus, could elicit this response even in cats which had been raised in isolation and had never attacked a prey before. The requirement for such stimulation to successfully elicit this response is simply the presence of the appropriate stimulus object in the environment.

57

That this is not a reflexive action has been demonstrated by Roberts and Kiess (1964) who showed that stimulation of this brain area would induce normal cats to learn to run a maze in order to reach a rat they could attack (cf. the discussions of mood states in Chapter 5 and in Section III).

The OR can also be elicited by brain stimulation (cf. Kaada, 1972). However, unlike species-specific behaviors, the performance of the OR does not seem to have motivational properties as evidenced by the difficulty of using it as the unconditioned response in a classical conditioning experiment. This is probably because the unconditioned stimulus capable of evoking the OR is any unexpected event. Once the event is repeated a few times, it is no longer unexpected.

## Species Specific Behaviors and Learning

It was mentioned previously that each of the response classes could be distinguished on the basis of its effects on the information processing capacity of the IPM. As we saw, the OR was instrumental in facilitating information processing and seemed to be a necessary prelude to learning about the stimulus environment. The performance of species-specific behaviors, however, appears to have a negative impact on the concurrent processing of information.

It was noticed some years ago that some responses are less sensitive to reinforcement contingencies than others. Breland and Breland (1961), in the course of training various animals for commercial purposes, noted that the operant technique of providing food reinforcement after the occurrence of a particular response did not always lead to an increase in the occurrence of that response. For example, a raccoon rewarded for putting tokens into a piggy bank would start to rub and wash them instead of depositing them in the bank. Breland and Breland noted that natural or species-specific food-gathering responses would often intrude into the target response that was being reinforced. This new response would usually involve more effort than the rewarded response and would delay reinforcement, yet the animal would often persist in performing the species-specific response. Timberlake et al. (1982) showed that the misdirection of behavior from reinforcers to stimuli associated with reward was the result of Pavlovian conditioning. The stimuli such as the tokens become incentive objects eliciting components of the species-specific appetitive behaviors related to food obtainment (cf. Bolles, 1970; Shettleworth, 1978).

The species-specific pecking response of some birds to small, high contrast objects can also be seen in the phenomenon of auto-shaping. In this paradigm, pigeons will peck at a lighted key which is non-contingently associated with food. The food may be presented at regular intervals during which the key is continually lit. However, the key has no connection with the presentation of the food. Pigeons will, nevertheless, consistently start to peck the lighted key (Brown & Jenkins, 1968). The species-specific response is so strong that it can override reinforcement contingencies. Williams and Williams (1969) showed that this pecking would continue even when it reduced the amount of reinforcement available to the pigeon.

It is important to note that within these general categories some response patterns display these characteristics more than others. The behaviors that immediately precede the occurrence of the reinforcer in natural situations seem to be the most refractory to conditioning by other reinforcers and most likely to interfere with the learning of incompatible responses (cf. Shettleworth, 1972; Staddon & Simmelhag, 1971).

What is interesting about these findings is that it has long been noted that increases in arousal (drive) increase the likelihood of dominant responses at the expense of less dominant responses (e.g., Hull, 1943). For example, Spigel (1964) showed that a response learned with difficulty by turtles, initially walking away from a reinforcer blocked by an obstruction in order to circumvent the obstruction, could be performed only when they were calm. Turtles that were given tranquilizers were able to perform the response; however, if under normal conditions they became agitated, then performance of the response quickly broke down. It was generally replaced by a response directed at the reinforcer and thus into the obstruction.

Species-specific responses are necessarily the most dominant organismic response to the controlling reinforcers and their performance is indicative of at least moderately high levels of arousal. In this connection it is well known that organisms performing the terminal components of species-specific responses or under high arousal are less disrupted by or sensitive to the introduction of irrelevant or novel stimuli (Denny & Ratner, 1970; Nevin, 1974; Bahrick, 1954). In other words, they are less likely to display ORs to these stimuli. Since, as we have seen, the OR is an essential prerequisite for learning about a stimulus, it follows that processing capacity is diminished when species-specific (emotional) responses are being performed. This is a subject that receives more attention in later chapters.

Species-Specific Responses in Humans

One of the most striking differences between animals and humans is the qualitatively different nature of the species-specific behaviors in each group. Animals, even primates, have a wide variety of species-specific behaviors in sexual, social, feeding, and drinking response categories which are elicited by relatively

59

standard environmental stimuli and which appear in roughly the same form in all normal members of the species. Although socio-biologists (e.g., Morris, 1977) have pointed out that humans also have behavioral patterns that seem to have an innate component, language acquisition perhaps being the prime example, a close examination indicates that the majority of these response patterns either are present only in infants (e.g., suckling response), are dependent on basic autonomic or anatomical characteristics (e.g., licking one's lips because of a reduction in salivation due to fear) or are simple behavioral reactions to stimuli (e.g., the consistency of facial expressions to sweet, sour, and bitter-tasting stimuli; cf. Steiner, 1979). In precisely those areas that one sees the most elaborate integrated species-specific behaviors in animals, human behavior shows convincing evidence of great varia-bility. This variability could perhaps be due to the invasion of verbal-symbolic mediation which can create significance in stimuli that have no necessary biological or evolutionary importance, although the direction of causality is of course an open one. For example, rodent sexual behavior is controlled by a precise sequence of stimuli which elicit particular responses given the appropriate level of hormones. If the correct stimuli are not present or if the particular response performed is prevented, then the whole behavior is disrupted. It is hard to think of an equivalent example with regard to human motivated behavior. Even the suckling response of infants is readily modifiable through operant conditioning (Crook, 1979). In particular, there is the complete arbitrariness of linguistic symbols. There is no species-typical language, just as every word in every language is an arbitrary symbol.

Actually, humans display many of the visceral components of species-specific behaviors. For example, the human autonomic re-sponse to fear-evoking stimuli bears many similarities to that found in animals; what is different is that there are few consistent stimulus conditions that are causally linked to the elicitation of these emotions. In other words, few stimuli act as "releasers" for particular overt behavior. Instead, there is more freedom in terms of the stimuli which arouse fear, or social behavior or anger and more variability in the overt responses that are actually exhibited to those stimuli. In the context of the present theory, the commonality of the visceral components of species-specific behaviors and human emotions will be seen to provide the basis for predicting similar effects of such behavior on the concurrent information processing capacities of the IPM.

The voluntary response class has necessarily received some mention in the discussion of the other two response classes, in order to define their properties more clearly. Voluntary responses are generally those responses which do not have a fixed relationship to particular environmental stimuli and is not meant necessarily to suggest conscious control.

Behavioral Characteristics

In terms of the behavioral identification of voluntary responses, we can apply criteria which are essentially the converse of those applied to species-specific responses. Responses which do not appear in experimentally naive organisms are obviously prime candidates for inclusion. Response patterns which do not occur immediately prior to consummatory acts will more likely fall into the category of voluntary responses. Presumably, those responses which are less bound to specific regulatory processes or stimulus releasers are the most likely to be under voluntary control (cf. Black & Young, 1972).

Although a precise definition of voluntary responses which cover all possibilities is not yet attainable, a useful generalization would define voluntary responses as those responses which are not stereotyped components of any response sequence performed by experimentally naive organisms. By stereotyped we mean response components which are performed in a consistent manner from occurrence to occurrence or which have a fixed position in an overall response sequence.

It is highly probable that voluntary responses developed from species-specific responses. As the species-specific behaviors developed evolutionarily and became less stimulus bound, behavioral patterns became more anticipatory and thus more extended in the pursuit of reinforcement. Although the initial responses in the sequence were necessarily less under the control of releasing stimuli, they were still closely connected with related consummatory responses.

Perhaps for this reason, the precise degree of voluntary control over a particular behavior can be difficult to ascertain in animals. Even with relatively clear examples of voluntary responses such as the pigeon's keypeck, the empirical evidence would suggest that the pigeon can more easily perform it to obtain positive reinforcement such as food than it can to avoid aversive reinforcement such as shock (Bolles, 1972b). It may well be that only humans and perhaps some primates can exhibit voluntary behavior in its pure form, i.e., responses which can be arbitrarily interchanged to achieve a similarly arbitrary reinforcer.

61

Since the other two response classes have been defined in part by their influence on the stimulus processing capacity of the IPM, it can be asked what influence voluntary responses have on the IPM. The evidence supports the idea that the performance of voluntary responses has a neutral effect on stimulus processing in contrast to species-specific responses which diminish stimulus processing and the OR which facilitates it. The performance of a voluntary response is more likely to come under the complete control of different reinforcement contingencies than are species-specific responses, which provides an indirect indication that stimulus processing is not curtailed during their performance. The effect on stimulus processing would provide an independent way of determining the response class to which a particular response belonged.

Although the existence of voluntary responses is beyond question in mammalian species, it is a matter of theoretical concern that the distinction between species-specific responses and voluntary responses can become rather tenuous on occasion. Given this ambiguity, it would be extremely valuable if some independent confirmation could be gained of the distinction between species-specific and instrumental behaviors.

Neurological Characteristics

One possible independent measure of voluntary behavior is the theta wave which is generated from a limbic system structure, the medial septum, and which can be recorded in another limbic structure, the hippocampus. A number of researchers have shown that in rats, rabbits, cats, and dogs, voluntary types of movements such as walking, running, turning around, climbing, and postural changes are all accompanied by certain kinds of hippocampal theta wave activity (Vanderwolf, 1971; Winson, 1972).

Two forms of the theta wave have been demonstrated: Type I theta is associated with movements that are not integral components of species-specific behavior (such as locomotion, or sniffing). It has a frequency range of 6.5 to 12Hz and is resistant to the administration of atropine. Type II theta is associated with alert immobility (ORs) to stimuli in various sensory modalities. It has a frequency range of 4 to 9 Hz and is sensitive (i.e., blocked) by atropine (Komisaruk, 1977; Vanderwolf et al., 1975; Winson, 1972).

Bland et al. (1983) have shown that the discharge rates of theta cells in the hippocampus are significantly higher during Type I behaviors compared with Type II behaviors even when theta frequencies are identical (over the part of the range that overlaps), suggesting that discharge rates code the speed of initiation of movement. It has been noted that there is a relation between the extent of the movements performed and the amplitude of the corresponding theta wave activity (Vanderwolf, 1971). However, individual theta cells in the hippocampus have been shown to discharge during both Type I and Type II behaviors (Sinclair et al., 1982).

When rats remain motionless, the theta pattern is much reduced; often an irregular wave pattern is displayed. This irregular wave activity can also be seen during certain behaviors of rats which involve movement; however, the nature of these behaviors seems very different from those kinds of voluntary responses that are correlated with theta waves. They would appear to fall under the category of species-specific responses as defined previously. Some of the motor patterns correlated with hippocampal irregular waves were chewing, licking, salivation, urination, face washing, scratching, pelvic thrusting and ejaculation, vocalization, etc. (e.g., Whishaw & Vanderwolf, 1971).

Even when the species-specific behaviors correlated with irregular wave activity are used in a more or less voluntary fashion, the theta wave still does not appear. For example, Black and Young (1972) trained rats to drink water either to avoid shock or to obtain food. In neither case was the drinking response accompanied by hippocampal theta waves. This would indicate that it is the response itself and not the use to which it is put that determines whether theta waves will be produced.

These findings are important to the present discussion because they suggest that the nervous systems of at least some species do make a functional distinction between responses that fall into the categories defined here. Theta activity can be demonstrated in monkeys and humans as well; however, it is much more difficult to record in these species and seems to occur in briefer bouts (Brazier, 1972; Crowne & Radcliffe, 1975). It is unclear at the present time how strictly linked this theta activity is to motoric responses.

It should be noted that simply because a species does not display theta with all voluntary responses it cannot be assumed that no functional distinction exists between species-specific and voluntary responses. The theta wave in the rat may simply provide a particularly clear indication of functional differentiation which exists in other species without such a definite theta correlation with voluntary responses. An analogy might be with Aplysia, which provides a particularly good preparation for studying neuronal activity because of the large size of its neurons. However, the action of its neurons is highly similar to that found in less easily studied species.

# Chapter 5
## Motivational Processes

Now that we have presented the general stimulus analyzing and response factors of the present theory, it is necessary to examine two fundamental motivational mechanisms which interact with the IPM in determining the form and direction of behavior. These motivational processes will, of course, have particular significance for the expression of species-specific behaviors. However, they also have a direct impact on the form of learned behaviors and stimulus analysis.

MOOD STATES

Definitions

A mood state is defined as the product of the effects of a neurotransmitter/hormone on specific brain areas combined with the neural processing of particular reinforcing stimuli. The mood state is a relatively sustained response which provides the support for an integrated series of species-specific behaviors to take place over time.

Evolutionarily speaking, a major problem for organismic survival has been the development of the capacity not only to make appropriate responses to environmental and internal events, but to anticipate them as well. A certain level of adaptiveness certainly can be said to exist in organisms low on the phylogenetic scale, but the adaptiveness generally takes the form of reflexes or taxes to events which have already occurred. For example, an insect such as the isopill will increase its degree of activity when light falls upon it until its motion takes it to a dark area, whereupon it will stop. However, it doesn't travel in a directed manner to the dark spot (Denny & Ratner, 1970). Thus, two essential characteristics of reflexive behavior are its lack of anticipation of events and its lack of variation once the reflex is initiated (cf. Teitelbaum, 1977).

As we move up the phylogenetic scale, some of the greatest advances have been in precisely these two areas. Mammalian behavior, in particular, is characterized to a great extent by its anticipatory and situation-specific nature. Rather than waiting for an event to occur, mammals engage in complex behaviors prior to the occurrence of the reinforcer, either to avoid or obtain it. Furthermore, the response to stimuli is not invariant but instead is greatly dependent on the context in which the event occurs. For example, a rat will ordinarily flee a larger animal but if it is cornered, it will turn and fight. A cat stalking a rat engages in a complex series of responses which can extend over an appreciable period of time. The components which comprise the stalking behavior are highly dependent on the particular events which occur during this time in the environment (e.g., the rat's movements, other animals in the area, the physical topography, etc.).

The internal environment can also function to initiate species-specific responses in anticipation of physiological needs. For example, it would be counterproductive to have an organism seek water only when its tissues were in an actual state of water deficiency. At this point, the physical strength of the organism would be diminished. It would be far better for internal stimuli which precede such a state (e.g., dry mouth) to have the capacity to initiate water-seeking behavior.

We are faced with two problems that must be solved in order to create the complex and variable pattern of species-specific behaviors connected with the attainment of important reinforcing objectives. First, what mechanism can connect the exteroceptive stimulus occurring in the environment with the performance of particular species-specific response patterns? Second, how is the entire integrated pattern of responses comprising the species-specific behavior performed by the organism in the absence of specific learning of the response requirements?

Although the precise mechanism in molecular terms are still unclear, the available evidence provides a relatively consistent picture of the overall way in which these objectives are achieved. Particular reinforcing stimuli, when they are processed through the IPM, activate neurons in neurochemically distinct pathways. The activation of these pathways results in the release of appropriate hormones and also activates the initial response of the species-specific behavioral pattern. It is the performance of the initial response which then makes the succeeding response more probable, if inhibiting factors are not present. Conversely, the performance of these components tends to inhibit competing responses and make them less probable. In other words, only events of potentially high significance can interrupt the initiated response (cf. Gallistel, 1980; Mogenson & Phillips, 1976).

Neurotransmitter Systems

It has long been known that the neurons, constituting the essential working structure of the brain, affect and interact with each other through the release of chemical substances or neurotransmitters across the small space or synapse which exists between the axon of one neuron and the receptor dendrites of contiguous neurons (e.g., Eccles, 1973). The absolute identification of the particular neurotransmitter a neuron releases has been a difficult experimental problem in the brain because of the density of the neurons. However, converging evidence and logical inference from the results of psychopharmacological studies permit a number of relatively firm conclusions that are relevant to the present discussion.
First of all, it seems almost a certainty that individual neurons release only one type of neurotransmitter (Dale's Principle). Secondly, there is strong evidence supporting the idea that there are at least several, and possibly more, neurotransmitters that function in the brains of animals and humans. The more likely candidates are acetylcholine (ACH), dopamine (DA) and norephinephrine (NE) (catecholamines), and serotonin (5HT) (Warburton, 1975).
As we would expect, neurotransmitters have excitatory and inhibitory effects on receptor neurons. It is quite possible that individual neurotransmitters exert both excitatory and inhibitory influences depending on the neural region and the type of neurons which are being affected. For example, NE is an agonist (facilitator) at its own receptors but acts as an antagonist for ACH receptors (Kruk & Pycock, 1983).
From these two assumptions, we can draw the conclusion that one way the brain can prevent excitation or inhibition of one neuron from spreading to adjacent neurons is by giving them a different chemical coding or receptiveness. This chemical specificity would enable the neuron to be insensitive to inappropriate excitation and sensitive to appropriate excitation. Thus, we could have parallel neuronal systems existing in very close proximity without any unwanted interaction between the two. This would allow some order to emerge from the potential chaos of billions of neurons firing in close proximity to each other.
In our discussion, we concentrate on the neurotransmitters just mentioned, because they do seem to have a critical role in many

instinctive and homeostatic behaviors. However, it should be noted that the total percentage of synapses involving ACH, DA, NE, and 5HT is well below half of all brain synapses. Thus, there must be at least several and possibly more additional neurotransmitters (possibly glycine, taurine, and aminobutyric acid) (see Fig. 5-1).

ACH. ACH is located in several central pathways in the brain: (a) a diffuse, ascending system, originating in the mesencephalic reticular formation and reaching the thalamus and cerebral cortex associated with arousal, (b) a diffuse system between the septum and other limbic and neocortical structures, and (c) a diffuse intracortical system. In addition, there are cholinergic synapses in the caudate nucleus, amygdala, and hypothalamus which appear to be directly involved in the expression of species-specific behaviors such as sexual activity. For example, in vitro experiments have shown that the release of luteinizing hormone and follicular stimulating hormone from anterior pituitary tissue is dependent on the interaction of ACH and the hypothalamus (Kamberi, 1973). These hormones play a key role in the occurrence of sexual behavior in birds and mammals.

Cholinergic agonists injected into the hypothalamus or amygdala generally facilitate or induce predatory biting attacks or threat behavior while cholinergic antagonists such as atropine suppress these behaviors (Cooper et al., 1982). Stimulation of the neural structures comprising these chemical pathways can be accomplished by electrical current as well. Lateral hypothalamic stimulation in cats can evoke rat stalking and killing behavior (Egger & Flynn, 1963).

A key question is whether the species-specific behaviors elicited by stimulation of subcortical sites bear the same characteristics as when they are evoked under normal circumstances. Electrically induced eating has the same properties as normal eating, such as sensitivity to bitter (Terren & Miller, 1964) and sweet tastes (Chisholm & Trowill, 1972). Wise and Albin (1973) showed that feeding induced by electrical stimulation of the brain (ESB) reflected preferences established through learning.

The predatory behavior of the cat shows a similar correspondence in its normal and ESB elicited forms. McDonnell and Flynn (1966) introduced an unreachable mouse into view of cats. The presence of the mouse caused a reflex turning of the head of the cat to the side of a muzzle touch while a touch near the lips evoked biting (i.e., components of the stalking and biting behaviors). In contrast, when stalking behavior has not been activated a touch to the muzzle elicits head turning away from the direction of the touch. The same pattern of reflexes was seen when predatory attack was induced by ESB. This example also shows how the induction of a particular motivational state activates certain reflexes and responses while inhibiting incompatible responses.

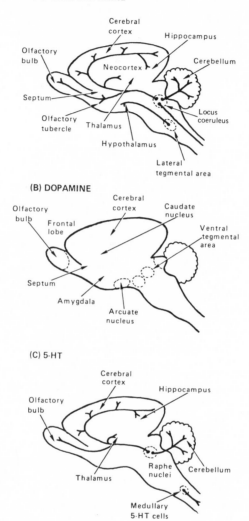

(A) NOREPINEPHRINE

Cerebral
cortex
Hippocampus

Olfactory
bulb
Cerebellum

Neocortex

Septum

Olfactory
tubercle    Thalamus

Locus
coeruleus

Hypothalamus

Lateral
tegmental area

(B) DOPAMINE

Cerebral
cortex    Caudate
nucleus

Olfactory
bulb
Frontal
lobe

Ventral
tegmental
area

Septum

Amygdala

Arcuate
nucleus

(C) 5-HT

Cerebral
cortex
Hippocampus

Olfactory
bulb

Raphe
nuclei    Cerebellum

Thalamus

Medullary
5-HT cells

**Fig. 5-1 . Neurotransmitter Systems .** Some of the neural pathways containing norepinephrine, dopamine, and 5-HT. From Kuffler, Nicholls, and Martin, From neuron
to brain , 1984. Copyright Sinauer Associates 1984. Reprinted by permission.

Catecholamines and Serotonin. The catecholamines (NE and DA) are contained in large part in pathways originating in the brainstem. The dorsal NA bundle projects from the locus coeruleus to the thalamus, dorsal hypothalamus, hippocampus, and neocortex. The ventral NA bundle arises from cells in the medulla and pons and projects to the hypothalamus and limbic system. Major DA pathways include (a) the nigro-neostriatal pathway which originates in the substantia nigra and projects to the caudate nucleus, (b) the meso-limbic system originating close by the nigro-neostriatal pathway and projecting to the amygdala, frontal and cingulate cortex, and (c) the tubero-infundibular system originating in the arcuate nucleus of the hypothalamus and terminating in the median eminence.

On a general level, the catecholamines appear to be involved in the response to stress, the sleep-wake cycle and the response to reinforcers. Increased noradrenaline activity is associated with the occurrence of unexpected events. DA agonists increase the rate of responding for rewards while DA antagonists decrease it. Higher concentrations of NE facilitate affective aggression (fighting), but inhibit predatory aggression which is usually accompanied by relatively low arousal (Reis, 1974).

It should be emphasized at this point that a particular behavior is undoubtedly influenced by the effects of more than one transmitter or hormone. For example, DA seems of fundamental importance to voluntary locomotor behavior, but NE is a significant modulatory influence. In fact, it is likely that many neuromodulators are present in the brain which are not neurotransmitters (cf. Sabelli et al., 1974). One possible modulator is phenylethylamine (PEA), a neuroamine which is present in significant concentrations in the brain. It acts as a behavioral stimulant and, interestingly, urinary levels of PEA are reduced in depressive patients and elevated in manics. Thus, a multiplicity of modulators may be exerting their influence at synaptic receptors along with the actual neurotransmitter.

Serotonin (5HT) is distributed diffusely in pathways originating in the brainstem such as the midline raphe nuclei in the pons which innervate the hypothalamus, thalamus, and the limbic system. Serotonin is also concentrated in the pineal gland which produces enzymes under the control of external factors such as the day-night cycle. Serotonin seems to exert an inhibitory influence in many cases, perhaps opposing the effect of cortical NE. For example, injections of 5HT into the anterior hypothalamus of monkeys produce hyperthermia while NE injections into the same site produce hypothermia. Similarly, 5HT inhibits affective aggression while NE facilitates it (Reis, 1974).

Although the varied effects of the neurotransmitters and modulators are complex, there may be more systematicity than is apparent on a superficial basis. It must always be remembered that behavior occurs as an integrated unit, not as disconnected components. As such, a particular behavioral pattern will always involve the simultaneous activation of certain visceral and motor responses and the inhibition of others. For example, activation of the sympathetic component of the autonomic nervous system by noradrenaline results in increases in heart muscle contraction but decreases in intestinal contractions. Activation of the parasympathetic component by ACH has the opposite effect. Thus, evaluation of the influence of neurotransmitters, modulators, and hormones must not be based on their effect on isolated responses. Instead, the affected response must be evaluated in the context of the species-specific behaviors in which it plays a role.

Neuroendocrine Systems. It should be noted that hormones, produced in certain endocrine cells or glands, have some similarities with neurotransmitters in that they can interact with neuronal receptors and affect their reactivity. For example, estrogens seem to affect sensory thresholds for hearing, smell, and taste (Reinis & Goldman, 1982). The hypothalamo-pituitary system is the most prominent site of interaction between neural and endocrine systems involved in species-specific behaviors. The hypothalamus is a neural structure which has typical neuronal functions but also possesses secretory hormonal functions, while the pituitary gland is often termed the master gland since it releases hormones into the bloodstream which affect the release of other hormones. Hypothalamic and pituitary peptides are common to both the hypothalamus and the anterior or glandular region of the pituitary. It has been shown that the anterior pituitary must have direct blood flow from the hypothalamus in order to function.

Secretory hypothalamic neurons produce specific releasing hormones (oxytocin and vasopressin) which are stored and released in the posterior or neural portion of the pituitary. These and other hormonal substances are found in several other proximal structures (e.g., the mammillary bodies, infundibulum) which affect the secretion of six hormones from the anterior pituitary: (1) ACTH which controls the adrenal stress response, (2) growth hormone, (3) thyroid stimulating hormone, (4) follicle stimulating hormone, (5) luteinizing hormone, and (6) prolactin (Reinis & Goldman, 1982; Weiner & Ganong, 1978).

The catecholamines and serotonin are important to hypothalamic secretory function. The DA concentrations in the median eminence, an area of the hypothalamus with close humoral connections with the anterior pituitary, are among the highest in the brain. DA is a known inhibitor of prolactin secretion. Three major noradrenergic pathways are directly involved in the control of hypothalamic secretory functions. Serotonergic fibers originating in the raphe nuclei regulate the secretion of growth hormones.

70

At this point, it is useful to examine the processes of mood states in the context of a few specific examples which show the interrelationship of environmental stimulation and induction of motivational states underlying species-specific behaviors. The first example is the adrenal stress response, regulated by the release of ACTH from the hypothalamo-pituitary axis. Adrenal function is characterized by two types of responses: circadian fluctuation of hormonal levels and the ACTH produced response to stressful events. ACTH affects the metabolism of serotonin and increases turnover rates of brain DA and NE (cf. Hennesy & Levine, 1979).

Injection of ACTH and its related peptide fragments into the cerebral ventricles can elicit exaggerated grooming in rats which is similar to normal grooming in the sequence of actions characterizing the grooming response (Dunn et al., 1976). ACTH facilitates visual memory in human males but auditory and verbal memories in females, suggesting that ACTH emphasizes dominant responses at the expense of subordinate responses for the individual. Visual memory in females has been found to be impaired by ACTH administration (Urith et al., 1978).

Environmental conditions in turn can affect ACTH response. Denying or restricting access to positive reinforcers produces an increase in corticosterone levels (Smotherman et al., 1977) particularly when there is a mismatch between response performance and the absence of the expected reinforcing event (Davis et al., 1976). Interestingly, the performance of stereotypical (species-specific) behaviors often has an inhibitory effect on ACTH secretion. Conner et al. (1971) reported that when rats were shocked in pairs, permitting shock-induced stereotypical fighting, they exhibited reduced ACTH secretion compared to individually shocked rats.

Another example of the interaction between environmental stimuli and neurochemical processes is the control of maternal and nesting behavior in the rat. The presence of pups stimulates dams (and eventually even virgin females) to release various hormones such as prolactin which are intimately involved with the expression of maternal behavior, particularly in the second week after parturition (Simpson et al., 1973). Prolactin stimulates the secretion of ovarian and adrenal steroids in dams mediating the normal cycle of nesting times. If these steroids are suppressed at parturition, the normal decline in maternal nesting over time is also suppressed i.e., their gradual decline as the pups grow older. Prolactin increases the dam's internal temperature. This increase in metabolic activity and internal temperature supports milk production and also leads to initiation of the nest bout.

The general question of exteroceptive control over motivated behaviors is more closely examined in Chapter 11. However, a topic that is best treated at this time because of its importance to the

71

general functioning of mood states is that of opponent processes, or the interaction between different species-specific behaviors and different chemical pathways.

## OPPONENT PROCESSES

We have seen that the performance of particular species-specific behaviors inhibits the performance of competing responses. More generally, it can be argued that such inhibition of competing responses occurs because of a general inhibition of the motivational state which controls the expression of those responses; e.g., a fearful organism is unlikely to feel hungry at the same time. Many experimental studies have in fact revealed an interaction in the performance of various species-specific behaviors. Hess (1957) showed that stimulation of subcortical sites in the rooster which produced apathy of response also produced an aftereffect of relatively "euphoric" behavior in which the rooster would crow and exhibit a lively interest in its surroundings. Gallistel (1980) cites a study by Beagley in which medial forebrain bundle stimulation that produced eating, drinking, or locomotion would also produce grooming as an aftereffect. The aftereffect is seen up to a few minutes after the stimulation has stopped. Stimulation of the septal region in humans produces immediate cessation of pain and a general euphoric feeling (cf. Valenstein, 1973). Many behavioral examples can be found in the ethological literature where they are termed displacement activities. These typically occur when a species-specific response sequence is interrupted, after which the organism will display irrelevant components of other species-specific behaviors.

### Definitions

A good way of thinking about opponent processes is to view them as one manifestation of homeostatic processes designed to keep an organism in physiological equilibrium. An organism has to engage in a variety of different behaviors in order to survive, as well as resting those structures and organs that have become fatigued through use. It should be noted that opponent processes are evident in phenomena other than motivation, for example, in color perception. Viewing a pure color for an extended period of time will induce a complementary colored afterimage (cf. Hurvich & Jameson, 1974). This finding suggests that the extended use of a particular set of visual neurons results in their fatigue and permits the dominance of visual neurons which have not been in use (i.e., complementary color sensitive neurons). However, at this

72

point, it is uncertain whether the opponent processes involved in perception are identical to those in motivated behavior.

At the outset, the relationship between mood states and opponent processes should be clearly understood. Mood states are the neurological substrates of species-specific behaviors. Opponent processes are the forms of the interactions between different mood states. As might be expected, these interactions are quite complex and reflect both the ecological requirements imposed on the organism and its physiological characteristics. For example, it is well known that thirst tends to inhibit hunger or conversely that eating tends to facilitate drinking. These interactions can be seen to proceed from obvious physiological bases. Some mood states tend to suppress or inhibit each other as we saw previously while others complement or facilitate each other. In this regard, it should be emphasized that the term opponent processes does not imply a specific inhibitory interrelation between different mood states but is meant to refer to all the possible forms of mood state interaction.

Opponent process theories have been developed by a number of researchers who postulate that a reinforcer initiates a primary affect (mood state) "A" which is correlated with the intensity of the reinforcer. The initiation of the "A" process in turn arouses an opponent process (mood state) "B", whose strength is directly related to that of the "A" process and whose effect is opposite to the "A" state (cf. Schull, 1979; Solomon, 1980). It has been argued that opponent processes serve to disengage an organism from a particular motivational sequence, particularly during those times when the probability of satisfying the dominant mood state "A" is low (e.g., Staddon, 1975).

Solomon and Corbit (1974) and Solomon (1980) hypothesize that the time course of the "A" state is coincident with the presentation of the reinforcing stimulus and dissipates very soon after its removal. However, the "B" state is assumed to have a more gradual time course, both with respect to recruitment and decay. In addition, there is evidence that the strength of the "B" process is inversely related to the interstimulus interval (e.g., Starr, 1978). In other words, the longer the interval between presentations of the reinforcing stimulus (inducing the "A" state), the weaker the opposing "B" state.

Solomon and Corbit noted that repeated presentation of the reinforcer leads to diminution of the organism's response to it (i.e., a reduction in the "A" state) but also a concomitant increase in the strength of the "B" state or aftereffects. This phenomenon reflects the homeostatic impulse to reduce affective disturbance. The physiological response of tolerance to addictive drugs is a common example of this putative process.

Schull (1979) has extended the idea of opponent processes to conditioned stimuli (CS) as well as the US. By pairing a CS with a

73

US ("A" state) the CS elicits a CR associated with the US mood state but also induces the associated opponent processes. Conversely, when a CS is paired with the non-US ("B" state) it gains the capacity to inhibit the "A" state (cf. Siegel, 1977).

Thus, the introduction of a US causes an affective disturbance whose strength is directly related to the strength of the US. The organismic response to affective disturbance is homeostatic, an attempt to reduce the disturbance by compensatory metabolic and behavioral processes. By association, the CS can elicit the responses and affective characteristics of the "A" state, but in so doing it provokes the appearance of (conditioned) opponent processes (see Fig. 5-2).

The stronger the "A" state, the greater the strength of the opponent processes needed to restore affective equilibrium. The sudden removal of the stimuli evoking an intense "A" state permits the unimpeded expression of the similarly intense "B" state causing an affective disturbance opposite in sign to that originally produced. Under normal circumstances, the induced "A" state is much more moderate in its intensity and therefore its removal results in an unopposed "B" state which is similarly moderate in intensity. It is argued that in these situations opponent processes subserve the normal change in motivational states and associated behaviors over time.

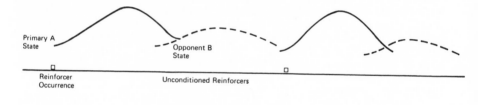

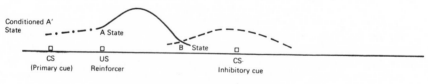

**Fig. 5-2 . Mood States .** The occurrence of unconditioned or conditioned reinforcers induces an associated mood state (A) in the organism. The activation of the A state leads to the activation of opponent (B) states which are in reciprocal interaction with it. All mood states subserve species-specific responding. The interactive organization between mood states maintains homeostatic and behavioral balance.

74

It should be noted that these theories have viewed opponent processes in the narrow sense of mood states directly inhibiting each other. In the current view, this restriction is misleading since it obscures the more comprehensive nature of mood state interactions which insure that the organism engages in its complete repertoire of behaviors over time (cf. adjunctive behaviors: Chapter 10).

## Affective Interactions

There is evidence that some opponent processes are opposite in their affective quality to the hedonic state associated with the "A" state. For example, LaBarbera and Caul (1976) showed that rats were less likely to suppress drinking when a CS for shock was presented if the CS had been preceded by another CS for shock. This finding suggests that the first CS induced an aversive "A" state which was followed by a hedonically positive aftereffect which interacted with the succeeding aversive "A" state. Thus, the overall aversiveness of the second CS was reduced.

Ross and Randich (1984) found that rats exposed to electric shock showed significantly longer latencies to respond to subsequent thermal stimulation than non-shocked controls. The strength of the analgesic aftereffect was systematically related to the shock intensity with stronger shocks producing a greater analgesic effect (cf. Maier et al., 1983; Fanselow, 1984). Domjan et al. (1980) studied the aftereffects of lithium-conditioned stimuli on drinking behavior. Lithium chloride typically suppresses drinking and cues paired with lithium treatment exhibit the same effect. However, when drinking behavior was evaluated after a delay (5 or 25 min) from the presentation of the lithium-conditioned cues, drinking levels were enhanced.

The development of tolerance to drugs seems a classic example of opponent processes. Siegel (1977) has argued that tolerance reflects classical conditioning of opponent processes under the control of the cues that accompany drug administration. The associative cues that accompany the administration of drugs such as morphine and pentobarbital exert control over the appearance of tolerance to these drugs (Cappell et al., 1981). In addition, morphine tolerance is acquired more quickly when distinctive cues are paired with its delivery (Tiffany et al., 1983). However, there have been a number of reports of failure to obtain compensatory opponent responses to morphine analgesia from the morphine-paired cues when presented alone (e.g., Sherman, 1979). In addition, in nondistinctive environments morphine tolerance is exhibited, although it displays somewhat different parametric characteristics (Kesner & Cook, 1983).

Poulos and Hinson (1984) suggest that a possible explanation for these effects is that tolerance involves both homeostatic regulation and classical conditioning. For example, they found that tolerance to scopolamine-induced adipsia in rats depended on their exposure to water while under the influence of scopolamine. Rats not exposed to water during this period did not develop tolerance. Thus, the authors argued that tolerance to a drug is dependent not on its homeostatic presence per se but rather on its ability to induce a homeostatic disturbance. Tolerance therefore requires some initial affective disturbance. However, once tolerance is induced, then the associated cues can evoke the opponent process.

It should be emphasized that the present theory does not assume that the opponent process is a qualitatively different phenomenon from the "A" state. Both the "A" and "B" states are viewed as mood states that are in reciprocal interaction with each other. The initiation of one mood state sets up a physiological and neurological chain of events which results in the induction of reciprocal mood states. It should further be noted that the same mood state can function as either an "A" or "B" state. In both contexts, it is not simply an internal affective state but also has behavioral implications, i.e., the species-specific behaviors that are a function of the mood state.

## SUMMARY

At this point, the most general properties of the IPM have been introduced and discussed along with the basic response and motivational mechanisms with which it interacts. Now we are ready to proceed with an examination of how these basic variables interact with more specific variables to produce observed behavior in particular situations.

It has been proposed that all mammals, including humans, possess a common IPM (information processing mechanism). The IPM processes and encodes a representation of the environment which can contain precise and detailed information about exteroceptive events. The precise encoding of the environment takes place relatively automatically in both animals and humans, although greater processing effort will result in even more detailed stimulus encodings than occur normally. The encoded representation preserves some of the essential stimulus characteristics of the exteroceptive stimulus in analogical form. The nature of these encoded characteristics is determined by the particular perceptual operations which were performed on the stimulus as it was being processed.

Exteroceptive information is analyzed through a match-mismatch process in which the processed stimuli are compared with internal representations. When the overlap between the attributes of both representations achieves a criterion value a match occurs. The nature of the perceptual capacities of particular sensory modalities will determine the way in which the match-mismatch process operates the comparison of representations (e.g., parallel or sequential processing).

The IPM interacts with three response classes in the expression of behavior, namely, the OR, species-specific responses, and voluntary responses. Each of these response classes involves responses with both motoric and visceral components. The response classes are best differentiated in a functional sense by their differing effects on the stimulus analysis capacities of the IPM. The OR is a response which occurs as the result of a mismatch between an internal representation and the stimulus environment and which functions to facilitate the processing of information. It is an essential prerequisite for associative learning to occur; however, once learning takes place it is no longer exhibited. The strength of the OR is inversely related to the probability of an event in a given situation--the less probable the event, the stronger the OR.

Species-specific responses are behaviors that are controlled by a particular set of stimuli in the absence of specific learning. They are common either to all normal members of a species or to all species members of the same sex. The performance of species-specific responses results in a decreased capacity for stimulus analysis on the part of the IPM, due to inhibition of the OR.

Voluntary responses are those responses which have no fixed or necessary relationship with particular exteroceptive stimuli. This response class is composed of all learned responses not exhibited by naive organisms as well as a small class of relatively unlearned motoric behaviors such as locomotion which are not terminal components of species-specific behavioral sequences. These responses are neutral in their effect on stimulus analysis.

The performance of species-specific responses is directly controlled by the action of two fundamental motivational mechanisms, the mood state and opponent processes. A mood state is the product of the effects of a neurotransmitter on specific brain areas combined with the neural processing of a particular reinforcing stimulus. It is a relatively sustained response which provides the support for an integrated series of behaviors to take place over time. Opponent processes operate to disengage the organism from the influence of a particular mood state during those times when the probability of goal attainment is low as well as preserving homeostatic balance. This is accomplished by facilitation of competing mood states which subserve different species-specific behaviors.

77

Although these processes are common to all mammals, including humans, the latter species displays additional behavioral properties because of the presence of rule-based behaviors in addition to match-mismatch processes. Rule-based behaviors interact with all the processes mentioned; however, the evocation of the OR is particularly affected in this way. The OR in humans can be evoked by the same conditions as with animals but it can also be evoked through verbal-symbolic mediation. This significantly expands the possibilities for associative learning in humans as a result.

One other noteworthy difference in human behavior relative to other mammals is the change in the nature of species-specific responses. Although the visceral components of such responses are similar in nature between humans and animals, in humans they are dissociated from specific motoric responses and are not under the control of releasers except in a few cases.

It should be re-emphasized that the eight factors discussed are assumed to be fundamental principles of mammalian and, to a large extent, vertebrate behavior. Their influence should extend to virtually all behavioral phenomena in which they could logically be expected to operate and their interactions should determine much of the form and direction of behaviors. Obviously, they are not an exhaustive list of all the basic processes of learning and motivation and additional principles are proposed. Nevertheless, these factors are found to permeate the discussion of specific behavioral and cognitive phenomena presented in the following chapters.

78

# Section III
# The Behavioral Analysis Division of the IPM

One of the primary aims of the present section is to examine the reasons why some stimuli lead to the habituation of responding while others lead to motivated behavior. Match-mismatch theory assumes that in the mammalian brain there are two major divisions devoted to stimulus analysis. The first consists of sensory-perceptual analysis which is handled by the major sensory systems. The second division consists of neural structures, i.e., the fronto-reticular system and intermediary structures, devoted to the categorization of stimuli based on their behavioral implications. This does not involve perceptual analysis per se. Match-mismatch theory assumes that this latter division is handled by two distinct but interrelated systems which are termed the reinforcer system and the habituative system. It should also be noted that the reinforcer and habituative systems do not directly subserve response output. The functions that they do control are our first order of business. The reader is asked to reserve judgment on the plausibility of the hypothesized reinforcer and habituative systems at least until the entire section is read. It is recognized that since these are hypothetical constructs relating to the internal characteristics of the organism, much evidence needs to be amassed in support of their existence.

Before examining the hypothesized properties of these systems individually, it is necessary to examine the general relationship existing between the sensory-perceptual division and the behavioral analysis division of the IPM. Exteroceptive stimuli first are processed through the initial sensory receptors and their corresponding registers (e.g., the retina-iconic register) which provide

79

the initial transformation and filtering of the sensory information. After passing through the appropriate sensory registers, the processing of the stimuli is less easy to chart on an a priori basis because of the changes that can occur through experience. However, the general factors of precision and analogic encoding are assumed to hold true despite this variability.

From this assumption, we can anticipate that stimuli will differ in the kind and amount of analysis which is needed in order to identify or recognize them perceptually, both as a function of their inherent attributes and the organism's prior experience. Once the perceptual identification of a novel stimulus or recognition of a previously presented stimulus has been accomplished, this information is relayed to the division of the IPM concerned with behavioral analysis. It should be emphasized that the perceptual information can be relayed from different points in the sensory systems corresponding to the kinds of analyses performed.

The behavioral analysis division receives the information relayed from the sensory-perceptual division and determines its behavioral relevance. It fosters the connection of motivationally significant stimuli with appropriate organismic responses and inhibits organismic response to non-significant stimuli. This process of analyzing the behavioral implications of stimuli can have feedback influences on the operation of the sensory-perceptual division by affecting the degree and kind of sensory analysis performed on subsequent stimulus events. The OR is the mechanism through which the behavioral analysis division exerts its influence in this respect. This feedback process has important implications for the memorial characteristics of incoming stimulus information. Thus, the two main divisions of the IPM should not be viewed as a linear system because of the constant reciprocal interactions which occur between them.

# Chapter 6
# The Reinforcer and Habituative Systems: Theory and Definitions

Although in previous sections we showed how the IPM could process the stimulus environment in rather precise detail, no distinctions were made in terms of the relative significance of various stimuli. Now we are faced with situations where it is clear that some stimuli have a qualitatively different effect on the organism than do other stimuli, i.e., reinforcing versus non-reinforcing stimuli. The simplest solution to this in terms of the structure of the IPM would be a component which processed reinforcers and one which processed non-reinforcers. Let's examine the properties of the reinforcer system first.

The Reinforcer Representation

The reinforcer system processes reinforcing stimuli and controls the induction of appropriate mood states which subserve species-specific responding. How are reinforcing stimuli distinguished from non-reinforcers and the connection made with the response systems controlling species-specific responses? In more primitive organisms, the reinforcing stimulus is completely innate in that its first presentation will evoke the appropriate species-specific behaviors in fully developed form. In terms of the present theory, the reinforcers in these cases are stimuli which have at least some critical dimensions present in a neural model prior to the organism's exposure to them. The match-mismatch process can be applied in straightforward fashion in such cases. The reinforcing stimulus is compared to an already present stimulus model. If the two match in behaviorally relevant variables, then the appropriate response patterns are initiated. Otherwise, they are not.

Mammalian species seem to follow a more complicated procedure with regard to encoding neural models of reinforcers for later recognition. For example, Melzack and Scott (1957) raised Scottish terrier puppies in restricted environments and tested their reaction to shock, burns, and pinpricks when mature. In general, the restricted environment dogs required many shocks to avoid the shock apparatus and ran aimlessly around the test area when shocked. Their reaction to the other painful stimuli was similar; the most noticeable aspect was that they seemed to show little fear and would not move away from the source of the painful stimuli unlike normal dogs.

Although most mammalian and avian species would seem to be born with few, if any, preset neural models of specific reinforcers, the identification of reinforcers is quickly learned, suggesting genetic prepotency. Preferences seem to be established quickly and are firmly based on a few initial experiences. For example, weanling rats prefer to eat an unpalatable diet that the adults have been trained to eat rather than a palatable diet which the adults have learned to avoid (Burghardt, 1967; Galef & Clark, 1972). Research by Hogan (1975, 1977) on the development of food recognition in chicks indicates that the pecking response is controlled by rather specific cues, e.g., small high contrast objects, but apparently is related to a motivational system (hunger) only through experience. The consequences of pecking food versus sand had an effect on the chicks' pecking behavior only when specific pecking experience previously had been allowed.

It is useful to remember that we are almost never training or testing a totally naive organism. By the time an organism is old enough to test in typical learning studies it has had sufficient experience to be able to categorize and recognize reinforcers successfully. When the reinforcer does occur, the IPM should encode it in much the same way that it does other stimuli; in other words a precise internal representation is constructed within the perceptual limits of the organism.

Since stimuli which evoke ORs or URs are processed through the IPM, its three general stimulus analyzing processes must exert their effect on stimuli processed through the reinforcer system. The precision and analogical encoding processes largely take place in the sensory-perceptual division prior to the relay of the processed information to the reinforcer system. The match-mismatch comparison processes, however, are more evenly divided between the sensory-perceptual division and the behavioral analysis division.

82

Phylogenetic Considerations. At this point we have to examine the
way these general processes come into play in the context of
reinforced learning, but to do this requires some consideration of
the phylogenetic changes which are embedded in the mammalian central
nervous system. It is obvious that as we go up the phylogenetic
scale, the information processing capacities of organisms show
variety and expansion. This is not to say that there is a linear
relationship between phylogenetic level and information processing
capacity; however, we do see the addition of new neural structures
and the functional development of phylogenetically older structures.

Since the process of evolution doesn't encourage the scrapping
of the older brain and the redesign of a new brain each time a
functional advance is made, the brains of phylogenetically more
recent species such as mammals have new neural structures overlaid
on older structures. Thus, cortical areas extend and control the
functioning of older subcortical structures rather than replacing
them. Since learning (conditioning) can be demonstrated in simple
organisms or preparations (e.g., the cockroach or the spinal cord)
the existence of neural structures with varied lineages within the
individual brain can have important implications.

It is argued that conditioning mechanisms have been modified
in the course of phylogenetic development and that separable
processes exist at different levels of the brain, particularly in
avian and mammalian species. The distinguishing feature between
these conditioning processes is the potentiation of organismic
response to reinforcing stimuli by upper level structures of the
reinforcer system with respect to lower level structures (cf.
Fig. 6-1).

The mechanisms underlying associative learning in lower level
structures involved changes in synaptic and cellular responsiveness
in individual or groups of neurons through the mechanism of the
early components of the OR. These neuronal changes are based upon
stimulus repetition and develop gradually. In addition the unconditioned response to the reinforcer controlled at this level has
limited affect as indexed by the sustainment of visceral and neurochemical response components.

In contrast, the potentiation of the response to reinforcers
by upper level structures of the reinforcer system affects both the
late EEG component of the OR and the UR and thus influences all
levels of stimulus processing as well as response output. The potentiation involves both the intensity and duration of these responses
and produces several important effects. First, the increased
strength of the OR to reinforcing stimuli leads to a greater degree
of stimulus processing in the sensory-perceptual division of the
IPM. Second, there is an enhancement of the affective response to
the reinforcer, i.e., the visceral and neurochemical components of

83

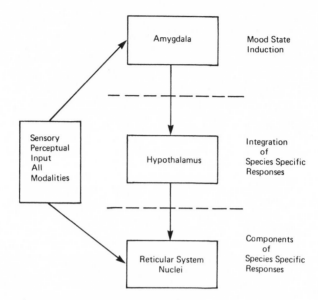

**Fig. 6-1 . The Reinforcer System .** Some of the major neurological structures of the reinforcer system and its functional organization. This system fosters the connection between exteroceptive reinforcing stimuli and appropriate species-specific or learned behaviors.

the UR. This affective response enhancement or mood state produces selective increases in response probability for the behavioral components of the appropriate species-specific response pattern over an extended period of time.

Memorial Characteristics. By considering the actions of the rein-forcer system in conjunction with the general processes of the IPM, we should be able to derive some additional implications for learning and memory. If precision encoding is a general process of the IPM, then the affective response to a reinforcing stimulus should be represented in the internal representation of that stimu-lus in the same manner as the sensory attributes. Thus, there is no inherent reason why both affective and sensory attributes and, for that matter, motoric memories should not be contained in the internal representation or memory of the stimulus event. As Maki et al. (1977) have shown, the same interference conditions in delayed match-to-sample responding lead to deficits in the retention of memories for stimuli, reinforcers, and responses, indicating the existence of some common processes in the retention of stimuli and responses (cf. D'Amato, 1973; Herman, 1975).

84

If the affective response to a reinforcer is potentiated by the reinforcer system then we can assume that such response attributes will be salient elements in the memorial representation. However, if we consider the operation of the analogical encoding process, it should be clear that these affective attributes cannot be localized in the same pathways producing the sensory analyses. The well-known findings from neocortical stimulation which show no affective response support this idea. From this effect, we can infer that match-mismatch comparisons should be occurring in the reinforcer system with respect to the affective attributes of a stimulus. That is, a stimulus can be recognized on the basis of its sensory attributes in the sensory-perceptual division of the IPM but must go through another comparison process in the reinforcer system in order for its affective attributes to be "recognized."

This sequential comparison implies that the reinforcer system has at least some structures or neurons which can respond to the perceptual qualities of reinforcers which activate the various sensory channels (i.e., they are multi-modal stimulus processors). Such units are receivers of already processed stimulus information and are not engaged in perceptual analysis per se. These units' reactivity is modified by stimuli that produce or occur concurrently with affective responses and through this process encode the critical parameters of the reinforcer. The extent of this experience-based encoding will be determined by the nature of the species and the particular reinforcer measured. In many cases, the units will be programmed to respond to particular sensory reinforcers without the necessity of environmental experience. Lower level sensory units of the reinforcer system are more likely to receive stimulus information connected to reflexively based responding (e.g., tactile/pain sensation) while upper level units are more likely to receive stimulus information requiring extended and/or anticipatory behaviors (e.g., visual).

It is argued that it is best to view conditioning or instrumental learning as the memory of motivational events. To the extent that the memories or internal representations of CSs and other cues are fully re-accessed (retrieved) from memory then the organism will display maximal conditioning given the circumstances of training. Experimental manipulations or other factors which tend to diminish the retrieval of these representations will lead to reduced behavioral expression of conditioning.

In avian and mammalian species, conditioning and other stimulus learning is achieved through the mechanism of the OR. As we have seen, the OR is evoked by unexpected changes in the stimulus environment and gradually habituates as the changed conditions become more predictable to the organism. This characteristic has important implications for stimulus learning since it means that the organism is actively processing information when unexpected changes occur in the stimulus environment. Such information processing gradually diminishes as an internal representation incorporates the novel attributes which can be used in the comparison process. In other words, the OR and thus stimulus learning is inhibited by stimulus predictability. With respect to reinforcer system functioning, changes in the occurrence of reinforcers or temporally proximal stimuli that evoke or re-evoke the OR will lead to changes in the conditioning of these stimuli.

Conditioned Reinforcers

Up to now we have been considering the activation of the reinforcer system by unconditioned reinforcers, which are minimally dependent on environmental experience for their capacity to produce affective responses (mood states). However, reinforcing stimuli can also be produced which are dependent on experience for their affect-inducing properties, i.e., conditioned reinforcers. If we are to be consistent we have to assume that these reinforcing stimuli are also processed through the reinforcer system, and actually, we need hypothesize no additional processes in order to accommodate them.

Unconditioned reinforcers produce affective responses in the organism which become part of their memorial representation through the process of precision encoding. However, organisms rarely are processing only one stimulus during even a brief span of time. Thus, other stimuli are being processed when the reinforcer is presented and the affective responses are evoked. Precision encoding operates on these temporally proximate stimuli the same way that it does on the reinforcer. Their memorial representation contains not only their sensory attributes but also the affective attributes that are evoked by the reinforcer. By this logic, only stimuli which are being processed or whose presentations are otherwise retrieved at the time of reinforcer occurrence can share its affective attributes.

Now, in classical conditioning and in discriminative instrumental learning there is a particular stimulus which precedes the occurrence of the reinforcer, i.e., the CS. While the reinforcer is being encoded, the CS is also becoming encoded in an internal representation. However, the interval between CS and US needs to be relatively brief or the CS would no longer be in working memory. The longer CS-US intervals that Pavlov (1927) and others have demonstrated were accomplished under unusual circumstances in which no other interfering stimuli intervened in the CS-US interval or when there were special cuing relationships between the US and CS, e.g., taste aversion conditioning (Revusky & Garcia, 1970). It is through this processing that the association of the CS with the US is begun and maintained. In this connection it should

86

be noted that the potentiation of response to the reinforcer by upper level structures increases the magnitude of conditioning that can accrue to temporally proximate stimuli. In other words, the greater the affective response to the reinforcer, the greater the potential response to associated CSs. Since the affective properties of the conditioned stimulus are much weaker in the case of lower level conditioning, it has less capacity to act as a conditioned reinforcer. What is the specific nature of this association between the reinforcer and contiguous stimuli?

One possibility that has been long noted is that the CS and US have the UR in common, in that the UR occurs while both the CS and US are in working memory. In this view the CS would be a part, albeit a highly discriminable part, of a total stimulus complex which includes the affective (species-specific) response of the organism occurring at that time. Of course the CS will temporally precede at least part of the organismic response to the US depending on its onset and termination parameters. From this perspective, the re-presentation of the CS should enable the organism to re-access some of the other details of the stimulus environment concurrent with the CS. In other words, the CS becomes a redintegrative cue for the CS-US complex in memory. Presumably, the more salient elements of the stimulus context will predominate in such a representation.

From this account we would expect the presentation of the CS, after a number of CS-US pairings, to elicit some of the same responses evoked by the US, i.e., those responses which are not directly dependent on the physical presence of the US. In other words, the CS should assume some of the psychological properties of the reinforcer without sharing its physical properties. We would expect at least a small degree of difference between responding to the CS and to the US for this reason. In addition, the CS, as a stimulus, will tend to elicit its own response pattern from the organism.

Mood State Induction

It was noted previously that the induction of a mood state led in time to the appearance of an opponent process. Essentially the opponent process is another mood state in reciprocal interaction with the original (A) mood state. Since the reinforcer induces a mood state by its presentation, it follows that after the removal of the reinforcer, an opposing mood state will appear. This becomes important when it is considered that stimuli processed through the reinforcer system at this time will, through the same process as outlined above, become associated with the existing organismic state, i.e., opponent state. This suggests that such stimuli will

87

have psychological properties that are different, if not opposite, from those stimuli which were paired with the "A" state.

One other characteristic of reinforcer system processing is that habituation is inhibited. It is clear that if habituation were not inhibited no conditioning could occur because the CS or other cues to reinforcement would never acquire associative strength from the proximity to reinforcement. It is the induction of the mood state which leads to the inhibition of habituation in more complex organisms.

In summary, the reinforcer system processes all stimuli which innately or through learning have the capacity to induce a mood state in the organism. Through a match-mismatch process, the reinforcer system identifies such stimuli by comparing them with internal representations. The activation of the reinforcer system by a reinforcing stimulus leads to the registration of the contents of working memory at the time of its occurrence. In addition, the induction of an appropriate mood state by the reinforcer inhibits habituation of these stimuli. As a result of the initial mood state, an opponent "B" state will appear immediately following the cessation of the "A" state. Stimuli processed through the reinforcer system at this time will become associated with the "B" state and its organismic effects.

THE HABITUATIVE SYSTEM

Since we have hypothesized that one component of the IPM is involved in processing reinforcers and associating them with other stimuli, it seems logical to hypothesize another component to handle the extinction or habituation of stimuli that are not followed by reinforcers (see Fig. 6-2).

Our basic assumption will be that any stimulus evoking the OR which is neither a reinforcer (at the time of its presentation) nor signals the occurrence of a temporally proximate reinforcer will be processed through the habituative system of the IPM. From our discussion on the reinforcer system, we will have to add the qualification that this does not entirely apply to stimuli signaling the non-occurrence of a specific reinforcer (whether positive or aversive). This qualification can only apply when a reinforcer is occurring in the same situation at some other time.

It can be deduced from this proposition that the habituative system must generally be processing nonsalient stimuli. If the reinforcer system is basically sensitive only to reinforcing stimuli while the habituative system is sensitive to any stimuli capable of evoking the OR on the organism, it would seem necessary to hypothesize that the habituative system is more sensitive to environmental

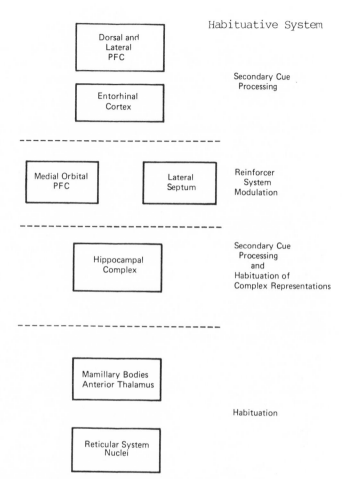

Fig. 6-2. The Habituative System. Some of the major neurological structures of the habituative system and its functional organization. This system processes nonsalient stimuli which are either habituated or function as secondary cues.

stimuli (i.e., has a lower threshold with regard to stimulus change) than the reinforcer system.

It should be clear from the habituation studies that it is necessary to hypothesize the same precision-encoding capacity and match-mismatch process in the habituative system as with the reinforcer system. The same problem of recognition of a certain class of stimuli is present in both systems; the difference simply being the category towards which each is sensitive.

As with the reinforcer system, stimuli are first processed through the sensory-perceptual division of the IPM in which the general processes of precision encoding, analogical encoding, and match-mismatch (perceptual) comparisons are functioning. The kinds of perceptual analyses performed on the incoming stimuli will vary as a function of their inherent attributes and the organism's prior experience. Thus, the relaying of perceptual information to the habituative system will occur at different points of the sensory-perceptual systems involved in the analysis of the stimulus.

Since there are a number of situations in which the habituative system operates, let's start with the most straightforward one, the habituation paradigm. A novel neutral stimulus (e.g., a light) is presented which evokes an OR from the organism. On repeated presentations the sensory-perceptual division of the IPM encodes a stimulus model of the stimulus. Since it is not a reinforcer in this situation, the stimulus is processed through the habituative system. In this system a match between the external stimulus and the stimulus model leads to the partial or complete habituation of the OR and other organismic responses to the stimulus.

Habituation is a stimulus-specific learning process which produces a decrement in responding to stimuli which have been repeatedly presented to an organism. In a real sense, habituation can be regarded as the most basic (and ubiquitous) form of opponent processes. In this view, habituation opposes the disturbance which a novel stimulus creates in an organism (i.e., the OR, its concomitant attentional demands, and the interruption of on-going activities) by reducing the salience of the stimulus to the level where it no longer evokes a response or evokes only an irreducible UR.

To the extent that stimulus repetition is a critical requirement for habituation there are other situations in which it should operate apart from the presentation of novel stimuli. Habituative processes could play a role in moderating organismic responses to USs with the proviso that the greater the affective disturbance (mood state) induced by an exteroceptive stimulus, the more difficult it is to eliminate responding to it. However, partial reduction in response strength could be expected except for the most intense stimuli. In these cases, habituation would be inadequate as a means of restoring homeostatic balance and more powerful opponent processes would be necessary.

In this connection, it should be noted that species-specific differences can be expected in the habituability of particular stimuli because of the induction of mood states. Since the interactions between exteroceptive stimuli and neurochemically organized pathways vary from species to species, stimuli will necessarily vary in their arousal value and thus their relative habituability.

Phylogenetic Considerations

In the discussion of reinforcer system functioning, the importance of considering the phylogenetic development of its component
structures was noted. Since habituation is perhaps the most widespread and primitive form of learning, the existence of neural
structures with varied lineages can have important implications
for the expression of habituation. One of the distinguishing
features of organisms of phylogenetically higher levels of development is the range of stimuli which evoke a response (e.g., the
OR). That is, such organisms are more sensitive to changes in the
stimulus environment particularly with respect to stimuli which
are not strongly arousing and don't control a species-specific
response pattern.

In the previous chapter, a case was made for the functional
division of the OR and species-specific responses. It is predicted
that this functional difference will manifest itself in habituation.
With respect to species-specific responses, habituative mechanisms
are located in habituative interneurons in lower level structures
of the habituative system as well as in reflexive pathways and the
reinforcer system. Habituation involves a comparison of the
previous pattern of neural excitation with that induced by the
presented stimulus. When the two patterns match, then habituation
increases or is maintained asymptotically. Dishabituation occurs
as the result of a mismatch producing sensitization (or mood state
induction) which facilitates other related responses, in addition
to the habituated response, above their normal levels. This implies
that only mismatches which can induce sensitization or mood state
induction will cause dishabituation. Mismatches which involve
decreased stimulation compared with that provided by the habituation
stimulus will not be able to alter habituation to the decremented
response.

The OR to affectively neutral stimuli is more sensitive to
stimulus change because of the greater involvement of upper level
structures of the habituative system. With this response, habituation results from the matching of an internal representation against
a repeated or expected stimulus. However, dishabituation occurs
as the result of a mismatch caused by a change in the pattern of
stimulation, even when a decrease in stimulus intensity is involved.
Thus, dishabituation of the OR is a stimulus-specific loss of
habituation which does not involve increases in the level of other
responses.

It was noted previously that the temporal characteristics of
the stimulus are encoded along with its physical properties in the
internal representation used in the habituative process. If there
is a discrepancy in the temporal pattern of the stimulus, then
dishabituation of the OR typically occurs. The question arises as

to the manner in which the temporal patterning attributes of the internal representation can be applied in the habituation situation to inhibit responding.

The most plausible (and widely shared) hypothesis is that the internal representation is primed or retrieved into working memory or into some preattentive (subcortical) location by predictive cues immediately prior to the reoccurrence of the stimulus. In other words, the cues, through their association with the habituated stimulus, function as retrieval cues for the target's internal representation. A mismatch in these circumstances results when the internal representation is not primed appropriately. In the present theory, this kind of priming is applicable in the case of OR habituation but has minimal or no impact on the habituation of species-specific responses controlled by reinforcing stimuli because of the different habituative mechanisms underlying the latter case.

Learning Procedures Involving
Habituative System Processing

The habituative system can be evoked in three different situations outside of the standard habituation paradigm if our basic assumption is correct that the system operates whenever reinforcing stimuli are not present. The most obvious circumstance would be in extinction. An organism has become conditioned to a CS which precedes the arrival of shock and thus is responding to the tone as well as the shock. Now we discontinue the shock and just present the CS tone.

Since the reinforcer (US) is no longer occurring, the habituative system is not inhibited by the reinforcer system. Thus, the stimuli present in the environment, including the CS, now begin to be processed through the habituative system and habituated. The only difference between the CS and a typical habituated stimulus is that an internal representation exists of the CS that was formed through the reinforcer system. Although processing through the habituative system will result in the habituation of response to a stimulus, this process cannot erase the internal representation of the CS as an excitatory stimulus already present. Therefore, although the organism should cease to respond to the CS when it is repeatedly presented without the US, there should be latent differences between the extinguished CS and stimuli which have never been associated with a reinforcer.

The second situation that the habituative system should be active in, if we follow our basic assumption, would be the processing of higher order cues that are temporally distant from the occurrence of reinforcement (e.g., a CS2 which precedes the occurrence of the CS). The reinforcer system is sensitive to reinforcing stimuli and simply processes all the contents of working memory at the time of reinforcer occurrence. This permits it to process temporally contiguous stimuli such as the CS. However, temporally distant stimuli, while they may signal reinforcers in an indirect sense, generally are not in working memory at the time of reinforcer occurrence. If we examine this point carefully, it can be seen that these stimuli, when considered from the organism's point of view, really have a number of similarities with the type of stimuli which the organism normally processes through the habituative system and therefore habituates. The most crucial point, of course, is the lack of close connection between their occurrence and the occurrence of the reinforcer.

Perhaps the clearest example that can be offered would be the learning of a maze-running response. The parts of the maze closest to the goal box containing the reinforcer are the strongest conditioned reinforcers, while those parts closest to the starting point show the least conditioned reinforcing properties. Often these latter cues show no reinforcing properties at all. Of course, this phenomenon is the well-known goal gradient effect.

If the habituative system is hypothesized to process these maze stimuli temporally distant from reinforcement, why aren't they habituated instead of becoming higher order cues to reinforcement? Actually, it is well known that even a moderate delay between the occurrence of a primary cue (CS1) and the US typically makes conditioning difficult if not impossible. Yet organisms display facility in learning a CS2 - CS1 - US relationship in which the CS2 or higher order cue is temporally distant from the US. The answer lies with the existence of the CS1.

A crucial point is that the CS2 cannot be stably conditioned by the organism until the CS1 - US relationship has been established. According to the assumptions of match-mismatch theory, the CS1, because it is in working memory at the time of reinforcer occurrence, is processed with it through the reinforcer system. In the encoding process, it becomes associated with the representations of the other stimuli and responses occurring at that time. Through this process, the CS1 acquires the capacity to activate the reinforcer system, albeit relatively weakly, prior to the occurrence of the reinforcer.

The weaker activation of the reinforcer system by the primary cues (CS1) also results in diminished inhibition of the habituative system, in particular the OR to nonsalient stimuli. Therefore, nonsalient stimuli can be processed through the habituative system both prior to and to some extent during the presentation of the primary cues. However, as these stimuli are being processed through the habituative system, the primary cues are occurring and beginning their activation of the reinforcer system. The habituation of the nonsalient or secondary cues is thus progressively inhibited. Instead, they are encoded in association with the primary cues. Thus,

93

the internal representation of these higher order or secondary cues cannot function in a habituative match-mismatch process, but instead become cues to the CS1. Since they are processed through the habituative system, however, they cannot acquire the conditioned reinforcing properties of the CS1. This property is reserved for cues processed through the reinforcer system in working memory at the time of the reinforcing event.

The third situation in which the habituative system has to be hypothesized to function is the partial reinforcement situation. By definition, on a certain percentage of trials no US will occur, despite the presence of stimuli and/or responses that signal the US. According to our assumptions, the habituative system will begin processing any stimulus that is not a reinforcer or in correlated temporal proximity to a reinforcer. Thus, we have to assume that the habituative system is activated on non-reinforced trials in the partial reinforcement situation. The IPM should function as follows: In the trials where the CS occurred immediately preceding the US, it would begin to be conditioned because of its processing through the reinforcer system. On those trials where the CS occurred by itself in the absence of the US, the reinforcer system would not be able to inhibit the habituative system and thus the CS would be processed through the habituative system. Since conditioning can occur with partial reinforcement in either classical or instrumental conditioning we are forced to assume that the reinforcer system can increment the associative value of a stimulus at least somewhat faster than the habituative system can decrement it. However, the associative strength of a partially reinforced stimulus should be less than that of a continuously reinforced stimulus.

It may be asked how the habituative system can know on which occasions the CS is to be followed by the US and on which it is not. Actually, simple cuing procedures can probably account for the role of the habituative system in its intermittent processing of the partially reinforced stimulus. To the extent that there is a regular pattern of CS and CS-US presentations, of course, the identity of any particular trial can be predicted on the basis of the immediately prior trials. For more irregular patterns, the division of CS processing between the reinforcer and habituative systems will be more under the control of the local pattern of CS-US presentations at any given time.

The Processing of Secondary Cues

In the previous section, it was noted that the activation of the reinforcer system led to the inhibition of habituation of the stimuli being processed. Actually, as we have seen here, the habituative system comprises both stimulus processing functions and habituative functions. If the activation of the reinforcer system inhibits the operation of the habituative system then we have to assume that both the stimulus processing functions and the habituative functions can be inhibited at this time.

The greater the magnitude and frequency of reinforcement that occurs on a reinforcement schedule, the less probability that stimulus processing will occur through the habituative system. Conversely, the lower the frequency or magnitude of reinforcement, the greater the probability of stimulus processing through the habituative system. Furthermore, since reinforcement is occurring occasionally, the stimuli processed through the habituative system in these circumstances can be assumed to be registered as secondary cues to reinforcement rather than habituated because of the occasional activation of the reinforcer system. The implications of this process are examined in detail during the course of this section.

Let's examine the nature of stimulus processing through the habituative system to see the implications of such a position. The habituative system has to be sensitive to any stimulus capable of evoking the OR, otherwise such stimuli would never be habituated. From this, we can conclude that the habituative system has to be able to process nonsalient stimuli since the OR can be evoked by very subtle changes in the stimulus environment.

In addition to discrete exteroceptive stimuli that are not reinforced, secondary stimuli are likely to fall along three main dimensions of the stimulus environment: temporal attributes, spatial attributes, and nonsalient features of discrete exteroceptive stimuli. By temporal attributes, we mean the memorial tagging of events such as stimulus presentations or response performance with temporal or stimulus features so that their sequence of occurrence with other events can be discriminated and retained.

Spatial attributes are stimulus features which permit the memorial representation of visual information in some two-dimensional or three-dimensional framework and are obviously dependent on the level of analysis of spatial information in the sensory-perceptual division of the IPM for a particular species. Nonsalient features of discrete exteroceptive stimuli are those dimensions of the stimulus which are less likely to predominate in the internal representation in the absence of explicit discriminative contingencies i.e., stimulus hierarchies. To use a simple example, a red triangle used as a discriminative stimulus might be encoded with the color as the predominant feature controlling the response while the form would be a less salient feature. Verbal stimuli can be encoded with respect to a variety of features such as their semantic meaning, orthography, pronunciation, etc., some of which predominate in any particular representation at the expense of other features.

Response Functions

What relation do the habituative and reinforcer systems have to the three proposed response systems? It is clear that responses falling into the category of species-specific behaviors are going to be controlled by reinforcers or by stimuli such as CSs which have conditioned reinforcing properties. Thus, the reinforcer system will control such responses. Voluntary responses are more problematical. Reinforcers can control the probability of such responses; therefore, the reinforcer system has at least partial control over their occurrence. However, it is also true that voluntary responses are exhibited in the absence of reinforcing stimuli and thus it seems likely that they can be controlled through the habituative system as well, i.e., through secondary cues. Therefore, voluntary responding would seem to be controlled through both systems.

The same reasoning should apply to the OR response class. It is clear that both reinforcers and non-reinforcers are capable of evoking the OR. Therefore, the involvement of both the reinforcer and habituative systems in the control of the OR is indicated.

In summary, the habituative system processes stimuli not in temporal proximity to reinforcement. This processing occurs in the standard habituation paradigm, in partial reinforcement schedules, and with temporally distant cues to reinforcement. In situations devoid of reinforcement, these stimuli are asymptotically habituated. In reinforcement situations, the occurrence of primary cues processed through the reinforcer system can inhibit the habituation of temporally distant stimuli and lead to their registration as secondary cues to reinforcement. This effect is due to the inhibition of habituative system function while the reinforcer system is activated. Partial reinforcement results in the alternating processing of a primary cue between the reinforcer and habituative systems, which reduces its asymptotic conditioning level. Secondary cues processed through the habituative system can control voluntary, but not species-specific, responses. Primary cues can control both types of response.

## THE RELATION OF THE REINFORCER AND HABITUATIVE SYSTEMS TO CLASSICAL AND INSTRUMENTAL CONDITIONING

At this point we are ready to give some consideration to the question of how the two hypothesized processing systems of the IPM relate to the classical-instrumental learning distinction. Since match-mismatch theory hypothesizes a single IPM with general stimulus analyzing processes, an appeal cannot be made to two fundamentally different stimulus learning processes. However, the existence of two processing components in the behavioral analysis division of the IPM allows the possibility that the two learning paradigms tap different interactions of these two components.

An organism in a typical classical conditioning experiment is more likely to exclusively utilize the reinforcer system during acquisition and the habituative system during extinction or non-reinforcement. In addition, since there are reduced response selection requirements, species-specific behaviors are more likely to occur. As we have seen, such responses have significantly different properties from those of voluntary responses.

In the instrumental learning paradigm, it is more likely that both the reinforcer and habituative systems will be in operation during acquisition. The reinforcer system is engaged when reinforcers or primary cues are presented in the instrumental paradigm. However, since voluntary responses, unlike species-specific responses, can be controlled by cues processed through the habituative system, it is also possible for the habituative system to play a positive role in the acquisition of instrumental behaviors. Lower magnitude or frequency of reinforcement lessens the inhibition of the habituative system by the reinforcer system. In these circumstances nonsalient stimuli can be processed through the habituative system because of reduced inhibition of the OR controlled by it. The intermittent presence of primary cues and reinforcers inhibits their habituation while the internal representations of these nonsalient cues incorporate some common attributes with the cues processed through the reinforcer system. Since the unconditioned reinforcer is temporally distant, affective attributes cannot play a critical role in the representation of the secondary cues. Instead, their own sensory attributes are associated with concurrent organismic responses and/or the sensory attributes of the primary cues.

The non-affective properties of the secondary cues have three direct effects. First, it makes them incapable of controlling species-specific responses which depend upon mood state induction by reinforcing stimuli. Second, their control over voluntary responses is less affected by the presence or absence of an appropriate mood state in the organism since their association with these responses is not based upon affective attributes. This property stands in contrast with the control of primary cues over species-specific or voluntary responses, which is dependent on the appropriate mood state. Third, the control over voluntary responses by secondary cues is more susceptible to disruption by external events than is the comparable control by primary cues. This phenomenon is due to the lessened capacity of secondary cues to inhibit the OR to stimuli.

During extinction, of course, the situation is the same as in classical conditioning since only the habituative system can operate

97

in such circumstances. This does not necessarily mean that extinction will be identical in all instances between instrumental and classical conditioning since the nature of what is learned during acquisition can affect the parameters of extinction. According to match-mismatch theory, therefore, the differences found between learning parameters in the classical and instrumental paradigms are due to the greater occurrence of species-specific responses in the classical paradigm and the division of cue processing between the reinforcer and habituative systems in the instrumental paradigm.

## DEFINITION OF THE UNCONDITIONED REINFORCER

In the classical conditioning paradigm, it is obviously the US or reinforcer which maintains the behavior of the organism. Although, as we shall see, associative learning is possible in the absence of a US (or at least in the absence of an obvious US), the reinforcer seems to evoke a qualitatively different response by the organism compared with more neutral stimuli. The problem is how to define a reinforcer so that we can always distinguish it from a non-reinforcer.

The operational definition of a reinforcer which is generally used is that a reinforcer is any stimulus which increases the probability of a response. As has been noted (e.g., Meehl, 1950) the definition is quite circular as it stands since there is no mention of how to define a reinforcer apart from its effect on a response. The usual way out of this circularity is to state that a reinforcer can be identified by its effect on a variety of organismic responses in natural settings or in other situations. Meehl (1950) has argued that there are great practical difficulties in coming up with an adequate definition of a reinforcer so that it can be categorized as such before testing its effect. In fact, he concluded that there quite probably was no way of a priori determining whether a particular stimulus would be a reinforcer. It can be useful at this point to briefly go over some of the reasons for this difficulty.

First of all, there are no inherent stimulus properties which are inextricably linked with reinforcers, even intensity along a particular stimulus dimension. In large part this is simply a function of the different sensory systems which various organisms possess. Pigeons are very sensitive to visual stimuli and relatively insensitive to olfactory stimuli, while rats and mice have more or less the reverse stimulus hierarchy. What would be an intense stimulus to one would not necessarily be so for the other.

This fact leads us to the second point, namely, that reinforcers are more a function of the characteristics of the organism than anything else. Although a more complicated matter than that of inherent stimulus characteristics, this would not be an insuperable difficulty if we could find some basic factor common to different organisms which determines the reinforcing value of a stimulus. Of course, the drive reduction hypothesis by Hull (1943, 1952) and others was an attempt in this direction. Essentially, a reinforcer exerted its effect by diminishing a drive related to the tissue needs of an organism. If the organism sought out the reinforcing stimulus, it was viewed as a reward and if the organism sought to avoid or escape the stimulus it was viewed as a punisher. In the absence of drive reduction, no learning could occur according to this viewpoint.

These notions were upset rather dramatically when it was discovered that animals could learn to respond for stimuli which did not seem to alleviate biological needs in any apparent fashion. Girdner (1953), Kish (1955), and Marx et al. (1955), all showed that rats would learn to barpress merely to produce the onset of a light. Butler (1953) found that rhesus monkeys would learn a discrimination in order to have a 30-second view of the laboratory environment from a dark experimental cage. Additionally, strong species-specific differences were found in preferences for different kinds of stimuli. For example, Baron (1959) found that presentation of response-contingent auditory stimuli depressed responding by mice, indicating that they found the sounds aversive, even at moderate intensities. On the other hand, monkeys had strong auditory exploratory tendencies (Butler, 1957). These and other studies demonstrated that for many species, simple stimulus change could function as a reinforcer.

Actually, for some organisms such as primates (not to mention humans) the problem is more one of deciding what stimuli are not reinforcers rather than which ones are. The variety of stimuli that will sustain learning is extremely broad as we saw in the examples of sensory reinforcement. Organisms lower on the phylogenetic scale seem to respond to a smaller proportion of such stimuli. It is perhaps for this reason that the concept of reinforcement is used less frequently by psychologists studying human or primate behavior. The problem then is that reinforcing stimuli do not necessarily involve biological needs and they vary from species to species. It is interesting that the increase in the kinds of reinforcers that we see as we progress phylogenetically is paralleled by an increase in the kinds of stimuli which can evoke the OR.

As we saw previously, the OR is a non-specific response to stimulus change, whether or not this involves the introduction of a novel stimulus or simply changes in the characteristics of an already present stimulus. There are a few key points that should be noted about the OR in connection with the present discussion.

First of all, it apparently can be found in some form in all vertebrate species so that it qualifies as an extremely general property.
Second, the stimuli which evoke the OR can vary from species to
species. Species such as amphibians and reptiles seem responsive
to stimuli which are either very obvious kinds of reinforcers (e.g.,
food) or to stimuli with species-specific functions (e.g., threat
postures from conspecifics). There is little response to stimulus
novelty or change per se. With mammals there is a vast increase in
the reactivity to novel stimuli, even when they are completely neutral in their effects on the organism. Of course, humans display
the greatest degree of sensitivity to stimulus change (cf. Glickman
& Sroges, 1966).

It is suggested that any stimulus capable of eliciting an OR
on the part of an organism can function as a reinforcer for that
organism under certain circumstances. Thus, the same stimulus can
be a reinforcer and non-reinforcer on different occasions. When a
stimulus is functioning as a reinforcer it induces a homeostatic
change in the organism. Defining a reinforcer in this way allows
us to take advantage of the points about the OR noted in the preceding paragraph. Additionally, this view of the reinforcer can
comfortably accommodate both the Hullian notion of the drive reducer
and the more recent thinking which suggests that a reinforcer is
a contextually determined property of a stimulus (e.g., Premack,
1971).

Some years ago, it would have been argued that the OR to novel
stimuli was much too broad and non-specific to be of much applicability in terms of identifying reinforcers. In essence, reinforcers
were considered to be a small subclass of the total number of stimuli to which an organism would devote attention. The research picture at this juncture looks very much different. A wide variety of
stimuli have been found to sustain learning and responding in many
different species. In addition, there seems to be a phylogenetic
factor in the number of different reinforcers that are found in a
species. Primates and humans will respond to, and learn to obtain
(or avoid), a very broad range of stimuli, most of which infraprimates find relatively or totally uninteresting. Thus, it is very
much an open question as to whether or not reinforcers do represent
merely a small subset of the total number of stimuli to which the
organism is responsive. In the present view the more difficult
problem is to define the conditions under which a particular stimulus functions as a reinforcer. It is clear that such a definition
requires a much greater knowledge of the biology of the organism
than we currently possess if it is to completely specify the relevant parameters.

In summary, any stimulus capable of evoking the OR in an
organism can function as a reinforcing stimulus for that organism.
However, each stimulus has certain contingent conditions which

must exist in order for it to have reinforcing properties at a particular time.

## INHIBITION OF THE HABITUATIVE SYSTEM BY THE REINFORCER SYSTEM

Another critical theoretical point with regard to establishing the existence of two different stimulus analyzing systems is the postulated interaction between the reinforcer and habituative systems. Match-mismatch theory assumes that the activation of the reinforcer system inhibits the operation of the habituative system. From a logical standpoint, there can be no disagreement over the fact that habituation of stimuli has to be inhibited when they signal reinforcement, otherwise the organism could never learn anything. Unfortunately this point alone has only a marginal bearing on the current concerns, since there are a number of plausible ways that this result could be achieved.

### Inhibition of Secondary Cue Processing

The current theory actually has a somewhat stronger prediction to make in this regard. The habituative system does not simply habituate stimuli, it also functions as a stimulus analyzing system. In other words, it both processes and habituates stimuli that meet its operating characteristics. If the activation of the reinforcer system inhibits the operation of the habituative system then we should note changes in behavior relating to both functions. That is, not only inhibition of habituation but inhibition of cue processing should be seen. As explained previously, the habituative system only processes stimuli with certain characteristics (i.e., non-reinforced or non-salient). Thus, we would expect changes in the processing of these kinds of stimuli but not in those processed through the reinforcer system. There are a few areas of research in both animals and humans which may have some relevance to this point.

Nevin (1973, 1974), in trying to formulate a consistent interpretation of response strength in operant responding, developed the idea that the disruptability of such responding might be the best measure of response strength. He found that under conditions of high motivation (i.e., frequent activation of the reinforcer system by reinforcing stimuli), animals were much less likely to notice novel stimuli. Bruner et al. (1955) pretrained rats on a discrimination problem with multiple, correlated cues. One group was food deprived for 12 hours while the other was food deprived for 36 hours. The rats were then trained to use only the less salient cues to obtain reinforcement. The 36-hour group showed

101

the least benefit from pretraining when less salient cues were subsequently made the key discriminative stimuli.

Similar findings have been reported in a number of classic human information processing studies. Bahrick et al. (1952) studied cue utilization on central and peripheral tasks under different motivational conditions. Three peripheral tasks varying in relevance to the central task (continuous tracking) were used. Half of the subjects were told that the task was only for practice while the other half were given monetary bonuses for high scores on all the tasks. The latter group was superior on the central task but inferior on the peripheral tasks even though they were losing money as a result.

In a further experiment Bahrick (1954) varied motivational levels as before and compared the two groups on learning of a series of colored geometric forms. After training, subjects were tested for their incidental learning of the colors. Results were similar to that of the previous study; i.e., incidental stimuli were less well-learned under strong motivation. Conversely, Siddle (1971) has shown that ORs to irrelevant stimuli reduce cue processing in the central task.

Easterbrook (1959) on the basis of these and other studies developed the idea that the range of cue utilization in any situation tends to become smaller with increases in emotion or motivation. It should be emphasized that the restriction in cue utilization is not uniform since those cues most strongly associated with performance on the central task are learned as well and often times better under strong motivation as under weak. The loss tends to be concentrated on less salient stimuli. Bacon (1974) has shown that this loss is due to a drop in sensitivity to these items rather than a result of changes in response bias. Incidentally, these results argue against any simple notion of restriction of cue utilization by an increase in threshold sensitivity on the part of a single stimulus analyzing system. The increased sensitivity to central cues cannot be accommodated with these ideas. These results are easy to accommodate within match-mismatch theory however.

Interactive Effects in Human Motivation

Social Facilitation. A basic phenomenon of current research interest in social psychology which can be viewed as the result of the operation of the interactive characteristics of the reinforcer and habituative systems is social facilitation. Social facilitation refers to the enhancement of an organism's (animal or human) dominant responses by the physical presence of other members of the species. This facilitation of dominant responses is not dependent on any informational or interactional influence. One of the interesting things from the standpoint of the current theory is that social facilitation is a ubiquitous phenomenon which is found not only in a variety of social situations in humans but also can be found in a wide range of animal species. This, of course, provides a strong indication that some basic structural process lies at the heart of this effect.

Zajonc (1965) and Zajonc et al. (1969) proposed a drive theory interpretation of this effect. Drive theory predicts that increases in drive facilitate dominant responses or habits at the expense of weaker habits or responses. In fact, social facilitation facilitates performance on easy tasks while performance on hard tasks is impaired. (It is important to note that social facilitation applies to the performance of the individual in the presence of others, not to group performance [cf. Markus, 1978].)

It should be clear how match-mismatch theory accounts for social facilitation. It has been shown that the activation of the reinforcer system tends to inhibit the functioning of the habituative system; the stronger the activation, the more complete the inhibition. This inhibition of the habituative system has two effects: the cessation of habituation of stimuli being processed in the presence of the reinforcing stimuli and the inhibition of secondary or nonsalient cue-processing. The performance of difficult tasks is generally dependent to a greater extent on more subtle or nonsalient cues or cue dimensions, exactly what is being inhibited. However, processing of salient cues continues in normal fashion through the reinforcer system. These latter cues and the responses they control are more likely to be associated with over-learned types of behaviors, exactly the type which are facilitated by the presence of others.

It is of interest to note that group problem solving is generally inferior to individual problem solving when complex or subtle issues have to be analyzed. It has been argued that time is lost in such groups when individuals with a greater grasp of the problem have to bring other members up to their level of understanding (cf. Maier et al., 1963). This is highly plausible; however, another contributing factor may simply be social facilitation effects which diminish the full functioning of the higher level structures of the habituative system.

It should be noted that the present interpretation of social facilitation is consistent with any hypothesis of this effect which assumes that the presence of others can act as a reinforcing stimulus capable of activating the reinforcer system. We would assume that more complex environmental determinants of this phenomenon exist in humans than in animals, but the underlying basis of the effect should be the same for all mammals.

103

Intrinsic Motivation. Another phenomenon that would seem to be explainable in part as the result of the interacting characteristics of the reinforcer and habituative system is intrinsic motivation. Intrinsic motivation is often defined in the human literature as the performance of an activity for which the reinforcing consequences are contained in the performance of the activity itself rather than in the attainment of any biological or monetary reward (e.g., Deci, 1975; Lepper & Greene, 1975). Hobbies are one example of this. Actually, under most definitions of intrinsic motivation, animals can be included as well as humans. For example, as we have seen, monkeys will often engage in exploratory or manipulative activities which result in no apparent biological reinforcement.

Intrinsic motivation has generally been contrasted with extrinsic motivation which includes the more conventional types of reinforcing outcomes such as money or biological reinforcers. Most theories (e.g., Deci, 1975; Lepper & Greene, 1975; Ross, 1976) assume that there is an inverse relationship between the extrinsic reinforcing outcomes which can be obtained by performing an activity and the degree of intrinsic motivation to perform the task. This overjustification hypothesis assumes that extrinsic rewards lower intrinsic motivation to the extent that they are viewed as controlling the behavior and as a sufficient reason for engaging in the activity. For example, people who get a good income for performing a job will attribute their performance to the monetary reward more than to their own intrinsic interest in the job (Lepper & Greene, 1975). When the reward is discontinued therefore, the person will be less likely to engage in the behavior (i.e., will show extinction) compared with a person who engaged in the behavior without extrinsic reward.

Ross (1975) had young children, aged 3 to 5 years old, play with a drum under conditions of either nonsalient or salient reward. In the salient reward condition, the child was told that the reward was located under a box in front of the drum. In the nonsalient condition the child was not told the prize was under the box. The child's intrinsic interest in the drum was measured by the amount of time spent playing the drum in a subsequent 5-minute freeplay period in which no rewards were forthcoming. Children in the nonsalient reward condition played the drum for a significantly longer period of time than the salient reward group. The latter results were found to be due to a decrease in intrinsic interest because of the high salience of the reward. Ross et al. (1976) provided evidence that the effect was not due to the task becoming aversive through a delay of reward process. Scott and Yalch (1978) showed that rewards undermined intrinsic interest to the extent that subjects interpreted their behavior as being motivated by the reward (cf. Deci et al., 1975; Lepper et al., 1973).

One of the implications of the view that intrinsic and extrinsic motivation are in basic opposition to each other in their effects on behavior is that it may be unwise to extrinsically motivate people to perform tasks in many situations. Two situations where extrinsic motivation is viewed as unwise are learning situations and situations where the maintenance of behavior is important and external rewards may not be uniformly available.

Schwartz (1982) conducted a series of experiments in which he analyzed the effects of extrinsic reward on complex response sequences involving rule-discovery and problem solving. Extrinsic reinforcement fostered the development of stereotyped sequences even under conditions permitting variability. In addition when novel response sequences were required for reinforcement, naive (nonrewarded) subjects were better able to master the contingency than subjects with a history of reinforcement and were better at rule-discovery.

In general, reinforcement seems to encourage repetition of the responses that resulted in reinforcement. This was certainly the case with animal subjects and appears with humans as well (Condry & Chambers, 1978). Children rewarded for complex discrimination performance take longer to learn and make more errors than unrewarded children (McGraw & McCullers, 1974). In concept attainment tasks which involve identification of the target stimulus dimension in a set of stimuli varying on a number of different dimensions, rewarded adolescents perform more poorly than when unrewarded (McGraw, 1978). Creativity in general seems impaired when performance is directly rewarded (Kruglanski et al., 1971). In addition, intrinsic interest is also lowered. McGraw and McCullers (1979) had college students solve a series of ten water jar problems and were either rewarded or non-rewarded. The first nine problems established a set for a relatively complicated three-jar solution. The tenth was a set breaker which required a simple solution. Rewarded subjects performed more poorly on the last problem but not on the first nine.

It has been noted that intrinsically motivated behavior seems more stable and persistent than extrinsically motivated behavior. There would seem to be two main reasons for this. First of all, it is difficult to insure consistent external reward for an activity over a long period of time. Thus, the reinforcement contingencies are more likely to change for extrinsically motivated than intrinsically motivated behavior. Second, the reinforcing outcomes associated with intrinsically motivated behavior are generally less salient than for extrinsically motivated behavior. In other words, it is generally less clear exactly what reinforcing outcomes are maintaining the intrinsically motivated behavior both to the observer and to the individual. In fact, as we have seen (e.g., Ross, 1975) extrinsic rewards made less salient often result in an apparent increase in the persistence of the behavior.

It would seem that so-called intrinsically motivated behavior displays some strong similarities with partially reinforced behavior. In the latter situation the lack of any cues with 100%

correlation with reinforcement leads to the processing of additional cues because the associative mechanism cannot shut off (cf. the discussion of partial reinforcement in Chapter 10). In addition there is greater likelihood that the cues processed under partial reinforcement will be secondary cues since there is less proximity to reinforcement at any given time. The conditions supporting intrinsic motivation are similar in that there are no salient reinforcing outcomes that are associated with the occurrence of particular cues. Thus, the behavior is likely to come under the control of more diverse cues than an extrinsically reinforced behavior.

A growing number of researchers have warned against the use of extrinsic rewards to teach behaviors, particularly when the behaviors are complex or when it is undesirable or impractical to constantly reward them. A common example is good comportment on the part of a child. It is argued that if a child is taught to behave only because he/she receives extrinsic rewards, the child will not learn good comportment when extrinsic reinforcement is not available, as in later life. This is a legitimate concern of course, and stress has always been placed on the internalization of attitudes and standards of behavior.

The problem, as I see it, is in carrying this idea of an inverse relationship between intrinsically motivated and extrinsically motivated behavior to the extreme. Carried to such a point, we would end up with the principle that extrinsic rewards should never be used whenever we want people to do something more complex than pressing a button. How can the views of a direct inverse relationship between intrinsic and extrinsic motivation be squared with the common observation that people will engage in tremendous amounts of creative effort to achieve large rewards, e.g., commercial inventors, entertainers, business entrepreneurs, etc. It is true that extrinsic rewards can have an informational value over and above their reward value, but it would seem highly questionable to assume that if the reward value of money were removed from its informational content, the same degree of creative effort would be seen in these endeavors from these individuals.

Evidence is accumulating that extrinsic rewards do not necessarily have a negative impact on intrinsic interest in a task. For example, Calder and Staw (1975) found that extrinsic rewards enhanced favorable attitudes toward a task if the task was uninteresting to the individuals. Williams (1980) argues that if extrinsic rewards necessarily decreased intrinsic interest in a task, then effective rewards should produce this effect much more than ineffective rewards. However, in his own study it was found that the more effective the reinforcer in increasing task performance, the greater the degree of intrinsic interest that was created (cf. Hamner & Foster, 1975; Davidson & Bucher, 1978). It was concluded that the behavior-constraining aspects of a contingency are likely to produce the typical intrinsic motivation effect while the reward value aspect leads to an increase in intrinsic interest and post-contingency performance. The importance of behavior constraints on the intrinsic motivation effect is illustrated by studies that show that the effect can be produced by nonreward procedures that put constraints on target performance (e.g., Amabile et al., 1976; Swann & Pittman, 1977).

Bem (1972) has argued that individuals discount internal motivation as a cause of behavior if plausible external rewards are present. To the extent that rewards are expected and salient, they should be so perceived. It is interesting to note that a potential discounting cue not involving reward, i.e., adult surveillance of children, has the same effect on behavior as incentives; that is, it decreases intrinsic interest (Lepper & Greene, 1975).

How can we reconcile the findings that reward seems to harm creative activity and other kinds of complex behavior with the findings above that effective rewards do not necessarily undermine intrinsic interest in a task? I believe that the interaction between the operation of the reinforcer and habituative systems can provide some insight into this question. The more activated the reinforcer system is by external reward, the more it inhibits the operation of the habituative system, both with regard to habituation and nonsalient stimulus processing. More complex cognitive behavior is heavily dependent on the normal functioning of the habituative system's stimulus processing capacities which permit the subtle nonsalient stimulus processing and manipulation required in more complex tasks (cf. Section V). To the extent that a person is given salient effective reward for engaging in a task, it is clear that there is an increased likelihood of habituative system inhibition, thereby making more complex and varied behavior less likely.

Conversely, however, the habituative system is not closely tied to motivational processes. When reward is completely absent, of course, the nonsalient stimuli are processed only to be habituated. It is only when there are primary cues or reinforcers of some kind in the environment that habituative processes will be inhibited. We can see from this line of reasoning that nonsalient cue processing is likely to be most effective under conditions where reward is expected but either temporally removed or not overly salient. If this is the case, then both the operant extreme of constant external rewards and the intrinsic motivational extreme which advocates the non-use of external rewards for any behavior that needs to be intrinsically motivated would not be supported.

External rewards are important in order to induce strong enough motivation to give the person's behavior direction in the face of distractions, including other external rewards which control behavior incompatible with attainment of the target outcome. Therefore,

107

it would be inadvisable to discontinue or minimize the attainment of external rewards even when it is desirable for behavior to occur in the absence of rewards. However, it should be noted that social reinforcement and reduction of uncertainty outcomes, because of their lessened susceptibility to satiation, are perhaps better able to sustain behavior over extended periods of nonreward than are sensory-biological rewards. What is required is that the expected rewards be made relatively infrequent in occurrence and temporally distant. For example, people voluntarily engage in complex learning in college with only the generalized expectancy that such an education will result in a greater probability of attaining important outcomes (e.g., greater income, more desirable work, social prestige, etc). Under these conditions, there is little need for concern that extrinsic rewards will have unwanted effects on persistence and intrinsic interest.

In summary, the functions and interactions of the reinforcer and habituative systems seem to have important implications for human motivated behavior. Although the presence of verbal-symbolic mediation materially affects the form and direction of human moti-vated behavior, it does not cancel the match-mismatch functions of the IPM. These latter functions will continue to express themselves in human behavior in situations where verbal-symbolic mediation does not specifically work against them. As an example of this process, the behavioral properties of intrinsic motivation were shown to be based in large part on the development of conditions favorable to secondary cue processing and the subsequent control of behaviors by such secondary cues.

## HABITUATION AND EXTINCTION

The reader will have noticed that there has been at least a partially implicit assumption that the decremental process in extinction is similar if not identical with that occurring in habituation. Although both phenomena involve the reduction of response strength or probability, there has nevertheless been a lack of attention given to the assumption that the two are based on the same process. The reason for this lies not only in the belief that habituation is a more primitive form of learning and that extinction belongs with more advanced forms, but also because there are a number of significant differences between the habituation of a response and the extinction of a response to stimuli associated with reinforcement. The point that will be argued here is that these differences are not due to different response-decrementing processes, but rather to memorial factors which are independent of the habituative process.

There are both logical and empirical reasons for postulating a common identity to extinction and habituation. Logically, there would seem to be little use for having two separate processes which would diminish responding to stimuli depending simply on whether the stimuli had or had not been associated with reinforcement. Habituation involves the decrementing of response to a repeating stimulus not associated with reward or punishment for the most part (although there is probably some small amount of habituation even with reinforcers, cf. Randlich & LoLordo, 1979) while extinction involves the decrementing of a response to a stimulus that formerly has been paired with reinforcement. While the methodological and procedural differences between the two are clear, this would seem to be a slim basis for the development of two separate response-decrementing processes to handle these two situations. In addition, as we have shown, almost any stimulus capable of evoking the OR is also capable of acting as a reinforcer under certain conditions.

It would seem more parsimonious to assume that the response-decrementing process is the same in both cases, but that the different procedures happen to differentially involve additional factors which then create the observed response differences. It should be emphasized at this point that there are many similarities as well as differences between habituation and extinction. Additionally, some apparent differences have not held up well under closer examination.

A good example of a supposed difference between habituation and extinction is the relative permanence of each process. Habituation was assumed to be a relatively short-term process of response decrementing in which the habituated response would soon recover its initial strength. In other words, spontaneous recovery of the habituated response occurred relatively quickly and restored the response to its original level. On the other hand, extinction was considered a relatively permanent process which showed only partial spontaneous recovery of the extinguished response, and even this partial recovery was soon extinguished itself. Once extinction was complete, spontaneous recovery was not seen and the response would be emitted in the presence of the stimulus only at the level that was sustainable by the stimulus before it was paired with reinforcement.

More recent evidence, however, suggests that habituation may be a more long-lasting phenomenon than was originally thought. There is evidence for both a short-term and a long-term component of the habituation process. Kimmel and Goldstein (1967) studied the GSR of human subjects in response to visual and auditory stimuli. Each subject received repeated presentations of one or the other stimuli until the GSR was habituated. Afterwards, the subjects were instructed to return 7 and 14 days later at the same time and be tested again. All three sessions were identical to

109

one another.  The results showed that the number of trials needed
to reach the habituation criterion declined from session to session
in highly significant fashion, indicating a savings of habituation
from the previous session (cf. Bishop & Kimmel, 1969).

Retention intervals longer than a week have been found in a
number of infrahuman species.  For example, Leaton (1976) tested
the long-term retention of habituation in the rat's startle response
and found that habituation was retained without detectable loss in
intervals ranging from 30 seconds to 30 days.  He found evidence
for both short-term and long-term response decrements which seem
to act independently of each other.  Logan and Beck (1978) tested
habituation in the contraction response of intertidal sea anemones
and found significant retention 72 hours later.  An absence of
spontaneous recovery and a potentiation of habituation were the
key determinants of habituative savings.  Carew et al. (1972)
found retention of habituation in Aplysia 21 days after original
habituation training.  Cheal et al. (1982) showed evidence for long-
term habituation of conspecific odors in gerbils up to 4 weeks later.

The emerging consensus is that habituation is a much more long-
term process than was originally believed.  However, there is
still a difference between the moderately long-term retention of
much habituation and the seemingly permanent retention of extinction.  A closer examination of this issue is useful in determining
some of the reasons for these apparent remaining differences.

First of all, not all reinforcing cues display apparently
permanent conditioning.  Conditioned inhibitors seem to undergo a
somewhat spontaneous extinction over the course of weeks or months
(Rescorla, 1979).  Second, the retention of habituation may be in
part a function of the particular response measure.  For example,
the OR is very sensitive to stimulus change.  Any stimulus occurs
in a given situation or context; the more time that passes, the
more likely the context or situation also changes.  We have seen
that the IPM is entirely capable of processing detailed contextual
information in addition to the target stimulus.  If the OR is
sensitive to changes in stimulus context as it appears to be, then
long-term retention of OR habituation would be difficult to show,
not because it does not exist, but simply because it would be
difficult to keep the stimulus context similar enough to forestall
dishabituation.

Another point to consider with regard to habituation and extinction differences in retention is that the antecedent stimulus
history is vastly different in the two situations.  In the case of
extinction, generally speaking, a formerly neutral stimulus is
paired with reinforcement and then the stimulus is presented in
the absence of reinforcement.  The habituation paradigm is simply
the repeated presentation of a neutral stimulus in the absence of
reinforcement.  It would be surprising if this difference did not

reflect itself in some way when the CS was placed in extinction, i.e., placed in a situation which is procedurally similar to the standard habituation procedure.

In the extinction situation, the psychological properties of the stimulus have been changed by the association with reinforcement. Thus, if we picture a baseline level of occurrence for a particular response to a particular stimulus, we can see that extinction is a procedure whereby an artificially raised response probability is reduced to baseline level. In habituation, the organism learns to decrease the response to this stimuli below what the stimulus initially evokes normally. Strictly on logical grounds, we would expect extinction to be more permanent because of the inherent nature of the situation in which the response is now at the original baseline level. In the absence of any change in the stimulus and its relation to other significant events, we would expect this situation to continue. The habituated stimulus is in an unstable situation in the opposite direction. We would expect a reversion back to the baseline level of responding in the absence of its repeated non-reinforced presentation. By not presenting the stimulus we are restoring its novelty and thus its capacity to evoke the OR.

For reasons mentioned above, the parallel between habituation and extinction has not received detailed attention at the behavioral level. There is one line of evidence that may be promising as a means of testing this point. Some research has gone into the question of whether an extinguished stimulus acts as a true conditioned inhibitor or not. If habituation and extinction are based on the same fundamental process, then the extinguished stimulus should not be a conditioned inhibitor. Unfortunately, not much investigation into this matter has yet been done; however, what evidence there is does suggest that conditioned inhibition, if it plays a role at all, does not figure as the primary cause of the loss of excitatory strength caused by the extinction procedure. Rescorla (1975, 1979) has summarized the state of the research up to this point and his reviews bear examination on a number of important issues that can create interpretational problems.

Rescorla (1975) notes, first of all, that direct tests of extinguished stimuli do not show them to be net inhibitory stimuli. Another possibility is that the extinguished CS retains its excitatory potential but that inhibition is superimposed over it. Spontaneous recovery and the rapid reacquisition of the response to an extinguished stimulus are cited in support of such an interpretation. As I noted previously, an extinguished stimulus certainly has a different antecedent history than a habituated stimulus. The simple fact of quicker reacquisition of an extinguished stimulus does not necessarily indicate inhibition superimposed over excitatory tendencies. Two plausible alternatives would be either a

111

competing response theory or the retention of memories of the
original training. For example, in extinction an organism may
simply learn to perform a different response than the originally
rewarded one. No postulation of inhibition is necessary in such a
case.

An alternative more consistent with match-mismatch theory would
be an assumption that the internal representation of the stimulus-
response complex associated with reinforcement undergoes changes
in extinction. The organism almost certainly retains some representation of these events in long-term (inactive) memory whether or not
they are extinguished. The memory of such an event cannot disappear
from long-term memory once it is formed. However, new representations can supersede it. A number of studies (e.g., Rescorla & Heth,
1975; Rescorla & Cunningham, 1979) suggest that changes in the
internal representation of the stimulus and reinforcer may occur
in extinction. The extinguished stimulus does seem to retain at
least a latent excitatory quality (cf. the discussion on memorial
processes and interference in Section IV).

While the behavioral evidence linking extinction and habituation is thin, it is definitely not negative. Moreover, at the
neurological level there is more positive evidence for the idea
that a common decremental process is at work in both learning
situations. The hippocampus, which we have seen to be linked
with habituative processes in mammalian species, is also clearly
linked with extinction as well. One well-known finding after damage
to the hippocampus is impairment of extinction (e.g., Kimble, 1968;
Isaacson, 1974). On the other hand, habituation also seems impaired
(e.g., Douglas & Pribram, 1969). What is most interesting from
the present viewpoint is that hippocampal damage does not appear
to have an effect on the formation of conditioned inhibitors
(Solomon, 1977). This is exactly what we would expect if extinction
and habituation were related but both were distinct from conditioned
inhibition. While this kind of evidence does not provide definitive
evidence for a common decremental process between habituation and
extinction, it does provide significant negative evidence that
extinction is a form of conditioned inhibition which is conceptually
distinct from habituation.

# Chapter 7
# Habituative Processes

In this chapter we examine more closely the nature of the habituative process. In doing so, empirical evidence which relates to the assumptions of match-mismatch theory concerning habituative function is presented and analyzed. A particular focus is the question of whether differential habituative processes exist for species-specific responses and the OR and what the nature of these differences might be.

## HABITUATION OF SPECIES-SPECIFIC RESPONSES

### Dual Process Theory

Since the appearance of species-specific responses antedates that of the mammalian OR phylogenetically speaking, it is possible that the corresponding habituative processes for these responses are more fundamental than OR habituative processes. As we will see, the habituative process for species-specific behaviors can function in the absence of complex neural structures, indicating the existence of fundamental mechanisms that can be contained within an individual neuron or small group of neurons.

The foremost theory of response habituation at these levels is the dual process theory developed by Thompson and associates (Groves & Thompson 1970; Thompson et al., 1973, 1979). Dual process theory assumes that the observable behavior of organisms in the habituation paradigm is the result of an interaction between two opposing processes, habituation and sensitization. Habituation is caused by a decrease in synaptic transmission due to presynaptic depression of transmitter release within a stimulated pathway. Sensitization or state refers to the general excitatory state (or tendency to respond) of an organism and it is produced by stimuli of sufficient intensity to instigate heterosynaptic facilitation in diverse pathways. These two processes are assumed to be tied down at the neural level to two distinct groups of interneurons, one of which produces habituation and the other sensitization. Sensitization is assumed to increase on the initial presentations of a stimulus and then decline, with the degree of sensitization directly related to the intensity of the stimulus. Obviously, intense stimuli should increase the arousal or sensitization level more than moderate or weak stimuli. At low or moderate stimulus intensities, sensitization may be entirely absent.

One of the major differences between the dual process theory and stimulus comparator theories is that in the former theory dishabituation is assumed to be the imposition of sensitization over the habituative process and not an actual change in the level of habituation for a stimulus. Thus, when dishabituation occurs, according to this view, we should see not only an increase in the level of response to the formerly habituated stimulus, but a general increased level for other responses as well.

Behavioral Evidence. There is quite a bit of behavioral evidence congruent with these assumptions. Kimble and Ray (1965) reported obtaining either habituation or sensitization of the wiping reflex in frogs to tactile stimulation depending on the precise form of the stimulation. Goodman and Weinberger (1973) showed that changes in state in the salamander Necturus produced short periods of dishabituation to stimuli which gradually decayed. In another study, Ewert and Ingle (1973) demonstrated separable habituation and sensitization of prey catching by toads.

Thompson and his associates have shown that similar results can be shown for simplified preparations such as spinal cats or frogs. Groves et al. (1970) showed that the flexor twitch of the spinal cat demonstrated many of the parametric characteristics of habituation. In addition, the connection of sensitization with dishabituation was clearly demonstrated. After habituation of the response, shock was applied in a different location on the skin in order to produce sensitization. When the original stimulus was presented, there was an initial increase in the habituated response. If re-presentation of the original stimulus was delayed, however, there was no increase in the habituated response, which indicates that sensitization has its own intrinsic decay time. Farel et al. (1973) also demonstrated these properties of habituation in the isolated frog spinal cord (cf. Fig. 7-1).

114

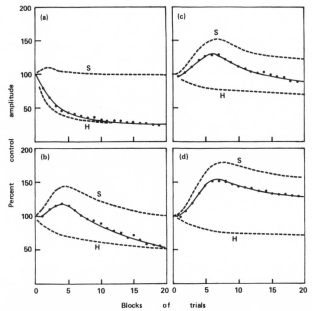

Fig. 7-1 . Dual Process Theory of Habituation . Dashed lines represent the hypothesized processes of sensitization (S) and habituation (H). The center line is based
on data from hindlimb flexion responses in spinal cats. The boxes (a - d) show
increasing levels of US shock intensity. Sensitization is hypothesized to increase
while habituation decreases to increasing stimulus intensity. From Groves & Thompson,1970. Copyright 1970 by the American Psychological Association. Reprinted
by permission.

The evidence supporting the dual-process theory extends to
neurological as well as behavioral data. Much of the confirmatory
evidence has come from investigations of simple organisms or spinal
neurons. This use of simple preparations has the advantage of increasing experimental control and thus improves replicability; the
disadvantage is that it is unclear to what extent generalizations
can be made from these preparations to more complex organisms,
including humans. This latter point is dealt with later in this
chapter.

Neurological Evidence. Major neurological research on habituation
has been performed by Kandel and his associates on the mollusc
Aplysia, which is ideal for such investigations on account of the
large size of its neurons. Many of the neurons have been labeled
as distinct entities which can be found reliably in each individual
organism. The response most typically studied in habituation
research with Aplysia is the gill withdrawal reflex to tactile

115

stimulation. Carew et al. (1972) demonstrated that this response was subject to both habituation and dishabituation.

One of the key points of the dual-process theory is that dishabituation is the result of a superimposed sensitization process and does not represent a change in the habituation level itself. Carew and his associates examined this question at the behavioral and neurological level in Aplysia. Carew et al. (1971) first demonstrated the independence of the gill withdrawal reflex from siphon stimulation from that of mantle stimulation. Habituation of the reflex to one form of stimulation, in other words, did not affect responsiveness to the other. However, the application of a dishabituative stimulus facilitated not only the habituated response but also the unhabituated response above their previous control levels. This directly supports the idea that sensitization is superimposed on a habituative process.

Studies of individual neuronal response provide more details as to the nature of the habituative response in Aplysia. A number of studies have shown that habituation and dishabituation of neural response are independent of receptor adaptation or motor fatigue (Carew et al., 1974; Byrne et al, 1974). Other studies indicated that the loci of habituation and dishabituation are on synapses between sensory cells and interneurons or motor cells (Kirk & Wine, 1984). Habituation is evidenced by a homosynaptic depression at the presynaptic terminals while dishabituation involves heterosynaptic facilitations of those terminals. The mechanism by which those changes are accomplished is apparently a change in the amount of transmitter substance that is released. During habituation the quantal packets of transmitter released at presynaptic sites decline in number. Correspondingly, dishabituation creates an increase in the number of transmitter packets that are released presynaptically (Castelluci & Kandel, 1976). In confirmation of the behavioral findings about dishabituation, Carew et al. (1971) showed that the excitatory post-synaptic potential was facilitated by a dishabituative stimulus in both depressed (habituated) and non-depressed synapses. Habituation seems to take place in a particular pathway while sensitization seems to involve a wider network of pathways. This finding is in line with the concept of sensitization as a determinant of the arousal level of the organism.

In species higher on the phylogenetic scale such as the cat, the site of habituation seems to be largely or entirely in the interneurons rather than in sensory cells (cf. Groves & Thompson, 1970), at least at subthalamic levels (Pribram & McGuinness, 1975). In the cat spinal gray area of the spinal cord, two types of interneurons were located. The first type displayed only habituative properties even when a strong dishabituator was presented. The other type was sensitive to repeated strong stimulation, showing higher output than was reflected in the behavioral response itself.

Thus, habituative and sensitization processes seem to have their own set of interneurons in the cat's spinal gray area. Additional supportive evidence for dual process theory has been obtained using the rat's startle response (Marlin & Miller, 1981) and human responses to intense auditory stimuli (O'Gorman & Jamieson, 1975).

A comment about the sensitization process is in order here. In dual-process theory, arousal is considered to be a unitary state accounting for sensitization (Thompson et al., 1979). However, there is little evidence for a unitary arousal or drive process even for lower organisms. If sensitization is the direct result of a unitary arousal process, then US (e.g., food) or associated cues should increase the tendency to perform other unrelated responses as well. However, the evidence is quite clear that there is no such general arousal for mammals (e.g., Trapold, 1962) or invertebrates (Castelluci & Kandel, 1976). In addition, according to match-mismatch theory, arousal in mammals is generally controlled by the induction of mood states which do not have a uniformly facilitatory or inhibitory action on organismic responses.

Dishabituation. The nature of dishabituation in dual process theory deserves discussion because of the theoretical controversies which surround this phenomenon. As we saw, habituation of a response could be counteracted by a superimposed sensitization process which facilitated other responses in addition to the habituated response. One implication of this effect is that dishabituation should show an asymmetrical effect on the dimension of stimulus intensity. That is, dishabituation should occur when a stronger stimulus than the habituated stimulus is presented but not when a weaker stimulus is presented. A stronger stimulus induces sensitization because it activates more neurons than the habituated stimulus did; on the other hand, a weaker stimulus would activate fewer. Thus, the weaker stimulus would not produce sensitization or dishabituation of the response. Actually, this dishabituative pattern makes a great deal of sense in the case of species-specific responses. To the extent that an organism is able to habituate to a recurring US, it would make little sense to dishabituate to a weaker stimulus.

One service that dual-process theory has provided is to focus on the interplay between arousal and habituation. In the present theory, the interaction between the reinforcer and habituative systems has important implications for the habituative process. The presentation of stimuli which control species-specific responses activates the reinforcer system which induces a graded inhibition of the habituative system, particularly with respect to higher level structures (e.g., hippocampus). The lower levels of the habituative system, however (thalamus and below), are less affected by the inhibition along with the habituative interneurons which

117

exist outside the habituative system. This mechanism is responsible for the limited amount of habituation which does occur to the US in accordance with the process described previously.

Species-specific responses, particularly the visceral components, when they do habituate, recover relatively rapidly. Heart rate acceleration in rats in response to handling decreased within sessions but recovered completely between sessions a day apart (Black et al., 1964). Evans and Hammond (1983a, 1983b) presented rats with a recording of a conspecific distress squeal or a simulated mimic squeal at 80 and 100db. Recovery of orienting after rest periods of 1 or 7 days was greater to the distress squeal. The rats did not seem to habituate completely, appearing to display vigilant behavior even after their emotional behaviors had ceased. In addition, habituation to the distress squeal was specific to the context in which it first appeared, whereas the mimic squeal showed generalization of habituation across different contexts.

The relatively slower habituation of species-specific response to stimuli with signal value compared with the OR or voluntary responses may not have process implications for habituation because of the differences in the arousal value of the respective stimuli controlling these responses. However, different components of the same response often show different rates of habituation; this finding holds across the different response classes. For example, a stimulus eliciting startle initially induces gross bodily movements. Upon repetition, these larger movements tend to drop out while less vigorous components remain (Graham, 1979). Szlep (1964) showed that the prey-catching response of the webweaving spider contained a number of separate components which habituated at different rates. The response consists of spreading the legs to touch different radii of the web after vibrations have been detected. Then the spider runs toward the vibrational center, circles the object on the web, and attacks. Repeated presentations of a vibrating stimulus to the web first result in general retardation of all response components. Later, however, the running toward the stimulus is the first component to be omitted (habituated) while leg movements are still present.

Thus, the habituation of motoric response components quite likely proceeds according to the effort required to make the response. A progressive decrease in the number of activated neurons could achieve this result with the simple assumption that more vigorous response components require greater neuronal activation. In addition, visceral components of a response should habituate roughly in accordance with the rate for the overall response since in large measure they are fitted to the requirements of the overall exertion involved in making the total response.

Turning from the habituation of species specific responses to the habituation of the OR is akin to changing from a blunt instrument to a scalpel. Species-specific responses habituate to repeated stimulation in order to conserve an organism's energy for more critical events; the performance of these responses is generally effortful both autonomically and motorically. The response requirements of the OR are much less than for the typical species-specific response, so this isn't as great a consideration for the initiation and maintenance of its habituation. The function of the OR is to alert the organism to stimulus changes in the environment, particularly where these do not involve strong affective reactions. (In the latter case the organism would probably be performing species-specific responses anyway.) Thus, the habituative and dishabituative mechanisms associated with the OR have to be fitted to permit this general function.

With species-specific responses, habituation proceeds through the action of habituative interneurons in the reinforcer system and through lower level structures of the habituative system because of the inhibition of higher level habituative system structures. Habituation of the OR, on the other hand, involves the entire habituative system because of the reduced or absent inhibitory action of the reinforcer system.

With dishabituation, we find differences in the sensitivity with which stimulus changes can re-evoke the OR as opposed to species-specific responses. There are two reasons for this effect: first, the development of the habituative system in structures such as the hippocampus permits a greater representational capacity in defining the internal model and comparing it with processed stimuli. Second, with stimuli which do not induce affective responses in the organisms and consequently do not strongly activate the reinforcer system, these habituative system structures can operate with reduced inhibition from the reinforcer system.

Models of OR Habituation

Let's turn our attention at this point to several models of habituation which deal with the more complex situations characterizing habituation and dishabituation of the OR. It should be noted that these theories were formulated as general theories of habituation. However, in the current view they are really more descriptive of OR habituative mechanisms than of those involving species-specific responses.

Additional research led Sokolov (1975) to adopt a more precise description of the habituative process. Sokolov hypothesized that the encoding of a stimulus is accomplished through the activation of a particular pattern of neuronal responses in the sensory analyzing areas of the cortex. Each perceived stimulus parameter would be encoded by a particular subset of the activated neurons and the discharge density of the neuron would indicate the "weight" of that parameter in the integrated response of the organism. The more times the stimulus is presented the more stable the response pattern becomes (see Fig. 7-2).

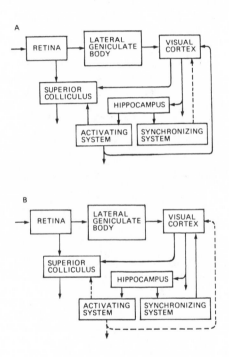

**Fig. 7-2 . Sokolov's Comparison Process .** A) Novel stimuli are processed through the sensory systems and activate novelty (mismatch) detectors in the hippocampus. As a result, the excitatory response of the reticular activating system to the cortex is increased and the inhibitory or synchronizing system is suppressed, thus producing an OR. B) Habituating stimuli no longer excite the hippocampal novelty detectors while inhibitory neurons continue sustained activity. The activating system thus becomes depressed and the synchronizing influence on the cortex becomes more pronounced. Solid lines are active connections in the situation depicted while dashed lines are inactive connections. From Sokolov,1975. Copyright 1975 by Lawrence Erlbaum Associates. Reprinted by permission.

Cortical output neurons representing the analyzed stimulus trigger hippocampal activating neurons and interneurons. With stimulus repetition, the action of the inhibitory interneurons on hippocampal cells is potentiated, leading to the inhibition of these cells. The inhibition of the hippocampal cells interrupts the transmission of excitatory information to the reticular system. Instead, the inhibitory neurons' output becomes dominant, causing an increase in synchronization (reduced arousal) of the reticular activating system.

Under conditions of stimulus change which cause a mismatch between the pattern of output transmitted from the cortical cells and the pattern of potentiated and inhibited hippocampal neurons, the hippocampal response matrix is disrupted. This allows excitatory input to flow through to the reticular system, re-evoking arousal (i.e., the OR). Neurological evidence suggests that excitatory potentials simply override the action of the inhibitory interneurons rather than directly inhibiting them (Dichter & Spencer, 1969; Thatcher & Purpura, 1973). This finding is interesting in light of our prior discussion of dual-process habituative functions in which sensitization overrides habituation rather than inhibiting it directly.

The key difference in the present situation is that it is the pattern of stimulation which is crucial to the maintenance or the disruption of habituation. The presentation of a weaker stimulus than the originally habituated stimulus activates different neurons and thus a different response matrix is constructed. The properties of neurons in the sensory areas are compatible with this basic idea (cf. Rose et al. 1963; Thatcher & John, 1977). For example, some duration-sensitive neurons respond strongly to stimuli appearing at short duration while others are more sensitive to long durations. Because of these complex stimulus analyses, a wide variety of stimulus changes are capable of producing dishabituation.

If this scheme is accurate, and it has much to recommend it at a general level, why do species-specific responses also not display these dishabituative properties? According to the present theory, the activation of the reinforcer system exerts an inhibitory effect on the habituative system, particularly at the level of the hippocampus and higher structures. Thus, the cortical-hippocampal-reticular loop would not come into being in such circumstances or would have a much more circumscribed effect. Instead, habituation occurs at lower levels in the habituative system or in inhibitory interneurons in reinforcer system structures. To some extent these can exert an effect on OR habituation too.

Wagner (1976, 1978) has proposed a comparator theory of habituation which incorporates a few additional assumptions to the basic Sokolovian position. One of the ideas used by Wagner as a starting point was derived from the Atkinson and Shiffrin (1968) model of human memory processes. They proposed that when an item was present in short-term (STM) or working memory, there could only be one representation of that item even if it were presented twice. STM is generally defined as a memory store for items currently or recently in working memory (cf. Chapters 12, 13). Let's say that a series of five two-digit numbers were presented to a subject, e.g., 24, 68, 37, 51, 19. If a sixth number duplicated one of the original five, e.g., 37, it would not exist separately in short-term memory but would be combined with the duplicate.

Wagner (1976) proposed that habituation exists when a representation of a stimulus already exists in short-term memory at the time the stimulus itself is encountered or presented. This pre-representation of the stimulus in STM reduces the degree of stimulus processing which would ordinarily take place to the incoming stimulus if it were not prerepresented in STM. In colloquial terms, when a stimulus is prerepresented we can define it as being expected and when it is not, we can define it as surprising, at least in a limited sense. The prerepresentation of a stimulus in working memory can occur in one of two ways: by retrieval from permanent memory because of the presence of predictive cues for the stimulus or because it has just been entered into STM due to a recent environmental occurrence. Wagner terms the first situation retrieval-generated priming of STM and the second as self-generated priming of STM. In the current context we can rephrase all this by noting that since the OR is evoked by uncertainty and unanticipated stimulus change, then to the extent that a stimulus is anticipated the OR will be inhibited (habituated).

One serious problem with Wagner's formulation is that all stimuli which have become habituated in the environment must be prerepresented in working memory. This would require a very large capacity in working memory and simply doesn't seem plausible. Ohman (1979), in putting forth a similar theory of habituation, has argued that the comparison process takes place through pre-attentive mechanisms as long as there is a match. Only a mismatch causes the stimulus to be transferred to working memory, resulting in the appearance of an OR.

Evidence has accumulated in favor of some limited amount of pre-attentional processing of stimuli (cf. Egeth, 1977; Posner, 1979). The early evoked components prior to the occurrence of the P300 wave may be an indication of such pre-attentional processing. It is plausible, especially given some parallel processing assumption, that the match-mismatch process could take place pre-attentionally in the case of a fully habituated or very familiar stimulus (cf. the discussion in Chapter 12 on pre-attention).

Experimental Evidence

In Chapter 3 we briefly discussed some of the evidence supporting a sophisticated stimulus comparator mechanism involved in the habituative process. Dishabituation of the OR was shown to occur as a result of changes in stimulus modality (Ginsberg & Furedy, 1974), tone pitch changes (Van Olst, 1971), decreases in stimulus intensity (Fredrickson et al., 1984) and changes in the pattern of stimulation (Yaremko et al., 1970). While these findings are generally accepted, there are four issues that merit specific examination with respect to the underpinnings of comparator theories: (1) dishabituation without sensitization, (2) the effect of stimulus omission, (3) the effect of stimulus priming of working memory, and (4) generalization of habituation.

OR Dishabituation. Stimulus comparator theories, unlike the dual-process theory, make a distinction between sensitization and dishabituation. Dishabituation is assumed to be specific to the habituated response and does not involve a general response facilitation. This of course is due to the working of the comparison process in which a mismatch causes dishabituation whether or not the mismatch comes about from a weaker or stronger stimulus. Thus, we need to see if dishabituation is specific to the habituated response.

Whitlow (1975) tested the stimulus specificity of short-term habituation in the rabbit to tones using the vasoconstriction response. Whitlow found that the effect was indeed stimulus specific, but more important to the present discussion, dishabituation could be produced by a mild stimulus (a flashing light-electrotactile stimulus sequence) which did not cause a corresponding increase in other nonhabituated responses. In other words, the dishabituator did not seem to have a sensitizing effect. Other evidence similarly suggests that in more complex situations a dishabituator is not necessarily a sensitizer. A good example is those studies which used a dishabituator which was less intense than the original habituated stimulus (e.g., Edwards, 1975; Sokolov, 1963). Presumably, sensitization cannot occur to a less intense stimulus than the one already habituated.

Maltzman et al., (1978) presented college students with a list of common words repeated over 5 daily sessions. A particular word acted as the CS and a 110 db noise was the US. Two to four filler words were interspersed between stimulus presentations. On the fourth and fifth days, the room lights were dimmed for 1/2 second either 5 seconds prior to the CS or simultaneously with it. The response measure used were the GSR and vasomotor responses.

Habituation of these responses occurred rapidly to the repeated presentation of a common set of words. The light dimming produced a large dishabituation of the OR, particularly when the novel stimulus occurred simultaneously with the CS word. Importantly, there was no increase in response to the control word that followed the CS word and light dimming, which precludes a sensitization effect. These results are in line with those reported by Whitlow (1975).

Megela and Teyler (1979) found that in humans early components of the EP which preceded the P300 components, such as N100, displayed a dishabituative pattern which was asymmetrical in the way predicted by dual-process theory. Dishabituation occurred to stimuli of greater intensity than the habituated stimulus but not to stimuli of weaker intensity. However, the P300 component did not show asymmetrical generalization; instead, symmetrical generalization around higher and lower intensities was found as predicted by stimulus comparator theories.

It should be remembered that the P300 wave seems to be involved in what might be described as the more cognitive aspects of initial stimulus processing while the early components are more sensitive to basic stimulus characteristics (cf. Schandry & Hoefling, 1979). Habituation of the P300 wave is more dependent on the presentation sequence of the stimulus events than on the intensity and proceeds significantly slower when stimuli occur at irregular as opposed to regular ISIs (Fitzgerald & Picton, 1981). This finding is more difficult to obtain when autonomic measures are used however (e.g., Kimmel et al., 1979). This pattern of results suggests that different factors are at work in the habituative process in these domains.

It is interesting to note that much of the data that have been used to support the dual process theory have come from more primitive organisms or preparations while stimulus comparator theory has been based almost entirely on data from human studies. The different interpretations that have arisen, and they are not all that extreme, seem perfectly reflected in the data from Megela and Teyler. More basic, noncognitive habituation seems to display many of the characteristics proposed by dual-process theory while more complex habituative processing follows stimulus comparator models.

Stimulus Omission. A related issue is the question of whether dishabituation occurs to complete stimulus omission as opposed to a decrease in intensity. The experimental evidence is mixed on this point, although the confusion is more evident when peripheral measures of habituation such as the electrodermal response are used than with central measures such as evoked potentials or EEG (cf. Siddle et al., 1983). The occurrence of dishabituation after the omission of an expected stimulus has been clearly shown in studies of the P300 wave as we have seen. Additionally, the effect has been found when the omitted stimulus has been part of a stimulus compound even when peripheral measures have been employed (e.g.,

124

Ohman, 1974). It may be unrealistic to expect a large autonomic or motoric response to the complete absence of a stimulus, particularly when it has been habituated. The apparent solidity of the EEG and the stimulus compound data would seem to bear out this contention.

Priming in STM. With respect to the role of STM priming in observed habituation, Wagner and his associates have conducted a number of experiments which provide some evidential basis for the main points above. Whitlow (1975) tested the idea that response decrements characteristic of habituation should occur only when the stimulus input matches the contents of STM. Two tones were presented to rabbits in sequences for a number of separate trials. On one half of the trials the tones were the same (either 530 or 4000 Hz). On the other half, they were different (530-4000 or 4000-530). Using the vasomotor response, Whitlow examined whether decremental effects were specific to the trials in which the same tone was presented twice in sequence. Additionally, the temporal distance between the two tones in sequence was varied from 30, 60, or 150 seconds in order to test the transience of the memory. If the stimulus input is in STM then it should be sensitive to temporal factors which limit the maintenance of an item in STM without constant rehearsal.

The results indicated that repetitive stimulation did produce greater response decrement than the different tonal sequence. Importantly, however, this response decrement was dependent to a great extent on the temporal distance between the two sequential tones; that is, the more time elapsed between the first and second tones, the smaller the difference in response decrement between repetitive versus different stimulation. This is what we would expect if the stimulus input of the first stimulus was part of a transient trace which was being compared with the second tone.

In a second experiment, Whitlow found that presentation of an innocuous stimulus in the interval between $S_1$ and $S_2$ could produce the same dishabituative effect that was found in the preceding experiment from increases in the temporal distance between the stimuli. The intervening stimulus is assumed to displace the memory of $S_1$ from STM, thus reducing the match between $S_1$ and $S_2$ even when the two stimuli are the same. Since appropriate controls were made for fatigue and adaptation effects, there is presumptive evidence that a memorial process was involved.

The Whitlow study provides an example of what Wagner terms self-generated priming. There is also the question of retrieval-generated priming, which more closely approximates the standard habituation paradigm. In this situation we expect that cues associated with the occurrence of the habituated stimulus will retrieve the internal representation into STM. One implication of this position is that anything which affects the retrieval effectiveness of the cues associated with the habituated stimulus

125

should also interfere with its habituation. Grant et al. (1983) showed that pigeons exhibited enhanced post-perceptual processing of surprising stimuli in a matching-to-sample task which involved retrieval-generated priming of STM.

Wagner (1976) reports a study on this topic done in conjunction with Whitlow and Pfautz. One group of rabbits was tested for retention of habituation to a tone after being placed in the experimental chamber between initial training and post-test two days later. The other group was simply left in their home cages during this time. The apparatus cues which were associated with the presentation of the habituated stimulus should become less able to evoke its representation since the animal has been placed in the apparatus after training, when the habituated stimulus was not presented. In effect, the cues to habituation are being extinguished in this situation. The other group, however, does not come in contact with the cues except when the habituated stimulus is also being presented. A significant difference was found between the two groups on the habituation retention test, with the group receiving the exposure to the cues in the absence of the habituated stimulus showing much less habituation than the group which received no such exposure to the cues. Similar findings have been reported by researchers in latent inhibition, incidentally (cf. Lantz, 1973; Anderson et al., 1969). (The latent inhibition paradigm consists of the preexposure of a stimulus later used as a CS in a standard conditioning paradigm. The prior presentations of the stimulus occur in the absence of any reinforcement, i.e., the standard habituation paradigm.)

These latter findings have been the subject of some controversy, however. Marlin and Miller (1981) found that habituation of the startle response in rats was greater if they had habituated to both the target stimulus and the experimental context. Baker and Mercier (1982) were able to exhibit the dishabituation effect after contextual extinction in the latent inhibition paradigm but only when a continuous reinforcement (CRF) schedule was used. Latent inhibition of the stimulus was not reduced by contextual extinction when a partial reinforcement (PRF) schedule was used.

With respect to the Marlin and Miller study it should be noted that the startle response was used instead of the OR. According to the present theory, this could make a significant difference because of the activation of the reinforcer system. The operative habituative mechanisms would to a greater extent be those delineated in dual-process theory since the habituative system itself would be in a state of partial inhibition. Dishabituation would tend to be more a function of sensitization or mood state induction rather than a true mismatch process. The study by Baker and Mercier provides partial support for the priming hypothesis in a situation which involves the OR. The differential effect as a result of the reinforcement schedule is an important finding but it raises issues

126

that are best left to the point in the section where stimulus selection and latent inhibition are discussed.

Generalization. The final topic that merits discussion is the question of the generalization of habituation. Although this question has a number of facets, the point to be discussed at this time involves the phenomenon in humans of generalization of habituation with verbal materials. The ability of humans to habituate to a class of stimuli in addition to a single repeating stimulus is a phenomenon which has been found by a number of different researchers (e.g., Lovibond, 1969; Unger, 1964). For example, habituation of the OR was found by Unger when presenting numbers seriatim. After habituation, the presentation of a number out of sequence caused dishabituation of the OR. As Velden (1978) notes, the OR can apparently habituate to stimuli which are constantly changing in their physical properties. This raises questions about the role of a match-mismatch process of stimulus comparison given stimuli which are constantly changing. Velden suggests that deviations from expected stimuli, rather than previously presented stimuli, are the cause of dishabituation of the OR.

It will be remembered in the section on the OR in humans that the P300 wave could be evoked by just such disconfirmations of expected events. Velden regards the information value of the stimulus and its motivational implications to be key additional factors in the occurrence or dishabituation of the OR to that of stimulus change per se. In this view, two different stimuli could convey the same information and thus be processed similarly. With regard to motivation, stimuli may be informative but motivationally trivial or meaningless. Although Velden argues that these factors interact in multiplicative fashion to produce the OR, other evidence suggests an additive relationship between stimulus significance and stimulus change in the evocation of the OR (e.g., Siddle et al., 1979).

This general viewpoint is echoed by Maltzman et al. (1979) who note that the occurrence of the OR is not only a function of stimulus changes but also of cortical set. They distinguish between involuntary ORs to surprising stimuli and voluntary ORs to stimuli of some particular significance to the subject.

Habituation of Verbal-Symbolic Stimuli. It is important to closely analyze studies such as those described above in order to better define the similarities and differences between habituation in humans as opposed to other vertebrate species. The basic thrust of habituation theories involving stimulus comparison is that information in working memory which matches the input from external stimuli can effectively forestall additional processing of that stimulus input. As Wagner noted, there are two ways that such

127

information can come to reside in working memory; it can either be retrieved from long-term memory through the mechanism of retrieval cues or it can be in working memory because of a prior presentation of the stimulus.

Let's look at the example of habituation to a series of non-repeating stimuli such as seriatim numbers. It might be asked how a match-mismatch process can apply to stimuli which are continuously changing in their physical parameters, whether presented visually or auditorially. How does an internal representation match up with the stimulus input? One thing that can be noted at the beginning is that in presenting numbers or words to subjects we are not dealing with novel stimuli in the same sense that we are with many stimuli presented to animals. The subjects in these experiments already have internal representations of these verbal-symbolic stimuli before the experiment has begun. On the other hand, an animal may not have ever heard a pure sine tone before. Thus, in the case of items already represented in the organism, there is no need to build up or construct a stimulus representation from a number of repetitions of the items.

Therefore, the key question is whether or not the pre-existing representations can be primed in working memory at the same time that they are occurring externally. Of course, when numbers are presented consecutively, as in the experiment by Unger, we have an ideal retrieval situation. The presentation of each item also acts as the cue for the next item. Therefore, habituation can occur with constantly changing stimuli if they are pre-represented in permanent memory and if there are strong cues for their retrieval at the appropriate time.

The above example is a clear-cut case; however, there are many situations which are more ambiguous with regard to the mechanism of habituation. The most striking differences between human habituative behaviors and those of animals are the range of stimuli which can be habituated and the kinds of discrepancies from past stimulation that produce dishabituation. In layman's language, we can perhaps say that humans' expectancies about what is consistent with past stimulation and what is not are qualitatively different from those we see in animals.

Pendery and Maltzman (1977) demonstrated that habituation of the orienting component of the electrodermal response can be obtained in verbal conditioning once the CS word's relationship with the (innocuous) US is detected. Maltzman et al. (1979) have demonstrated that latent inhibition can also be found in semantic conditioning. Different groups received presentations of either 0, 20, or 40 words other than the CS word prior to the first pairing of the CS with the US. The responding to the CS was diminished in those groups which received presentations of words prior to conditioning.

In addition, the groups differed in the magnitude of their response to the omission of the US in extinction.

In this experiment subjects habituated to a series of common words. Insofar as was possible, the words selected were associatively unrelated to each other. As the authors note, habituation to these common words proceeded relatively rapidly. As in the experiment by Unger, we have habituation occurring to stimuli which are changing. Unlike that experiment, however, individual items were not good retrieval cues for the following items. Maltzman et al. noted that habituation occurred on the first day despite the fact that none of the words were repeated. It seemed that the subjects were habituating to a class of stimuli rather than to particular stimuli. Furthermore, the class of stimuli is a rather arbitrary one, the class of common words. This is a more abstract class than say a series of tones of similar frequencies.

An analysis of this effect reveals certain things. The subject has to have a fairly good idea as to what constitutes the class of stimuli that are to be presented. Obviously, in the case of common words, we have highly overlearned items. Thus, the definition of the class would seem to be one necessary factor for habituation to occur. In this regard Ben-Shakhar et al. (1982) showed that habituation could generalize across different stimuli provided they belong to the same general category. The generalization was not indiscriminate, however, as it did not extend across categories. Perceptual attributes, incidentally, were not found to be crucial in determining categories.

In these kinds of examples we are probably encountering cognitive strategies on the part of subject. If this is the case, then it is clear that habituation should be able to proceed in any situation which can be verbally or symbolically mediated by the subject so that stimulus events are primed into working memory (or pre-attention).

One bit of evidence in favor of the idea that these results are due to cognitive strategies is that there are great individual differences reported in this type of research. To the extent that strategies are invoked, we would expect more idiosyncratic responses and general differences in response bias to occur. For example, different people would necessarily have somewhat different ideas as to what constitutes the class of common words.

These considerations may help shed some light on the often confusing literature on human habituation. For example, Kimmel et al. (1979) found that habituation sometimes proceeded slower to tones presented with constant intertrial intervals (ITI) than with variable ITIs. In another case, variations in tone frequency retarded habituation but variations in the shape of visual stimuli produced no effect. A variability effect for visual stimuli was found with color changes, however. Other researchers have also

129

occasionally found slower habituation with an unvarying stimulus than with changing stimuli. Sokolov (1969) found that habituation occurred after a moderate amount of exposure to an unvarying stimulus, but as the stimulus continued, dishabituation occurred. Thus, subjects may simply expect a certain amount of stimulus variability in the occurrence of exteroceptive stimuli and be surprised by too much stimulus invariance. These points lead to the idea that humans, by virtue of the complexity of their expectations, may simply be a poor species in which to obtain consistent results in habituation.

## SUMMARY

In summary, different habituative processes seem to exist for species-specific responses as compared with the OR. The habituation of species-specific responses is most congruent with the assumptions of dual-process theory in which habituation is caused by a change in synaptic transmission due to presynaptic depression produced by habituative interneurons. Dishabituation is caused by sensitization which overrides habituation and elevates other response levels besides the habituated response.

In terms of match-mismatch theory, these habituative processes are located in isolated interneurons in the reinforcer system and in the lower level structures of the habituative system. Since species-specific responses inhibit upper level structures of the habituative system, the habituative processes subserved by those regions does not operate in the habituation of species-specific responses.

The habituation of the OR is most congruent with stimulus comparator theories in which habituation is produced by a match between an internal representation and the exteroceptive stimulus and dishabituation is produced by a mismatch. Dishabituation can be produced by stimulus changes of greater or lesser intensity and salience than the habituated stimulus. In addition, dishabituation is specific to the habituated response and does not involve changes in the level of other responses.

In terms of match-mismatch theory, the entire habituative system is operative during the habituation of the OR. The upper level structures of the habituative system, because of their expanded information processing capacities, are mainly responsible for the different properties of OR habituation as compared with species-specific response habituation.

# Chapter 8
## Affective Properties of Cues

CONDITIONED REINFORCEMENT

Previously we examined some of the properties of the unconditioned reinforcer. In this chapter we turn our attention to conditioned reinforcers, or the cues in temporal proximity to reinforcement. Conditioned reinforcement is the result of a procedure in which a formerly neutral stimulus, through association with an unconditioned reinforcer, comes to control behavior in its own right in much the same way as the reinforcer. It has, of course, been recognized that this conditioned reinforcing property could be maintained only through a continued cue-reinforcer relationship.

There have been a number of criteria used to establish the existence of conditioned reinforcing properties in a stimulus (cf. Deese & Hulse, 1967; Schwartz & Gamzu, 1977). Perhaps the strictest requirement is that a conditioned reinforcer have the same effect on behavior in all situations as an unconditioned reinforcer. This definition has not been supported (e.g., Mackintosh, 1983). However, other more limited criteria are possible.

One strong criterion for a conditioned reinforcer would be to use it to train a completely new response that it could not reinforce inherently. Another criterion would be the enhancement of resistance to extinction. Presumably, the presence of the conditioned reinforcer would provide at least some reinforcement in the extinction situation to compensate for the absence of the unconditioned reinforcer. In other words, a conditioned reinforcer should

131

have the capacity to maintain responding. A variant of this maintenance technique can be found in the chain schedule, in which a sequence of responses, each sequence paired with a different stimulus, leads to primary reinforcement. Finally, responding to a conditioned reinforcer should be sensitive to the same parametric considerations as those found with unconditioned reinforcers. For example, a stimulus associated with a large reward should function as a stronger conditioned reinforcer than a stimulus associated with a small reward. The basic criteria outlined above have been supported in a number of classic studies (e.g., Miles, 1956; Saltzman, 1949).

## Associative Attributes of Primary Cues

If we can summarize the implications of match-mismatch principles for the psychological properties of the CS or cue in close temporal proximity to the US, they would consist of two main points. First, the processing of a US involves the contents of working memory at the time of US occurrence. Any cues in close temporal proximity to the US or retrieved into working memory at this time will therefore be processed along with the US as will the organism's mood state and responses. These cues are termed primary cues. Since the cues are being processed while the organism is in a particular state caused by the US, they will be encoded in association with the particular qualities and affect produced by it. In other words, the CSs will function as redintegrative cues which, upon presentation, can retrieve the total stimulus complex of which they are a part. However, the second point limits the functional identity between the CS and US. The CS, even when it acts to retrieve the US representation cannot stimulate the same pathways as the US. Thus, there will be a certain amount of interaction and competition between these factors in determining the final organismic response to the CS.

Response Aspects. Pavlov (1941) noted that a dog, trained to respond to a metronome acting as a CS for the occurrence of food, would lick and attempt to bite the metronome as if it were food. Farris (1967) used a buzzer as a CS for the presentation of a female Japanese quail to a male. Conditioning proceeded rapidly, but more important, the CS began to elicit part of the courting behavior and display that constituted the male UR to the presence of the female. Peterson et al. (1972) also found similarities between the responding to a CS and the UR to a US. Rats had electrodes implanted in the lateral hypothalamus which, when stimulated, acts as a potent positive reinforcer. Stimulation was signaled by the insertion of a (CS) lever into the experimental chamber. The rats showed directed responses to the CS that were correlated with the kind of responses shown during stimulation (i.e., licking, gnawing, or exploratory activities).

A similar correspondence between the forms of the CR and UR has been found using the autoshaped keypeck response in the pigeon. Jenkins and Moore (1973) demonstrated that the form of the pigeon's keypeck depended on the type of reinforcer used. When water was the reinforcer, the keypecks resembled drinking movements, while food reinforcement tended to produce keypecks resembling pecking for food. Additionally, it was shown that the deprivational state was not a determinant of the form of the response. When two keys were used each associated with a different reinforcer (i.e., water and food) the responses to each key were appropriate to the kind of reinforcer obtainable on that key (cf. Dunham, 1977).

The interesting thing about these and similar studies is that the whole behavior of the organism is being studied. As we noted before, in early classical conditioning studies one specific response component was selected as the UR and then measured as the CR. The studies just described indicate that there is a good deal of correspondence between the responses to a US and to its associated CS even when we consider the overall behavior of the organism.

The correspondence between CR and UR can be disrupted when the CS is not a neutral stimulus. For example, Grant (in Hearst, 1975) used a conspecific rat as a CS for food. The experimental rats learned the CS-US relationship; however, they did not respond to the CS conspecific as they did to food, although they did orient and approach the CS. Instead of eating movements they displayed sniffing and social contact responses; in other words, they displayed those behaviors appropriate to the CS when presented by itself. A similar effect can be seen in counterconditioning studies in which food is a CS for shock or vice versa. Although the CS-US relationship is learned, organisms rarely display a correspondence between CR and UR (Pavlov, 1927).

Stimulus Aspects. It has been stated that cues in temporal proximity to the US are processed with it through the reinforcer system and thus acquire its reinforcing properties. A natural question is how long-delay conditioning can be observed in certain circumstances. The best known example is the taste aversion paradigm in which gustatory cues paired with the ingestion of substances associated with gastric illness (US) can become conditioned reinforcers even when the interval between cues and illness (US) is several hours (e.g., D'Amato, 1973; Lavin, 1976; Revusky & Garcia, 1970). Other types of cues which do not have gustatory properties (e.g., tones) cannot become conditioned with delays of this length.

133

What must be kept in mind is that the process of conditioned reinforcement is dependent on the concurrent processing of cues and reinforcer through the reinforcer system. Placing cues in temporal proximity to the US is a useful procedural way of insuring that such concurrent processing occurs. However, an alternative mechanism is for an internal representation to be retrieved into working memory during the processing of the reinforcer (e.g., retrieval-generated priming: Chapter 7). This priming can occur if cues or reinforcers in the environment match with pre-existing internal representations and thus retrieve them. In other words, gastric illness may be a particularly good retrieval cue for gustatory representations (cf. Spear, 1978). In principle, however, long delay conditioning can happen in any circumstance in which the stimuli present at the time of US occurrence function as retrieval cues for pre-existing internal representations. To avoid circularity, the retrieval relationship should be established independently of long-delay conditioning.

There is substantial evidence that the representation of the CS is not only precise in its own right but also evokes the correspondingly precise US representation which is associated with it. Flaherty and Checke (1982) showed that rats reduced their intake of saccharine when it was used as a cue for 32% sucrose but not when it preceded 2% sucrose. Thus, rats not only learn that saccharine predicts the occurrence of sucrose but it also appears to evoke specific attributes of the sucrose. In this connection, Holland and Forbes (1982) have shown that the representations evoked by CSs can substitute for the exteroceptive stimulus in the control of conditional discrimination performance. In addition, these expectancies are context specific rather than general emotional or motivational arousal (Baxter & Zamble, 1982).

A study by Holland (1978) would seem to indicate that even when there are different unconditioned responses to two different CS's, the underlying associative basis between them is quite similar if not identical. Holland, using a second-order conditioning procedure, showed that although different CSs evoked differing responses, they established similar second order conditioning to a $CS_2$.

Results such as these are not theoretically surprising. A CS that also is a US in its own right will command the reinforcer system of the IPM and, as it is processed, will release the species-specific responses which constitute the organism's UR. It should be emphasized that the observable correspondence between CR and UR does not constitute the essential basis for the association between CS and US. When the CS is neutral, the particular attributes of the US incorporated into the CS representation are free to evoke the inherent response to the US. When the CS is not neutral, there will be interference and competition between the respective species-specific responses evoked by the two stimuli. Nevertheless, the

CS is still processed in association with the US because the US typically represents the dominant motivation at that particular time. That is, the non-neutral CS is still less favored than the US in the attributes comprising the CS-US representation.

If primary cues processed along with positive reinforcers acquire some of their qualities, then similar effects should be observed for cues associated with aversive reinforcers. It should be noted, however, that there is more of a measurement problem with such cues than with the positive cues, since the organism is presumably going to try to avoid any cues which carry aversive qualities. Thus, it will be more difficult to differentiate between different types of aversive stimuli on the basis of the response made to the aversive CS.

Organisms exposed to aversive USs typically display what might be called a fear reaction (cf. Bolles, 1972b). Components of this fear reaction are also evident to the cues which signal the occurrence of the aversive US (cf. Schneider, 1972). Fear reactions and freezing to cues signaling aversive USs occur in many different situations, not just classical conditioning. One of the most prominent situations is the conditioned suppression paradigm in which an aversive CS (AvCS) is presented while the organism is engaged in some instrumental behavior. Typically, the presentation of the AvCS results in freezing or inhibition on the part of the organism (cf. Blackman, 1977; Millenson & de Villiers, 1972).

Another aspect to the acquired aversive properties of cues associated with the presentation of aversive USs has stemmed from the insight that the removal of positive reinforcers might have much the same aversive implications to an organism as the presentation of actual negative USs (cf. Daly, 1974; Amsel, 1972). If this is the case, we should see some evidence that cues associated with the absence of positive reinforcement have aversive qualities to the organism.

Wasserman et al. (1974) compared the behavior of pigeons to a CS+ and a CS- for positive reinforcement. All the birds exposed to the CS+ soon began approaching and pecking it (keylight). Control pigeons exposed to backward conditioning trials (i.e., US-CS) or CS- only presentations did not display the approach behaviors found in the positive group. Those pigeons exposed to the CS- spent most of the time during its presentation on the side of the chamber opposite the key; that is, withdrawing from the stimulus. When the nature of the relationship between the stimulus and the US was changed, the birds' behaviors were also changed in the appropriate direction. Hearst and Franklin (1977) noted similar findings and further discovered that the amount of time that pigeons spent withdrawing from the CS- was a direct function of the rate of reinforcement in the absence of the cue.

135

Similarly, discriminative learning is impaired if a distinctive feature distinguishing the S- from the S+ was shown only on S-trials, the feature positive effect (cf. Hearst, 1978). Newman and Hearst (reported in Hearst, 1978) studied the feature positive effect using college students as subjects. Symbols or nonsense syllables were used as the discriminative stimuli. The students were less likely to notice the distinctive feature when it occurred on S-trials. If organisms tend to withdraw from or avoid stimuli associated with reinforcer omission, then it would seem likely that less stimulus processing will occur with such stimuli compared with those associated with positive events.

Holmes (1972) showed that a CS- for food could function in much the same way as the AvCS in a conditioned suppression situation. In Holmes' study, pigeons keypecked on a RI 1' schedule for food over which a CS- signaling a one minute period of no food (i.e., extinction) was occasionally presented. All the pigeons showed nearly complete suppression of responding during the CS- despite the obvious fact that food reinforcements were being lost due to non-responding. D'Andrea (1971) made a more detailed examination of the correspondence between the psychological properties of the CS- for food and the AvCS+. Rats could postpone periods of no food reinforcement (timeouts) by leverpressing. Similar effects were displayed under withdrawal of positive reinforcement as compared with the presentation of aversive reinforcers (cf. Daly, 1974; Rilling et al., 1969; Terrace, 1971).

Although studies using humans have been less conclusive in this area, Coughlin (1972) notes that the reinforcers used in such studies often have less incentive value than those used in animal studies. Therefore, the omission of such reinforcers would be expected to produce equivocal results. It should be noted that better results have been found with children (Bauer, 1962; Willoughby, 1969) than with adults (Baron et al., 1967).

The Law of Effect and Negative Law of Effect

Considerable evidence has accumulated in support of the notion that affective properties of primary cues (CSs) can be grouped into either an appetitive (positive) reward class or an aversive (negative) reward class whether they signal the presentation or omission of a reinforcer. From the evidence just cited we have seen that primary cues associated with rewarding stimuli such as food evoke approach tendencies, while primary cues associated with aversive stimuli such as shock evoke withdrawal tendencies. More counterintuitive were the findings which indicated that primary cues associated with the omission of rewarding stimuli seemed to have the same kind of aversive affect as cues associated with the actual presentation of aversive stimulation.

We can rephrase these effects in terms of their match-mismatch properties. In a reward situation, the affective properties of the primary cue (ApCS+) are maintained by a match between the internal representation of the associated reinforcer and the occurrence of that reinforcer in the environment in accordance with the established expectancies. In a punishment situation, the affective properties of the primary cue (AvCS+) are also maintained by a match between the exteroceptive reinforcer and the internal representation of the associated reinforcer.

On the other hand, the affective properties of primary cues associated with reward omission (ApCS-) are maintained by a mismatch between the expected occurrence of the reinforcer (as specified by the internal representation) and the non-occurrence of the exteroceptive reinforcer. To complete the picture we need to hypothesize that the affective properties of primary cues associated with punisher omission (AvCS-) are maintained by a mismatch between the expected occurrence of the punisher and its environmental non-occurrence.

The experimental evidence indicates that the AvCS- as expected does not show aversive properties to the organism. A warning stimulus for shock which permits a successful avoidance of the pending punisher does not function as an aversive stimulus when the organism reliably performs the avoidance response (e.g., Starr & Mineka, 1977). Only cues paired with unavoidable shock acquired aversive properties. Furthermore, stimuli which signal the omission of shock (e.g., safety signals) seem to have positive affect in that they have been shown to summate with an ApCS+ (Goodman & Fowler, 1983).

Following loosely after Mowrer (1960) we can thus graph the relationships:

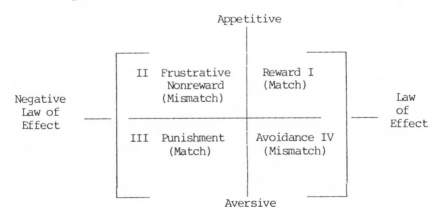

137

Reward and avoidance are both examples of the Law of Effect because both serve to increase the probability of a response. Why should a mismatch be the basis for the registration of responses in an avoidance situation whereas it is a match which serves this function in reward situations? The reason for this is based on no more profound fact than that organisms seek to avoid unpleasant stimuli and seek out pleasant stimuli.

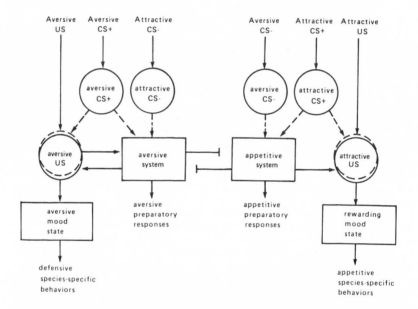

**Fig. 8-1 . Affective Properties of Cues.** Cues gain affective properties from the mood state which they activate. The aversive CS+ and the appetitive CS− activate the same aversive state and its associated species-specific behaviors while the appetitive CS+ and the aversive CS− both activate the same appetitive state. Model by Dickinson & Dearing,1979. Copyright 1979 by Lawrence Erlbaum Associates. Reprinted by permission.

On the other hand, both frustrative nonreward and punishment serve to decrease the probability of response, on the basis of reward omission and aversive reinforcer presentation respectively. Thus, the behavior, whether species-specific or arbitrary voluntary responses, should be suppressed when it is associated with a match between the stimulus model and the punishing stimulus, in much the same way that positive reinforcers directly increase the probability of the associated responses (cf. Fig. 8-1).

## Inhibition

At this point, we need to take a closer look at the concept of inhibition as it is behaviorally expressed with the ApCS- and the AvCS- because we have been skirting some difficult issues. We have seen that stimuli negatively correlated with positive or negative reinforcers take on conditioned reinforcing properties opposite in sign to temporally proximal cues to these reinforcers.

Match-mismatch theory states that only stimuli processed through the reinforcer system can become conditioned reinforcers. However, such stimuli need to be in working memory at the time of the reinforcer's occurrence to be processed in this way. If they fall outside the temporal limits set by the reinforcer system, they are then processed through the habituative system. In this case, the stimuli are either habituated or registered as secondary cues (discriminative stimuli) to reinforcement. And yet Rilling et al. (1973) have shown that pigeons will learn to peck a key simply to turn off a CS light on another key which signals the omission of food. Even more dramatically, Hutchinson et al. (1968) have shown that monkeys will display aggressive biting behaviors both when they are shocked and at the start of appetitive extinction.

As Mackintosh (1983) notes, inhibitory conditioning seems to result from the omission of an expected reinforcer. A strong way to disconfirm such expectations is to present the organism with a $CS_A$ previously paired with reinforcement, in conjunction with a second stimulus ($CS_B$) and then omit the reinforcer. Strong inhibitory conditioning accrues to the $CS_B$ under such circumstances (e.g., Marchant & Moore, 1974). If inhibitory conditioning were limited to this situation it would not be overly troublesome to explain. The $CS_A$ evokes the representation of the CS-US internal representation. With the memory of the US now retrieved into working memory, reinforcer omission causes a mismatch in the presence of the $CS_B$.

However, inhibitory conditioning can also be demonstrated in the procedure in which reinforced trials to the $CS_A$ are alternated with non-reinforced trials to $CS_B$ (e.g., Gaffan & Hart, 1981).

At no time does the $CS_A$ occur concurrently with the $CS_B$. Although it is true that such inhibitory conditioning is weaker than occurs with the concurrent presentation of $CS_A$ and $CS_B$, the fact remains that inhibition is developing without any specific cues predicting reinforcer occurrence. Generalization of excitatory conditioning from $CS_A$ to $CS_B$ leading to an initial expectation that $CS_B$ will be reinforced has been ruled out as an explanation for this effect (e.g., Karpicke & Hearst, 1975). Thus, we have the development of conditioned reinforcers without temporal proximity to the US.

It is clear that the relationship between the reinforcer and inhibitor is critical since inhibitory properties accrue to non-reinforced stimuli only in situations where reinforcement is present (Rescorla, 1975). Otherwise, these stimuli would simply be habituated, and habituated stimuli do not possess inhibitory qualities. Unfortunately, what we seem to have is action at a distance and this is as theoretically intolerable in psychology as it is in physics.

One of the key points brought up in the previous section was the complex nature of the organismic response to the reinforcing stimulus. The reinforcer not only evokes species-specific behaviors, but also, due to its induction of a mood state, leads to the appearance of an opponent mood state or "B" process. Although the reinforcer is not temporally proximal to the occurrence of a $CS_B$ in the procedure described, its effects on the organism take a certain amount of time to run their course. Thus, in a reinforcement situation, the effects of a reinforcer on the organism are not limited to the moments of its occurrence.

Given our knowledge of opponent processes, it seems likely that the organism, during periods of low reinforcement probability or non-occurrence, experiences a shift in the basic underlying motivational state. Although this shift is dependent on the occurrence of the appropriate reinforcer, it occurs at a time that is temporally distant from the reinforcer. The mechanism should be clear at this point: the power of the primary cues to maintain the psychological state appropriate to the reinforcer cannot be extended over long periods of time.

Thus, when the S- comes to be associated with periods of reinforcer non-occurrence, it can be predicted that the organism is experiencing a shift in its motivational state. In short, the S- comes to be associated with this opposing state and acquires reinforcing properties as a result. The transformation of a neutral stimulus into an excitatory stimulus occurs because of the emotional or motivational affect induced by the reinforcer. On the other hand, inhibitory properties develop in a stimulus because of the aftereffects of the mood state induced by that reinforcer.

140

From our discussion of opponent or reciprocal processes in the organism, it will be remembered that the motivational aftereffects of a particular mood state often resembled that found in the opponent state. Thus, the "B" state of some positive event often seemed to resemble a negative state and vice versa. From this we might infer that an inhibitory stimulus will induce a motivational state opposite to that induced by the reinforcer whose absence it signals. A strong interpretation would assume that an inhibitory stimulus for an aversive state would have much the same properties as an excitatory stimulus for a positive or appetitive state. Similarly in this view, an inhibitory stimulus for a positive state would have psychological properties akin to that found in excitatory stimuli for an aversive state.

An associative connection formed between the conditioned inhibitor and the reinforcer (more specifically, its aftereffects on the organism) has been postulated. If this is in fact the case then we should see an association between the conditioned inhibitor and the US but not between the conditioned inhibitor and the conditioned stimulus. Rescorla (1975) used a transfer design to test this idea in which a conditioned inhibitory stimulus, acquired in a setting of a CS(A) – US1 pairing, was tested with another CS(B) also followed by the US1. Substantial transfer of inhibitory power would indicate a S-(-)US association while minimal transfer would indicate a S-(-)CS association. The results of both studies supported the former possibility.

Baker (1977) demonstrated a further connection between conditioned inhibition and the reinforcer by showing that conditioned inhibition develops in a stimulus only when that stimulus occurs at a time when the reinforcer is expected. This expectation can be mediated by conditioning to background cues or other predictive cues (cf. Schull, 1979).

Thus, inhibition can be seen to flow out of the basic processes of learning and motivation that have been enunciated previously. In the present view, inhibition is not action at a distance by the reinforcer, but instead is a direct result of the extended effect of the reinforcer on the organism. It is produced when the affective state induced by the reinforcer or its associated cues is diminished by the omission of expected reinforcement or the occurrence of temporal intervals with lower reinforcement probability. The reduction in strength of the A state leads to the appearance of the opponent B state in the organism. The strength of the B state is directly proportional to the strength of the A state. Stimuli which are correlated with the omission or lowered probability of reinforcement become associated with the concurrently occurring B state. Since the B state is a mood state in its own right (although of opposite sign to the A state) the reinforcer system is activated and the associated cues are processed through it, acquiring conditioned reinforcing (inhibiting) properties as a result.

## SECONDARY CUE CHARACTERISTICS

Match-mismatch theory postulates the existence of two distinct cue types because of the processing characteristics of the behavioral analysis division. We have examined the characteristics of primary cues in discussing conditioned reinforcement. Now we will turn to an analysis of secondary cue characteristics.

Behavioral phenomena such as second-order conditioning, sensory preconditioning, and operant chain schedules are highly relevant to the question of the existence and form of secondary cues because the extended sequence of behavior necessarily increases the temporal interval to reinforcement, thereby reducing the activation of the reinforcer system.

Classical Conditioning

The basic paradigm for second order conditioning was established by Pavlov (1927). A CS1 was paired with a US such as food or shock. Once the CS1 had reliable control over the CR a CS2 was then paired with the CS1. (The US was no longer presented to avoid possible direct conditioning of the CS2 with the US.) Pavlov found that the CS2 came to control a CR, although its associative strength was well below that of the CS1. An interesting phenomenon that has not been noted frequently is that higher order conditioning seemed somewhat dependent on whether an appetitive or aversive US was used. The use of shock as the US enabled conditioning of third and fourth order stimuli (i.e., CS3 and CS4). However, Pavlov was unable to establish higher than second-order conditioning using the salivation response to food.

The weakness of the second (or higher) order CS led to some skepticism about the reality of the effect; however, it should be noted that the second-order conditioning paradigm established by Pavlov has great similarities to an inhibition paradigm. The US never occurs in the presence of the CS2, even when the CS1, which formerly signaled reward, is present. Thus, it is not surprising that second-order effects were variable and ephemeral.

Rescorla (1973b; 1980), by modifying the second-order conditioning procedure slightly, has produced more robust effects and in so doing has been able to analyze the characteristics of second-order conditioning much more analytically. For example, Rizley and Rescorla (1972) demonstrated second-order conditioning using conditioned suppression to a CS paired with shock as the response measure. First, a light was paired with shock, then after conditioning occurred to the light, a tone was paired with the light. Pavlov's procedure was modified by the introduction of "refresher" trials in which the CS1-US sequence was presented intermixed with CS2-CS trials. The CS2 was never presented with the US, but the US was not totally removed from the conditioning situation. Although this can be an inhibitory paradigm as well, it seems that inhibiting qualities develop more slowly to the CS2 in this situation. The results of this study showed quite clearly that second-order conditioning did exist and could be substantial in magnitude (cf. also Maisiak & Frey, 1977). Holland and Rescorla (1975) displayed similar second-order conditioning using appetitive instead of aversive USs. In general, second-order conditioning seems to display the same parametric effects as first-order conditioning with regard to temporal variation and predictiveness (cf. Leyland & Mackintosh, 1978).

Nature of the Association. Given the existence of second-order conditioning, we can ask more analytical questions. The chief one that concerns us here is the nature of the association between the second-order stimulus (S2) and the first-order stimulus (S1). That is, is there any qualitative difference between the CS2 - CS1 association and the CS1 - US association?

Rizley and Rescorla (1972) first examined the notion that the strength of the S2 is dependent on the strength of the S1. After extinguishing the response to the S1, they found that the organism continued to respond to the S2. Importantly, this was not the case with the S1 when the US (noise) was habituated. In this latter situation the strength of the S1 was also found to be largely diminished. Thus, there seems to be a qualitative difference between the S2-S1 association and the S1- US association. As a matter of fact when the $S_1$ is extinguished the S2 can be used to reestablish some conditioning to the S1.

Holland (1978) has found that although different S1s evoked different responses on the part of the organism (even when the US was the same) the behavior to the S2 was similar in both instances. Thus, the S2 is associated with the S1 but is not dependent on the particular sensory or response attributes of the S1.

These and similar findings are of crucial importance, not only with respect to the particular point in match-mismatch theory that we are addressing, but also in their implications for behavioral expression in a wide variety of situations. It is for this reason that we need to examine them in as detailed fashion as possible.

Rescorla and his associates have conducted a number of analytical studies of second-order conditioning subsequent to the Rizley

143

and Rescorla study (cf. Rescorla, 1980). One strategy has been to carry out second-order conditioning and then manipulate various aspects of the reinforcer to see what effect this has on the association between events. The logic of this approach is that manipulation of factors of the reinforcers essential to the association between cues and reinforcer should result in the disruption of the association. If a factor can be changed without appreciable effect on the association then it can be regarded as incidental.

One such experiment involved another test of the dependence of S2 on the current strength of S1. Two groups of pigeons were given S1-US training in which the S1 was a compound stimulus of colors and line orientation. The response measure was the autoshaped keypeck. After this training the pigeons received second-order conditioning in which another compound stimulus was used (a black X and a blue light). This compound stimulus was paired with the compound S1. The results showed that maintaining the value of an S1 component similar to S2 resulted in greater performance than maintaining a dissimilar element, when the other S1 component was extinguished. For example, if the line orientation element of the S1 was extinguished, this would have more effect on decreasing responding to the black X element of the S2 than on the blue light element. These results indicate that S2 can be sensitive to the current value of S1 in contrast to the Rizley and Rescorla results (cf. Rashotte et al., 1977). Rescorla does note that the changes in S1 strength had only incomplete effects on S2, however.

I think that results such as these should be interpreted cautiously, for two reasons. First, it is unclear what the implications are of making the S1 and S2 similar to each other. Although simple generalization was ruled out, the possibility of special cuing relationships remains. In this connection, it should be noted that research has indicated that similarity between elements of the stimuli used as primary cues can facilitate within-compound associations in which the different stimuli are processed more as a single unit than as separate elements (e.g., Marlin, 1982; Rescorla, 1982). Nairne and Rescorla (1981) in a second-order conditioning study found that when a visual S2 was paired with a visual S1, the associative strength of S2 was affected by S1 extinction. However, this was not the case when the visual S2 was paired with an auditory S1.

Second, a wide variety of independent evidence using different methodologies and species supports the idea that qualitative distinctions generally do exist between the S1 and S2. Cheatle and Rudy (1978) demonstrated that the strength of the S2 remained unaffected by extinction of the S1 using neonatal (7-day-old) rats. Holland and Rescorla (1975) reported similar findings when the value of the S1 was reduced by satiation or extinction procedures (cf. Razran, 1971).

Response Class. Another point that is important to our discussion of classical second-order conditioning is the effect of using different response measures on the appearance and strength of conditioning of higher order cues. For example, Popik et al. (1979) studied second-order conditioning with both the conditioned suppression and the eyelid response. The researchers found good second-order conditioning using the former but virtually none using the latter. In eyelid conditioning the S2 seemed to inhibit responding to the S1, perhaps because of the inherent nature of operation of the eyelid reflex.

Previously we have seen the important role that different responses can play in the character of learned behavior, particularly when we move across the functional response classes that have been described. The distinction between species-specific and voluntary responses plays a central role in understanding the processing of secondary cues which occurs in the classical and instrumental learning paradigms.

In terms of match-mismatch theory, the performance of species-specific responses indicates the activation of the reinforcer system since these behaviors can be controlled only by primary cues. In addition, the activation of the reinforcer system inhibits stimulus processing of secondary cues through the habituative system. Thus, in the classical conditioning paradigm, which mainly involves primary cue learning and the performance of species-specific behaviors, the degree of stimulus processing through the habituative system will be limited outside of the extinction procedure.

Pavlovian second-order conditioning, because of the methodological difficulties in isolating learning to the S2 from direct association with the US, is basically tested in an inhibition paradigm as was noted. Thus, the excitatory properties of the S2 are relatively transitory and with continued training the S2 becomes a conditioned inhibitor. Conditioned inhibitors have conditioned reinforcing properties as we have seen, and their inhibitory strength is based on the extended action of the reinforcer. Therefore, they are processed through the reinforcer system.

The development of inhibitory properties indicates that an S2 could only be transitorily processed as a secondary cue in the habituative system before again being processed through the reinforcer system. Actually, there is reason to doubt that Pavlovian second-order stimuli (S2) are ever processed as secondary cues when an S2 is dependent on an S1 for its associative strength and when species-specific responses with few voluntary components are being performed.

145

It is interesting to note that a strong similarity between the inherent characteristics of the S2 and S1 facilitates the development of an S2 dependent on the S1. Such findings support the idea that conditioning is essentially the memory of affective events. Manipulations which affect such encoding and retrieval will affect conditioned performance. To the extent that two stimuli have many congruent elements, the construction of an internal representation which incorporates both stimuli into an integrated unit is facilitated.

Such a process would mean that the S2 would activate an internal representation which contained both it and the S1. Since the S1 is an affective stimulus because of its pairing with the US, the S2 would also come to control (briefly) an affective response. Furthermore, the use of a species-specific response or response component restricts the probability that stimuli can be processed through the habituative system at that time. In such situations, the S2 is processed through the reinforcer system. Initially, it has excitatory strength because of the concurrent processing of the affective S1, but as training progresses the non-occurrence of the US leads to the assumption of inhibitory properties in the S2.

In other situations, however, we have seen that the S2 is not dependent on the current strength of the S1. This phenomenon seems to occur when the S2 and S1 are qualitatively different stimuli and when response measures are used which are more likely to contain voluntary response components. This last statement requires some explanation. The classical conditioning procedure is ideally defined by two characteristics: the non-contingent occurrence of the US and the performance of a CR which is, a component of the UR to the US. For example, Pavlov used the dog's salivary response as his response measure to a food US (and the CS) rather than using the dog's approach to a food tray or some similar measure. However, most contemporary research uses response measures which are not clear-cut components of the UR. In addition, aversive USs are often used which enhance the likelihood of various voluntary movements (e.g., postural adjustments) occurring as part of the CR (UR).

To the extent that voluntary movements rather than species-specific responses are occurring then there is an increased likelihood that secondary cue processing can take place through the habituative system. In addition, the second-order paradigm reduces the occurrence of the reinforcer, or to put it another way, increases the temporal interval between US presentations. This also enhances cue processing through the habituative system. In these circumstances, the S2 is more likely to be processed in the habituative system as a secondary cue. As such, it will not function as a conditioned reinforcer but instead as a discriminative stimulus

146

for the non-species-specific response components associated with
it. Thus, it will no longer be dependent on the affective strength
of the S1 for its expression.

Higher Order Instrumental Conditioning

Chain Schedules. Another line of evidence relevant to the distinction between primary and secondary cues comes from research on two
operant (instrumental) schedules, namely the chain schedule and the
tandem schedule. In the instrumental procedures, the use of voluntary responses increases the probabiliity of habituative system
processing. The most common instrumental procedure for investigating higher order learning has been the chain schedule (cf. Gollub,
1977). Chain schedules are sequences of responses that lead to
reinforcement, in which each response component is associated with a
different external stimulus and only the final response terminates
with presentation of an unconditioned reinforcer. A typical chain
schedule might be a FR20 FI1' schedule. On this schedule the
organism would have to make 20 responses and then make at least
one response after an additional minute had elapsed to receive
reinforcement. Different external stimuli would be present while
each component was in force. Thus, for example, while the animal
responds on the FR20 schedule, a red light would be on. When the
schedule requirement for this component was completed (i.e., 20
responses) the red light would go off and a green light would come
on in association with the start of the FI1' schedule.

Responding by an organism in the individual components of a
chain schedule is basically controlled by two factors: the instrumental schedule in that component [e.g., FR (fixed ratio), VI
(variable interval), DRL (differential reinforcement of low rate),
etc.] and the temporal location of the component with respect to
presentation of the unconditioned reinforcer (cf. Staddon, 1972).
That is, a response component can be temporally distant or temporally proximal to the reinforcer. The nature of the schedule will
basically determine the response characteristics displayed by the
organism on that component while the temporal position of the component with respect to the reinforcer tends to affect the response
rate or strength of responding.

For example, organisms will display the typical scalloping
effect found on FI schedules regardless of whether they are in the
terminal component or the initial component; however, the rate of
responding would differ within that general pattern of response.
The closer the component is to primary reinforcement, the more one
can expect overall response rate increases given the same type of
schedule. Responding in the initial components tends to be more
irregular; that is, responding is often interrupted by long pauses

147

(cf. Ferster & Skinner, 1957). A number of studies have indicated that the rate of responding in the initial components is dependent on the frequency of food delivery in the terminal component (Findley, 1962; Kaufman & Baron, 1969).

An important finding is that the extent to which responding is maintained in the initial components depends to a great extent on the temporal distance of the components to food reinforcement. Essentially, response rate is a decreasing exponential function of the time from reinforcement (Gollub, 1977). The effects of a given temporal distance are greater for FI than for equivalent VI schedules apparently because of the occasional short intervals that can occur on the VI schedule (Kendall, 1967). Segmenting a given FR schedule into different numbers of components has a more deleterious effect on responding in initial components than does segmenting on interval schedules (Jwaideh, 1973). This is probably due to the pausing behavior which typically occurs after completion of a given ratio requirement which would, of course, lead to lengthening of the temporal distance to reward.

An explanation of these results is provided by examining the way in which the associated stimuli in these schedules function to control behavior. One controversy has been over the exact nature of these stimuli correlated with particular response components, namely, whether the stimuli function as conditioned reinforcers or discriminative stimuli. As Gollub (1977) notes, there have been essentially four different methods used to examine this question using chain schedules: (1) omitting stimulus changes with otherwise identical schedule contingencies (tandem schedules); (2) changing the order of presentation of the component stimuli; (3) scheduling the sequence of stimuli independent of responding; and (4) presenting the component stimuli for brief response dependent exposures.

Tandem Schedules. Comparisons between tandem and chain schedules are useful since the tandem schedule is similar to the equivalent chain schedule. The sole exception is that the stimuli associated with different chain response components are absent. Thus, differences in responding can be attributed to the properties of the component cues. Generally speaking, response rates in the terminal component of chain schedules exceed that for comparable tandem schedules (Thomas, 1967). However, the response rates in the initial and middle components of chain schedules are generally lower than on comparable tandem schedules. Jwaideh (1973) found that the post-reinforcement pause on FR schedules was longer in chain schedules than for tandem schedules. In addition, the rate of responding was lower initially on the chain schedules.

These results suggest that the stimulus associated with the terminal component in the chain schedule does have conditioned reinforcing properties since response rates were elevated in its

148

presence. The terminal component on the tandem schedule has precisely the same temporal proximity to reinforcement yet has lower response rates. The lower response rates on the initial components of the chain schedule suggest that the associated stimuli may well possess some inhibitory (aversive) qualities since, in their absence on the tandem schedules, response rates in these components increase somewhat.

Cue Characteristics. If the terminal stimulus is a conditioned reinforcer, it should pass some of the tests we have set for defining reinforcing properties. Thus, responding should be maintained for a while even when the conditioned reinforcer is presented in the absence of primary reinforcement. Kendall (1972) studied this question by segmenting a FI-3' interval into three equal parts with three associated stimuli. For example, a white light might be associated with the first minute of the interval, a green light with the second, and a red light with the third and final minute. Pigeons could peck one of two keys; the first key produced food on the FI-3' schedule while the second produced a two-second presentation of white, green, or red light in the first, second, or third minutes of the interval.

After training had progressed, pecks on the second key were programmed either to produce red during the final minute and no other stimuli at any other time or produce only white and green lights during the first and second minutes. Pecks on the second key were maintained only when the terminal (red) stimulus could be produced either as one of three stimuli or by itself. Responding was not maintained on the second key when only the initial stimulus could be produced. Similar results were found by Marr (1969) who used a more complex one-key procedure. Brief presentations of the terminal stimulus maintained higher rates of responding than presentations of the initial stimulus. As Gollub (1977) notes, these results support the idea that reinforcing functions of stimuli are dependent on direct association with primary reinforcement. It should be noted that information was provided by all three stimuli concerning the occurrence of reward, yet only the stimulus in close temporal proximity with food developed positive conditioned reinforcing properties.

The question has been raised on whether the discriminative properties of such associated stimuli can fully account for the results obtained. Stubbs and Cohen (1972) demonstrated that brief stimuli presented at the completion of the requirements of each component of the chain enhanced responding even when they never appeared in the terminal component and thus were never associated with primary reinforcement. The pairing procedure used was the simultaneous pairing of the brief stimulus and food (but see Rescorla, 1972, on simultaneous conditioning). Cohen et al. (1979) studied the properties of briefly presented stimuli using multiple schedules. Responses in one schedule produced food according to a second-order schedule with FI components, in which food or a brief stimulus occurred with equal probability. In the second schedule, responses produced only the brief stimulus on a FR schedule. Under various conditions, the brief stimulus in the first schedule was (a) paired with food; (b) not paired with food; (c) partially omitted; and (d) scheduled simultaneously with the second-order schedule and an independent VI schedule. The results showed that both paired and non-paired brief stimuli maintained similar response patterns in the second-order schedule. However, only paired stimuli maintained responses in the FR schedule. This suggests that non-paired brief stimuli engender response patterning because of their discriminative properties which can mask reinforcing properties (cf. Wilson et al., 1981)

How do these results support the current theory? According to match-mismatch theory, the reinforcer system processes salient cues in correlated temporal proximity to the reinforcer and imparts conditioned reinforcing properties to them. On the other hand, the habituative system processes cues that are nonsalient and temporally distant from reinforcement and registers them as discriminative stimuli when the occurrence of primary cues inhibits their habituation. Thus, we would expect two types of cue properties, and this division should be dependent in part on the temporal relation of the cue with reinforcement. As we saw on chain schedules, those stimuli in conjunction with reinforcement (i.e., terminal component stimuli) definitely displayed conditioned reinforcing properties since the animals would maintain responding to produce these stimuli and thus meet the definition of primary cues. On the other hand, initial stimuli decreased response rates from the level that occurs in their absence or functioned as discriminative stimuli.

Behavioral Implications. One issue that was remarked upon in the discussion of second-order conditioning was the independence of the CS2 from the current strength of the CS1. This question has not been systematically examined in the context of chain or tandem schedules. However, there exists research using other instrumental procedures which has some bearing on this point.

Response chaining has been studied using barpressing and running in the alleyway as the response measures (e.g., Miller, 1951; Zimmerman, 1959). First, the animal is taught to run down the alleyway for food. Then it is required to barpress on some operant schedule (e.g., FR10) and only when the schedule requirements are completed is the running response reinforced.

In this situation, the extinction of these responses does not occur simultaneously. When reward is discontinued, the running response extinguishes fairly rapidly; however, the initial bar-pressing response is unaffected by the extinction of the running response and continues for a long period of time. More generally, all chains of behavior seem to extinguish backwards, with the responses closest to reinforcement delivery the first to disappear. Thus, similar results appear in both classical and instrumental paradigms.

If we think about it behavior has to be arranged in this way. If the discontinuation of reward affected the second (or higher) order stimuli before the first-order stimuli or even at the same time, the whole learned sequence would collapse completely. If the S2 extinguished first, it would disrupt responding to produce a still potent S1, which seems anomalous. With the present situation, the animal can continue to engage in behaviors that have been associated with reward in the past for extended periods. This allows the organism the possibility of overcoming a "fallow" period and be in a position to notice a return of the original contingencies, i.e., a return of the reinforcing stimulus. Thus, these results make perfect sense in terms of the organism's survival.

It seems that evolution has created these cue-processing capacities in the organism to achieve this result. The dependence of the S1 on the reinforcer makes it sensitive to the reinforcer's withdrawal from the organism's environment. However, it also provides a strong motivating function to the S1 which has assumed the psychological properties of the reinforcer (US). On the other hand, the secondary cues processed through the habituative system, while emotionally less controlling, are less sensitive to fluctuations in the occurrence of the reinforcer and thus promote stability in behavior. It should be noted in this connection that extinction in the typical Pavlovian procedure is rapid. In these situations we have predominantly S1-US relationships, processed through the reinforcer system.

The alert reader will probably have realized that there exists a problem of interpretation with respect to the initial stimuli on chain schedules, namely, the apparent inhibitory qualities of these stimuli. Stated succinctly, a discriminative stimulus processed through the habituative system should not possess conditioned reinforcing properties. It is clear that the initial stimuli on the chain schedule represent a problem in this context since they are temporally distant from the occurrence of the reinforcer and yet display conditioned reinforcing properties.

If the theory is correct, we would have to hypothesize that stimuli with true inhibitory properties are in fact processed by

the reinforcer system and are not secondary cues as defined here.
Thus, there must be other stimuli present in the initial component
of the chain schedule which function as secondary cues to reinforcement; otherwise, the organism would not respond at all.

It should be noted that the procedure used to associate exteroceptive stimuli with chain components typically do not involve
formal discrimination training. In other words, a stimulus is
presented with a particular response component which eventually
leads to reward; however, the organism is not repeatedly exposed
to the condition in which absence of the stimulus is associated
with non-reward despite the occurrence of the same responses.

This lack of explicit discriminative training possibly plays a
part in the observed results. From the organism's standpoint,
reward always follows responding on the chain components and never
follows the absence of responding. On the other hand, the external
stimulus paired with the initial response component has a more
ambiguous status. It is temporally distant from reward and the
organism is rarely exposed to the condition in which its absence
results in reward omission despite continued responding. It seems
likely that under those conditions the instrumental response and
background cues which are continually present will be better cues
for eventual reward than the initial chain stimulus. Since the
latter is associated with delay of reinforcement (or low reinforcement probability) its tendency to become a conditioned inhibitor
would be enhanced.

A comparison with second-order conditioning is instructive at
this point. As we saw, the second-order stimulus came to control
a conditioned response which was similar in some respects to that
found when the first-order stimulus is presented. In other words,
it was definitely not an inhibitory stimulus. It is clear, however,
that if continued training was given in the classical paradigm, the
second-order stimulus would in fact become an inhibitory stimulus.
Many more trials are typically given the organism in an instrumental
procedure than in Pavlovian conditioning, so inhibitory properties
are more likely to develop to stimuli temporally distant from
reward.

In the case of chain versus tandem schedules, we saw that even
at the same temporal distance from reinforcement, response rates
were higher in tandem as compared to equivalent chain schedules.
It should be emphasized that the absence of explicit and salient
exteroceptive stimuli on the tandem schedule does not mean that
there are no stimuli controlling initial responding. However,
these stimuli are likely to be more subtle, i.e., less salient.
Since the habituative system needs to be more sensitive to stimulus
change than the reinforcer system, it seems logical to assume that
the less salient a stimulus, the more likely it will be processed

152

through the habituative system. In addition, many stimuli on this schedule will be contextual or background stimuli which are present at all times; i.e., both when reward is temporally distant and at the moment of reinforcer occurrence. This should reduce their acquisition of inhibition.

It should be noted that some elements of the stimulus environment or context can be processed through either the reinforcer or the habituative system depending on their relative salience in the learning procedure. If very salient discrete stimuli are presented (e.g., a loud tone) then the relative salience of background stimuli will be low. If no such salient stimuli are presented, then the organism has a tendency to divide the stimulus background into elements with higher and lower relative salience (e.g., the bar might be more salient than the ceiling of the operant box). This point is discussed in more detail in the next chapter.

## SUMMARY

The existence of two separate stimulus processing systems has been supported by a variety of behavioral evidence related to cue processing in both animals and humans. The reinforcer system is hypothesized to process unconditioned and conditioned reinforcing stimuli. Stimuli in close temporal proximity to an unconditioned reinforcer are processed in conjunction with it through the reinforcer system which registers the stimulus complex. Stimuli acquire conditioned reinforcing properties because they become redintegrative cues for the organismic response which occurred to the reinforcer. They thus acquire the capacity to activate the reinforcer system and institute mood states similar to those controlled by the associated reinforcer. Greater conditioning is likely to accrue to the more salient elements of the stimulus complex.

The habituative system processes stimuli that fall outside the limits of reinforcer system processing, either because they are not associated with reinforcement or because they are nonsalient. If reinforcement is not present, then these stimuli are habituated. When reinforcement is present, these stimuli are registered as secondary cues to reinforcement. However, because they have been processed through the habituative system, they do not have the capacity to act as redintegrative cues for the reinforcer affect; i.e., they are not conditioned reinforcers.

The activation of the reinforcer system by reinforcing stimuli tends to inhibit the functioning of the habituative system. This results in the inhibition not only of habituation to processed stimuli, but also the inhibition of stimulus processing through the habituative system. The stimuli which meet the requirements for habituative system processing are therefore less likely to be processed by the organism.

A reinforcing stimulus initiates a mood state which is followed, after removal of the reinforcer, by an opponent mood state. The sequence of organismic effects induced by the reinforcer is used to explain the phenomenon of conditioned inhibition.

# Chapter 9
## Stimulus Selection

In the previous chapter we found that cues could possess either or both conditioned reinforcing properties and discriminative properties. Since the focus of the discussion was on the psychological nature and effect of cues, we necessarily examined the reinforcing or motivational properties more closely. However, the discriminative properties of cues are as important and probably more important as one goes up the phylogenetic scale. In these latter species, the capacity to learn about cues not closely linked to the occurrence of primary reinforcement is vastly expanded. Thus, discriminative properties of cues are often more relevant for an understanding of more complex behaviors in these species.

The term "discrimination" is used in its broadest sense and is meant to refer to the whole question of stimulus selection, which perhaps is a better term to use for such phenomena. The fundamental question being examined here is the basis for the control of behavior by only a part of the stimulus field: Why is a behavior controlled by one stimulus (complex) and not another one? As in most things, it is best to start at the beginning or at least at the most fundamental level, which in this case I believe to be the Rescorla (1967) study on correlation effects in conditioning.

## CORRELATION AS A FUNDAMENTAL CUE LEARNING FACTOR

Like many germinal studies, the Rescorla (1967) article had implications that went far beyond its original purpose, which was

155

an analysis of the proper control procedures to use in order to assess the degree of Pavlovian conditioning accruing to the CS. However, these implications were only fully revealed in conjunction with certain other studies which were performed shortly afterwards, namely, the articles by Kamin (1968, 1969) on the phenomenon known as blocking.

Rescorla attempted to test the idea that temporal proximity or contiguity in and of itself was insufficient for conditioning to occur to a neutral stimulus paired with a US. Instead, Rescorla argued that there must be some predictive relation between the occurrence of a CS and the US before significant conditioning could accrue to the CS. For example, if the CS and US were independently programmed to occur at random with respect to one another, we might expect that by chance the CS would occur on occasion in temporal proximity to the US; however, overall, the probability of US occurrence would be just as likely when the CS was absent as when it was present. This situation is quite distinct from what occurs in a partial reinforcement situation. In the latter situation the CS only imperfectly predicts the occurrence of the US; however, the US only occurs when the CS does. Thus, we can say that the CS is partially correlated with US occurrence but that the US is perfectly correlated with CS occurrence. As it turned out, the results supported Rescorla's basic contention that there must be some predictive relation between the CS and US for conditioning to occur; in short, the CS must serve a discriminative function. Thus, the existence of a conditioned reinforcer seems to be dependent on its discriminative properties, rather than on simply its pairing with a reinforcer. This does not mean that there is no difference between a conditioned reinforcer and a discriminative stimulus but that the affective attributes of the conditioned reinforcer are dependent on some positive or negative correlation with the US.

Previous studies of classical conditioning had basically conceived the associative process underlying the CS–US pairing to be a simple reflection of the co-occurrence of these two stimuli. However, the finding that the overall correlation of CS and US occurrences in relation to their independent occurrences determined conditioning made it clear something else was involved. This other factor is the conditioning that accrues to stimuli other than the CS in the conditioning situation. It is useful to follow the logic of this process more closely.

An organism is in an experimental situation in which a CS and a US are presented. We arrange it so there is zero correlation between the occurrences of the CS and the US; in other words, one is as likely to occur without the other as with the other. On the first trial, by chance, the CS and the US occur together and thus some conditioning accrues to the CS. However, on the next trial the US occurs in temporally distant fashion from the CS and thus no conditioning occurs to the CS on that trial. We cannot regard this as a null trial in the absolute sense, though, since a significant stimulus (i.e., the US) has occurred in the presence of the organism. It is obvious that whatever process underlies conditioning does not depend for its operation on the foresight of the experimenter to provide an explicit CS for the occurrence of the US. The US is always being presented in a stimulus field whether or not the experimenter has made an explicit decision to include specific cues.

It should be clear that the organism will associate whatever cues are present with the US; in this particular case, the cues will probably be situational or background cues, i.e., the sensory stimuli of the apparatus or the room in which the US has been presented. Thus, these cues receive conditioning on the trials when the CS does not co-occur with the US. The fact that conditioning does not accrue to the CS when there is zero correlation between it and the US suggests, if this interpretation is right, that somehow conditioning to the background cues can prevent conditioning to a CS which on occasion is paired with the US. Dweck and Wagner (1970) showed that, in the correlational procedure, background stimuli do indeed become conditioned. Rescorla (1972) further showed that the absence of conditioning to the CS in the uncorrelated procedure, rather than being due simply to the lack of relationship between CS and US, is dependent upon conditioning accruing to other stimuli present on that situation, i.e., the background stimuli. This fact was demonstrated by presenting a second stimulus in advance of the US on all CS-US trials. Conditioning accrued to the second stimulus and at the same time diminished to the background cues. Baker and Mackintosh (1977) showed that uncorrelated preexposure resulted in an even more severe retardation of conditioning to the CS than is found in the latent inhibition paradigm, i.e., where the CS is habituated.

We can see from these experiments that there seems to be an interaction among available cues in terms of the conditioning of cue learning which takes place to the stimuli in temporal proximity to the US. This phenomenon was shown in dramatic fashion by the Kamin (1968, 1969) studies. Kamin examined the situation in which a CS with a prior history of correlation with a US was compounded with another stimulus and then reinforced. Thus, in the first stage of training, stimulus "A" is paired with the US and acquires conditioning. Then in the second stage, "A" is presented along with a new stimulus "X" and the AX compound is paired with the same US. In this situation very little conditioning accrues to the new stimulus "X" despite the fact that it is perfectly correlated with US occurrence. In other words, prior conditioning to

157

"A" seems to block conditioning to "X" when it is presented concurrently with "A."

There are a number of factors which can affect the amount of
blocking that occurs in this procedure. For example, Kamin found
that the amount of blocking could be attenuated if there was some
change in the reinforcement delivered after compound AX trials
compared with that delivered in the first stage after "A" alone
trials. Conditioning occurred to "X" if "A" was followed by a
one ma shock while AX was followed by a 4 ma shock. Blocking
was also attenuated when "A" was partially extinguished before AX
trials, when fewer conditioning trials were given to "A" and when a
weak stimulus was used as "A." This latter condition is akin to
the phenomenon known as overshadowing (Pavlov, 1927) in which a
strong stimulus acquires more conditioning than a weak stimulus
under equivalent pairing with a reinforcer.

Kamin (1969) advanced the view that one of the critical determinants of conditioning is the surprise value of the reinforcer.
A reinforcer that was unexpected could provoke a backward scanning
of recent stimulus input or might alert the animal to be more
attentive to succeeding events. In the blocking situation, the
reinforcer is fully predicted by stimulus "A"; therefore it has no
surprise value. This would inhibit the formation of conditioning
to stimulus "X" when it is presented concurrently with "A." On
the other hand, changes in the US would again increase the surprise
value of the US. As we saw previously, in this case, blocking to
"X" was in fact diminished. To put it informally, a reinforcer
only sustains new conditioning when there is uncertainty about its
occurrence. Once it is fully predicted, the organism will no
longer continue to associate other stimuli with the US.

The Rescorla-Wagner Model

In an attempt to add precision to Kamin's hypotheses as well
as to tie together all the studies investigating correlational
effects in conditioning, Rescorla and Wagner (1972) developed a
theory which summarized the relevant variables in the form of an
equation. The basic notion was that the effect of a reinforcement
on learning depends not upon the reinforcement itself but on the
degree to which the reinforcement received corresponds to the reinforcement expected. Thus, the same reinforcer, depending on the
situation, may support learning or be totally ineffective in this
regard.

Rescorla and Wagner also sought to account not only for the
asymptotic performance of animals in the above situations, but
also the development of that performance on a trial-by-trial basis.
The following equation was offered as a formal statement of the
ideas expressed above:

$$V_A = a_A \, B_i \, (\lambda_i - V_{AX})$$

where $V_A$ represents the change in the associative strength of a stimulus "A" on a given trial (increasing or decreasing ); "$a$" represents a learning rate parameter of stimulus "A" which is roughly equivalent to stimulus salience; "B" is the learning rate parameter associated with the particular US; $\lambda$ is the asymptotic level of conditioning which each US will support and is related to US magnitude, and $V_{AX}$ is the associative strength of stimulus A and X to the US and is assumed to be equal to $V_A + V_X$.

The fundamental expression determining changes in associative strength is $(\lambda - V_{AX})$ which is the difference between the asymptotic level of conditioning and the current level of conditioning to AX. Rescorla and Wagner basically left to one side the "$a$" and "B" parameter effects and so we will do the same.

It can be seen that the closer $V_{AX}$ gets to the asymptotic value $\lambda$, the smaller the potential increment for $V_{AX}$ on each trial. Thus, this equation can handle the common observation that the learning curve is negatively accelerated. Large changes in associative strength occur on initial trials but gradually the increments decline in size as learning proceeds. Non-reinforcement is represented by a $\lambda$ of 0 $(0-V_{AX})$ and the extinction curve is negatively accelerated. Since at the start of extinction the strength of the formerly reinforced cues is positive, they exceed the value for $\lambda$. No cue can stably possess a value greater than $\lambda$ so $V_{AX}$ would start to decrement until it reached 0.

This straightforward idea has been found to handle the results of many classical conditioning studies quite well, including of course the correlation studies. It is useful to see how the model deals with a few of the studies in a more detailed way, starting with the Kamin study. An animal is first exposed to pairings of stimulus "A" with the US, which results in $V_A$ approaching the asymptote $\lambda$. Necessarily, $\lambda - V_A$ must be a small number in this situation indicating that there is little additional conditioning that can be supported by the reinforcer. In the next stage, the compound AX is presented and followed by the same reinforcer. This leaves $\lambda$ unchanged and since $V_{AX} = V_A + V_X$, $\lambda - V_{AX}$ is still a small number. Thus, little conditioning can occur to stimulus "X" because "A" has used up most of the possible associative strength for that US. Informally speaking, there is competition among stimuli for the associative strength based on a US; when one stimulus gets a head start, it can forestall conditioning to others. On the other hand, if there is no prior conditioning to "A," then $\lambda - V_{AX} = \lambda$. Reinforcement following the compound AX would be expected to increase the associative strength of both "A" and "X" since both would be starting at the same low point.

159

We saw that blocking to "X" could be attentuated if the US magnitude, and therefore $\lambda$, were increased. This also follows from the model. If $V_A$ is close to then $V_{AX}$ is close to $\lambda$ and little conditioning can occur to "X". However, if another, larger $\lambda$ is substituted, then substantial capacity for conditioning is left.

One of the strengths of the R-W model has been its capacity to successfully predict not only the results of novel classical conditioning situations but also counterintuitive effects. To take just one example, the model predicts that when two different CSs are asymptotically conditioned separately to the same US and then are presented together, they will lose associative strength even when reinforced by the US. The model shows that two different CSs paired independently with the same US can have their associative strengths reach $\lambda$. It is clear that when they are presented concurrently as a stimulus compound $V_{AX}$ must exceed $\lambda$ since $V_{AX} = V_A + V_X$. Since $V_{AX}$ can never stably exceed $\lambda$, there must be a reduction until it reaches the asymptotic limit set by $\lambda$. Kremer (1978) found that this predicted decline in response strength to the separately conditioned elements presented in compound did in fact occur. The loss was a positive function of the number of compound CS-US pairings. In addition, if a previously neutral stimulus was added to the compound at the start of the compound trials, it became a conditioned inhibitor indicating that it absorbed the decline in associative strength, again in conformance with the model (cf. Rescorla, 1972).

The R-W theory has also been extended to a number of different phenomena which lay outside the immediate area for which the model was developed. Some notable examples are the observed preference for signaled as opposed to unsignaled aversive events (Fanselow, 1980) and the ability of independently established aversive or appetitive cues to aid discriminative learning (Fowler et al., 1977).

Problems with the Rescorla-Wagner Model

As with all psychological theories the Rescorla-Wagner model, while highly successful, nevertheless encountered a number of predictive failures which cast doubt on some of its assumptions. Some of these problems perhaps stem from a lack of connection between the equations and process assumptions. For example, the model assumes that inhibition is the symmetrical inverse of excitation more on the basis of ease of handling in the model than on empirical demonstrations that such symmetry exists.

Three major lines of criticism have surfaced in the experimental literature against assumptions inherent in the R-W model. The first centers around the trial-by-trial contiguity process assumed by the R-W theory to underlie correlation effects. That is, correlational effects are assumed to occur in conditioning not because the organism ignores the contiguity between a CS and US on any given trial, but because it takes into account the contiguity relations of all other concurrent stimuli with the US. In other words, the model does not simply take into account trials where the CS and US are contiguous and treat as null those trials where the CS and US are not contiguous. Instead, all US and CS presentations are considered as affecting conditioning. Those trials in which the US occurs without the CS result in the conditioning of those stimuli which are contiguous with the US on that trial, thereby reducing the available conditioning that can possibly accrue to the CS. On the other hand, CS alone trials result in the extinction of associative strength to the CS.

Prokasy and Gormezano (1979) examined these assumptions using the partial reinforcement paradigm in classical conditioning. According to the R-W model, the organism should respond as follows on a 50% (FR2) reinforcement schedule in classical conditioning. On trials where the CS is followed by the US, conditioning should occur to the CS as long as the asymptote has not yet been reached. On trials where the CS is not followed by the reinforcer, however, there should be a reduction in strength to the CS, since $\lambda = 0$, in the absence of the US. Thus, compared with 100% reinforcement there should be some oscillating pattern of associative strength accruing to the CS in the 50% schedule with its final value of "V" somewhere beneath what it would be on continuous reinforcement.

In the Prokasy and Gormezano study, rabbits were given 100% or 50% reinforcement of the CS, using either an aversive or an appetitive US. A detailed analysis of the trial-by-trial results indicate that the major effect of partial reinforcement in the aversive condition was to increase the length of time in the initial phase, during which CR response likelihood remains at its initial value. Only a small proportion of subjects showed effects from US omission during the learning phase (i.e., a reduction in CR strength). However, in the appetitive situation the major effect of US omission was in the second, or learning, phase.

Another experiment by Gormezano and associates (Gibbs et al., 1978) also examined the details of conditioning in classical partial reinforcement schedules. Although response decrements were noted on 15% reinforcement schedules, the level of response was still substantial. In addition, the performance decrements noted did not seem to be caused by the immediate effects of even three consecutive non-reinforced trials. Substantial decrements were found, however, on 5% reinforcement schedules.

What are the implications of these findings? First of all, Prokasy and Gormezano note that associative strength seems to be acquired faster than it is extinguished (cf. Berger & Thompson, 1978a; Prokasy, 1965). Thus, we would not expect zero conditioning on a FR2 schedule, i.e., conditioning on one trial and an equivalent extinction effect on the next. If conditioning does accrue very rapidly to a stimulus once it gets started, then we would expect some inertia in the organismic response to non-reinforcement. It is clear that this represents a departure from a strict interpretation of the R-W model since the effect of US non-occurrence will probably be different on the 12th consecutive non-reinforcement than on the first. However, on an intuitive basis this seems more like messy reality intruding rather than an outright disconfirmation of the pertinent assumptions by the model (cf. the section on the partial reinforcement effect in the next chapter).

The second objection to the R-W model is its handling of inhibitory relations. As we have seen, the model treats inhibition as the symmetrical inversion of excitation. A number of studies have raised questions about this assumption, however. For example, the R-W model predicts that inhibition can be extinguished by presenting the inhibitor in the absence of any reinforcer present in the experimental situation (i.e., nonreinforcement). Zimmer-Hart and Rescorla (1974) failed to find any confirmation of this prediction, however, since conditioned inhibition was not extinguished under these conditions. Another prediction of the R-W model is that an inhibitor, paired unreinforced with a neutral stimulus, should produce excitation to that stimulus. Again, no confirmation was found for this prediction (Baker, 1974). This does not imply that the R-W model has been completely unsuccessful in predicting the formation of conditioned inhibition (e.g., Baker, 1977); however, some direct predictions have not been confirmed in this area.

If we examine this prediction in the light of match-mismatch processes we can see that there is no different consequence as a result of the procedure establishing the inhibitor and the one extinguishing it. In both cases, the inhibitor is paired with the absence of the US. Thus, the internal representation matches the environment as long as the stimulus is not followed by the reinforcer. In the extinction situation applied by the R-W model, this same consequence exists as well (cf. Schull, 1979). The whole point of extinction is that it signals the opposite relation between a stimulus and reinforcer that existed during acquisition. In appetitive conditioning CS-US learning is extinguished by CS-US trials, i.e., where the extinction trials create a mismatch between the stimulus model and the environmental stimulus. Thus, for an inhibitor to be extinguished some mismatch must be established between the stimulus model and the exteroceptive stimulus.

The third major criticism of the R-W model concerns the definition of the asymptote of conditioning, $\lambda$ . As we will recall, $\lambda$ was assumed to be a direct function of the reinforcer magnitude; the stronger the reinforcer, the higher the asymptote. In some of the studies conducted by Kamin and Rescorla, it was shown that when a CS had reached the level set by $\lambda$ , further conditioning did not occur to it without increasing the reinforcer magnitude. In that case, the level of $V_A$ would once again be below $\lambda$ and additional conditioning could occur. Essentially, the R-W model assumes that the reinforcer becomes ineffective in inducing conditioning to a stimulus once that stimulus reaches $\lambda$ (i.e., is perfectly correlated with the US). Thus, in the blocking paradigm, the novel redundant element "X" does not become conditioned because the US has been rendered ineffective in producing conditioning by the previously conditioned stimulus "A."

This line of argument has been called into question by a number of experiments. Dickinson and Mackintosh (1979) showed that conditioning would accrue to the redundant stimulus paired with US shock both when an unexpected shock 8 seconds after the compound trial was presented and when an expected shock was omitted after a trial. The addition and omission of free food after such trials had no such effect. Similarly, when food was used as the basic reinforcer for a response, the addition or omission of food after compound trials resulted in conditioning accruing to the novel element (i.e., there was a reduction in blocking). However, presenting the equivalent manipulations of shock had no effect in this situation on blocking.

Now, it is possible for the R-W model to account for conditioning to "X" when additional shock or food is presented through the possibility that $\lambda$ has been raised. However, this reasoning breaks down in the case of reinforcer omission. There is no way for the R-W model to account for the fact of increased conditioning to X when there is less reinforcement and hence a smaller $\lambda$ than existed when "A" was paired with the US. In fact, "X" should become an inhibitor in this situation.

A number of theorists have proposed modifications to the R-W model in order to account for these and similar kinds of results (e.g., Hall & Pearce, 1979; Mackintosh, 1978; Wagner, 1978). A basic thread to the new formulations is that conditioning is based on changes of effectiveness not so much (or not entirely) because of changes in the effectiveness of a US to support further learning but rather because of changes in the associability of a CS.

For example, Hall and Pearce (1979) showed that prior associations of the CS to other stimuli could reduce the readiness of the stimulus to enter into new associations. Pfautz and Wagner (1976) demonstrated that the prior presentation of the CS on a trial could depress the CR to that CS when presented again. Rehearsal of the CS could be inhibited by its prior representation in STM. On the other hand, prior presentation of a different CS augmented the CR to the target CS. Thus, the associability ($a$) of a stimulus is dynamic and changes with the organism's experience (cf. Frey & Sears, 1978; Terry & McSwain, 1984).

163

In this section, an interpretation of the stimulus selection studies presented above is offered in the light of the principles developed in match-mismatch theory. However, before we begin, I would like to make a few comments about the development of equations to describe behavioral phenomena.

As a number of researchers have noted (e.g., Hall & Pearce, 1979), one of the best things about the R-W model has been the emphasis on qualitative rather than quantitative predictions. Of course, it is true that in the absolute sense qualitative analysis is necessarily inferior to quantitative analysis. However, there has been the realization that for a model to make quantitative predictions at this stage is only to invite immediate disconfirmation, which inevitably leads to elaborations of the model to fit all of the empirical difficulties.

It may be humbling, but it seems more prudent to realize that in the absence of a qualitative understanding of the basic psychological variables underlying phenomena, it is virtually impossible to construct quantitative equations which can apply to more than a few studies. Qualitative analysis at least lets us see if we are able to tell the general direction behavior is going to take and lessens the impact of idiosyncratic or unrelated variables that will affect its precise form.

We have seen that even the qualitative R-W model has encountered difficulties because of inadequate conceptualizations of certain basic variables or phenomena. The present section does not contain any quantitative formulation meant to replace the R-W models. Instead, an attempt is made to define the kinds of variables that have to be considered in the construction of these kinds of equations for classical and instrumental conditioning.

One hindrance to the interpretation of conditioning studies, I believe, has been the failure to consistently apply the notion that conditioning is essentially the memory of affective experiences, and therefore, any manipulation which affects the organism's capacity to encode and retrieve particular stimuli or stimulus associations will affect their control over conditioned behavior. At this time, then, we will try to apply several straightforward memorial principles in the context of reinforcer and habituative system function to see if certain issues in stimulus selection can be clarified.

OR Occurrence and Conditioning

The reader should have been struck with the similarity between the conditions under which the OR is evoked and the conditions in which changes in stimulus selection occur. As we saw in a number of Russian studies beginnning with Pavlov, conditioning accrues to a

CS only when the stimulus has evoked the OR. Once conditioning reached asymptotic levels, the OR dropped out. Thus, the OR seems to be necessary for changes in conditioning strength to stimuli but not for the maintenance of such strength.

The OR is evoked by stimulus novelty and by changes in the occurrence or relationship of familiar stimuli and rapidly habituates once the organism has encoded enough of the stimulus attributes to be able to perform a match-mismatch comparison. It is re-evoked when further changes occur in the stimulus environment and in this connection it should be emphasized that the OR seems to habituate whether or not the stimulus is reinforcing or non-reinforcing.

For example, Schrier and Povar (1979) found that monkeys' eye movements between discriminanda reached a maximum during acquisition of the task but when asymptotic levels were attained, these movements declined to a level merely sufficient to locate the CS. Kaye and Pearce (1984) studied orienting toward a CS light using various classical conditioning procedures. Rats oriented toward the light more strongly during initial training trials, but as the CR increased in magnitude the OR declined. At the start of extinction, however, the OR was re-evoked. The use of partial reinforcement, in which the US followed the CS only 50% of the time, resulted in a retardation of OR habituation compared with CRF. Reversing a discriminative contingency of a CS+ light and CS-tone so that the tone was followed by the US also re-evoked the OR.

Similar findings have been obtained in human classical conditioning. Prokasy and Ebel (1967) demonstrated three types of electrodermal response to CS-US pairings: a first interval anticipatory response (FAR) related to CS onset; a second interval response (SAR) related to US onset and third interval response (TOR) to stimulus omission. FARs are most commonly reported in differential classical conditioning rather than in simple conditioning (e.g., Maltzman et al., 1977; Ohman, 1971). FARs are obtained in subjects who correctly verbalize the differential CS-US contingency, between trials or post-experimentally (Dawson, 1970). The FAR usually habituates over trials and is re-evoked by stimulus change (Ohman, 1971). Thus, this peripheral measure bears many of the characteristics of a (verbally mediated) OR.

Obviously, the OR is not the sole basis for all of the stimulus selection findings that were reviewed above. There are several factors that I believe are fundamental to many of the observed effects. First, the circumstances of OR evocation in the particular procedures used will determine when changes (excitatory or inhibitory) in stimulus strength occur either within a specific stimulus or between concurrent stimuli. Second, as the R-W model specifies, the reinforcer magnitude defines the asymptotic limit of conditioned reinforcing strength which can accrue to correlated CSs. Thus, if more than one CS is correlated with the US the multiple CSs must divide up the _affective_ response strength so as not to exceed $\lambda$. It should be emphasized that it is the affective properties which are limited by $\lambda$; as we will see, $\lambda$ does not set the limit for secondary cue learning. Third, changes in the circumstances of cue or reinforcer presentations produce interference between different internal representations. Since internal representations have been constructed for the previous relationships and the current relationship, environmental cues can activate either or both of these representations until the more recent one achieves predominance through continued training. This interference will reflect itself in deficits in the conditioning of the changed cues relative to cues which do not have conflicting internal representations. Fourth, the operating characteristics of the reinforcer and habituative system determine the level of affective response strength to correlated primary cues and the relative mix between primary and secondary cue control over responding.

We can use the basic blocking procedure as a simple example. In the first stage of the blocking paradigm, we have nothing more than the most basic classical conditioning situation, namely the pairing of a stimulus "A" with some reinforcer. The first presentation of the reinforcer is going to evoke ORs and other URs specific to its stimulus properties. Since it is an unconditioned reinforcer, the reinforcer system of the IPM will be activated. The reinforcer and the other stimuli which are in STM at the time of reinforcer occurrence will thus be processed through this system.

For a significant stimulus such as a US, the process of forming a stimulus model of the US proceeds quickly. Since the $CS_A$ is in temporal proximity to the US, it is processed along with the US and a stimulus model of it is also formed. After a few presentations of $CS_A$-US, the organism has constructed a stimulus model which contains the predictive correlation of the CS and US as well as the information about the characteristics of the stimuli themselves. This representation of the A-US complex is thus available for comparison with further presentations of the CS-US pair.

As conditioning proceeds, the ORs drop out and the organism responds exclusively with a CR or UR depending on the stimulus represented. Of course, by this time the $CS_A$, having been processed through the reinforcer system, has acquired conditioned reinforcing properties. Thus, in the first stage of the blocking paradigm, after asymptotic conditioning has been reached, the organism possesses a detailed internal representation of the A-US sequence. Since a match is occurring while the reinforcer system is activated, the stimuli are controlling the induction of an appropriate mood state which in turn is controlling species-specific responding to the stimuli. If we refer back to the R-W model at this point, we can see that the OR is most likely to occur on those initial trials which typically involve large changes in associative strength (V).

166

The R-W model predicts that the initial changes in $V_A$ will be greater than those that follow, i.e., a negatively accelerated learning curve. At asymptote we can see that in terms of match-mismatch theory, the ORs to the A-US pairings have ceased. In the R-W model, changes in V have also ceased at this point.

The second stage of the blocking paradigm contains within it the same stimulus relationship as existed in the first stage (i.e., A-US). However, an additional stimulus is now paired with the asymptotically conditioned "A," namely "X." On the first compound trial AX-US, a change in the stimulus situation has occurred in that "X" is a novel element occurring within a familiar stimulus sequence. Perceptible changes in the stimulus field generally result in the evocation of the OR, thus we should expect the additional element "X" to evoke an OR on the part of the organism. The strength of the OR to the added stimulus will be affected by its relative salience compared to the existing CS. However, there is a big difference between the circumstances of the first AX-US trial compared to the first A-US trial. The relation A-US has been incorporated into a stimulus model at this point. In the compound trial, the A-US relation still exists. In other words, there is a match between the stimulus model and the presented stimulus-reinforcer relation. As we know, ORs are inhibited when a match exists between environment and stimulus representation. The OR occurs to the first AX presentation for the simple reason that the US has not yet occurred and thus some temporary uncertainty is induced by the novel added element. However, on succeeding trials, this uncertainty has been removed because of the match that occurred on the first AX trial. Thus, ORs are inhibited and in consequence further changes in associative strength or V do not occur.

How does match-mismatch theory conceptualize the correlational studies which show no conditioning accruing to stimuli uncorrelated though contiguous with the US? Actually, the present theory is supportive of the existing R-W conceptualization in this regard. To the extent that a stimulus is in temporal proximity to a reinforcer, it should gain conditioning; to the extent that it occurs in the absence of the reinforcer, whatever conditioning has accrued to it should start to extinguish. As we saw in the Prokasy and Gormezano studies, there is good reason to believe that excitatory and extinctive functions are not symmetrical. Conditioning seems to proceed more rapidly than extinction, and extinction does not necessarily begin until a few non-reinforced trials have occurred. However, over the course of a number of sessions, the stimulus with a zero correlation with the US is essentially going to possess little or no conditioning because of the balance of contiguous and noncontiguous occurrences with the US. In terms of match-mismatch processes, we can see that in the zero correlation studies, the organism can never establish a consistent match between the CS and

167

US. The only match that can be developed is the pairing of the background cues with the US.

In general, changes in associative strength for various cues occur on trials when some form of mismatch has been arranged between the internal representation and the exteroceptive stimulus conditions. The precise nature of the stimulus changes can vary from study to study in part because of differences in the details of such mistakes. It is clear that the effect of the mismatch depends on the particular prior training that the organism has received as well as the particular stimulus change that has been introduced on the critical trial.

## Latent Inhibition

It is worthwhile to examine the operation of these stimulus processing factors in the latent inhibition paradigm. As we saw, the basic latent inhibition procedure is to first present a non-reinforcer (e.g., a light or tone) repeatedly to an organism. After this sequence of unpaired presentations of stimulus A the organism is then presented with a sequence of conditioning trials in which stimulus A is paired with a US. The typical finding is that stimulus A acquires conditioned reinforcing properties more slowly in these circumstances than it would have if it had not been previously presented in non-reinforced fashion (Best & Gemberling, 1977; Lubow, 1973; Rescorla, 1971).

Let's examine the effect of these procedures on the factors which were outlined above. In the first phase of the latent inhibition paradigm, we have a typical habituation procedure in which a non-reinforcing stimulus A is repeatedly presented to an organism. As we have seen, the OR rapidly habituates to the stimulus in such circumstances; whatever other organismic responses (URs) are evoked by stimulus A will also habituate, albeit more slowly.

Thus at the end of the first phase, we have a stimulus which has been processed through the habituative system and habituated. In the process, an internal representation of the stimulus has been constructed in the sensory-perceptual and behavioral analysis divisions of the IPM. Since the stimulus is not a reinforcer, its internal representation will not contain affective features. In addition, the internal representation will have only the background stimuli as additional elements to the stimulus features themselves since no other stimulus occurred contiguously.

In the second phase, we have a pronounced change in the stimulus environment, namely the introduction of a US following the presentation of stimulus A, which is now a predictive cue for US occurrence. However, since stimulus A has already been habituated, it is being processed through the habituative system at the time the US is occurring. Thus, on the first presentation of the US, stimulus

A does not evoke an OR. Consequently, no change in its associative properties takes place and it remains a habituated stimulus. On succeeding trials, however, the changed stimulus circumstances can re-evoke the OR to stimulus A and concurrent contextual stimuli.

The re-evocation of the OR to stimulus A permits changes in its associative strength to occur; however, since the stimulus has occurred previously, it is able to retrieve an existing (habituative) internal representation. The previously established internal representation obviously differs in important respects from the current situation in which stimulus A is paired with a US and processed through the reinforcer system. Thus, there is interference between the internal representation of the current conditioning phase and the previous habituative phase (cf. interference effects: Chapter 14). Pearce and Kaye (1984) in fact showed that the OR to a previously habituated light CS was greatly reduced on the first conditioning trial relative to non-preexposed conditions. On the other hand, renewed ORs to the light by the preexposure group, tended to persist longer before finally habituating again (cf. Hall & Pearce, 1979; Baker & Mackintosh, 1977).

Wagner (1978), in his theory of habituation, argues that in latent inhibition as with habituation, the presence of predictive cues for a stimulus results in a retrieval-generated priming of working memory which diminishes the further processing of the stimulus. Latent inhibition is significantly greater when stimulus preexposure takes place in the same stimulus environment as the later conditioning (e.g., Lantz, 1973). Conversely, extinguishing the contextual cues by presenting them in the absence of the stimulus results in reductions in latent inhibition at least when CRF is used (Baker & Mercier, 1982). Contextual extinction did not reduce latent inhibition however when PRF schedules were used. The nonreinforced trials on the PRF schedule may act to reinstate the previously established habituative internal representation. The differences between stimulus processing on PRF as opposed to CRF schedules actually have a number of important ramifications which we will address next.

The Asymptote of Conditioning

In the R-W model, the asymptote of conditioning or $\lambda$ is an important determinant of stimulus selection since it sets the overall limit of conditioning which concurrent predictive cues must divide among them according to such parameters as stimulus salience or degree of correlation with the reinforcer.

Match-mismatch principles suggest that the identification of $\lambda$ with reinforcer magnitude may be only partial accurate. If we use reinforcer magnitude we are implying that associative strength and reinforcing strength are in direct correspondence. That is, the larger the reinforcer, the more conditioned reinforcing strength it can impart to associated cues. In the case of primary cues processed through the reinforcer system, this correspondence can be said to exist. However, primary cues are not the only cues which the IPM can process. Secondary cues processed through the habituative system possess discriminative properties based on their correlation with reinforcer occurrence; however, they are not assumed to simultaneously possess reinforcing properties too.

The potential for associative changes in primary cues is dependent on the occurrence of a situation in which ORs are evoked, i.e., where a mismatch occurs between the stimulus model and the environment. The discriminative aspect of primary cues, or their predictive utility for reinforcer occurrences, must be considered as an aspect separate from their conditioned reinforcing properties even though these two dimensions will eventually converge. For secondary cues, we can obviously expect no such convergence because they do not have conditioned reinforcing properties. These considerations become particularly important in instrumental learning.

The R-W model, while quite accurate in many instances in explaining classical conditioning results, has been shown to break down when applied to instrumental conditioning. The model predicts that blocking will be exhibited to a novel redundant cue "X" if "A" is presented with an equal or greater rate of reinforcement than AX. However, both Feldman (1971) and Neely and Wagner (1974) did not confirm this prediction with instrumental procedures (lever pressing).

In Feldman's study, one group of rats was pretrained so that responding to stimulus A was reinforced 100% of the time (CRF) and the other group was pretrained on 25% reinforcement with A (PRF). Then each group was divided so that half received 100% reinforcement to a stimulus compound AX containing a novel redundant cue and the other half received 25% reinforcement to AX. Thus, there were four conditions of training: A-100%, AX-100%; A-100%, AX-25%; A-25%, AX-25%; and A-25%, AX-100%.

Blocking to X was observed when the percentage of reinforcement remained the same between trials on A and AX (i.e., A-100%, AX-100%; A-25%, AX-25%). However both groups which received a shift in reward conditions showed a reduction in blocking. The R-W model can account for the fact that more responding to X was observed when the reinforcement changed from A-25% to AX-100% by noting that $\lambda$ has increased. It is not able to explain why blocking should be reduced to X when the change in schedule is in the opposite direction (A-100%, AX-25%) when $\lambda$ has presumably been reduced.

Neely and Wagner (1974) replicated Feldman's findings. However, they also showed that if training to A alone was given contemporaneously with AX trials in the same sessions, there was no attenuation of blocking. It should be noted, though, the R-W model predicts

170

that X should become an inhibitor in this situation an effect which wasn't observed.

The common factor creating the attenuation of blocking in both of the changed reward schedules is the match-mismatch process; the change in reinforcer occurrence in both instances creates a mismatch in which the OR is evoked. This paves the way for changes in associative strength among the cues. Up to this point there is no difference between the behavior in the two situations. However, the differing tendencies on the part of classical and instrumental procedures in tapping the two components of the behavioral analysis division of the IPM must now be considered. Match-mismatch theory assumes that classical conditioning tends to involve cue processing mainly through the reinforcer system while instrumental learning has more likelihood of a division of cue processing between the reinforcer and habituative systems.

Let's imagine a situation in which stimulus "A" is reinforced 100% of the time and the compound AX is reinforced 5% of the time. In the classical paradigm, the tone and the reinforcer have been processed through the reinforcer system. Since the CR is a species-specific response, activation of the reinforcer system inhibits the habituative system. Thus, the cue processing functions of the habituative system are inhibited, preventing secondary cues from being processed. Now the organism is presented with a concurrent compound stimulus consisting of the tone "A" plus a light "X." In this situation little conditioning would be exhibited to the redundant stimulus "X" if the compound was also followed 100% of the time by food as "A" alone. However, in our example only 5% of the AX trials are followed by food. If the Gibbs et al. study (among others) is any guide, we would expect a substantial response decrement to take place to the AX compound compared to "A" alone. In fact, asymptotically we would expect "X" to become a net inhibitor. This is because the conditioned reinforcing asymptote would be in effect greatly reduced because of the large number of trials where $\lambda$ would be 0, i.e., AX-US trials.

Let's look at the equivalent situation in instrumental learning. An animal is exposed to a tone "A" in the presence of which it can press a bar on a FR1 (CRF) schedule. Again, tone "A" accrues conditioned reinforcing strength close to $\lambda$. At this stage, a compound AX is introduced, reinforced on a FR20 schedule. According to the R-W model the same thing that happened in the classical conditioning paradigm should occur here. That is, since the asymptote is reduced when AX is presented, the conditioned response strength should decline as well to AX. The Feldman and Neely-Wagner studies indicated, however, that instrumental responding continued undiminished in the presence of both "A" and "X." Blocking to "X" only occurred if "A" and AX were trained contemporaneously in the same sessions, in other words, when the organism can make a comparison

171

between reinforcement under A and AX. As Neely and Wagner note, the failure to find a decrease in response to AX is not surprising in light of the partial reinforcement effect in instrumental learning.

These results are explainable in terms of the properties of the reinforcer and habituative systems and the conditions which evoke the OR. The reinforcer system processes the primary cues that are in correlated temporal proximity to the reinforcer as well as the reinforcer itself. This is true in both the classical and instrumental paradigms. However, the instrumental paradigm tends to make greater use of cues processed through the habituative system, i.e., temporally distant, nonsalient, or background cues. This increased use of habituative system cue processing is possible because of the greater performance of voluntary responses and the increased temporal distance of the reinforcer from the initiation of responding. The habituative system is thus able to process the kind of stimuli that it would normally process in a situation where reinforcement was not present. The only difference is that in a reinforcement situation these stimuli become registered as secondary cues because the primary cues inhibit their habituation.

The difference between classical and instrumental conditioning in this situation is that the CR would suffer a response decrement to a 5% reinforcement schedule, but the instrumental response does not. What can account for this difference? According to match-mismatch theory, the maintenance of instrumental responding in this situation is due to the increased activation of the habituative system in instrumental conditioning compared to classical conditioning. Secondary cues do not have conditioned reinforcing properties and therefore are not nearly as sensitive to changes in $\lambda$. Since secondary cues can control voluntary responses, the instrumental response can be maintained even when $\lambda$ is declining.

It should be noted that while the voluntary response may be maintained while $\lambda$ is declining, this does not mean that the conditioned reinforcing properties of the primary cues are unaffected. The reinforcing properties of the primary cues can be expected to decline in the same way in the instrumental paradigm as they would in classical conditioning. However, since the CR to the primary cues is rarely measured in instrumental learning it is generally overlooked.

In a previous chapter, we saw how the activation of the reinforcer system tended to inhibit the functions of the habituative system. This inhibition has a twofold effect of course, as it not only stops habituation of processed stimuli but also prevents the habituative system from processing the nonsalient stimuli which become secondary cues to reinforcement. The critical point to remember is that the habituative system becomes inhibited not only by reinforcers and primary cues, but also by the species-specific (emotional) responses they initiate and control. As we saw, there

172

is a functional distinction between innate motivationally significant behaviors and more voluntary responses.

Thus, in the classical paradigm, to the extent that the CR is a species-specific response, it is going to inhibit the processing of secondary cues whether or not the CS is followed by the US on a particular trial. In this situation, it is clear that the CR is only going to be under the control of primary cues, which as we know derive and maintain their reinforcing strength strictly on the current strength of the US. When we reduce the occurrences of the US as in partial reinforcement, we decrease the strength of the associated primary cues, which in turn affects the magnitude of the CR (cf. Fig. 9-1).

Instrumental performance has been shown to be much less affected by satiation and other changes in the motivational state of the organism (Morgan, 1974). Capaldi and Myers (1978) showed that this instrumental response independence was particularly strong when PRF schedules were used. The use of CRF schedules tended to make the instrumental response more susceptible to motivational changes (Krieckhaus & Wolf, 1968; Holman, 1975). This is not surprising in the current theory because the influence of primary cues is going to be higher on CRF than on PRF schedules.

It should be clear now why the instrumental response does not suffer decrements in the face of diminished reinforcement. When AX is presented at a lower rate of reinforcement than "A" alone, "X" gains excitatory power through the process discussed above. However, as conditioning progresses, the total amount of reinforcing strength will decline in AX to the level set by $\lambda$ for the new reinforcement rate. It must be remembered that in this second stage there is now no primary cue in perfect correlation with the US, unlike in the first stage where "A" was 100% correlated with the US. On every reinforced trial, we have a match between AX and the US, but on every nonreinforced trial we have a mismatch. As we know, a mismatch between a CS and a US evokes ORs on the part of the organism.

With the reinforced system not in a state of activation, the organism can process secondary cues. These cues can come to control the occurrence of voluntary responses which in the present example constitutes the class from which the contingent response comes. When the primary cues occur again (i.e., AX) the secondary cues are preserved from habituation. When the US occurs, the primary cues, which presumably have not been totally extinguished, regain some of their excitatory strength.

Once the secondary cues acquire discriminative control over the instrumental response, we know that they are not nearly as dependent on a particular motivational state for their proper expression. Thus, they are less affected by the relatively frequent absence of the reinforcer at the 5% schedule. Although the same

173

evocation of ORs occurs when the US is omitted in the classical paradigm, it does not lead to the same effect since the secondary cues cannot gain direct control over the species-specific response evoked by the CS or US. Thus, the CR declines as the strength of the primary cues declines. In line with this interpretation, Holman and Mackintosh (1981) have shown that a discriminative stimulus (SD) for lever pressing does not block conditioning to a concurrent CS for food nor does a CS block a concurrently presented SD or the acquisition of another (redundant) SD. Primary cues and secondary

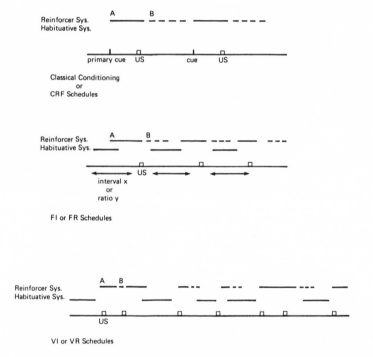

Fig. 9-1 . Differential Activation of the Reinforcer and Habituative Systems on Various Reinforcement Schedules. High rates of reinforcement and high cue-reinforcer correlations favor reinforcer system activation. Habituative system activation is fostered by omission of reinforcers and low cue-reinforcer correlations.

174

cues do not compete with each other because they are processed through different systems and because secondary cues do not use up any conditioned reinforcing strength.

## SUMMARY

In summary, the characteristics of stimulus selection are largely determined by the interactions of the basic information processing and response variables described in Section II. The association of particular elements of the stimulus field with the reinforcer in an internal representation is dependent on the pattern of ORs evoked by the stimulus presentations, the characteristics of the existing stimulus model (if any), the asymptote of conditioning supportable by the particular US (reinforcer) used, and the nature of the organismic response being performed. The affective and behavioral properties of the associated cues to reinforcement are determined by the relative salience of these stimuli and the temporal interval between their occurrence and the occurrence of the US (reinforcer) since these factors affect the assignment of stimulus processing to the reinforcer or habituative systems.

Changes in the level of association of particular stimuli with reinforcers are dependent on the occurrence of ORs, which permit modifications in the characteristics of the activated internal representations. Interference develops when a change in the pattern of stimulation conflicts with existing internal representations. This interference produces a delay in the attainment of the asymptotic reinforcing or discriminative value. In accordance with the R-W model, primary cues must compete for affective (conditioned reinforcing) strength from the available quantity set by $\lambda$ or the reinforcer magnitude.

Cues which are salient and in close temporal proximity become primary cues processed through the reinforcers. Their affective properties are dependent upon and derived in large part from the US representation. Salient cues which are associated with reinforcer omission are also processed through the reinforcer, but, as conditioned inhibitors. Nonsalient cues to reinforcement, particularly those which are temporally distant from reinforcer occurrence, are processed through the habituative system and registered as secondary cues. Since they do not possess affective reinforcing properties, they do not compete with primary cues for the affective properties whose limit is $\lambda$. However, they are subject to overshadowing from concurrent primary cues because of their lower relative salience.

175

# Chapter 10
## Behavior on Reinforcement Schedules

A consideration of the interaction between responses and reinforcement has been the heart of operant analysis. This may be due to the original Skinnerian position that operant behavior was emitted rather than evoked. That is, stimuli were not viewed as controlling operant behavior in the way they did with species-specific or respondent behavior (Skinner, 1938). While it is true that eventually Skinner modified his views and acknowledged the importance of stimuli which at least "set the occasion" for the operant response, the response bias has generally been maintained in theoretical analyses of operant responding (e.g., Herrnstein, 1970; Zeiler, 1979). I have no intention of minimizing the importance of response variables, particularly in the molecular structure of operant responding. However, I do hope to show that a consideration of motivational and stimulus processing variables is also warranted in analyzing responding to obtain positive reinforcement or avoid aversive reinforcement.

To this end, this chapter focuses on several issues that illustrate the importance of the variables already discussed in previous sections. First, we examine the effects of motivational variables on anomalous (i.e., not determined by the prevailing reinforcement contingencies) phenomena such as adjunctive behaviors and the pausing after reinforcement on FR schedules. Second, there is an examination of stimulus processing variables on the acquisition and extinction of reinforced behavior, including a detailed look at the partial reinforcement effect. Third, the way in which humans respond to the presentation of reinforcers is examined, with particular attention paid to the interaction of rule based behaviors with match–mismatch processes.

Adjunctive Behaviors

Adjunctive behaviors are motivated behaviors which occur in times of low reinforcer probability on the reinforcement schedule (Falk, 1969). The behaviors seem to be part of species-specific responses governed by reinforcers different from that being obtained on the schedule itself (e.g., water-seeking behavior at times of low reinforcer probability for food). Adjunctive behaviors have attracted interest, not only because they represent the intrusion of unplanned motivated behaviors into the seemingly well-ordered operant environment, but also from their occasional irrational quality (e.g., the excessive drinking seen by animals on many partial reinforcement schedules).

In the context of match-mismatch theory, the ubiquity of adjunctive behaviors gives credence to the hypothesis that they represent some very fundamental organismic factors which may well be present in mammals and birds as a whole. Since they do not seem to be under the control of the prevailing reinforcement contingencies, it seems reasonable to assume that they reflect motivational rather than information processing mechanisms. In Chapter 5, two fundamental motivational factors were identified as general properties of mammalian (and avian) organisms, namely, mood states and opponent processes. For the sake of parsimony, it would be highly desirable to show that these factors underlie the display of adjunctive behaviors.

Actually, the identification of adjunctive behaviors with opponent processes in the organism is not a novel one, although it is not completely noncontroversial. Staddon (1977) and Staddon and Simmelhag (1971) have argued that on periodic schedules of reinforcement, different motivational states exist in the terminal and interim segments of the interreinforcement interval which are in reciprocal interaction; i.e., they are opponent processes to each other. The authors relate this effect to an ecological function; changing an organism's goal-oriented behaviors when the goal is not likely to occur at that time. For instance, in situations or times where food is not available it makes adaptive sense to look for water or engage in other activities that also promote survival. Reciprocal interaction between motivational states could help achieve this distribution of organismic effort and time over the range of goal-directed behaviors necessary for survival.

It is clear that if this interpretation of adjunctive behaviors is to have plausibility, it is going to be necessary to show that adjunctive behaviors do display fundamental similarities with the appropriate motivational behaviors seen in more typical circumstances. Since schedule-induced polydipsia, or the excessive drinking of water when food reinforcers are not imminent, has been the

177

most intensively studied adjunctive behavior, the discussion will center on its determinants. However, it should be noted that the nature and characteristics of schedule-induced polydipsia do not seem to be unique in theoretically significant ways from properties of other adjunctive behaviors (cf. Cherek et al., 1973; Knutson & Kleinknecht, 1970; Richards & Rilling, 1972).

When water is freely available in the operant box, schedule-induced drinking generally occurs immediately after food is delivered except when the interval between food reinforcement is large. Rosselini and Burdette (1980) showed that the food reinforcer magnitude and the intermeal interval interact in their control over drinking. Small meals (pellets) support drinking only when the interval is relatively short. To maintain drinking at larger intervals, the reinforcer magnitude had to be increased. Flory (1971) and Falk (1969) provide evidence that the higher the food rate the higher the drinking rate; that is, larger reinforcer magnitudes support more drinking than small magnitudes at a given rate of reinforcement. At low food rates, drinking drops sharply. However, the more motivated (i.e., the more food deprived) the organism, the greater the tendency towards polydipsia. Thus, there seems to be an inverse relationship between body weight and polydipsia (cf. Staddon & Ayres, 1975). The control of the reinforcer over induced drinking does not seem basically attributable to its role as a discriminative stimulus, but instead seems a direct function of its reinforcing or motivational properties (Corfield-Sumner et al., 1977).

These studies provide particular support for the concept of opponent processes since a variety of factors correlated with motivation for food all seem to affect the amount of schedule-induced drinking. More important, the stronger the original motivation for food, the stronger is the corresponding opponent motivation for water. This ties in very well with other evidence that we examined in Chapter 5 concerning the operation of opponent processes, namely, the stronger the "A" process, the stronger is the opponent "B" process (cf. Solomon, 1980).

The occurrence of drinking only in times of low reinforcer probability is another indication of reciprocal motivational states in the organism. In this connection it is interesting that on random interval (RI) schedules polydipsia is reduced compared with FI or VI schedules (Millenson et al., 1977). The same is true for noncontingent food reinforcement on random time (RMT) schedules as opposed to fixed time schedules (Lashley & Rossellini, 1980). These results are probably due to the fact that on RI or RMT schedules, there is no temporal certainty regarding the delivery or non-delivery of food. Thus, it is difficult for the organism to ascertain periods of low reinforcement probability. In such cases, it is not surprising that the opponent process would be inhibited compared with schedules in which periods of nonreinforcement were more discriminable (cf. Shurtleff et al., 1983).

To what extent does the schedule-induced drinking resemble the motivational state of water deprivation or thirst? Many of the variables that affect thirst also affect schedule-induced drinking in much the same way (cf. Falk 1969, 1971). For example, access to water prior to performance on the schedule reduces the acquisition of induced drinking. Second, both rats and monkeys will learn a response that leads to access to water during the interim period. If the food reinforcer contains substantial amounts of water then induced drinking is also reduced (Mendelson et al., 1972; Bond & Corfield-Sumner, 1978).

Increasing attention has been paid to the interaction of various species-specific response patterns over the course of the interreinforcement interval (IRI). Staddon and Simmelhag (1971) differentiated between terminal responses and interim responses in the IRI. Terminal responses essentially correspond in the present theory to species-specific responses and appear in temporal proximity to reinforcement. They are governed by the mood state generated by the appropriate reinforcer. Interim activities represent a more complex situation. As Staddon (1977) later realized, there are two types of responses which seem to occur in periods of low reinforcement probability on the FT schedule: interim activities, which are essentially adjunctive behaviors, and facultative responses which in the present theory correspond to the arbitrary, voluntary responses.

Match-mismatch theory makes clear that both the adjunctive and terminal behaviors belong to the class of species-specific behaviors whose basic expression is governed by mood states. On the other hand, the facultative behaviors are voluntary responses that can be relatively independent of an underlying mood state.

Staddon and Ayres (1975) studied the interaction of some of these response patterns in polydipsic rats. They found that the drinking rate increased with food rate; however, the rate of wheel running decreased. This possibly indicates that the latter response is suppressed by drinking (adjunctive) behavior. Staddon (1977) goes on to note that the evidence would indicate that running is not schedule-induced because it increases in frequency during extinction. Roper (1978) studied various responses in the FI interval. He noted that a number of different adjunctive behaviors were exhibited by rats depending on the interval between reinforcements. One other important finding was that the substitutability of different activities for one another (e.g., drinking as a replacement for running) was limited by the tendency of these different responses to occur in different segments of the IRI (cf. Penney & Schull, 1977). These studies tie together a number of points that have been made previously.

179

When the US is occurring at definite times (or is accurately predicted by certain cues) the organism can determine not only when the US will occur but also when it will not occur. The salient stimuli that occur during the times when reinforcement probability is low should eventually become inhibitory in nature because they become associated with non-reward. As we saw, the development of inhibition and the occurrence of an opponent process to the prevailing reinforcer seem to be closely linked if not causally related. The opponent process exhibits itself when the reinforcer and its associated primary cues are absent from the stimulus environment. In this situation, motivated behaviors that were inhibited because they were not congruent with the species-specific responses induced by the reinforcer are free to occur given appropriate stimulus support. That is, an organism in a low probability interval for food will drink water when it is made available but will not engage in drinking responses in the absence of water. Actually, the opponent process, since it is induced by the action of the reinforcer, provides a motivational impetus to such behaviors. This is why the repeated presentation of the food reinforcer can lead to the organism drinking in excess of what it would under ad-lib conditions.

It is the presence of the reinforcer which sets in motion the adjunctive behaviors that occur in its absence. Presenting a brief stimulus instead of the reinforcer reduces adjunctive (but not facultative) behaviors. According to the present theory, this is because the action of the reinforcer on the reinforcer system is the essential event from which these other behaviors flow. The differential effects on adjunctive and facultative behaviors are also understandable in the present theory. The adjunctive behaviors, since they are species-specific responses controlled by the mood states, are dependent on the activation of the reinforcer system for their expression. However, the facultative behaviors, or voluntary responses, are not assumed to be dependent on mood states for their expression and can be controlled by secondary cues processed through the habituative system. Both the Penney and Schull and Roper studies provide support for the non-commonality of these different types of responses in terms of the effects of the reinforcement schedule. Of course, this ties in very well with the basic distinction made earlier between species-specific responses and voluntary responses. The studies of adjunctive behavior provide good support not only for this distinction but also for the hypothesized basis for the difference.

It seems quite clear that motivational factors are involved in the expression of adjunctive behaviors in reinforcement schedules where their occurrence is not required as part of the operant contingencies. Thus, they are in no way mysterious or counter-intuitive if it is kept in mind that the organism is necessarily an intact whole when placed in an operant situation. Although the reinforcement contingencies and the experimental situation may manipulate certain organismic and information processing variables more than others, it must be recognized that the other variables still are present and will be exhibited whenever the situation permits them to occur. Although occasionally those behaviors will act to prevent contingent responses or cause the organism to behave in a counterproductive way, as in omission studies, they are nevertheless controllable to some extent by differential reinforcement contingencies. This should not be surprising since in normal circumstances the organism will learn contingent responses to attain the adjunctive reinforcer as well.

Pausing Behavior

Another phenomenon that has been a puzzle from the theoretical standpoint for much the same reasons as adjunctive behaviors has been the FR pause. After reinforcement is delivered on an FR schedule, the organism usually pauses for some length of time before starting to respond on the fixed ratio again. The interesting aspect is that the pausing is in excess of the time spent in approaching and consuming the delivered reinforcer. That is, the time the organism spends eating a pellet is only a part of the total time in which responding ceases. Thus, pausing goes against the maximization of reinforcement on FR schedules.

There are several pieces of evidence which confirm that the pause cannot be attributed to theoretically trivial factors such as reinforcer consumption. First of all, the pause is much reduced or eliminated on VR and VI schedules and yet reinforcement is equivalent (cf. Ferster & Skinner, 1957; Shull, 1979). Second, the length of the pause is directly related to the size of the FR ratio. Of course, there is a confoundment between FR size and the amount of time that elapses between reinforcements. Obviously, it takes a rat longer to press a bar 100 times than 10 times. Thus, the relationship between pause length and the size of the ratio may well be due to the interval between reinforcements instead of the number of responses emitted per reinforcement (cf. Griffiths & Thompson, 1973; Rider, 1980).

Actually, the pause in responding that occurs after delivery of the reinforcement is not unique to FR schedules. As is well known, substantial pausing occurs after reinforcement on FI schedules. Usually, the pause amounts to about half of the entire fixed interval. Once responding begins, the rate gradually accelerates until it reaches a maximum around the time the interval lapses (cf. Zeiler, 1977, 1979). The pause on the fixed interval schedule, although possessing some interesting aspects as we shall see, has not seemed as prickly from the theoretical viewpoint because it does

181

not interfere with the delivery of reinforcement as in the FR schedule.

A possible reason for this effect has been provided by Williams (1965) in a comparison of FI and FR performance and the correlation of operant responses with more autonomic responses (e.g., salivation). Williams found that on FI schedules both operant responses and the conditioned species-specific responses tended to occur more or less in tandem. That is, once operant responding began about halfway into the fixed interval, the autonomic responses started to appear at about the same time. However, on FR schedules this correspondence was not found. In the latter schedules, operant responding tended to occur prior to the appearance of the conditioned emotional responses.

In terms of the hypothesized workings of the IPM, the conditioned reinforcing stimuli or primary cues control responding on the FI. As we saw in a previous section, the motivational level seems to rise as the interval progresses since it becomes increasingly difficult to suppress terminal responding (cf. Lyon & Millar, 1969). Thus, it seems that primary cues with their conditioned reinforcing properties control the occurrence of the operant responding prior to the lapsing of the interval. It should be remembered that the primary cues can control both species-specific responses and voluntary responses. It could be said that the responses that occur prior to the end of the interval are due not so much to timing errors as to the motivation to perform responses associated with positive reinforcement given appropriate stimulus support (cf. Dews, 1962, 1970).

Responding on DRL schedules offers an interesting comparison with that of FI schedules. The major difference between the two types of schedules is that on DRL schedules, the responses themselves must be separated by a certain interval before reinforcement is delivered, while on FI schedules the interval is imposed independent of the organism's responses. Thus, in the former schedule, response output can be said to be relatively constrained by the schedule parameters while in the latter, it is relatively unconstrained.

The constraint on responding in DRL schedules is quite direct since a response that quickly follows another response delays reinforcement. On the other hand, responding on the FI schedule can never delay reinforcement. It can be said, in terms of the present theory, that the FI schedule provides an opportunity for the organism to reveal the underlying motivational propensity through the operant response. To the extent that primary cues induce a motivational state reflective of that produced by the unconditioned reinforcer, the associated response can express itself at a rate appropriate to the cues' reinforcing strength.

If this analysis is applied to DRL schedules, we should see that the constraint on responding would seem to reduce the rate below that which the primary cues would support and encourage. Thus, the response output and motivation induced by the primary cues would not be congruent on this schedule. One of the salient characteristics of DRL responding is, in fact, the tendency to respond at a rate higher than the optimum. That is, responses occur too closely spaced together to provide the maximum number of reinforcements available. The average number of responses per reinforcer tends to increase as the minimum time permitted between reinforced responses is increased from small values up to approximately one minute (Richardson & Clark, 1976).

It has been commonly assumed (e.g., Ferster & Skinner, 1957; Reynolds, 1968) that the overresponding on DRL schedules is a function of the reinforcement principle; i.e., reinforcement increases the probability of any response which precedes it. In this view, when a reinforcer is delivered, the tendency to perform the preceding response increases, thus increasing the response rate.

As Zeiler (1979) notes, this interpretation encounters some problems when the responding on DRL schedules is examined more closely. One of the more anomalous findings is that longer inter-response times (IRT) are more likely to occur right after reinforcement than shorter times, which goes directly counter to the idea that the reinforcer simply raises the rate of the contingent responses. Of course, this finding is in line with the idea that cues associated with low probability periods of reward become conditioned inhibitors and depress the contingent response. In addition, the IRTs do not seem to display the consistent pattern that one would expect if reinforcement was directly operating on the spacing of responses. Although the schedule parameter specifying the minimum reinforced IRT determines the spacing of responses in the overall distribution, particular times appear to be random in that distribution (cf. Harzem et al., 1975).

In the present view, the overresponding on DRL schedules occurs for the same reason that organisms overrespond on FI schedules, namely, the tendency for the conditioned reinforcing strength of primary cues to set the motivationally optimal rate for the responses they control. The fact that this motivated responding does not conform to schedule requirements simply proves one of the central points of the current theory—information processing interacts with motivational mechanisms and the two are not necessarily congruent in their behavioral influences.

It was mentioned that, contrary to reinforcement principles, pausing (longer IRTs) is found after reinforcement on FR schedules. Shull (1979), in his analysis of the FR pause has noted that the tendency to begin responding in an interval terminated by reward is fundamentally determined by the work time associated with attainment

183

of that reward. Shull regards the FR pause as composed of two parts: unmeasured terminal behavior associated with receipt of the reinforcer and a true pause consisting of nonterminal behavior. The amount of time spent in the latter behavior can be regarded as an index of the reward value of the reinforcer. Presumably, the more powerful the reinforcer, the smaller the time spent in noncontingent behaviors.

There appears to be evidence for these two factors in this kind of pausing behavior. Both Innis and Honig (1979) and Harzem et al. (1978) have shown that the delivery of reinforcement per se has a suppressive effect on behavior immediately following its occurrence. This effect is independent of its discriminative function in signaling a low reinforcement probability immediately after its occurrence.

The suppressive function of reinforcer occurrence is also indicated by the enhancement of responding when an expected reinforcer is omitted, i.e., the well-known reinforcement omission effect in extinction (cf. Deese & Hulse, 1967). The omission of reward results in an increased response rate that often exceeds the rate found under asymptotic conditions on the schedule itself. Harzem et al. note as well that on FI schedules, when a brief stimulus is presented instead of the reinforcer, the post-reinforcer pause is shorter (cf. Staddon & Innis, 1969; Zeiler, 1972).

The second factor governing pausing after reinforcement is the temporal characteristics of reinforcer occurrence. When a reinforcer occurs in a definite temporal relationship with certain cues or with previous reinforcer occurrences, the internal representation of the reinforcer can be retrieved at systematic intervals. Thus, an organism has a way of determining the temporal distance of the next reinforcer occurrence. If the time between occurrences is long enough, we know that the effective limits of the reinforcer system will be exceeded. When this occurs, two things generally result: (1) a change in the underlying motivational state with the concomitant possibility of inhibitory stimuli being established in the period of low reinforcement probability; and (2) the possibility of secondary cue control over instrumental responding through the functioning of the habituative system, which in this situation is freed from inhibition by the reinforcer system.

It should be noted that these processes are basically opposing actions. The presence of inhibitory stimuli will tend to reduce responding associated with the prevailing reinforcer while the secondary cues can control the occurrence of contingent instrumental responses for that same reinforcer. Interestingly, the data would seem to indicate the presence of just such conflicting tendencies on the part of an organism in this situation. On chain schedules with FR components, organisms in the initial components display very irregular patterns of responding, oftentimes with long

184

interruptions before the FR requirement for that component is completed. In this connection, it is interesting to note that FI schedules can support more responses than can FR schedules. Zeiler (1977) showed that pigeons which could average 800-1000 responses per interval on FI-40' would stop responding on FR 600. From the present standpoint, we can note that FI schedules permit the organism to respond only when primary cues are present, while FR schedules force the organism to respond during low probability periods of reward.

This analysis indicates that the anomalous behavior of organisms on reinforcement schedules can only be considered as such when all behavior is viewed as being under the direct control of the prevailing reinforcer. However, if the basic motivational and information processing variables identified by match-mismatch theory are considered, then the behaviors can be seen to be consistent with these fundamental factors.

INFORMATION PROCESSING VARIABLES
IN ACQUISITION AND EXTINCTION

In the first part of the chapter we examined several behavioral phenomena occurring on reinforcement schedules which were shown to result from basic motivational factors interacting with contingent responding. In this section, we examine the operation of the information processing factors controlling the occurrence of the contingent response. The acquisition of the contingent response has always been ascribed to a specific learning process of some kind; however, extinction has always been viewed more ambiguously. The focus of this section is mainly on extinction, but it is contended that a real understanding of extinction, in particular the partial reinforcement effect, depends to a great extent on the conditions under which the contingent response was learned.

Extinction, when considered as a procedure, is the sustained omission of an expected reinforcer. Such reinforcer omission typically results in a decline in the probability of the contingent response which produced reinforcement. An important factor that can affect resistance to extinction is the similarity of the conditions presented in extinction with those present in the acquisition of the contingent response (Skinner, 1950; Welker et al., 1974). To the extent that conditions remain the same, resistance to extinction is greater than when some change is introduced in extinction.

One of the best documented findings concerning the conventional extinction procedure is that it tends to foster variability in an organism's behavior (cf. Staddon & Simmelhag, 1971). In this respect, it displays opposite effects to the introduction of reinforcement. For example, Schwartz (1980) trained pigeons to peck on a five-by-five matrix of lights. A keypeck on one key moved a light down a row while keypecks on another key moved it over a column. To obtain reinforcement, pigeons had to peck four times on each key, i.e., move the light to the lowest row and last column. Five pecks on one key resulted in reinforcer omission. In this situation, there are 70 different sequences of keypecks which will result in reinforcement. However, each of the pigeons developed particular stereotyped sequences which they exhibited to the general exclusion of the other possibilities. When extinction was introduced, however, the stereotyped responding was replaced by substantial increases in sequence variability. Wong (1977) using naturalistic observational methods of reinforced runway responding in the rat found that extinction produced increases in exploratory behavior. This was followed by displacement (adjunctive) behaviors and finally goal avoidance. In other words, the reinforcer system's inhibition of the stimulus processing functions of the habituative system are reduced in such situations.

## Extinction in Classical Conditioning

Extinction of classically conditioned responses seems to display some differences from instrumental extinction, but in ways which have been difficult to define in any systematic or satisfactory way. According to the present theory, the two paradigms tend to activate the reinforcer and habituative systems in different proportions. The classical paradigm generally activates the reinforcer system in acquisition and the habituative system in extinction. In the instrumental paradigm, both the reinforcer and habituative systems can be active in acquisition because of the performance of voluntary responses which do not inhibit the processing capacities of the habituative system.

In classical conditioning, we would expect the organism to display lower response amplitudes to partially reinforced primary cues since decrements in associative strength should be occurring on non-reinforced trials. The data concerning asymptotic levels of classically conditioned responses with partial reinforcement of primary cues are quite inconsistent, however. In some studies, a lower asymptote of conditioning has been reported when partial reinforcement has been given in acquisition; in others, the asymptote is essentially the same as that found in continuous reinforcement (Hartman & Grant, 1962; Hilton, 1969; Thomas & Wagner, 1964). The most systematic investigation of this effect is probably the Gibbs et al. (1978) study mentioned previously. Asymptotic response levels remained relatively undiminished on schedules of reinforcement higher than 25%. In addition, the performance decrements that did occur could not be attributed to the immediate effects of three or less consecutive nonreinforced trials. This would seem to be an example of the conservatism of the IPM with regard to reinforcement.

Gibbs et al. did find substantial response decrements when the schedule of reinforcement dropped to 5%, however. It should be noted that this is equivalent to an instrumental random ratio schedule of 20. Instrumental ratios of this kind do not cause instrumental response decrements. Thus, the classically conditioned response seems sensitive to partial reinforcement in acquisition, particularly when the schedule departs substantially from 100% reinforcement. It seems likely, though, that evolutionary considerations would act to modify acquisition processes towards a more conservative stance vis à vis reinforcement and the associative strength of the processing cues. In the natural setting, the occurrence of reinforcement is usually a life or death matter. If a reinforcer occurs in a particular situation, it would be counterproductive for the organism to become too easily discouraged by reinforcer omission. Obviously, in the real world there are rarely two events which are 100% correlated in terms of their occurrence. We would expect to see such conservatism, particularly when the reinforcer does occur on a good proportion of the cases, say, 25% or 50% of the time. In such cases, the habituative system may continue to be inhibited by the associated primary cues sufficiently to prevent much loss of conditioning on non-reinforced trials.

Since the strength of the partially reinforced primary cues remains roughly equivalent in the classical conditioning procedure with moderate departures from a CRF schedule, it would be predicted that the extinction rate should be roughly comparable as well. In fact, with large departures from CRF (e.g., 10% or less reinforced trials) we would expect faster extinction since the strength of the primary cues is significantly reduced on such schedules.

Gibbon et al. (1980) note that the partial reinforcement extinction effect (PREE), in which partial reinforcement leads to longer responding in extinction than continuous reinforcement, is inconsistently found in classical conditioning (in contrast to its ubiquity in instrumental learning). The PREE is typically measured by the number of trials before the CR (or contingent response) is extinguished. Using this measure, a PREE would be claimed if, for example, it took the organism 40 trials to extinguish after a 25% schedule of reinforced trials, but only 10 trials after continuous reinforcement. However, if the same data are analyzed from the point of view of the number of expected reinforcers, we see that the difference disappears. That is, an organism on a 25% schedule would "expect" only 10 reinforcements for every 40 CS presentations. In other words, the same number of mismatches would be occurring in both situations.

Gibbon et al. reanalyzed the data from studies reporting a PREE in the Pavlovian paradigm. Almost invariably, the PREE disappeared when the different groups' extinction responding was analyzed in terms of the number of expected reinforcers. In terms of the current theory, the organism has encoded the temporal characteristics of the US occurrences and only registers a mismatch on trials that were associated with reinforcement on the acquisition schedule. Without a mismatch occurring, the stimuli controlling the CR will not evoke the OR and be switched from the reinforcer system to the habituative system. The representations of the US should be retrieved into working memory only at those times specified by the controlling retrieval cues, which can be cues such as an exteroceptive CS or temporal cues in the interreinforcer interval. It is well-known that extinction does not occur in the absence of the cues which predict reinforcement (cf. Deese & Hulse, 1967; Nevin, 1974).

The nature of the response is important to the above analysis, in that the reasoning applies to the performance of species-specific responses but not fully to voluntary responses. However, the discussion of this response effect is best dealt with in the context of the analysis of the instrumental PREE.

Extinction in Instrumental Learning

As we have discussed, instrumental learning tends to involve two factors that are minimized in the classical procedure, the voluntary response and secondary cues. It is these two factors which account for the differences in extinction behavior in the two paradigms. In particular, we will see why the number of mismatches in instrumental learning may not produce the same extinction rate as would occur in classical conditioning.

Let's use a concrete example to illustrate the workings of the IPM in the acquisition and extinction of a contingent response. An organism receives food each time it presses a bar. To make the correspondence with the classical conditioning procedure greater, reinforcement is only delivered after the contingent response is performed in the presence of a tone. In other words, a discriminant operant procedure is used.

The action of the reinforcer is much the same in its effects in both procedures. When the bar is first operated either by accident or through the organism's free operant behavior then the reinforcer is delivered and the reinforcer system is activated. The activation of the reinforcer system acts to preserve the information residing in working memory and also the response information. Thus, the tone cue, the sequence of responses prior to reinforcement and the contextual stimuli all are processed by the IPM. Upon repetitions of reinforcement delivery the associative strength of these stimuli and responses of course will increase through their processing through the reinforcer system.

The reinforcer evokes the species-specific responses and mood state appropriate to it, exactly as in the classical paradigm. The stimuli processed through the reinforcer system along with the unconditioned reinforcer (US) thus become associated with that mood state and with those species-specific responses (i.e., they become conditioned reinforcers). There is one large difference, obviously, between the instrumental paradigm and the classical paradigm, in that the organism now has to perform some voluntary contingent response. The performance of such responses can be controlled by the primary cues. In the example used here, it is clear that with discriminative training the organism will perform the particular instrumental response of pressing the bar mainly when the primary cue (i.e., the tone) is present. The nature of the associative connection probably differs between the primary cue and the instrumental response compared with the species-specific responses. The conditioned reinforcing property of these cues is undoubtedly more relevant to the performance of the species-specific responses than the voluntary responses.

The importance of the voluntary responses is that their performance does not inhibit the functioning of the habituative system. The increased possibility of secondary cue processing has important implications for instrumental learning. A stimulus will be processed by the habituative system when it is nonreinforced and when it is nonsalient. The first instance is not relevant to secondary cue processing so we will concentrate on the second condition.

Salience or nonsalience is a difficult stimulus quality to define precisely. It is clear that to a large degree it is a relative matter dependent on the particular context in which a given stimulus occurs. In different situations, the same stimulus might be salient and nonsalient. This is not to say that the saliency of a stimulus in a situation is not measurable, but simply that a priori assignment of a stimulus into one or the other category is not likely in the absolute sense. Contextual salience of a stimulus is properly defined in terms of organismic effect rather than on inherent stimulus properties such as intensity. Many stimuli which are nonintense can nevertheless be highly salient to an organism (e.g., stimulus releasers for species-specific responses). One other point is that stimuli generally have a number of encodable dimensions, some of them more salient than others. For example, an organism might notice the color of a red triangle more than its shape.

We have already discussed why the habituative system does not habituate nonsalient stimuli that are temporally distant from reinforcement. The action of the primary cues tends to activate

189

the reinforcer system which in turn inhibits the operation of the habituative system. It is well-known that response chaining and the association of stimuli occur backwards from the reinforcer. The cues temporally closest to the reinforcer are learned first and then more temporally distant cues are acquired (cf. Gollub, 1977).

Temporally distant cues therefore can be processed either by the reinforcer or habituative system depending on their salience. The more salient the cue the more likely its eventual processing through the reinforcer system as a conditioned inhibitor. Less salient cues will be processed through the habituative system as discriminative stimuli devoid of conditioned reinforcing properties (whether excitatory or inhibitory). The absence of conditioned reinforcing properties actually is an advantage for cues that are temporally distant from reinforcement since they are not subject to the various organismic effects induced by the reinforcer. Thus, they can control voluntary responding which leads to reward without becoming inhibitory stimuli.

Marcucella (1981) studied both operant responding on a VI schedule combined with noncontingent responding to a brief signal associated with reward (i.e., a conditioned reinforcer). As we would expect, the pigeons increased their rates of pecking while the primary cue was present compared to the rest of the schedule, but only as long as the stimulus was correlated with reinforcement. Pecking during the signal was eliminated when the correlation was reduced to zero. The most interesting finding was that noncontingent pecking to the stimulus displayed different properties from contingent responding. The operant behavior was relatively insensitive to differing rates of reinforcement compared to the noncontingent pecking which was highly sensitive to these same reinforcement rates.

How does this division of cue processing operate on typical instrumental schedules of partial reinforcement? When an organism barpresses for food on a CRF schedule, the cues associated with barpressing have a 100% correlation with the occurrence of food. In terms of R-W theory, the available cues are at the asymptotic value. In terms of match-mismatch theory, the organism has an internal representation which matches each time with the stimulus environment. Thus, additional cue processing would be inhibited whether through the reinforcer or habituative system. In the classical paradigm, the processed cues would be primary cues with conditioned reinforcing properties. In the CRF instrumental situation, the nature of the associated cues is not quite as definite. The primary cues because of their high correlation with reinforcement will be close to the asymptotic limit. However, the performance of the voluntary response does not inhibit the habituative system the way that the species-specific responses do. In these

190

circumstances, there is somewhat more probability of limited secondary cue processing than in the classical procedure.

This analysis suggests that there is not that much difference between the CRF schedules in instrumental and classical conditioning. The extinction data would seem to bear this out. Extinction generally occurs rapidly after CRF schedules (cf. Deese & Hulse, 1967; Kimble, 1961) in instrumental as well as classical paradigms. When extinction begins in the instrumental paradigm, a mismatch occurs between the stimulus environment and the internal representation. In terms of stimulus processing, the mismatch is going to evoke the OR on the part of the organism. The absence of reinforcement allows the habituative system to begin processing and habituating the stimuli present in the environment which have associative strength above the level supportable by nonreinforcement. Each time the cues associated with reinforcement occur and are nonreinforced, reductions in associative strength occur. As can be seen, this differs very little from the situation in classical conditioning. The similarity in extinction rates is reflective of this basic correspondence in the information processing and motivational factors present in both situations.

On the FI schedules, the cues controlling responding are likely to be primary cues since there is no need for the organism to respond during times of low reinforcement probability. To the extent that responding is controlled by a few well-defined primary cues, extinction should be relatively rapid. Extinction rates for FI schedules are in fact relatively rapid (cf. Deese & Hulse, 1967; Reynolds, 1968) and sometimes are not that much different from the extinction rates on instrumental CRF schedules.

Fixed ratio schedules present a somewhat different picture depending on the size of the FR. For small fixed ratios (e.g., < 10) the contingent relationships would seem to be fairly easy for organisms to encode even when symbolic mediation could not be used to count the number of responses necessary for reinforcement. Despite this ease in encoding contingent relationships in some cases, the fixed ratio schedule is more likely to promote control over responding by secondary cues than the fixed interval schedule since the schedule contains a conflict between motivational factors and maximization of the available reinforcement. To the extent that responding during low probability of reinforcement probability periods increases reinforcement, there will be an increased tendency for the organism to initiate such responding. The motivational factors will be strongest initially during the low reinforcement period as we have seen in the FR pause. However, as the initial postreinforcement effects diminish, the organism will again respond. With the contingency to respond early, the pause will be as short as the organism can control. Responding that begins during a period when inhibitory stimuli are still present, however, must be controlled by the secondary cues. Thus, on the FR schedule it is more likely that secondary cues will control at least the initiation of ratio responding. On very small ratios these factors should be minimized because of the short minimum time between reinforcements that is attainable. The larger the ratio, however, the more these factors should come into play.

Why don't inhibitory cues, which are conditioned reinforcers, inhibit the habituative system's processing of secondary cues? The answer would seem to be twofold. First, the inhibitory stimuli are not that strong on these schedules, and second, conditioned inhibition is fairly slow to develop (Rescorla, 1979). By the time the inhibitory stimuli have acquired conditioned reinforcing properties, the secondary cues have already been processed.

Partial reinforcement schedules with unpredictable reinforcer occurrences (e.g., VR, VI) pose a somewhat different problem for the organism's IPM. Partial reinforcement schedules, in general, obviously have less correlation between their primary cues and the occurrence of reinforcement than CRF schedules do, with random reinforcement representing one extreme. Since the primary cues are occurring sometimes with the reinforcer and sometimes not, the correlation of such cues is typically less than asymptotic. The OR will be evoked when there is a mismatch between the stimulus model and the stimulus environment. Changes in associative strength of stimuli can only occur when the OR occurs. To the extent that the available cues are not perfect predictors of reinforcement, a mismatch will occur. Presumably, the alternation of reinforcement and nonreinforcement on a FR2 schedule is an easy enough relationship for most organisms to grasp. If this is the case, then with extended training a mismatch will not occur on the nonreinforced trials because the available cues will predict reinforcement on every second presentation of the CS and will predict it in consistent fashion. In such circumstances the cues associated with the nonreinforced response in the ratio should become inhibitory or negative conditioned reinforcers. In fact, organisms have been shown to run less vigorously in the alleyway on these alternating nonreinforced trials compared to the reinforced trials (Capaldi, 1967).

However, variable or random ratio schedules for large fixed ratio schedules (that exceed the organism's counting ability) should present greater difficulties for the IPM simply because the available cues do not permit the precise identification of the temporal characteristics of reinforcer occurrence. The theory would predict that there would be more ORs on these latter kinds of schedules than there would be on FI, FR, or CRF schedules because there would be an increased number of mismatches between the internal representation and the environmental events.

Interestingly, the rate of extinction on these schedules seems to parallel the degree to which we would expect mismatches (and ORs) to occur in acquisition. Extinction proceeds most quickly on the CRF schedule, next quickest on FI and low FR schedules, and slowest on comparable variable and random-ratio schedules (cf. Reynolds, 1968; Nevin, 1974).

Match-mismatch theory contends that the rate of extinction on a particular schedule is dependent in large part on the nature of the cues processed during acquisition. Generally speaking, the lower the strength of the primary cues in relation to the attainable asymptote, the more likelihood of secondary cue processing. In such a situation, the density or magnitude of reinforcement is low and there are no cues which have a high correlation with reinforcer occurrence. With larger elapsed times between successive reinforcers, the temporal limits of the reinforcer system would be exceeded. This would free the habituative system from inhibition. Therefore, we should expect more opportunity for secondary cue processing.

For example, Amsel et al. (1964) showed that PRF schedules promote faster running speeds in the early portions of the alleyway compared with CRF schedules, while the opposite relation holds in the terminal portions of the alley. This is exactly what we would expect from the present theory. Wong (1977) has shown that the inferior acquisition speed on PRF schedules compared with CRF schedules results from greater response variability on the part of the subjects rather than slower running per se. PRF subjects were more likely to sniff (ORs) and engage in collateral behaviors such as drinking or digging.

Since the stronger the reinforcer system is activated, the more it inhibits habituative system functioning, the reward magnitude should play an important role in determining the degree of reinforcer system activation. The larger the US, the stronger the UR and the more motivated the organism becomes. To the extent that large rewards activate the reinforcer system more strongly, they should inhibit secondary cue processing more strongly during acquisition.

The effect of reward magnitude on later extinction has been known since the Zeaman (1949) studies which showed that responses reinforced with large magnitude rewards tended to extinguish faster than when reinforced by small magnitude rewards. Morris and Capaldi (1979) studied the effects of different reward magnitudes on PRF and CRF schedules and found that increased numbers of large rewards reduced resistance to extinction to a greater extent than did small rewards (cf. Capaldi et al., 1976). In other words, large magnitude rewards tend to make the instrumental paradigm more like the classical paradigm, in terms of cue processing effects. Thus extinction proceeds more rapidly with large magnitude rewards in this situation. A point in favor of this interpretation is the difficulty of obtaining this effect in the classical conditioning paradigm in which secondary cue processing is minimized (Wagner, 1961).

The addition of secondary cues acts to extend extinction responding in two ways. First, it increases the number of associated cues controlling the response. Although this does not extend extinction per se, the variability of these cues is an important factor in doing so. It should be noted that the secondary cues have not been specified by the experimenter but are the consequence of the continual mismatches that are created by unpredictable reinforcement. Thus, the secondary cues processed on the schedule are necessarily of a somewhat idiosyncratic nature, although they will be specified in a general way by the nature of the schedule and the stimulus environment.

The second factor at work in extending extinction responding on such schedules is the qualitative nature of the secondary cues themselves. The primary cues, while potent in their ability to control behavior, are very susceptible to changes in the motivational state of the organism due to temporal distance from reinforcement. As we saw previously, changes (e.g., habituation) in the value of the reinforcer had profound effects on the primary cues. Secondary cues, while controlling behavior less strongly in the sense that the behavior is more easily disrupted (e.g., Lyon & Millar, 1969), are also more impervious to motivational changes.

The secondary cues should thus be more resistant to the changes in reinforcer value associated with extinction, which is simply the reduction of reinforcer magnitude to zero. The primary cues, dependent as they are on the continued strength of the reinforcer, will decline. However, the secondary cues, acting as discriminative stimuli, will continue to evoke the responses which have become associated with them. Actually, responding to the secondary cues may well cease more because the organism has come under the control of new stimuli during extinction than because they have lost control over the associated response (e.g., Wong, 1977). It should be remembered that in naturalistic settings, organisms are more likely to be exposed to a variety of motivational influences which would disrupt responding in extinction. The typical experimental setting probably fosters longer extinction because of the absence of competing stimuli.

The secondary cues are thus the reason why extinction in instrumental learning does not follow the apparent rule found in classical conditioning; i.e., similar extinction rates as a function of expected reinforcement occurrence. Their lack of dependence on the presence of affective attributes in the representations of the primary cues and US gives them more persistent control over associated responses.

In summary, important aspects of behavior on operant schedules appear to be determined by the fundamental behavioral factors described in Section II. The extended motivational effects produced by the occurrence of reinforcers can be used to explain anomalous aspects of schedule behavior such as adjunctive responses and pausing which either have no effect on reinforcement delivery or act to reduce the amount of reinforcement. The relative balance of control by primary and secondary cues creates important schedule differences. Secondary cues are more likely to be processed under conditions of low reward frequency and magnitude when the reinforcer system has a reduced tendency to inhibit habituative system processing. The control over responding by secondary cues tends to prolong responding in extinction because of the reduced sensitivity of these cues to motivational changes induced by reinforcer omission. However, behavior under the control of secondary cues is more subject to disruption by competing stimuli. Conversely, primary cues are more sensitive to motivational changes produced by changes in reinforcer occurrence, but the behaviors they control are resistant to disruption by competing stimuli.

HUMAN CONDITIONING

It has been noted in a variety of situations that language, symbolic behavior, cognitions, etc., constitute an important qualitative difference between humans and infrahumans. For example, Pavlov (1955) talked of the "second signal" system (i.e., verbal-symbolic behavior) and the possible interaction of these processes with the presumably more fundamental learning processes examined in animals. As he noted, the second signal system could enhance, inhibit, or have no effect on these basic learning processes. In another context, MacLean (1970) talked about the "grafting" of cerebral function onto more primitive or at least phylogenetically older brain structures.

The key point in these various notions is that verbal-symbolic processes exist in tandem with other information processing factors that are not dependent on the existence of language. In the present theory, this distinction is contained in the idea that humans have two potential controls over behavior: verbal-symbolic rules, and match-mismatch processes. As Pavlov noted, the possibility for complex interactions exists between verbal behavior and other learning processes and this interaction necessarily complicates the analysis of human behavior. In predicting human behavior, we have to consider not only the interaction between the various match-mismatch variables that are operative but also the additional interaction of rule-based behaviors or cognitions. This is not to conclude that human behavior is beyond analysis. There are a number of simplifying factors that enhance the possibility of prediction,

195

e.g., the dependence and constraint of rule-based behaviors by match-mismatch processes.

If we assume that the rule-based system has been added to an existing IPM based on match-mismatch processes, we can conclude that humans should have the potential of exhibiting the same kinds of behavioral processes seen in infrahumans. Furthermore, these behaviors can be manifested for the same reasons that they are in animals, i.e., the operation of match-mismatch processes. Whether they do occur, of course, is dependent on the operation of the rule-based system in those particular circumstances. Thus, to the extent that we minimize verbal symbolic behaviors in a situation, the more clearly the behavior should reflect match-mismatch processes.

How can we conceptualize the interaction between match-mismatch processes and verbal symbolic processes? Actually, the solution is probably a very straightforward one: verbal symbolic rules simply add new contingencies to the situation. For example, the establishment of a retirement or pension fund is a clear case of a verbal-symbolic contingency contravening match-mismatch processes. Obviously, there is a direct contingency between spending money and the obtainment of particular kinds of reinforcing stimuli. Although animals can be taught to bypass small immediate rewards for larger delayed rewards, this only occurs when the conditioned reinforcing properties of stimuli associated with the delayed reward outweigh the reinforcing properties of the stimuli associated with immediate small reward (Rachlin, 1976). However, in the case of the retirement fund, not only is there no comparable outweighing of conditioned reinforcing cues on the side of delaying reinforcement, but also the delayed reward has never been experienced. It is clear that such behavior can be sustained only by verbal-symbolic mediation.

Nevertheless, human behavior should be conceptualized as an interaction between match-mismatch and rule-based processes. Let's examine the previous example a little more closely. While it is quite true that people will act according to a more or less dominant verbal-symbolic contingency, it is also the case that the more the rule-based behavior contravenes match-mismatch processes, the more difficult it is for humans to engage consistently in the behavior. To take the establishment of pension systems, many behavioral supports are typically provided for people to engage in such behavior. For example, retirement systems in an organization are generally compulsory, with established rates of payment into the fund. In addition, such payments are often in the form of payroll deductions so that the person does not have to actually perform the action of putting aside money for the future.

It can be inferred that in general, the more a verbal-symbolic contingency contravenes match-mismatch processes, the more likely it is that a person will eventually come under control of the latter. In talking about verbal-symbolic contingencies and their effect on behavior, we necessarily must confront the question of whether such contingencies are actually controlling the observed behavior or are simply epiphenomena or rationalizations for behavior controlled by other means. We are all familiar with saying we will act in a certain way prior to experiencing the controlling contingencies and then finding out that we are acting in a quite different way than our verbal behavior suggested, for example.

The obvious question at this point is how do we distinguish verbal-symbolic behavior with mediational properties from those verbal-symbolic behaviors that are merely epiphenomenal? Unfortunately, to state the question is not to provide the answer. One thing that can be said is that we will not be able to decide even ex post facto what class a particular verbal-symbolic behavior falls into until we are able to define what behaviors we would expect from match-mismatch processes alone.

## Match-Mismatch Conditioning Processes in Humans

The match-mismatch processes present in the classical and instrumental paradigms of animal behavior also can be found in humans, although the presence of rule-based behavior can obscure this fact. As I see it, more work is going to have to be done with human populations possessing minimal verbal-symbolic behavior (e.g., retardates and young children) in order to establish this hypothesis more firmly. Although there are numerous studies of human conditioning, most provide no clear dissociation of rule-based and match-mismatch processes.

There have been a number of basic conditioning studies showing similar kinds of learning processes in humans compared with those found in animals. For example, Hovland (1937) showed a typical negatively accelerating learning curve in GSR conditioning in humans with shock as the US and a vibrating stimulus as a CS. Studies by Kimble et al. (1955) and Spooner & Kellogg (1947) showed the most effective conditioning in humans to occur with 500 msec CS-US intervals as with animals. Grings and his associates (1961, 1962) studied electrodermal response conditioning in both of the special populations specified above. In the first study, totally deaf pre-school age children were compared with normal college studies. The deaf children were able to condition the GSR as rapidly and reliably as the college students, indicating that simple conditioning is not dependent on the level of verbal-symbolic capacity. Similarly, when two groups of retarded adolescents with average IQs of 63 and 34 were exposed to GSR conditioning procedures, they exhibited rapid and reliable conditioning as well. In a more recent study, Grings et al. (1979) reported some of the same correlational effects in human conditioning as found with animals. At a somewhat more complex level, Kendler and Kendler (1968), in a well-known study, showed that children and adults differed in the way they learned certain discriminations. By examining the kinds of errors made in reversal situations, it was shown that children basically learned discriminations on an individual or case-by-case basis rather than on some higher rule, whereas the adults were more likely to engage in the latter activity. Interestingly, the pattern of errors shown by children on such tasks was very similar to the kinds of errors made by animals such as rats.

Those kind of studies provide evidence for the idea that basic learning processes found in animals also exist in humans. Indeed, it would be extraordinary if an IPM that took millions of years to come into existence would suddenly be thrown out. The neurological evidence confirms the general viewpoint that, typically, new functions are integrated with phylogenetically older functions rather than replacing them. I believe that a more careful and analytical examination of human populations with minimal verbal-symbolic activity will show a large degree of correspondence with the learning processes found in animals.

Interactions Between Rules and
the Response to Reinforcers

Rule based behavior has been shown to exert a significant effect on the response to reinforcers in humans. In the classical conditioning paradigm, for example, clearcut differences have been obtained between subjects who have verbalized the CS-US relationship and those who have failed to do so (Nelson & Ross, 1974; Zagano et al., 1974).

Cerewicki et al. (1968) presented words forming part of a set or category as CSs. The members of one set were followed by the US, while the members of the other set were not. The size of the set and the relatedness within the set of words were varied. The performance of all subjects in differential responding decreased as set size increased when unrelated words were used. However, when related words were used, performance depended on whether the subjects verbalized the relationships or not. Voluntary form responders (Vs) had short latency, high amplitude responses sustained through US presentation (air puff to the eye). Conditioned form responders (Cs) had less effective lower amplitude responses with gradual recruitment. The Vs tended to perform better when words were related; the Cs performed the same in both cases (cf. Maltzman et al., 1977; Pendery & Maltzman, 1977).

Cognitively oriented research has also shown strong interactions between rule based behavior (e.g., attributions) and the response to sensory reinforcers. One line of research has been in the area of cognitive dissonance. Cognitive dissonance is hypothesized to be a motivational state brought about when a person has cognitive elements that are in conflict or have contradictory elements. As an arousal state, it persists until cognitive behavior lowers the relative number or importance of relevant cognitions discrepant with the elements that are most resistant to change (i.e., overt behavior). The cognitive activity can consist of adding consonant cognitions, increasing the importance of consonant cognitions, subtracting dissonant cognitions, and decreasing the importance of dissonant cognitions.

Cognitive dissonance has been found to induce properties akin to physiological excitation (Gerard, 1967; Zanna & Cooper, 1974). In addition, it can influence biological drives such as hunger, thirst, and pain (Zimbardo et al., 1969). For example, Brehm and Crocker (1962) had subjects go without lunch or breakfast prior to the experimental session with the understanding that they would eat there. However, when they arrived they were asked to commit themselves to additional hours of fasting. In the high dissonance group, nothing was offered for the additional fasting while in the low dissonance group the subjects were offered five dollars. At the same time the subjects were asked how many sandwiches, cookies, and pints of milk they would have later on. High dissonance subjects desired significantly less food than the low dissonance group.

Baumeister (1982) argues that cognitive dissonance is arousing not so much because of inconsistencies in one's cognitions but because telling lies about one's feelings or attitudes is arousing, particularly when done by choice for an inadequate reward. In line with this view is the finding by Higgins et al. (1979) that the motivating factor in dissonance reduction is unpleasantness of affect rather than arousal per se. In this connection, it is interesting to note that dissonance reduction behavior has been shown to be greater for subjects possessing high self-esteem and presumably more concerned about the possibility of negative perceptions of their behavior (cf. Glass, 1964; Jorgenson & Papciak, 1981).

The explanation of cognitive dissonance in terms of the pressures induced by social motivations is supported by a pattern of findings concerning the conditions under which cognitive dissonance and dissonance reduction occurs (cf. Goethals et al., 1979). In particular, it has been shown repeatedly that such factors as choice and responsibility are crucial to obtaining dissonance-like effects. Brock and Buss (1962) gave different groups of male subjects a choice or no choice in administering shock to a confederate. Those subjects given a choice to participate changed their attitudes so as to evaluate the shock as less painful after administering it than before. However, the no-choice group perceived the shock as being more painful than before. Similarly, Greenbaum et al. (1965) had subjects either choose or be assigned to complete a task for which they received negative performance feedback. Only the subjects in the choice condition showed an increase in liking for the performed task (Cooper, 1971).

It is of interest to note that cognitive dissonance behavior goes counter to reinforcement theory in that the smaller the reward is, the greater the attraction of the outcome to the subject. In fact, there are many findings which show just the opposite effect, namely, the greater the reward the greater the liking and acceptance of the attitude discrepant actions (e.g., Mischel et al., 1969). Gerard et al. (1974) argued that insufficient justification for an action is what leads to dissonance reduction behaviors, while oversufficient justification produces incentive or secondary reinforcement effects.

Interactions Between Rules and Instrumental Learning

Instrumental learning is even more apparent in human behavior than is classical conditioning; thus, no mention need be made of the particular tasks and responses that humans can learn. More interesting in the present context is whether or not human instrumental learning is based on the same kind of processes underlying infrahuman instrumental learning.

Operant performance has been a favorite area to investigate human instrumental behavior and possesses the favorable characteristic of a large body of systematic data from animals that can be compared with human performance. If both groups are learning instrumental behavior based on similar information processing factors, then the details of their learning performance should correspond with each other to a large extent, particularly since there is a good deal of correspondence between animal species.

This predicted correspondence has not in fact been exhibited in almost all of the human operant studies for which such comparisons can be made. For example, as Lowe (1979) notes, humans show two kinds of responding on FI schedules, neither of which is characteristic of animal responding on these schedules. In animals, a typical FI scallop of pausing and responding in the fixed interval is generally seen. Humans, however, can show a steady high response rate throughout the interval more reminiscent of VR responding in animals (e.g., DeCasper & Zeiler, 1977; Lippman & Meyer, 1967) or a low rate pattern with just one or two responses at the end of the interval (Leander et al., 1968; Weiner, 1969). In particular, this last response pattern would seem to reflect verbal-symbolic activity since it is exactly suited to the requirements of the schedule as rationally determined. In addition, the duration of the FI seems to have little effect on human response patterning. Human FR performance also diverges from that found in animals, particularly in the lack of the FR pause after reinforcement (Weiner, 1972; Zeiler & Kelley, 1969).

On the other hand, reinforcement contingencies are occasionally found to be ineffective until the relevant contingencies are verbally described. Studies of token economies (often used with mental patients), which specify the relationship between responding and reinforcement, have led to appropriate behavior that was not exhibited when the relationship was not made explicit (Ayllon & Azrin, 1964; Kazdin, 1973). Thus, humans can be insensitive to contingencies that are well within their comprehension when described; this leads to the idea that verbal-symbolic activity can actively interfere with the normal operation of match-mismatch processes. In this case, it might be due to attentional factors.

Another difference between human and animal instrumental performance is that information seeking seems to provide reinforcement intrinsically since it is engaged in even when it has no use in obtaining reinforcement. For example, Lanzetta and Driscoll (1968) showed that individuals will seek (useless) information about an uncertain outcome that is unavailable. Lanzetta (1963) showed that individuals seek to lower subjective uncertainty to some criterion level before stopping the acquisition of information or making a choice between alternatives.

An experiment by Brigham (1979) examined the degree of motivation to exercise control or choice behavior. Children were given the opportunity to press a key for token reinforcers under several schedules of reinforcement, which were either self-selected or experimenter-selected (but the same in each condition) (cf. Brigham & Stoerzinger, 1976). In a multiple schedule where experimenter-selected and self-selected consequences alternated, the children earned equal numbers of tokens in both conditions. This demonstrates that the consequences themselves were essentially equivalent in the two conditions. However, when a concurrent schedule was used which permitted a simultaneous preference choice between the two, the children worked almost exclusively for self-selected reinforcers. Most importantly for the present discussion, this preference was maintained even when the schedule requirements were higher in the self-selected chain than in the experimenter-selected chain. Thus, the reinforcing outcome after engaging in choice behavior is sufficiently strong to compete with other types of reinforcing outcomes, even when this results in a direct cost for those other outcomes.

Humans show a pronounced reliance on the use of cognitive schemes, attitudes and attributions to interpret events and their interrelationships (Carlson, 1980; Cohen & Ebbesen, 1979). If attributions are based on cognitive schemas that help interpret the events occurring in a person's environment, then we should see a motivation to use such cognitive schemas whenever possible in order to simplify and make coherent these various events. If the motivation is strong enough for cognitive control or reduction of uncertainty, we should see behaviors or cognitions used even if they result in a distortion or misinterpretation of the events. Of course, we would expert such distortion to incline in the direction of attitudinal consistency since distortion in the other direction would only increase uncertainty. Chapman and Chapman (1967) have shown that subjects' prior beliefs about causal relationships between events can affect the intake and processing of information even when there is a reward for accurate observations. Subjects were given drawings purportedly by people who were under clinical observation. It was found that preconceived ideas about the relationship between features of drawings (e.g., large eyes on people) and clinical syndromes (e.g., paranoia) were highly resistant to disconfirmatory evidence (cf. Staff & Katkin, 1969).

Jenkins and Ward (1965) using a button press response as a means to obtain particular rewarding outcomes showed that regardless of the instructions given, subjects' judgments of the degree of contingency between response and outcomes were unrelated to the actual degree of contingency. Subjects relied instead on the number of successes or reinforced responses to judge the degree of contingency. Producing a desired event was seen as an indication that the subject was controlling outcomes even when this occurred rarely (cf. Fischoff, 1976).

SUMMARY

In summary, this sample of studies makes it clear that human performance in learning paradigms cannot be predicted solely on the basis of the match-mismatch processes governing animal behavior. Although the old view that a direct extension from animal learning principles to the prediction of human behavior is almost certainly incorrect, it would be unwise to veer too much in the opposite direction. Much human learning is based on match-mismatch principles in part. As we saw, special populations lacking in verbal-symbolic mediation of behavior should perform basically according to match-mismatch principles. Even in the normal population, it would be predicted that whatever behavior is not under the control or mediation of rule-based contingencies would also display characteristics congruent with match-mismatch processes.

# Chapter 11
# Neurological Substrates of the Reinforcer and Habituative Systems

Although a substantial amount of behavioral evidence supports the existence of two different stimulus processing systems possessing the hypothesized characteristics of the reinforcer and habituative systems, additional evidence is required from neurological studies before we can have confidence in these constructs. There are many possible constructs that can be developed to explain the same behavioral phenomena; however, only one has biological existence. Therefore, there has to be a conjunction of evidence from both behavioral and neurological research, all pointing to the same hypothesized construct, to be sure that it is not only plausible but also actually in operation in the brain.

Ideally, an identification of the precise neural pathways and structures corresponding to each of the proposed stimulus processing systems would be the goal of such an analysis. The present state of knowledge concerning neural interconnections in the mammalian brain does not make this goal feasible, however. A more limited but correspondingly more realistic goal is to identify at least one major component of each system and then show that different neurological interventions produce the hypothesized changes in behavior. The latter approach is taken in the present chapter.

The focus of the discussion centers on the limbic system, an interrelated group of neural structures comprising the "old" cortex (Papez, 1937); in particular, around the three most studied limbic structures: the amygdala, the septum, and the hippocampus. The limbic system provides a convenient level of analysis for the functioning of the reinforcer and habituative systems (cf. Figures 11-1, 11-2). First of all, it is present in all mammals; although

203

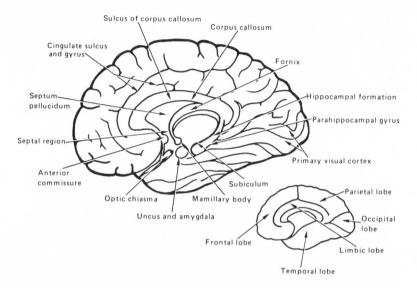

Fig. 11-1 . Location of the Limbic System in the Human Brain . From Noback, The Human Nervous System. Copyright 1981 by McGraw-Hill. Reprinted by permission.

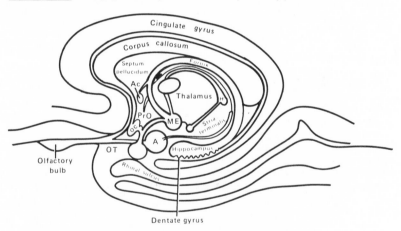

Fig. 11-2 . Configuration of Structures Within the Limbic System.
A, amygdala; Ac, anterior commissure; H, habenula; MB, mamillary bodies; Oc, optic chiasma; Ot, olfactory tract; Pro, preoptic area of hypothalamus. From Noback,1981. Copyright 1981 by McGraw-Hill. Reprinted by permission.

204

naturally there are phylogenetic differences between species, there exists a basic correspondence of structures. Second, the limbic system constitutes an important high-level region for motivational expression, unlike the neocortex. Third, there has been a great deal of research directed at determining the function of these structures.

The chapter is organized in the following manner. First, there is a sequential discussion of three key limbic system structures: the amygdala, the hippocampus, and the septum. The connection between these structures and the normal operation of the reinforcer and habituative systems is given at the start of their respective sections. This is followed in each case by an analysis of the data base which led to the formulation of those principles. Following this, a basis for understanding some of the major interconnections of these three structures is offered.

THE AMYGDALA AND THE REINFORCER SYSTEM

Principles of Operation

Match-mismatch theory assumes that the amygdala is a component of the reinforcer system with the following properties:

1.  It processes all unconditioned reinforcers, and the primary cues which occur in temporal proximity to the reinforcers, by augmenting neural and endocrine response to their occurrence. This process results in the formation of an appropriate mood state. The action of the reinforcer triggers the system to "fix" all of the salient details of the situation surrounding its occurrence by extending the duration of this information in working memory (cf. the reinforcer system: Chapter 6).

2.  Since the primary cues must be residing in working memory when the reinforcer is processed, relatively short temporal limits between the occurrence of a primary cue and the reinforcer foster cue processing through this system (cf. Chapter 8).

3.  The cues in correlated temporal proximity to the unconditioned reinforcer take on the psychological properties of the reinforcer. This is due to the evocation of appropriate species-specific behaviors by the reinforcer while the primary cues are being processed. The primary cues become redintegrative cues for the cue-reinforcer representation in memory. This becomes the basis for their conditioned reinforcing properties and it

205

is through this means that primary cues gain control over species-specific responding (cf. Chapter 9).

4. It influences certain homeostatic functions, but only in modulatory fashion, through its processing of motivationally significant stimuli.

5. Its activation inhibits the normal operation of the habituative system, including stimulus processing and habituative functions (cf. the interaction between the reinforcer and habituative systems: Chapter 6).

Amygdalar Involvement in Stimulus Processing

Logically speaking, the effects that a particular neural structure has on behavior can be due to its influence on the processing of stimuli that control these behaviors or on the actual responses themselves. Theories of limbic system function have often wavered between assigning to limbic structures an involvement in stimulus processing or response functions (e.g., Douglas & Pribram, 1966; McCleary, 1966; Vanderwolf et al., 1975). Since the present theory contends that the amygdala is part of a stimulus analyzing system rather than being directly involved in the elaboration of responses, it would be useful to present some of the data which support this point.

First of all, there are neurons in the amygdala which are variously sensitive to simple and complex sensory stimuli in different modalities (O'Keefe & Bouma, 1969; Jacobs & McGinty, 1972). Sanghera et al. (1979) have shown that there are neurons in the dorsolateral amygdala which have sustained responses to visual objects which remain in the effective visual field. These amygdala neurons are not particularly sensitive to the simple physical properties of the stimulus. This information is already processed in the primary sensory areas of the brain, in this case, visual cortex. Instead, the amygdala neurons seem to display stimulus processing characteristics which are intermediate between initial sensory analysis and final assignment of motivational significance seen in hypothalamic neurons sensitive to visual input (Rolls et al., 1976). The response latencies of these neurons do in fact fall between latencies of neurons in the inferotemporal cortex, which have output to the amygdala, and neurons in the lateral hypothalamus, which have input from the amygdala. This relationship raises the possibility that these structures are part of a connected system involved in stimulus analysis.

Electrical stimulation of certain areas of the amygdala commonly elicits orienting responses (OR) from unanesthetized animals (Ursin & Kaada, 1960; Ursin et al., 1967). It is important to

note that the elicitation of the OR does not seem to be of a direct
motoric nature since the animals can respond appropriately to
stimuli presented during stimulation. Additionally, the elicited
OR is generally a fully integrated response which is similar in form
to those occurring in normal animals; i.e., there is an initial
arrest or pause in ongoing activities, followed by arousal, and then
general searching or exploratory behaviors commence as if to locate
an object.

More generally, any theory positing a direct amygdalar involvement in response elaboration or sequencing has to cope with two
findings in the experimental literature, namely, the wide variety
of integrated behaviors known to be influenced by damage or stimulation to the amygdala and the lack of any obvious difficulties in
performing a particular response when it does occur (cf. Goddard,
1964; Kaada, 1972; Kling, 1972). As we shall see, it is the sheer
variety of behaviors that are affected by amygdalar damage or stimulation that make it more parsimonious to hypothesize a stimulus
processing function instead of a response function for the amygdala,
especially since the behavioral responses reveal no structural or
topographic similarities.

Amygdalar Involvement in Mood State Formation

We noted in previous chapters that the performance of species-
specific behaviors seemed dependent on the formation or evocation of
an appropriate mood state in the organism. A mood state was defined
as the product of the effects of a neurochemical on specific brain
areas with the neural processing of particular unconditioned stimuli. The reinforcer system was hypothesized to be the mechanism
through which unconditioned reinforcers were processed, leading to
the evocation of mood states and species-specific behaviors. If
the amygdala is an important component of the reinforcer system,
then its normal functioning should be an essential substrate of the
expression of appropriate species-specific behaviors. It should be
emphasized that since the reinforcer system (and the amygdala)
processes the general class of stimuli which meet its processing
characteristics, we should note a correspondingly general effect on
species-specific responding from the functioning of these neural
structures.

The amygdala's connection with species-specific or emotional
behaviors has been widely noted by researchers and theorists alike
(e.g., Hughes & Andy, 1979; Kaada, 1972; Kling, 1972) and, in fact,
feeding, flight, defense, and sexual behaviors have all been elicited by stimulation of various sites in the amygdala. Since these
motivated behaviors can still be induced in an organism with all
tissue above the hypothalamus removed (Hess, 1957), a high-level
involvement seems a logical description of the amygdala's role in

207

Amygdala and the Reinforcer System

these behaviors.  In this connection, Gloor (1972) has speculated that the amygdala and other temporal lobe structures provide the link between the memorial representation of information in the neocortex and fundamental motivational mechanisms residing in the hypothalamus.  Thus, there is widespread general agreement that the involvement of the amygdala in species-specific behaviors is important and a central part of its function.  Let's examine specific evidence to see the form in which this involvement manifests itself.

Lesions to the amygdala can profoundly disrupt feeding, sexual, and social behaviors, although these disruptions do not seem to be related to simple changes in drive level, especially since homeostatic functions can be largely unimpaired in some instances (Grossman, 1964).  For example, Schwartzbaum (1961), in studying amygdaloid hyperphagia, found that amygdalectomized monkeys were less selective about what they ate, but at the same time were less responsive to prolonged food deprivations (cf. Czech, 1973; Leung & Rogers, 1973).  In this connection, it has long been noted that amygdalectomized animals are more likely to put non-food items in their mouth as well as food, as if they had increased difficulty in distinguishing between them (cf. Kling, 1972).

The same kind of defect can be seen with sexual behavior. Aronson and Cooper (1979) tested the sexual response of male amygdalectomized cats in two different settings.  The first involved the standard test of placing the male with an estrus female, while the second involved the sequential presentation of various sexually inappropriate objects arranged in a presumed gradient of attractiveness (i.e., stuffed toy, moving toy, tranquilized rabbit, male, and estrus female).  In the standard test, the amygdalectomized cats, compared with controls, displayed an increased tendency to mount inappropriate objects, but no increases in sexual drive or level of performance were found.  These cats still retained preferences when given a simultaneous choice between objects. This so-called amygdaloid hypersexuality has been noted in other species including rats, monkeys, and humans, although there are species-specific differences (Kling, 1972; Narabayashi, 1972; Schreiner & Kling, 1953).

Amygdaloid lesions in rats and mice have been shown to cause less fear to novel situations or objects as well as diminished flight tendencies (Slotnick, 1973; Ursin & Divac, 1975), perhaps leading to the observed increase in open field activity.  This apparent reduction of fear arousal can be used to explain the finding that amygdalar lesions in the rat can decrease the severity of ulcers caused by physical restraint (Henke, 1980).

Many social behaviors are profoundly affected by damage to the amygdala.  Tarr (1977) found that normal patterns of social behavior exhibited by the iguanid lizard (sceloparus occidentalis) were abolished by bilateral amygdaloid lesions.  Dominance and submissive behavior no longer occurred in appropriate fashion. Shipley and Kolb (1977) noted changes in territorial aggression in Syrian golden male hamsters following amygdalectomy. Amygdalectomized monkeys often display an increase in the amount of fear (or confusion) during social interactions which can affect dominance relationships and lead to withdrawal from social contact (Kling et al., 1970; Thompson et al., 1977). A simple reduction in aggressive behavior does not seem likely as an explanation since even appropriate submissive gestures are lacking (cf. Bunnell et al. 1970).

Many of these general kinds of deficits are noted in humans with damage to the amygdala. In this connection, it is useful to note that the arrangement of nuclei in the amygdala displays significant consistency across most mammalian species including humans (cf. Crosby & Humphrey, 1941; Girgis, 1972). Stimulation of the amygdala can often evoke fear (Penfield & Perot, 1963) and, sometimes, rage (Mark et al., 1972). Pleasant emotions have also been evoked on occasion using chronic implanted electrodes or from epileptic discharge in the area (Daly, 1958; Stevens et al., 1969). Lesions of the amygdala seem to decrease general emotional expression (Narabayashi, 1972; Scoville et al., 1953). Hughes and Andy (1979) studied responses to odors in nine patients receiving amygdalotomy for control of seizures. Lesions to the amygdala eliminated EEG fast background activity to odorants and caused a temporary increase in identification errors of odors. Clinical seizures which involved the amygdala were also studied, with the finding that they were associated with both increased errors in odor identification and an increased tendency to judge odors as intense or unpleasant. Of course, since the number of species--specific behaviors is much reduced in humans, the behavioral changes seen after amygdalar stimulation or damage will be in the learned behaviors which have become associated with the particular mood states affected.

Amygdalar Processing of Unconditioned Stimuli

With regard to the amygdalar principles of operation, there are a number of points in particular which should be involved in the organism's ability to appropriately express species-specific behaviors. Since we are dealing with behaviors that are common to members of the species and possess a substantial genetic component, the amygdala's processing of unconditioned stimuli is the focus of attention. According to the theory, the amygdala is assumed to augment the neural and endocrine response of the organism to unconditioned stimuli and to modulate related homeostatic functions. The studies cited above provide suggestive evidence that the amygdala is importantly involved in processing unconditioned stimuli; however, more specific data are available.

Amygdala and the Reinforcer System

Holmes and Egan (1973) and Pagano and Goult (1964) have shown
that particular kinds of electrical activity in the amygdala,
specifically, 30-40 Hz spindling, seem to be correlated with a
variety of species-specific behaviors and reinforcers (e.g., the
presence and odor of food and sexual activity in the female cat).
Norton (1970) reported increases in the amplitude of amygdala
electrical activity which occurred after reinforced barpresses but
not after non-reinforced barpresses (cf. Kesner & Andrus, 1982).
Rolls (1972) demonstrated that individual amygdala neurons could be
directly activated by stimulation of lateral hypothalamic sites
which were associated with rewarding brain stimulation, eating, and
drinking.  Importantly, the firing pattern of these amygdala neurons
did not appear to be significantly correlated with general arousal.
As Margules and Olds (1962) have shown, there is often a correspondence between self-reward and food systems in the hypothalamus.

Lesion studies involving the amygdala present the same picture.
Barrett (1969) and Downer (1961) have studied the effect of unilateral amygdalectomy in the split brain monkey.  In this preparation, since the optic chiasm is cut visual input can only go to the
ipsilateral hemisphere.  If the monkey looks only through the eye
on the side of the amygdalar lesion, then visual input is processed
without benefit of the amygdala.  Visual input processed through
the other eye, however, can be processed by the intact amygdala on
that side.  In both studies, the behavior of the monkeys with respect to positive or negative reinforcing stimuli was altered
dramatically when visual input was restricted to the lesioned
hemisphere.  For example, the monkey studied by Downer had preoperatively shown a high degree of aggressive behavior towards humans in
his presence.  When visual input was restricted to the lesioned
hemisphere, these aggressive behaviors disappeared and the monkey
acted quite tame.  However, the opening of the other eye led to a
return of the aggression towards humans.  These studies clearly
show that a general emotional change in the organism cannot explain
the deficit to emotion-producing stimuli in animals or humans with
amygdalar damage.

Other studies provide evidence that the changed reactions to
these reinforcing stimuli are not associated with simple attentional
deficits.  Rolls and Rolls (1973) demonstrated altered food preferences in rats with damage to the basolateral region of the amygdala.
The amygdalar rats ate much more of novel, palatable food than did
control rats; however, the differences in preferences were not
connected with food-sampling differences between groups.  The rats
with amygdalar damage sampled from all the food as did the controls,
but the controls stayed with the more familiar foods until a number
of sessions had been run.  It was as if the normal neophobia to
different foods was eliminated by damage to the amygdala.  In addition, changes in fear level or arousal had no effect on either

group's food preferences. Belluzi (1972) showed that injections of carbachol or eserine, which potentiate cholinergic transmission, into the amygdala caused deficits in one way avoidance but left performance of an appetitive visual discrimination unimpaired. In fact, animals and humans with amygdalar damage are quite capable of learning many different kinds of tasks, some of which can be quite difficult (cf. Andersen, 1978; Douglas & Pribram, 1966). Thus, an explanation involving a generalized attentional deficit would have to explain why it would not be exhibited in these latter situations as well. Finally, it should be noted that amygdalar damage does not seem to affect the organism's ability to distinguish painful from pleasurable reinforcing stimuli; for example, rats with amygdalar lesions will flinch when receiving electric shock even though they do not avoid it the way control rats do (Kellicut & Schwartzbaum, 1963).

The implications of this distinction between motivating and sensory properties of the reinforcer are worth examining. As we saw, simultaneous preferences among reinforcers seem to be retained after amygdalar lesions. Aggleton and Passingham (1982) showed that monkeys retained post-operative preferences between three highly palatable foods, although the authors note that there did seem to be a diminution in the apparent aversiveness of unpalatable substances. In addition, the monkeys' performance on a progressive ratio schedule, in which the size of the response ratio becomes larger and larger, was sensitive to size and type of reward (cf. Schwartzbaum, 1961).

First of all, since the amygdala is a higher level structure of the reinforcer system, we would not expect it to be critical to the processing and interpretation of the elemental sensory properties of reinforcers. These attributes presumably would be processed at more initial stages of sensory analysis. Second, it should be remembered that the reinforcer system (including the amygdala) is the essential substrate for the performance of species-specific responses but does not have the same role with respect to voluntary responses. It is probably no accident that the general behavior of organisms with amygdalar damage is more deranged to aversive and social reinforcing stimuli than to appetitive stimuli because it is precisely in the former reinforcer classes that we see the most elaborate species-specific responses. In contrast, food-seeking behavior typically contains more voluntary components, thus permitting an increased control over behavior by secondary cues. Undoubtedly, this is due to the fact that the organism has to seek out food in the environment, whereas it can react to aversive and social reinforcers as they occur.

Taken together, these studies provide evidence that the amygdala is importantly involved in the processing of reinforcers. Although organisms without a functioning amygdala seem to retain perceptions of the sensory qualities of reinforcers, somehow they are not able to remember how they should feel about them in an emotional sense. It should be noted that this latter interpretation of the deficit from amygdalar damage has received as much considera- tion from researchers as any that have been advanced (cf. Holmes & Egan, 1973). One general point which lends credence to this posi- tion is that the amygdala tends to receive its strongest sensory projections from the modality most involved in the identification of unconditioned stimuli for a particular species. Animals such as the rat, which depend heavily on olfactory stimuli for the expres- sion of a wide variety of behaviors, have strong olfactory projec- tions to the amygdala. On the other hand, species which depend most heavily on vision, such as the primates, including humans, have strong visual projections to the amygdala.

Amygdalar Mechanisms in the
Response to Unconditioned Stimuli

Even if we assume that the amygdala does play a role in con- necting external reinforcing stimuli with appropriate emotional or species-specific behavior, there still remains the discovery of the actual process by which a functioning amygdala achieves this result. The theory states that the reinforcer system, including the amyg- dala, processes reinforcers by augmenting the neural and endocrine response to them. This augmentation provides the means by which appropriate species-specific (emotional) behaviors will occur to unconditioned stimuli. Of course, the augmentation can be in an excitatory or inhibitory direction, depending on the nature of the reinforcer. Since we are dealing with unconditioned stimuli, the neural and endocrine response presumably produces behavioral or homeostatic responses which, from the start, are adaptive to the stimulus.

There are two issues, then, that we need to explore: first, to what extent does the amygdala affect neural and endocrine re- sponses, and second, how does this effect produce appropriate behavior? Since the total amount of material relevant to these points is voluminous, to say the least, a necessarily selective but hopefully representative sample will be examined.

With regard to the first issue, the relationship of the amygdala and hypothalamus is probably the best place to start. The amygdala has two strong projections to the hypothalamus, namely, the stria terminalis and the ventral amygdalofugal pathway (VAF). Dreifuss et al. (1968) demonstrated strong evoked responses could be obtained in the ventromedial hypothalamus after stimulation of cortical and central amygdaloid nuclei (cf. Egger, 1967; Murphy et al., 1968). Lesions of the ventromedial hypothalamus counteract the effects of amygdaloid stimulation (White & Fisher, 1969).

The connection between the amygdala and the ventromedial hypothalamus has important implications since this provides strong
evidence that the amygdala is involved in the modulation of activity
in the tuberal hypothalamus and thus the pituitary axis. Some
neurons in the tuberal hypothalamus have both typical neuronal functions and also secretory functions in which they produce, store,
and release hormones (cf. Martini et al., 1970).

The amygdala has been shown to have a specific effect on a
number of different hormones controlled by this region, for example,
growth hormone and the sex hormones. With regard to growth hormone,
Ehle et al. (1977) demonstrated that stimulation of the amygdala
in monkeys that provoked after-discharge produced large increases
in plasma growth hormone. Stimulation that was subthreshold for
such after-discharge produced smaller increases. Additionally,
stimulation of the hippocampus did not produce these increases even
when the electrical activity spread to the amygdala, which indicates
that direct stimulation of amygdalar neurons was critical. As Meyer
and Knobil (1967) have shown, noxious environmental stimuli can
affect the levels of growth hormone released. Since amygdala damage affects the response to such noxious stimuli, it is reasonable
to assume that the amygdala is involved in the mediation of growth
hormone level by environmental unconditioned stimuli.

The sex hormones have been intensively studied, both with respect to the influence of the amygdala on their release and the
effect of other stimulus factors (cf. Pfaff et al., 1973; Zolovick,
1972). These hormones are useful in the present context because
mating behavior in rats and other rodents is directly dependent
upon them. Furthermore, the response components of mating seem to
be highly stereotyped and under the external influence of particular
stimuli. For example, the lordosis response of the female rat is
dependent on estrogen and progesterone levels and on specific
external stimulation such as the male's forepaws on her flanks.
Thus, changing the levels of the female sex hormones could reduce
the incidence of lordosis even with the appropriate stimuli present.

The amygdala has been shown to have a significant impact on
these sex hormones in both the male and female. First of all, the
amygdala along with the hypothalamus-pituitary axis seems to be a
principal site for uptake of the female sex hormone estradiol
(McEwen & Pfaff, 1970; Stumpf & Sar, 1971). These and other studies
indicate that some neurons in these regions have receptor sites
which bind molecules of the hormone. Second, these hormones have
been shown to alter the excitability of amygdala neurons, which
display an inverse relationship with hippocampal neurons in this
respect (Terasawa & Timiras, 1968). Third, lesions of the amygdala
institute distinct changes in the levels of secretion of these
hormones (Eleftheriou et al., 1967). Amygdalectomized female rats
that had been ovariectomized did not show facilitated lordosis

213

behavior after being treated with estradiol benzoate, in contrast to olfactory or septally lesioned female rats. Interestingly, this facilitation seen after septal lesions could be attenuated by amygdaloid lesions, indicating that the amygdala might be mediating the increased sensitivity to estrogen found in the septal rats (McGinnis et al., 1978).

Evidence that the amygdala is mediating the effect of at least some kinds of external stimulation on sex hormone levels is provided by Pasley et al. (1978). Grouped or singly caged male and female mice were given lesions of the amygdala and compared to controls on several measures of reproductive functions. The intact female mice that had lived in groups under crowded conditions displayed reduced ovary weights relative not only with their singly caged counterparts but also with the amygdalectomized females that had lived in the group cages. In fact, there was no difference in ovary weights between the amygdalectomized females that had lived singly or in groups under crowded conditions. The same pattern was seen in the seminal vesicle weights of the males. Intact and sham operates living in groups had reduced vesicle weights compared to amygdalectomized males living in similar conditions. Levels of plasma luteinizing hormone also corresponded to the morphological data. These data strongly suggest that amygdalectomized mice show a diminished response to stressful stimuli relative to normal mice and that this in turn can affect sex hormone levels.

There is strong evidence to suggest that the amygdala has an important role in the processing of stimuli that increase stress in the organism through its influence over the pituitary-adrenal system. In particular, a number of researchers have examined amygdalar modulation of adrenocorticotropin hormone (ACTH) secretion and plasma corticosterone levels. It has been clearly shown that adrenocortical secretion increases in response to stimuli which are associated with fear and anxiety such as shock or novel stimuli (cf. Hennesy et al., 1977a; Redgate, 1970; Smith, 1973), although such secretion is not graded according to stimulus intensity (Bassett et al., 1973; Hennesy et al., 1977b).

Although the degree of corticoid response is not sensitive to a number of stimulus parameters such as intensity, it nevertheless is the case that the history of the organism, in a general sense as well as with a particular stimulus, plays an important role in such responses (cf. Hennesy & Levine, 1979). For example, handling of rats in the first 3 weeks after birth can permanently attenuate the adrenocortical response to novel stimuli compared to non-handled rats (Denenberg & Haltmeyer, 1967), presumably through some sort of habituative process. On the other hand, monkeys who were judged highly aggressive had higher corticoid responses to training on an operant avoidance task than less aggressive monkeys (Levine et al., 1970). Gibbons and McHugh (1962) found that severely depressed humans tend to have higher levels of plasma corticoids than mildly depressed humans. Dallman and Jones (1973) have demonstrated an apparent increase in responsivity of ACTH-releasing mechanisms to repeated exposure to stressful stimuli.

Corticoid response to unconditioned stimuli presentation or omission has been observed in learning paradigms. The omission of reward in an operant task increases pituitary-adrenal activity (Coover et al., 1971) as does changing from FI to VI schedules (Davis et al., 1976). Interestingly, changing from VI to FI schedules does not cause such increases, perhaps because of the increased predictability of reinforcer occurrence. Adrenocortical response in avoidance situations can be increased by modifying the avoidance contingency so that on some trials shock no longer can be consistently avoided (Hanson et al., 1976). However, in situations where active avoidance behavior has stabilized and is successful, attenuation is found in the pituitary-adrenal response. Koranyi et al. (1967) demonstrated that mice receiving ACTH prior to the delivery of shock in the passive avoidance paradigm showed greater suppression of approach behaviors than did controls. Guth et al. (1971) injected ACTH 10 minutes prior to the delivery of punishment and obtained significantly greater response suppression than with controls.

Taken together, these results support the idea that adrenal corticoid response is increased when an organism is exposed to a more stressful situation and that such activity can be related to learning about stressful events. In turn, it can be shown that the amygdala plays a profound role in the kinds of pituitary-adrenal activity discussed.

Allen and Allen (1974) studied the effect of unilateral and bilateral lesions of the amygdala on the release of ACTH to stress following leg break, ether, or the application of a tourniquet. Bilateral lesions blocked increases in ACTH in response to the leg break but not to the other two stressors, indicating that the amygdala is important to the ACTH response to neurogenic, but not systemic, stress. In other words, the amygdala is more likely involved in the response to direct, external stress than to changes in the internal milieu. These results were not found after unilateral lesions. Allen and Allen (1975) showed that the VAF pathway between the amygdala and hypothalamus was critically involved in the ACTH response to stress.

Electrical stimulation of the amygdala has been shown to increase adrenocorticotropic activity in a number of species, including humans (Rubin et al., 1966). Bouille and Bayle (1975) have shown that stimulation of the avian amygdalar homologue, or archistriatum, in pigeons has a similar effect. The injection of ACTH into amygdalectomized rats has been found to reverse the deficits in passive avoidance caused by amygdaloid lesions (Bush et al., 1973).

Burt and Smotherman (1980) showed that ACTH injection could reverse a deficit in conditioned taste aversion in rats with bilateral amygdalar lesions. In this connection, it should be noted that the role of ACTH in acquisition and recovery of conditioned taste aversion has been independently established (Smotherman et al., 1976).

Werka et al. (1978) demonstrated that amygdalar lesions in rats led to deficits in one-way avoidance, with the greatest deficit appearing in rats with lesions in the central area. Lesions of the central amygdala lower corticosterone levels and reduce freezing (Coover et al., 1973). Thus, the deficit in one-way avoidance is probably due to reduced fear to shock. As Werka et al. note, the findings of improved avoidance by Grossman (1972) could very well be due to the difficult task used; reduced fear in this case would facilitate learning relative to controls.

The evidence cited above clearly indicates the involvement of the amygdala in the neural and endocrine responses to stressful or arousing stimuli. How might damage to the amygdala produce the disruption of species-specific behavior that has been noted in numerous studies?

It is hypothesized that the augmentation of response to reinforcers and stressful stimuli enables the formation of a mood state in the organism which increases the probability of response of particular behaviors. As we have seen, the mood state is a relatively sustained response which provides the support for an integrated series of species-specific behaviors to take place over time. For example, stimulation of certain hypothalamic areas can produce a complete defense response, including all autonomic and postural elements. However, the defense response in the animal terminates the moment the stimulation is stopped. Amygdalar stimulation can also produce a defense reaction but this develops slowly during stimulation and outlasts the period of stimulation by several minutes (Hilton & Zbrozyna, 1963).

It is becoming increasingly clear that many motivated behaviors are under the control of external stimuli as much as they are under the control of internal homeostatic forces, if not more (cf. Fitzsimmons, 1972; Mogenson & Phillips, 1976). To take just one example, it has been shown that the urine odor of a strange or novel male mouse can block prolactin secretion and thus terminate an early pregnancy in a female mouse (Bronson, 1968). Many sexual behaviors are under the control of various pheromones in rodents.

This line of argument indicates that the amygdala is responsible for the processing of external unconditioned stimuli by augmentation of the neural and endocrine response to them. This augmentation leads to the creation of a mood state which makes certain species-specific behaviors more likely to occur. The destruction of the amygdala interrupts this process by inhibiting the formation of an appropriate mood state and this creates a situation where these behaviors are not made prepotent. This accounts for the common observation of inappropriate species-specific responding on the part of organism with amygdalar damage.

## Amygdalar Processing of Primary Cues

The principles of operation for the amygdala indicate that it processes not only unconditioned stimuli, but also primary cues in close temporal proximity to the occurrence of the reinforcer. The processing of the reinforcer acts to preserve the information that exists in STM at the time of its occurrence. Two related points flow out of the processing of stimuli that are in temporal proximity to the reinforcer, namely, the conditioned reinforcing properties of these stimuli and their ability to control species-specific behaviors.

We have already examined the nature of conditioned reinforcement in some detail in previous chapters. As we noted, the primary cues become redintegrative cues for the cue-reinforcer representation in memory. This representation contains a record of the attributes of the stimuli that were in working memory at the time of reinforcer occurrence as well as the response state of the organism itself. One proviso is that it is the stimuli correlated and not just contiguous with the occurrence of the reinforcer that are contained in the representation, constructed over a series of trials.

In the previous sections, it was shown that the amygdala played an important role in the processing of unconditioned stimuli and thus, in the elaboration of many species-specific behaviors. The current theory hypothesizes that the amygdala also plays an important role in the association of primary cues with the reinforcer, particularly with regard to their conditioned reinforcing properties. Since the reinforcer imparts certain properties to the primary cues which make them functionally similar to the reinforcer, it seems highly possible that the amygdala's response to the reinforcer is a substrate for this phenomenon. If this is in fact the case, damage to the amygdala should impair the process by which primary cues become conditioned reinforcers and functionally similar to the co-occurring reinforcer.

Cohen (1974, 1975) showed that lesions of the posterior-medial regions of the archistriatum in pigeons produced severe decrements in the conditioning that accrued to a visual stimulus paired with electric shock. Other limbic structures, with the possible exception of the septum, seemed to play little role in the development of conditioning to the primary cue. Kellicut and Schwartzbaum (1963) reported that formation of a CER to a tone paired with shock showed a severe deficit in rats with amygdaloid lesions, indicating that the tone had not acquired significant conditioning. Even increasing

217

the shock intensity or duration failed to have an effect. The responding of amygdaloid rats for food during the CS period could only be diminished by punishing each response. McGowan et al. (1972) demonstrated that rats with amygdalar lesions were deficient in acquiring conditioned suppression of drinking when a CS noise that had been paired with shock was presented. They were also deficient in acquiring an aversion to a flavor associated with illness. Bermuden-Ratton et al. (1983) showed a similar disruption of the association between odors and illness after injection of the amygdala with novocaine. Spevack et al. (1975) demonstrated that amygdalectomized rats that displayed deficits in CER formation had normal habituation to the stimulus used as CS. This last study would seem to indicate that the deficit in conditioning in amygdala-lesioned organisms is not due to attentional factors. Could the ineffectiveness of the CS paired with shock in suppressing food-motivated behavior be the result of an increased motivation for the food? This seems highly unlikely since there is no evidence that amygdala-lesioned animals display increased responsiveness to food or other appetitive reinforcers (Aggleton & Passingham, 1982; Schwartzbaum, 1961).

Additionally, animals with amygdalar damage seem to be less affected by cues associated with reinforcement delay or omission (Goomas et al., 1980; Henke, 1973). Somewhat more indirect evidence is provided by McDonough and Manning (1979) who studied amygdalectomized rats on an appetitive FI schedule. The presentation of noncontingent reinforcement on the FI schedule reduced the contingent responding of the amygdalar rats significantly more than controls, indicating that the conditioned reinforcers on the schedule had less control over behavior.

A similar effect has been found with amygdalectomized monkeys tested on visual discrimination tasks. Douglas and Pribram (1969) found that amygdalectomized monkeys displayed abnormally high distractibility on sequential discriminations to at least occasionally reinforced irrelevant cues. Non-reinforced irrelevant cues did not affect amygdalar-lesioned monkeys any differently than controls (Douglas et al., 1969).

This inability to keep focused on a task also shows up in humans with amygdalar damage. Andersen (1978) investigated the cognitive functioning of human patients before and after they received amygdalotomy for the treatment of epileptic seizures. Although their general intelligence remained at about the same level post-operatively, performance on certain tasks declined markedly. For example, in continuous graphic performance, where the patients had to copy out a particular repeating pattern indefinitely, there was a large difference between controls and amygdalectomized patients in the ability to correctly repeat the pattern, although deficits in pattern reproduction per se or in motor

218

performance were not evident. In verbal recognition and recall tasks, subjects tended to improve their performance when given a second test some time after an initial test of memory. That is, if they were asked to distinguish list words from distractors, they were helped in a second recognition test by seeing the targets and distractors on an initial recognition test. There is some evidence to suggest that amygdalar-damaged humans have trouble bringing memories to consciousness (cf. Kling, 1972).

These various results suggest that the amygdala does not affect all cue processing since even certain difficult tasks are acquired quite well, but instead selectively affects the processing of those stimuli which most strongly control performance on a task. Since amygdalectomized monkeys were most affected by irrelevant cues that were at least occasionally reinforced, it is logical to assume that the amygdala is involved in keeping attention focused on the cue(s) which has the closest relationship with the reinforcing stimulus. The present theory suggests that the disruption of the process by which primary cues acquire conditioned reinforcing properties is the basis for the increased distractibility of the amygdalectomized monkeys in discrimination performance. The amygdalectomized monkeys do not come under strong stimulus control from the main relevant cue and thus divide their responding among the various cues that co-occur at some point with the reinforcer.

By implication, a similar deficit contributes to the poorer performance of amygdalar-damaged humans on cognitive tasks which involved concentration on particular operations as a requisite for successful performance. It was noted previously that humans, perhaps because of verbal-symbolic mediation, have the capacity to regard any stimulus event as if it were a reinforcing stimulus. This process would seem to necessitate some mechanism to focus and maintain attention on a stimulus or task. By the same token, to retrieve less well-known items from memory would seem to involve more concentration or effort than for highly over-learned items. The loss of reinforcer system function reduces the extent to which such cognitive behavior can be effectively demonstrated for these reasons.

These studies also support the idea that the normally functioning amygdala and reinforcer system act to inhibit the processing of less salient cues and cue dimensions. Damage to the system, therefore, makes such inhibition less effective, with the result that the organism is more likely to orient to such cues while being reinforced. Since the reinforcer system is not activated when a reinforcer is not present, we would not expect such cue processing differences to occur in non-reinforcement situations.

As we saw in Chapter 6, the reinforcer system (and thus, the amygdala) are not involved in cue processing which does not meet the requirements of the reinforcer system's operating principles.

219

Thus, the processing of secondary cues and non-reinforced stimuli would not be assumed to be directly affected by amygdalar damage. It is the primary cue which is heavily dependent on the current strength of the reinforcer, unlike the secondary cue (Rizley & Rescorla, 1972).

The last principle unmentioned is that habituation is blocked when the reinforcer system and amygdala are activated. This point needs little elaboration since the positive results of every conditioning experiment support it.

## THE HIPPOCAMPUS AND THE HABITUATIVE SYSTEM

### Principles of Operation

Match-mismatch theory assumes that the hippocampus is a component of the habituative system with the following properties.

1. It processes stimuli that are not in temporal proximity to reinforcers and habituates (extinguishes) them. This can occur either when novel, nonreinforced stimuli are encountered, or in the extinction situation where reinforcement is no longer paired with the conditioned stimuli or discriminative stimuli which preceded it (cf. the habituative system: Chapter 6).

2. It reduces the associative value of cues in declining correlation with the occurrence of reinforcement to a level sustainable by the new correlation between cue and reinforcer (cf. Chapter 9).

3. It processes secondary cues that are not in close temporal proximity to the reinforcer and which thus fall outside the limits of the reinforcer system. Nonsalient and background stimuli are also possible secondary cues. The secondary cues initially are processed in the same way as the nonreinforced stimuli; however, they are registered as cues to reinforcement when primary cues are present to inhibit habituative processes. (Primary cues are processed through the reinforcer system whose activation inhibits habituation.) (cf. Chapter 8.)

4. It cannot impart conditioned reinforcing properties to the secondary cues since only stimuli processed through the reinforcer system can acquire such properties. The secondary cues function only as discriminative stimuli. Therefore, the stimuli processed through this system cannot gain direct control over non-arbitrary species-specific responses, but only over arbitrary

220

voluntary responses. This is in contrast to reinforcing stimuli which can directly control both types of behavior.

5. It receives information concerning the performance of conditioned or reinforced responses. This information is used to identify the controlling stimuli that signal the occurrence of a reinforcer, not as a means of modulating motoric output. This process results in the protection of those stimuli from interference or habituation as long as the reinforcer system is activated.

6. The hippocampal theta waves occurring during various activities in different species, most typically with voluntary movements, are a reflection of a general capability of cue processing through this system. It is a nonspecific state in that the theta waves indicate processing capability, not necessarily actual processing of changes in the associative strength of stimuli.

7. It has primarily an indirect role in motivational or homeostatic functions resulting from its general habituative function.

Hippocampal Involvement in Stimulus Processing

Since it is contended that the hippocampus, like the amygdala, is part of a stimulus processing system, some evidence should be provided to support that basic assumption. Vinogradova (1975) has shown that the majority of neurons in the dorsal hippocampus are sensitive to stimuli in a number of different modalities. Green and Machne (1955) showed that bursts of neuronal activity which were correlated with the hippocampal theta rhythm could be evoked for all types of sensory stimuli. Adey et al. (1960) and Vinogradova (1975) reported electrical changes on initial learning trials which gradually faded. Any of the stimulus changes used by Sokolov (1969) to cause dishabituation could make these evoked responses reappear. Stimulation of the hippocampus can create changes in the activity of neurons in other areas of the brain which process sensory information. Hippocampal stimulation has been shown to modify evoked responses to appropriate stimuli in the auditory cortex (Parmeggiani & Rapisardi, 1969), the visual cortex (Fleming & Bigler, 1974) and hypothalamic neurons sensitive to olfactory stimulation (Komisaruk & Beyer, 1972).

As with the amygdala, a number of researchers have hypothesized a direct involvement of the hippocampus in the elaboration of response output (e.g., McCleary, 1966; Vanderwolf et al., 1975). This hypothesis has more direct support in the case of the hippocampus if only because the neuronal activity of this structure seems to be correlated with a number of overt responses (cf. Berger & Thompson, 1978a and b, Vanderwolf, 1971). The problem with viewing this response-related activity as essential to the behavioral response is quite simply that damage or disruptive stimulation to the hippocampus does not seem to affect response output per se, even when the specific neuronal activity correlated with the responses is eliminated. Livesey (1975) showed that stimulation of the hippocampus did not have an apparent effect on the execution of a response in a simultaneous discrimination task. However, it did affect cue selection. Similar findings have been reported after hippocampal lesions (Spevack & Pribram, 1973; Ross et al., 1984). Salafia et al. (1977) have shown that post-trial electrical stimulation of the hippocampus immediately after CS-US pairings causes massive disruption of conditioning compared to controls. The stimulation exerts its effect through postponement of CR emergence. Once the CR begins to occur, conditioning seems to proceed normally even with continued stimulation. Thus, the hippocampus seems to be importantly involved in stimulus processing, since in its functional absence cue selection and processing seem fundamentally altered. Later on, we will consider the question of why response-related activity is found in the hippocampus at all.

Novel Stimuli and the Hippocampus

From the principles of operation it can be seen that the hippocampus is assumed to play an important role in the processing of non-reinforced stimuli. As it turns out, the nonreinforcement of a stimulus can come about in a number of ways, e.g., in the extinction situation, on nonreinforced trials on a partial reinforcement schedule or simply with stimuli which have not been associated with reinforcement to begin with, such as those encountered in exploratory activities. This last category is the focus of this section.

If the hippocampus is involved in the processing and habituation of novel, nonreinforced stimuli, this process should reflect itself in exploratory and investigatory tendencies at the behavioral level (cf. Douglas 1967, 1972; Kimble, 1968). Hippocampectomized rats habituate more slowly in an open field situation and engage in more repetitive behaviors than do normal rats (Blanchard et al., 1977). In general, hippocampal lesions result in increased levels of motor activity although the evidence would suggest that this is a secondary effect of disturbed stimulus processing. Wickelgren and Isaacson (1963) found that the introduction of a novel but relatively inconspicuous neutral stimulus, irrelevant to a reinforced running response, failed to inhibit the running of hippocampally lesioned rats. In fact, Raphaelson et al. (1965) showed that the introduction of a novel visual cue increased the running speed of hippocampal rats while slowing the running of normal rats.

On the other hand, hippocampal responding to a novel stimulus is relatively normal when no dominant response is being performed (e.g., Crowne & Riddell, 1969). In terms of the present theory, the reinforcer system is capable of inducing orienting to novel stimuli, but only when primary cues or reinforcers are not present.

Interestingly, locomotion by hippocampectomized mice is greater in the dark than during the day (Isaacson & McClearn, 1978). Iuvone and van Hartesveldt (1977) have demonstrated that hippocampal lesions in rats result in a disruption of their normal diurnal fluctuation in activity, primarily by increasing the amount of activity observed in the morning before the onset of light. Suess and Berlyne (1978) showed that light-related response decrements in exploratory behavior towards different novel stimuli could be found together with impaired habituation in hippocampally lesioned rats.

In terms of the present theory this effect could be due to the operation of the reinforcer system acting without the inhibitory balance provided by the habituative system and hippocampus. If the hippocampus is processing and habituating novel stimuli, then damage to it should disrupt this process. To the extent that the novel situation is slightly fear evoking, which initially it typically is (Blanchard et al., 1974), the reinforcer system is engaged. If this initial fear reaction is not habituated normally, then exploratory behavior should be inhibited as a result. However, in the dark there is a reduction of sensory stimulation which should lead to a decrease in arousal and fear, particularly in a nocturnal animal such as the rat. Thus, the hippocampectomized rat is more likely to engage in exploratory behaviors at this time.

Spontaneous alternation is a rather specific example of the general exploratory tendency to avoid exposure to the same stimulus environment (Dember, 1956). The test is usually conducted in a "T" maze where normal rats strongly tend to explore alternate arms from trial to trial, choosing a different maze arm from the previous trial approximately 85% of the time. Hippocampally lesioned rats seem to prefer the same maze arm on the next trial about 60% of the time, however (Douglas, 1975). In line with the current theory is the fact that lesions of the amygdala do not have any material effect on spontaneous alternation (Douglas, 1975).

Hippocampal Involvement in the Reduction of
Associative Strength of Stimuli

The involvement of the hippocampus in habituation and extinction has been perhaps the most common property ascribed to this structure (cf. Douglas & Pribram, 1966; Kimble, 1968). There is a wide body of empirical evidence supporting this general assumption. For example, Ellen and Wilson (1963) demonstrated extinction deficits on several operant schedules in hippocampally lesioned animals.

Similar findings of increased resistance to extinction have been found in discrimination tasks (Douglas & Pribram, 1966), in classical conditioning (Schmaltz & Theios, 1972) and in both spatial and non-spatial reversal tasks (Becker & Olton, 1980; Lash, 1964). Powell and Buchanan (1980) showed that the acquisition of eyeblink and electromyographic CRs in hippocampectomized rabbits proceeded normally, although extinction was impaired. Interestingly, the magnitude of the HR-CR was enhanced relative to controls. The Becker and Olton study provides support for the idea that the reversal deficit in hippocampectomized animals is of a general nature and not confined to spatial tasks.

Kohler (1976a) has reported that hippocampectomy of rats delayed habituation of the OR; however, it seemed to have no effect on habituation of locomotor activity, rearing, or the startle response. This would seem to contradict assertions that the hippocampus is, in fact, involved in habituative processes. The present theory makes clear, though, that it is the habituation of stimuli that is mediated by the hippocampus. Thus, a novel stimulus or former cue to reinforcement has its motivational or discriminative value decreased by the action of the hippocampus. However, the performance or non-performance of motor activity such as locomotion or rearing per se are not considered directly under the control of the hippocampus since it is part of a stimulus analyzing system.

In this context, it is significant that habituation of the OR was affected since the OR has been shown to be intimately involved in the processing and learning of environmental stimuli (cf. Sokolov, 1969). It would have to be shown that nonreinforced stimuli habituate normally after hippocampal damage, which is opposite to what has been obtained empirically. For example, rats with hippocampal lesions display deficits on latent inhibition. Normal animals have reduced conditioning to the habituated CS. Solomon and Moore (1975) have shown, however, that hippocampectomized rabbits do not habituate as readily to the novel stimulus and thus do not display the normal reduction in conditioning when it is used as a CS. Ackil et al. (1969) found a similar effect when using an avoidance task. Conversely, low-level hippocampal stimulation augmented latent inhibition (Salafia & Allan, 1982).

Data from studies of hippocampal unit responses also support the idea that the hippocampus is involved in habituative processing. (Harris et al., 1978; White et al., 1979). Habituative decrements have been observed in cells in the CA3 or regio inferior fields which correspond very closely to the characteristics of behavioral habituation (Vinogradova, 1975). Interestingly, both habituation and potentiation can be produced in hippocampal pathways depending on the frequency of the stimulation. Higher frequencies of stimulation result in neuronal response potentiation (Segal, 1973) while lower frequencies lead to habituation, at least in certain neuron populations such as the CA3 field (White et al., 1979). A similar differentation of neuronal response can be created by pairing or not pairing a stimulus with a reinforcer (e.g., Hirsh, 1973; Berger & Thompson, 1978).

The present theory assumes that the hippocampus is involved in habituation and extinction in a very precise and well-ordered way. Unlike most theories dealing with this function, the current theory assumes that the habituative and extinction processes of the hippocampus are not limited to the typical situations discussed previously; instead, it is hypothesized that a continual analysis of the relationship of cues to reinforcement is being made throughout the learning situation, in acquisition as well as extinction. Cues that initially controlled responding can be attenuated or extinguished as the organism finds better, more correlated cues to reinforcement.

This prediction is derived in part from the findings discussed in Chapter 9, indicating that the associative strength of a stimulus depends on the existing associative strength of all other concurrent stimuli as well as on its own association with reinforcement. For example, a reinforcer which is perfectly predicted by a cue (100% correlation) is unable to sustain conditioning to a novel concurrent cue even though the new cue is itself perfectly correlated with the reinforcer. If the first cue was lowered to a 50% correlation with the reinforcer then its associative strength would decline to an appropriate level. If the new cue had a higher correlation with the reinforcer, then it would gain some of the associative strength lost by the first cue. Thus, the total amount of associative strength supported by the reinforcer would remain the same but it would be split between the two cues.

The present theory argues that the hippocampus and habituative system are engaged whenever a cue loses strength in relation to another cue, or when a completely redundant cue is presented. Thus, if a cue was correlated 50% with reinforcement and then dropped to 40%, the hippocampus would decrease the associative value of the cue to an appropriate level even though the cue is still being occasionally rewarded. In addition, orienting to redundant stimuli would be inhibited if other cues had appropriated the associative strength supportable by the reinforcer.

Solomon (1977) has shown that damage to the hippocampus disrupts this process. Rabbits with bilateral hippocampal damage tended to orient to redundant novel cues while control rabbits only responded to the old cue. This provides evidence that hippocampal damage makes the animal less able to appropriately ignore or reduce the strength of salient stimuli (processed by the reinforcer system).

Hippocampal Involvement in
Motivational and Homeostatic Mechanisms

Given the proposed set of principles of hippocampal function it would seem logical to assume that the hippocampus is less involved with homeostatic or motivational behaviors than the amygdala. Whatever changes do occur should result indirectly from the loss of proposed functions. For example, failure to habituate normally to environmental stimuli could increase stress to novel situations. The homeostatic changes resulting from this case would clearly not be due to direct loss of control over them by the hippocampus.

Olds' (1956) study of self-stimulation in rats with chronic electrodes provides an appropriate starting point. Olds found that self-stimulation by rats with electrodes in the hippocampus occurred at significantly lower rates than those with electrodes in the amygdala. The lack of a large rewarding effect does not seem to be due to aversiveness of such stimulation either. Finch et al. (1978) showed that the predominant response of hippocampal neurons in cats to stimulation of mesencephalic and pontine stimulation was inhibitory in nature. In humans, stimulation of the hippocampus has very little of the emotional affect found upon amygdalar stimulation. The usual effect produced by damage to the hippocampus in humans is a severe memory and learning deficit (Valenstein, 1973).

Studies investigating changes in motivation and homeostasis after hippocampal damage have been fairly negative in their findings (Kaada et al., 1971). Beatty and Schwartzbaum (1968) demonstrated that hippocampal lesions failed to exaggerate consummatory reactivity either positively or negatively to the taste properties of solutions. Similarly, on FI schedules, terminal rates in the fixed interval were enhanced for the septally lesioned, but not the hippocampally lesioned subjects. Kapp et al. (1978) showed that hippocampal stimulation disrupted the response contingent aspects of passive avoidance but not the noncontingent fear conditioning aspects. Other studies have shown that lesions of the hippocampus do not create deficits in CER conditioning (Nadel, 1968) nor does hippocampal stimulation (Gustaffson et al., 1975).

A number of studies have seemed to show an inhibitory effect of the hippocampus on the pituitary-adrenal system in both animals and humans (Casady & Taylor, 1976; Rubin et al., 1966) although the evidence is quite mixed (Micco et al., 1979; van Hartesveldt, 1975; Wilson & Critchlow, 1973). Some of the confusion possibly stems from a lack of consideration of the learning variables that the hippocampus can affect. For example, Endroczi and Zissak as reported in Bohus (1975) showed variable effects of hippocampal stimulation on adrenal response depending on the stimulus frequency. However, when the animals were habituated to the stimulus the various changes induced previously were not observed. Mixed results have also been obtained with respect to hippocampal involvement in food and water consumption (Jarrard, 1973) and species typical behavior in cats (Nonneman & Kolb, 1974). In the latter study, some affective responses were enhanced and others were diminished.

It should also be noted that autonomic changes induced by hippocampal ablation or stimulation could exert their effect through disruption of septal circuits which act as way stations between the hippocampus and brain stem (Anchel & Lindsley, 1972; Raisman, 1966). In short, the hippocampus seems to influence homeostasis and motivation to a lesser extent and in a more indirect way than the amygdala.

Secondary Cue Processing and the Hippocampus

The hippocampal principles of operation state that in addition to being involved in the habituation of nonreinforced stimuli, the hippocampus plays an important role in the registration of secondary cues to reinforcement. Secondary cues are those cues which are not in close temporal correlation with the occurrence of reinforcement or are nonsalient, background cues. For the moment, we will defer the question of how the hippocampus is involved in the registration of secondary cues as well as habituation in order to consider the evidence which supports the assertion of hippocampal involvement in the former process.

Plunkett and Foulds (1979) demonstrated that hippocampally lesioned rats, unlike those with amygdalar lesions, were deficient on discrimination tasks that had a low level of cue distinctiveness. However, the hippocampally lesioned group performed similarly to control groups when the task contained highly distinctive cues. Cue utilization by hippocampally lesioned rats in a complex maze was studied by Winocur and Breckinridge (1973). It was found that these rats could learn a fixed response sequence as well as cortically lesioned or control rats if highly conspicuous cues were used. When the cues were removed after acquisition, only the performance of the hippocampally lesioned group deteriorated (cf. Kimble & Bre-Miller, 1981). Similar findings have been obtained in a delayed match to sample task (Sinnamon et al., 1978). Devenport (1979, 1980) showed that hippocampally lesioned rats displayed strong contiguity effects in an operant learning task compared to controls.

This deficiency in processing nonsalient cues after hippocampal damage helps explain the puzzling finding in the literature that hippocampectomized rats seem to have generally facilitated performance in two-way active avoidance tasks but deficits in one-way active avoidance (Duncan & Duncan, 1971; Lovely et al., 1971). It should be noted that facilitated shuttle box performance is associated with reduced fear elicited by situational cues except for the CS since the animal must return to a place associated with shock

(McAllister et al., 1971). Since hippocampectomy was shown to disrupt processing of nonsalient cues the hippocampally lesioned groups are more strongly under the control of the primary cues than normal rats.

On the other hand, in one-way active avoidance one site is consistently associated with shock and one site is consistently shock free. In this paradigm, both primary and secondary cues are congruent with the learned response. Normal animals learn this response very quickly, sometimes in a single trial (Bolles, 1972b). Since the hippocampals have diminished stimulus support for the response compared to normals, it is not surprising that they would show some deficit in responding, particularly given the high performance level of normals.

This proposed function is able to account for the O'Keefe and Nadel (1978) hypothesis of hippocampal behavior which assumes that spatial information is being analyzed in the hippocampus. Their idea is based on findings that tasks involving spatial components are usually adversely affected by damage to the hippocampus, at least with animals. In the present view, such spatial information typically falls into the category of secondary cues, which are processed through the habituative system. In other words, the ability to process spatial information is specifically disrupted by habituative system damage; however, this represents only part of the deficit created, since the capacity to process non-spatial secondary cues is also diminished. Morris (1983) showed that a place navigation task which normal rats learned in a few trials was never acquired by hippocampal rats even after extensive trials. Jarrard and Elmes (1982) found that hippocampal rats preoperatively trained on a 12-arm radial maze task selectively lost previously learned information about the spatial location of previously rewarded arms. However, they still showed retention of the general task requirements.

Electrophysiological evidence also supports the idea that spatial information is routed through the hippocampus. Kubie and Ranck (1983) found that phasic increases in complex spike cell response were related to place information in different environments. The background response rate of these neurons was specific to a given environment. Other units fire preferentially while the animal is moving irrespective of final destinations, i.e., displace units (O'Keefe & Nadel, 1978).

Other research has shown that performance on non-spatial tasks is also disrupted. For example, Olton et al. (1979) tested hippocampal rats in a cross maze in which spatial cues were minimized and salient visual cues differentiated each of the four arms. The rats have to choose a different arm on each trial until all four arms have been chosen. Hippocampal lesions produced a severe deficit on this task. In general, hippocampal animals have particular difficulty in remembering cues which appear on one trial as opposed to cues which are consistent across trials (Olton & Pappas, 1979). The evidence supports the idea that hippocampally lesioned animals do display deficits in processing nonsalient stimuli compared to controls, especially while engaged in some reinforced behavior. How can this function be reconciled with the well-supported finding of hippocampal involvement in habituative processes?

Essentially, it is argued here that hippocampal involvement in secondary cue processing proceeds directly from its processing capabilities with regard to the novel and/or nonreinforced stimuli which it habituates. The novel stimuli associated with, say, exploration are of a more subtle kind than those salient stimuli occurring together with reinforcers which are processed through the reinforcer system. Therefore, the hippocampus needs to be more sensitive to relatively small changes in the stimulus field in order to respond to and process these stimuli. Secondary cues, by definition, have a more distant or less correlated relationship with reinforcement and thus share some of the characteristics, in this respect, of the nonreinforced stimuli.

The next question is why the hippocampus, after processing these cues to reinforcement, simply does not habituate them since they are often temporally removed from the occurrence of the reinforcer. In this case, it is the action of the primary cues which prevent their habituation and preserve their registration as secondary cues to reinforcement. It will be remembered that the primary cues which are processed through the reinforcer system acquire some power to activate the reinforcer system on their own. The activation of the reinforcer system tends to inhibit habituative processes in turn. Thus, the secondary cues that are processed through the hippocampus are preserved from habituation because of the presence of primary cues processed through the reinforcer system. It should be noted that when stimuli are temporally removed from reinforcement, registration as secondary cues takes place after conditioning has occurred to the primary cues (Gollub, 1977).

The habituative system, by allowing the organism to process the secondary cues, serves to improve the stability and persistence of reinforced behaviors over a longer period of time. Interestingly, the capacity to process nonsalient stimuli also gives the organism greater flexibility by allowing shifts in attention to occur to stimuli which would pass unnoticed by the reinforcer system. Thus, depending on the situation, the processing of nonsalient cues can serve two functions.

Discriminative Stimuli and the Hippocampus

The current theory ascribes specific properties to the secondary cues, namely, that they have no conditioned reinforcing properties. As was noted before, Rizley and Rescorla (1972) among others showed that the strength of a second-order stimulus was not dependent on the current strength of either the $CS_1$ or the US. The $CS_1$ seemed to have a direct shared relationship with the US which was qualitatively different from that of the $CS_2$. The primary cues (e.g., $CS_1$) are processed through the amygdala and reinforcer system, which has strong afferent connections to affective areas as well as producing affective reactions itself. On the other hand, the secondary cues are processed through the hippocampus, which is less involved with emotional responses. Thus, the secondary cues are, in a sense, divorced from the emotions.

There is a large body of evidence which points out that a conditioned reinforcer and discriminative stimulus are not necessarily the same thing (cf. Gollub, 1977; Morgan & Firsoff, 1970). Some neurological studies (e.g., Schwartzbaum & Gay, 1966) have been able to dissociate the affective responses to reinforcers from instrumental responding on operant schedules. It should be mentioned in this regard that many cues on an operant schedule are discriminative stimuli, but not conditioned reinforcers (Williams, 1965).

These observations can shed light on the findings of a number of studies. For example, Winocur and Black (1978) studied the effects of hippocampectomy on passive avoidance performance. After training rats to run to a goalbox to obtain food, shock was delivered in the goalbox. Hippocampectomized rats showed a greater deficit in inhibiting their approach behavior than normal rats, which is the usual finding. The rats were then given a retention test 24 hours later. However, before the retention test for passive avoidance was given, the rats were noncontingently exposed to shock, related stimuli, or neutral stimuli as a reminder of the previous treatment. When the hippocampally lesioned subjects were exposed to shock or related stimuli they performed the same as controls. Exposure to the neutral stimuli left the deficit unchanged.

Winocur and Bindra (1976) found that the essential difference between the hippocampally lesioned rats and control rats on a passive avoidance task was not the number of shocks they received but the point at which the approach behavior to the food was inhibited (cf. Cogan & Reeves, 1979). Hippocampals would proceed about two-thirds of the way down the alley before stopping, while controls would stop shortly out of the start box.

It is well known from behavioral research that the conditioned reinforcing properties of cues at any point in a runway leading to food are directly dependent on the distance of that part of the alley from the food, i.e., the reinforcement gradient (Grice, 1948). Applying this fact to the above two studies indicates that the hippocampally lesioned rats are being guided by the primary cues present in such a task but are unable to make use of the secondary cues as the control rats do. The reminder technique used by Winocur and Black involved the presentation of the reinforcer or primary cues and thus the hippocampally lesioned rats were able to make use of this information and improve their performance.

A further indication that this division of cue processing actually exists is provided by Solomon (1977) who demonstrated that hippocampal damage had no effect on the formation of conditioned inhibitors. This paradigm involves the pairing of a CS+ with reinforcement and a CS- with nonreinforcement. In terms of the present theory, the conditioned inhibitors are being processed through the reinforcer system. The evidence for this statement is based on the finding that they seem to possess negative conditioned reinforcing properties (Terrace, 1971). As was previously noted, the reinforcer system is involved in the acquisition of conditioned reinforcing properties and is unaffected by hippocampal damage.

Given that primary cues and secondary cues have different properties and that the reinforcer system processes the former and the habituative system the latter, what reasons are there for such a division of cue processing? As we have seen, salient stimuli which are too far removed from the occurrence of reinforcement seem to take on inhibitory qualities. This could create problems for an organism in terms of its ability to carry out long-range strategy to achieve reinforcement. The hippocampus has little direct involvement in motivational functions when compared to the amygdala. Thus, it is less affected by such considerations. Although the secondary cues control behavior less strongly than the primary cues in the sense that an animal's behavior under secondary cues is more easily disrupted (Lyon & Millar, 1969), they have the advantage of working in more difficult circumstances, allowing the organism to engage in behaviors that will eventually lead to reward.

The Hippocampus and Response Information

An important line of inquiry into hippocampal function has been initiated by studying hippocampal unit response to simple classical conditioning procedures (Berger et al., 1976; Berger & Thompson, 1978a, 1978b). Units were recorded in the dorsal hippocampus of rabbits while presenting a CS tone paired with air puff to the cornea. Differential responses of neurons were discovered to occur very early in the course of conditioning. This initial response preceded the occurrence of the unconditioned response by approximately 30 msec. The general topography of the neuronal response also appeared to match that of the behavioral response. The truly important finding of these studies lay in the fact that unpaired presentations of the CS and US did not lead to this pattern of neuronal response, although there was some slight activity to presentations of the US alone. Thus, the activity of these neurons seems directly related to learning variables.

231

Hoehler & Thompson (1979, 1980), in further investigations of this phenomenon, manipulated certain variables in the classical conditioning procedure. Changes in CS-US interval created changes that were consistent at both the behavioral and neuronal levels. When the CS-US interval was too short to yield behavioral conditioning to the CS (i.e., 50 msec), neuronal response was also absent. However, behavioral and neuronal responses were evident at 150 msec and 250 msec intervals; when the CS-US interval was shifted from 250 to 500 msec, the peak neuronal response moved in tandem with the peak behavioral CR. At the human level, there is also some evidence that neurons in the hippocampus are sensitive to responses, in this case, verbal responses (Halgren et al., 1978). Hippocampal neurons have also been shown to be sensitive to body orientation in space, approach to food and water, and general orienting (O'Keefe & Dostrovsky, 1971; Ranck, 1973).

As Moore (1979) notes, the puzzling aspect of the animal data is that the hippocampal sensitivity to responses at the neuronal level does not lead to a response deficit after damage to this area. It might also be noted that neither does hippocampectomy disrupt basic classical conditioning. There is not even a discernible short-term loss which might indicate relearning or recovery of the function through other brain areas.

Thus, after damage in just those regions of the hippocampus which receive extensive response information, we see no actual response-related deficits (cf. Solomon & Gottfried, 1981). However, we do see pronounced deficits in stimulus processing capacities. This kind of evidence compels one to believe that the response-related activity of hippocampal neurons is not due to their functioning as the substrate of the CR or other responses, but rather is present because it serves some purpose with regard to the stimulus processing capacities of the hippocampus.

Moore (1979) hypothesized that this response information is used to preserve the functional integrity of the CS-US relationship and provide a means by which irrelevant stimuli could be blocked out. Translated into the context of the present theory, this hypothesis achieves the following form: Response information related to learning is transmitted to hippocampal neurons so that the relative correlation of stimulus cues with the reinforcing event can be evaluated. The learned response is probably an ideal way of identifying relevant stimuli for the hippocampus since in a learning situation there may be any number of stimuli which are occurring at some time during the trial. A match between the CS-US representation and the exteroceptive sequence inhibits the habituation of the CS, therefore, because a consistent response follows its occurrence. Through the same mechanism, other stimuli, which are irrelevant to the match between the internal representation and exteroceptive stimuli, can be identified and habituated (or at least not attended to, as in blocking). Lynch et al. (1978) showed that neurons in the dentate gyrus were particularly responsive to situations in which there were both positively and negatively correlated cues to reinforcement, firing strongly to the positive cue and inhibiting their response to the negative cue. Firing rates to the CS+ - US relationship, when presented alone, were reduced in comparison. That said, an additional question suggests itself: What relationship does the activation of the reinforcer system have with the transmission of response information to the hippocampus? One phenomenon relevant to this problem is the hippocampal theta wave.

The Hippocampal Theta Wave

No discussion of hippocampal function can be complete without mention of the role of the hippocampal theta wave, which is a rhythmical slow wave, nearly sinusoidal in character. It varies in frequency between 6 and 12Hz in the rat and also has a widely varying amplitude. There are basically two forms of theta waves: one that is sensitive to atropine and one that is atropine resistant. This latter type is associated with behavioral movements (Robinson & Vanderwolf, 1978; Vanderwolf, 1971).

This EEG pattern has been linked to just about all possible behavioral variables, including arousal, attention, learning, motivation, and motor behavior (cf. Bennett, 1970; Black & Young, 1972; Nadel & O'Keefe, 1974). There are distinct species differences in the characteristics of these waves. Rats, cats, and dogs seem to display somewhat similar theta patterns; however, theta in monkeys and humans is noticeably different from these species (Halgren et al., 1978). One main difference is that the occurrence of theta in monkeys and humans is briefer in duration and occurs less frequently (Brazier, 1972; Crowne & Radcliffe, 1975).

Vanderwolf (1971) and Arnolds et al. (1979) have shown that at least for the rat and dog, the theta waves are basically dependent on the motor activity of the animal, although there is evidence for some type of theta during immobility (Frederickson et al., 1980; Winson, 1972). The mobility-related theta waves accompany voluntary, arbitrary movements such as walking, running, climbing, and head movements. Steady motor activity is correlated with a lower frequency than occurs at the initiation of movement but the theta waves themselves continue as long as the movement, even up to 8 hours (Whishaw & Vanderwolf, 1970). Thus, the hippocampus receives response-related information not only about the CR, but also about instrumental, voluntary responses. The latter information seems to be transmitted to the hippocampus irrespective of their connection with reinforcement.

Anatomically, the hippocampal theta activity is strongest in the $CA_1$ region and dentate gyrus and weak or non-existent in the

233

$CA_3$ region, the latter region being closely associated with habituative processes as we have seen (cf. O'Keefe & Nadel, 1978). The theta wave is generated from neurons in the medial septum which control the activity of all hippocampal theta neurons (Stumpf, 1965; Rawlins et al., 1979). A secondary generator is the entorhinal cortex, at least with respect to atropine-resistant theta (Vanderwolf & Leung, 1983) which indicates that theta activity can be controlled from both lower and higher regions from the level of the limbic system.

Other types of hippocampal theta waves such as the large, irregular waves are correlated with behavioral immobility, but interestingly, also appear with species-specific behaviors such as licking, cleaning, drinking, urination, shivering, etc. Vanderwolf (1971) and Black and Young (1972) support a dichotomy between arbitrary, voluntary responses and consummatory, autonomic behaviors based on this phenomenon. It is obvious, of course, that motor behavior is occurring in those species-specific behaviors, yet theta waves are not generally displayed. Thus, the theta is correlated with only certain kinds of motor activity.

Despite the strong correlation between the atropine-resistant theta and voluntary movements, many researchers have argued that the theta wave is directly related to attentional or learning variables (cf. Bennett, 1970; Isaacson, 1974) and evidence has been found linking theta with modulation of sensory processing (Fleming & Bigler, 1974; Komisaruk & Beyer, 1972). Nadel and O'Keefe (1974) hypothesized that the hippocampus is involved in processing spatial information and the theta is correlated with movements as the animal moves through space (Hill, 1978).

Crowne and Radcliffe (1975), working with monkeys, have provided evidence for a rather clear dissociation between theta and movement in this animal. Many apparently voluntary movements do not display theta in the monkey. On the other hand, theta is not especially correlated with attentional responses to novel stimuli either. The authors did discover, however, that theta did seem to occur more frequently in the extinction situation. The theta bursts generally occur at the beginning of the cessation of reward, sometimes noncontingently with responses. Joseph and Engle (1981) and Joseph et al. (1982) have provided evidence that theta activity may have components linked to both attentional and motor behavior, which perhaps may correspond to the distinctions between atropine sensitive and resistant theta.

Crowne and Radcliffe (1975) argue that the theta wave is associated with changes in the valence of stimuli. They hypothesize that this process is closely coordinated with physical movement in the rat but that higher up the phylogenetic scale this correspondence declines. Komisaruk (1977) has put forth a hypothesis which states that the theta rhythm may reflect the organization of

234

sensorimotor processes into sequential patterns. He advances the interesting idea that each theta cycle is composed of discrete periods in which different activities are more probable than at other points in the cycle. For example, Semba and Komisaruk (1978) showed that the performance of an operant response is more probable at the negative peak of the cycle than at other times, although there is no invariable correlation between the operant response and the negative peak.

In the present theory, a slightly different approach is taken. It is argued that the occurrence of the theta wave represents a capability of cue processing by the habituative system in certain species. It should be stressed that capability here does not mean that cue processing will necessarily occur when theta waves occur. However, in the absence of theta waves, cue processing by the habituative system of the normal animal should be greatly reduced or nonexistent. Cue processing by the reinforcer system should remain, though. This processing state of the habituative system is perhaps best understood by comparing it to cortical EEG. It is well known that in the awake organism cortical EEG patterns such as desynchronization are correlated with a broad class of behaviors rather than with any specific behavior. For example, cortical desynchronization is not dependent on movement or learning or motivational factors even though all of these can occur with it. Instead it seems to be related to a general capacity to engage in certain activities. Additionally, it should be remembered that EEG patterns can be abolished without necessarily disrupting behavior either at the cortical or limbic system level (Key & Bradley, 1959; Vanderwolf & Vanderwart, 1970). This is a reminder that it is the neurons underlying a particular EEG pattern that are responsible for behaviors, not the electrical activity they emit as a consequence of this.

The presence of hippocampal theta waves in the awake, normal organism indicates a capacity to process cues through the habituative system that is not present when hippocampal fast wave activity is seen. This in no way goes against the finding that in some species motor activity of a certain kind is correlated with theta waves. It is entirely possible for a processing capability to be tied to the occurrence of these particular activities even though it may not always be engaged or operative. Similarly, mental concentration is correlated with cortical desynchronization, although desynchronization can occur without mental concentration.

It may be possible to illustrate more precisely the hypothesized workings of the habituative system by analyzing some of the theta wave induction literature. Gray (1970) noted that the theta wave frequency of rats was correlated with different situations. When rats are exploring a novel environment or when they are exposed to frustrative non-reward the theta frequency is about 7.5–8.5 Hz.; when they consume a reward the frequency falls to 6–7.5 Hz; running

235

is associated with a 8.5-10 Hz frequency. This is consistent with Vanderwolf's findings of theta frequency correlation with degree of activity.

In this study, Gray administered sodium amobarbitol to the rats and measured the effect on septal driving at the theta rhythm. Stumpf (1965) had shown that it was possible to drive the theta rhythm by stimulating the medial septal cells. Lesions to this area blocked the theta rhythm (Donovick, 1968). Gray found that sodium amobarbitol selectively raised the driving threshold for theta at 7.7 Hz., but had little or no effect at other frequencies. It will be noted that 7.7 Hz. falls inside the range which normally accompanies frustrative non-reward and exploration in the rat. Behaviorally, the rats took longer to extinguish a rewarded response.

Since amobarbitol retards extinction and raises the driving theshold of 7.7 Hz. theta waves, it is reasonable to assume that artificially producing these theta frequencies during extinction should increase the rate of extinction; this is what Gray found. Additionally, Gray found that amobarbitol administered during acquisition in a partial reinforcement schedule could block the partial reinforcement extinction effect. Conversely, driving the theta rhythm of 7.7 Hz during acquisition on continuous reinforcement produced a pseudo partial reinforcement extinction effect. Thus, opposite effects are produced by theta driving or blocking depending on whether they are administered during acquisition or extinction (cf. Glazer, 1974a, 1974b). Landfield (1977) obtained similar results using active avoidance and passive avoidance (cf. Gray, 1982).

According to the present theory, it is possible to reconcile the findings with those of Vanderwolf and others. First of all, there can be little doubt that, in the rat, theta activity is correlated with arbitrary, voluntary movement and not particular learning or motivational variables. However, it should be noted that the 7.7 Hz frequency is also the frequency that occurs in rats placed in a novel environment or in extinction. One of the things that rats do when they are exposed to novel stimuli is to make orienting responses to them. The theta frequency in this instance is probably reflecting the occurrence of the motor aspects of the OR, at least with rats. The frequency and amplitude are about right since these movements are fairly small. In the case of frustrative non-reward, ORs are also occurring.

Interestingly, evidence does exist for the idea that theta frequencies between 7 and 8 Hz may be special because this zone represents a transition between the action of atropine-sensitive theta associated with frequencies below 7 Hz approximately and atropine-resistant theta associated with frequencies above 7 Hz (Gray, 1982).

It is hypothesized that amobarbitol raises the threshold of this particular frequency by suppressing the processing capabilities of the habituative system in the rat. The rat can no longer process the secondary cues and novel stimuli that are usually processed by this system. The loss of this processing capability in turn leads to a diminution of ORs to these stimuli. The increased driving threshold is thus a reflection of the increased threshold for ORs to occur. Amobarbitol can be said to functionally ablate this capacity of the habituative system at least temporarily. However, the action of the reinforcer system is left intact. This is why amobarbitol affects behavior during frustrative non-reward, but not during acquisition. When it is administered during extinction, it serves to inhibit habituation by inhibiting the processing of the now non-rewarded cues through the habituative system. In addition ORs to novel nonsalient cues underlying response shift tendencies are also inhibited. It should be emphasized that amobarbitol is having this affect because it is directly affecting neuronal response in this system and not because it is changing the theta wave per se.

The converse is true for theta driving in extinction. Here the conditions necessary for cue processing in the habituative system are being artificially induced. Thus, the animal has an increased capacity for processing novel and nonsalient cues in extinction. The response shift tendencies of the hippocampus in a non-reward situation are enhanced.

There remains the problem that when amobarbitol is administered during acquisition, it speeds up subsequent extinction instead of retarding it. Theta driving during acquisition retards later extinction, on the other hand. How does the processing of cues through the habituative system relate to these extinction effects, in brief?

In an instrumental partial reinforcement setting, the normal animal is processing secondary cues through the habituative system in addition to the processing of primary cues through the reinforcer system. This secondary cue processing is hypothesized to enable the animal to gain increased resistance to extinction in low reward conditions. This processing occurs because the primary cues are no longer perfectly correlated with reward (cf. Rescorla & Wagner, 1972). As we saw in the previous chapter, the lower density of reinforcement results in an increasing temporal separation of reinforcer occurrences. This permits the acquisition of more secondary cues which gain control over the contingent response in these periods. In the absence of disruptive influences, the secondary cues can maintain control over the response longer in extinction than can the primary cues because their own associative strength is not as dependent on the current strength of the reinforcer.

The normal animal has a decreased resistance to extinction under conditions of high reward because there is little chance for additional cue processing to take place through the habituative system. These primary cues are already highly predictive of reward and thus equal the asymptote of conditioning by themselves.

The animal with a disrupted habituative system, on the other hand, tends to have increased resistance to extinction under conditions of high reward because the processing of novel stimuli in extinction is inhibited. Thus, the response shift tendencies induced by such processing in extinction are absent, leading to increased perseverative responding to the correlated primary cues processed through the intact reinforcer system. Such an animal has decreased resistance to extinction under conditions of low reward because the additional cue processing that should have taken place during acquisition never does. Since the primary cues are weakly correlated with reinforcement, extinction is fairly rapid.

Theta driving would accentuate the normal workings of the habituative system. Additional cue processing in acquisition would tend to lengthen later extinction. This is due to the longer times needed for the various cues to occur in the presence of nonreinforcement. Thus, a pseudo partial reinforcement effect could be exhibited in a continuous reinforcement schedule. As was noted above, theta driving in extinction speeds up extinction because of the enhanced response shift tendencies.

## THE SEPTUM IN LEARNING AND MOTIVATION

### Principles of Operation

The present theory assumes that the septum is a coordinating structure between the reinforcer and habituative systems with the following properties:

1. It is composed of two functionally distinct regions: the medial and lateral septum. The medial septum transmits information from the reinforcer system to the hippocampus, while the lateral septum receives information from the hippocampus.

2. The lateral septum reduces the motivational properties of sensory information to avoid having the organism respond too powerfully to their positive or negative qualities. Thus, it has a reciprocal relationship with the action of the amygdala in controlling organismic responsiveness to motivationally significant stimuli.

238

3.  The lateral septum decreases the conditioned reinforcing properties of primary cues associated with reinforcement. Through the same process it inhibits frustrative responses to cues partially reinforced or frustratively non-rewarded.

4.  The medial septum controls processing through the hippocampus and habituative system by means of its pacemaker cells for the theta wave.

5.  The medial septum acts as a relay for information from the reinforcer system to the habituative system. Information about the presence of significant stimuli is relayed through this septal area, which then sends appropriate signals to the hippocampus.

Septal Involvement in Motivation and Homeostasis

The septum, in its role as intermediary between the reinforcer and habituative systems, necessarily has a strong effect on the processes of both systems. In this section, we examine its effect on the amygdala and therefore the reinforcer system.

The principles of operation indicate that the lateral septum acts as an opponent to amygdalar processes involved in the processing of reinforcers. Since the amygdala tends to augment neural and endocrine response to such stimuli, the septum should counteract the operation of the amygdala, acting as a negative feedback loop in restraining an otherwise excessive increase in responsivity.

Abbot and Melzack (1978) demonstrated that electrical stimulation of the lateral septum which produced after-discharges led to analgesia in rats, although fear reduction may play a role in this effect (Grauer & Thomas, 1982). Medial septal stimulation did not have this effect nor did amygdalar stimulation. Septal stimulation also has an analgesic effect in humans (Valenstein, 1973). Lateral septal stimulation has been shown to suppress aggressiveness and reactivity by almost 80% compared to baseline response in rats. Again, medial stimulation had no such effect (Brayley & Albert, 1977). Septally lesioned rats reach successively higher levels of discrimination between odorants faster than controls, suggesting that the septum has an inhibitory role on the olfactory bulbs (Von Saal et al., 1975).

Increased reactivity to the taste properties of stimuli is also evident after septal lesions (Beatty & Schwartzbaum, 1968). Rats with septal lesions completely inhibit drinking when a quinine solution is the only choice available, although they tend to consume more water than controls when it is unadulterated (Gittelson et al., 1969). Although both of the above studies employed total septal lesions, Munoz and Grossman (1980) have shown that destruction of medial septal neurons had no significant effect on sucrose

239

or saline preference, making the lateral septum the likely site of the change in reactivity. This does not mean that the medial septum has no influence on any motivational or homeostatic behaviors (cf. de Castro et al., 1978) but it should be much less than that of the lateral septum.

Septally lesioned rats seem to have exaggerated reactivity to other kinds of stimuli. For example, septally lesioned animals spend less total time in the light than control animals (Zuromski et al., 1972); display increased activity in the openfield (Poplawsky & Isaacson, 1983) and after shock, although detection thresholds are normal (Lubar et al., 1970); spend more time in contact with conspecifics and display more social behaviors (Booth et al., 1979); are more aggressive outside of the home territory (Marsden & Slotnick, 1972) and show a consistent augmentation of defensive behaviors as a result of threat from conspecifics (Blanchard et al., 1979). This last study showed that the defensive enhancement was not due to an increase in attack behaviors or general reactivity. Amygdalar lesions abolished this enhancement of defensive behaviors.

A similar pattern is displayed in changes of endocrine response to septal lesions. A number of studies have investigated pituitary-adrenal function following lesions of the septum. A number of other studies have found elevations of plasma corticosterone levels in response to stress after lateral septal lesions (Usher et al., 1974), which sometimes occur to stimuli not found stressful by controls (Uhlir et al., 1974). Basal levels of such hormones tend to remain at normal levels, however. Stimulation of the lateral septum does not show a consistent effect on corticosterone levels (Bouillé & Baylé, 1975) nor do septal lesions block hypersecretion of ACTH following adrenalectomy, unlike amygdala lesions (Allen & Allen, 1975).

It is important to point out that the septum is not viewed in the current theory as a sort of negative amygdala. Although it is directly involved in motivational expression, it does not control the occurrence of species-specific behaviors in the way that the reinforcer system and amygdala do. The septum acts to restrain the augmentation of response produced to significant stimuli rather than directly controlling or inhibiting species-specific behaviors themselves. For example, Thomas and Evans (1983) showed that animals would perform a learned response to obtain septal stimulation only when they were experiencing concurrent aversive stimulation. Thus, it is not surprising that basal levels of pituitary-adrenal hormones remain relatively unchanged after septal lesions but that the specific response to stressful stimuli is elevated. The lateral septum seems to be part of ascending and descending pathways, which makes it a likely candidate for the motivational and homeostatic changes exhibited after septal lesions (DeFrance et al., 1976).

In the current theory, disruption of species-specific responding after total septal lesions should be the result of unrestrained
action by the reinforcer system and/or the loss of function by the
habituative system.  For example, Fleischer and Slotnick (1978)
found that septal lesions prior to mating totally disrupted maternal
behavior in female rats; female rats with pups did not build nests
or nurse them.  Retrieval behavior of the mother was extremely
persistent but the pups were rarely gathered into a common location.
Female rats septally lesioned after parturition became hyperrespon-
sive and quickly cannibalized their pups.  Virgin female rats that
had maternal behavior induced in them by the presence of foster
pups displayed similar but less marked effects.

We saw with pituitary-adrenal function that the effects of
septal lesions including the lateral region seem to be focused most
strongly on organismic response to significant stimuli rather
than on basal levels of hormones.  This finding is echoed in the
Fleischer and Slotnick study since septal lesions in virgin female
rats disturbed maternal behaviors less severely than it did the
actual mothers.  Presumably, the maternal behaviors are more highly
motivated in the actual mothers because the appropriate sensitizing
hormones are present.

The action of the amygdala is unrestrained with the destruction
of the septum.  Since the reinforcer system is differentially sensitive to salient, motivationally strong stimuli, it is precisely
this response which will be abnormally expressed to the greatest
degree.  Retrieval behaviors prompted by dispersal of the pups were
perseverative in the septally lesioned rats.  Again, the authors
note that the female rats seemed highly motivated to carry out the
retrieval behaviors, but seemed to have difficulty inhibiting the
behavior once it was started.  Support for this interpretation is
provided by the finding that septally lesioned rats trained on FI
schedules and in the runway for food did not show the typical
perseverative effect when trained under satiated conditions (Henke,
1975; cf. also Fallon & Donovick, 1970).

Destruction of the septum would also be expected to disrupt the
functions of the habituative system, since information to and from
the hippocampus is being interrupted.  Derangement of nest-building
could be due to a deficit in the processing of spatial cues; the
rat is unable to settle on a home territory.  The septally lesioned
mice in the Marsden and Slotnick study seemed to have such deficits
in connection with aggressive behaviors which, in the normal animal,
are confined to the home territory.

This analysis points up the fact that total septal lesions are
likely to disturb a number of functions in the reinforcer and habituative systems by virtue of the intermediary role of the septum.
One must agree with Numan (1978) that in the future researchers must
make distinctions between lesions of the lateral and medial septum

in order to obtain theoretically useful results. The present theory makes it clear that these two regions are performing very different functions which achieve unity only in the sense that they are both involved in the exchange of information between two important stimulus analyzing systems.

Septal Involvement in the Response
to the US in Learning Paradigms

If the lateral septum has a reciprocal relationship with the amygdala with regard to reinforcers, this should reflect itself in changes in response to reinforcers used in learning paradigms. Septal rats show a deficit in one-way active avoidance (McCleary, 1966). As Bengelloun (1979) demonstrated, this deficit is related to handling of the animal at the end of each trial in this paradigm. When no handling occurs, the septally lesioned rats show no deficit in acquiring one-way avoidance. In shuttlebox active avoidance tasks where handling is not a factor, septal lesions facilitate avoidance learning. The animal's behavior seems much more strongly controlled by the primary cues (Sodetz, 1970).

DeNoble and Caplan (1977) studied the effect on septally lesioned rats of response-independent food superimposed on a baseline schedule. Normal animals increase response rates in the schedule temporarily to noncontingent food on a DRL schedule while decreasing their rates to noncontingent food on DRH schedules. Septal lesions greatly enhanced the acceleration or suppression of responding in these schedules.

Passive avoidance deficits are another common result of lesions to the lateral septum (Hamilton et al., 1970). It has been shown that before the introduction of shock the approach tendencies of the septally lesioned rat are stronger than those of controls. A relative measure of suppression which took this stronger approach tendency to food into account revealed equivalent degrees of response suppression between controls and septally lesioned rats (Kasper-Pandi et al., 1969).

If septal lesions in animals are causing stronger approach tendencies toward the positive reinforcer in the passive avoidance situation, then we should expect to see greater tolerance of aversive stimulation before the approach response is inhibited. This effect has been found in a number of studies (Poplawsky & Hoffman, 1979; Schwartzbaum & Spieth, 1964). The largest difference between the behavior of controls and septally lesioned rats seems to be with moderate levels of shock; in this situation the normal rats suppress the approach response while the septal rats continue to engage in it. At stronger shock intensities both groups suppress. It should be remembered in this connection that septal lesions do not affect detection thresholds of shock; the septally lesioned

242

animal presumably experiences the same painful stimulation as the normal animal but has a greater motivation to perform the punished response.

It may be objected that if the septally lesioned animal is reacting more strongly to reinforcers because of the non-restrained reinforcer system, then it would be just as reasonable to expect them to react strongly to the shock and suppress the approach response as it would the other way around. Actually, septal rats do exhibit little or no deficit in passive avoidance if the approach response has not been established before the introduction of shock. In the Schwartzbaum and Spieth study, for example, the septally lesioned rats were no different than controls on the first shocked session if the response had not been well established. Wishart and Mogenson (1970) made a more precise test of this notion by making septal lesions before and after passive avoidance training had been initiated. The lesioned rats which received post-operative approach training before punishment was introduced did not learn to passively avoid. However, the lesioned group that received punishment from the start did acquire the passive avoidance response.

These results suggest that septally lesioned animals find it difficult to suppress a previously learned habit rather than having a specific passive avoidance deficit. This is not to say that they do not react more strongly to positive reinforcement than normal animals, but that this exaggerated response can occur to negative reinforcement as well. This aspect of septal damange is due to loss of control over the amygdala and reinforcer system. The deficit with regard to inhibiting a previously learned response is due to interruption of habituative system functioning. It will be remembered that damage to the hippocampus caused a very similar syndrome with regard to inhibition of previously learned responses, but not to reactivity to reinforcers.

Cue Processing and the Septum

According to the current theory, both the medial and lateral areas of septum are involved in the processing of cues, although in different ways. The medial septum influences the initiation of processing by the hippocampus and habituative system while the lateral septum receives the output from the hippocampus.

Wetzel et al. (1977a, 1977b) studied EEG activity in freely moving rats with implanted electrodes in the dorsal hippocampus. Stimulation of 7 Hz to the medial septum led to the establishment of typical theta waves and behaviorally always resulted in ORs such as sniffing, exploration, and searching. In line with this finding, Semba and Iwahoras (1974) demonstrated that rats with medial septal lesions were less likely to display ORs to novel stimuli while engaging in drinking than controls (cf. Solomon & Gottfried, 1981).

243

Evoked activity of single neurons in the hippocampus was studied by Miller and Groves (1977) who compared the neuronal activity of normal rats with those receiving medial septal lesions. In the normal rat, almost half (41%) of the hippocampal neurons studied displayed inhibition following peripheral stimulation. This percentage was halved in the rats with medial septal lesions.

With regard to the lateral septum, we would expect to see deficits relating to hippocampal output (i.e., deficits in habituation or extinction). Burton and Toga (1982) showed that lateral septal lesions decreased latent inhibition. Kohler (1976b) demonstrated that rats with lateral septal lesions displayed impaired habituation of the OR to auditory stimuli unlike rats with medial septal lesions. The lateral septal rats also took longer to habituate to the test environment. Thus, medial septal lesions cause diminished cue processing or ORs, while lateral septal lesions prolong ORs, exactly what we would expect from their functions in the present model.

Another property of cues is their conditioned reinforcing strength (if any). The principles of operation predict that septal damage will lead to an augmentation of the conditioned reinforcing properties of primary cues, since as has been demonstrated, these cues are processed through the amygdala. Carlson et al. (1976) demonstrated that septal lesions increased the appetitive value of a secondary reinforcer associated with food. Septally lesioned rats displayed an enhanced response rate in the last 10 seconds of a FI-1 interval compared to controls (Ellen & Powell, 1962), while septally lesioned mice ran significantly faster than controls on reinforced trials but significantly slower on non-reinforced trials (Carlson, et al., 1972). Henke (1977) showed that septally-lesioned rats displayed a frustration effect after non-reinforced trials that was abolished by lesions of the amygdala.

Septally lesioned animals tested in the runway for food reinforcement display increased resistance to extinction following CRF training but decreased resistance to extinction following partial reinforcement (Henke, 1977). Feldon and Gray (1979) have shown that the lateral septum is the probable site for this effect as we would expect from the current theory. Medial septal lesions had inconsistent effects.

Lancaster and Johnson (1976) provide supporting evidence for these findings. Rats with lateral or medial septal lesions were studied on various FR schedules. It was found that the response rates of septally damaged rats increased more rapidly than controls as a function of increasing food deprivation. More importantly, although lateral septal lesions enhanced FR performance and prolonged extinction, medial septal lesions had no such effect. There were no significant differences between the medial septal group and the control animals; however, there was a distinct trend for the medial septal group to have the lowest response rates and to show the lowest FR strain point. Thus, medial and lateral septal lesions display contrasting effects on cue processing in keeping with their theoretically assigned functions.

## Cue Selection and the Septum

One of the most noted findings with regard to septal damage is that lesioned animals seem to display a different pattern of cue selection than do normal animals. For example, Dalland (1970) has shown that septally lesioned rats are more likely than controls to perseverate toward external stimuli in a maze arm instead of using proprioceptive information. Similar findings were reported by Clody and Carlton (1969) and Thomas (1972). In the latter study, perseveration in a spontaneous alternation test occurred when olfactory and visual cues were placed in conjunction. Placement of these types of cues in opposition to each other eliminated perseveration.

Krantz and Mitchell (1977) showed that the perseveration displayed by septally lesioned rats is not specific to a particular kind of stimulus (i.e., external versus proprioceptive). Normal and septally lesioned rats were trained on a behavioral chain where both exteroceptive- and response-produced cues were relevant. In extinction, when the two sets of cues were placed in conflict, the septal rats relied mainly on the response-produced cues while normal rats displayed random preference.

Changes in the nature of cue selection would be expected on the basis of the septal principles of operation. Damage to the lateral septum would be expected to disrupt the habituative output of the hippocampus and release the amygdala and reinforcer system from inhibition. Hamilton (1969) tested cats with lateral septal lesions on cued active avoidance using several different response measures i.e., jumping on a shelf, one-way jump hurdle, and two-way shuttle box. Facilitation of two-way avoidance was reported and there was no difference between septals and controls on the jump hurdle. The septally lesioned cats showed a consistent deficit on the shelf jump task, however.

The author noted that in the latter task the initial probability of the shelf-jumping response was not high, even in normal cats, unlike the other two response measures. However, the normal cats, after first making escape responses to the shock, eventually came under control of the cue and displayed avoidance. The septal cats learned to make short latency escape responses but never did come under the control of the CS in this task. In the other two tasks the response probability was relatively high and the septally lesioned animals, if anything, seemed to come more strongly under the control of the CS. The pattern of behavior seems to be due to

245

the difficulty septally lesioned animals have in changing control of behavior from one set of cues to another.

Supporting evidence can be found in a number of studies. For example, Ellen et al. (1977) studied extinction behaviors of septally lesioned rats on different operant schedules, some of which involved noncontingent delivery of food. On contingent schedules such as DRL, FI, FR, and VI, the lesioned group barpressed more both in acquisition and extinction, although they were sensitive to the general response contingencies in effect. However, response rates on free operant testing and on a VT schedule did not show any evidence of enhancement. As the authors note, the necessary factor for overresponding seems to be a contingency between the response and reinforcement. Fewer behaviors can apparently be initiated and maintained by delayed reinforcement as we would expect from a reinforcer system acting with a disrupted habituative system.

The enhancement of contingent responding after septal damage is most clearly displayed in DRL schedules, which reinforce a low rate of response. Septal animals do particularly poorly on these schedules because they overrespond and delay reinforcement (Braggio & Ellen, 1976). The addition of cues can facilitate the performance of these animals, but it may do so by changing the essential nature of the schedule. Interestingly, the improved performance with the cue is not maintained after its removal unless it is slowly faded out (Ellen et al., 1977). These deficits tie in very well with the cue processing functions of the septum as outlined here.

If cue shift tendencies are reduced after septal damage, we would expect fewer deficits to occur in reversal tasks which require attention to be spread among a number of different cues rather than just on one or two. To the extent that the reinforcer system and amygdala can increase the strength of a few cues, attentional behavior after septal damage should be more tightly circumscribed since novel cue processing and cue habituation are affected by total septal lesions. Donovick et al. (1979) found that septally lesioned rats were deficient on discrimination tasks that involved the use of newly relevant cues. The lesioned rats failed to attend to such cues and their behavior did not come under their control. The degree to which this deficit was exhibited depended on the difficulty level of the task; the more difficult the task, the less deficient was the performance (Schwartzbaum & Donovick, 1968). Easy discrimination reversals apparently cause the most problem for septally lesioned animals (Chin et al., 1976).

Since spatial cues fall into the category of secondary cues processed by the habituative system, total septal lesions should disrupt such behavior as well. Beatty and Carbone (1980) showed that septal lesions caused performance deficits in an eight-armed radial maze. The task involved the sequential choice of each of the eight arms since reinforcement could be obtained only once in each arm. The addition of external stimuli to make the cue arms distinctive did not help the septally lesioned rats' performance on this complex spatial task. Visual cues did not help improve septal rats' performance in another complex spatial task, the three table reasoning test (Hermann et al., 1980).

Septal Coordination Between the Amygdala and Hippocampus

Although a hypothesis of the septal function has been proposed along with hypotheses of amygdalar and hippocampal function, the interrelationships between the three structures have only been discussed tangentially. It is interesting to speculate on the reasons these structures are interconnected as they are (cf. Figure 2-3).

The septum and the hippocampus have very strong interconnections, both afferent and efferent; the amygdala has a strong efferent connection with the septum; but there is only an indirect connection between the amygdala and hippocampus. The present theory provides a basis for exploring these particular interconnections.

The amygdala processes reinforcers and primary cues, and influences the inhibition of habituative processes in the hippocampus to secondary cues and conditioned reinforcers. It seems to do this indirectly, through neurons in the septum. Swanson and Cowan (1979) have shown that the amygdala has efferent connections running from its medial and central portions to the medial septum via the stria terminalis.

Ranck (1973, 1975) has studied individual neuronal firing patterns in the septum and hippocampus. He found two major types of cells in the nuclei of the medial septum: theta cells and tight group cells. The theta cells fired in the theta rhythm at various times. The tight group cells, however, fired during specific consummatory behaviors. This is important because the amygdala seems to have an efferent connection to this part of the septum (Brazier, 1972; Klinger & Gloor, 1960). It should further be noted that Ranck found cells in the dorsal hippocampus which fired during any consummatory behavior with the exception of paradoxical sleep. Interestingly, these cells seemed to make no distinction among different consummatory behaviors, firing at the same rate for all of them. Berger & Thompson (1978b) have obtained similar findings for neurons in the medial septum, which may drive the hippocampal neurons. Miller & Groves (1977) showed that the medial septum also plays a crucial role in inhibiting neuronal firing of hippocampal neurons after peripheral stimulation.

The septum and hippocampus restore behavioral flexibility in a two-stage process. First, the septum acts to decrease the emotional and motivational differences between reward and nonreward. Second, the hippocampus operates to decrease the value of stimuli and

247

responses that are in declining correlation with reinforcement and processes novel stimuli. The septum needs to be in constant communication with the hippocampus to be able to inhibit its cue processing at appropriate moments. It accomplishes this through its efferent connections to the hippocampus from the medial septum via the dorsal fornix and fimbria, and through the efferent fibers from the hippocampus routed to the lateral septum (Swanson & Cowan, 1977, 1979). Conversely, the hippocampus needs to send information to the septum when rewarded stimuli are no longer being reinforced in order to lift such inhibition. Thus, a strong flow of information between these structures is constantly required (cf. Segal, 1979).

It is apparent from the diagram that the amygdala is somewhat isolated from the other two structures especially when compared to the strong septohippocampal interconnections. This is necessary to protect the functional integrity of the reinforcer and habituative systems. For example, input to the amygdala from the hippocampus could disturb its capacity to recognize reinforcing events. Direct output from the amygdala to the hippocampus could overwhelm its ability to extinguish uncorrelated stimuli and responses. However, the amygdalar output to the septum is crucial, since there must be some way of informing the septum when consummatory behaviors are being performed and reinforcers are being processed in order to suppress unwanted processing by the hippocampus (cf. Buser & Bancaud, 1983).

One other piece of evidence for the current theory is provided by the interconnections between the inferotemporal cortex and the limbic system. The inferotemporal cortex is involved in high-level visual processing. Some aspects of the Kluver-Bucy syndrome of hyperorality and hypersexuality are known to be due to destruction of inferotemporal cortex as well. The inferotemporal cortex has efferent connections to the amygdala and hippocampus but not the septum (Jones & Mishkin, 1972). This is exactly what is required by the present theory. The amygdala and hippocampus would have to receive high-level visual information in order to know whether a reinforcing stimulus, habituated stimulus or novel stimulus had been encountered. On the other hand, in the current theory there is no reason why such information would need to go directly to the septum as well.

SUMMARY

In summary, we can see that the limbic system is composed of two major stimulus processing systems. One system processes salient stimuli such as reinforcers and primary cues and is strongly tied to motivational factors. The other system processes nonsalient stimuli and either registers them as secondary cues if there is inhibition of habituation from primary cues or habituates (extinguishes) them. This division of cue processing is shown to be helpful in explaining certain qualitative differences between cues as well as the dissociation between motivational changes and operant behavior that can often be obtained.

The amygdala is identified as belonging to the system processing salient stimuli, while the hippocampus is placed in the system processing and/or habituating nonsalient stimuli. The septum is regarded as a coordinating structure handling the flow of information between these two structures.

The reinforcer system and its opponent processes in the septum are assumed to be principally involved in the flow of information to the hypothalamus because of its strong involvement in species-specific behavior. The hippocampus is assumed to be more divorced from motivational considerations.

# Section IV
## Memorial Processes of the IPM

In the previous section, we discussed in some detail how the behavioral analysis division of the IPM relates aspects of the stimulus environment with their response consequences (or non-consequences) to the organism. In performing this function, this division necessarily plays an important role in memory formation, particularly with respect to the stimulus dimensions attended to and the affective properties which are integrated into the stimulus representation. However, the term memory is most commonly used in reference to sensory-perceptual processes which involve the manner in which stimulus information is encoded and retrieved and the way in which such memories are functionally organized within the brain. In the present section, we implicitly adopt this more restricted definition in discussing memorial processes, without forgetting that memory formation in reality is the result of an interplay between the behavioral analysis division and the sensory-perceptual division of the IPM.

Because of methodological (and ethical) considerations, infrahumans are the favored means of investigating the functions of the behavioral analysis division. Conversely, methodological considerations make verbal humans the favored means of investigating memorial processes. Thus, many of the studies that are cited in this section use adult humans as subjects. Although the sensory-perceptual division of the IPM is assumed to have substantial similarities across mammalian species, the use of adult humans does pose two problems with respect to the generalizability of the findings from these experiments to other species. The first problem is the obvious species-specificity of sensory-perceptual systems.

However, it is doubtful if basic sensory-perceptual processes (e.g., vision) are completely different from species to species in the mammalian order. The second and more serious interpretive problem in understanding fundamental memorial processes lies in the distinction between structural processes and control processes (cf. Atkinson & Shiffrin, 1968).

In their model of human information processing, Atkinson and Shiffrin argued that such behavior could be due either to the actual structural capacities of the nervous system (e.g., STM capacity, iconic or echoic storage) or to voluntary control processes (e.g., labeling, organization, voluntary attention to one item at the expense of another). Thus, a subject cannot change the amount of STM capacity or the operation of iconic memory, but can affect the amount of organization that a list of words are subjected to during learning. (Although Atkinson & Shiffrin use the term control processes to refer to these voluntary behaviors, I prefer to use the term strategies since it emphasizes their voluntary nature.)

Although the distinction is reasonable and intuitive, and has been accepted by most if not all researchers in human learning, strangely enough it has not had much practical impact either on the orientation or interpretation of research conducted in this area. For example, contradictory results between different studies mean very little in and of themselves if strategies are involved since different people could engage in different strategies.

Battig (1975, 1979) notes that there is a great deal of inconsistency in subjects' approach to learning a list of items for recall, not simply between subjects but also within subjects. Subjects can use two or more different types of strategies for different items in the same list or for two different presentations of the same item (cf. Mathews et al., 1980). Logan & Zbrodoff (1982), using a speeded word discrimination task, showed that subjects' strategies changed in accordance with the informational structure of the task environment and their own cognitive abilities.

In contrast, structural processes must be shown to exist in all normal people and be more insensitive to direct voluntary control. For example, the capacity of iconic or echoic storage cannot be increased in a direct sense (cf. Crowder, 1976). It should be noted that most human learning research is really examining strategies as much as, if not more than, structural processes. Of course, any strategy employed will necessarily interact with the basic processes of the IPM. However, to the extent that the focus is on strategic behavior, there is always the danger that their essentially open-ended nature will be forgotten; i.e., there are an infinite number of rules that can potentially guide behavior. If the distinction between strategies and structural processes is lost sight of, the information processing characteristics of the human IPM will seem more complex than they are.

251

Underwood (1972) in an article entitled "Are We Overloading Memory?" questioned the proliferation of different terms and processes that have developed in the last few decades on human learning and memory. Although he did so from the vantage point of the associationists it is a point worth examining here. From the preceding discussion it should be clear that the answer to Underwood's question will depend on whether we are talking about strategies or processes. If the former, then there is no need to be concerned about a variety of terms to explain the behavior of subjects in particular learning situations. However, if we are talking about processes, then it is highly unlikely that there are many more (if any) additional processes possessed by the IPM in the human species that are not present in some form in animals as well, the one overriding exception being the process underlying symbolic-verbal behavior. In short, it seems probable that there are only a small number of structural processes and it would be wise to emphasize parsimony in our theorizing unless forced by substantial evidence to add factors.

What then are the guidelines we can follow in trying to distinguish the effects of structural processes from those of strategies or rule-based behavior in human learning and memory situations? The first point to consider is whether a particular phenomenon is present in animals as well as humans in substantially the same form. To the extent that it is, we should consider the possibility that essentially the same substrate exists for the phenomenon across animals and humans. Obviously, if there are additional structural processes present in humans this approach will underestimate the number of such processes in humans. However, at this point it is probably better to be conservative in the identification of memory processes in humans anyway.

A second point to consider is the generality of the effect across different types of material, particularly within a specific modality. In human learning experiments, verbal materials of one sort or another are usually the materials presented (e.g., nonsense syllables, words, phrases, sentences). A basic process should, if it exerts an effect on one form of verbal material, exert it on the rest even if not to the same extent. The same logic should apply to pictorial or auditory materials, etc. It is harder to draw conclusions about a lack of generality across modalities simply because major differences in the sensory systems may be responsible. However, if generality is found across different modalities, it provides even stronger support for the existence of some fundamental information processing factor at work.

Generality across different types of subjects is also indicative of a basic process although we have to add the caveat that this may be limited to the normal adult population. Differences in children or the elderly, not to mention the retarded, might well be due to neurological differences between them and the normal adult population. However, we would have to question whether a factor was a structural process if it was found to vary with educational background or sociocultural factors. Although these considerations may seem commonsensical, they are not often applied to the analysis of data to determine if a phenomenon is simply a strategy devised by the subject or is the reflection of an actual structural process.

The third point that should be considered is whether a neurological basis for the phenomenon can be identified or plausibly postulated. Obviously at our present state of knowledge, it can be difficult to specify what neurological substrate might exist for a hypothesized process; however, at a minimum, such processes should not be neurologically implausible.

This discussion of the distinction between strategies and processes is a necessary prelude to the examination of the human learning literature as well as for the foundations of cognitive abilities. Though some discussion is made of strategic behaviors, the focus is more on the interaction of these strategies with the basic structural processes of the IPM.

253

# Chapter 12
## The Structural Processes of Memory

In this chapter, we examine the memorial processes assumed to operate within the sensory-perceptual division of the IPM. Using the same basic approach taken in Chapter 6, we make a few basic assumptions and see how far they and their direct implications can carry us. In so doing, we draw upon the three stimulus analyzing processes that were first discussed in Section II, namely, precision encoding, analogical encoding, and the match-mismatch retrieval process. In addition, two additional processes are included in the theoretical analysis: unrestricted memory formation and indirect activation/inhibition. As in Chapter 6, only a limited amount of empirical data will be presented in this chapter. Such research will be intensively analyzed in the remaining chapters of the book.

### UNRESTRICTED MEMORY FORMATION

Our first assumption is that information processed through the initial stage of sensory analysis (i.e., iconic memory, echoic memory, etc.) is retained in some form permanently in the nervous system (cf. Bernbach, 1969). We will call this process unrestricted memory formation.

Since simple but sweeping statements usually contain a number of implicit assumptions, it is essential that we analyze this idea further and in so doing, deal with the obvious objections that arise. The first point that we want to check is whether such a policy of profligate memory formation will overtax the storage

254

capacity of the nervous system, human or otherwise. On this point there seems to be general agreement that the number of neuronal interconnections known to exist in the human brain are quite sufficient to store a lifetime's amount of memories. As Booth (1973) has noted, even if only one in $10^4$ neuronal interconnections in the human brain were permanently modifiable because of learning there would be ample representational capacity to allow for a steady rate of memory formation.

Second, why is there a distinction between, for example, iconic memory in which some stimulus information is permanently lost and later stages of stimulus processing in which all the information is permanently encoded in some form? It is accepted that before a stimulus can be identified it must be subjected to an initial perceptual analysis of its sensory features. Neisser (1967) defined these precategorical stages of sensory analysis in the visual and auditory systems as iconic and echoic memory respectively.

Research on iconic memory have identified a number of properties which distinguish it from other kinds of memory. For our purposes there are two iconic characteristics which are of interest: a high rate of stimulus processing and a peripheral locus for such processing. Sperling (1963) obtained evidence that visual information can be entered into the iconic store at rates approximating 100 characters per sec, i.e., 10 msec per character. However, the amount of information retained (or at least reported) by the subject is far less, on the order of six characters per second (Von Wright, 1972).

Additionally, iconic memories contain the physical features of the visual stimulus, but not its categorical or semantic attributes (von Wright, 1972). This suggestion of a peripheral processing locus is supported by data indicating that the retinal receptor cells are the site of the iconic store (Sakitt, 1975; Turvey, 1973). Thus, it would seem that the iconic store (and the other sensory registers) represent the initial transformation of stimulus information into a sensory code which is then relayed to the brain. The amount of concurrent information in the stimulus field is greater than the capacity of the central nervous system to process all of it, so that only a part of this information is forwarded at any moment in time. Since it is the receptor cells which are involved in this process, information which is not immediately relayed to higher processing levels will be masked or written over by incoming stimulus information.

The third question that arises from the assumption of unrestricted memory formation for stimuli which have passed through the sensory registers is the status of the short-term memory concept. Up to this point, we have tacitly accepted the idea that short-term memory is something distinct from long-term memory; however, the assumptions put forth in the section on unrestricted memory formation require a more careful analysis than before. Short-term memory has been defined either in terms of the number of discrete items that can be held there or in terms of some temporal limit, e.g., 5+2 items or items that have been entered into memory within the last minute or so (Deutsch & Deutsch, 1975; Miller, 1956).

As we noted above, however, permanent memory formation is assumed to begin almost immediately after the stimulus has been processed through the sensory registers. Thus, in the present IPM, there would seem to be little basis for a neurological or structural distinction between short- and long-term memory at least in the sense of a transient versus permanent store. Empirical evidence nevertheless shows quite a few functional differences between memories of stimuli that have been processed within the previous minute or two and those that have been processed further in the past (Crowder, 1976).

The present theory assumes that once an item passes through the sensory registers it can be in one of two states: working memory and/or permanent memory. Working memory is not quite the same thing as short-term memory since it consists only of those items that are completely activated. Typically no more than two or three distinct items can be kept fully activated at any particular moment. In this view, short-term memory consists of working memory plus those items that have just been entered into permanent memory. Items in working memory are in a complete state of retrieval while those recently entered into long-term memory are not. These latter items have facilitated retrieval properties, however, due to their recency (cf. the later discussion on retrieval processes). All items in short-term memory that have left working memory have a permanent representation of some kind in the brain. In the case of a novel stimulus which has just entered working memory from the sensory registers, a permanent representation would be formed within a very short interval (e.g., 1 or 2 seconds).

One important question about the nature of short-term memories does need to be focused on, this being the apparent permanent loss of memories that are only processed briefly. On an intuitive level, we have experienced the apparently irretrievable loss of items that were recently processed for at least a few seconds, but in transitory or superficial fashion. In the present theory, this would be due to the nature of the precision-encoding capacity of the IPM. If the nature of the memory trace is determined by the neural areas involved in its processing, then stimuli which are processed in more elemental ways are not likely to receive the kind of processing which cross-indexes their features in any systematic way (e.g., cross-modal integration, association). Given match-mismatch retrieval principles, it then becomes extremely difficult to access such a stimulus trace again.   If the item is re-presented, processing may well be more extensive and fail to match for that reason.   On the other hand, if a subject is trying to free recall the trace, it is almost impossible to generate retrieval information or cues which are fragmentary in nature.   Generally speaking, verbal or symbolic cues are used which are well-integrated traces themselves.   Thus, retrieval of elementarily processed traces can, for all practical purposes, be impossible for the subject to retrieve.

## PRECISION ENCODING

Once stimulus information has passed through the sensory registers, it has been transformed into a neural code.   However, memorial encoding of this information is accomplished at later stages of processing in the sensory-perceptual division of the IPM. At this point, two processes discussed in Section II play a major role, namely, precision encoding and analogical encoding.   In this section, we examine the former process.

Precision encoding, as previously discussed, refers to the detailed encoding of the stimulus environment to which the organism has oriented.   The encoded details comprise both intentional or salient attributes of the stimulus field as well as incidental or nonsalient attributes.   Although we have seen considerable evidence for the detailed encoding of the stimulus field in both animals and humans, it is demonstrably true that even the most detailed encoding generally comprises only a part of the total amount of stimulus information present in the environment.   Furthermore, even when we consider just that information which actually impinges on the sensory registers at any moment, research shows that only a small percentage can actually pass on to higher levels of processing (e.g., Sperling, 1963).   What then are the mechanisms that allow organisms to display such sensitivity to the characteristics of the stimulus environment?

One obvious way of overcoming limitations on the amount of information that can be concurrently processed is to engage in successive episodes of encoding the stimulus field.   A common example would be the successive eye fixations that occur when people are presented with a picture to remember (e.g., Vurpillot, 1968). In this way, much of the information contained in the stimulus field can be encoded despite sensory processing constraints.

Another approach to overcoming processing limitations is to recognize that some stimulus attributes contain more information than others.   The informational value of stimulus attributes is complexly determined, of course.   Intense stimuli have high informational value for psychophysical reasons.   Most other stimuli have

257

more contextually determined informational value based on the organism's previous exposure to them and to their association with other stimulus events. Nevertheless, through experience, an organism is able to determine with considerable accuracy those elements of the stimulus field which carry the most information with respect to the selection of appropriate behaviors.

At the neurological level, the process of precision encoding is dependent to a significant degree on the interacting properties of the reinforcer and habituative systems. The processing characteristics of these two systems permit the efficient encoding of both salient and nonsalient attributes of the stimulus environment. It should be noted that this extended range of stimulus processing is not assumed to be due to an increased capacity for simultaneous processing or for working memory per se. Instead, it is based on the processing characteristics of the reinforcer and habituative systems. The constraints on working memory are largely determined by the processing characteristics of the sensory modalities.

ANALOGICAL ENCODING

The Structure of Sensory Systems

The second process operating in the formation of the memorial code is analogical encoding. If it is the case that analogical similarities exist between the external stimulus and the internal representation, this must be due to the perceptual analysis that takes place. Classical thought concerning sensory analysis in humans generally involved the idea of a hierarchical sequence of sensory, association and motor cortex (cf. Diamond, 1979; Merzenich & Kaas, 1980). Stimuli were given elementary sensory analysis in the appropriate sensory modality at subcortical and cortical sensory areas and then integrated in association cortex. The integrated perception then triggered the appropriate impulses to motor cortex which resulted in adaptive behavior.

However, recent research has altered this picture considerably. The emerging picture indicates that the sensory systems in mammals, including humans, are composed of a number of parallel ascending projections coupled with the workings of relatively discrete but interacting systems of analysis. For example, Diamond (1979) has shown that the auditory cortical field in the tree shrew contains parallel pathways which overlap in orderly fashion (cf. Oliver & Hall, 1978). Projections from the auditory thalamus are directed to the auditory cortex. Since the thalamic nuclei are relay centers, it follows that the auditory cortex in the tree shrew qualifies as primary sensory cortex rather than as sensory plus association cortex. Merzenich et al. (1976) demonstrated that the squirrel has two topographically complete representations of the cochlea projected to the cortex. Owl monkeys have four such cochlea representations (Imig et al., 1977) while rhesus monkeys have six (Merzenich & Brugge, 1973).

In other words, there seems to be an increase in the number of cortical sensory representations as we move up the phylogenetic scale. These overlapping sensory projections do not seem to be completely redundant, however. For example Randolph and Semmes (1974) demonstrated that removal of one of the parallel cortical areas for somatosensory analysis would create a quite specific deficit. Destruction of the representation of the hand in area 1 of the monkey's somatosensory cortex caused deficits in tactile discriminations involving texture while a similar lesion of the hand representation in area 2 created deficits in form discrimination. The human neurological literature provides many examples of highly specific deficits resulting from cortical damage (cf. Luria, 1980). Thus, the parallel pathways, more than simply creating analytical redundancy, seem to provide the opportunity for more complex and discriminative analysis of the external stimulus.

In addition, there is increasing evidence that the visual system is composed of a number of interacting but somewhat independent systems. The most studied system extends through the geniculate area through to striate cortex. Formerly, this system was viewed as essential to sight since humans seemed to be blind after lesions to the striate cortex (Anderson & Williamson, 1971). However, other evidence casts strong doubt on this contention since animals have been shown to retain a surprising amount of visual function including localization and discrimination after total extirpation of striate cortex (Humphrey, 1970; Sprague et al., 1977).

A system that has been found to remain functional after geniculo striate system damage is the pulvinar-colliculus prestriate system. Projections from the pulvinar nucleus in the thalamus to prestriate cortex have been found to exist (Diamond et al., 1970; Glendenning et al., 1975). This latter system seems critically involved in localization of visual objects in space. As Humphrey (1970) has noted, there is a great deal of correspondence between the reach and grasp behaviors of monkeys deprived of visual striate cortex and the prey-catching behavior of the toad, which of course has no visual cortex but does possess the pulvinar system.

In humans, recovery from cortical blindness after striate lesions follows a pattern that supports this interpretation of two interacting visual systems. First, perception of light recovers, then movement. Only after this does color and form perception return. One cortically blind patient discussed by Hecaen and Albert (1978) who claimed to be unable to see anything was found to be able to grasp moving objects as we would expect if the pulvinar-prestriate system was still operative. Perhaps most interesting was the finding that he was unable to see or accurately grasp immobile objects regardless of their size. This is strikingly parallel to the prey-catching response of frogs and toads who only strike at moving objects and totally ignore the same objects when immobile.

These kind of findings support the idea that the evolution of the nervous system occurs by the addition of function rather than by the reorganization and the elimination of phylogenetically older functions. Thus, we should not expect sensory analysis to proceed in a simple hierarchical progression of elementary sensory analysis followed by integration and association further on in the system. Instead, certain types of analysis can take place in parallel within a sensory modality either through functionally independent systems as with vision or simply with pathways performing overlapping but somewhat unique discriminations of sensory information as with audition or touch.

## Forms of the Internal Representation

In match-mismatch theory, we have made a point about the encoding of stimulus properties which incorporates in analogical form their relevant characteristics. The evidence that a sensory system can perform a number of at least partially independent analyses on a stimulus provides the basis for potential variety in the nature of its internal representations. To the extent that different kinds of stimuli have different analytical and perceptual processes activated during their processing, we should see systematic differences in the nature of their respective internal representations as well. We would naturally expect this to be the case with stimuli presented in different sensory modalities, but it may also occur within a sensory modality if different dimensions are involved (e.g., form, location, color).

With humans the potential variety of encoding differences is likely to be accentuated because of the interaction of verbal-symbolic processes with the basic perceptual-sensory processes. Thus, through verbal mediation different aspects of the stimulus can be encoded or different kinds of associations can be evoked which transform the stimulus. For example, a concrete noun (e.g., "Boat") might be presented as a spoken word. The subject can of course encode the word as an auditory stimulus. However, the word "Boat" may evoke a visual image of a boat and this could become encoded with the auditory stimulus.

In addition, we would expect systematic processing changes upon repetitions of the stimulus. A completely novel stimulus would be encoded less efficiently since the most economical processing of the differentiating dimensions of the stimulus would be lacking.

Any systematic change in the nature of the perceptual processes used to analyze the incoming stimulus should be expected to result in similar and corresponding changes in the characteristics of the internal representation.

Neurological evidence supports this hypothesis. Yoshii et al. (1957) demonstrated that evoked response wave shapes of CSs recorded from different brain areas became more similar as conditioning proceeded. John (1967) has also shown that an increase in stimulus significance increases ERs in different brain areas. Conversely, when animals acted confused or uncertain, the homogeneity of the ERs deteriorated (cf. Segal & Olds, 1972). Thatcher (in Thatcher & John, 1977) conducted four experiments with variations in the duration of a CS followed by foot shock. As CS duration increased, the heterogeneity of wave patterns across different neural structures also increased. In other words, there was greater complexity in the global representation considered across the brain as a whole. A comparison of the wave form data with behavioral data showed that significantly fewer animals exhibited a CER as the CS duration increased. Thus, increasing complexity of the internal representation was correlated with greater variability of responding (cf. Gabriel et al., 1980).

In some cases, stimulus repetition can lead to automatization of encoding or responding. Automatization refers to the development of fast, accurate and relatively unvarying encoding or responding to a repeatedly presented stimulus or set of stimuli. Consistency across stimulus presentations is critical to the appearance of automatization. With stimulus or response variability automatized encoding does not develop even after extended practice (Kristofferson, 1972; Schneider & Fisk, 1982).

In the current theory, automatization is one aspect of the process of analogical encoding. In such situations lower neuronal regions assume greater control over recognition and responding to a repeated stimulus, which was originally controlled at higher processing levels. In this view, the development of automatization is simply a reflection of the more limited processing capacities of these lower level neurons (which can be cortical or subcortical).

At higher processing levels, neurons are receiving information sufficient to perform the most complex perceptual analysis (encoding) and discriminations of which the organism is capable. Some perceptual or discriminative tasks are so difficult for the organism that even with increasing familiarity all of the sensory-perceptual resources allocated to the task at the beginning of training must remain allocated at essentially the same levels. More typically, however, as a stimulus or set of stimuli become increasingly familiar to an organism, the perceptual operations of encoding the stimulus (set) become more efficient as do the contingent behavioral responses.

261

What is implied when we say that encoding (or responding) has become more efficient?  In general, efficiency involves the reduction of unnecessary encoding operations or response elements. It is this mechanism which is largely responsible for the increased speed characteristic of automatization.  Increases in speed of the individual processing or response operations themselves are assumed to play a minor role at best.  Automatization can develop when increasing stimulus familiarity permits the reduction of the most complex encoding operations on the presented stimulus and this "reduced" stimulus fully specifies a particular behavioral act. The reason for this is simple:  the encoding and response requirements have been reduced to a level which is appropriate to the processing capacities of lower level neurons.

The more elemental the analyses, the more elemental the representation that should be formed.  By this line of thought, the analogical representations formed in automatized processing and responding are quite different from those formed during non-automatized processing.  Repeated presentation of a stimulus leads to increases in its speed of retrieval from memory even when degree of learning (recognition accuracy) is controlled for (Dosher, 1984). Corbett (1977) showed that word pairs studied by rote repetition had faster retrieval speeds but lower asymptotic accuracy than word pairs studied with a visual image mnemonic strategy.  Over multiple testing, however, the retrieval speeds of the mnemonic pairs increased to equal those found in the rote repetition condition.  In the present view, the increases in retrieval speed are due to the reduction of operations needed to encode the presented item or to retrieve it rather than to changes in the rate of retrieval per se.

The related concepts of precision and analogical encoding provide a basis for understanding why individual memories are so resistant to loss as the result of brain damage (cf. Lashley, 1950). If a stimulus is analyzed through a number of different perceptual operations, then memories will be formed which retain the characteristics of those perceptual operations.  These memories will be stored in the neurons and neural regions which perform those perceptual operations.  Almost any stimulus that has been presented a number of times will have various internal representations corresponding to the different analyses performed on it during its reoccurrences.

Brain damage to a particular region can cause the loss of those representations of the stimulus contained in that region but it does not affect other representations located elsewhere.  In this connection, it is important to note that the stimulus is not necessarily represented in numerous identical memories.  Instead, different representations of the same stimulus (set) most typically are distinct ways of encoding their characteristics.  Thus, memories are not so much protected by formal redundancy as by different but overlapping representations stored in the neural regions involved in their encoding.

## THE MATCH-MISMATCH RETRIEVAL PROCESS

To be useful to an organism, a memory which has been encoded and stored must be retrievable under some set of circumstances. From previous discussions it is clear that the match-mismatch process must play a dominant role in memory retrieval. The retrieval of an internal representation requires the presence of a processed or generated retrieval cue that matches part or all of its encoded attributes. This process is assumed to govern all retrieval from memory, whether in animals or humans. Furthermore, it is argued that the match-mismatch process functions with verbal-symbolic material at any level of complexity regardless of the conditions under which retrieval must occur (e.g., recall, recognition).

The requirement of a match between the internal representation and the retrieval cue makes it clear that the nature of the encoded representation will determine what cues can be effective in retrieving the item (cf. Tulving, 1976). In situations where strategies are not likely to be used (e.g., with animal subjects or very young children) we can more safely assume that an unchanging stimulus will be encoded in roughly the same way (i.e., with emphasis on its nominal attributes) across representations, assuming equivalent environmental contexts. This cannot be assumed to be the case in more complex human learning situations. Subjects, using appropriate strategies, can encode the same item differently on different presentations. This creates a potentially difficult circumstance for experimental analysis. If we have trouble knowing precisely what was encoded about a stimulus, it becomes difficult to independently establish the validity of a match-mismatch process at the time of retrieval. The dangers of circularity are quite apparent: If a retrieval cue successfully elicits a particular item we can say that the internal representation contained at least one common attribute. If the cue does not elicit the item then we say there was no overlap. Of course, the problem is that we have no way of independently verifying the encoded attributes of the item independently of the retrieval cues which successfully elicit it.

In this situation, the process of convergent and divergent validation becomes especially critical. The closer the pattern of retrieval cue effectiveness approximates what we would predict from such a position, the more faith we can have in its existence even though no single experiment can demonstrate its validity. For example, we would expect that items which are more difficult to recode or less likely to be recoded due to the circumstances should

263

demonstrate more consistent elicitation by retrieval cues that overlap the nominal attributes. The converse should be demonstrated with items easy to recode or more likely to be recoded.

It should be emphasized that we are only discussing the match-mismatch process itself and not the possible relations between retrieval cues and the encoded trace and the different strategies that can be used by subjects to accomplish a match. There are a potentially large number of contingent factors which can affect the probability of a match between retrieval information and a specific item in memory. However, it must be kept in mind that these contingent factors, while operating on a process, are not structural processes themselves. For example, different instructions at the time of encoding can bias the weight given to various attributes of the TBR item. In addition, a subject can use a retrieval cue which has no direct relationship with a target trace but which does have a match with an attribute of a mediator trace which in turn overlaps with the target trace. However this does not change the fact that the actual retrieval of the target is due to a direct match between at least some feature or attribute of the (mediator) cue with the target trace (cf. Fig. 12-1).

The match-mismatch process might be thought to fit the recognition paradigm comfortably since the retrieval cue in this case is the item itself, even if the contextual information is often changed from what was encoded. Recall, on the other hand, might be viewed as not falling so easily into the hypothesis of a match-mismatch retrieval process which controls all retrieval from memory. In this situation, there are minimal exteroceptive cues or information that are present to match against the target traces. For example, when we are asked to recall a list of words that have been presented, retrieval of the words must take place only with the general retrieval cue "Recall the words that you learned" (in context or situation X).

The apparent lack of a direct match-mismatch process in recall is illusory. Such processes do operate, but within the subject, who generates the appropriate retrieval cues internally. As a number of researchers have noted, the instructions to recall include mention of a particular context (cf. Brown, 1976; Tulving, 1976). In learning a list of words or other stimuli to recall, the items have to be processed in conjunction with a particular context, including possibly the other items to be learned. Thus, a match-mismatch process could occur between memory traces and recall instructions, not in a direct sense but through the elicitation of the particular context by the instructions. The contextual attributes can then be compared directly with memory traces which may contain them. Obviously, this contextual comparison does not offer the best basis for a successful match, but this is only to point out that free recall is in fact a procedure with variable and often quite low retrieval rates.

**Indirect Activation and Inhibition**

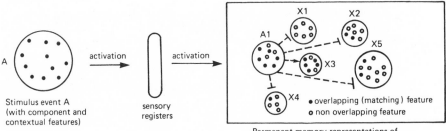

**Mediation**

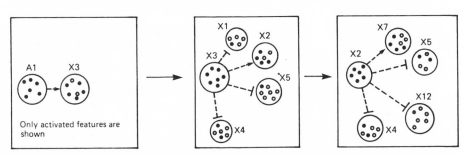

**Fig. 12-1 . Indirect Activation/ Inhibition .** A) The activation of one internal representation (A1) leads to the activation of another representation which has the greatest degree of overlap (X3) and the inhibition of other less-related representations. B) Mediation can occur through the mechanism of the match-mismatch process. A retrieval cue (A1) does not directly match the target representation (X7), but does match X3 which matches X2 which matches X7.

## INDIRECT ACTIVATION/INHIBITION

One other memorial structural process is the indirect activation (priming) or inhibition (damping) of other internal representations by a previously activated representation. Firm neurological

265

evidence exists for the idea that the activation of one (or multiple) neurons leads to the activation or inhibition of certain other neurons. For example, lateral inhibition, in which one neuron inhibits a neighboring neuron, is known to operate in the sensory systems as a means of enhancing contrast between stimuli (cf. Walley & Weiden, 1973).

Since we are postulating the analogical encoding of stimuli in the sensory systems, it follows that the internal representations of stimuli, whether verbal-symbolic or not, should also be affected by the process of indirect activation or inhibition. Our basic assumption about the memorial effects of indirect activation/inhibition is that the initial activation of a particular internal representation causes a decrease in the latency to achieve response threshold in closely associated internal representations and an increase in response threshold latencies to the others (cf. Lorch, 1982). A related assumption is that the simultaneous activation of multiple internal representations leads to a mutual inhibition which decreases the probability that the response threshold of any individual representation will be reached.

Let's examine some of the implications of these assumptions. When a retrieval cue is presented to the subject, the match-mismatch process runs a comparison of the features or attributes of the cue with the contents of memory. The internal representation whose response threshold is most rapidly attained will become activated and thus be retrieved from memory. This representation will obviously be the item in memory corresponding to the retrieval cue itself. The activation of this representation will in turn partially or fully activate closely associated representations. We can conceive of these partially activated representations as part of a larger set of associated representations. Depending on the context in which the retrieval cue is occurring, a particular subset of these associated representations will be partially or fully activated. The context, of course, is simply an additional set of stimuli and could comprise verbal instructions, additional discriminative stimuli, background cues, etc. (cf. Becker, 1979; Meyer & Schvaneveldt, 1971).

Representations can be associated either through contiguity (correlation) or by the sharing of features/attributes. Since any particular representation comprises multiple features, the subset of featurally related representations activated at any particular time will be more dependent on changes in the contextual environment surrounding the retrieval cue than will contiguity-related representations. Contextual changes would produce changes in the relative weights assigned to the features of the internal representation. On the other hand, item associations based on contiguity would not be as sensitive to the particular features biased by a

266

given occurrence of the retrieval cue, since that is not the basis of their relationship.

The size of the subset of associated representations that are primed must be narrow if the two theoretical assumptions are to hold. If it were not narrow, then multiple representations would be retrieved simultaneously. However, by our second assumption such multiple activation would produce mutual inhibition which would prevent the representations from attaining their response threshold. Also, the rarity of intrusions of unrelated or distantly related memories during retrieval would argue against this notion (cf. Underwood, 1983). In fact, there is considerable evidence that increasing the number of unrelated facts about a concept makes recall or recognition of any individual fact more difficult i.e., fan effects (Anderson, 1983; Whitlow, 1984). A study by de Groot (1983) indicates that the priming stimulus can activate only its direct associate with further automatic spread ruled out. Conversely, an increase in the number of related primes presented to the subject produces increases in recognition latencies for the target item (Neely et al., 1983; cf. Watkins, 1979).

It is important to note that the particular encoding strategies engaged in by a subject will play a critical role in determining which representations will be primed (or inhibited) by a retrieval cue. For example, it comes as little surprise that the semantic attributes of a word used as a priming stimulus are a far stronger determinant of recognition latencies for target words than are its orthographic or other physical attributes (Meyer et al., 1974). However, functional distinctions such as these are not based on structural mechanisms and thus could be modified or reversed with appropriate instructions or practice.

Summary

Five structural processes critically involved in the encoding and retrieval of memorial representations have been discussed. Initial registration of information occurs through the unrestricted memory formation process, which preserves information remaining in active memory past some criterion value (generally, a few seconds). Such information may enter active memory either through the sensory registers or through retrieval from permanent memory. Memories become organized through the continual formation of traces with overlapping attributes. The form that such representations take is a function of the precision encoding process and its related analogical encoding capabilities. Each different perceptual-analytical operation on the processed trace leaves its own representation in appropriate neural areas. This means that stimuli are represented in multiple, non-identical representations throughout the brain. Memories are retrieved through the operation of the match-mismatch retrieval process, either through the direct match of retrieval information with the target trace or through a mediated chain of such matches. The activation of a memorial representation leads to the activation of closely associated representations and the inhibition of other representations through neuronal processes such as collateral and concurrent inhibition. In addition, through the same processes, the simultaneous activation of multiple representations causes mutual inhibition which prevents individual representations from attaining response threshold (retrieval).

THE FUNCTIONAL CHARACTERISTICS OF MEMORIES

In this part of the chapter, we are going to examine some of the ways in which the five memorial processes interact with each other and produce some of the most general features of the memory system. In particular, the focus will be on the way that the functional characteristics of memories change as they become associated with other memories, subjected to interference, or increase in abstraction. As part of our discussion, the concept of study-phase retrieval will be introduced. This mechanism, directly derivable from the structural processes of memory, involves the retrieval of items from memory while another representation resides in working memory.

The Formation of Memorial Associations

One of the most salient features of the memory system is that memories have varying degrees of association with each other. Differences in interitem association are characteristics of animal as well as human memory (cf. Hulse et al., 1978; Underwood, 1983). However, since research on human memory has been much more extensive than that with animals (at least until recently) we will concentrate on the literature using human subjects.

In the most popular current view, the human memory system is described as a complex network of interrelated memory modes (e.g., Anderson, 1983; Kintsch, 1974). Retrieval of one memory trace provides differential access to other memory traces depending on the degree of association between them.

The network models assume that individual concepts or propositions are contained in memory nodes. Related concepts or nodes have stronger or more extensive interconnections. When new information is processed, it tends to activate memory nodes that are related to it. For example, a new fact about Abraham Lincoln would activate at least some of the existing memory nodes which contain propositions dealing with Abraham Lincoln. The new datum would be stored in its own memory node but would have interconnections with those nodes that it had activated during processing. Most of these network theories assume that contextual information (e.g., the circumstances in which the new datum about Abraham Lincoln was learned) are attached to the relevant memory node in some way. However, the connection between node and attached context is not infallible (i.e., one can activate the memory node on occasion without activating the surrounding contextual information or vice versa).

It is fair to say that network theorists have been most concerned with developing models which predictively simulate the semantic organization and retrieval capacities of the human memory system. There has been less attention or interest in the degree of correspondence between the operating assumptions of the model and the actual structural processes of human memory. However, in the present view, it is going to be difficult to develop predictively accurate memory models in the absence of a clear knowledge of these structural processes. With this in mind, we will see if the hypothesized processes in the present theory provide a plausible basis for the construction of an organized memory store. As was noted above, two kinds of associative relationships can be identified: those based on featural relationships and those based on contiguity (correlation). It is argued that these two associative relations involve different interactions of the hypothesized memorial processes. For this reason, they represent a good way to begin our examination of process interactions.

Featural Associations. Memories can be associated with each other because they share a common feature or attribute. Such common attributes are typically perceptual in nature. With these associations, we have a relatively straightforward interaction of the precision and analogical encoding processes with the match-mismatch comparison process at the time of retrieval. For example, in encoding the list of words fire-engine, strawberry, cherry, stoplight, we could emphasize the perceptual feature of color (i.e., red) as an associative mechanism. Thus, the nature of the encoding is critically important to the formation of featural associations since the weight assigned to the different attributes of the items' representation will determine the set of featurally associated items.

It should be noted that featural associations can be formed in the absence of any objective or subjective contiguity between two items. The critical factor is whether the same retrieval cue can independently match each item's representations. Because of this, the featural association between two items may be first established, even to the subject, at the time of retrieval by the capacity of a retrieval cue to elicit both items (cf. Slamecka, 1968). By

269

reducing the number of distinct retrieval cues needed to match the traces, the number of matches required for retrieval of the items is reduced. This kind of "revealed" association is more likely with featural associations based on common perceptual attributes than with common conceptual attributes.

Contiguity-Based Associations. Although featural associations based on common perceptual and conceptual attributes play an important role in the association of memories, they cannot account, by themselves, for the powerful memorial organization found in humans. The other mechanism by which humans can associate various internal representations is based on contiguity (correlation), both objective and subjective. By objective contiguity, we mean the correlation of two stimulus events in the environment; subjective contiguity (study-phase retrieval) is the correlation of two internal representations in the working memory of the subject (Hintzman, 1976; Jacoby, 1974). While one stimulus is being processed, other memories can be activated or retrieved from memory and thus be placed in conjunction with the processed stimulus in working memory.

The mechanism of study-phase retrieval and subjective contiguity can be shown to flow directly from the hypothesized memorial processes. When a stimulus acting as a retrieval cue is entered into working memory, it will activate closely associated representations in memory through the process of indirect activation or priming or it will contain attributes which directly match particular representations. If such associates are retrieved from inactive memory, they are entered into working memory. However, the retrieval cue is also in working memory. By the principle of unrestricted memory formation, this conjunction of items now residing in working memory will be encoded as another representation and it will be added to the set of representations in permanent memory. The precise set of associations will be somewhat idiosyncratic from subject to subject since each person will have a somewhat different pattern of study-phase retrieval of items from memory elicited by the items being processed.

There is quite a bit of experimental evidence for the study-phase retrieval of items from memory. The study of implicit associative responses (IAR) has demonstrated not only that they occur, but also that they exert an influence on memory for the items which elicit them (cf. Underwood & Schulz, 1960). For example, cross associate lists are more difficult to learn than control lists in which the stimulus or response terms are not associated (Spence, 1963). In the cross-associate list, highly associated word pairs are used, but each term is randomly paired with a term from another pair (dog-chair; cat-table). The increased difficulty of the cross-associate lists can be accounted for by the occurrence of IARs to the related terms.

270

The occurrence of IARs can also exert a positive influence on learning when the conceptual relationships are not made deliberately interfering (e.g., Underwood et al., 1975). It is argued that such study-phase retrieval of related information from permanent memory plays an important role in organizing domains of information or stimulus materials. Such organization develops through the constant overlap of presented material with previously encoded traces that have been elicited by the input stimulus.

The process being outlined here implies that there is much duplication of memories. Let's say that a subject is sequentially presented with five sentences containing factual information about Abraham Lincoln not previously known by him/her. From this set of circumstances, the subject will have a representation of the first sentence (A) which also contains whatever additional information was elicited from permanent memory during A's tenure in working memory. When the second sentence (B) is presented, the same process holds true except that information from the first sentence may also be contained in B's representation. It should be emphasized that only that information retrieved about A will be contained in the joint encoding. That is, the subject may only retrieve the gist or meaning of sentence A while studying B and it is this information which will be contained in B's representation.

It should be remembered that the process of unrestricted memory formation assumes that the subject forms a permanent representation of items in working memory whether they have been presented externally or recalled from permanent memory (cf. Klee & Gardiner, 1976). Of course, the subject may well be able to distinguish between representations formed in these two ways.

We will assume that the learning situations have established the following pattern of traces in permanent memory: "A," "BA," "C," "DB," "EAB." If we present item A again as a retrieval cue, it will most strongly match trace "A" in memory. However, it will also partly match traces "BA" and "EAB" in which "A" was study-phase retrieved in conjunction with the processing of other items. Once, say, the "AB" trace is retrieved by the subject it can be used in a match-mismatch process to retrieve trace "DB." The likelihood of a trace being retrieved is, of course, dependent on how good a match can be made between the active trace and the to-be-retrieved trace. In addition, in real life it is obvious that study-phase retrieval might also involve memory traces not directly acquired in the learning situation (e.g., there may be activation of memory traces of other people alive during Lincoln's life, of historical events not contained in the sentences, and so on).

It should now be seen how the content of the memory store can become organized: it is through the constant overlap of presented material with previously encoded traces that have been elicited either by or in the process of encoding the input stimulus. Thus, we can have an organized search through memory or even inferential reasoning while still retaining the requirement of a match-mismatch retrieval process for the activation of any trace stored in memory.

In the current conception, a functional interconnection of related concepts exists mainly because related items tend to be evoked during processing of new items and automatic memory formation then preserves this conjunction. Study-phase retrieval permits a more powerful organization of memories than featural association because it creates conjoint representations of diverse but related information rather than relying on the emphasis on a shared feature. This property permits the construction of associations in which the relations between representations are more complex or less clearly understood. Thus, study-phase retrieval permits the development of organized networks or domains of information that would overtax the capacity of a common featural attribute to function as a retrieval cue.

Transformations in understanding a subject matter can make use of these different traces by simply forming some additional traces with the new interpretation encoded in conjunction with some of the previous information. In that way, access to the information contained in the previous conceptualization or organization is assured. The retrieved information can then be evaluated in light of the new conceptualization without having to totally modify all the interconnections that previously existed.

## The Effects of Correlational Processing on Memories

In the previous section, we spent some time examining the way in which organisms display sensitivity to the correlation between stimulus events in conditioning paradigms. To the extent that conditioning is simply the memory for the circumstances in which emotion-producing stimuli occurred this phenomenon should have important implications for the characteristics of memorial representations.

Actually, study-phase retrieval is implicit in the perception of stimulus correlations. In order to assess the correlation between two stimulus events, the organism (human or animal) has to be able to evaluate current stimulus relations in the context of their previous occurrences. At this point, we will examine more closely the memorial effects of study-phase retrieval when an already encoded stimulus is presented again to an organism. Initially, we will deal with situations in which a stimulus, originally correlated with another stimulus event, is re-presented in correlation with a different stimulus event. Then we will turn to situations in which the same stimulus is simply re-presented to the organism.

Stimulus Interference. One of the more ubiquitous findings in the learning literature is the difficulty in learning new stimulus correlations which conflict with previously learned correlations of those same stimuli. Reversal learning (A-B, C-D -> A-D, C-B), blocking (A-B -> AX-B), paired associates (A-B -> A-D) and contingent to non-contingent discriminative responding (A-B -> Ā-B) are some of the procedures which involve changed stimulus correlations, and in each, organisms display deficits in learning the new correlation of stimulus events, i.e., proactive interference (PI). In addition, once the new stimulus correlations are learned, organisms display increased forgetting of the original stimulus correlations compared to situations with no change in stimulus correlations i.e., retroactive interference (RI).

If the approach taken here is correct, then all these interference effects should be the result of the operation and interaction of the same structural processes of memory. For simplicity's sake, lets focus on the standard verbal learning interference paradigm in which the subject learns different response terms to the same stimulus term (A-B -> A-D).

We will start off by assuming that a series of A-B associations have already been learned by a subject and that the A-D list is now being presented. First of all, we can make the assumption that the presentation of the "A" term again will lead to some intrusions (covert or overt) of the previously learned A-B association. Presentation of the "A" term should make contact with the trace(s) containing the recent A-B association in a significant proportion of cases and lead to its study-phase retrieval. If the "B" term is retrieved while the subject is studying the A-D pair, the provision of unrestricted memory formation predicts that the "B" term will have a significant probability of being embedded in the trace containing the A-D term. Whether it is embedded or not depends on the length of time it remains in primary memory and also the number of times it is retrieved during the relevant A-D presentations. However, since intrusion of the "B" term in A-D presentations diverts processing capacity from learning of the new association, the subject will try to suppress the occurrence of the "B" response unless instructed otherwise (cf. Ceraso et al., 1982).

In the present theory, the suppression of the "B" term is due to the operation of the habituative process( and thus the habituative system). The difference between the response suppression that typically occurs in verbal learning and that which occurs say, in extinction procedures, is the degree to which the subjects themselves supply the outcome of non-reinforcement. With biological reinforcers, the organism responds to the omission of a specific exteroceptive stimulus. In most verbal learning procedures, the nonreinforcement is more subtle for inappropriate responding. Nevertheless, in both situations inappropriate responding leads to non-favored outcomes (e.g., perceptions of poor performance, delays in finishing the task, etc.).

In such circumstances, the habituative system is activated and the stimuli and/or responses which lead to non-favored outcomes (i.e., the "B" terms in our current example) are processed through this system. It should be remembered that the habituative process suppresses the retrieval of non-reinforced representations into working memory but does not erase those memories. If it did, then habituation would not occur because a match-mismatch process between the internal representation and the exteroceptive stimulus would be impossible. In addition, habituation will occur only for those attributes involved in the habituative comparison process. In the current example, the attributes of the "B" term which are retrieved from permanent memory and non-reinforced subjectively are habituated. Any other attributes of the representation which have not been retrieved, however, are not affected.

While the "B" term is being habituated, the subject is, of course, acquiring the new correlation of the "A" term with the "D" term. The acquisition of the A-D association is negatively affected by the processing capacity which is being devoted to the habituation of the "B" term, i.e., PI is occurring. It should be remembered that the "B" term is not a "neutral" stimulus since it has been highly correlated with "A." Thus, its habituation will take longer than if it were an unrelated term. When the acquisition of the A-D association has reached asymptotic or criterion levels, retrieval of the habituated "B" term becomes less probable (RI), because of the new high correlation between A and D.

This analysis suggests that the suppression of the "B" term is the major reason for the interference effects found in the A-B -> A-D paradigm. To the extent that the subject can learn the new A-D association without having to suppress the old A-B association, RI and PI should be reduced. Logically speaking, there are two ways in which the subject could attempt to perform this feat: integrate both the "B" and "D" terms into a unitary representation or encode the A-D association in a representation which is highly distinctive and discriminable from the A-B association (cf. Gilani & Ceraso, 1982; Lockhart et al., 1976; Nelson, 1979). By integrating the "B" and "D" terms, the subject can forgo suppressing the "B" term when it undergoes study-phase retrieval during A-D acquisition. By differentiating the A-B and A-D association, the subject minimizes the probability of retrieval of the "B" term during the A-D study phase or during attempted retrieval of the "D" term at the time of testing.

Another potential source for interference effects is the use of a retrieval cue which matches the attributes of a multiplicity of traces. In the present example, this would seem to be a less significant source of interference simply because there are only two such traces. In such a situation the process of indirect

274

activation/inhibition would not likely produce the complete inhibition of one or both traces through mutual interaction. However, in other situations with a multiplicity of common attribute traces, the retrieval cue might well be an important source of interference effects.

It is argued that interference effects in the different transfer paradigms are due to the operation of the same basic mechanisms discussed above. Each transfer paradigm will influence the degree to which each source of interference manifests itself in characteristic ways, but the basic mechanisms remain the same across procedures.

Stimulus Abstraction. Study-phase retrieval can involve not only the representations which have been associated with the retrieval cue but the representations of the retrieval cue (priming stimulus) itself, i.e., repetition effects. Numerous experiments and everyday experience confirm the importance of stimulus repetition in enhancing the retrievability of representations (e.g., Crowder, 1976). If the memorial processes are valid, then they should be able to provide some insight into the mechanism underlying this phenomenon. For now, we will focus on effects of repetition on the recognition of a stimulus item.

In match-mismatch theory, the basic abstractive processes are viewed as the result of the interaction of the correlational processing of stimulus information with the structural memory processes of the IPM. It is hypothesized that stimulus repetition increases the retrievability (recognizability) of that item's representation from permanent memory through the abstraction of its constituent attributes. In this view, repetitions of a stimulus permit the construction of a representation which contains fewer irrelevant attributes. The reduction of non-essential attributes permits the assignment of increased weights to relevant defining attributes of the stimulus event. Thus, the item's representation can be matched and retrieved with less complex or elaborate retrieval information.

Logically, what minimal conditions must exist for abstraction to be possible in a novel situation without the communication of a rule to the subject. First of all, there have to be at least two occurrences of an event or stimulus, since the unique event is not susceptible to appropriate information reduction. Second, the organism or subject would have to perceive some similarity or resemblance between the two events. This does not have to operate at the conscious level. However, the second event would have to initiate the study-phase retrieval of at least one representation of the prior event so that they could be processed in conjunction with each other. Third, there must be some mechanism by which the commonalities between the two events are emphasized at the expense of those features which are idiosyncratic to each (cf. Figure 12-2).

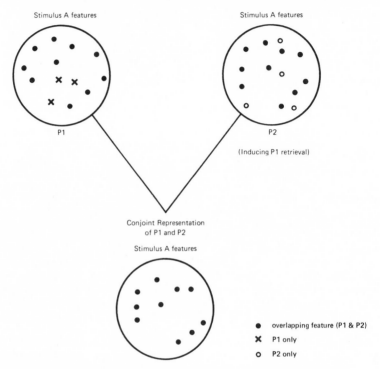

**Fig. 12-2. Stimulus Abstraction.** Through the correlational analysis of repeated stimulus events, features which are idiosyncratic to particular occurrences drop out in favor of features correlated across presentations.

A subject is presented with a TBR word that we will assume is completely novel. On the first presentation the subject encodes the word and whatever other stimulus information is present in working memory at that time. For example, if the word appears printed at the top of a page in a text, we would assume that this information would be encoded along with the word to some extent. There might be other contextual elements such as the room where the subject encountered the word, the sentential context, etc. In short, the structural process of precision encoding is operative.

Later, the subject encounters the word in a different situation, say, while reading a magazine at home. The word has been encoded so that the visual or auditory presentation of the same word can make at least a partial match with the original trace; in this case, we will assume that the visual presentation of the word does in fact result in a strong enough match with the trace that a retrieval of the item takes place. Since the item is being represented, we can term it a study-phase retrieval of the original trace. Since precision encoding is operative, the context of the second presentation of the item will again be processed.

There is a major difference in the processing of the second presentation of the item, namely, the presence in working memory of the first trace of the item. Let's assume that the second time the word appears, it again is at the top of a page of text, although this time it is in a magazine rather than a book. In addition, the same basic sentential context is present so that the meaning and connotation of the second presentation is close to that of the first. However, the other contextual features of the first trace are not present in the second.

Upon study-phase retrieval of the first trace, the subject now has available both traces at the same time in working memory. Given the recognition of the item, the subject is orienting most strongly on those aspects of the traces which matched, i.e., are common to both. Less salient details and idiosyncratic details that are not distinctive in some way will often receive less processing and less representation in memory. The reason for this lies in part with attentional processes but also in the operation of unrestricted memory formation. The common features will be represented in the traces of both occurrences of the item. They will also be represented in the conjoint trace. In this latter trace, the common features may be more salient than in the two individual item traces. As we know from perceptual organization or gestalt principles, there is a tendency for irregular elements to be modified in favor of a simpler, more coherent structure.

In the case of conditioned stimuli examined in the previous section, we have a clear-cut case of the favoring of repeated common elements in the acquisition of associative strength as opposed to idiosyncratic, unique elements. A stimulus element which occurs once in proximity to reinforcement will lose associative strength to those stimulus elements which occur repeatedly in proximity to the reinforcer. Thus, the greater the correlation of particular features or attributes of the stimulus situation across presentations, the more likely that such features will gain in associative strength relative to those features that do not display such correlation.

It is argued that the correlational principle of association can be applied to the stimulus attributes of the target stimulus in the same way as to the predictive or correlated cues which precede it. Those attributes or features of the target stimulus which are not highly correlated with it should lose associative or representational strength vis-à-vis more highly correlated features.

277

In the case of the associative relation of various attributes of the target to the target, we are dealing essentially with the question of trace characteristics. Thus, it would seem that the way to determine the correlation or associative relation between individual attributes and the target is to use memory tests which reveal trace composition. This can be done either by varying the nature of the retrieval cues used to elicit the item from memory or by varying these attributes in the target and seeing how recognition is affected (cf. Rescorla, 1980; Watkins, 1979).

From the above analysis it can be seen that repeated presentation of a stimulus results in the elimination of idiosyncratic or low-correlated attributes because of interference or habituation. Since the idiosyncratic elements vary from presentation to presentation they are likely to interfere with the prior contextual stimuli. On the other hand, the commonalities will match from presentation to presentation and will tend to predominate more and more in the new encodings for two reasons:  they will not suffer from interference, and the attention of the subject will be focused more and more on those recurring elements, resulting in less processing time for the less correlated attributes.

Given that the correlational process of association can result in the elimination of less correlated attributes of a stimulus or stimulus relationships, how does this affect the retrievability of the item?  It has been argued that retrieval probability is dependent on the accessibility of the item (i.e., the conditions under which the item can be retrieved).  Items which are retrievable only with atypical or multi-attribute retrieval information are generally going to be accessible under more restricted conditions than items which are retrievable through standardized retrieval information which is of simpler structure.  It is precisely the removal of idiosyncratic elements which can aid accessibility in more circumstances because of a reduction in the number or complexity of the cues necessary to achieve a match with the stored trace. Indirectly, this process also aids the organization of memory by making it easier to usefully categorize the item.

SUMMARY

The fundamental processes of memory interact with each other to form the substrate of the observed characteristics of memory. The neurological structure and interconnections of the sensory systems are shown to exert a powerful influence on the nature of stimulus encodings.  The level at which a stimulus is processed in a sensory system determines the degree to which automatization can develop.

    Particular kinds of process interactions are hypothesized to underlie the phenomena of memorial associations, interference (negative transfer) and repetition effects. The mechanism of study-phase retrieval is shown to be a natural consequence of the operation of the structural processes of memory. Its importance in producing a structured memorial content and its role in the occurrence of stimulus interference and abstraction is described.

279

# Chapter 13
## Encoding and Retrieval

In this chapter, we examine some of the research on encoding and retrieval operations with particular emphasis on the human literature. In so doing, we see what support can be gained for the theoretical arguments presented in the previous chapter. First, we see if one of the main tenets of unrestricted memory formation can be maintained, namely, the permanent registration of information passing through the sensory registers. For this to be true, there cannot be a structural difference between STM and permanent memory although there may well be functional differences. Next, the process implications of encoding strategies and imagery are discussed. Finally, we turn our attention to the interaction of encoding and retrieval operations in the context of such phenomena as encoding specificity, recall and recognition, and rehearsal effects.

### THE NATURE OF STM

The possibility that the functional distinction between STM and LTM is based on different underlying structural processes has been under consideration since William James (1890). In large part, this idea has been based on the many observed differences between short- and long-term retention. However, such differences may be due to the operation of different contingent factors that operate only at short- or long-term retention intervals. Therefore, if a separate STM is assumed to exist, it must be shown that there is at least one structural process unique to it. If STM is essentially part of the same memory system as LTM, then the different results should be ascribable simply to contingent factors. It should be emphasized that working memory is not equated with STM in the current theory. A structural difference is assumed to exist between working or fully active memory and permanent or inactive memory. STM, as typically measured, includes not only fully active items but also items recently processed in the preceding minute or two.

Waugh and Norman (1965) and Atkinson and Shiffrin (1968) both proposed a memory system containing separate short- and long-term stores. In both of these models perceived information is first represented in a limited capacity, primary memory system. Some information is lost while in the short-term store, but other information is rehearsed and transformed into secondary or permanent memory. Atkinson and Shiffrin contended that it is processing capacity rather than storage capacity that is limited. Complex encoding operations are likely to reduce the available storage capacity for even routine tasks.

Information must pass through STM before it can be stored in LTM. Loss of information from the short-term store is assumed to be permanent but is based on standard interference principles, i.e., the number or character of intervening items. One of the most important ways in which information is transferred from STM to LTM is through the mechanism of rehearsal, which allows more time for coding operations to take place. Thus, one of the key assumptions inherent in this approach is the slow consolidation of memories into a permanent form. This issue will receive our attention at this point.

Consolidation

The assumption that memories must remain in STM for some period of time before transfer can take place into LTM implies that permanent traces cannot be formed or initiated immediately after initial perceptual processing. Instead, a certain fixed or variable time must elapse while consolidation (presumably chemical or neuronal in nature) takes place (e.g., Hebb, 1949).

A wide variety of electrical and chemical interventions have been studied in order to see if the process of permanent trace formation could be delayed or prevented. For example, electroconvulsive shock (ECS), or the application of an intense electrical stimulus to the brain, has been found to result in deficits of memory formation in both humans and animals (e.g, Spear, 1978; Kihlstrom & Evans, 1979). ECS can dramatically accelerate forgetting of events up to one hour prior to its administration. The basis for such forgetting is not clear, however, since ECS has multiple physiological effects. A single ECS has been shown to produce heart rate changes and weight loss (Routtenberg & Kay,

1965) and decreased intake of food and water (Layden & Birch, 1969). ECS also has profound biochemical consequences such as the reduction in total RNA in certain neural areas, and a general decrement in protein synthesis, both of which have been suspected as prime determinants of memory formation.

Since loss of an item from STM is assumed to be total, if an ECS prevents consolidation, there should be no savings in relearning the material. However, after a second sequence of administration of amnestic agents, animals often behave as if they had not received any amnestic treatment at all (Kesner et al., 1970; Riccio & Stiles, 1969) even with adaptation effects controlled (Jensen & Riccio, 1970). In addition, there is a surprising number of different experiences that will serve to prevent retention deficits. For example, Jensen and Riccio (1970) showed that the amnesic effects of hypothermia following passive avoidance training were prevented in rats exposed to other avoidance tasks (cf. Hinderliter et al., 1975).

The finding that memory becomes progressively less vulnerable to disruption is well-documented in both humans and animals (Barbizet, 1970; McGaugh & Herz, 1972). The period of so-called consolidation is surprisingly variable, ranging from seconds (Chorover & Schiller, 1965) to hours (Kopp et al., 1966) and perhaps years (cf. Cohen & Squire, 1984). In addition, some selectivity in amnesic effect has been noted depending on whether the response measured is motoric or autonomic in nature. For example, ECS after Pavlovian conditioning clearly results in amnesia for skeletal responses but not for HR (Mendoza & Adams, 1969). However, Davis and Holmes (1971), using fish, showed that ECS after Pavlovian conditioning of brachial pump movements induced amnesia for this autonomic response. Springer (1975) showed that studies demonstrating amnesia for both skeletal and autonomic responses had used higher levels of ECS than those that showed no amnesia for autonomic responses. He demonstrated that a steeper gradient exists for autonomic responses (cf. Gold & King, 1974).

One might expect older memories to be invulnerable to the effects of amnestic agents since the consolidation process should presumably have been long completed. However, results by Squire (1974) indicate that memory over 20 years old can be disturbed. In addition, many studies support the idea that amnestic agents, rather than stopping the process of memory formation, simply slow it down (Mah et al., 1972). Recovery from amnesia also does not seem consistent with a long-term consolidation process. Amnesic effects from such agents often retreat from loss of memory for events an hour to a few seconds before the administration of ECS (cf. Kihlstrom & Evans, 1979).

The evidence thus is quite mixed concerning the existence of some consolidation process lasting longer than a second or two prior to which memories are lost permanently and subsequent to which they are retained permanently. Strictly behavioral evidence also provides little support for such a slow consolidation process. Smith et al. (1971) found that imagery instructions in contrast to repetition instructions led to increased recall of the prerecency portion of a list of noun pairs. However, the repetition group had higher primary memory scores. This creates a logical problem since transfer from STM to LTM is supposed to depend on the degree to which the memory is stored in STM. On the other hand, high autonomic arousal can impair STM but facilitate LTM (Kleinsmith & Kaplan, 1963).

Kesner and Connor (1972) provide data from rats which seem to rule out serial STM-LTM transfer. Rats were given foot shock contingent on a well-learned barpressing response and 4 seconds later received stimulation to the medial reticular formation or hippocampus. The MRF group failed to exhibit normal suppression when tested one minute later but exhibited normal suppression 24 hours later. The hippocampal group showed just the opposite pattern. This makes parallel STM-LTM processing the only viable option, although it is puzzling why there would be separate STM-LTM stores if processing is occurring automatically in parallel.

A study by Wickelgren et al. (1980) raises questions about the distinction between short-term and long-term memories in another way. Subjects saw 16 consonants presented serially. Following a blank interval, a test consonant was presented which subjects judged to be present or not present on the previous list. Memory strength, as assessed by speed-accuracy tradeoff responding, declined over a 6-second interval containing 12 items. However, the priming of retrieval dynamics was found only for the last item in the set. Thus, active memory may only exist for the one or two different items which can be held simultaneously in a completely active state. This would imply that the other items in STM may be differentially accessible but may not constitute active memory in the strict sense (cf. Balota & Engle, 1981).

This evidence relating to the consolidation and transfer of information from short-term to long-term stores casts doubt on the notions that short-term memory is identical with active memory and represents a structurally distinct memory system from LTM. In addition, there seems to be little solid evidence in favor of a serial transfer of information from STM to LTM.

Differential Retrieval Characteristics of STM Versus LTM

Much evidence suggests that the loss of items from STM may be due to interference rather than to some decay process peculiar to STM (cf. Tulving, 1968; Jacoby, 1974). Items in STM are more accessible because of a number of factors having a bearing on retrieval. First of all, there is little change of contextual cues and thus no diminution in context matching of retrieval cue and trace. Second, there are fewer items which have occurred after the targets' presentation, thereby reducing the probability of retroactive interference (RI). Third, there is greater opportunity for use of temporal cues in differentiating items.

Tulving and Patterson (1968) gave subjects serial lists that had four highly related words in the middle or end of the list or had no such words. The related words were recalled better than the controls when in the middle of the list but not at the end. The authors suggested that temporal cues were used for retrieval of end items, while organizational, associative cues were used for retrieval of middle items (cf. Buschke, 1974; Ritter et al., 1974).

One line of evidence used to support the idea of a structurally distinct STM has been the recency effect in serial position learning. Typically, the last few items on a serial list are remembered better than the other items, particularly those in the middle of the list. Items at the beginning are remembered better than the middle items but generally not quite as well as the last items. (This so-called primacy effect is assumed to be due to greater processing given the first few items.) The recency effort can be handled quite easily by the above models, such as Atkinson and Shiffrin's 1968 version, by assuming that the last few items are still in STM while the rest are in LTM.

This interpretation is supported by the large number of differences in the effects of various factors on recency versus prerecency items. For example, a number of variables have a strong effect on the retention of the prerecency portion of the list but very little on the recency portion such as slower presentation rates of items (Glanzer & Cunitz, 1966); item familiarity (Sumby, 1963); and list length (Murdock, 1962). A complementary situation occurs in free recall when recall is tested for a list following an interpolated task. Gardiner et al. (1974) showed that with long and difficult distractor tasks, a reversal of the recency effect can be obtained, i.e., poorer recall of the last few items than for the others.

Nevertheless, recency effects are also congruent with a retrieval interpretation of STM properties for the reasons presented above. In addition, the phenomenon of long-term recency uncovered by Bjork and Whitten (1974) is difficult to account for if STM is assumed to be fundamentally different than permanent memory. Glanzer and Cunitz (1966) had shown that the recency effect could be eliminated by interpolating a distractor task after list presentation. However, Bjork and Whitten showed that the recency effect could be restored by placing additional distractor tasks between the presentation of pairs of words in a 26-word list. This paradoxical result can be explained by assuming that the insertion of

284

the distractor activity between item pairs helps the subject keep the items temporally separated even after a delay. Retrieval of the items through temporal cues becomes possible once again through these means. Glenberg et al. (1983) have shown that the size of the long-term recency effect is a logarithmic function of the ratio of the interitem interval to the retention interval (cf. Glenberg, 1984). Thus, not only is there little neurological evidence for an extended consolidation of impermanent representations into permanent form, but the behavioral evidence is similarly weak.

Although it is not possible to be dogmatic about the nature of STM at this time, I believe that the overall evidence presents serious problems for a structural dichotomy between STM and LTM. One can argue, as does Crowder (1976), that a functional distinction can be made between the two, whether or not a structural distinction exists. While this is true, if there is no structural difference it is probably wise to rethink the precise way in which we want to make such a functional distinction.

It does seem likely that STM may differ in its characteristics because it presents the subject with more optimal retrieval conditions. This would indicate that the main difference between STM and LTM lies in the nature of the contingent factors that exist in the circumstances comprising immediate retention rather than in some structural process unique to either type of memory. There does seem to be a special status for fully activated memories, i.e., those one or two items which are in direct and immediate consciousness, but this specialness may simply lie in the fact that these are items that do not need to be retrieved to be fully available to the subject.

It would seem to me that if there is some structural difference between STM and LTM it might lie in the neurological properties of recently activated neurons. That is, there might be special properties to a neuron activated within the past minute or so that make such a memory trace inherently more retrievable (i.e., a lower firing theshold, or some characteristic which allows a subject to search successfully for recently activated neurons). However, such a finding would not constitute evidence for a temporary STM store.

In closing, it should be noted that we have not addressed the question of how information is transferred from working memory to permanent memory. However, this question is best handled in the context of neurological evidence which is presented in Chapter 15. What can be said at this time is that such transfer is assumed to take place very quickly and does not involve the kind of slow chemical or neuronal consolidation process advanced in theories of STM.

In this part, we are going to consider some of the more common encoding strategies that humans use in order to make more effective use of their memory system. Although these strategies are largely voluntary in nature, their characteristics do provide insight into the operation of the structural processes of memory.

## Rehearsal

Rehearsal can be defined as the repeated self-presentation of information by a subject. Although Atkinson and Shiffrin essentially treated rehearsal as a unitary strategy in terms of its effects, recent research has indicated that two types of rehearsal exist: Type I rehearsal involves rote rehearsal (e.g., simply repeating a TBR word over and over again), while Type II rehearsal involves elaborative or associative processing, e.g., organizing items into a number of categories or associating them with an existing memory concept structure or other concurrently processed items (cf. Lachman et al., 1977).

In essence, rehearsal is a means of amplifying the memorial effect from the presentation of a stimulus. We took the position that all information passing through the sensory registers into working memory will be encoded in permanent form. In this respect, it makes no difference how the information entered working memory, i.e., whether it was subject generated or was a perceptually processed exteroceptive stimulus. Each such entry into STM resulted in the formation of another trace, particularly when at least a small amount of time intervened between items (cf. Johnson et al., 1979). This can explain how we can not only recall a stimulus but recall that we previously recalled it. If different items are presented in STM at the same time, it is possible that they will become conjointly associated in a memory trace. Thus, each time an item is presented or rehearsed another duplicate encoding is made of the item; however, the retrievability of the duplicate trace will be dependent on a number of additional factors such as the nature of the processing which it receives (e.g., McFarland & Kellas, 1974; Tzeng, 1976).

A study by Klee and Gardiner (1976) sheds some light on this problem by examining the extent and accuracy of subjects' knowledge of previous recall and recognition performance. In the first experiment, subjects were given a sequential recall and recognition test in which all the originally presented words were re-presented. The subjects had to discriminate those items they had recalled from those they had not. In the second experiment, the subjects were given the same recognition test after an initial recognition test. It was shown that subjects were more aware of their previous recall performance than their previous recognition performance.

In addition, while memory for previous recognition was independent of the item's serial position, memory for previous recall was worse for recency items compared with nonrecency items. Thus, memory for subject-generated traces seems to depend on the amount of output-monitoring decisions performed on the retrieved item, assuming that recall involves more effort than recognition (cf. Underwood & Malmi, 1978; Whitten & Leonard, 1980). The characteristics of the rehearsal trace are, therefore, going to fluctuate because of its strategic nature.

An important issue, then, is the nature of the differential effects from Type I and Type II rehearsal. Woodward et al. (1973) demonstrated that rehearsal which simply involved maintaining the item in STM pending the presentation of a cue signaling whether to forget or remember it had little or no effect on final recall probability for those items. This held true for rehearsal periods of 0 to 12 seconds. However, the rehearsal interval did have a direct relationship with recognition performance.

Glenberg et al. (1977) showed that increases in Type I rehearsal improved recognition regardless of whether one or three words were maintained in STM at one time and independently of the associative value of CVC syllables used. Glenberg and Adams (1978) had subjects overtly rehearse pairs of words 1, 5, or 10 times with rehearsal intervals from 1.3 to 13.3 seconds. Recognition errors of the subjects for these targets suggested that Type I rehearsal was differentially strengthening acoustic phonemic features of the words rather than semantic or associative components. The latter point was indicated because co-rehearsed words did not effectively cue one another's recall. More recent evidence indicates that long-term memory effects are produced mainly from the early segment of a period of maintenance rehearsal (Nairne, 1983). This finding is not surprising given the properties of the OR. The initiation of maintenance rehearsal of an item represents a change in the contents of working memory, unlike continued maintenance rehearsal periods.

Type II rehearsal represents a somewhat more difficult analytical problem because it requires more processing operations by the subject and thus makes it more difficult for the subject to externalize the mental processes involved. For example, in maintenance rehearsal, we can ask the subject to rehearse overtly; however, Kellas et al. (1975) have shown such overt rehearsal does disrupt many of the cognitive activities normally utilized by the subject. In particular, it resulted in an increase in serial processing and required greater study time than covert rehearsal presumably because overt production is slower. This may not represent a source of difficulty in Type I rehearsal, but it almost certainly affects the more complex functions assigned to Type II rehearsal, such as elaboration.

287

Some connection between overt rehearsals and later recall performance have been found when subjects expected a delay test (Brodie & Prytulak, 1975; Rundus, 1971). Free rehearsers tended to show advantages at immediate as well as delayed intervals (Bandura & Bachica, 1974; Wetzel, 1979). Dark and Loftus (1976) showed that items freely rehearsed during the Brown-Peterson retention interval showed better delayed recall than did items where rehearsal was prevented. The greater the interval, the better the performance on rehearsed items, but with nonrehearsed items the performance was constant over the retention interval. As we would expect, subjects can use rehearsal time to increase the accessibility not only of newly processed information but also of traces already in permanent memory (Lachman & Mistler, 1970).

## Organizational Strategies

In this part and the next, we examine encoding strategies that appear to be widely utilized by subjects particularly in recall procedures. For now, we concentrate on organizational strategies, such as categorization.

As we noted earlier, organization of traces can act to reduce the number of retrieval cues needed to overlap the target traces and thus retrieve them. This is particularly the case with featural association or organization in which different traces are encoded so that the common feature is made more salient. Contiguity association or organization requires more effort to develop a retrieval plan since there are few or no useful common attributes in these situations. One of the most important determinants of organizational strategy is of course the memory limits of STM which constrain the number of separate items that can be held in consciousness or in easily retrievable form at any one time. Techniques that can pack extra information or increase the retrievability of items in STM will obviously increase the total amount of usable information that can be processed (cf. Miller, 1956; Postman, 1971; Watkins, 1979).

Empirical evidence for the use of organizational strategies on the part of subjects has been clear for some time, e.g., Birnbaum, 1975; Bousfield, 1953; Cohen, 1963). The disputes have been over the form in which organization exists in memory and to some extent whether or not organization is the cause of improved memory rather than simply a correlate or epiphenomena. Arguments have centered on whether organization is hierarchical with control elements (superordinates) and exemplars (subordinates) or can simply be explained as the result of interword associations without invoking multiple levels (cf. Puff, 1979).

This question has been investigated for a number of years and a general consensus has arisen that control elements or category

words do exist in hierarchical fashion; however, these are themselves treated as any other item in memory would be. For example,
Cohen (1963) found that with study time controlled, words and
categories had comparable recall. Mandler and Pearlstone (1966)
showed that a very high correlation existed between the number of
categories used (2 to 7) and mean recall.

If control elements or category words are processed as are
other items, they should be subject to the same memory restrictions
themselves. That is, subjects should have trouble retaining a
number of categories exceeding the limits of STM, and recall of
categories should follow the same course as recall within categories
(cf. Tulving, 1968). Tulving and Pearlstone (1966) presented
subjects with lists of words belonging to categories along with the
category names and asked them to recall the category instances.
Providing the category names increased recall significantly over
noncued recall of the category instances. From this we can derive
the principle that subjects can recall only a limited number of
category names. Increases in free recall performance, therefore,
reflect an increase in the size rather than the number of higher
order units. Mandler (1967) showed that this relationship between
set size and recall was similar for both the recall of categories
and items within categories (cf. Cohen, 1966). Wood (1971) showed
that the formation of larger memory units is similar to the formation of small units, in that reorganization of the units produces the
same negative effect in both instances (cf. Mandler & Pearlstone,
1966).

The same kind of organizational effects can also be seen with
prose passages as well as word lists. Buschke and Schauer (1979)
showed that text-based story recall involved the retrieval of
distinct memory units which are clustered together. The recall
units correspond with the propositional units of the story and the
organization of recall corresponds to the propositional units
organized by a story schema (cf. Thorndyke, 1977). Black and Bower
(1979) showed that the recall of actions within story episodes
depended on the length of that episode but not on the lengths of
other episodes. This indicated a discrete structure akin to separate categories. Adding more actions to an episode did not affect
the recall of other episodes. Another experiment showed that the
more subordinate actions in an episode, the more likely a statement
(control element?) summarizing those actions is to be recalled,
providing a link with the finding of increased recall with increasing size of categories. Thus, there seem to be parallels in the
organizational strategies used with prose materials to that of word
lists, indicating their general mnemonic utility. One other indication of this generality is the apparent equivalence of instructions
to organize materials and instructions to recall (Mandler, 1967).

Instructions to recall make no difference in performance if subjects are told to categorize and vice versa.

Although organization can serve to increase the number of representations accessible by a single retrieval (category) cue, this property can have negative as well as positive retrieval consequences. One such negative consequence is the within-category inhibition of recall first noted by Slamecka (1968, 1969). Two groups of subjects received a 30-word list to free recall. At test, the experimental group received 15 words from the list and were asked to write down the remaining words. The control group was simply given a blank sheet of paper and asked to write down all the words. Contrary to expectations, the performance of the two groups was equivalent.

In studying categorized lists, moreover, items within a category actually inhibit each other in recall. Once access to a category is achieved, providing additional list items inhibits the recall of the others (Roediger, 1973, 1974; Slamecka, 1975). Hudson and Austin (1970) showed that list items serving as retrieval cues could facilitate recall but only by providing access to unretrieved higher order units. Brown (1981) examined the retrieval dynamics of multiple retrievals from a semantic category. Cumulative inhibitory effects were seen after five consecutive retrievals using letter cues and picture cues (cf. Rundus, 1973). Blaxton and Neely (1983), in a study of semantic priming effects, showed that when both primes and targets were generated, RTs increased, with an increase in the number of related primes presented to the subject.

Watkins (1975) presented subjects with categorized word lists and then tested recall with the category names provided as cues. Recall of the items was impaired when the category name was accompanied by extra-list categorical cues (i.e., cues belonging to that category which were not part of the word list). The impairment was comparable in magnitude to that found in the Slamecka type studies. In addition, attention to the extra-list cues depressed recall to a greater extent than presenting them as part of the study list itself.

A number of points are relevant here. First, organization is highly useful in reducing the number of retrieval cues needed to retrieve list items. However, there is a limit to how many items can be linked to one cue and still have their retrieval probability remain high (cf. Watkins, 1979). This may be the reason that the association of uncategorized items to a particular context, as occurs in free recall, does not exert much of a cuing effect for an extended series of items.

Second, the grouping of items within a category enhances the probability of indirect inhibition between them. Through the process of priming, the activation of one category item will raise

290

the level of activation of its closest associate but also causes the inhibition of less associated category members. Raaijmakers and Shiffrin (1981) note the importance of providing a random sample of list items as cues, since intra-list cues will increase the recall of highly associated words (e.g., Roediger, 1978). It seems likely that output interference is due to the repeated recall of already retrieved items (Rundus, 1973). As more items are retrieved, there are more chances that a retrieved item will have already been recalled. When a certain criterion of successive failures to recall has been reached, then recall stops. In line with this argument, providing more time does increase recall performance (Fuld & Buschke, 1976).

A third point is that organizational effects conform to the structural processes of the IPM in the sense that they do not contravene their normal expression. Higher order units display the same basic characteristics as any other processed stimulus for example. Their usefulness is due to their making more effective use of the existing processes than would otherwise occur. This is the result of strategic behavior on the part of the subject. Although organizational strategies can show consistencies between subjects, there is no necessary reason why such strategies will occur in precisely the same form on each occasion.

Imagery and Memory

In the second chapter we examined the evidence in favor of analogical characteristics for memory traces derived from perceptual stimuli. Thus, for example, visual stimuli would be encoded so as to retain in analogical form some of their visual properties. In this connection, we noted that mental imagery, in the sense of a non-verbal or propositional memory system, has often been proposed as an important phenomenon of cognitive activity. However, its exact functional role in memory has been highly controversial (cf. Paivio, 1971; Pylyshyn, 1979; Seymour, 1979).

Let's examine a representative selection of studies examining the role of mental imagery in retention and retrievability of memory traces. First of all, there is a clear gradient of memorability as we proceed from pictures to concrete words to abstract words as measured both in free recall and recognition (e.g., Bevan & Steger, 1971; Paivio & Csapo, 1973). Concrete adjective-noun phrases are better remembered than abstract phrases (Kusyszyn & Paivio, 1966). In such cases, the imageability of the cue is more important than the response term in determining recall levels (Yuille et al., 1969). Although the nouns in such phrases are better recalled than the adjectives (Horowitz & Prytulak, 1969), Begg (1972) has provided evidence that recall performance differences are eliminated when imageability is equated for adjectives and nouns.

291

Imagery may produce more distinctive features in the encoding of an item, whether visual or verbal (cf. Richardson, 1980). This cannot be the whole explanation, however, because instructions to the subject to use bizarre images have little additional effect on retention other than at immediate testing (Hertel & Ellis, 1979; Wood, 1967).

When recall is used (cued or free), the role of imagery seems clearly linked to increases in the organization and integration of different items (cf. Gilani & Ceraso, 1982). Instructions to produce separate mental images for each item often produced no improvement in performance (Begg, 1973; Bobrow & Bower, 1969). This effect of interactive imagery is not found with recognition.

Paivio (1963) suggested that the degree to which the stimulus term of a paired associate redintegrates the mediator (image) linking the stimulus and response term will determine the latter's retrievability. The imagery value of the stimulus term is thus more important than that of the response term. This is sometimes known as the conceptual peg hypothesis, which has had significant applied success (e.g., Atkinson, 1975; Pressley et al., 1980). Richardson (1980) argues that it is the ease with which a stimulus item evokes an interactive mental image which is critical in this case.

In the studies examined so far, we have seen clear differences in the memorability of pictures and verbal stimuli rated as high in imagery compared with low-imagery stimuli. However, the way in which these kinds of imageable stimuli exert their effect seems little different than the ways in which other kinds of stimuli are encoded and retrieved. In other words, while imageable stimuli apparently contain characteristics conducive to their retrieval, it is not necessary to assume that any special principles or processes are operating exclusively with these kinds of stimuli.

A number of experiments would seem to bear out the contention that special principles are not needed to account for differences in retention. For example, Nelson and Brooks (1973) tested the idea that imageable items are represented in a dual code of visual representation and a verbal label which thus increases their probability of retrieval (Paivio, 1971). They presented subjects with pictures and their verbal labels in a paired associate format as stimulus and response terms respectively. Label similarity (e.g., parrot, puppet) impaired acquisition when instructions required the naming of the pictures out loud. Pictorial similarity could be ruled out as an explanation because the objects clearly do not look alike. When the instructions made no mention of having to name the pictures, high label similarity failed to produce any interference (cf. Nelson et al., 1973).

Thus, the naming of a picture seems to be a secondary process which may or may not occur. Nelson et al. (1976) also found that the superiority of picture recognition could be reduced with high visual similarity at a slow study rate and completely eliminated at a fast study rate.  Again, if verbal labeling of visual stimuli is automatically occurring, then at least at the slow study rate visual interference should be reduced by implicit naming of the pictures.

Gillund and Shiffrin (1981) had subjects free recall lists of abstract words, complex pictures, or both.  Presentation of the pictures and words were mixed or blocked, according to stimulus category, and recall was free or blocked.  By increasing the length of the list, the recall properties decreased whether the increase was accomplished by adding items of the same type or the other type.  The list length effects were obtained regardless of presentation or test condition.  This provides strong support for the idea that the cross-modal effects of pictures or words are accomplished by a single process or similar set of processes regardless of the particular form of the encoding for each type of item.

It is important to emphasize that even if imagery exerts its effects through structural memory processes that are general to all types of stimuli, this does not affect the arguments for analogical representation.  Analogical encoding permits the efficient and compact representation of perceptual attributes which would be difficult to encode otherwise.  However, retrieval processes are the same for all stimuli and thus the same contingent factors can be found to operate with different kinds of stimuli.

Summary

Humans make use of their verbal-symbolic capacities to mitigate the processing constraints of the IPM.  Some widely used encoding strategies have been examined in order to better understand the interaction of strategies and the structural processes of memory. Rehearsal increases the functional presentation rate of an item and provides the opportunity for it to become processed in conjunction with various other representations.  Organization or categorization strategies reduce the number of retrieval cues needed to match a group of items.  In somewhat similar fashion, imagery mnemonics foster the integration (simultaneous processing) of discrete stimulus events.

THE RETRIEVAL CHARACTERISTICS OF RECOGNITION AND RECALL

Recognition and Recall Procedures

Recognition and recall, as currently measured, are not unitary procedures; a number of variants of each exist.  The most widely

293

used recognition procedures are contextual familiarity and discriminative recognition, while recall is measured under cued or free (non-cued) conditions. In the case of contextual familiarity, the subject has to decide whether the presented items at test have occurred in a particular context such as on the second of three word lists. (It is rare to test for non-contextual recognition in which the subjects would be asked if they had ever seen the TBR item previously.) The TBR items are presented in conjunction with previously unpresented items functioning as distractors. The subjects can be given a forced choice or a yes-no test of the TBR items. In forced choice, the subject is given a pair of items, one TBR item and one distractor, and is supposed to identify the TBR item. In yes-no testing, the subject is presented one item at a time and indicates whether it is old (TBR) or new (distractor). Discriminative recognition requires the subject to recognize TBR items as belonging to one of two categories (e.g., correct or incorrect) rather than distinguishing between them on the basis of familiarity (cf. Underwood, 1983).

Free recall is a simple memory procedure in which subjects are presented with a list of TBR items and then asked after a prescribed delay to recall the items in any order. In cued recall, the subject is given a cue or priming stimulus, which is associated in some manner with a TBR item(s), and then asked to recall that TBR item(s). Paired-associate recall generally uses two arbitrary items as cue and TBR item and creates an association through the correlation of the two items in the course of the experiment. Cued (semantic) recall makes use of previously established semantic or featural relationships between items.

Associative and Discriminative Factors

The Distinction Between Recognition and Recall. Recognition and recall represent significantly different procedures for testing memory performance. More important, however, the pattern of performance in these procedures seems to be qualitatively different. For example, given a set of TBR items, there is little correlation between recognition and recall performance on those items. That is, items which are recognized may not be recalled and vice versa (cf. Flexser & Tulving, 1978).

As with classical and instrumental learning, a great deal of controversy has arisen over the nature of the performance differences found in recognition and recall procedures. Are the procedures different in their underlying processes or do they simply foster different interactions of the same set of processes?

One common argument has been that recognition performance is based on the capacity to make discriminations between traces, while recall performance is based on interitem associations (e.g., Norman,

294

1968). Underwood (1983) has argued that frequency discriminations lie at the heart of the recognition process (cf. Mandler, 1980).

Actually, the research literature is quite supportive of this conceptualization. Nelson et al. (1975) found that stimulus similarity (i.e., an associative factor) in paired-associate learning disrupted stimulus recognition but not contingent recall. In this connection, Galbraith (1975) has shown that the memory trace can contain both an associative and a frequency attribute simultaneously but with little interaction between the two.

Rare (low-frequency) words are recognized better than common words, while the reverse is true in recall. This word frequency effect can also be explained as a consequence of these two variables. Rare words have distinctive orthographic features which are aids in discriminating them from other words, while common words do not. On the other hand, common words have many associates, while rare words have few. Thus, rare words have discriminative attributes fostering recognition, while common words have many associations fostering recall. Procedural changes which provide better associations for low-frequency words have been found to increase their recall (Matthews, 1966; May & Tryk, 1970).

Bahrick (1969, 1970) demonstrated the importance of interitem associations for recall performance of words by using extra-list word cues. The subject is presented with a list of words and asked to free recall as many as possible. After this, extra-list cues (prompts) are given for those list words as yet unrecalled. The extra-list cues are novel to the subject; however, they have some predetermined probability of eliciting the target word, e.g., the word "fountain" generated "water" 44% of the time. Bahrick reasoned that if the subject failed to free recall a list word, he/she would use the extra-list cue to implicitly generate a series of associates in accordance with the pre-existing structure of memory. Bahrick's results fit this hypothesis in that strong extra-list cues were more effective than extra-list cues with moderate or low association. In addition, the results indicated that the generation process was not random. Correct responses were more likely to be generated and recognized early in the retrieval interval and this was especially true with the strong associates.

In the interest of parsimony, attempts have been made to account for the effects of both discrimination and association in terms of just one of these factors. Jacoby and Craik (1979) have regarded trace distinctiveness or discrimination as the crucial factor in both recognition and recall. It has been suggested that distinctiveness is the basis of associative effects in retrieval in the sense that a distinctive feature restricts the number of possibilities that need to be searched. In the same way, elaboration between traces which fosters an interrelated network or adding more information to the trace is viewed as increasing its distinctiveness (cf. Klein & Saltz, 1976). To the extent that a particular trace contains features which are unique or low in frequency relative to the set of traces to be discriminated, a retrieval cue containing such a feature should contact that trace more strongly than the competing traces.

Stein (1978) showed that congruous elaborations could either decrease or increase memory performance. A base sentence such as "The tall man purchased the crackers" could be elaborated either with a congruous phrase such as "that were on the top shelf," or an incongruous phrase such as "that were on sale." Elaborations such as the latter decreased cued recall of associated target words relative to the first kind of elaboration, which increased the significance of the concepts expressed. As Bransford et al. (1979) note, elaboration seems to be most effective when it permits some relatively unique interpretation or specification of invariant relationships.

This line of argument can account for the once surprising finding that orthographic or structural features of words could be as well retained as semantic features, given that they were equally distinctive (e.g., Nelson & Vining, 1978; Winograd, 1981). It had originally been thought that structural attributes of words are typically forgotten more than semantic features because they are processed less fully (cf. Craik & Tulving, 1975). The research indicating that structural information could be retained just as well led to the notion that deeper or more extensive processing exerts its effect not by making the trace more durable, but by making it more discriminable (cf. Moscovitch & Craik, 1976).

Actually, the recent results are more in accord with the processing assumptions of the IPM than the original formulation of qualitative differences in the encoding of structural and semantic attributes. Precision encoding and the related capacity for analogical representation would be equally applicable to both kinds of attributes and unrestricted memory formation insures that whatever information resides in active memory for a minimum time will be stored permanently. The basis of differential retention should therefore not lie in a factor incompatible with these processes. The loss of structural information due to lower distinctiveness or greater interference from other such information would be congruent with these processes, however.

Postman et al. (1978) have objected to the lack of a clear operational definition of the concept of distinctiveness and note that the experimental literature strongly supports the idea that trace distinctiveness will be of variable aid in memory retrieval. Free recall is favored by similarity rather than distinctiveness. Distinctiveness is helpful in learning stimulus terms in paired-associate learning but has inconsistent effects on response terms (Nelson et al., 1971).

296

The attempt to view distinctiveness as the essential factor underlying associability or elaboration between items has also been attacked by Anderson and Reder (1979), who offer examples of two passages describing a dog and a chair which are equally distinctive. However, one has greater semantic content and integration than the other and is retained better. The general importance of meaningfulness is well documented with a variety of stimuli. Goldstein and Chance (1971) showed that two types of distinctive material (faces versus snowflakes) were quite different in their effect on recognition performance. The faces were much better remembered and yet each snowflake represents a unique and distinctive pattern. Similarly Bower et al. (1975) demonstrated that ambiguous cartoons resembling doodling were remembered better when they were given a meaningful interpretation (cf. Tulving & Patkau, 1962).

Theoretical Interpretation. If there is a strong impression that we are essentially moving in circles, I believe it to be accurate. The problem, as I see it, is the failure to distinguish between factors which are invariable to the expression of particular phenomena and those which are important to the expression of those phenomena depending on the circumstances. In other words, there are central variables which form the basis for phenomena and there are contingent variables which often affect the particular behavioral form in which it expresses itself. It should be emphasized that we are not necessarily talking about the processes-strategies distinction. These contingent variables may or may not be under the control of the subject. For example, the flight path of an airplane is affected by the force and direction of wind currents; however, the flight of the airplane itself is not dependent upon wind per se. Variations in contingent variables will thus affect the particular results one obtains in any given situation; however, by changing the situation, these effects can be minimized or changed from facilitating to detrimental or vice versa. In the present case, discriminative and associative variables can be viewed as contingent factors in memory performance. To the extent that the situation under which memory traces have to be retrieved favor either factor, then a facilitatory effect will be shown. In a different situation where the procedural circumstances mitigate their usefulness there will be a negative relation between them and memory performance. For example, very distinctive material is oftentimes better remembered at relatively short intervals after presentation than less distinctive material. However, at longer intervals very distinctive material is often less well remembered, particularly if it is not integrated in some way with other material (cf. Fisher, 1981). As Eysenck (1979) notes, distinctiveness of a particular trace depends on the existing content of memory. The similarity and

297

quantity of prior encodings of that and related items are obvious determinants of an item's distinctiveness. These factors can logically operate at the time of encoding as well as retrieval. At encoding, the presentation of a stimulus can induce study-phase retrieval of previous encodings of the item as well as related items which then tend to get processed with it (cf. Underwood, 1983). This can have a positive or negative impact on retrieval depending on the nature of the information required at retrieval. With recognition, we would expect impairment because we have to discriminate one trace from all the others. With recall, we would probably see facilitation, because making contact with appropriate traces is more difficult on the average than discriminating between them. That is, similarity exerts a negative impact in both recognition and recall, to the extent that the target trace is retrieved with a set of similar items. However, this negative effect in the recall situation is outweighed by the strong positive effect of retrieving the target trace in the first place.

Encoding Specificity. Tulving (e.g., 1976) has been an effective advocate of the idea that recognition and recall involve the same processes. He and his associates demonstrated that recall and recognition procedures could not be distinguished on the basis of different retrieval processes (e.g., Wiseman & Tulving, 1976; Watkins et al., 1976). It had been previously argued that in recognition, unlike recall, access to the internal representation by the copy cue was automatic and thus did not involve retrieval or search through memory. The recognition decision was based on a discrimination of familiarity or frequency. Recall, however, involved both search (retrieval) and a recognition decision. Such theories were termed generation-recognition models (e.g., Kintsch, 1974). However, Tulving showed that there were many conditions in which recognition failure occurred for words which were subsequently recalled using cues (e.g., Thomson & Tulving, 1970; Wiseman & Tulving, 1976).

Subjects were given a cued recall task in which TBR words were presented in conjunction with high or low associates. For example, the TBR word BLACK was presented in conjunction with a low-associate cue such as train. In a significant proportion of cases subjects are not able to recognize the TBR word even though they can recall it when given the associated cue presented at the time of encoding. Since the subjects in recalling items were both locating and recognizing the items, it makes no sense for recognition failure to occur unless retrieval also plays a role in recognition. Thus, in some situations a cue for a word might prove to be more effective in retrieving the contextually appropriate representation than the word itself.

From those kinds of results, Tulving (1976) formulated the encoding specificity principle which states that no cue, no matter how highly associated to a target word, can be an effective aid in retrieval unless it has been encoded with the target at input. Thus, retrieval, whether in recall or recognition, is dependent on reinstatement of the precise way in which the item was encoded. In this view, the basic principles involved in the recollection of an event are the same whether or not the testing procedure used is free recall, cued recall, or recognition. The only difference, according to encoding specificity theory, is that in cued recall and recognition the subject is given more retrieval information than he/she gets with free recall.

From our previous discussions we can see that the retrieval process hypothesized by encoding specificity is a rather rigid application of the match-mismatch retrieval process. Tulving (1979) views all variables as essentially irrelevant to determining the retrieval of an item apart from the relation between the target and the retrieval cues presented to the subject. As far as this goes it is consonant with the present position; however, a confusion often exists in the specification of the retrieval cue. Just as we may have a difference between the nominal stimulus and functional stimulus at the time of encoding, so may we have a difference between the nominal and functional retrieval cue. If we keep this in mind, there is no necessary or fundamental conflict between either encoding specificity or generation-recognition mechanisms with respect to retrieval.

In ES the match-mismatch retrieval process is viewed as a structural process and does not involve the use or interaction of strategies in conjunction with it. In this respect, it is essentially the same retrieval process used by all mammalian species. The match is determined by the overlap between the retrieval cue presented and the target memory trace. Generation-recognition assumes that the nominal cue is the initiator of the retrieval process rather than necessarily making direct contact with the TBR's trace. However, there is no barrier to assuming that a match-mismatch retrieval process can occur because of an overlap between a generated retrieval cue and the target trace. Obviously, such a situation must involve search strategies of some kind in memory and presumably operate in accordance with the associative structure of memory.

The existence of both types of retrieval situations (i.e., direct overlap and inferential or generated overlap) has been demonstrated. Camp et al. (1980) presented questions that could be answered either by direct access through memory or required inferential reasoning or search. Responses to inferential questions took longer than to direct access questions, as we would expect. Importantly, subjects who failed to retrieve an answer on direct

access attempted retrieval through inferential strategies, whether
or not the question was solvable on that basis (cf. Rabinowitz
et al., 1979).

There are a number of parallels in the recall and recognition
controversies to what we concluded about classical and instrumental
conditioning. Recall and recognition are procedures which share
the general structural memory processes of the IPM such as match-
mismatch retrieval, unrestricted memory formation, precise encoding,
and analogical encoding. However, they differ in the extent to
which various contingent factors are emphasized or operative in
their respective procedures. Since the recognition procedures as
currently constituted primarily ask the subject to select a particular subset of traces of an item from the total number, it is clear
that important determinants of performance are going to include the
detail in which the critical stimulus dimensions have been encoded
in the target trace and the number of traces with similar features
or attributes. On the other hand, free recall primarily asks the
subject to locate a subset of traces using an indirect match-
mismatch process. In this case, it is clear that perceptual variables are minimized since the subject has to move from the initial
retrieval cue, which does not generally contain features capable of
directly triggering the retrieval of the target to intermediary
traces which are capable of doing so. Instead, formulation of a
chain of partially overlapping traces is necessary for movement
through the memory store. To the extent that particular variants of
these procedures change particular task contingencies then the
importance of these factors will shift as well. Thus, to argue over
whether contingent factors such as distinctiveness or elaboration
is more important is to ask questions which are not particularly
useful in understanding the structural processes of memory.

## SUMMARY


In this chapter we have examined a variety of memorial phenomena relating to the encoding and retrieval of representations
including short-term memory, encoding strategies, and the distinction between recognition and recall. In so doing, there were two
aims: to provide support for the memorial processes described in
Chapter 12 and to show the way in which the voluntary memorial
strategies employed by humans interact with and extend the operation
of these processes. Neurological and behavioral evidence was
provided in support of the idea that the distinctive attributes of
short-term memory are due to special conditions of retrieval rather
than to structural properties of the IPM. As a result, the tenet
of unrestricted memory formation was confirmed. Several common

encoding strategies were examined and their properties were found to be congruent with the operation of the hypothesized structural processes. The procedures of recall and recognition were analyzed and their memorial differences were shown to be explainable on the basis of contingent factors which affected the interaction of memorial processes in characteristic ways.

# Chapter 14
## The Functional Characteristics of Memories

In this chapter we focus on representations which already exist in permanent memory, with respect to changes in their characteristics and their interactions with other representations. First, we examine the effects of repetition on the functional character of the internal representation. As is well known, repetition or practice has profound effects on memories and is closely connected to the experience of familiarity and recognition. Thus, an understanding of what factors underlie the "strength" of a memory is essential to even the sketchiest theory of memory. Second, the phenomenon of interference is studied. Although match-mismatch theory does not ascribe all forgetting or negative transfer to the effects of interference or response competition, it nevertheless plays an important role in memorial phenomena. Third, we analyze the apparent functional differences that exist between factual memory and what is commonly termed autobiographical memory, a distinction captured in the episodic-semantic memory dichotomy popularized by Tulving. As we will see, the concepts of episodic and semantic memory have ramifications with respect to several issues raised in this section such as the effects of repetition, the nature of memorial associations, and encoding and retrieval strategies.

### THE EFFECTS OF STIMULUS REPETITION ON MEMORIES

Although the most obvious memorial consequence of stimulus repetition is an increase in its familiarity or recognition latency, this is by no means the only effect that is produced. Repetition

or practice increases the retention (retrievability) of representations, reduces their susceptibility to interference and provides
partial protection from various amnestic conditions produced by
neural damage or pharmacological agents. In addition, these effects
are not limited to humans, but are just as ubiquitous among animals
including invertebrates (cf. Miller & Marlin, 1984; Underwood,
1983).

In many situations, variations in the temporal conditions of
practice do not exert differential effects on retention as long as
the total study time is held constant (Cooper & Pantle, 1967).
Thus, if a subject studies a 20-item word list four times, taking
three sec for each item, performance is about the same as if it had
been studied six times taking 2 sec for each item. The major
exception to this total time law is the case of massed versus distributed practice (cf. Hintzman, 1976). In this situation, massed
training, or the repeated consecutive presentation of a stimulus
event for one period of training, typically results in lower long-
term retention than the same amount of training in which the stimulus
repetitions are spaced apart in time (e.g., Vandermeer & Amsel,
1952).

To begin, we analyze more closely the assumptions of the
present theory on the memorial consequences of stimulus repetition.
Then, we examine some relevant research literature on the integration of information, automatization, and distributed practice.

## The Abstraction of Memorial Representations

In the discussion of memorial processes and their interactive
effects contained in Chapter 12, it was noted that the operation of
study-phase retrieval of related representations from permanent
memory while exteroceptive information was being entered into
working memory provided a mechanism for the correlation of discrete
stimulus events. Let's examine this process interaction in terms
of its implications for repetition effects.

When a subject is presented with a list of items (words,
pictures, etc.) to remember, the encoding processes of the IPM are
activated. Through the operation of precision and analogical encoding, the subject forms representations of the stimulus environment
existing at the time of stimulus presentation. We have seen that
representations are formed not only of the specified target stimulus
events but also of the context in which they occur (cf. Chapter 3).

A number of researchers have assumed that the representation
of some stimulus event can be characterized by a population of
related and interrelated features or attributes. The various
attributes of the stimulus event are encoded along with certain
attributes of the stimulus context. For example, Lovelace and
Southall (1983) showed that the recall of words from a prose passage

could be cued by their within-page spatial location and vice versa (cf. Bower, 1972; Tversky, 1977).

We will now assume that the subject receives another presentation of the list of words immediately after the first presentation. It is inevitable that some changes in the stimulus context will occur over even limited periods of time. In the present case, the subject may be thinking of something different at the start of the second presentation than he/she was at the start of the first, or an airplane may be passing overhead, etc. However, since the repetition is immediate (massed) there is little time for much stimulus fluctuation to occur or for the item to leave working memory. Thus, the stimulus features should be quite similar between the two presentations.

From our knowledge of the properties of the OR, we can predict that the OR should be reduced in those cases where the second presentation (P2) of a stimulus differs little from its first presentation (P1) particularly if the item is residing in working memory. To the extent that some features are present on P2 that were not present on P1 there will be interference; however, massed repetition would minimize the chances of this occurring. Also, most of the features of P1 will also be present on P2. In other words, most of the features of the context (and stimulus itself) will be correlated across presentations, and thus there is little opportunity for the correlational process to reduce the association of a significant proportion of the contextual attributes.

Let's change our procedure so that the subject receives a delayed repetition. The greater the interval between P1 and P2 the greater the probability of substantial change in the contextual attributes surrounding the stimulus event. In addition, there is an increased probability that the item will have left working memory and be present only in a representation in permanent memory (Cuddy & Jacoby, 1982). In such cases, the occurrence of the stimulus at P2 can produce a study-phase retrieval of the representation encoded at P1. At this point, the joint presence of the P1 and P2 representations again creates the potential for correlational processing. The effect of correlational processing will be greater in the case of distributed or spaced repetitions than with massed repetitions since a higher proportion of the attributes will not be correlated across stimulus occurrences.

In essence, we can say that distributed practice favors correlational processing, which in turn tends to favor encoding of consistently occurring attributes of the stimulus and inhibit the encoding of less correlated or uncorrelated attributes. Thus, the representation of a stimulus which has occurred in distributed fashion becomes increasingly abstract in the sense that it contains only those attributes which are common to most or all of the stimulus' representations. Posner (1969) notes two different types of abstraction. The first involves the selection of certain portions or aspects of an event, presumably because of their greater importance or definitional character. The second involves the classification of a stimulus as part of a wider or more inclusive superordinate category.

We can view these two types as first-order and second-order abstraction since the categorization of stimuli in broad categories would seem to require the first kind of abstractive process as a prerequisite. Posner has termed abstraction a process of information reduction; however, such information reduction must have a quite specific character which selectively eliminates those idiosyncratic or redundant features which do not have generality or definitional power. Thus, abstraction must involve not only the identification of stimulus invariants but also emphasize those invariants which best distinguish the abstract class, category, or prototype.

It should be emphasized that the abstraction of the representation discussed here is not synonyous with the concrete-abstract verbal dimension widely used in verbal learning research (cf. Paivio, 1971). In the current formulation the representations of any repeated stimulus, whether a concrete word such as apple or an abstract word such as truth or non-verbal stimuli such as lights or tones, undergo the abstractive correlational process discussed above.

Given that such an abstractive process takes place, what role does it play in the expression of the memorial consequences of stimulus repetition such as ease of retrieval, protection from interference, etc.? From our knowledge of match-mismatch principles and the experimental findings of encoding specificity, we know that the conditions under which retrieval can occur are strongly influenced by the attributes which have become incorporated in an item's representation.

If an item does not undergo correlational processing, then attributes idiosyncratic to a particular occurrence are not removed from the current representation. By remaining in the representation, they can continue to play a role in the match-mismatch comparison. Thus, in order to retrieve a non-abstracted representation, the retrieval cues need to contain a greater number of attributes which are idiosyncratic to a particular occurrence of the item than they would for the equivalent abstracted representation.

It should be noted that the abstracted representation of a word or other stimulus in no way replaces or erases the non-abstracted representation formed because of the stimulus' particular occurrences (cf. Hasher & Griffin, 1978). Both kinds of representations co-exist for any repeated stimulus. However, the abstracted representation has a tendency to become the most probable representation to be retrieved when the stimulus is re-encountered unless additional retrieval information is present which matches the idiosyncratic attributes contained in one of the non-abstracted representations. Another way of viewing it is that the retrieval of abstracted representations is less affected by changes in the retrieval context since only the most correlated attributes need to be present.

For example, when a subject is presented with the word apple, the abstracted representation formed from the repeated correlational processing of the word or object "apple" will be retrieved first. To retrieve particular instances when the word or object "apple" was encountered requires additional retrieval information, either self-generated or given; e.g., the last time I saw an apple was at the supermarket on Tuesday (cf. Rao & Proctor, 1984).

The increasing tendency for only highly correlated attributes to remain in a recurring stimulus fosters a greater degree of integration of the remaining attributes (cf. Mandler, 1980). In addition, the accessing of the abstracted representation biases the encoding of the current occurrence of the stimulus in favor of those correlated attributes. It is this process which is the basis for the feeling of familiarity or item strength.

Study Phase Retrieval and Information Integration

A principal contention of the discussion concerning the effects of repetition has been that representational abstraction depends upon the integration of information across occurrences (representations) of a particular stimulus event. This phenomenon has been studied in connection with the formation of simple concepts.

Specifically, the researchers have analyzed the way in which subjects form an idea of a category or prototype from the presentation of a series of exemplars which bear some less than total resemblance with the prototype on which they are based. Such simple concepts are often nonverbal in nature and comprise geometric or other kinds of pictures or figures which can be varied systematically on particular dimensions.

Posner and Keele (1967) trained subjects to identify and associate four distortions each of four unseen prototypes of dot patterns. The subjects were then transferred to a list of patterns consisting either of the prototypes they had never seen, old previously learned distortions, or control patterns which were equated so that they had the same mean variation as the original distortions. In the transfer task, it was found that the prototypes were correctly classified significantly more often than any of the control patterns, even those equated for variation. The authors suggest that whatever process underlies the classification of the prototypes appears to be unique to them.

Posner and Keele (1968) used the same test described above but with a delay of a week interposed between the stimulus presentation and transfer task.  The results indicated that the unseen prototype or schema pattern was recognized at least as well as the original four distortions.  Furthermore,  correct classification of the prototype showed no loss over the week while performance with the original patterns suffered significantly.  Thus, extraction of information concerning central tendency takes place during learning and is not thereafter mediated by the individual patterns.  The prototype seems to be more resistant to forgetting than the individual presentations from which it was derived.

Homa (1978) used figure drawings of ill-defined forms to investigate category abstractions.  Subjects initially classified 18 different patterns into three categories which contained 3, 6, or 9 members.  Following this, a transfer test was given in which old, new, prototype, and random patterns were presented.  In another experiment, categories were defined by 4, 8, 16, or 32 exemplars followed by a transfer test which contained unrelated and new patterns based on the categories at each of six distortion levels. In both studies, prior training on numerous exemplars enhanced transfer over training on a few.

Using dot pattern stimuli, Homa et al. (1973) showed that the development of stimulus categories was dependent on exemplar experience (cf. Medin et al., 1984).  The boundary of an ill-defined category is widened by increasing the variation in the exemplars. Importantly, category abstraction seems dependent on the detection of common features in the category exemplars as well as the analysis of the distinctive features among categories (Homa & Chambliss, 1975; Reed, 1972).

A number of studies have investigated the development of simple concepts using verbal material.  Clark (1978) notes that the integration of information in concept learning involves several component processes:  (a) a concept has to be accessed in memory; (b) the concept and related propositions have to be retrieved; and (c) the information responsible for activation of the concept has to be stored or associated with the concept in some usable way. Bransford and Franks (1971) showed that subjects spontaneously integrated the information contained in a series of semantically related ideas and stored this as a structurally integrated memory representation.

Studies of anaphoric reference (e.g., using a pronoun to refer back to a previously mentioned subject) reveal evidence for the importance of study phase retrieval processes in the integration of information.  Yekovich et al. (1979) argued that the integrative process involved in anaphoric reference was composed of identification of a potential antecedent from a context sentence and relating an appropriately marked anaphor from a target sentence back to the candidate.  This interpretation was supported by subjects' comprehension times involved in the integration of two sentences under

307

varying degrees of relational ease. Garrod and Sanford (1977) showed that anaphoric references are affected by the semantic distance between the two sentences to be integrated. Haberlandt and Bingham (1978) showed that certain inferences are activated by the first sentence of the set and that subsequent sentences are processed faster if their content is consistent with these inferences.

There are other lines of evidence which also support the idea that study-phase retrieval is involved in the integration of information across stimulus occurrences. For example, reactivation of prior stimulus traces in the test phase of study-test cycles facilitates later recall in the recall and paired-associate learning (e.g., Darley & Murdock, 1971: Izawa, 1970). Loftus and Loftus (1980) have shown that reactivation of established memories makes them vulnerable to modification making the original memory representation more inaccessible. In this connection, it has been demonstrated that reactivated prior knowledge takes up processing capacity in working memory like other items (Britton & Tesser, 1982).

These studies taken together provide significant support for the general principles outlined previously. Subjects are sensitive to similarities across different presentations of the same or related stimuli, resulting in the study-phase retrieval of that information. As a result, the new information is integrated with other information already present in memory. Relevant or significant information is retained by formation of a new cohesive unit with the old material; on the other hand, irrelevant information is less likely to be encoded in the new unit. Importantly, the perception of similarities across different presentations is affected by a number of contingent factors in intuitively reasonable ways, which in turn affects the degree of integration of related concepts or propositions.

The Spacing Effect

The effects of distributed practice in verbal learning have been analyzed under the term "the spacing effect" (cf. Hintzman, 1976), which refers to the increase in retention found with spaced re-presentation of items. The spacing effect seems to asymptote at around a 15-second interval between repetitions of an item, although this interval is somewhat task dependent. For example, when subjects are asked to judge the frequency with which an item occurred on a list, the 15-second asymptote is almost always found. However, on a paired-associate task, the asymptotic interval is somewhat longer and the function tends to form an inverted U-shape overall. In free recall, the spacing effect seems to increase monotonically with increasing spacing far past 15 seconds—this is sometimes called the lag effect.

308

Massed Practice and the OR. From our knowledge of the principles of OR evocation, we could surmise that massed practice which involved the immediate repetition of stimuli would be likely to lead to learning deficits compared with spaced practice. This effect has been conclusively demonstrated in a number of studies. Hintzman et al. (1973) showed that when the first and second presentations of an item were presented in different modalities in massed practice it was the second occurrence that suffered the most in terms of processing and later retrieval. Johnston and Uhl (1976) tested the processing of massed items by requiring subjects to monitor and respond to faint sounds while studying a word list with massed and spaced repetitions of items. It was found that the reaction time to the sounds decreased monotonically over massed repetitions of a word but not for spaced repetitions, again indicating that the subject devotes less processing capacity to the immediate repetition compared to the spaced repetition.

Ciccone and Brelsford (1974) found that when subjects were allowed to program their own sequence of item repetitions they generated lag values almost identical with experimentally determined optimum values. Subjects overwhelmingly preferred to be tested on items at or near the limit of STM. This suggested that the accessibility of an item in memory is an important determinant of the effectiveness of repetitions. Presumably, massed repetitions are ignored because the item is well within STM (cf. Cuddy & Jacoby, 1982).

Although substantial evidence has accumulated implicating attentional changes to the $P_2$ presentation of a massed item as the basis of the spacing effect, studies which had attempted to manipulate changes in attention directly did not find changes in the spacing effect. The redefinition of attention as an OR helps to uncover the basis for these failures. For example, Hintzman et al. (1975) tried and failed to show that habituation was responsible for the decrement of attention to the massed $P_2$ presentation. They manipulated the exposure time of the $P_1$ occurrence, varying it from 2.2 to 5.2 to 8.2 seconds, but found no difference in the spacing effect. They had assumed that the longer the $P_1$ duration, the more habituation would result to the item. By increasing the duration of exposure to an item it was assumed that this would by itself cause more habituation. However, whether the duration of the $P_1$ occurrence is 2.2 or 8.2 seconds makes no difference in terms of whether an OR will occur to the item initially, or whether there will be a diminished OR to the $P_2$ of an item, since the occurrence of the OR depends on a change in the situation. A massed repetition represents no more change after a 2-second $P_1$ exposure than an 8-second $P_1$ exposure and thus we would expect this test not to show any difference in terms of the spacing effect.

Underwood et al. (1976) note another problem of interpretation by pointing out that in nearly all experiments some subjects will not show a spacing effect. Additionally, the magnitude of the spacing effect is not reliable for individual subjects. They conclude that this must result from measurement deficiencies since it is difficult to see how such a widespread effect could not have same degree of reliability of magnitude.

Actually, this is not unexpected given the nature of the materials used in the majority of spacing studies. The occurrence of the OR is going to be occurring on more subtle, idiosyncratic bases with verbal material than with other types of stimuli. For example, almost everyone will turn around when they hear a loud noise behind them or orient to a sudden flashing light. However, orienting reactions to words must necessarily be more individual since they are dependent more on the personal history of the subject than the other stimuli. A dog lover may react to the word spaniel much more strongly than someone totally uninterested in dogs. Even with nonsense syllables there must be a large individual component to the reaction depending on whether some correlate is thought of; e.g., dart may be thought of when the subject is presented with DRT. Reducing the cognitive level of the materials should produce more consistent evocations of the OR.

The condition of massed practice has negative implications for OR evocation to stimulus repetitions which do not exist when an interval of time (and presumably intervening events) separates such repetitions. However, the occurrence of the OR does not specify the effectiveness of distributed repetition per se.

In the present view, first-order abstraction increases the retrievability of representations because they tend to contain those stimulus attributes which are likely to possess stability across occurrences. A match can, therefore, be more reliably attained than when the internal representation contains many features not present in the re-occurrence of the item, given that the retrieval situation is at least partially changed from the conditions at encoding. If the retrieval information is highly similar to the encoded attributes of a non-abstracted trace, though, this argument would not hold. In these cases, the abstracted representation of the item would have fewer matching attributes than the non-abstracted representation. In fact, massed presentation does provide superior retention in short-term memory tasks, which have high similarity between encoding and retrieval conditions (Peterson, 1963).

Variable Encoding in Distributed Processing. A number of researchers have argued that the superiority of distributed practice over massed practice can be attributed to an increased variability of encoding which occurs with spaced repetitions of a stimulus, thus

affording more independent retrieval routes to the items' representation (Bower, 1972; Martin, 1972). These encoding variability
theories assume that the more independent the encodings, the more
different types of cues or contexts are associated to the item. As
applied to the spacing effect, encoding variability explains it by
the further reasonable assumption that the longer the interval
between repetitions of an item, the more likely that there will be
a change of context. Thus, a different encoding of the item on the
second presentation will result.

There are two basic types of encoding variability theory with
regard to the spacing effect. The first type assumes that it is
changes in the semantic interpretations of items which cause the
effect (Melton, 1970). The second type postulates that it is
variability of the surrounding context that is responsible for
the spacing effect and not necessarily just semantic variability
(Anderson & Bower, 1974; Bower, 1972).

Madigan (1969) used homographs presented twice at different
spacings (massed or distributed). The degree of spacing is determined by the number of intervening items. The homographs were
presented in company with cue words which either biased the same
interpretation of the homograph or a different one (e.g., fever-
CHILL...fever-CHILL or fever-CHILL...snow-CHILL). An encoding
variability interpretation would predict that CHILL would be better
remembered at massed presentations if two different meanings were
biased as opposed to the same meaning. Also, there should be less
advantage for distributed practice over massed practice when two
different meanings are biased in both cases. The results confirmed
both predictions. A flattened spacing curve was obtained when two
different meanings were biased.

The encoding variability position has also been applied to the
lag effect. The difference between the lag effect and the spacing
effect is that in the lag effect recall is a monotonic function of
spacing between items, while in the spacing effect it is a nonmonotonic function. The lag effect seems to occur mainly in free recall
tasks, but can also occur in paired-associate tasks with a large
retention interval between $P_2$ and test. In terms of encoding
varability, long lags between $P_2$ and test conditions decrease the
overlap between item encodings but so too does the free recall
condition at even moderate intervals because of the reduction of
retrieval information in this procedure (Glenberg, 1976).

A number of other studies have been conducted which provide
partial but not total support for the encoding variability position.
For example, Thios (1972) showed that varying the interpretation
of repeated homographs in sentences resulted in improved recall
over the same meaning. However, similar interpretations of the
homographs, but not identical repetitions, resulted in better recall at all spacings than both the varied or identical repetitions.

311

A somewhat different variation was performed by D'Agostino and De Remer (1973), who measured the free recall of object phrases in sentences using massed or distributed practice. The same object phrase was either in the same sentence and repetition or was in two different sentences, which were presented at separations of 0, 5, 10, or 20 intervening items. A typical spacing curve appeared with repetitions of the object phrase in the same sentence but a flattened curve like that of Madigan's appeared with the object phrase being repeated in different sentences.

These and other studies would seem to provide some support for semantic variability of encoding contributing to the spacing effect; however, there are some difficulties. First of all, retention in the different encoding condition was superior to the same encoding condition only at 0 spacing. Encoding variability theory predicts a superiority for variable encoding at all spacings.

A second problem is that Martin (1972) has suggested that one reasonable criterion of encoding variability might be the failure to recognize an item on the second presentation ($P_2$) as having occurred before. The more different the encoding, presumably the more difficult it is to identify it as the same item on both $P_1$ and $P_2$. A number of studies cast doubt on this as a factor in the spacing effect, however. Belleza et al. (1975) showed that items recognized on $P_2$ and therefore encoded in roughly the same way were better recalled than those not recognized on $P_2$. In addition, they found that the spacing effect was virtually identical for both CVC trigrams and CCC trigrams even though semantic encoding of the latter is inherently more variable (Martin, 1968).

In a more complicated task, Johnston and Uhl (1976) measured encoding effort and variability by measuring reaction time to light signals scattered throughout the aural presentation of words, and also measured the latency to detect word repetitions. Longer reaction time implied greater processing effort of word encoding, and increases in word detection latencies implied greater encoding variability. The results showed that RT increased somewhat across four distributed presentations of a word and decreased across four massed presentations. In addition, a negative correlation was obtained between recognition latencies on $P_2$ and probability of free recall. The spacing effect only occurred for words correctly recognized on $P_2$.

DeRemer and D'Agostino (1974) and D'Agostino and DeRemer (1973) found that when rehearsal and organization were restricted for the $P_2$ of an item, the lag effect was eliminated. Restrictions at $P_1$ had no effect, however. Even when the lag effect was eliminated, the spacing effect remained, indicating that the two are at least partially separable. If rehearsal and organizational processes are crucial to the lag effect, this must mean that context elements which are not susceptible to these processes cannot even

312

theoretically contribute to variability of encoding here, e.g., random environmental events, stream of consciousness, physiological stimuli.

Thios and D'Agostino (1976) and Hintzman (1976) have argued that the reason for these effects is that the second occurrence of an item must induce study-phase retrieval of the $P_1$ occurrence for better retention of that item to occur. In other words, the $P_2$ occurrence is viewed as a retrieval cue for the $P_1$ occurrence. Thios and D'Agostino had subjects free recall a list of object phrases each repeated twice. A 2-, 6-, or 12-second intervening task between successive presentations was used in order to prevent rehearsal. Subjects at the time of the second occurrence were required to retrieve $P_1$ information in the retrieval condition. In the nonretrieval condition, $P_1$ information was provided at $P_2$. A significant spacing effect was found only with the retrieval condition.

Correlation versus Contiguity. Encoding variability theory is essentially derived from Bower's (1972) stimulus sampling theory. The argument is that the context surrounding an item can be conceptualized as composed of a large number of elements, be they stream of consciousness, systematic cues, or random environmental events. When an item is repeated, different kinds of contextual elements are attached to the target item through contiguity. Better performance on distributed practice results from the greater change in context occurring between repetitions as compared with massed practice, increasing the number of associated elements.

If correlation is assumed to be as necessary as contiguity for stimulus association to occur, however, the above analysis will not hold. The elements that become most strongly associated with the TBR item are those which are recurrent with its repetitions. Those elements idiosyncratic to any one presentation are habituated or subjected to interference; thus, there are not increasing numbers of stimulus elements becoming associated with the target on repetitions. If so, recall probability cannot be tied systematically to the number of stimulus elements conditioned to the TBR item (cf. Ross & Landauer, 1978).

Semantic variability as in the Madigan study improves retention after massed practice because it insures that the subject will attend to the repeated item. The large difference in the emphasized attributes of the word between $P_1$ and $P_2$ mitigate its nominal repetition and under conditions in which $P_2$ is certain to re-evoke $P_1$.

Under relatively favorable retrieval conditions such as those found in recognition and cued recall with moderate retention intervals, there will be substantial but not total overlap between the retrieval attributes and the encoded trace. The abstracted representation produced by spaced repetitions will have an advantage over the non-abstracted repetition produced by massed repetitions because of its lessened susceptibility to changed retrieval conditions. The non-monotonic function, i.e., the decline in retention at longer spacings between $P_1$ and $P_2$, can be attributed to increasing failure to recognize $P_2$ as a repetition (cf. Hintzman, 1976).

Under less favorable retrieval conditions such as those found in free recall or cued recall with long retention intervals, repetitional abstraction is not as useful in insuring retrieval of an item. In these situations, associative elaboration or organization is also needed to increase the probability of retrieval since even correlated attributes of a target trace may be absent at test. The monotonic function obtained in these circumstances is probably due to the expectancies induced by long lags between $P_1$ and $P_2$. Subjects who encounter a long interval between $P_1$ and $P_2$ are going to have a greater expectation of being tested after a longer interval and thus will devote more Type II rehearsal to such an item than they would after a short lag.

Zimmerman (1975), in studying processing time devoted to items presented at different lags, found that differences in recall level to items with long lags as opposed to short lags could be explained on the basis of more processing time devoted to long-lag items. However, study-time differences could not support the differences in recall between massed and distributed items. Zimmerman notes that subjects spent almost 50% more time studying massed repetitions of an item than for a single item and yet recall levels were virtually identical for both types (cf. Elmes & Bjork, 1975).

Summary

The effects of stimulus repetition on an item's representation in memory were examined. The reoccurrence of the stimulus, through the match-mismatch process, retrieves the traces of previously stored items which it overlaps (directly or indirectly) on some feature, i.e., study-phase retrieval. The juxtaposition of the two traces in working memory allows the formation of a conjoint trace containing elements of both items. Since common elements are the basis for the study-phase retrieval of items, these will typically receive more processing than idiosyncratic elements. Conditioning will accrue to repeated elements at the expense of non-repeated elements, resulting in the systematic elimination of idiosyncratic elements from the representation. As the process continues, representations of the stimulus will retrieve the abstracted representation rather than the original traces of the item. Thus, more and more representations will be formed which do not possess the idiosyncratic elements contained in the first representations of the item. The operation of this abstractive process was examined in the areas of simple concept formation and the spacing effect.

We have seen that the repetition of a stimulus in varied form or in a changed context can produce interference between uncorrelated attributes of its different representations. At this time, we will more explicitly examine the operation of interference or competition between memorial representations during encoding or retrieval.

It should be emphasized that in the present theory, interference is not the sole means by which memories can be rendered inaccessible. In fact, it is quite likely that representations are more often forgotten simply because the information present at retrieval is not sufficient to match their critical features. We can consider these cases as examples of contextual forgetting in which items, not retrievable in some circumstances, can be retrieved with more appropriate cues. One example we saw previously in the encoding specificity studies by Tulving in which items could be recalled using cues but not recognized.

Logically speaking, interference between memories can exert its effect either retroactively or proactively. In the former case, memories learned more recently decrease retention of those learned previously. In the latter case, previously learned stimuli or responses decrease retention of those more recently learned. First, we examine the nature of retroactive interference (RI) and then proceed to proactive interference (PI). The discussion of these two procedures will be divided since there is good reason to believe that they involve at least somewhat different interactions of the structural processes of memory.

Retroactive Interference

The standard paradigm for examining RI has been the A-B, A-D paradigm in which the subject was given an initial paired-associate (P-A) list which was learned to criterion. Following this, a second P-A list was presented to the subjects in which the stimulus terms remained the same but new response terms were paired with them. Almost invariably, negative transfer in learning the second list is shown relative to the control condition A-B, C-D, where subjects learn new stimulus and response terms in the second list. However, it should be noted that negative transfer does not always occur when measured against an absolute (rest) control (cf. Postman, 1976).

Although there is slower learning of the A-D list, once it has been learned, subjects display decrements in their ability to recall the original response terms (i.e., A-B). It is this retention loss of the "B" terms which is evidence of RI. To what factors can we attribute this RI affect? Let's examine this problem in the context of a specific example developed from the discussion of interference effects in Chapter 12.

A subject has first learned the paired-associate APPLE-TABLE so that presentation of the stimulus term or cue APPLE leads to the retrieval of the response term TABLE. Now a second set of response terms is being learned such that APPLE is paired with TAPE. When the stimulus APPLE is presented during second list learning, it may retrieve the "B" term TABLE. If so, the subject in trying to encode APPLE-TAPE will experience interference between the response terms TABLE and TAPE. In this situation, the subject has several options. First, it is possible to directly suppress the incorrect response TABLE although this can be relatively costly in terms of processing effort. A second option would be to integrate both response terms into a common representation. Again, this strategy may be relatively costly in processing capacity. A third option would be to increase the correlation of APPLE with TAPE and thereby decrease the correlation of APPLE with TABLE, e.g., by rehearsing the APPLE-TAPE association or by extending the practice with the second list.

From this line of reasoning we can infer that there is no necessary relation between negative transfer in learning A-D and the degree to which the "B" term becomes inaccessible. Negative transfer occurs in the first two cases because the subject is having to devote processing capacity to reduce the interference from the "B" term on acquisition of the A-D association. However, in the second option, the integration of the terms is actually reducing the probability of retrieval failure of the "B" term. Conversely, in the third option, there is little negative transfer but increasing inaccessibility of the "B" term.

This is an important point since interference theories have expended much effort to show a consistent correlation between negative transfer and the retention loss (unlearning) of first list items and have failed to do so (cf. Underwood & Lund, 1981). In addition, as Petrich (1975) notes, the lack of consistent correlation between the relative associative strengths of the A-B, and A-D terms and RI can be accounted for by storage of "B" term intrusions during A-D learning. This effect would fit in well with the current notions concerning unrestricted memory formation.

Experiments in which two different responses are learned simultaneously to the same stimulus show both negative transfer and unlearning; however, these effects depend on the nature of the alternation between "B" and "D" responses. Frequent changes from one response to the other tend to decrease the observed amounts of both negative transfer and unlearning (Popp & Voss, 1965; Postman & Parker, 1970).

In considering the literature on RI, good support can be provided for the idea that changes in the retrieval effectiveness of the "B" term features lies at the heart of RI effects. In line with this reasoning, Reynolds (1977) showed a significant reduction in RI in the A-B, A-D paradigm when the "B" terms were instances of higher order semantic categories and the cues were names of the higher order categories.

The interference between different representations can be reduced by increasing the relative distinctiveness of one or more of their features. Underwood (1945) advanced the concept of list differentiation (LD) or the ability to identify the list membership of responses. He argued that LD varied directly with both the absolute and relative strengths of the competing associations and inversely with the length of time between final testing and learning of the second list. These hypotheses were confirmed experimentally (McCrystal, 1970; Winograd, 1968).

Unlearning or RI is essentially eliminated when there is a high degree of distinctiveness between the different lists. This can be accomplished by having a clear temporal separation between A-B and A-D learning. Underwood and Ekstrand (1966, 1967) found that when learning of A-B is conducted under wide distribution and A-D learning is massed, there is very little unlearning of A-B associates. This held true even after a high degree of A-D learning (cf. Postman & Underwood, 1973).

Greenspoon and Ranyard (1957) showed reduced PI when the second list is learned in an experimental setting which is greatly changed from that present during first-list learning. Conversely Deese and Marder (1957) showed that when a long delay was interposed before final testing, increases in between-list errors were found, presumably because of a decrease in the temporal separation between lists (cf. Runquist & Runquist, 1978).

Given the idea that individual representations are comprised of a number of features, it follows that only part of the set of features may be subjected to interference. In this case, the representation should be retrievable through the unaffected features. Recognition and recall of the same set of items show little correlation which indicates that different item attributes are used. We might expect to see differences in RI across those procedures therefore. Postman and Stark (1969) studied the degree of RI when recognition tests were used at both acquisition and test, using a multiple-choice procedure. Three interference paradigms were used, namely, A-B, A-D; A-B, C-D; and A-B, A-Br (A-B, A-Br involves rearranging the "B" terms with different "A" terms on the second list). Only in the latter paradigm did RI appear. However, substantial negative transfer did occur in both the A-D and A-Br lists compared to C-D. Specific associations seem highly resistant to unlearning as measured by recognition except where negative transfer is persistent and heavy. In a recall test using the same

317

materials and procedures, RI was greater for the AB-AD condition than AB-ABr (cf. Anderson & Watts, 1971; Bower & Bostrom, 1968; Wickelgren, 1967).

Motor Associations. An interesting question is the relative lack of evidence for RI in animals after specific interference of the A-B, A-D type, where two different responses are learned to the same stimulus, compared with the strong evidence for nonspecific RI of the A-B, C-D type (cf. Spear, 1978). For example, Wickens et al. (1977) found that in cats trained on two different classically conditioned responses with one or two different CSs, RI was greater when interpolated learning consisted of a different stimulus and response than when the same stimulus was used (A-B, A-D). Nonspecific RI is particularly evident after relatively high degrees of interpolated learning and long retention interval (e.g., Honig, 1974; Parsons & Spear, 1972). Although RI does occur in the A-B, C-D paradigm with humans it is almost always less than in the A-B, A-D paradigm. Keppel (1971), for example, showed very little evidence of RI under intense but nonspecific interpolated learning of 45-minute duration.

First of all, there are practical difficulties in testing for RI in animals using the A-B, A-D procedure since it is difficult to instruct them to go back and perform the originally learned response. In other words, animals are controlled by the most recent contingency arranged under a particular stimulus. Second, it may not be irrelevant that the nature of the responses being tested with animals is quite different from those tested with humans. Clearly, animals can only be asked to produce responses that are motoric or glandular in nature; although a human producing a verbal symbolic response is also engaged in some motoric activity, the nature of the response would seem to bear crucial differences from non-verbal responses. For example, a response term in a paired-associate is no different than the stimulus term in any inherent properties. The designation of one term as the response and the other as stimulus is purely arbitrary, unlike instrumental or classical procedures in which a tone and a barpress cannot be arbitrarily defined as stimulus and a response depending on the whim of the experimenter.

The study of perceptual-motor responding has long found important differences in retention and forgetting of such responses when compared with verbal-symbolic material (cf. Adams, 1964; Bilodeau & Bilodeau, 1961). For example, Jahnke and Duncan (1956) showed no evidence of a retention loss over a 4-week retention interval for a pursuit-motor tracking task. More complicated tasks have shown only marginal losses over a 3-month retention interval (Lewis & Lowe, 1956). Barch and Lewis (1954) showed

318

that it was extremely difficult to produce in perceptual motor performance the kinds of RI and PI found in verbal learning.

Actually, when forgetting does occur in motor learning, it can often be ascribed to loss of verbal-symbolic information controlling the occurrence of the response. Bilodeau et al. (1962) showed that response learning which involved remembering feedback of results such as a knob positioning task can suffer losses in retention. Bilodeau et al. (1964) analyzed such responding in terms of the response made, the knowledge of results, and an alternative response for a few trial series. The greatest interresponse correlates were between the original response and the first reproduction of it. The smallest correlations were between the final reproduction and the original response. The retention loss is best characterized as a random deterioration of the form of the response since changes are irregular and random between individuals. As Bilodeau et al. note, it is as if people attempted to reproduce the original response, but do so with decreasing success due to random changes in the form of the motoric representation.

The forgetting of feedback (verbal-symbolic) information followed a different course, however. Proximate recall attempts correlated more highly with each other than with more separated trials; thus, it seems that previous reproductions are remembered rather than the original material. The reason for the retention differences of verbal-symbolic material and perceptual-motor responses is not entirely clear at this point. However, it may simply be due to greater distinctiveness between motoric responses and/or fewer responses that have to be learned compared with verbal stimuli.

This view suggests that forgetting of verbal-symbolic material may be forgotten more readily than motoric responses simply because verbal material places a tremendous burden on the memory system. Humans try to remember an enormous amount of very detailed information which is often quite similar in character, use, or form to other information. Thus, it is not surprising that a certain amount of this information becomes inaccessible due to the operation of the contingent factors discussed previously (e.g., contextual change, trace distinctiveness).

Proactive Interference

Proactive interference is the enhanced forgetting of new material due to the action of previously learned information compared with what would be forgotten if there had been no such prior learning. Although PI was recognized at the outset as a possible factor in forgetting, it was viewed as a weaker factor than RI (e.g., McGeoch, 1942). However, Underwood (1945) corrected this impression by showing that PI could indeed produce significant forgetting.

It was argued that PI was due to response competition and failures of list differentiation (cf. Underwood and Postman, 1960). One of the problems with this view was the apparent low level of interference from exposure to English in the years preceding the subject's exposure to the verbal lists. If cumulative PI was such an important determinant of PI levels, why didn't the subject's exposure to written and spoken language cause massive PI? Eventually, it was determined that PI was greatly reduced when A-B learning is widely distributed (Underwood & Ekstrand, 1966, 1967). Thus, prior verbal experience does not interfere with laboratory learning because such experience is gained under conditions involving wide distribution of practice. In other words, list differentiation can mitigate PI as well as RI. Underwood and Ekstrand (1967) tested their idea by repeating some of the first-list responses in the second list. The advantage of distributed practice was greatly reduced in such a situation.

The relation between list differentiation and PI has been intensively investigated in both short- and long-term retention studies. Perhaps best known are the release from PI studies of short-term retention by Wickens and associates (Wickens, 1972; Wickens et al., 1970). Subjects were given a number of short-term memory trials with items from one or several categories. It was consistently found that PI built up rapidly when items were all from the same category. However, a shift between different categories provided a reduction or release from PI for those items. The categorical shift could be quite subtle and still produce reduction in PI (e.g., garden versus wildflowers). Bird (1977) showed that a shift from semantic to structural processing or vice versa produced more release from PI than did shifting from one semantic task to another. Similarly, no release from PI was obtained with two related structural tasks (Bird & Roberts, 1980).

Controversy has developed over whether the release from PI found after categorical shifts is an encoding or retrieval process (cf. Wickens et al., 1981; Dillon & Bittner, 1975). From the standpoint of match-mismatch principles, it would seem unlikely that release from PI would be due exclusively to either encoding or retrieval operations. As we have seen, given the operation of the match-mismatch retrieval process, encoding and retrieval are inextricably linked in producing memory performance. Thus, operations which affect either the encoding or retrieval of items should potentially have an effect on PI.

Encoding Deficits. It has been more recently suggested that PI may be partly attributable to a learning deficit on later lists or items. Lockhart et al. (1976) argue that increased practice on list learning results in changes in the ease with which subjects acquire the new associations. That is, the subject does not learn the second

320

list as well as the first list, and thus inevitably shows poorer retention compared to subjects who did not have specific prior learning.

For example, fewer trials to criterion are needed by subjects on lists presented later in the session compared to the number required at the start. They argue that such learning set behavior is a result of the reduction in processing effort or number of operations needed to successfully encode the items. Therefore, the amount of learning cannot be equated between successive lists by conventional methods such as equal training on both lists (cf. Underwood, 1964). Warr (1964) equated the amount of study time (i.e., exposures) to the list and found a large decline in the amount of PI.

Hasher and Johnson (1975) and Postman et al. (1974) examined the idea that in procedures such as the A-B, A-D paradigm where the same stimulus is used twice, the subject employs the more effective mediators in establishing the A-B association and thus, has less useful mediators to use for A-D learning. Hasher and Johnson showed that mediators used by subjects in learning the A-D list produced more forgetting in subjects who had to use them in learning a single list (A-B).

This is an extremely interesting possibility from the standpoint of match-mismatch principles since it dovetails neatly with the idea that stimulus traces reflect the characteristics of the neural areas involved in their encoding. To the extent that familiarity or meaningfulness varies the nature of stimulus processing, then there is a strong possibility that situations in which experience with particular tasks or stimuli is gained affect the nature of the encoding operations used. Thus, subjects may not be encoding stimuli the same way at the end of the task that they were at the beginning. In particular, contextual attributes may be adversely affected. Perhaps most important, many of the same memory processes and strategies already discussed seem to play a substantial, if not predominant, role in the characteristics and conditions underlying the appearance or nonappearance of RI and PI.

## THE ASSOCIATIVE STRUCTURE OF MEMORY

The associative structure of memory has been a central interest of experimental psychology from the beginning; however, the complexity of the subject matter led psychologists to study association in more manageable contexts such as the paired associate paradigm. This concern was well founded since the associative structure of human memory necessarily involves not only structural processes but also the personal experiences and knowledges of the individual organized with the aid of voluntary and occasionally idiosyncratic strategies. Be that as it may, one outgrowth of the information processing and cognitive movement was the renewed interest in studying associative structure as it existed in the adult human (e.g., Collins & Quillian, 1969; Rips et al., 1973).

## Semantic and Episodic Memory

One concept that has been widely used as a heuristic tool in studying the structure of memory is the distinction between episodic and semantic memories advanced by Tulving (1972). Episodic memory stores encodings of all autobiographical events in temporally dated form. Items in episodic memory are strongly bound to the specific context in which they occurred and are relatively unconnected to each other. Episodic memory is contrasted with semantic memory which contains a network of interrelated factual knowledge.

For example, an episodic memory might be the image of a sea-shore visited on a holiday or a list of nonsense syllables learned in an experiment. Semantic memory could contain axioms of geometry, meanings of words, or a knowledge of law. Information in semantic memory necessarily plays a role in the laying down of a trace in episodic memory. However, the two types of memory are basically independent of each other in terms of storage.

The exact nature of the episodic-semantic distinction is an open question at this time. However, it is doubtful if different structural processes underlie the two kinds of memory since there is no hard and fast rule for deciding whether a particular memory is episodic or semantic in nature. For example, a semantic memory such as the meaning of a word was first learned in an episodic context such as a vocabulary lesson. Researchers have obtained conflicting experimental results concerning a process distinction (e.g., Shoben et al., 1978; Muter, 1978). Since there is no strong reason to believe that different structural processes are involved we will move on to more interesting questions concerning episodic and semantic memory.

There are three issues that bear examination in this section. First, how are semantic memories organized? Second, how do the structural processes affect the form and utilization of semantic memory? Third, what is the nature of the relationship between episodic and semantic memories?

## The Organization of Semantic Memory

Semantic memory must contain representations of objects with their conceptual and/or perceptual referents, their relationships (semantic, physical, logical, etc.) with each other, and rules which specify the operations (cognitive or physical) which can be performed on them. To be even minimally useful, these elements of semantic memory must be organized in such a way that the individual can retrieve them at the appropriate time with the typical cues likely to be available (cf. Glass & Holyoak, 1976; Smith et al., 1974).

In the present discussion, we will focus principally on the character and organization of the semantic representations of objects. This restriction is not due to the lesser importance of the other elements of semantic memory, but is more a result of our rather dim understanding of how these logical relations and rules are to be represented memorially and how they are organized within semantic memory. In addition, the largely strategic nature of these representations heavily obscures the operation of the structural processes on which they are based.

For example, Tversky tested the idea that similarities between stimuli are based on a feature-matching process, i.e., a linear combination of the measures of their common and distinctive features. Twelve types of vehicles were the stimuli used (e.g., bus, car, truck). One group of 48 subjects rated the similarity between all 66 possible pairs of vehicles on a scale from 1 to 20. A second group was instructed to list the characteristic features of each, of which 100 were shared between two or more terms.

For every pair of vehicles, the number of features attributed to both and the number of attributed to only one were counted. The number of subjects that listed each common or distinctive feature was computed. The product moment correlation between the average similarity of objects and the number of common features was .68.

It could be further suggested that the degree of semantic association between words is mainly based on the way one word biases the meaning or feature selection of another and is not generally a function of frequency of co-occurrence. When a high probability feature of one word is shared by another, the two are viewed as high associates. When a low probability feature is shared, then the two words are viewed as low associates. Since non-associates do not share features, they are encoded with the features that would be used if presented alone. In somewhat the same vein, redundancy is the biasing of a word's dominant feature, e.g., royal-KING. To illustrate these points a few examples follow.

"Table" and "Chair" are considered to be high associates of one another. According to the present interpretation this is because one causes the selection of a high probability feature in the other; with the above two words the feature selected is obviously their use as pieces of furniture. On the other hand, "Glue" and "Chair" are low associates because it is a low-probability feature of "Chair" to think of it as a collection of pieces of wood held together by glue. In the case of non-associates like "Glue-Sheep" or "Mustard-Truth" neither word generally biases the feature

323

selection of the other in a direction different than what would occur if the two were presented by themselves.

To what extent are semantic categories characterized by featural relations? Rosch (1973) and Smith et al. (1974), in a series of experiments, studied the properties of semantic categories and their relation to exemplars. In analyzing the structure of categories such as birds or furniture, the authors found certain factors important to membership. These included (a) defining features, which are essential for category membership (e.g., birds have wings); (b) characteristic features, which are often possessed by category exemplars (e.g., birds often perch in trees); and (c) typicality, which is a function of the congruence of features between a word and a category and sometimes is termed family resemblance (cf. Kemler-Nelson, 1984).

Since defining features are common to all category members, they are not so useful in making comparisons within categories as characteristic features. The latter can function as continuous dimensions on which different category members can be arranged. For example, the dimension of size can be used as a measure of the typicality of particular bird species. Small birds are considered more typical than large birds (Battig & Montague, 1969). The time to make comparative judgments between category members has been found to be a function of the relative difference or distance along such dimensions (cf. Mervis & Rosch, 1981). For example, it takes longer to judge the smaller of SPARROW/CROW than of SPARROW/OSTRICH.

It should be noted that such semantic organization is not unique to well-established or socially prevalent categories. Barsalou (1983) showed that similar category structure could be detected in ad-hoc categories created at the time of the study, e.g., things to sell at a garage sale. Typicality gradients were as salient as in established categories even when category and exemplar relationships were variable in nature. Thus, the structure and character of semantic categories seem to be quite consistent over a wide range of conditions. This observation leads us to a consideration of the influence of memory processes on the structure and properties of semantic memories.

Memory Processes and Semantic Memory

Semantic memories, like any other memorial representations, should reflect the operating characteristics of the structural processes. One way of examining this question is to see whether more adaptive or efficient semantic structures achieve their advantage because they more precisely meet the operating characteristics of the hypothesized structural processes.

Recent research in the areas of expertise and schema formation indicates that subject matter experts are able to achieve economies

324

of encoding and retrieval due to their semantic memory structures (cf. Anderson, 1983; Norman & Bobrow, 1975). A number of studies have shown that the level of prior subject matter knowledge can have a direct effect on the speed of encoding as well as the degree to which such information can be retrieved (e.g., Chiesi et al., 1979; Johnson & Kieras, 1983). In the latter study, level of technical knowledge was positively related to recall of passages in forced pace and incidental tasks but not in self-paced tasks in which subjects could take extra time to acquire unfamiliar information. In the Chiesi et al. study, baseball experts had a higher probability of recognizing new domain relevant material and needed less contextual information in order to make such recognition decisions than did low-knowledge subjects (cf. Klatzky et al., 1982). Importantly, the high knowledge subjects were better at recalling event sequences in the presented material because of their greater capacity to relate successive segments of input information.

These and other studies suggest a close connection between the usefulness of a schema and its capacity to aid study-phase retrieval of relevant semantic information while new information is in working memory. For example, Perfetto et al. (1983) in studying performance on a problem solving task showed that failures were mainly due to the subjects inability to retrieve such information on their own. There was no significant rejection of information which had been successfully retrieved (cf. Gick & Holyoak, 1983).

Thus, while the particular micro-characteristics of schemata and semantic memory will vary widely from individual to individual and even from domain to domain within individuals, these variations are simply contingent responses to the processing constraints and characteristics of the IPM. Each individual has variations in his or her processing aptitudes and skills and each knowledge domain favors certain processing and organizational strategies over others.

The Interaction Between Episodic and Semantic Memory

Tulving (1976) has claimed that the basis for encoding specificity effects is the separation of episodic and semantic memories. Thus, the presentation of a TBR item such as GROUND on a word list results in the formation of an episodic trace which is quite separate from the representation of GROUND in semantic memory. More generally, factual knowledge is assumed to be separate from autobiographical knowledge.

Precisely because episodic memories are representations of uniquely occurring events there is the possibility that features are present which are not part of the normal feature pool for an item. As an extreme example, the semantic features of "Stick" would probably be rarely used in the episodic encoding of a "Stick" used as a magic wand. Thus, episodic encodings contain information which differs at least partially from that contained in semantic memory for those items. The difficulty that can exist in accessing episodic events, using the pre-existing structure of memory, is therefore understandable.

However, by the same logic, to the extent that episodic encodings contain features contained in semantic memory, they should be accessible through semantic representations. This idea offers a possible resolution of studies which do or do not show a close connection beween episodic and semantic memories.

Sometimes, when a person encodes words, he/she makes use of a typical set of semantic features comprising the item. On other occasions semantic features are used which do not exist as part of the normal semantic feature pool for the item. To the extent that the information contained in semantic memory is utilized in episodic memory, it should be seen that the pre-existing structure of memory is useful in retrieving the item. Thus, a generation-recognition strategy on the part of the subject would be successful. On the other hand, the more atypical the semantic features used, the more difficult it would be to retrieve the item through the pre-existing structure of memory.

This suggests that the real difference between semantic and episodic memory lies not so much in the type of information stored in each, but the way such information is encoded. To be useful, knowledge of facts or relationships needs to be retrieved in changing circumstances. It is counterproductive to encode them in such a way that they can only be recovered in the particular situation in which they occurred. On the other hand, many situations in life have no apparent future usefulness, at least outside of their specific context. In one sense, tying events to a particular context is a useful way of preventing confusion. Retrieval would probably be an extremely difficult operation to perform if all information was encoded so as to be available in situations and with retrieval cues other than the ones encoded at input. Many memory traces would be interfering with each other during any retrieval process. Conversely, the more distinct the memories are, the less confusion between similar items.

This interpretation of the semantic-episodic distinction flows naturally out of the basic memory processes discussed previously. Episodic memories are a direct consequence of the precision encoding of the contents of active memory. Each presentation of a stimulus or event occurrence will be registered in accordance with unrestricted memory formation, although some stimulus presentations will be processed to a greater degree than others. Semantic memories are formed in the same way; e.g., learning the meaning of the word "Apple" occurs at a particular time in a particular way. However, semantic memories are generally encoded with respect to a standard retrieval cue which is not contextually bound. In addition, semantic memories are likely to be activated a number of times by repetitions of the same stimulus or retrieval cue. Episodic memories are less likely to be accessed to the same degree with all that this implies for the development of representational abstraction.

The associative structure of human memory is shown to be the result of interactions between organizational strategies and the processing characteristics of the IPM. The organization of semantic categories through featural relationships is shown to explain a number of semantic memory phenomena such as comparison judgments and category verifications. The development of expertise in knowledge domains is seen to be a function of schemata in semantic memory which facilitate encoding speed and also provide more optimal retrieval routes for factual information. Semantic memory is distinguished from episodic memory on the basis of characteristics encoding differences rather than on content per se.

SUMMARY


In this chapter, we have examined the way in which existing representations in memory are organized as well as the changes and interactions which can occur to such traces. Semantic categories were seen to be organized through featural relationships which specified the typicality or congruence between exemplars and category prototypes. These featural relationships were shown to affect performance on a number of semantic memory tasks such as verifications and comparison judgments. Stimulus repetitions were shown to change the nature of the existing memorial representation of the item through correlational processing of its features. Repetition fostered the development of an abstracted representation containing only highly correlated attributes. The influence of massed and distributed practice on this process was examined. Interference at encoding was shown to be due to the study-phase retrieval of existing representations which cannot be integrated with the contents of working memory. Interference at retrieval was shown to be due to declining correlations between items and between constituent features of single items, thereby reducing the number of effective retrieval cues which could access their representations.

# Section V

## Cognitive Functions and the IPM

In a sense, the previous chapters are preparatory for the subject matter of the present section since the information processing and cognitive capacities of the human brain are undoubtedly the most complex and perhaps the most difficult to analyze in the animal kingdom. In previous chapters I have proposed that the IPM is common to all mammalian species. This Section will put that proposition to its sternest test, but the boundary conditions set on the statement should be remembered. In humans, match-mismatch processes interact with rule-based behavior to produce human behavior. We now examine more closely the nature of this interaction, but one point should be clear at the outset, namely, that the cognitive capacities of humans (i.e., that which constitutes human intelligence) must ultimately rest on match-mismatch processes.

There are three main issues that are analyzed. First of all, an analysis of some of the cognitive changes that occur in childhood and old age is conducted in the light of the proposition that habituative system functioning also changes at these times. In addition, the amnesias produced by habituative system damage due to senility or disease are discussed. Needless to say, all developmental changes are not ascribable to changes in habituative system functioning.

The second issue is a tentative identification of several basic information processing capacities as the substrate for the expression of general intelligence or $g$. In particular, interrelationships between the OR and correlational processing underlying basic abstraction are examined. Again, it is not contended that these are the only factors underlying $g$.

The third issue is a discussion of the way in which particular aptitudes interact with general intelligence. The basis of some of these specific aptitudes is sought in the fundamental construct of analogical encoding. Human intelligence is viewed as the result of an interaction between the processes comprising $g$ and the analogical processes related to perceptual-analytical processing.

# Chapter 15
## Developmental Changes in Cognitive Function

It is a common fact of experience that people's cognitive and memorial abilities do not remain perfectly constant throughout life. Although such characteristics do exhibit remarkable consistency from adolescence through middle age, there are substantial changes that occur in old age and in early childhood. The critical dates for these changes do exhibit a fair degree of consistency across individuals, suggesting that some basic developmental process or processes are involved concerning neural function. In childhood, there seems to be a critical difference in the information processing capacities between children below the age of 5 and those between 5 and 7 (cf. White, 1970). Perhaps it is no accident that the age of 5 or 6 is when serious schooling for the child commences in practically all countries. In old age, the demarcation line for information processing changes is not so sharply drawn; however, the ages between 65 and 70 seem to be a critical period here (cf. Schonfield & Stones, 1979). Again, it may be more than coincidence that retirement ages are set in this span. Nor can it be argued that purely physical or morphological reasons dictate such retirement since many of today's jobs involve minimal physical exertion.

If, indeed, the changes in information processing capacity that occur are the result of some consistent sequence of neurological changes, then it becomes of interest to identify the brain areas which might be underlying these changes. Of course, there are undoubtedly changes in all brain areas during these critical periods, however, since some capacities seem to be more affected than others there is the strong possibility of differential effects of growth and aging on particular neural structures.

330

One line of research that has potentially great implications for these issues is the study of the human amnesic syndromes produced by damage to the neural structures associated with the habituative system. Interestingly, the memorial and cognitive changes seen in these syndromes seem to be more extreme manifestations of some of the changes seen in aging populations. To ascertain a relation between particular information processes and the state of neural structures at these stages of development is thus the critical question. Since it is best to start at the beginning, we will first examine the changes that occur in childhood.

## COGNITIVE CHANGES IN CHILDREN

### Nonsalient Cue Utilization

Researchers in children's learning capacities have detailed a number of interesting changes that occur starting around the age of five. If there is a common thread between these various changes, it would seem to be an increased capacity to make use of less salient stimulus attributes, perhaps because of an increased sensitivity to them.

Very young children tend to perseverate rather than spontaneously alternate with positional choices (Jeffrey & Cohen, 1965; Pate & Bell, 1971). In addition, they have a greater tendency to make perseverative errors in walk-through mazes compared with older children (cf. White, 1970). Hale and Morgan (1973) showed that 4-year-olds were more likely to attend to single features of stimuli than were 8-year-olds. Perhaps as part of the same syndrome, children under 5 tend to process stimuli as integral wholes rather than in more featural fashion (e.g., Kemler & Smith, 1979). Conversely, older children were better able to select the relevant cue when only one stimulus dimension was made relevant, presumably because they attended to the range of stimulus dimensions in the beginning and thus, were better able to determine which dimension was relevant.

White (1966) attempted to disrupt perseverative responding based on position by varying the position of cues independently of their reinforcement, thus demonstrating the irrelevance of position. Older children (second and third graders) benefited from the demonstration of the irrelevance of position on correct responding. However, the same manipulation with young children only enhanced the salience of position as a cue, regardless of its demonstrated irrelevance. Thus, they responded even more strongly on the basis of positional cues (cf. Brown et al., 1972).

Scott and House (1978) demonstrated a similar kind of stimulus bound responding by young children on oddity problems. In this

331

situation, three or more stimuli are presented and the subject is supposed to pick the one that is different from the others. This paradigm is moderately difficult in that the correct stimulus on one trial can be the incorrect stimulus on the next. For example, on trial 1, the subject might be shown two circles and a triangle, with the latter stimulus being the correct choice. On the second trial, the subject could be shown two triangles and a square, in which case the square would be the correct choice. Scott and House showed that 3-year-old children were particularly deficient in mastering this problem even with training with non-repeated stimuli. Repeated stimuli across trials would be expected to focus more attention on specific rather than on the necessary relational cues. Five-year-olds benefited more from the training and in fact demonstrated transfer of training from nonrepeated stimulus sets to repeated stimulus sets. Thus, young children tend to be controlled by more obvious perceptual qualities of stimuli.

Mackworth and Bruner (1970) examined the visual exploration of pictures by 6-year-olds and adults by recording spontaneous eye movements to slides presented at one of three levels of optical resolution. When the optical resolution was sharp, the children tended to fixate longer and have shorter distances between successive fixations compared with adults. Under unfocused conditions, however, children made much longer initial shifts of fixation than did the adults, who spent the time fixating informative details (cf. Abravanel, 1968, on haptic exploration in children). Thus, young children seem to perseverate even in their visual exploratory tendencies except when the salience of the stimului is reduced, in which case they seem to display more aimless or distractible searching.

The reduced effectiveness of nonsalient attributes or dimensions other than the one which is perseverated to also shows up in memorial tasks in young children. It would seem that even children in the critical age span of 5 to 7 years continue to have trouble with memorial tasks which necessitate more flexible or less salient retrieval attributes of traces even when there is improvement in the ability to process nonsalient exteroceptive stimulus information.

Ceci and Howe (1978) studied differences between children aged 4, 7, or 10 in their ability to shift retrieval strategies. The children were presented with 25 line drawings of familiar objects which could be organized both thematically (e.g., Life in the Arctic) and categorically (e.g., animals). During an initial training phase, all the subjects demonstrated the ability to classify the drawings into both modes. Following this, the children were then given a cued recall test designed to determine the characteristics of the encoded trace and then a free recall test. Older children not only recalled more items, but they also demonstrated a greater amount of mode switching during recall. For example, after

332

recalling a number of items under one of the thematic codes, a child could try to recall additional items by using one of the categorical cues as an implicit retrieval cue or vice versa.

Although younger children retained enough attribute information to retrieve items based on both modes, they did not seem to be able to shift (i.e., stop perseverating) response modes. In general, young children recalled more items encoded thematically (salient mode) than on nonsalient modes, e.g., categorical (cf. Hasher & Clifton, 1974; Melkman & Deutsch, 1977).

Howard and Goldin (1979) studied the allocation of processing resources by kindergarten children on visual discrimination tasks. On each trial, the children were presented with an array of one, two, or four items. The children were given a verbal cue either before or after presentation of the stimulus array which designated one, two, or all of the items as relevant. When the cue was given prior to the array presentation, the children showed considerable control over their attentional and processing strategies. However, when the cue followed the presentation of the array, they were deficient in selective allocation of processing for items already encoded (cf. Bray & Ferguson, 1976; Eimas, 1970).

Paris and Lindauer (1976) showed that young children were worse at constructing and remembering inferred relationships which they were capable of understanding if made explicit. Implicit cues for sentence recall were much less effective compared with explicit cues for the 6- and 7-year-olds than for the 11-12-year-olds. However, instructions to initiate the actions described in the sentences improved the sentence memory of the young children to the implicit cues (cf. Perlmutter & Ricks, 1979). Fisher (1979) showed that preschoolers had reduced ability to use internal frames of reference when external cues were presented.

Relation to Hippocampal Function

The reader should have been struck by the similarity of many of these findings with the data concerning animals and adult humans with habituative system damage or incapacitation. As we saw, the habituative system was critically involved in shifts of attention to and the processing of nonsalient cues or stimulus dimensions in addition to habituation. With regard to the latter principle, it was seen that animals with habituative system damage were much more likely to perseverate along previously reinforced responses to particular stimuli than normal organisms.

The mere fact that young children's behavior has some resemblance in its characteristics to organisms with incapacitated habituative systems is of course insufficient to make a causal connection between developmental changes in the habituative system and more "adult" ways of responding and thinking. There are two key findings that we need to establish before taking this idea seriously. First, of course, we must see major developmental changes in the habituative system structures such as the hippocampus at about the same time as response and cognitive modes change to a more adult pattern; second, the types of information processing handled by the reinforcer system should follow an independent course with respect to habituative system processing since the two systems are structurally independent.

A number of researchers have pointed out that changes in hippo-campal development in the rat and human child do seem to occur at about the same time postnatally that more adult modes of behavior begin to appear (cf. Douglas, 1975; Rose, 1980; White, 1970). Altman (1967) and Bayer and Altman (1975) showed that 85% of one type of hippocampal neuron was generated postnatally. The level of hippocampal development necessary for full functioning in the rat seems to occur at about 30 days of age which is when rats begin to be fully capable of the kinds of nonsalient stimulus processing that adult rats can perform (cf. Isaacson & Kimble, 1972; Hirsh, 1974). Habituative system development in humans seems to occur primarily in the ages from 5 to 11 or 12 (cf. Luria, 1980), which is the same span for the behavioral changes that take place.

Preweanling rats display some of the information processing characteristics that we would expect from this line of reasoning. For example, they are less likely to exhibit blocking to redundant cues to reinforcement (Solheim et al., 1980) and are more deficient at tasks with successive stimulus presentation than with simultaneous presentation (Rudy & Cheatle, 1979).

It is obvious that experiental factors are also going to play an important role in determining which behaviors and cognitive strategies will be demonstrated by children. However, if one believes in some systematic relationship between brain and behavior, it would seem equally clear that an appropriate neural substrate must exist for experiences to be registered and interpreted in the appropriate way.

The second point that needs to be demonstrated is that the developmental changes in neural function cannot be ascribed to some general factor operating on the brain as a whole. Since the reinforcer system is hypothesized as independent from the habituative system, it would be nice to see a dissociation in the developmental changes in the two systems. We have already examined evidence showing that classical conditioning can be demonstrated in very young infants. This would suggest that the reinforcer system is quite functional at this early age since reinforcers and primary cues need to be processed through it for conditioning to occur. Similarly, Rudy and Cheatle (1979) reported taste aversion learning in rats only 2 days old. In general, there are many studies showing basic conditioning in very young mammals, whether they are altricial or precocial. Thus, it would seem that the changes occurring in children's cognitive and behavioral capacities between 5 and 11 cannot be ascribed to some general neuronal maturational factor.

Infantile Amnesia

The functional maturation of the higher level structures of the habituative system provides a possible explanation for the interesting phenomenon of infantile amnesia (cf. Campbell & Coulter, 1978). The young of certain species, including humans, display increased forgetting of memories compared with the degree of retention found in later childhood or adulthood. In humans, infantile amnesia is nearly complete for the first 2 years or so of life; somewhat reduced amounts are found in the next 3 or 4 years of life.

Various explanations have been offered for the inability to recall many events from infancy or early childhood; however, since retention of memories can usually be demonstrated for at least a day or two after acquisition it is unlikely that storage problems are causing the memory deficit. Most recent accounts of infantile amnesia have focused on the possibility that retrieval difficulties form the basis of the effect (cf. Spear, 1978). In this view, the immature organism encodes and stores the trace, but in such a way that later retrieval becomes more difficult or impossible. Since we are dealing with immature subjects, nonfunctional encoding, if this is in fact occurring, would have to be ascribed to particular structural processes operating in infancy rather than to inappropriate encoding strategies. This point is strengthened by the finding that nonverbal organisms such as the rat also display infantile amnesia.

Since infantile amnesia in the rat does seem to display substantial similarities to human infantile amnesia, the rat presents a good preparation with which to analytically examine the effect. The time course of infantile amnesia in the rat seems to extend from birth to about 20 to 25 days of age. Since the immature rat in the first 2 weeks of life is a difficult preparation to test due to sensory and motor limitations (unopened eyes, poor locomotion), most studies have tested retention in the 15- to 25-day period.

A number of carefully controlled studies have shown that immature rats show increased rates of forgetting over long retention intervals than adult rats (cf. Spear, 1979). Nagy (1975) demonstrated similar findings for 9- to 13-day-old mice (which mature faster than rats).

Interestingly, the degree of infantile amnesia can be reduced by distributed practice. For example, Coulter et al. (1976)

distributed CER training for rats 17-22 days old over 3 days and showed no retention deficit although still younger rats did display the effect.

One of the most significant findings in the animal experimentation on this phenomenon was demonstrated by Campbell et al. (1974), who compared infantile amnesia in the rat with that in the guinea pig. The theoretical significance of this comparison lies in the different development of the young organism in these respective species. The rat, when newborn, is quite helpless and is sensorily deficient. In addition, substantial neural development in the brain occurs in the first 3 weeks or so after birth. In contrast, the neonatal guinea pig is mobile, with opened eyes, and has practically complete neuronal development of the brain. Campbell et al. showed that in two learning tasks over a variety of retention intervals, the young guinea pig showed no evidence of infantile amnesia. Thus, infantile amnesia seems to be linked with neuronal development of the brain after birth. As we have seen, human children exhibit substantial neuronal development up to 11 or 12 years after birth, but particularly so in the first 5 or 6 years of life.

Spear (1978) has suggested that the development of the brain might lead to systematic changes in the way that the organism perceives and encodes stimuli. If this were so, it might make it difficult to retrieve the trace after development is complete because the event or object is no longer perceived as it was when it was first learned. Thus, contact would not be made with the stored trace.

I would like to suggest that it is the functional development of the habituative system which is the primary cause of infantile amnesia. Infantile amnesia is much reduced after about 25 days or so in the rat and after about 4 or 5 years in the human child, approximately the same time at which hippocampal development is nearing completion in these respective species (although frontal cortex development is still ongoing in humans). The importance of a functional hippocampus in the encodings of nonsalient stimulus attributes has been amply demonstrated in both animals and humans, cf., the discussion on amnesic syndromes later in this chapter. If we combine this fact with the idea of a match-mismatch retrieval process, it is clear that the functional addition of an operative habituative system will not only change the way an organism perceives novel events, but it will also change the way in which familiar stimuli are perceived. If we hold to the principle that a match must take place between the encoded trace and the retrieval information, it is clear that retrieval of memories stored before the onset of higher level habituative system functioning will be made very difficult by this process.

In keeping with the general rule of last in, first out, the human hippocampus is one of the structures affected earliest by aging processes, which reduce the number of neurons and change dendritic formations (cf. Landfield & Lynch, 1977; Malamud, 1972). Interestingly, such changes are also demonstrated in the hippocampi of aged rats as well (Scheibel & Scheibel, 1977; cf. Pettit, 1982). Progressive declines in components of the OR (e.g., N200, P300 amplitudes) are also seen (Brown et al., 1983; Thompson et al., 1978).

The behavioral evidence is consistent with these neural changes in the elderly. Progressive changes in cognitive and memorial function are not uniform across all tasks as would be expected if aging were producing a general decline in brain function. Instead, such deficits are accentuated for particular kinds of tasks. Verbal intelligence scores remain fairly constant even in advanced old age; however, cognitive tasks involving spatial components show pronounced declines (cf. Schonfield & Stones, 1979). It will be remembered that spatial performance (as opposed to spatial perception) was disrupted in animals with habituative system damage. The same decline in spatial performance occurs in aged rats (Wallace et al., 1980).

On the other hand, no large decline in primary memory is seen in either aged humans (e.g., Craik, 1977) or aged rats (Wallace et al., 1980). Animals with habituative system damage also showed deficits in ignoring salient irrelevant cues (e.g., Douglas & Pribram, 1969). Hoyer et al. (1979) presented elderly subjects (mean age of 72.6 years) a matching task in which one dimension (e.g., color, form) was relevant and three were irrelevant. The elderly subjects made more errors than younger subjects and exhibited a disproportionate increase in both RT and errors with increasing levels of irrelevant information (cf. Kausler & Kleim, 1978).

The most studied age related deficit is undoubtedly the increased likelihood of forgetting that elderly humans exhibit. The loss is greatest for more recently acquired information. The pattern of memory deficits is quite interesting from the present standpoint as well. Although recognition is somewhat more stable than recall (e.g., Schonfield & Robertson, 1966), declines in recognition are found after age 65 (Erber, 1974). Aged subjects are particularly deficient on recognition performance on a second list (Gordon & Clark, 1974) suggesting that the distractors on the first test cause PI for the second list. Smith (1975) showed that semantic association between targets and distractors caused somewhat greater problems for aged subjects.

Rankin and Kausler (1979) tested subjects aged 19, 45, and 70 on phonological and semantic false recognition rates. The task was continuous recognition with moderate (4-second) or slow (8-second) presentation rates. Both middle-aged and elderly displayed a greater false recognition rate for both rhymes and synonyms (cf. Harkins et al., 1979; Wickelgren, 1975).

Memory deficiencies are particularly pronounced when recall is used (e.g., Schonfield & Stones, 1979). Elderly subjects, especially over 65, show substantial deficits when compared with young adults or middle-aged adults. Interestingly, the elderly show significant improvement when given cued recall tests. For example, Lawrence (1967) showed that aged (x = 75 years) subjects could perform as well as young adults on a 36-word list consisting of exemplars from six categories when the category cues were available at the time of recall.

In paired-associate learning aged subjects do particularly well when the pairs have high associative strength. Decreasing the associative strength of the pairs or creating unusual or bizarre pairs results in accentuated differences according to age (Boyarsky & Eisdorfer, 1972; Lair et al., 1969). The aged seem to display a general deficit in retrieving less familiar or less well-learned memory traces. The digit substitution test of the WAIS which requires the substitution of particular symbols for digits shows substantial age-related deficits, for example (Storandt, 1976; Schonfield & Robertson, 1966).

On the other hand, the aged showed little deficit on well-learned and over-rehearsed memories and cognitive skills. Charness (1981) tested young and old chess players of varying skills on problem solving and memory tasks related to chess. On such problem-solving tasks as choosing a move or a speeded end game, skill level was the only significant predictor of performance. Age was a factor on an unexpected recall task, although it interacted with skill to determine final performance. Similarly, aged subjects are quite able to use many organizational and rehearsal techniques to improve their recall levels when instructed to do so. Interestingly, they seem less likely to engage in these actions spontaneously, however.

Many of these findings bear a great deal of similarity to those found in patients with habituative system damage, although the deficits are much less severe as a consequence of aging than those found with pathological conditions. The elderly have reduced ability to deal with nonsalient stimuli, are more likely to perseverate on salient dimensions, and suffer from encoding and retrieval deficits as a consequence. These are all suggestive of the operation of a normal reinforcer system combined with diminished habituative system functioning.

To speculate a bit, it may well be that this combination of factors in the elderly accounts in part for the lessening of creativity that usually accompanies old age, even among the most

338

talented individuals. It has long been noted anecdotally (cf. Koestler, 1964) that significant insights often come about during a period of temporary disengagement from thinking about a particular problem or subject. In fact, there are a number of French expressions which express this phenomenon, e.g., pour inventer il faut penser à côté (to invent you must think aside) and reculer pour mieux sauter (step back the better to leap forward). The essential point is that sometimes sustained and intense concentration on a subject can render fresh viewpoints less likely. By lowering the level of goal-related activity, even if only temporarily, less obvious relationships can be found.

This process is highly suggestive of the way the reinforcer and habituative systems are assumed to interact in humans. The reinforcer system is assumed to focus attention and processing capacity on motivationally salient stimuli and cognitions, while the habituative system is concerned with the processing of less salient stimulus dimensions and habituation of responding to nonreinforced stimuli. It will be remembered that the activation of the reinforcer system tended to inhibit the operation of the habituative system. The more strongly the reinforcer system was activated, the more the habituative system was inhibited.

If this interaction does take place as specified, then it is clear why insights can become less likely when a person is strongly engaged in a particular task, i.e., through the inhibition of habituative system functioning. Of course, the young and middle-aged adults can relax their concentration and, thus, reduce this inhibition. However, if older individuals have a diminished habituative system, the process of reculer pour mieux sauter may be made much less likely because the relaxation of concentration does not lead to the variety of nondominant cognitions needed to achieve problem solution in novel situations or circumstances. In addition, the diminished functioning of the habituative system would make it more difficult to disengage from salient activity because of the lack of a counteracting influence on the operation of the reinforcer system. Thus, there would be an increasing rigidity in the thought process along dominant, well-learned dimensions, which is quite often the case in aged individuals.

## THE HIPPOCAMPAL SYNDROME IN HUMANS

If the kinds of memorial and cognitive effects seen from aging are due to developmental changes in the habituative system, then we should see at least some of the same effects from other forms of diminished function in these structures. Damage to upper and lower level habituative system structures such as the mammillary bodies and the hippocampus does occur from various experiential factors such as disease, alcoholism, or impact trauma. Obviously, deficits arising from those causes are likely to be much more severe than any we would expect from normal aging, but we should see some correspondence if our reasoning is correct.

A fascinating question concerning hippocampal (and habituative system) function has been the relative lack of correspondence between the deficits displayed by humans and animals following hippocampal damage. Typically, bilateral damage to the hippocampus in humans seemed to result in an almost total incapacity to learn new information, at least in long-term memory. Short-term memory remained relatively unimpaired (Talland, 1965). On the other hand, deficits displayed by animals, while considerable, did not approach the level seen in humans. Additionally, the pattern of losses in humans and animals seemed to be different, leading to the possibility that the hippocampus assumed new functions in humans. The present theory contends, however, that there is no appreciable difference in the function of the hippocampus in humans and animals, although humans do process types of information that animals do not.

Before dealing with the specifics of the losses, it will be useful to provide a possible reason for the very extensive nature of the human hippocampal deficit. One of the most striking differences between humans and animals is the qualitatively different nature of the emotional or motivationally significant behaviors in each group. Humans show very few of the species-specific behaviors that are found in even the most intelligent primates. We saw the disruptive effect of amygdalectomy on monkeys' interpretation of social behavior (Thompson et al., 1977). The social signals used by monkeys are fairly invariant across members of the species. This is not the case with humans to anywhere near the same degree.

Now it will be remembered that the reinforcer system was assumed to process reinforcing stimuli and primary cues, providing the means for their capacity to evoke species-specific behavior. On the other hand, secondary cues without conditioned reinforcing properties seemed to be processed through the hippocampus and habituative system. If there is a lack of fully integrated species-specific responses, as there seems to be, and if humans possess the capacity for a wide variety of arbitrary, voluntary responses controlled by discriminative stimuli which are not conditioned reinforcers, as is known, then the relative importance of the reinforcer and habituative systems should reflect this fact. That is, the habituative system should be more important relative to the reinforcer system in humans than it is in animals. In mammals, the reinforcer and habituative systems seem to be fairly evenly balanced in terms of their importance. With humans, this balance is gone because of the reduction in species-specific behaviors and because so many cues are discriminative stimuli without emotion-evoking properties.

Thus, it seems clear that destruction of the hippocampus and other habituative system structures could cause a broader, more severe deficit simply because a greater percentage of information is being processed through it. Animals process much information through the amygdala and reinforcer system, which should remain intact after hippocampal damage. It is now time to examine the exact nature of the deficit in humans, to see if it can be accounted for in terms of the hippocampal principles of operation listed above.

Although earlier studies (e.g., Talland, 1965) indicated an almost total long-term memory deficit for non-motor tasks, more recent evidence suggests that long-term memory per se is still intact (e.g., Squire & Slater, 1978; Warrington & Weiskrantz, 1968). It should be noted at the outset that since amnesic syndromes in humans are almost always produced through environmental rather than surgical traumas, the precise nature of the damage is not easy to ascertain. Nevertheless, there appears to be broad support for the existence of at least two types of amnesic syndromes produced by habituative system damage (cf. Huppert & Piercy, 1982; Squire & Cohen, 1984). The first type, often called Korsakoff's syndrome, is associated with damage to diencephalic structures such as the mammillary bodies and mediodorsal thalamus which have close connections with the hippocampus. The hippocampus itself is minimally affected, although diffuse damage to the prefrontal cortex often exists. The second type is produced by damage to the hippocampus and limbic cortex because of encephalitis, hypoxic ischemia, and, perhaps, electroconvulsive therapy.

In previous discussions, we have noted that functional distinctions exist between lower and upper level structures of the habituative system. Lower level structures in the diencephalon were primarily involved in habituative functions with less control over the processing of nonsalient stimulus information. Upper level structures from the hippocampus to the prefrontal cortex had a larger role in nonsalient stimulus processing than in habituative function although the hippocampus, true to its medial position, had a roughly equal role in both. Thus, the amnesic syndromes should differ in their memorial effects according to which set of habituative system structures are damaged.

Korsakoff's Syndrome

Damage to the diencephalic structures indicated in Korsakoff's syndrome produces a learning and memorial deficit characterized by (1) increased proactive interference; (2) retrograde amnesia for events prior to the onset of clinical symptoms; (3) poorer encoding of contextual attributes; and (4) normal forgetting rates (cf. Aggleton & Mishkin, 1983; Butters & Albert, 1982; Cermak & Reale, 1978; Zola-Morgan & Squire, 1982).

Cermak and Reale (1978) have suggested that the amnesic effect found with patients with Korsakoff's syndrome is due to deficient encoding abilities. Winocur (1979) argues for a related idea, namely, that the deficit is in the encoding and retrieval of contextual cues. Although the amnesic patients have the ability to encode verbal material on either a semantic, acoustic, or associative basis, they tend to perseverate on one particular encoding dimension in a task (Oscar-Berman, 1973). Korsakoff patients seem to attend to fewer stimulus dimensions of the test stimuli compared to control subjects (Dricker et al., 1978). Conversely, it has been shown that such amnesics perform consistently better on paired-associate and free recall tasks when distinctive external cues are used to aid recall. The control subjects, on the other hand, perform effectively with minimal external cuing (Winocur & Kinsbourne, 1978). Similarly, amnesics' performance on recall and recognition improves as they devote more effort in the acquisition or learning phase (Cermak et al., 1976).

To the extent that the encoding of the target items is unidimensional or otherwise impoverished, it reduces the number of interassociations and other retrieval cues which can effectively elicit the item. This would make retrieval more difficult in many circumstances since only those retrieval cues which in some way relate to the encoded dimensions of the target are useful (Anderson & Bower, 1974; Tulving, 1976).

Warrington and Weiskrantz (1968) provided evidence that the severe memory deficit found in Korsakoff's syndrome is associated with severe interference effects. In a paired associate task, the learning rate for the amnesics was very poor on the second list but relatively normal on the first list. The amnesics showed a very high intrusion rate, in that words from the first list were recalled instead of words from the most recent list. In other words, there was an abnormal amount of proactive interference (PI). Kinsbourne and Winocur (1980) showed that the deficit in list 2 performance was not related to the level of overt intrusions, although this finding is not surprising.

Additional research indicated that the deficit on the second paired-associate list occurs mainly after the first recall attempt (Warrington & Weiskrantz, 1978). That is, the first attempt to recall the A-D list revealed a similar deficit in both normal and amnesic subjects, with high false-positive rates. It was on subsequent recall trials that the normal subjects showed substantial improvement, whereas the amnesics remained at nearly the same initial level of performance. Amnesics can remember items that are kept in STM, but when a distractor task intervenes before recall, intrusion rates from previously learned material increase significantly (Meudell et al., 1978).

Recognition tasks clearly reveal the inability to suppress previous information. Huppert & Piercy (1976) studied recognition performance on familiar and unfamiliar items and found a high false-positive rate with regard to familiar items. Interestingly, amnesics were more accurate in recognition of unfamiliar items than of familiar items, unlike the control subjects. Owens and Williams (1980) note that in recognition tasks amnesics tend to accept as to-be-remembered items anything which evokes a dominant response (i.e., a sense of familiarity) because of past usage. Interestingly, patients with amygdalar damage seem to benefit from exposure to previously presented targets and distractors with regard to recognition tasks, which is the opposite of what is found with Korsakoff patients (Andersen, 1978).

Korsakoffs also display retrograde amnesia for memories established prior to the onset of amnesia, although severe cases seem due to additional brain damage outside of the regions under consideration (cf. Squire & Cohen, 1984). Patients with more localized lesions have a mild retrograde deficit (Cohen & Squire, 1981). The retrograde deficit is typically graded in that the loss of memories becomes progressively worse for more recent time periods (Butters & Albert, 1982).

Interestingly, when the Korsakoffs do learn material, their retention rates are comparable to normal subjects. Huppert and Piercy (1978) used a picture recognition task in which initial recognition rates were equalized between groups by lengthening the item presentation time for the Korsakoffs. Delayed recognition tests conducted one day and one week after training showed comparable forgetting curves for both normal and amnesic subjects.

How is the present theory able to account for this pattern of results after habituative system damage? It will be noted at the start that the exhibited deficits seem to relate either to processing of secondary, nonsalient cues or to the failure to habituate previously learned responses--deficits that were found in animals with habituative system damage.

Thus, the amnesics should show deficits to the degree that nonsalient stimulus attributes must be encoded or used to retrieve existing items in memory. For example, Warrington and Weiskrantz (1982) showed that amnesics were significantly worse on paired associate learning in situations in which the stimulus and response terms were not highly associated with each other compared with highly associated pairs. In contrast, control subjects had roughly equivalent levels of performance on the two types of material. Similarly, Cermak et al. (1978) demonstrated that Korsakoffs have particular difficulty in retrieving less typical members of a

343

semantic category but are relatively normal with typical category members.

The second specific point made by the present theory concerns the increased intrusion of previously learned materials in situations where the response to a stimulus has been changed. It was stated before that the hippocampus and habituative system were involved in all stimulus strength reduction whether or not this occurred in the extinction situation. If this is the case, then it is obvious why previously learned material should have such a powerful interference effect for the amnesics. Any verbal response they have learned in a particular situation tends to be extremely persistent and stable in terms of its associative strength. New material must compete with all this previous material in terms of encoding and retrieval.

We saw how this mechanism exerted its effect in the discussions of interference phenomena. Through the operation of match-mismatch retrieval, the presentation of a cue evokes the representations of its closest associates. If the subject has to learn to associate a new item with the cue, the retrieval of the existing associate into working memory reduces the capacity to process the new item. Because of the damage to regions involved in habituative processes, the Korsakoffs are unable to inhibit the retrieval of highly associated episodic representations of the item. For example, if the amnesic sees the item DOG, the semantic representation of the item will be retrieved. From this, the amnesic can access the meaning of the item and also recognize it as familiar. However, other representations will not be accessible because of their lower associative strength or decreased attribute similarity with the retrieval cue.

It should be noted that this effect in Korsakoffs is limited to existing semantic information and associations. The acquisition of new semantic information would run into the same problems as does the acquisition of new episodic information since it necessitates the formation of associative relationships which are not present in the pre-existing structure of memory. However, once such new associative relationships are learned by the Korsakoffs, they should be retained in comparable fashion with the pre-existing representations.

Medial Temporal Amnesic Syndrome

Patients with damage or dysfunction to the limbic system coupled with relative sparing of diencephalic regions display an amnesic deficit which differs somewhat from the Korsakoffs (cf. Huppert & Piercy, 1982; Lhermitte & Signoret, 1976). The characteristic deficits of this amnesic syndrome are (1) abnormally rapid forgetting and (2) temporally limited retrograde amnesia. In contrast with diencephalic amnesia, there is little evidence of

344

excessive interference or extensive remote memory impairment, at least when damage is confined to the limbic system.

Patients with lesions to the hippocampus and amygdala, and patients who have received bilateral electroconvulsive shock, show very rapid forgetting of newly learned information even after relatively short retention intervals compared with both controls and Korsakoffs (e.g., Drachman & Arbit, 1966; Huppert & Piercy, 1979). The forgetting is not associated with intrusions of prior material; instead, there appears to be a total inability to remember certain kinds of material, such as lists of words or pictures, once they leave working memory (e.g., Gabrieli et al., 1983).

Similar results in monkeys with limbic lesions have been obtained in studies by Mishkin and his associates using procedures for testing these animals which approximated the tasks used in studying human amnesia (cf. Mishkin et al., 1982). For example, Mishkin and Delacour (1975) tested monkeys with combined amygdalar and hippocampal lesions on an object recognition task in which food reward could be obtained only by choosing the novel object in an object pair. However, the other object had been seen only once by the monkey, namely, on the previous trial. In other words, this task has a delayed non-match to sample requirement. Control monkeys' performance was nearly perfect, while the limbic monkeys performed only slightly better than chance. Thus, the limbic monkeys had a severe amnesia with respect to the occurrence of a specific item recently seen.

The sharp temporal limitation of the retrograde amnesia seen in limbic patients and those receiving electroconvulsive therapy indicates that damage to the hippocampus and amygdala can affect more recently acquired information, generally within one or two years of the trauma, without having an effect on older memories (Milner et al., 1968; McGaugh & Gold, 1974). These findings indicate that more recent memories are more fragile in some way than older memories and give rise to the thought that some consolidation processing is occurring. The problems with this notion are that several years is a long time for consolidation to occur and that, as we saw, the process of consolidating representations in working memory into permanent form apparently can take place in a matter of a few seconds.

What is the basis for the differences in the diencephalic and limbic amnesic syndromes? In starting out, it should be noted that many of the traumas found in limbic patients have produced damage, or in the case of shock therapy, temporary dysfunction, in both the amygdala and the hippocampus. From the present point of view, this dual loss would be expected to cause particularly severe amnesia since both the reinforcer and habituative systems are being disrupted. However, there is reason to believe that the amnesia produced by damage to the hippocampus may be due to the same

345

mechanism as that produced by amygdalar damage even if the class of memories affected is distinct in each case (cf. McGaugh et al., 1984).

Both the amygdala and the hippocampus are critically involved in the OR to stimulus events, the amygdala to reinforcers and the hippocampus to nonsalient stimuli or to mismatches between external events and internal representations. Both structures are extremely sensitive to seizures and abnormal electrical activity. In addition, there is evidence that amygdalar- and hippocampal-evoked potentials to stimulus events which typically produce the OR are volume conducted to the scalp where they are recorded as the late component of the OR wave complex i.e., the P300 wave (Halgren et al., 1983; Okada et al., 1983).

In the current theory, the late components of the OR are essential prerequisites to the constructions of representations in the cortex and to modifications in the associative strength of memories, although they are not essential to perceptual motor memory formation. The function of these limbic components of the OR is to protect the contents of working memory from being written over by other irrelevant environmental or internal events at the time a significant stimulus event has occurred.

The absence of this control over the encoding process in limbic amnesics creates a situation in which no part of the stream of environmental stimulation entering working memory is assigned preferential attentional capacity. More highly correlated attributes are not associated with affective attributes because of amygdalar dysfunction, and less correlated attributes do not have their associative strength reduced because of hippocampal dysfunction. In addition, many secondary cue attributes will not be attended to at all.

We have seen that representations are formed in the hippocampus (and entorhinal cortex) which contain the associative and response attributes of stimulus representations analyzed in the sensory-perceptual division of the IPM. The CA1 region of the hippocampus and particularly the entorhinal cortex which are strongly interconnected, have neuronal populations which have stimulus specific firing (Andersen, 1978; McNaughton & Miller, 1979; Vinogradova & Brazhnik, 1978). It is argued that on the basis of the associative and response attributes of a stimulus event, the amygdala and hippocampus will potentiate or habituate the behavioral response of the organism. However, irrespective of the behavioral outcome, the activation of the amygdala or hippocampus in mismatch situations always results in the potentiation of the neuronal responses concurrently occurring in the cortical regions of the sensory perceptual division. The potentiation of the sensory-perceptual response pattern permits the registration of the stimulus by increasing the consistency of that firing pattern against the background neuronal responses (cf. John et al., 1973; Spinelli & Pribram, 1966).

The basis for the rapid forgetting characteristic of limbic lesions is therefore the reduction in the potentiation of the stimulus specific firing patterns of neurons in the sensory-perceptual neocortex. In diencephalic amnesia, this potentiation still exists so that the registration of sensory-perceptual information in the neocortex still can occur. The deficient habituative process makes such registration more difficult, however. In passing it should be noted that these deficits are due to a dissociation between working memory and long-term memory rather than between short-term memory and long-term memory. Thus, there should be clear differences between the short-term memory performance of normal subjects and the medial temporal amnesics.

The limited retrograde amnesia characteristics of limbic amnesia must also be due to the loss of a functional amygdala and hippocampus. The close connection between the appearance of retrograde and anterograde amnesia in the same individual suggests as much. The analytical problem is that the retrograde amnesia usually extends back one to three years prior to the trauma. The fact that relatively recent memories are affected but not older memories implies a lengthy consolidation process, so lengthy that it approximates the life span of a number of mammalian species. In addition, the length of consolidation exceeds any estimate of a short-term memory store. What is clear is that fundamental difference exists between the way that old and relatively new memories are accessed in permanent memory. Old memories do not depend on amygdalar and hippocampal function during the match-mismatch retrieval process, while relatively recent memories do.

One crucial point that has not been adequately examined in either humans or animals is whether the amount of reactivation (retrievals) of a recent internal representation has any bearing on the speed with which the memory trace becomes protected from the results of limbic system damage. If the amount of practice is the primary factor in determining the degree to which a recent memory is susceptible to limbic system damage, it would suggest that a change in the nature of the representation rather than a consolidation process on the original trace is responsible.

We have already examined in the abstractive process and in automatization two mechanisms that can alter the neural regions which are activated in the match-mismatch comparison process. By this line of reasoning, repeated activation of a representation alters its constitutent attributes in such a way that the representation can be accessed without the aid of the limbic system. Studies such as Gabriel et al. (1980) have shown that with practice learned stimulus associations which are represented in neurons in limbic cortex gradually are transferred to thalamic neurons. Even with

347

representations that remain strictly within the neocortex such as verbal stimuli, through repetition they can become more differenti- ated from other neuronal response patterns. Thus, the potentiation produced by amygdalar or hippocampal activation is not necessary to the reinstatement of the appropriate neuronal response pattern.

Thus, the retrograde amnesia of limbic or diencephalic amnesics may well be due to the differences in the way that repeated events are encoded compared with events which have occurred only once or a relatively few times. The failure to access newer memories would thus not mean that these representations had been lost from perma- nent memory.

## Spared Capacities for Learning and Memory in Amnesics

In the beginning of this section, it was noted that a number of learning capacities seemed to remain in relatively normal form in amnesics. These include perceptual motor learning, rudimentary classical conditioning, associative semantic priming, memory for older events and some kinds of rule learning (cf. Cohen & Squire, 1980; Corkin, 1965; Kinsbourne & Wood, 1975). For example, both diencephalic and limbic amnesics displayed normal learning rates in a mirror reading task in which words were presented in reflected form in a tachistoscope. Amnesics similarly display normal per- formance on semantic priming tasks, in which word fragments are presented and the amnesic has to identify the full word, as well as on perceptual priming tasks in which the prior activation of a representation facilitates its later retrieval (Graf et al., 1984; Warrington & Weiskrantz, 1968).

A number of attempts have been made to properly characterize the distinction between the tasks that amnesics succeed on and those which they are unable to perform (e.g., semantic-episodic, procedural-declarative) but it is fair to say that most involve labels rather than process descriptions. In trying to identify the processes underlying the different memorial properties of these preserved and deficient capacities it is useful to consider what the unaffected regions of the brain are in amnesics.

Damage to the diencephalon and limbic system leaves a number of areas relatively unaffected even with respect to interrupting their interconnections. The sensory-perceptual division of the IPM can function normally, at least with respect to the match-mismatch comparison of its existing representations with the exteroceptive environment. The prefrontal cortex is left intact in the amnesics, although Korsakoff's syndrome is often accompanied by prefrontal damage. Nevertheless, prefrontal damage does not cause amnesia (cf. Squire & Cohen, 1984); it does lead to deficits in planning behaviors and the ability to use verbal cues to control behavior (cf. the discussion on prefrontal function in Chapter 16).

One other unaffected region is the striatal complex, lying above the level of the diencephalon, with strong connections with the reticular system nuclei. Interestingly both the sensory cortex and the prefrontal cortex have extensive interconnections with this region which bypass the areas indicated in the amnesic syndromes (e.g., Pribram, 1960). Mishkin has argued that these cortical connections with the brain stem provide the substrate for perceptual-motor learning and perceptual discriminations (Mishkin & Petri, 1984). This view is supported by the deficits that occur in these tasks when these connections are interrupted (e.g., Zola-Morgan & Squire, 1982).

In addition, it should be remembered that neurons in the sensory systems have been shown to encode perceptual features even when the animal has been anesthetized (e.g., Blakemore & Cooper, 1970). This finding provides strong evidence that perceptual analysis and memory formation per se are not dependent on limbic mechanisms. However, the perceptual-motor learning that does occur is limited by the processing capacities of the cortico-striatal system. In the case of humans, this means that verbal cues cannot be acquired because they require the representational or modeling properties of the hippocampus and higher limbic cortex neurons. Similarly, the cortico-striatal system has little capacity to encode complex conditional cue-response associations. Thus, the conditions under which amnesics can acquire perceptual-motor responses approximate the conditions under which automatized responding develops, i.e., consistent cue-response relationships. Amnesics display normal performance on semantic and perceptual priming tasks because these only make use of existing representations in the sensory-perceptual division which have been accessed on many occasions prior to the amnesia-inducing trauma.

In summary, the amnesic syndromes are shown to result from damage to diencephalic and limbic structures which interrupts processing through the reinforcer and habituative systems. The particular deficits exhibited depend on the level at which damage is sustained. Damage to diencephalic regions of the habituative system creates severe deficits in habituative processes but relatively mild encoding deficits. Damage to limbic structures such as the amygdala and hippocampus creates severe deficits in the formation of complex internal representations and associative relationships but milder deficits in habituative functions. Preserved learning capacities in amnesics stem from the preservation of sensory-perceptual regions, prefrontal cortex, and the brain stem whose interconnections bypass the limbic system and diencephalon.

# SUMMARY

It is argued that the habituative system follows the biological principle of "last-in, first-out" with respect to its developmental functioning. The continuing post-natal development of habituative system structures such as the hippocampus and frontal cortex is the primary basis for changes in the cognitive capacity of young children and in altricial mammals. Prior to full habituative system development, these organisms exhibit cognitive and memorial behaviors typical of a functional reinforcer system interacting with a diminished habituative system, e.g., reduced ability to process nonsalient stimuli, to shift from previously rewarded behaviors, and to make use of spatial cues in controlling responding. Aging individuals of these species show similar behavioral patterns and also exhibit neuronal changes in their habituative system structures characteristic of declining neural function. These habituative system changes occur prior to and are more severe than the morphological changes occurring in reinforcer system structures. Amnesic syndromes are shown to result from damage to the reinforcer and habituative systems, with the precise deficits dependent on the level at which damage is incurred. Lower level damage creates greater deficits in habituative function while upper level damage creates greater memorial and cue processing deficits.

# Chapter 16
## General Intelligence

The concept of general intelligence is undoubtedly as ancient in origin as that of specific aptitudes and talents, although its formal definition awaited this century (Spearman, 1923). Over the years there has been a great deal of controversy about whether human cognition or intelligence should be described as basically consisting of one general factor $g$ with a few other less important specific aptitudes or whether numerous specific factors exist without any important contribution from a general factor (cf. Nunnally, 1978; Guilford, 1967).

Part of the difficulty in settling this question as to the number and importance of particular cognitive factors is the nature of factor analysis. This statistical technique does not provide unambiguous solutions to these kinds of problems. However, the principal reason for the arguments, I believe, is that both general and specific aptitudes do exist. In the absence of specific experimental manipulation and analysis of the structural processes comprising cognitive activity, the interrelations can be sufficiently complex as to prevent firm conclusions on either side.

In this chapter and the next, we try to identify some of the structural processes that underlie general intelligence and specific aptitudes. However, the discussion does not concern itself with the specific ways in which people successfully perform on particular item types in cognitive aptitude tests (cf. Hunt, et al., 1975; Sternberg, 1977). This is because performance on such tests has such a large strategic component.

It should be noted that there is no essential disagreement with the idea that cognitive behavior should be experimentally analyzed in terms of the constituent or component information processing capacities which may underlie performance on one or more verbal-symbolic tasks. However, human behavior other than that found in infants must be regarded as the product of structural processes interacting with rule-based strategies and knowledge. The difference between the behavior of the very young child and older children and adults is reflected in the differing validities of intelligence tests given at these respective stages of life. Infant intelligence scores are poor predictors of future intelligence scores (cf. Vernon, 1979) in part because the tasks are not that representative of the tasks or intelligence tests given from the age of 5 on, e.g., psychomotor, imitation, simple discriminations (cf. Bayley, 1949; Lewis, 1976; McCall, 1977). Of course, this dichotomy is also predictable from the discussion of the neural development of the habituative system around the age of 5 years.

Thus, when "typical" intelligence tests can be given to an individual, we are already dealing with significant interactions between verbal-symbolic behaviors and whatever other factors may underlie cognitive performance. When the components or processes which together comprise the cognitive activity involved in performance on such tasks are identified, therefore, we have then to decide whether a particular component is a result of strategic rule-based behavior or is the expression of structural processes (or perhaps what is more likely, to what extent each of these possibilities contributes to task performance).

## STRUCTURAL PROCESSES UNDERLYING GENERAL INTELLIGENCE

There can be little doubt that performance on such item types as induction, deduction, vocabulary, numerical operations, measure developed intelligence and provide only the most indirect clues as to the nature of the structural processes which necessarily must be involved. Logically, all rule-based behavior must be based on particular information processing capacities which are not themselves rule-based since otherwise we would be unable to account for the first rule which came into existence. It is obvious that the principles governing language acquisition must be of vital importance, but since many cognitive activities seem at least partially dissociable from language (e.g., music, mathematics) this cannot be viewed as the structural basis for $g$. Perhaps an even more telling point in this regard is that we can generally agree on a phylogenetic scale of intelligence for nonverbal organisms.

What are the considerations that should be taken into account in identifying the structural processes which permit the development of the $g$ factor? First of all, phylogenetic progression in intelligence is likely to be relevant because the idiosyncracies of particular species' behavioral and information processing capacities (including language) are partialed out when considering the phylogenetic ladder as a whole. A factor which was specific to one species would be a less promising candidate than one which could be shown to vary across species in correlation with their phylogenetic position. Second, the factors would need to show developmental changes in the life of the individual organism since it is clear that g can vary developmentally. Third, the factors would have to be highly compatible with rule-based behaviors in the sense that they would in some way be shown to directly facilitate the development of rule-based behavior. Fourth, if there are several structural processes underlying the capacity for g, then they must be highly intercorrelated with each other in terms of their functioning; otherwise we would not find evidence for a unitary g factor at all. Fifth, the structural processes must show individual differences. This is an unfortunately long list of conditions that must be met by a potential factor underlying g, but it at least narrows the field of possibilities that need to be considered.

Let's start our discussion by considering some phylogenetic evidence. As we proceed from animals with simpler nervous systems to those of greater complexity, are there any systematic changes in learning factors that seem to be phylogenetically correlated? We will accept for the moment that there is some relationship between intelligence as commonly conceived and learning capacity (Thomas, 1980). Unfortunately from the point of view of simplicity, we cannot make any claim that learning capacity per se varies systematically as we ascend phylogenetically. Many lower animals such as bees, wasps, and ants show highly developed capacities to learn relationships among events in particular species relevant domains (cf. Seligman & Hager, 1972).

Bitterman (1964) has examined phyletic differences on a number of different types of reversal tasks (i.e,. the subject has to respond to a previously non-reinforced stimulus and stop responding to a previously reinforced stimulus). One of the principal findings was that while rats and pigeons show progressive improvement in habit reversals, fish do not. The nature of the reversal was important for intermediate species such as turtles, which displayed reversal improvements on spatial but not visual discriminations. The interesting thing about these data is that they call to mind the evidence that mammals with habituative system damage also display more difficulty on habit reversals due to the unconstrained action of the reinforcer system. Another bit of relevant evidence is the progressive increase phylogenetically in the size and importance of higher level habituative system structures such as the hippocampus and frontal lobes (Luria, 1980).

353

Before we make any connection between habituative system function and intelligence there are two problems that need to be considered. First, as we noted, complex forms of learning can be
demonstrated in species low on the phylogenetic scale. Second,
complex learning can be demonstrated in animals and humans with
habituative system damage. As a matter of fact, the IQ scores of
people with such damage can be within the normal range.

With regard to the first point, Rozin (1976) offers the interesting suggestion that intelligence is the increasing accessibility
of subprograms which originated as specific solutions to specific
problems for the species. For example, the bee has a great deal
of learning capacity with regard to the location of pollen-bearing
plants, but this capacity does not seem to be usable for other
kinds of learning situations even when the same relations are to
be learned. With humans, the development of language in children
would be another example of a specific complex learning capacity
that does not seem to be available for other kinds of learning, at
least at that developmental state. Thus, the kinds of relations
and concept learning that a child displays in linguistic acquisition
are not shown in other areas even when the level of complexity is
no greater. As we ascend the phylogenetic scale, however, there
is greater likelihood that learning capacities demonstrated in one
situation will also be available in another.

As for the second point, it is possible that once certain
cognitive behaviors have been acquired, they are no longer totally
dependent on the structures which were employed in their initial
acquisition. For older children and adults, an IQ test is more of
an achievement test in certain respects than it is a pure aptitude
test since many of the necessary cognitive strategies have already
been acquired through experience and education. It is possible
that prior learning or meta-learning is less affected than would
be the capacity to learn new relationships and strategies (cf.
Chapter 15). This should be more true of human learning than for
animals since humans are more likely to learn strategies which are
not strictly tied to one type of learning environment and which are
verbally or symbolically mediated.

These points, taken together with the developmental studies of
the preceding chapter, provide at least suggestive evidence that
the habituative system has some connection with the growth and
development of intelligence both phylogenetically and within the
human species. They also indicate that there is not likely to be
some simple isomorphic relationship between the two. In addition,
to say that the habituative system is somehow involved in the development of intelligence does not precisely specify which specific
structural processes are most central to the effect, although it
does restrict the search space. It is this question to which we
will therefore turn our attention.

354

Habituative System Development and General Intelligence

According to match-mismatch theory, there are two main divi-
ions of the IPM: the sensory-perceptual division and the behavioral
analysis division. Since the sensory-perceptual division is composed of the various sensory systems, which have characteristically
different processing operations, it is difficult to envisage how to
conceptualize some general factor of intelligence existing within
its confines. On the other hand, the behavioral analysis division
is composed of two systems which are known to receive information
from all the sensory systems and to send back information to them.

In the preceding discussion, we singled out the habituative
system or at least its higher structures as critical to the expression of general intelligence rather than apportioning credit equally
between the reinforcer system and habituative system. The structure
of the amygdala shows greater structural consistency than the hippocampus and prefrontal cortex across mammalian species, including
humans. Since the amygdala is probably the highest level region of
the reinforcer system, this suggests that the reinforcer system
cannot be the major reason for the dramatic cognitive advances seen
in the primates, including humans. In contrast, such structures as
the hippocampus, entorhinal cortex, and prefrontal cortex show
dramatic increases in their volume, particularly in humans.

We noted that the upper level structures of the habituative
system seemed increasingly involved in the processing of nonsalient
stimuli as opposed to serving primarily as habituative structures.
By the logic of our position, then, we need to look at this process
as the basis for general intelligence.

It is hypothesized that the general function of the habituative
system structures from the hippocampus to the prefrontal cortex is
the establishment and maintenance of behavior under the control of
nonsalient cues. (The hippocampus also has a habituative function
which is not directly shared by higher level habituative system
structures.) The performance of this general function is based on
a number of subsystems in these structures which perform different
but interrelated tasks.

Given the existence of the reinforcer system, we can distinguish between two major activities that must be engaged in by the
frontal-hippocampal loop: selective inhibition or control of reinforcer system activation and the enhanced detection and maintenance
of attention to nonsalient cues which have behavioral significance.

The Control of Reinforcer System Activation Level

We have previously seen that high levels of activation of the
reinforcer system lead to diminished processing of nonsalient cues.
Thus, the proper functioning of the upper level structures of the

habituative system depends partially on their capacity to control the activation level of the reinforcer system.

Such control must be exercised carefully to avoid the problem of inadequate responses to motivationally significant stimulus events, however. Even at the level of the limbic system, the reinforcer system (amygdala) seems shielded from the direct intervention of hippocampal response, since there is almost no evidence of a direct link from the hippocampus to the amygdala.

In terms of the present theory, the habituative system up to the level of the hippocampus has a habituative function distinct from the processing of secondary cues. However, above this level, the habituative function drops out and only the involvement in non-salient stimulus processing remains. Thus, there is less danger from the intervention or control of these high-level structures on the proper functioning of the reinforcer system.

The control over reinforcer system function by habituative system structures such as the prefrontal cortex and entorhinal cortex has an aspect similar to the restraining influence that the (lateral) septum exerts on the amygdala; that is, they modulate amygdalar response without cancelling its effect. The difference is that the prefrontal cortex exerts its restraining influence on the basis of information from the highest processing levels of the sensory-perceptual division and the various areas of the prefrontal cortex itself. On the other hand, the septum exerts its effect on amygdalar response mainly as a function of the diencephalic and limbic output it receives.

The prefrontal control over reinforcer system function is strongest in those situations which contain secondary cues for the occurrence (expected or actual) of a behaviorally significant stimulus event. The inhibitory control over reinforcer system function in these situations reduces the magnitude of opponent processes that can develop in periods of low probability for imminent reinforcement and which tend to disrupt reward-directed behaviors (cf. the discussion on pausing and adjunctive behaviors). In addition, it reduces the probability of disruption from extraneous salient stimuli which occur in the presence of the secondary cues.

Cognitive Secondary Cue Processing

The maintenance of attention to cues complexly or distantly related to significant stimulus events is the other main activity that the prefrontal (and entorhinal) cortex are involved in. It is this activity which is most central to the expression of the general intelligence factor. Thus, we should see the greatest phylogenetic development in those areas of the prefrontal cortex subserving this capacity.

The extension of the secondary cue-processing capacities of the hippocampus to the prefrontal and entorhinal cortex permits more elaborate and extended processing of secondary cues with a concomitant increase in their control over voluntary responding. There are several aspects of this extension of cue processing capacity. First, in order to determine the connection between more complex stimulus events and motivationally significant outcomes for the organism, certain kinds of stimulus analysis are required. Most difficult tasks of analysis involve either the integration of information across successive events or the analysis of conjoint properties of the stimulus environment. Thus, the prefrontal cortex must have the capacity to assist these cognitive operations on sensory-perceptual information. It should be noted that these prefrontal operations are not sensory-perceptual analyses per se. Instead, they involve the organization of OR evocations to particular attributes of the stimulus environment, primarily on the basis of previous experience.

The second aspect of prefrontal cue-processing capacity is the potentiation of processing of secondary cues, either in the environment or retrieved from permanent memory. The latter capacity is particularly important in the context of human cognition because it enhances the control of verbal-symbolic representations over behavior.

The third aspect is the close connection that must exist between cognitive secondary cue processing and the performance of voluntary responses leading to motivationally significant outcomes. In situations in which these kinds of secondary cues are important, species-specific behaviors are unlikely to be of much utility.

## PREFRONTAL FUNCTION

Since we have hypothesized certain cognitive functions to the upper level structures of the habituative system, it behooves us to examine the neurological data pertaining to those structures. In particular, it is necessary to see evidence for the functional divisions that have been discussed above.

### Prefrontal Cortical Structure

The prefrontal cortex has not only undergone dramatic increases in volume in its phylogenetic development but also has been structurally reorganized. Research has revealed that corresponding structural areas of the prefrontal cortex between species may be functionally quite disparate. In discussing the results of prefrontal lesion studies, therefore, it should be understood that interspecies comparisons are based on functional correspondences rather than structural similarity (cf. Table 16-1 for a listing of some of the more probable corresponding regions). For example, the deficits shown after lesions of the dorsal bank of the rhinal sulcus in the rat, e.g., changes in locomotor activity and emotional behavior, are more characteristic of ventral orbital lesions in the monkey (cf. Rosenkilde, 1979).

In the monkey, at least five major subdivisions can be described, namely, the medial orbital cortex, the arcuate concavity, the inferior prefrontal convexity, the superior prefrontal convexity, and the sulcus principalis. The last two regions are sometimes grouped together as dorsolateral tissue. The prefrontal cortex of monkeys and humans contains large regions which are present only in incomplete form in infraprimate species (cf. Markowitsch & Pritzel, 1977). Interestingly, the growth has been primarily in prefrontal areas <u>lacking</u> connections with the amygdala (Porrino et al., 1981) (cf. Fig. 16-1).

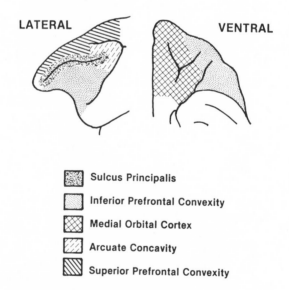

LATERAL     VENTRAL

▦ Sulcus Principalis

☐ Inferior Prefrontal Convexity

▩ Medial Orbital Cortex

▨ Arcuate Concavity

▧ Superior Prefrontal Convexity

Fig. 16-1 . Functional Regions in the Primate Prefrontal Cortex . From Rosenkilde, 1979. Copyright 1979 by Academic Press. Reprinted by permission.

Subregions of Monkey PFC and Some Homologous
PFC Regions in Dog, Cat, and Rat

| MONKEY | DOG | CAT | RAT |
|---|---|---|---|
| Sulcus principalis | Proreal gyrus | Presylvian gyrus | Medial |
| Inferior prefrontal convexity | | Proreal gyrus | Anteromedial |
| Arcuate concavity | Medial precruciate | Presylvian gyrus | |
| Superior prefrontal convexity | Medial precruciate | | |
| Medial orbital | Medial | | Sulcal |

Table 16-1

The Orbital Region and Reinforcer System Modulation. The medial
orbital region of the monkey's prefrontal cortex (and homologous
regions in other species) displays many of the properties required
for a modulator of reinforcer system activity. There are extensive
interconnections between this area and diencephalic and limbic
structures involved in motivational responses to stimuli such as
the hypothalamus, amygdala and basal ganglia (e.g., Krettek & Price,
1977; Nauta, 1972). Stimulation of the sulcal region in the rat
produced increases in quantities of food consumed compared with
medial regions (Cioe et al., 1980). Increasing levels of food
deprivation lead to significant increases in the rate of self administered ESB in this region (Koolhaas et al., 1977).
    Damage to this region often causes aphagia and adipsia in
the postoperative period, probably as a result of disruption of
diencephalic interconnections (e.g., Kolb et al., 1977). Although
homeostatic changes in food regulation can be chronic, more generally there is recovery. In such cases, however, permanent changes
in food preferences still remain (e.g., Brandes & Johnson, 1978;
Ursin et al., 1969). Eichenbaum et al. (1980) showed that the
rhinal sulcus of the rat was involved in complex odor discrimination
but not detection.
    Changes in learned behaviors following medial orbital lesions
are congruent with the operation of an unconstrained reinforcer

359

system acting in conjunction with normal habituative system function. Lesioned animals show an increase in the number of trials to extinction (e.g., Brennan & Wisniewski, 1982) and an increase in the stereotypy of learned responses (Crow & McWilliams, 1979) but are relatively unimpaired in object and spatial reversals (e.g., Iversen & Mishkin, 1970).

The Dorsolateral Regions and the Extension of Habituative System Function. While the medial orbital region or homologous structures modulate the reinforcer system directly, the rest of the prefrontal cortex displays qualitatively different properties and thus is not assumed to share this function. Instead, these remaining regions are assumed to extend the capabilities of habituative system structures such as the hippocampus and entorhinal cortex with respect to the processing of nonsalient information and its association with appropriate voluntary responding.

At the outset it should be noted that there is a great deal of functional diversity in the dorsal and lateral prefrontal areas. For example, neurons in the area of the arcuate concavity discharge in relation to eye movements, both before and during saccades (Bizzi & Schiller, 1970; Goldberg & Bushwell, 1981). This area has strong interconnections with the superior colliculus, as we would expect if it were involved in the attentional control of eye movements (King et al., 1980).

Other dorsal and lateral regions have different cortical and subcortical connections to the sensory-perceptual division of the IPM. The sulcus principalis has long been associated with performance in spatial delay tasks since lesions result in severe deficits in such tasks. Interestingly, however, performances on other kinds of tasks not involving spatial delay are relatively normal (e.g., Mishkin & Manning, 1978; Mishkin & Pribram, 1956).

Recent evidence has shown a close connection with parietal regions involved in spatial perception and this area of the prefrontal cortex. Goldman-Rakic & Schwartz (1981) showed that the principal sulcus of macaques received afferent fibers from the parietal lobe which alternated with projections from the opposite hemisphere of the frontal cortex. Similarly Jacobsen et al. (1978) showed afferent connections to the principal sulcus from the medial dorsal thalamic nucleus, also involved in spatial performance. Correspondences in firing patterns have also been demonstrated in these prefrontal and posterior regions during spatial delay performance in cats (Markowitsch & Pritzel, 1977). It should be noted that while lesions of dorsolateral areas create deficits on various delay tasks, such effects do not appear after ablation of medial orbital cortex (Fuster, 1973; Iversen & Mishkin, 1970).

As Rosenkilde (1983) and Gray (1982) have suggested, prefrontal regions may be functionally heterogeneous on the basis of which sensory-perceptual information they receive, but functionally homogeneous in terms of the supramodal processing operations which are performed on this sensory information. Maintaining cue representations for delayed responding or the detection of departures from elaborate motor programs are possibilities, suggested by Rosenkilde and Gray respectively, which would be examples of a supramodal prefrontal function.

In the present view, the dorsolateral regions of the prefrontal cortex are involved in these kinds of activities, but they must be understood in the context of habituative system function. The hippocampus increases the range of nonsalient stimuli which can evoke an OR in the organism. However, these secondary cues have properties which make them less able to control behavior in the face of competing stimuli than do the primary cues, namely, their lack of affective attributes. Thus, the extension of the capacity of secondary cues to control behaviors required the development of additional mechanisms.

It is hypothesized that the dorsolateral areas of the prefrontal cortex and the entorhinal cortex potentiate the neuronal response to secondary cues in working memory, both when they are exteroceptively present and when they have been retrieved from permanent memory. This action has two ramifications. By remaining at full strength in working memory, these cues make the entry of irrelevant stimulus information somewhat less likely. In addition, the continued processing reduces the subjective delay interval between the occurrence of the cues and the presentation of the reinforcing outcome. For example, dorsolateral lesions severely impair discrimination performance when irrelevant stimuli are introduced between cue presentation and the opportunity to perform the learned response (Bartus & LeVere, 1977). Conversely, low frequency stimulation of the gyrus proreus in cats reduced distractibility and improved delayed responding (Wilcott, 1977). In addition, dorsolateral neurons have been shown to be sensitive to nonsalient cues such as extrafoveal visual stimuli (Mikami et al., 1982).

Since neuronal potentiation has been observed in hippocampal tissue (e.g., Lee et al., 1980) it may be asked why the development of additional habituative system structures was required. The answer lies in the greatly increased connection between the prefrontal cortex (particularly the dorsal-lateral regions) and motor regions which permit secondary cues to exert stricter control over motor behavior. This control increases the efficiency of attentional behaviors as in the organization of eye movements controlled by the frontal eye fields of the arcuate concavity region (e.g., Collin et al., 1982; Crowne et al., 1981). In addition, it permits longer and more complex sequences of motor responses to be performed to obtain reinforcing outcomes (e.g., Glassman et al., 1981; Passingham, 1978).

361

The performance of voluntary behaviors must be guided by cost-benefit relationships of some kind for the organism. In other words, there must be an assessment of the efficacy of particular learned responses in the attainment of reinforcing outcomes. We have seen that the hippocampus is sensitive to conditions of mismatch; similar evidence exists with respect to prefrontal neurons. Sakai (1978) studied unit responses of selected dorsal prefrontal neurons in monkeys during visually guided motor tasks. The neuronal response was not correlated with forelimb movement or force but was sensitive to the reward contingencies. Similar findings have been obtained in complex go-no go discrimination and delayed conditional discrimination tasks (Kubota et al., 1980; Wantanabe, 1981).

Rosenkilde et al. (1981) showed that lateral neurons in the monkey change firing rates to specific cues as a function of both their stimulus attributes and their behavioral significance, showing particular responsiveness to stimuli requiring a behavioral response. Three types of neurons were identified based on their pattern of response in the interval between the learned response and the occurrence of the reinforcing outcome. Type I cells responded to the presence of reinforcers, whether or not the contingent response was performed. However, they were inhibited by the omission of expected reinforcers. Type II cells changed firing rates after nonreinforced trials but not when expected reinforcers occurred. Inhibition was observed when unexpected reinforcers were delivered, indicating a possible mismatch detection function for these cells. Type III cells were inhibited after all discriminative choices by the monkey, whether reinforced or not, and were inhibited to a lesser extent after unexpected reward (cf. Niki & Wantanabe, 1979; Markowitsch & Pritzel, 1977).

The Frontal Syndrome in Humans

Damage to the prefrontal cortex in humans leads to many of the same kinds of deficits which have been shown in animals. Frontal patients show attentional deficits in detecting and responding to novel stimuli (e.g., Salmaso & Denes, 1982). Knight et al. (1981) have shown that patients with dorsolateral lesions have reduced ORs during performance on selective attention tasks. Perseverative responding is very common among such patients, who will continue to perform a dominant response in the face of changed conditions (Luria, 1980; cf. Mattes 1980).

One deficit that deserves a close examination is the dissociation often observed in these patients between their motor behavior and their verbal behavior (cf. Luria, 1980). Verbal commands, even when uttered by the patients themselves, often have no effect on the performance of voluntary responding. This deficit is most noticeable when the patient has to stop performing a dominant or

362

well-practiced response. Other deficits which may well have their basis in this dissociation are an inability to consider their actions objectively or from another's viewpoint and an inability to plan their actions for any long-term goals (cf. Deutsch et al., 1979; Shallice & Evans, 1978).

In the present view, the dissociation of verbal and motor behavior is the consequence of the diminished processing of secondary cues. Most verbal cues or stimuli have a weak or distant relationship with motivationally significant outcomes. Since the dorsolateral prefrontal cortex has strong interconnections with voluntary motor regions, any damage to this area will interrupt secondary cue control and thus verbal control over voluntary responses. It is probably no coincidence that children do not fully display adult patterns of verbal behavioral control until the age of 12 or later when their habituative system development has been completed.

It should be noted that there is one striking difference between human and animal syndromes after frontal lesions. In contrast to animals, humans display very little deficit on delayed response tasks, at least insofar as the delay is concerned (Luria, 1980). One possible reason for this is that typically no overt behavior is required during the delay interval. Since verbalization and ideation per se are not significantly impaired by frontal lesions, the patient can verbally represent the reward that will later occur without having to perform additional responses to obtain it. In this connection, frontal patients have long been known to have deficits in working toward long-range goals.

Summary

The prefrontal cortex is shown to have two major functional divisions. The medial orbital region in monkeys and homologous structures in other species modulates the activation of the reinforcer system so as to minimize the inhibition of secondary cue processing. The dorsolateral regions are direct functional extensions of the habituative system. They potentiate neuronal responses to secondary cues and thus increase their capacity to control voluntary behaviors leading to motivationally significant outcomes. In humans, verbal cues extend the effectiveness of frontal mechanisms. By increasing the capacity of relevant secondary cue control over behavior, the potential for extended response patterns and anticipatory planning is enhanced.

INDIVIDUAL DIFFERENCES IN GENERAL INTELLIGENCE

Up to now we have considered the criteria which hypothesized factors underlying general intelligence must meet and it has been argued that the upper-level structures of the habituative system provide the substrate for the g factor. To review quickly their functions, we have seen that they increase the initial processing of nonsalient stimuli as measured by the strength and latency of the late EP components of the OR. It should be noted that early EP components of the OR are assumed to be handled by lower level structures and thus are not dependent on hippocampal-frontal function. The frontal cortex potentiates and prolongs the neuronal response to secondary cues, thereby decreasing the subjective delay between their occurrence and a reinforcing outcome. Through their control of the late OR components, these structures are critical to all but the most elementary match-mismatch comparisons involving expected stimulus events. Additionally, since secondary cues can only directly control voluntary responses, the frontal cortex has greatly expanded the connections of the habituative system to the neural regions controlling voluntary resonses. Finally, all these functions are supramodal, being performed on information from all sensory modalities either separately or in multimodal convergence.

If these functions do in fact form the substrate of general intelligence, we should see individual differences in their expression. In particular we would need to see systematic and large differences in these factors between individuals in the normal range of the population and those individuals two or more standard deviations from the mean, i.e., <70 or >130 IQ points. Effects are not likely to show up within the normal range if only because our current measures of intelligence are not factorially pure enough to permit such fine discriminations. Since the bulk of relevant research has been conducted with the lower end of the IQ range rather than the higher end, our discussion will be necessarily limited largely to an examination of deficits in the expression of the processes underlying g.

The OR and General Intelligence

One of the primary functions of the high-level structures of the habituative system is to increase the sensitivity of the organism to less salient stimuli or stimulus dimensions. At the most fundamental level, this must necessarily change the conditions under which the OR is evoked, since the occurrence of the OR is the necessary prerequisite of stimulus associative processing. Is the OR a plausible structural process to underlie the development of intelligence, both phylogenetically and developmentally?

To look at this question first phylogenetically, there does seem to be some connection between the range of stimuli capable of evoking the OR and the phylogenetic level of the organism. For example, reptiles and amphibians are likely to ignore many objects introduced into their cages that would evoke investigatory tendencies on the part of almost all mammals. Nor can this be laid to simple species differences in object salience and attractiveness, because the effect can be demonstrated with a variety of stimuli. This general phylogenetic trend is particularly well demonstrated in the studies of sensory reinforcement (e.g., Kish, 1955). Animals higher in the phylogenetic scale are more likely to engage in contingent responding to obtain exposure to stimulus change or objects which do not satisfy biologic or social needs. As we saw, the concept of the reinforcing stimulus as a separate class of stimuli becomes less useful as we move up the phylogenetic scale until it becomes almost identical with the total class of perceivable stimuli in the human species. Thus, the range of stimuli and stimulus relations which evoke the OR from the organism does seem to be correlated with the general level of intelligence that is commonly assigned to various species.

The evidence from human studies tends to support the idea of a relationship between the stimulus conditions which evoke the OR and the level of intelligence of the individual if we keep in mind that the late EP components such as the P300 are critical to these differences rather than earlier components responsive to the sensory attributes of the stimulus. Thus, the OR to simple salient stimuli such as loud tones should be relatively constant across low and high IQ levels, but differences should develop with respect to the OR to less salient stimuli.

Retarded children show particular trouble in attending to non-salient or less salient stimuli. Wilhelm and Lovaas (1976) gave groups of children with different IQ levels a picture discrimination task. Stimulus cards were presented which contained two or more pictures. At test, the pictures were presented singly in order to determine how many of the pictures on any one card were controlling the discriminative response. The lower the IQ, the fewer the number of pictures controlling the discriminative response. Reynolds et al. (1974) showed that autistic children attend to only some of the stimulus dimensions of speech. Spitz and Semchuck (1979) showed that in concept learning with geometric figures a few of the items accounted for most of the errors. These items were the ones most sensitive to inadequate scanning.

Brewer and Nettelbeck (1977) compared retardate and normal performance on an eight-choice RT task using a visual display. The removal of a mid-line dividing eight stimulus lights into groups of four slowed the retardates' response to the stimuli adjacent to the line. Conversely, the presence of an external verbal cue facilitates retardates' performance on paired-associate and concept learning tasks as does overt rehearsal (Gordon & Baumeister, 1971; Landau & Hagen, 1974).

Zeaman and House (1963) pointed out that retardates have unusual trouble with the initial phase of discrimination learning.

365

Simple discrimination learning often shows an initial phase characterized by chance levels of responding followed by a second phase
in which performance sharply rises toward asymptote. It is generally agreed that the subject first needs to attend to the relevant
stimulus dimension and then respond to the correct cue in that dimension. Interestingly, once the relevant dimension is attended
to, retardates perform at similar levels to normals. When stimulus
dimensions are selected which have high initial attentional value
for retardates such as position, then retardates perform quite
well. Switzky et al. (1979) showed that mentally retarded children
tended to explore objects of lower complexity than normal children
(cf. Weisler & McCall, 1976). Retarded children are more distractible than normal children, they show less attentive behavior and do
worse on vigilance tasks (Crosby, 1972).

Retardates are not deficient on all stimulus processing measures, since retardates show normal conditioning rates (e.g., Ross
et al., 1964), normal short-term memory (Belmont & Butterfield,
1971) and normal iconic memory (Hornstein & Mosley, 1979). Thus,
it cannot be contended that the particular deficits noted are part
of a general deficiency in all forms of stimulus analysis. Interestingly, retardates do show slower than normal habituation and
extinction rates for salient stimuli (Mosley & Bakal, 1976), yet are
sensitive to the fact that a change from acquisition conditions has
occurred (Mosley et al., 1975). In addition they seem to show
the capacity for sensory reinforcement and contingency awareness
(Haskett & Hollar, 1978). On the other hand, they habituate more
readily to innocuous stimuli, probably because of smaller initial
ORs (Kimmel et al., 1967)

As the reader should perceive, all these results are strongly
indicative of diminished habituative function combined with relatively normal reinforcer system function. Thus, we see an interesting parallel between the severe cognitive deficits displayed by
retardates and the mild deficits of the elderly and the very young.
It should be noted that the upper level structures of the habituative system are typically among the regions most severely affected
in mental retardation and senile dementia (cf. Pettit, 1982).

Although there appear to be appropriate differences in the OR
between retardates and normals, it is still necessary to establish
such differences between people of average and above-average intelligence. Unfortunately, there has been less research on this
question and the methodological difficulties are somewhat greater
as well. DeBoskey et al. (1979) studied the OR to innocuous stimuli
using the skin conductance response with both gifted and average IQ
children. The gifted children showed greater orienting reactivity
and slower habituative rates to the innocuous stimuli than the average children. Furthermore, the functional correlation between

intelligence and measured OR seemed similar to those obtained between average and retarded children by Kimmel et al. (1967).

An important finding in the Deboskey et al. study was that the slower habituation rate exhibited by the gifted children was only to the first presented stimulus series. On the second and third series there was very little difference between habituation rates of the gifted and average children. As the authors note, more intelligent children may be differentially sensitive to novel or unfamiliar stimuli, but once the nature of the stimulus is determined, its habituation can proceed even more rapidly perhaps than for average children.

As we have seen, the evocation of the OR in humans is more complexly determined than with animals. The kinds of stimulus change that will evoke the OR seem very much a function of the situation as we would expect if the OR could be controlled through verbal-symbolic means (cf. Beatty & Wagoner, 1978). Stimulus change per se does not necessarily evoke the OR (Berstein, 1969; O'Gorman et al., 1970) and is much more likely to do so under conditions where its significance or meaning is high or at least uncertain to the subject (e.g., Bernstein & Taylor, 1979; Voronin & Sokolov, 1960). Many of the typical laboratory tasks developed to study human information processing are used in part because they are well within the capacity of the average adult. Thus, if differences between people of average and above-average intelligence in the evocation of the OR are to be detected, it is going to be necessary to use tasks which are at the "limit" of average information processing capacity as suggested earlier.

To summarize, there would seem to be a good deal of support, both phylogenetically and developmentally, for some connection between the capacity for intelligent behavior and the conditions under which the OR can and will be evoked. This can hardly be the whole story, particularly with respect to human general intelligence since the OR merely ensures that the stimulus event will be attended to without specifying the nature of the stimulus analysis operations performed on it during encoding. It is obvious that these latter kinds of processing must play a key role in determining differences in g between individuals even if the exact way in which they achieve this is not yet clear.

Secondary Cue Utilization

It was argued previously that the prefrontal cortex was critically involved in enhancing the control of secondary cues over behavior. Since many verbal cues, whether exteroceptive or self-generated, can fall into this category, the ramifications of this process on human behavior should be extensive. Since this involvement of verbal cues in the control of behavior is such a crucial part of human intellectual behavior, it deserves a closer look.

With animals, the problem of distinguishing between primary and secondary cues is fairly easy since the temporal arrangements of the exteroceptive cues tend to be preserved in the internal representation. The verbal capacity of humans, however, makes it possible for internal representations to be far different in form or associative relation than the exteroceptive events that precipitated their formation. It is ironic that the increased capacity to process secondary cues possessed by the frontal cortex should make it possible for nominal secondary cues to become strong primary cues. This change can occur through the mechanism of mental contiguity in which the representation of the secondary cue is maintained long enough that it bridges the delay interval of the occurrence of reinforcement.

Verbal mediation makes this mechanism even more probable since symbolic reasoning can juxtapose distantly related exteroceptive events. To the extent that a representation is present at the same time as a motivationally significant event then it will share the affective attributes of that event. This may well be the process by which frontal activation facilitates anxiety and conversely why frontal lobotomies can reduce it.

Despite the reduced correlation between the relationship of exteroceptive events and the form of the internal representations, it is still possible to construct some guidelines as to the composition of the class of secondary cues in the verbal humans. Prefrontal function should be particularly important for cues, verbal or otherwise, which are (1) not currently present in the environment, (2) not closely associated with intense reinforcers, (3) secondary or atypical attributes of a representation, and (4) antagonistic to behavioral responses currently being performed.

Roaden et al. (1980) tested the degree to which varying properties of familiar animate and inanimate concepts could be accessed. Nonretarded and retarded children 8-16 years and 16 years old, respectively (the average mental age of the retarded was 10.7 years), were asked to verify four types of properties in these objects, namely, intrinsic action (e.g., sharks can swim), extrinsic action (horses can be ridden), static (turtles have shells), and superordinate (dogs are animals). The retarded subjects were particularly slow to respond to statements describing static properties of animate objects or intrinsic action properties of inanimate objects (cf. Mason, 1978).

McLean (1978), using a matching task, showed that the salience of stimulus compounds is higher than that of components for retarded subjects (cf. Butler & Rabinowitz, 1981; Cole, 1973). Richman et al. (1978) showed that the poorer performance of retarded subjects on discrimination and reversal learning was due to the greater

368

control of dominant dimensions over their responding. Meisel (1981) showed that in redundant cue discrimination tasks, stimulus overselectivity was reduced only by using cues in successive discrimination problems where previous training has not had a chance to exert its effect on attentional processes. As Butler and Rabinowitz (1981) note, one of the reasons why retarded children may have such trouble with redundant cue discriminations is that they learn them on a configurational basis. However, during testing the study configurations are broken down into their components to determine which elements control responding.

These studies provide strong indications that in at least some forms of mental retardation, there is differential damage to habituative system structures relative to reinforcer system structures. The lack of a fully functional habituative system in turn restricts the range and complexity of the correlational analyses of incoming information or reorganizations of already stored material since only dominant or typical dimensions are readily encoded or accessible. The operation of study-phase retrieval processes, therefore, are impoverished in their abstractive effects vis à vis normal individuals.

Sperber et al. (1976) studied retardates' knowledge of conceptual categories by semantic priming effects. This procedure involves presenting related items in succession and measuring whether RT decreases to the second item as a result of the prior presentation of the semantically related item. In this experiment, nameable pictures were used as the stimulus materials. Retardates did in fact show faster RTs to the second picture of related pairs, indicating that basic categorical information is encoded by them. However, in a concept usage task in which the subjects were tested on recognition and verbalization of categorical relationships, performance varied with IQ.

Retardates do seem particularly deficient in the kinds of internally generated reorganizations of encoded material that seem essential to the development of abstract knowledge structures. They show deficiencies in organization of items for recall (Brown, 1974; Ellis, 1970) when external aids are not provided (Glidden et al., 1977) and are less able to use intrasequence organizational structure (Holden & Winters, 1977). Byrnes and Spitz (1977) showed that retarded adolescents perform even more poorly than their mental age would indicate on tasks requiring some degree of logical foresight (internal cueing) such as the Tower of Hanoi puzzles. These tasks involve changing the placement of disks on poles while always keeping larger size disks below smaller size disks. Perseveration of responses was a frequent occurrence in the retardates relative to the normal children (cf. Spitz & Nadler, 1974).

Retardates are also deficient at transferring knowledge from one situation to a related but novel situation. Berger et al.

(1982) varied presentation formats of verbal tasks to promote the acquisition and generalization of a verbal abstraction strategy in retardates. The training program was able to impart the strategy to the subjects, but they could only use it on tasks very similar to the original task (cf. Bilsky et al., 1972). Brown (1978) showed some success in increasing transfer by training in multiple contexts.

It should be noted that the elderly show similar if considerably milder deficits in the utilization of such cues, as we saw in the previous chapter. One of the more counter-intuitive findings of this literature is that the elderly often fail to spontaneously use encoding and retrieval strategies which they are quite capable of employing (e.g., Perlmutter & Mitchell, 1982). The problem must lie in the generation of such information from permanent memory while attention is focused on the task being performed; such deficits provide an indication of declining prefrontal functioning.

The ability of individuals to work or wait for delayed reinforcement also shows a positive correlation with IQ levels. Clear developmental trends exist in the capacity of children to delay reinforcement with the most marked changes occurring around 8 or 9 years of age (e.g., Mischel & Metzner, 1962). Melikian (1959) argued that intelligence was a more crucial factor than age per se and in fact Mischel and Metzner found that subjects who preferred larger delayed rewards had significantly higher IQs than those preferring smaller immediate rewards. Levine et al. (1959) found a significant correlation between measures of cognitive inhibition and IQ, with the highest IQ subjects particularly likely to score high on cognitive inhibition.

Prefrontal Processes and the
Criteria for Factors Underlying g

To what extent do these prefrontal processes satisfy the requirements for consideration as variables underlying general intelligence? Phylogenetically, they accord well with what is known about species differences in intelligence. These processes seem to be ubiquitous among mammals and probably vertebrates as a whole. The conditions under which the OR is evoked seem to increase in range and variety as we move up the phylogenetic scale. Higher organisms display greater abstractive powers, as seen in their ability to integrate information across stimulus presentations or across different tasks. It is hard to think of a negative example, i.e., a species which shows diminished correlational analyses or less varied OR activity and yet acts at a highly intelligent level as well. Second, as we have seen, there are clear developmental changes in these factors both in childhood and in old age which are correlated with changes in intelligence test scores. The changes caused by old age are somewhat less systematic, but it is argued here that since the elderly can make use of already learned (some-times highly learned) skills and memories on many cognitive tests, their deficits are less clear-cut in terms of test scores.

Third, it is clear that these structural processes are quite susceptible to rule-based control or mediation. We have seen many instances of the OR coming under verbal-symbolic control. Addition-ally, internally directed reorganization and elaboration of encoded material will obviously determine the kinds of information under-going study-phase retrieval and thus, susceptible to correlational processes. Conversely the operation of these processes would be essential to the individual development of many of these personal strategies and knowledge structures.

Fourth, these processes are clearly highly intercorrelated in terms of their function. Correlational analyses cannot take place to unattended stimuli, while in turn the knowledge structures con-structed through such correlational analyses guide the individual in specifying the aspects of the stimulus environment to be attended to. It is hard to see how changes in one of these processes could fail to have a significant impact on the functioning of the others, in short.

Fifth, it is quite clear that individual differences do exist in the operation of these processes, and furthermore the individual differences seem to be correlated with differences in intelligence. Nor is it the case that all such structural processes vary with intelligence levels. Two prominent exceptions are the capacity of working memory and the operation of the reinforcer system which display very little change even over great differences in cognitive capacity.

A sixth point that might be added is that if these processes are a major determinant of $g$ we should not expect their effects to be localized within any one area or hemisphere of the brain. The mechanisms hypothesized to be governing the OR and correlational analyses are certainly bilaterally represented even if we consider only the habituative system.

There has not been a lot of research on this question, but a study by Zaidel et al. (1981) does provide some relevant evidence. They tested split brain and left or right hemispherectomized sub-jects (i.e., patients with one hemisphere surgically removed) on their performance on Raven's progressive matrices test. This is a cognitive measure (symbolic analogies) which is an often used index of general intelligence and which is not simply another measure of a more specific aptitude (i.e., visual-spatial or verbal). Zaidel et al. found little evidence for laterality effects on either group of subjects in that all the patients were able to perform at sub-stantial levels (cf. Kertesz & McCabe, 1975; Zaidel & Sperry, 1973).

In the split brain patients, the disconnected left hemisphere was slightly better than the right and approximated the problem-

371

solving ability of the brain as a whole. However, evidence was found for qualitatively different error patterns in the performance of the two hemispheres on the task, suggesting that different problem-solving strategies are used in each hemisphere. Spearman (1946) noted that both an analytic and synthetic strategy might be used in solving Raven's test. The left hemisphere proved particularly superior to the right on error correction, perhaps because the latter hemisphere most often engaged in holistic processing strategies.

Although there is broad evidence that the processes controlled by the upper-level habituative system structures are determinants of general intelligence levels, I do not wish to be dogmatic about whether there are additional factors which also comprise the basic phenomenon of $g$. However, we should be careful to distinguish between variables that can affect the final expression of $g$ and those which actually subserve it. For example, there can be little question that motivational factors will play some role in the development of an individual's level of intellectual functioning and capacity. However, such factors while having an influence on $g$ cannot be considered to form its structural basis. If there are other information processing capacities comprising $g$, they should conform to the basic considerations outlined above.

## SUMMARY

The structural processes underlying the psychometric factor of general intelligence are examined in the context of the phylogenetic development of the habituative system. The general function of the upper level structures of the habituative system is the establishment and maintenance of behavior under the control of nonsalient cues. The medial orbital region of the prefrontal cortex modulates the level of activation of the reinforcer system as a function of secondary cue occurrence. This mechanism minimizes the occurrence of opponent processes which can disrupt long behavioral sequences. The dorsal and lateral regions of the prefrontal cortex and the entorhinal cortex subserve the maintenance of attention to cues complexly or distantly related to significant stimulus events. These regions potentiate and prolong the neuronal response to secondary cues in working memory. In addition, they enhance the control of voluntary behaviors by secondary cues through their extensive interconnections with motor regions. These processes are shown to exert a major effect on cognitive activites in humans and appear related to individual differences in intellectual behavior.

# Chapter 17
## Specific Aptitudes

The same psychometric evidence that has provided support for the idea that a $g$ factor exists has also provided support for at least several and possibly many more specific aptitudes (cf. Guilford, 1967; Spearman, 1923). Let's start off with the assumption that there are, in fact, many different specific aptitudes but that some will be more significant than others either because of their greater usefulness in a variety of tasks and/or because human culture values certain abilities above others.

To go against parsimony requires good justification, so we should have sound logical and empirical reasons for hypothesizing many specific aptitudes which interact with general intelligence rather than just a few. If we consider physical talent, it is apparent that there are many different kinds of physical abilities, which can vary widely between individuals. Some people can run faster than others, some can lift more weight, some can jump higher, some can hit a ball with a bat better, and so on. It is clear that these are not entirely, or even mainly, due to some general motor ability since decathlon athletes, who are presumably the best all-around athletes in the world, are typically not the best in the world at any of the ten individual sports which constitute the decathlon.

Obviously, some physical abilities are simply due to the basic physical structure of the individual. For example, top running speed is determined in part by the relative proportions of leg bones and muscles. Yet it is also true that many physical abilities are what are usually termed psychomotor skills. Shooting a basketball through a hoop, catching a baseball or football, serving in tennis all require interactions between the analysis of perceptual information with skilled motor activity. Thus, it is not unreasonable to assume that individuals possess different aptitudes in perceptual analysis in addition to different physical aptitudes.

Recent research has indicated that extensive areas of the human cortex and primate cortex are involved in perceptual analysis in the different sensory systems. The different sensory systems project to the appropriate cortical areas in parallel and only partially overlapping systems. For example, in the somatosensory system one pathway may be capable of finer texture analysis than form analysis, while another projection is capable of finer form analysis than texture analysis. Individual differences in neuronal integration or structure in these two projections might allow one individual, given appropriate experience, to excel in the detection of textural differences in textiles while another would excel in the detection of irregularities in the shapes of objects that could not be seen. Presumably, the same process could apply in any of the sensory systems. Thus, some people would have excellent gustatory and olfactory capacities, others would be able to analyze sounds more accurately than others and so on.

The critical question for the current discussion is whether differences in perceptual aptitudes also reflect themselves in the performance of cognitive tasks. We saw in Chapter 3 that there was considerable evidence for the idea that cognitive tasks which required particular kinds of perceptually based manipulations of internal representations (e.g., imagery or mental rotation) activated the same sensory-perceptual regions as do similar stimuli presented exteroceptively.

In essence, the argued connection between specific cognitive aptitudes and sensory-perceptual processing should be seen as the product of the analogical encoding process. If the strong version of this construct is accurate, then we should see a neural fractionation of the processing required to perform integrated cognitive tasks when viewed at the behavioral level. To examine this question empirically, we will examine the neural processing of linguistic capacity as revealed by the aphasias.

THE APHASIAS AND ANALOGICAL ENCODING

It is important to see the extent to which the hypothesized analogical encoding process can explain the involvement of different cortical areas in linguistic and spatial behaviors. Linguistic and other verbal capacities, while restricted for the most part to the left hemisphere (LH) in lateralized individuals, have long been known to be affected by damage to a number of distinct regions in

374

that hemisphere. Undoubtedly the two best known regions involved with verbal function are Broca's area, located in the anterior portions of the temporal region, and Wernicke's area, located in the posterior infero-temporal region. Interestingly, the deficits produced by damage to these two regions are highly distinct, although both are involved with verbal functioning (cf. Fig. 17-1).

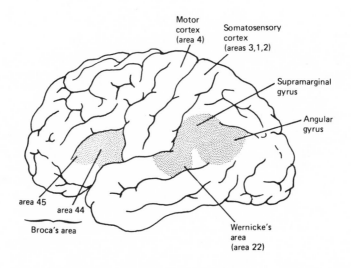

**Fig. 17-1 . Cortical Areas in the Left Hemisphere of the Human Brain Associated With Broca's and Wernicke's Aphasias .** From Kuffler et al., 1984. Copyright 1984 by Sinauer Associates . Reprinted by permission.

Broca's Aphasia

Broca's aphasia is characterized by difficulties in fluent speech, although these are not due to any motoric deficits in manipulating the organs of speech (cf. Locke et al., 1973; Lenneberg, 1973). In general such patients omit functional words and certain bound morphemes (e.g., prepositions, modifiers) while continuing to express nouns, verbs, and other content words. This gives their speech an oddly disjointed character often characterized as telegraphic speech. Zurif et al. (1972) showed that in a sorting task of words in sentences, Broca's aphasics coupled content words together in contrast to normals who coupled articles and nouns.

The patient with Broca's aphasia also has difficulty comprehending these functor words. Agrammatic aphasics have been shown to be incapable of retrieving the semantic information conveyed by determiners such as "a" and "the" (Goodenough et al., 1977). Caramazza and Zurif (1976) tested aphasics on a picture-matching task in order to gauge their understanding of sentences which varied in the extent to which inferential processes based on semantic information could be used as a substitute for lexical analysis. The patients were successful in understanding the sentences possessing constrained semantic relations (e.g., the apple that the boy is eating is red) but failed with sentences that were more ambiguous in the relation of the semantic constituents (e.g., The girl that the boy is chasing is tall).

Zurif et al. (1976) presented sentences to controls and Broca's aphasics which contained functors differing systematically in their communicative content. In contrast to the controls, the aphasics were unsure about the role of articles and grouped them inconsistently, violating the structural unity of the noun phrases in the sentences. Differences in functor usage were also evident. In sentences such as "Stories were read to Billy" and "Stories were read by Billy," the Brocas consistently linked the contiguous preposition with the final noun, Billy.

Broca's aphasics show uncertainty mainly for those functors which have little communicative content. In spelling, Brocas seem to depend more on the overall graphemic structure than on phonetic features (Wapner & Gardner, 1979; cf. Kohn et al., 1984). Interestingly, they seem to display difficulty in processing sequentially presented information (Benson, 1977). However, they can understand simple sentences because the range of possible relations between semantic items is often small.

Wernicke's Aphasia

The aphasic syndrome produced by damage to Wernicke's area demonstrates interesting differences from the typical effects seen in Broca's aphasia. Wernicke's aphasics, unlike Brocas, demonstrate fluent speech and show no difficulty with the functor words. However, they do have deficits on the content words (e.g., nouns) that the Brocas can successfully handle. Friederici and Schoenle (1980) presented both kinds of aphasics with an oral reading task of homophonic items which were all members of both vocabulary categories (e.g., wood-would). In the nonfluent aphasics, the functor items were disrupted while the fluent aphasics showed severe deficits with the lexical items. This was despite the good preservation of the same sounding grammatical items which sometimes possessed the exact same spelling. Wernickes are often unable to match an auditorily presented word to its equivalent picture when presented with an array of phonemically similar items (Blumstein et al., 1977). Goodglass and Stuss (1979) showed that while both fluent and nonfluent aphasics benefited in a naming task by being presented with a visual representation of the object, Brocas benefited most while Wernickes benefited least (cf. Pease & Goodglass, 1978).

Normal individuals seem to display differences in the way functors and semantic words are processed. It should be noted that functors belong to a small (closed) set while semantic items belong to a large (open) set of words. Bradley et al. (1980) examined whether open and closed class systems differed in their retrieval mechanisms by comparing them on frequency sensitivity and left to right scan order, factors that are strongly characteristic of open class performance. Word recognition of open class items is positively correlated with frequency of occurrence when heard with noise or in tachistoscopic presentation or in lexical decision tasks. (The superior recognition of low-frequency words occurs in retention tasks.) In contrast, no evidence for frequency effects or scan effects were found for closed class items. RTs are slower if the initial string of a nonword presented in a lexical decision task is a real word or stem (e.g., Toastle). This effect did not hold for closed class items. Thus, behavioral differences seem to exist between these word classes in normal subjects.

Neurological Differentiation and the Aphasias

If the hypothesized involvement of analogical encoding in linguistic processing is correct, it would suggest that the differences found in the aphasic syndrome as a function of the location of the lesion would be due to different processing characteristics of these respective areas. The comprehension deficits characteristic of Wernicke's syndrome relate to semantic referents above all. When speaking, these aphasics display paraphasia as well as omission of these kinds of verbal items in their speech (cf. Hecaen & Albert, 1978). It is interesting that the brain areas most typically associated with this deficit lie in a region bordering the association cortices of the visual, auditory, and somesthetic regions (i.e., in the angular gyrus, cf. Geschwind, 1980).

Patients with lesions in the border between the temporal and occipital region frequently show loss of memory for word meaning. They can carry out phonemic analysis, recognize pronunciations and differentiate between linguistic sounds while displaying a severe amnesia for their semantic interpretation (cf. Luria, 1980). Basso et al. (1980) described a patient who lost the capacity for mental imagery while still retaining other speech related functions. Besner and Coltheart (1979) demonstrated that normal subjects display differences between alphabetic and ideographic processing (e.g., one-1). Subjects were asked to judge which of two simultaneously displayed numbers was numerically larger. Irrelevant variations in physical size of the ideographic numbers influenced RT but this effect was not found with the same numbers printed alphabetically. Interestingly, brain-damaged patients have been found who can name numbers when they are printed ideographically but not alphabetically (Albert et al., 1973). Luria (1980) notes that the temporal occipital patients can copy drawings shown to them, but are unable to reproduce them when they are removed. It is highly significant in this connection that Wernicke aphasics perform more poorly on tasks with pronounced spatial components than do Broca aphasics (Dahmen et al., 1982).

These findings suggest that the characteristics of Wernicke's aphasia are due to the particular perceptual processing functions of the posterior region. Words which are encoded with features relevant to visuo-spatial features or other similar integrated representations are more likely to be processed in this particular neural area. Since memorial representations are formed in the areas that perform the encoding operations, damage to these areas will result in the differential loss of those memorial attributes of the stimulus.

Why are functor words differentially processed in the anterior region? Functor words are used linguistically in notably different ways. Some languages (e.g., Russian) do not even have the indefinite/definite article distinction. Many languages (e.g., English) show highly idiomatic use of prepositions such that completely different meanings are associated with the same preposition depending on its immediate verbal context. While nouns can have multiple meanings, it is almost always the case that the different interpretations refer to discrete and easily differentiable objects. This is not the case with functors, however, which often have an arbitrary relationship with the word phrase they precede (e.g., by the way, by golly, little by little, by the rules, by name).

If the notion of correlational abstraction has any validity here it is clear that this constant variation of prepositional (and other functor) usage should result in them becoming denatured of meaning to a large extent, particularly since they have no concrete perceptual or symbolic referents. In what way then can the individual encode these words? The remaining possibility is that they are encoded in terms of their own inherent stimulus properties, i.e., the auditory and kinesthetic features involved in pronouncing them or hearing them spoken.

If this is the case, then it is not surprising that damage to the area between the auditory and premotor areas produces a severe but selective deficit in the use and comprehension of this class of words, while leaving semantic meanings less affected. Luria (1980) has suggested that the deficit is due to the high degree of overlearning of such words and their consequent representation as motor plans or images. Actually, many common nouns are just as overlearned, yet they display quite different properties both behaviorally and in the neurological loci which seem to be involved with their processing. Rather, the difference in the aphasic syndromes is simply the outgrowth of the structural processes of precision and analogical encoding.

It should be noted that patients with either Broca's or Wernicke's aphasia very rarely have total destruction of the focal areas for these syndromes. Thus, the deficits they display on relevant tasks can show a high degree of individual variability. The use of semantic or functor representations is most severely impacted on tasks involving generation of these memory traces by the subjects themselves (e.g., Cermak et al., 1984; Kohn, 1984). As we noted in Chapter 3, the processing capacity of the IPM is taxed more severely in constructive or generative actions on internal representations (e.g., mental imagery) than it is on corresponding perceptual tasks involving exteroceptive stimuli. From this phenomenon, it can be predicted that the encoding of exteroceptive stimuli would be more resistant to damage in the corresponding sensory-perceptual regions than would more cognitive tasks.

Summary

Verbal capacity is shown not to be a unitary capacity of the human brain or even of the left hemisphere. Instead, the differentiation of some linguistic categories at the behavioral and linguistic level is shown to be paralleled by a neurological differentiation in processing these entities. Two well-known aphasic syndromes, Broca's and Wernicke's, show quite dissimilar patterns of linguistic deficits. In Broca's aphasia, damage to the area between the auditory and premotor areas in the LH produces a deficit in the use of functor words. Wernicke's aphasia is associated with damage to the angular gyrus and produces a deficit in the use of semantic relations. These specific deficits are shown to be related

to the operation of analogical encoding processes in these regions
of the sensory-perceptual division.

## THE VERBAL-NUMEROSPATIAL DISTINCTION

The factor analytic studies of cognitive test performance have
from the outset invariably shown at least two independent, although
somewhat correlated, specific aptitudes corresponding to verbal and
to numerical/spatial ability (e.g., Guilford, 1967). There are two
questions that concern us: (1) What kinds of processes might form
the basis of the verbal versus visuo-spatial cognitive aptitudes,
and (2) What is the relationship of these processes to cortical
regions involved in visual and auditory information processing?

### Analogical Encoding and Specific Aptitudes

The question of different processing factors accounting for
verbal as opposed to numerical/spatial aptitudes has for a long time
revolved around a possible dissociation between successive versus
simultaneous modes of information analysis. Verbal ability has been
hypothesized to be associated with successive or analytic processing
in the left hemisphere while numerical/spatial ability has been
hypothesized to be associated with simultaneous or holistic process
in the right hemisphere. A large body of evidence has related
mathematical ability to differences in visuo-spatial ability (e.g.,
Blade & Watson, 1955) in normal and retarded children and adults.

We saw in Chapter 3 that the mental operations employed with
memories formed from visually presented stimuli seemed to display
many of the same properties as those found with the perceptual analysis of visual stimuli (e.g., Kosslyn, 1980). The organization of
the cortex into different perceptual modality regions will inevitably distribute the processing and analysis requirements of a
complex task across different cortical areas.

It should be noted that, in this view, each distinct neural
area maintains its own basic information processing characteristics
regardless of the different tasks which involve it. Thus, developmental or lesion-induced changes of brain function affect the
relative involvement of various brain regions in the performance of
a task and do not affect the basic processing characteristics of
that region.

What is the nature of the connection between successive and
simultaneous processing modes and the concepts of analogical encoding and the verbal-spatial distinction? First of all, we cannot
expect an inevitable, rigid correlation between verbal and successive processing on one hand and spatial and simultaneous processing

on the other, although it does seem reasonable to say that these qualities or processing capacities are more likely to occur together than verbal-simultaneous and spatial-successive. Simply on logical and intuitive grounds, it can be seen that one can successively handle spatial information or information represented in a spatial framework. However, a spatial mode of processing is <u>particularly well suited structurally</u> for simultaneous processing just as a verbal analytical mode of processing is structurally suited for successive processing.

Second, the sensory and perceptual qualities inherent in spatial analysis by particular cortical areas, since they are analogical in nature, permit the individual to engage in the same kinds of activity during cognitive processing or ideation that are engaged in during the processing of exteroceptive stimuli within the limits set by the central capacity of working memory. However, we would not expect such capacity to be able to equal the total processing capacity for exteroceptive stimuli simply because full attentional resources must be employed in ideation, while much exteroceptive stimulus processing can be handled by preattentive mechanisms or through automatization processes.

Third, if verbal and visuo-spatial functioning or, alternatively, successive versus simultaneous processing, are relatively independent of each other in terms of brain region, then more neural volume allocated to verbal function compared to visuo-spatial function (or vice versa) should increase the capacity of that processing mode. A logical assumption is that individuals can recognize which processing modality is more easily and effectively employed by themselves in the performance of tasks. This would result in biases toward particular kinds of strategies. Thus, a person who finds that he or she has greater visuo-spatial than verbal capacity will try to perform tasks in such a way as to make use of processing strategies congruent with the favored processing modality. The end result may be that the cognitive activity of the individual assumes in general the characteristics of the favored modality.

Individual Differences in Simultaneous and Successive Processing

The preceding discussion suggested that verbal aptitude is related to the capacity to sequentially process related information while numerical aptitude is related to the capacity to manipulate information in parallel. A number of studies have shown that humans can employ configural (integral) or analytical (separable) modes of problem solving or perceptual analysis (e.g., Garner, 1974; Leiber, 1977). Such processing modes can be shown to differentially affect perception and performance. Kemler and Smith (1979) showed that this distinction could be extended to conceptual learning as well.

381

Subjects were asked to classify stimulus pairs dependent only on the relation between the pair items. Each of the stimulus pairs was composed of items identical on one dimension and different on another. Two types of stimulus conditions were used: integral (saturation and brightness) and separable (size and brightness). The study examined the ease with which a similarity-based rule can be abstracted from integral stimuli and a dimensionally based rule abstracted from separable stimuli. In the former case, the subject has to distinguish similar from dissimilar pairs, while in the latter, distinctions must be drawn between the stimuli differing on dimension "A" from those differing on dimension "B."

In fact, subjects were able to verbalize with clarity the rules they followed in the separable condition, but were not able to do so in the integral condition even though they were capable of correct judgments. Interestingly, subjects in the latter condition did not consistently employ either similarity judgment strategies or verbal rules in solving the problems.

Das and Cummins (1978) studied the correlation between simultaneous and successive processing and academic achievement and verbal and performance IQs in mentally retarded subjects. Simultaneous processing was measured using the integration of individual stimuli into quasi-spatial groupings, while successive processing was measured through the integration of individual stimuli into temporally organized successive series. Simultaneous processing ability was significantly correlated with WRAT arithmetic and WISC performance IQs whereas successive processing capacity was correlated with WRAT spelling and oral reading and negatively related to WISC performance levels. Silent reading and WISC verbal IQ were related to neither processing strategy.

Jarman (1978) has shown that the use of simultaneous and successive processing modes for particular cognitive tests seems to follow a similar pattern in both normal and retarded children (cf. Das et al., 1975). Cohn-Jones and Seimon (1978) studied the relationships of visuo-spatial ability in the development of numerical concepts in both normal and retarded children. The groups were matched for mental age and divided into high or low perceptual ability groups. Equivalent mental ages in the normal and retarded groups resulted in equivalent number performance. In both groups, regardless of variations in IQ and chronological age, visuo-spatial ability levels had a significant direct effect on number concept performance (cf. Brown, 1973).

Walker et al. (1975) showed that retarded children with deficits in auditory sequential memory also had related deficits in receptive and expressive comprehension. However, Kirby and Das (1977) showed a significant correlation between both simultaneous and successive processing and vocabulary and comprehension scores in fourth graders. Butler and Rabinowitz (1981) showed that younger children were more likely to encode discriminations on a configural basis while older children demonstrated more analytical learning even when given a simultaneous discrimination.

Shallice and Warrington (1977) presented data on two patients with an inability to read letters within a word that could be read as a whole. The impairment was found to be general to situations in which multiple items from the same category (e.g., numbers, letters) were simultaneously presented visually. This suggests a dissociation between perceptual classification systems operating in parallel with analytical systems operating serially (cf. Egeth et al., 1972).

Dyslexics, or people with reading impairments, show significant impairments on sequential verbal tasks. Holmes and McKeever (1979) showed that dyslexics have a significant deficit on serial reproduction tasks, although they were able to perform at normal levels on serial versions of a face memory task and on general verbal recall. Rudel et al. (1976) tested dyslexic and normal children matched for age, sex, and mean IQ on their ability to learn letter names of Braille configurations presented visually or tactually and on Morse code signals presented orally. The dyslexic children learned fewer letters in all three modalities although both groups found the visual-verbal method easiest. Thus, the dyslexic deficit was not due to specific modality dysfunction or to deficits in intersensory integration. However, the dyslexics did show severe deficits on the Morse code task which, of course, is totally serial (cf. Blank & Bridger, 1966; Sterritt & Rudnik, 1966). Vellutino et al. (1975) showed that nonverbal visual auditory P-A learning was unimpaired in dyslexics but they did show deficits on visual-verbal tasks.

## Laterality and Successive Versus Holistic Processing

There are a number of lines of evidence that do suggest some reciprocal interaction between levels of verbal and spatial aptitude in individuals, e.g., male and female differences. When carefully analyzed, most of the variables can be reduced to possible differences in hemispheric function, i.e., laterality effects. Therefore, it is to this factor that we will concentrate our attention to determine its potential influence of verbal and spatial aptitudes.

Since language function is often associated with left hemispheric brain regions, it has often been suggested that the left hemisphere (LH) is responsible for relational, analytical processing while the right hemisphere (RH) is responsible for holistic simultaneous processing and cognitive activity (e.g., Bever, 1980; Gazzaniga, 1975; Zaidel & Sperry, 1973). The LH was shown to be dominant for processing nonverbal temporal sequences in normal subjects using visual or auditory stimuli (e.g., Fontenot & Benton, 1972; Halperin et al., 1973). Kohn and Dennis (1974) found that an isolated RH can support more spatial processing capacity than an isolated LH.

Bever (1971) showed that subjects performed better on sentences heard in the right ear (and thus processed by the LH, given contralateral sensory projections). However, when the same word sets were reordered into random sequences of words, the right ear advantage disappeared. Bever (1976) showed that the time taken to recognize a syllable beginning with a particular sound (e.g., "b") is shortest for right ear presentation and right hand responding. There was no difference in RT to recognize an entire syllable. As the author notes, more relational processing is necessary to recognize a syllable in terms of its initial sound than to recognize the entire syllable, which can be accomplished with more holistic processing.

Temporal sequencing capacity has been examined in patients with either LH or RH lesions. Such capacity can be defined as the accurate perception of each discrete stimulus, perception of their presentation order and reproduction or identification of the stimuli in the correct sequence. Swisher and Hirsh (1972) and Carmon and Nachson (1971) examined the performance of such unilaterally brain-damaged patients on nonverbal sequencing tasks. They presented subjects with pairs of differently colored lights and tones of different pitches and asked them to identify which had occurred first. LH damaged patients were significantly more impaired than RH patients on these tasks. Goodglass et al. (1970) found similar sequential deficits in LH patients when using verbalizable pictures and objects.

Cohen (1973) presented subjects with two, three, or four letters to either the left or right visual field of their right eye. (Visual hemifields project contralaterally.) They were asked to judge whether all were the same or whether one was different. RT increased linearly for "same" decisions with increases in the number of stimuli in LH presentations while RH RTs remained relatively constant. This finding would imply more serial-like processing by the LH and more parallel-type processing by the RH. No hemispheric processing effect was found for different judgments, however. White and White (1975) did not find hemispheric differences in a similar task. However, Polich (1980) has shown that the LH is more adept at rapidly processing visual arrays containing variable numbers of stimuli than the RH in a same/different judgment task.

The RH has been shown, in turn, to be more proficient at performing more holistic tasks. For example, mental rotation of objects is performed more efficiently by the RH (Goldberg et al., 1978; Veroff, 1978). The RH is critically involved in face recognition (Milner, 1968) and performance on other spatial tasks (Gross, 1972).

These effects have been demonstrated with response learning as well. For example, Dalby (1980) had male and female students perform a unimanual task involving sequential finger movement alone or in conditions with concurrent cognitive activity. The two tasks that were predominantly spatial in character interfered with left hand (RH) activity more than with right hand (LH) activity. On the other side, the two verbal tasks interfered more with right than left hand activity. Right handers have been shown to perform better with their left hand than their right on tasks involving spatial cues (Kimura & Vanderwolf, 1970) and perception of Braille (Hermelin & O'Connor, 1967). Nachson and Carmon (1975) showed differential hemispheric effects on somatic responses only when both hands were engaged simultaneously on a competitive task.

Musical perception and analysis seems to occur in different hemispheres depending on the nature of the analysis. Musically untrained subjects show greater RH processing of musical relations and characteristics, but musically trained subjects show greater LH processing (Gates & Bradshaw, 1977; Johnson, 1977). EEG activity is also greater on the left side for musicians while greater on the right for nonmusicians (Hirshkowitz et al., 1978). Interestingly, skilled musicians show more pronounced RH superiority for holistic tasks such as chord recognition or familiar melody recognition than nonmusicians (Johnson et al., 1977).

Oscar-Berman et al. (1976) demonstrated that analyses of visually presented musical symbols may actively involve both cerebral hemispheres in subjects who have had formal musical training (cf. Bever & Chiarello, 1974). Peretz and Marais (1980) showed that nonmusicians did not exhibit ear asymmetry to melody recognition differing in local pattern, rhythm or both. However, subjects who discovered the relevant varying dimensions and tried to concentrate on constituent musical elements did show an increased tendency toward right ear advantage.

A similar differentiation in lateral assignment of stimulus processing has been found for different kinds of verbal materials. While articulate speech is usually largely confined to the LH (Zaidel, 1976), some auditory language comprehension does take place in the RH, particularly with simpler verbal constructions (Searleman, 1977). Spellacy and Blumstein (1970) found a right ear advantage (REA) for vowels embedded in a series of English words and a LEA for those same vowels embedded in a series with melodies and sound effects. Haggard and Parkinson (1971) demonstrated a LEA in subjects asked to concentrate on the emotional tone of a sentence while attention to linguistic or acoustic cues produced a REA. Greater average EPs for the production of speech sounds were found in the LH and greater average EPs for tongue-produced noises in the RH (McAdam & Whitaker, 1971; cf. Callaway & Harris, 1974).

It would be nice if the laterality effects unequivocally demonstrated that the LH was a sequential analytic processor and the RH was a simultaneous holistic processor. Unfortunately, too many discrepant studies have appeared in recent years to allow complacency in this matter. For example, DeRenzi and Nichelli (1975) found that while LH patients were deficient on verbal sequencing tasks, RH patients were deficient on nonverbal sequencing tasks, a finding which was replicated by Kean et al. (1980). Umilta et al. (1979) provided indications of RH serial-processing in a dot detection task in which subjects had to locate a solid dot among empty dots. Faster responses occurred to three- versus six-dot displays (cf. Davidoff, 1977). On a more conceptual level, it has been noted that there are difficulties in equating holistic modes of processing with parallel or simultaneous processing since the latter involves the simultaneous analysis of individual features (Cohen, 1973; Nickerson, 1972).

Part of the problem in interpreting laterality effects is that it is becoming increasingly clear that laterality is by no means a uniform phenomenon between individuals. Some population groups display much more laterality of function than do others. For example, men show greater laterality of language capacity than do women (e.g., McGlone, 1977) as do right handers compared to left handers (e.g., Silverman et al., 1966). One of the prime goals of recent research has been to see if such laterality differences are correlated with differences in verbal versus visuo-spatial performance.

To take male-female differences in laterality first, it has been found that aphasias are three times more frequently associated with LH lesions in men than in women (McGlone, 1977). This finding would indicate that women have more RH control of language function. Conversely, impaired spatial ability was not associated with lesions to one particular hemisphere in women. Men show a stronger REA for verbal stimuli in dichotic tasks (Lake & Bryden, 1976) and relatively greater RH desynchrony during visualization tasks (Ray et al., 1976). Females are hemispherically less specialized in tactile learning (Rudel et al., 1979) lateral eye movements (Bakan, 1977, and right-left side discrimination (Bakan & Putnam, 1974).

Bradshaw and Gates (1978) argued that some of the cortical areas of the RH devoted to visuo-spatial processing in men are involved in linguistic analysis in women. They showed that women exhibited RH superiority on a lexical decision task involving manual responses particularly early in training. On overt naming tasks, however, women showed LH superiority similar to males. Thus, secondary speech mechanisms may have co-opted RH regions devoted to spatial analysis in males. In turn, this would reduce the RH efficiency as a spatial analyzer. One of the more consistent findings is the relative visuo-spatial deficit of women relative to men (McKeever & Van Deventer, 1977; Waber, 1976). This line of reasoning leads to the prediction that the extent of lateralization should predict the level of spatial ability that an individual possesses. Zuccolotti & Oltman (1978) showed that young men 18-30 years old who did well on spatial tasks showed significant right visual field advantage while those who did poorly showed no hemifield differences.

The question of some degree of reciprocal interaction between verbal and spatial skills has been studied with dyslexic children who, as noted, display language- and reading-related deficits. Symmes and Rapaport (1976) found that intelligent children showing unexpected reading failure were above average in spatial ability. In the same vein, Witelson (1976) reported that dyslexic children show a preponderance of RH processing (Owen et al., 1971; Rourke, 1976). Gordon (1980) showed that on a cognitive laterality battery of tests, dyslexic children were consistently better on RH tasks. Interestingly, 90% of the first-degree family members of the dyslexic children also showed a similar RH dominance profile even though most claimed not to have a reading problem. The dyslexics were selectively impaired on reading tests involving sequential analysis (cf. Bakker, 1967). Although spatial ability shows some degree of inheritance, laterality does not (Bryden, 1975; Hartlage, 1970).

Processing Mode and Task Factors

Although there is considerable empirical evidence for the involvement of sequential and simultaneous processing in specific cognitive aptitudes, it is less clear what the relationship is between such processing modes and performance on specific tasks. As we saw from the examples cited above, while there was a general tendency for perceptual/numerical tasks to be correlated with a simultaneous or holistic processing mode and verbal tasks with a sequential or analytical processing mode, there was no absolute congruence between type of task and processing strategy employed. Thus, in some visuo-spatial tasks, sequential processing strategies were employed at least in part and in some verbal tasks, more holistic processing modes were found. Thus, we once again are faced with the flexibility of cognitive and perceptual analysis which humans can exhibit on tasks due to their verbal-symbolic capacity.

This does not nullify the conclusion that humans employ simultaneous and successive processing strategies, of course, but it does force us to display some caution in unequivocally linking performance on particular tasks with one or the other approach. Undoubtedly, some tasks are more conducive to one mode of perceptual or cognitive analysis than the other, but different subjects may employ idiosyncratic approaches to the problems and modifications or variations in the tasks themselves may result in changes in the processing strategy used.

Some dramatic examples of this point are provided by neurological studies which show that grossly abnormal hemispheric brain

387

development is not incompatible with language acquisition (e.g., Dennis, 1977). Smith and Sugar (1975) reported a patient with left hemispherectomy who possessed above-average language function with only a RH. This is a useful reminder that hemispheric differences are not based on rigidly prescribed taskrelated processes. In addition, more fundamental perceptual processing capacities appear common to both hemispheres; differentiation is more likely with higher order processing (Moscovitch et al., 1976; Proudfoot, 1982).

We should not take this to mean, however, that laterality effects are meaningless. The essential idea that we need to keep in mind is that there is often more than one way in which the brain can maintain or develop the capacity to perform a task, i.e., compensatory capacities or strategies. Thus, we should find that the way in which different brain regions handle the same task is suited to the way in which they normally analyze information. For example, Dennis and Kohn (1975) and Dennis and Whitaker (1976) have shown that in cases when the RH does subserve phonological and semantic capacities it nevertheless shows quite limited syntactic competence compared to the LH. The first two functions are capable of being performed through the use of semantic strategies which the RH seems more capable of performing; however, syntactic functions are not amenable to these strategies and thus, suffer performance deficits. Similarly, aphasias which develop after RH lesions in certain left-handed patients do not fit the typical taxonomies of aphasic syndromes (Gloning, 1977).

Changes in the way in which the LH and RH are utilized in a task may also exhibit developmental changes in normal subjects. For example, Tomlinson-Keasey and Kelly (1979) showed that RH specialization in a picture-processing task was positively associated with mathematical skill in the early elementary school years. However, this same relationship was not found to exist in seventh graders. As the authors note, more advanced mathematical tasks may require more of an interaction of sequential logical processing, with visuo-spatial processing rather than being susceptible to straightforward handling by visuo-spatial mechanisms alone.

Thus, differences in the brain regions which handle particular tasks may reflect themselves not so much in the performance levels of the criterion task itself but more in the way in which such performance is acquired and maintained. Of course, if we knew more about psychological processes our tasks would be much more revealing of the different methods of analysis which characterize different populations. However, since the behavioral tasks have been developed relatively independently of such knowledge they may or may not be revealing with regard to differences in processing approach.

## SUMMARY

Specific cognitive aptitudes such as verbal and numero-spatial ability are examined in the context of analogical encoding processes. Verbal ability is correlated with sequential processing capacities but only to the extent that linguistic analysis and production typically involves temporal integration of information. Aspects of verbal performance which do not rely on successive processing such as semantic judgments show more dependence on visuo-spatial processing. The differentiation of linguistic performance factors at the behavioral level is matched by corresponding neurological differentiation as seen in the aphasias of Broca and Wernicke. Mathematical ability is correlated with simultaneous processing capacities because this mode of processing information is apparently favorable to the manipulation of mathematical relationships which often involve simultaneous or concurrent relationships. Neurological differentiation is shown to be substantial between sensory-perceptual regions subserving numero-spatial performance and verbal ability.

## SECTION SUMMARY

The form and nature of intelligence is the result of an interaction between the structural processes underlying a $g$ factor with those underlying specific aptitudes. General intelligence is based on the operation of information processing factors controlled by upper-level habituative system structures which enhance the detection of nonsalient or secondary cues and enhances their control over goal-directed behavior. Variations in the functional effectiveness of the habituative system are correlated with variations in intelligence, both phylogenetically and developmentally.

Specific aptitudes are based on the functioning of the sensory-perceptual systems of the individual, from the most basic to the most complex levels of stimulus analysis. Specific aptitudes are held to exist for each of the discrete pathways of perceptual analysis, although some specific aptitudes will be more useful than others. The analogical encoding capacity forms the basis for the different specific aptitudes in that certain kinds of representational capacity are more useful with certain kinds of perceptual and cognitive activity than others. In humans, verbal-successive processing and visuo-spatial-simultaneous processing are the two most important specific aptitudes and they derive their character from the nature of auditory and visual processing respectively.

# Conclusion

Because the Appendix provides a convenient synopsis of the match-mismatch theory presented in this book, I will let it serve in place of a retrospective summary. However, in closing, I would like to make a few observations about the relationship between theoretical constructions and empirical investigations in experimental psychology.

1. A distinction should be made between the theoretical approach followed in this book and the results of that approach as realized in the specific theoretical constructs which have been presented. The theoretical accuracy or heuristic usefulness of match-mismatch principles is dependent on my own particular capacities or weaknesses and any deficiencies in this respect do not necessarily imply that the methodological approach taken is without value. I have argued strongly on behalf of a process of convergent and divergent validation of theoretical constructs across different areas or levels of behavioral analysis. The success or failure of this particular implementation of that approach would not affect my own belief in its necessity for theoretical constructions in behavioral analysis.

2. To a great extent, psychologists have very demanding (or optimistic) views concerning the degree of prediction capable by a theory of behavior. There is not simply a demand for what might be called predictions of a probabilistic or statistical nature but rather for predictions about the precise behavior

390

that will occur in each specific situation. This is not infeasible when the particular parameters of the situation have been studied; however, in some cases it may be difficult to predict the exact behavior that occurs on an abstract basis. To take the example mentioned in the introduction, it is possible to predict the rate at which an idealized object will cool, given a few basic variables such as temperature, pressure, etc. A physicist would be hard pressed, however, to predict the precise rate at which a cup of coffee will cool when placed on a kitchen table. The number of extraneous factors, of course, is vastly greater in the latter situation. As it turns out, the physical sciences can usually study or create situations which reduce the number of incidental variables and these artificial situations still can have great applicability to applied problems (e.g., a controlled environment is usually created for manufacturing processes involving chemical reactions). The problems that arise when such control is not possible can be seen in meteorology, a field, incidentally, which is rarely mentioned in discussions of the relative merits of the physical sciences over the behavioral sciences. Psychology, like meteorology, faces the problem that the particular situations for which prediction is desired are often those termed naturalistic or real-life where extraneous or idiosyncratic variables are rampant.

This is not a counsel of despair, but simply a statement that certain behavioral relationships may not be entirely due to the workings of an abstract principle which pervades the psychological domain, but rather to the operations of idiosyncratic organismic or environmental factors which cannot be estimated a priori. I should note that the domain of such factors is probably no greater in psychology than in any other area, but due to the focus of the field, it is possibly somewhat more visible.

3.  It would be exceedingly helpful if psychologists would be less dominated by task variables in talking about psychological processes. Many tasks which are in general use are at best quasi-analytical since they have no specific relationship to structural processes or even to major contingent factors (e.g., passive avoidance, paired associate learning, etc.). The emphasis on task factors is understandable psychologically since these tend to be concrete while the underlying processes are abstract. The problem is amplified by the non-standardized nature of the procedures which can be used in any single task by different investigators, who nevertheless use the same label to name the task.

4.  To state more positively the concerns expressed in the preceding paragraph, I would advocate that new tasks or procedures be developed which permit a more direct examination of the variables being measured. For example, if encoding processes are being studied, the task should permit the measurement of the encoding operations at the time they are occurring rather than estimate their characteristics indirectly at the time of retrieval when their effects are confounded with other processes (e.g., Johnston & Uhl, 1976). In the same vein, investigators should consider the process implications of the particular task procedures and modifications which they employ.

5.  It should always be remembered that a structural process will exert an effect on behavior whenever the task conditions permit its expression, regardless of whether the task has been designed to measure that process.

# Appendix

## Match-Mismatch Theory

The mammalian brain can be conceptualized as the control mechanism for three main functions: life maintenance, information processing, and motoric output. Life maintenance structures are mainly contained within the brain stem and are essential to vegetative functions which maintain homeostasis. Motoric output structures are present both subcortically and cortically and control the skeletal movements. The information processing mechanism (IPM) is composed of subcortical and cortical structures and controls information processing and analysis. The present theory describes (some of) the structural characteristics of the IPM, in terms of its intrinsic functions and its effect on life maintenance and motoric output structures.

### STRUCTURE OF THE IPM

The IPM has two major divisions: the sensory perceptual division and the behavioral analysis division.

The sensory-perceptual division is composed of the five sensory systems: visual, auditory, tactile, gustatory, and olfactory.

Each of the sensory systems has sensory registers, subcortical analysis regions and cortical analysis regions.

The sensory registers are the sites of initial sensory analysis which transduce sensory stimuli into neural signals. This processed modality specific information is transmitted in parallel through functionally independent systems or in pathways carrying overlapping, but partially unique sensory attributes.

Subcortical analysis regions in each of the sensory systems perform sensory-perceptual processing operations similar to those performed by homologous structures in inframammalian vertebrate species.

Cortical analysis regions in each of the sensory regions perform sensory-perceptual operations requiring greater representational capacity than subcortical regions possess as well as modulating subcortical response.

The behavioral analysis division has two components: the reinforcer system and the habituative system.

The reinforcer system is an integrated series of neural structures and pathways including the amygdala, medial septum, dorsomedial thalamic nucleus, hypothalamus and reticular nuclei.

The habituative system is an integrated series of neural structures and pathways including the prefrontal cortex, entorhinal cortex, hippocampus, lateral septum, mammillary bodies, anterior thalamic nucleus and reticular nuclei.

The septum is a coordinating structure handling the flow of information between the reinforcer and habituative systems.

The sensory-perceptual division has extensive interconnections with the behavioral analysis division. The two main pathways are cortico-limbic and cortico-striatal-reticular. The cortico-limbic pathway connects the cortex with the highest level structures of the reinforcer and habituative systems. The cortico-striatal pathway connects the cortex with the lower structures of the reinforcer and habituative systems but bypasses the mid- and upper-level structures.

Lower-level structures of the reinforcer and habituative systems perform attentional and motivational functions similar to those performed by homologous structures in inframammalian vertebrates. Upper level structures of the reinforcer and habituative systems perform attentional and motivational functions requiring greater representational capacity than lower level structures possess.


## STRUCTURAL PROCESSES OF THE
## SENSORY-PERCEPTUAL DIVISION OF THE IPM


All information passing through the sensory registers or otherwise present in pre-attention or working memory is encoded in permanent form in the nervous system.

Once a stimulus representation is transmitted by the sensory registers, it can be in one of three states: pre-attention (active), working memory (active), or permanent memory (inactive).

A representation which is being processed in subcortical regions is in the state of pre-attention.

A representation which is being processed in cortical regions is in working memory.

The same active state exists for representations activated from permanent memory and for exteroceptive stimuli being processed through the sensory registers.

Pre-attentional capacity is limited by the concurrent capacity of all of the sensory registers.

Working memory capacity is limited to two or three concurrent stimulus representations, with an inverse relation between the number of items and the amount of processing each receives.

The encoding of a stimulus takes the form of an analogical representation which reflects the nature of the sensory perceptual or cognitive operations performed during its processing through the IPM.

The encoding of a specific stimulus is accomplished by the establishment and maintenance of a particular pattern of neuronal response. Each stimulus parameter which has been transmitted through the sensory registers activates a subset of neurons in appropriate subcortical and cortical regions. The discharge density is correlated with the relative salience of that attribute.

The permanent internal represenation of a stimulus is stored in the neural structures which perform particular processing operations on it during encoding.

The relative density of neuronal response between lower and upper level processing regions in the sensory modalities defines the degree of complexity of the internal representation of a stimulus event. Complex internal representations are associated with less stable patterns of neuronal response. Conversely, simple representations are associated with highly stable patterns of neuronal response.

The retrieval of an internal representation from permanent (inactive) memory requires the presence of a stimulus representation (cue) in pre-attention or working memory which matches all or part of the encoded attributes of the permanent representation.

The simultaneous activation of multiple internal representations due to the action of a cue causes a mutual inhibition because only one neuronal pattern of response can exist at any one moment.

The activation of an internal representation produces a decrease in the latency to achieve retrieval threshold of a small subset of internal representations with which it is associated. Stimulus context determines the activated subset. Conversely, the activation of the target representation produces an increase in the latency to achieve retrieval threshold in the remainder of the target's associated representations.

Representations can be associated through temporal contiguity (correlation in active memory) or shared features or attributes.

## RESPONSES CONTROLLED BY
## SENSORY-PERCEPTUAL REPRESENTATIONS

Sensory-perceptual representations control the occurrence of two functionally distinct response classes: species-specific responses and voluntary responses.

Species-specific responses are integrated behaviors whose form and stimulus control has a substantial genetic component and which are common to all individual members (of the same sex) of a species or subspecies.

Species specific responses in humans are limited to visceral components.

Species specific responses are associated with increases in organismic arousal. The degree of arousal increases from initial to terminal components of a species specific response.

Species-specific behaviors can be elicited in fully integrated form (skeletal and visceral response components arranged in an appropriate sequence) by the stimulation of neural regions which induce the appropriate mood state.

A mood state is the product of the effects of neurotransmitters and hormones on specific subcortical structures combined with the processing of appropriate motivationally significant stimuli.

The mood state is a relatively sustained response which provides the support for an integrated species specific response pattern to be expressed over a period of time.

Voluntary responses are responses that do not have a fixed relationship with particular environmental stimuli or homeostatic (visceral) functioning.

## STRUCTURAL PROCESSES OF THE
## BEHAVIORAL ANALYSIS DIVISION

The behavioral analysis division of the IPM receives copies of internal representations processed through the sensory-perceptual division.

The behavioral analysis division fosters the connection of motivationally significant stimuli with appropriate organismic responses and inhibits organismic responses to stimuli with declining or nil motivational significance, through the mechanism of the orienting response (OR).

The OR is a response with characteristic electrophysiological and motor components which occurs as the result of a mismatch between pre-existing and newly entered internal representations in pre-attention or working memory.

The OR facilitates the processing of internal representations in pre-attention or working memory.

Early components of the electrophysiological OR, occurring within 200 msec of stimulus transduction by the sensory registers, are produced in lower level structures of the behavioral analysis division. These OR components are sensitive to the perceptual characteristics of the stimulus and respond on the basis of stimulus change.

Early components of the OR are essential to the formation of representations requiring the development and maintenance of neuronal response patterns involving different subcortical populations of neurons.

Late components of the electrophysiological OR, occurring after 200 msec from stimulus transduction by the sensory registers, are produced in the amygdala and hippocampus. These OR components are sensitive to stimulus expectancies rather than stimulus parameters. They are activated by mismatches between environmental events and the representations in working memory at the time of the event occurrences.

Late components of the OR are essential to the formation of representations requiring the representational capacity of cortical regions of the sensory-perceptual division (including verbal stimuli). The late OR components protect the contents of working memory at the time of occurrence of a significant stimulus event from interference from irrelevant environmental or internally generated stimulus representations. The amygdala and hippocampus potentiate the neuronal responses concurrently occurring in the cortical regions of the sensory-perceptual division as well as the concurrent affective (amygdala only) and motor responses. This potentiation permits the registration of complex stimuli and associative relationships by increasing the consistency of those neuronal response patterns.

The reinforcer system processes unconditioned reinforcers and conditioned reinforcers; salient stimuli with motivational significance (producing homeostatic changes).

Any stimulus which evokes an innate response or OR can be an unconditioned reinforcer given the appropriate contingent conditions at the time of its occurrence.

Innate reinforcers are stimuli with certain attributes preset in an internal representation prior to an organism's first exposure to them.

397

The preset internal representation of the unconditioned reinforcer is associated with a motivational state through experience with the stimulus.

Lower level structures of the reinforcer system (diencephalon and below) control the elemental association of non-complex internal representations and organismic responses (species specific or voluntary). This elemental associative process involves changes in synaptic and cellular responsiveness limited to individual or small groups of neurons.

Species specific responses controlled at this level are not dependent on the induction of a mood state but are coterminous with the duration of activation of the internal representation cueing their occurrence.

The amygdalar potentiation of the neuronal response to salient stimuli activates neurochemically specific pathways in subcortical structures inducing a mood state. The activation of these pathways results in the release of appropriate hormones and also activates the initial response of the species specific response pattern.

The performance of these initial components make the performance of later response components more probable.

The mood state inhibits the expression of incompatible responses by a general inhibition of the motivational (mood) state which controls these responses.

The mood state initiated by the processing of a reinforcer through the amygdala has an affective strength which is correlated with the intensity of the reinforcer.

The time course of the reinforcer-induced mood state A is coincident with reinforcer presentation and dissipates soon afterwords (within several minutes).

The A state induces the appearance of an opponent process B which is a mood state in reciprocal interaction with the A state, having its own associated species specific responses.

The B state has an affective strength directly related to the strength of the prior A state. However, its recruitment and decay is less rapid than its reciprocal A state.

The magnitude (intensity) of the US specifies the asymptotic limit of conditioned reinforcing (affective) strength that can accrue to concurrently processed (primary) cues and the motivational tendency to perform associated motoric voluntary responses.

The habituative system processes stimuli evoking the OR which are not unconditioned reinforcers (at the time of their occurrence) nor which are in temporal proximity to the occurrence of an unconditioned reinforcer.

The habituative system, particularly its upper level structures, is more sensitive to environmental stimuli (has a lower threshold to produce an OR to stimulus change or mismatch) than the reinforcer system.

398

Lower level structures of the habituative system are primarily involved in habituating the response to stimuli processed through them.

Habituation is a stimulus specific decrement in responding to a repetitive stimulus produced by a comparison of the previous pattern of neural excitation with that induced by the stimulus representation in active memory. When the two patterns match, and the reinforcer system is not activated, then habituation increases or is maintained asymptotically through the mechanism of presynaptic depression.

Lower level structures of the habituative system habituate stimuli processed at subcortical levels with limited representational complexity.

Dishabituation of the habituation produced by these lower level structures is the result of a mismatch producing sensitization or mood state induction which heterosynaptically facilitates other related responses above their normal level.

Some habituation occurs with species specific responses activated by reinforcers. The habituative mechanisms for these responses are located in habituative interneurons in lower level structures of the habituative system as well as in reflexive pathways and the reinforcer system.

Upper level structures of the habituative system have an expanded representational capacity to encode stimulus attributes and temporal patterning.

Dishabituation is produced by a mismatch between the hippocampal representational copy and the representations in working memory. The mismatch disrupts the output of the inhibitory interneurons, thereby releasing the reticular system from inhibition.

With stimulus repetition the stability of the copy in the hippocampus is increased. In turn, this potentiates the inhibitory interneurons' effect on hippocampal neurons, resulting in the habituation of the late components of the OR.

The inhibition of these hippocampal cells interrupts the transmission of excitatory information to the reticular system, thereby reducing the strength of the early components of the OR generated in these regions.

The maintenance of habituation to complex stimuli is dependent on the presence of a representational copy in the hippocampus which matches the representations in working memory.

The increased representational capacity of the hippocampus permits the detection of mismatches which do not involve increases in stimulus intensity. Thus, dishabituation at this level does not involve sensitization.

Excitatory strength is incremented by the reinforcer system at a faster rate than the habituative system decrements it.

The septum is a coordinating structure handling the interchange of information between the reinforcer and habituative systems at the level of the amygdala and hippocampus.

The medial septum transmits information from the reinforcer system concerning the presence or absence of motivationally significant stimuli to the hippocampus and entorhinal cortex. The medial septum controls the degree of hippocampal activation through this process.

The lateral septum receives habituative output from the hippocampus which it transmit to lower level structures in the habituative and reinforcer systems.

The lateral septum has a reciprocal relationship with the amygdala in controlling the organismic responses to reinforcers. It reduces the degree of amygdalar potentiation of neural response to motivationally significant stimuli.

Habituative system structures above the level of the hippo-campus such as the entorhinal cortex and prefrontal cortex (PFC), are involved in the maintenance of attention to non-salient stimuli and the construction of internal representations of secondary cues. They do not have a direct habituative function.

The medial orbital region of the PFC in primates (and homologous regions in infraprimates) modulates amygdalar and reinforcer system activity in a similar manner to lateral septal modulation. Medial orbital PFC exerts a restraining influence on the basis of information from the highest processing levels of the sensory-perceptual division and the other regions of the PFC, while the lateral septum acts on the basis of information from the dience-phalon and limbic system.

Medial orbital control over reinforcer system activity is positively related to the presence of secondary cues.

The dorsal and lateral regions of the primate PFC and homolog-ous regions extend hippocampal representational capacity with respect to nonsalient stimuli and secondary cues and receive information from all modalities of the sensory-perceptual division.

These regions potentiate the neural response to secondary cues and reduce the probability of irrelevant stimuli from entering working memory.

The dorsolateral PFC has close connections with voluntary motor regions because of its involvement in secondary cue proces-sing. Because of the status of verbal stimuli as secondary cues, verbal control over voluntary responses is dependent on dorsola-teral PFC.

# JOURNALS AND THEIR ABBREVIATIONS

| Abbr. | Journal Title |
|-------|---------------|
| ABN | Journal of Abnormal and Social Psychology |
| ABP | Journal of Experimental Psychology: Animal Behavior Processes |
| ACP | Acta Psychologia |
| AJMD | American Journal of Mental Deficiency |
| ALB | Animal Learning and Behavior |
| AMJP | American Journal of Psychology |
| ANB | Animal Behavior |
| ANE | Acta Neurobiological Experimentalis |
| AP | American Psychologist |
| APS | Acta Physiologica Scandinavica |
| ARCH | Archives of Neurology |
| B | Behavior |
| BBE | Brain, Behavior, and Evolution |
| BBIO | Behavioral Biology |
| BC | Brain and Cognition |
| BHVB | Behavioral Brain Research |
| BIP | Biological Psychology |
| BJP | British Journal of Psychology |
| BNB | Behavioral and Neural Biology |
| BPS | Bulletin of the Psychonomic Society |
| BR | Brain |
| BRES | Brain Research |
| BTEP | Behavioral Therapy and Experimental Psychiatry |
| C | Cognition |
| CD | Child Development |
| CJP | Canadian Journal of Psychology |
| COG | Cognitive Psychology |
| COMP | Journal of Comparative Psychology |
| COR | Cortex |
| CPSI | Comparative Psychiatry |
| DEV | Developmental Psychology |
| EBR | Experimental Brain Reserach |
| ECN | Electroencephalography and Clinical Neuropsychology |
| ENDO | Endocrinology |
| EXN | Experimental Neurology |
| HD | Human Development |
| HF | Human Factors |
| HLM | Journal of Experimental Psychology: Human Learning and Memory |
| HPP | Journal of Experimental Psychology: Human Perception and Performance |
| JCN | Journal of Comparative Neurology |
| JCON | Journal of Consulting Psychology |

| | |
|---|---|
| JCPP | Journal of Comparative and Physiological Psychology |
| JEAB | Journal of the Experimental Analysis of Behavior |
| JECP | Journal of Experimental Child Psychology |
| JED | Journal of Educational Psychology |
| JEP | Journal of Experimental Psychology |
| JEPG | Journal of Experimental Psychology: General |
| JESP | Journal of Experimental Social Psychology |
| JGER | Journal of Gerontology |
| JGP | Journal of General Psychology |
| JN | Journal of Neurophysiology |
| JNND | Journal of Neurology and Neurological Psychiatry |
| JP | Journal of Psychology |
| JPER | Journal of Personality |
| JPET | Journal of Pharmacology and Experimental Therapeutics |
| JPSP | Journal of Personality and Social Psychology |
| JSOC | Journal of Social Psychology |
| JVLVB | Journal of Verbal Learning and Verbal Behavior |
| LM | Learning and Motivation |
| LMC | Journal of Experimental Psychology: Learning, Memory, and Cognition |
| MC | Memory and Cognition |
| N | Neuropsychologia |
| NAT | Nature |
| NENDO | Neuroendocrinology |
| NEUR | Neurology |
| P | Psychophysiology |
| PBUL | Psychological Bulletin |
| PHAR | Pharmacological Review |
| PHB | Physiology and Behavior |
| PHYS | Physiological Psychology |
| PM | Psychological Monographs |
| PMS | Perceptual and Motor Skills |
| PP | Perception and Psychophysics |
| PR | Psychological Review |
| PREC | Psychological Record |
| PREP | Psychological Reports |
| PS | Psychonomic Science |
| QJEP | Quarterly Journal of Experimental Psychology |
| RCOM | Research Communications in Psychology, Psychiatry and Behavior |
| S | Science |
| SJP | Scandinavian Journal of Psychology |

# References

Abbott, F. V. & Melzack, R. (1978) EXN, 62, 720.

Abravanel, E. (1968) Soc. Rsch. Child Dev., 33, #118.

Ackil, I. E., et al. (1969) JCPP, 69, 739.

Adams, J. A. (1964) Ann. Rev. Psychol., 15, 181.

Adey, W. R., et al. (1960) ARCH, 3, 74.

Aggleton, J. P. & Mishkin, M. (1983) N, 21, 188.

Aggleton, J. P. & Passingham, R. E. (1982) JCPP, 96, 71.

Albert, M. L., et al. (1973) BR, 96, 317.

Allen, J. P. & Allen, C. F. (1974) NENDO, 15, 220.

Allen, J. P. & Allen, C. F. (1975) NENDO, 19, 115.

Altman, J. (1967) In G. Quartan, et al. (Eds.) Neurosciences.
New York: Rockefeller U.

Amabile, T. M., et al. (1976) JPSP, 34, 92.

Amsel, A. (1972) In R. A. Boakes & M. S. Holliday (Eds.) Inhibition
and Learning. London: Academic Press.

Amsel, A., et al. (1964) JEAB, 7, 135

Anchel, H. & Lindsley, D. B. (1972) ECN, 32, 209.

Andersen, P. (1978) In K. Elliott and J. Whelan (Eds.) Functions
of the septo-hippocampal system. Amsterdam: Elsevier

Andersen, R. (1978) N, 16, 439.

Anderson, D. C., et al. (1969) PS, 15, 54.

Anderson, K. V. & Williamson, M. R. (1971) PS, 24, 125.

Anderson, J. R. (1978) PBUL, 85, 249.

Anderson, J. R. (1979) PR, 86, 395.

Anderson, J. R. (1983) The architecture of cognition. Cambridge,
MA: Harvard U.

Anderson, J. R. & Bower, G. H. (1973) Human associative memory.
Washington, DC: Winston.

Anderson, J. R. & Bower, G. H. (1974) MC, 2, 406.

Anderson, J. R. & Paulson, R. (1977) JVLVB, 16, 439.

Anderson, J. R. & Paulson, R. (1978) COG, 10, 178.

Anderson, J. R. & Reder, L. M. (1979) In L. S. Cermak & F. I. M.
Craik (Eds.) Levels of processing. Hillsdale, NJ: Lawrence
Erlbaum Associates.

Anderson, R. C. & Watts, G. H. (1971) JVLVB, 10, 29.

Annable, A. & Wearden, J. H. (1979) JEAB, 32, 297.

Arnolds, D. E. A. T., et al. (1979) ECN, 46, 52.

Aronson, L. R. & Cooper, M. L. (1979) PHB, 22, 257.

Atkinson, R. C. (1975) AP, 30, 821.

Atkinson, R. C. & Shiffrin, R. M. (1968) In K. W. Spence & J. T.
Spence (eds.) The psychology of learning and motivation. V. 2.
New York: Academic Press.

Ayllon, T. & Azrin, N. H. (1964) JEAB, 7, 327.

Bacon, S. J. (1974) JEP, 102, 81.

Badia, P. & Defran, R. H. (1970) PR, 77, 171.

Bahrick, H. P. (1954) JEP, 47, 170.

Bahrick, H. P. (1969) JEP, 79, 213.
Bahrick, H. P. (1970) PR, 77, 215.
Bahrick, H. P., et al. (1952) JEP, 44, 400.
Bakan, P. (1977) N, 15, 837.
Bakan, P. & Putnam, W. (1974) ARCH, 30, 334.
Baker, A. G. (1974) LM, 5, 369.
Baker, A. G. (1977) ABP, 3, 144.
Baker, A. G. & Mackintosh, N. J. (1977) ALB, 5, 315.
Baker, A. G. & Mercier, P. (1982) LM, 13, 391.
Bakker, D. J. (1967) PMS, 24, 1027.
Balota, D. A. & Engle, R. W. (1981) JVLVB, 20, 346.
Bandura, J. R. & Bachica, D. L. (1974) J. Rsch. Pers., 7, 295.
Barch, A. M. & Lewis, D. (1954) JEP, 48, 134.
Bard, P. A. (1928) AJP, 84, 490.
Baron, A. (1959) JCPP, 52, 591.
Baron, A., et al. (1967) PS, 8, 329.
Barrett, J. W. (1969) N, 7, 1.
Barry, R. J. (1979) BIP, 8, 161.
Barry, R. J. (1982) P, 19, 28.
Barsalou, L. W. (1983) MC, 11, 211.
Bartus, R. T. & LeVere, T. E. (1977) BRES, 11, 233.
Bassett, J. R., et al. (1973) PHB, 24, 675.
Basso, A., et al. (1980) N, 18, 435.
Battig, W. F. (1975) In R. L. Solso (Ed.) Information processing
   and cognition. Hillsdale, NJ: Lawrence Erlbaum Associates.
Battig, W. F. (1979) In L. S. Cermak & F. I. M. Craik (Eds.)
   Levels of processing. Hillsdale, NJ: Lawrence Erlbaum Associates.
Battig, W. F. & Montague, W. E. (1969) PM, 80 (3, Part 2).
Bauer, D. M. (1962) JEAB, 5, 525.
Baumeister, R. P. (1982) PBUL, 91, 3.
Baxter, D. J. & Zamble, E. (1982) ALB, 10, 201.
Bayer, S. A. & Altman, J. (1975) JCN, 163, 1.
Bayley, N. (1949) JGP, 75, 165.
Beatty, J. & Wagoner, B. (1978) S, 199, 1216.
Beatty, W. W. & Carbone, C. P. (1980) PHB, 24, 675.
Beatty, W. W. & Schwartzbaum, J. S. (1968) JLPP, 66, 60.
Becker, C. A. (1979) HPP, 5, 252.
Becker, J. T. & Olton, D. S. (1980) PHB, 24, 33.
Begg, I. (1972) JVLVB, 11, 431.
Begg, I. (1973) CJP, 27, 159.
Belleza, F. S., et al. (1975) MC, 3, 451.
Belluzi, J. D. (1972) JCPP, 80, 269.
Belmont, J. M. & Butterfield, E. L. (1971) COG, 2, 411.
Bem, D. J. (1972) In L. Berkowitz (Ed.) Advances in experimental
   social psychology. New York: Academic Press.
Bengelloun, W. A. (1979) PHB, 22, 615.
Bennett, T. L. (1970) ECN, 28, 17.

Ben-Shakhar, G., et al. (1982) P, 19, 178.

Benson, D. F. (1977) ARCH, 34, 327.

Berger, A. L., et al. (1982) AJMD, 86, 405.

Berger, T. W., et al. (1976) S, 192, 483.

Berger, T. W. & Thompson, R. F. (1978a) BRES, 145, 323.

Berger, T. W. & Thompson, R. F. (1978b) BRES, 145, 293.

Bermant, G. & Sachs, B. D. (1973) In G. Bermant (Ed.) Perspectives on animal behavior. Glenview, IL: Scott Foresman.

Bermuden-Ratton, Z., et al. (1983) BNB, 37, 61.

Bernbach, H. A. (1969) In J. T. Spence & G. H. Bower (Eds.) The psychology of learning and motivation, V. 3. New York: Academic Press.

Bernstein, A. S. (1969) P, 6, 338.

Bernstein, A. S. & Taylor, K. W. (1979) In H. D. Kimmel, et al. (Eds.) The orienting reflex in humans. Hillsdale, NJ: Lawrence Erlbaum Associates.

Besner, D. & Coltheart, M. (1979) N, 17, 461.

Best, M. R. & Gemberling, G. A. (1977) ABP, 3, 253.

Bevan, W. & Steger, J. A. (1971) S, 172, 597.

Bever, T. G. (1971) In R. Huxley & E. Ingram (Eds.) Language acquisition. New York: Academic Press.

Bever, T. G. et al. (1976) N, 14, 175.

Bever, T. G. (1980) In D. Caplan (Ed.) Biological studies of mental processes. Cambridge, MA: MIT.

Bever, T. G. & Chiarello, R. J. (1974) S, 185, 537.

Biferno, M. A. & Dawson, M. E. (1977) P, 14, 164.

Bilodeau, E. A. & Bilodeau, I. M. (1961) Annual review of psychology, 12, 243.

Bilodeau, E. A., et al. (1962) PM, 76, #20.

Bilodeau, E. A., et al. (1964) JEP, 67, 303.

Bilsky, L., et al. (1972) AJMD, 77, 77.

Bird, C. P. (1977) MC, 5, 27.

Bird, C. P. & Roberts, R. (1980) MC, 8, 468.

Birnbaum, I. S. (1975) HLM, 1, 393.

Bisanz, J. H. & Resnick, L. B. (1978) JECP, 25, 129.

Bishop, P. D. & Kimmel, H. D. (1969) JEP, 81, 317.

Bitterman, M. E. (1964) AP, 20, 396.

Bizzi, E. & Schiller, P. H. (1970) EBR, 10, 151.

Bjork, R. A. & Whitten, W. B. (1974) COG, 6, 173.

Black, A. H. (1975) In R. L. Isaacson & K. H. Pribram (Eds.) The hippocampus V. 2. New York: Plenum.

Black, A. H. & Young, G. A. (1972) In R. M. Gilbert & J. R. Millenson (Eds.) Reinforcement. New York: Academic Press.

Black, J. B. & Bower, G. H. (1979) JVLVB, 18, 309.

Black, R. W., et al. (1964) JCPP, 57, 427.

Blackman, D. (1977) In W.K. Honig & J. E. R. Staddon (Eds.) Handbook of operant behavior. New York: Appleton-Century-Crofts.

Blade, M. L. & Watson, W. S. (1955) PM, 69, 69(12)
Blakemore, C. (1974) In F. O. Schmitt & F. G. Warden (eds.) The neurosciences: Third study program. Cambridge, MA: MIT.
Blakemore, C. & Cooper, G. F. (1970) NAT, 228, 477.
Blanchard, D. C., et al. (1977) PHY, 5, 331.
Blanchard, D. C., et al. (1979) JCPP, 93, 378.
Blanchard, R. J. & Blanchard, D. C. (1971) LM, 2, 351.
Bland, B. H., et al. (1983) PHB, 31, 111.
Blank, M. & Bridger, W. H. (1966) Am. J. Orthopsychiat, 36, 840.
Blaxton, T. A. & Neely, J. H. (1983) MC, 11, 500.
Blough, P. M. (1984) PP, 35, 344.
Blumstein, S. E. et al. (1977) BL, 4, 508.
Bobrow, S. A. & Bower, G. H. (1969) JEP, 80, 455.
Bohus, B. (1975) In R. L. Isaacson & K. H. Pribram (Eds.) The hippocampus V. 2. New York: Plenum.
Bolles, R. C. (1970) PR, 77, 32.
Bolles, R. C. (1972a) PR, 79, 394.
Bolles, R. C. (1972b) In G. H. Bower (Ed.) The psychology of learning and motivation. New York: Academic Press.
Bond, N. W. & Corfield-Sumner, P. K. (1978) ALB, 6, 413.
Booth, C. L., et al. (1979) PHB, 22, 931.
Booth, D. A. (1973) In J. Deutsch (Ed.) The physiological basis of memory. New York: Academic Press.
Bouillé, C. & Baylé, J. D. (1975) NENDO, 18, 281.
Bousfield, W. A. (1953) JGP, 49, 229.
Bower, G. H. (1972) In A. W. Melton & E. Martin (Eds.) Coding processes in human memory. Washington, DC: Winston.
Bower, G. H. & Bostrom, A. (1968) PS, 10, 211.
Bower, G. H., et al. (1975) MC, 3, 216.
Bowhuis, D. (1978) In J. Requin (Ed.) Attention and performance VII. Hillsdale, NJ: Lawrence Erlbaum Associates.
Boyarsky, R. E. & Eisdorfer, C. (1972) JG, 27, 254.
Bradley, D. C., et al. (1980) In D. Caplan (Ed.) Biological Studies of mental processes. Cambridge, MA: MIT.
Bradshaw, T. L. & Gates, E. A. (1978) BL, 5, 166.
Braggio, J. T. & Ellen, P. (1976) JCPP, 90, 694.
Brandes, J. S. & Johnson, A. K. (1978) PHB, 20, 763.
Bransford, J. D. & Franks, J. T. (1971) COG, 2, 331.
Bransford, J. D., et al. (1979) In L. Cermak & F. I. M. Craik (Eds.) Levels of processing. Hillsdale, NJ: Lawrence Erlbaum Associates.
Bray, N. W. & Ferguson, R. P. (1976) JECP, 22, 200.
Brayley, K. N. & Albert, D. J. (1977) JCPP, 91, 290.
Brazier, M. A. B. (1972) In B. Eleftheriou (Ed.) The neurobiology of the amygdala. New York: Plenum.
Brehm, J. W. & Crocker, J. C. (1962) In J. W. Brehm & A. R. Cohen (Eds.) Explorations in cognitive dissonance. New York: Wiley.

Breland, K. & Breland, M. (1961) AP, 16, 681.

Brennan, J. F. & Wisniewski, C. (1982) BHVB, 4, 117.

Brewer, N. & Nettlebeck, T. (1977) AJMD, 82, 37.

Briggs, G. E. (1974) MC, 2, 575.

Brigham, T. A. (1979) In L. C. Perlmuter & R. A. Monty (Eds.) Choice and perceived control. Hillsdale, NJ: Lawrence Erlbaum Associates.

Brigham, T. A. & Stoerzinger, A. (1976) In T. A. Brigham et al. (Eds.) Behavior analysis in education. Dubuque, IA: Kendall-Hunt.

Britton, B. K. & Tesser, A. (1982) JVLVB, 21, 421.

Brock, T. C. & Buss, A. H. (1962) ABN, 65, 197.

Brodie, D. A. & Prytulak, C. S. (1975) JVLVB, 14, 459.

Brodigan, D. L. & Peterson, G. B. (1976) ALB, 4, 121.

Bronson, F. H. (1968) In M. Diamond (Ed.) Perspectives in reproduction and sexual behavior. Bloomington: Indiana U. Press.

Brown, A., et al. (1972) JECP, 13, 283.

Brown, A. (1973) CD, 44, 376.

Brown, A. L. (1974) In N. R. Ellis (Ed.) International review of research on mental retardation V. 7. New York: Academic Press.

Brown, A. L. (1978) In R. Glass (Ed.) Advances in instructional psychology. Hillsdale, NJ: Lawrence Erlbaum Associates.

Brown, A. S. (1981) HLM, 7, 204.

Brown, D. L. & Jenkins, H. M. (1968) JEAB, 11, 1.

Brown, J. (1976) In J. Brown (Ed.) Recall and recognition. New York: Wiley.

Brown, W. S., et al. (1983) ECN, 55, 277.

Bruner, J. S., et al. (1955) JEP, 49, 187.

Bryden, M. P. (1975) BL, 2, 201.

Bunnell, B. N., et al. (1970) PHB, 5, 153.

Burghardt, G. M. (1967) PS, 7, 383.

Burt, G. S. & Smotherman, W. P. (1980) PHB, 24, 651.

Burton, H. A. & Toga, A. W. (1982) BNB, 34, 141.

Buschke, H. (1974) S, 184, 579.

Buschke, H. & Schauer, A. H. (1979) JVLVB, 18, 549.

Buser, P. & Bancaud, J. (1983) ECN, 55, 1.

Bush, D. F., et al. (1973) JCPP, 83, 168.

Butler, G. S. & Rabinovitch, F. M. (1981) CD, 52, 430.

Butler, R. A. (1953) JCPP, 46, 95.

Butler, R. A. (1957) JCPP, 50, 177.

Butters, N. & Albert, M. S. (1982) In L. S. Cermak (Ed.) Human memory and amnesia. Hillsdale, NJ: Lawrence Erlbaum Associates.

Bykov, V. D. (1965) In L. G. Voronin et al. (Eds.) Orienting reflex and exploratory behavior. Washington, DC: Am. Inst. of Biol. Sci.

Byrne, J., et al., (1974) JN, 37, 1041.

Byrnes, M. M. & Spitz, H. H. (1977) AJMD, 81, 561.

Calder, B. J. & Staw, B. M. (1974) JPSP, 31, 76.
Callaway, E. & Harris, P. R. (1974) S, 183, 873.
Camp, C. J., et al. (1980) JVLVB, 14, 583.
Campbell, B. A. & Coulter, X. (1976) Ontogeny of learning and
  memory. Cambridge, MA: MIT.
Campbell, B. A. et al. (1974) JCPP, 87, 193.
Campbell, D. T. & Fiske, D. W. (1959) PBUL, 56, 81.
Capaldi, E. D., et al. (1976) LM, 7, 197.
Capaldi, E. J. (1967) In K. W. Spence & J. J. Spence (Eds.) The
  psychology of learning and motivation V. 1. New York: Academic
  Press.
Capaldi, E. J. & Myers, D. E. (1978) LM, 9, 178.
Cappell, H., et al. (1981) PHAR, 74, 54.
Caramazza, A. & Zurif, E. B. (1976) BL, 3, 572.
Carew, T. J., et al. (1971) Int. J. Neurosc., 2, 79.
Carew, T. J., et al. (1972) S, 175, 451.
Carew, T. J., et al. (1974) JN, 37, 1020.
Carlson, N. R., et al. (1976) JCPP, 90, 780.
Carlston, D. E. (1980) JESP, 16, 303.
Carmon, A. & Nachson, I. (1971) COR, 7, 410.
Carter, D. E. & Werner, T. J. (1978) JEAB, 29, 565.
Casady, R. L. & Taylor, A. N. (1976) NENDO, 20, 68.
Castelluci, V. & Kandel, E. (1976) In T. J. Tighe & R. N. Leaton
  (Eds.) Habituation. Hillsdale, NJ: Lawrence Erlbaum Associates.
Ceci, S. J. & Howe, M. J. A. (1978) JECP, 26, 432.
Ceraso, J., et al., (1982) LMC, 8, 289.
Cerewicki, L. E., et al. (1968) JVLVB, 7, 847.
Cermak, L. S. & Reale, L. (1978) HLM, 4, 165.
Cermak, L. S., et al. (1974) BL, 2, 141.
Cermak, L. S., et al. (1976) BL, 3, 375.
Cermak, L. S., et al. (1978) BL, 5, 215.
Cermak, L. S., et al. (1984) BL, 12, 95.
Chapman, L. J. & Chapman, J. P. (1967) J. ab. psychol., 72, 193.
Charness, N. (1981) JEPG, 110, 21.
Cheal, M., et al. (1982) JCPP, 96, 47.
Cheatle, M. D. & Rudy, J. W. (1978) ABP, 4, 237.
Cherek, D. R., et al. (1973) JEAB, 19, 113.
Chiesi, H. L., et al. (1979) JVLVB, 18, 257.
Chin, T., et al. (1976) JCPP, 90, 1133.
Chisholm, D. L. & Trowill, T. A. (1972) PHB, 9, 277.
Chiszar, D. A. & Spear, N. E. (1969) JCPP, 69, 190.
Chorover, S. L. & Schiller, P. H. (1965) JCPP, 59, 73.
Church, R. M. (1978) In S. H. Hulse, et al. (Eds.) Cognitive
  processes in animal behavior. Hillsdale, NJ: Lawrence Erlbaum
  Associates.
Church, R. M. & Deluty, M. Z. (1977) ABP, 3, 216.
Ciccone, D. S. & Brelsford, J. W. (1974) JEP, 103, 900.

Cioé, J. D., et al. (1980) BPS, 16, 359.
Clark, H. (1978) In D. LaBarge & J. Samuels (Eds.) Basic processes in reading, perception, and comprehension. Hillsdale, NJ: Lawrence Erlbaum Associates.
Cogan, D. L. & Reeves, J. L. (1979) PHB, 22, 1115.
Cohen, B. H. (1963) JEP, 66, 227.
Cohen, B. H. (1966) JVLVB, 5, 182.
Cohen, C. E. & Ebbesen, E. B. (1979) JESP, 15, 305.
Cohen, D. H. (1974) In L. V. DiCara (Ed.) Limbic and autonomic systems research. New York: Plenum.
Cohen, D. H. (1975) JCN, 160, 13.
Cohen, G. (1973) JEP, 97, 349.
Cohen, N. J. & Squire, L. R. (1980) S, 210, 207.
Cohen, N. J. & Squire, L. R. (1981) N, 19, 337.
Cohen, N. J. & Squire, L. R. (1984) In N. Butters & L. Squire (Eds.) The neurophychology of memory. New York: Guilford Press.
Cohen, S. L., et al. (1979) JEAB, 32, 149.
Cohn-Jones, L. & Seimon, R. (1978) AJMD, 83, 9.
Cole, M. A. (1973) JECP, 16, 126.
Collin, N. G., et al. (1982) BBR, 4, 1977.
Collins, A. M. & Quillian, M. R. (1969) JVLVB, 8, 240.
Condry, J. & Chambers, T. (1978) In M. R. Lepper & D. Greene (Eds.) The hidden costs of reward. Hillsdale, NJ: Lawrence Erlbaum Associates.
Conner, R. L. et al. (1971) NAT, 234, 564.
Cook, R. G. (1980) ABP, 6, 326.
Cooper, E. H. & Pantle, A. J. (1967) PBUL, 68, 221.
Cooper, J. (1971) JPSP, 18, 354.
Cooper, J. R., et al. (1982) The biochemical basis of neuropharmacology. Oxford: Oxford U. Press.
Cooper, L. A. (1975) COG, 7, 20.
Cooper, L. A. (1980) In J. Requin (Ed.) Attention and performance VII. Hillsdale, NJ: Lawrence Erlbaum Associates.
Coover, G. D., et al. (1971) PHB, 6, 261.
Coover, G. D., et al. (1973) JCPP, 82, 170.
Corbett, A. T. (1977) JVLVB, 16, 233.
Corcoran, D. W. J. (1971) Pattern recognition. Harmondsworth, England: Penguin.
Corfield-Sumner, P. K., et al. (1977) JEAB, 27, 265.
Corkin, S. (1965) N, 3, 339.
Coughlin, R. C. (1972) PREC, 22, 333.
Coulter, X. et al. (1976) ABP, 2, 48.
Craik, F. I. M. (1977) In J. E. Birven & K. W. Schaie (Eds.) Handbook of the psychology of aging. New York: Van Nostrand.
Craik, F. I. M. & Lockhart, R. S. (1972) JVLVB, 11, 671.
Craik, F. I. M. & Tulving, E. (1975) JEPG, 104, 267.

Crook, C. K. (1979) In H. W. Reese & L. P. Lipsitt (Eds.) Advances in child development and behavior V. 14. New York: Academic Press.

Crosby, E. C. & Humphrey, T. (1941) JCN, 74, 309.

Crosby, K. G. (1972) AJMD, 77, 46.

Crow, L. T. & McWilliams, L. S. (1979) N, 17, 393.

Crowder, R. G. (1976) Principles of learning and memory. Hillsdale, NJ: Lawrence Erlbaum Associates.

Crowne, D. P. & Radcliffe, D. C. (1975) In R. L. Isaacson & K. H. Pribram (Eds.) The hippocampus V. 2. New York: Plenum.

Crowne, D. P. & Riddell, W. I. (1969) JCPP, 69, 748.

Crowne, D. P., et al. (1981) BHVB, 2, 165.

Cuddy, L. J. & Jacoby, L. L. (1982) JVLVB, 21, 451.

Czech, D. A. (1973) PHB, 10, 821.

D'Agostino, P. R. & DeRemer, T. (1973) JVLVB, 12, 108.

Dahmen, W., et al. (1982) N, 20, 145.

Dalby, J. T. (1980) COR, 16, 567.

Dalland, T. (1970) JCPP, 71, 114.

Dallman, M. F. & Jones, M. T. (1973) ENDO, 92, 1367.

Daly, A. B. (1974) In G. H. Bower (Ed.) The psychology of learning and motivation V. 8. New York: Academic Press.

Daly, D. (1958) Am. J. Psychiat., 115, 97.

D'Amato, M. R. (1973) In G. H. Bower (Ed.) The psychology of learning and motivation V. 7. New York: Academic Press.

D'Andrea, T. (1971) JEAB, 15, 319.

Dark, V. J. & Loftus, G. R. (1976) JVLVB, 16, 479.

Darley, D. F. & Murdock, B. B. (1971) JEP, 93, 66.

Das, J. P. & Cummins, J. (1978) AJMD, 83, 197.

Das, J. P., et al. (1975) PBUL, 82, 87.

Davidoff, J. B. (1977) COR, 13, 434.

Davidson, P. & Bucher, B. (1978) Beh. Thera., 9, 272.

Davidson, R. J. & Schwartz, G. E. (1977) P, 14, 598.

Davis, H., et al. (1976) PHB, 17, 687.

Davis, R. E. & Holmes, P. A. (1971) PHB, 7, 11.

Dawson, M. E. (1970) JEP, 85, 389.

DeBoskey, D., et al. (1979) In H. D. Kimmel et al. (Eds.) The orienting reflex in humans. Hillsdale, NJ: Lawrence Erlbaum Associates.

DeCasper, A. & Zeiler, M. D. (1977) JEAB, 27, 235.

DeCastro, J. M., et al. (1978) JCPP, 92, 71.

Deci, E. L. (1975) Intrinsic motivation. New York: Plenum.

Deci, E. L., et al. (1975) JPSP, 16, 294.

Deese, J. & Hulse, S. H. (1967) The psychology of learning. New York: McGraw-Hill.

Deese, J. & Marder, V. J. (1957) AJP, 60, 594.

DeFrance, J. F., et al. (1976) EXN, 53, 399.

DeGroot, A. M. B. (1983) JVLVB, 22, 417.

DeLong, R. E. & Wasserman, A. E. (1981) ABP, 7, 394.
Dember, W. N. (1956) JCPP, 49, 93.
Denenberg, V. H. & Haltmeyer, G. S. (1967) JCPP, 63, 394.
Dennis, M. (1977) In M. E. Blau, et al. (Eds.) Child neurology. New York: Spectrum.
Dennis, M. & Kohn, B. (1975) BL, 2, 472.
Dennis, M. & Whitaker, H. A. (1976) BL, 3, 404.
Denny, M. R. & Ratner, S. C. (1970) Comparative psychology. Homewood, IL: Dorsey Press.
DeNoble, V. & Caplan, M. (1977) JCPP, 91, 107.
DeRemer, P. & D'Agostino, P. R. (1974) JVLVB, 13, 167.
DeRenzi, E. & Nichelli, P. (1975) COR, 11, 341.
Deutsch, D. & Deutsch, J. A. (Eds.) (1975) Short term memory. New York: Academic Press.
Deutsch, R. D., et al. (1979) RCOM, 4, 415.
Devenport, L. D. (1979) S, 205, 721.
Devenport, L. D. (1980) BNB, 24, 105.
Devine, J. V., et al. (1977) ALB, 5, 57.
Dews, P. B. (1962) JEAB, 6, 369.
Dews, P. B. (1970) In W. N. Schoenfeld (Ed.) The theory of rein-forcement. Englewood Cliffs, NJ: Prentice-Hall.
Dewsbury, D. A., et al. (1982) JCPP, 96, 649.
Diamond, I. T. (1979) In J. M. Sprague & A. N. Epstein (Eds.) Progress in psychobiology and physiological psychology. New York: Academic Press.
Diamond, I. T., et al. (1970) JCN, 139, 273.
Dichter, M. & Spencer, A. (1969) JN, 32, 663.
Dickinson, A. & Mackintosh, N. J. (1979) ABP, 5, 162.
Dillon, R. F. & Bittner, L. A. (1975) JVLVB, 14, 616.
Dodwell, P. C. (1970) Visual pattern recognition. New York: Holt, Rinehart & Winston.
Dolin, A. O., et al. (1965) In L. G. Voronin, et al. (Eds.) The orienting reflex and exploratory behavior. Washington, DC: Am. Inst. of Biol. Sci.
Domjan, M. (1983) In G. Bower (Ed.) The psychology of learning and motivation. New York: Academic Press.
Domjan, M., et al. (1980) ABP, 6, 49.
Donovick, P. J. (1968) JCPP, 66, 569.
Donovick, P. J., et al. (1979) PHB, 22, 125.
Dosher, B. A. (1984) LMC, 10, 541.
Douglas, R. J. (1967) PBUL, 67, 416.
Douglas, R. J. (1972) In R. Boakes & M. Halliday (Eds.) Inhibition and learning. London: Academic Press.
Douglas, R. J. (1975) In R. L. Isaacson & K. H. Pribram (Eds.) The hippocampus V. 2. New York: Plenum.
Douglas, R. J. & Pribram, K. H. (1966) N, 4, 197.
Douglas, R. J. & Pribram, K. H. (1969) JCPP, 69, 473.

Douglas, R. J., et al. (1969) JCPP, 68, 437.
Downer, J. L. (1961) NAT, 191, 50.
Drachman, D. A. & Arbit, J. (1966) ARCH, 15, 52.
Dreifuss, J. J., et al. (1968) JN, 31, 237.
Dricker, J., et al. (1978) N, 16, 683.
Duncan, P. M. & Duncan, N. C. (1971) PHB, 7, 687.
Duncan-Johnson, C. C. & Donchin, E. (1977) P, 14, 456.
Dunham, P. (1977) In J. E. R. Staddon & W. K. Honig (Eds.) The
    handbook of operant behavior. New York: Appleton-Century-Crofts.
Dunn, A. J., et al. (1976) PBB, 5, 139.
Dweck, C. S. & Wagner, A. R. (1970) PS, 18, 145.
Easterbrook, J. A. (1959) PR, 66, 183.
Eccles, J. C. (1973) The understanding of the brain. New York:
    McGraw-Hill.
Edwards, C. A., et al. (1982) ABP, 8, 244.
Edwards, D. C. (1975) P, 12, 12.
Egeth, H. (1977) In G. H. Bower (Ed.) The psychology of learning
    and motivation V. 11. New York: Academic Press.
Egeth, H. & Blecker, D. (1971) PP, 9, 321.
Egeth, H., et al. (1972) COG, 3, 674.
Egger, M. D. (1967) ECN, 23, 6.
Egger, M. D. & Flynn, J. P. (1963) JN, 26, 705.
Ehle, A. L., et al. (1977) NENDO, 23, 52.
Eichenbaum, H., et al. (1980) BBE, 17, 225.
Eimas, P. D. (1970) JECP, 10, 319.
Eleftheriou, B. (1972) (Ed.) The neurobiology of the amygdala.
    New York: Plenum.
Eleftheriou, B. et al. (1967) J. Endocr., 38, 469.
Ellen, P. & Powell, E. W. (1962) EXN, 6, 1.
Ellen, P. & Wilson, A. S. (1963) EXN, 8, 310.
Ellen, P., et al. (1977) PHY, 5, 469.
Ellis, N. R. (1970) In N. R. Ellis (Ed.) International review of
    research in mental retardation V. 4. New York: Academic Press.
Elmes, D. G. & Bjork, R. A. (1975) JVLVB, 14, 30.
Engen, T. & Ross, B. M. (1973) JEP, 100, 221.
Erber, J. T. (1974) JGER, 29, 177.
Evans, J. G. M. & Hammond, G. R. (1983a) ALB, 11, 424.
Evans, J. G. M. & Hammond, G. R. (1983b) ALB, 11, 431.
Ewert, J. P. & Ingle, D. (1971) JCPP, 77, 369.
Eysenck, M. W. (1975) HLM, 1, 143.
Eysenck, M. W. (1979) In L. S. Cermak & F. I. M. Craik, Levels of
    processing. Hillsdale, NJ: Lawrence Erlbaum Associates.
Fagan, J. F. (1971) JECP, 11, 244.
Falk, J. L. (1969) Ann. N.Y. Acad. Sci, 157, 569.
Falk, J. L. (1971) PHB, 6, 577.
Fallon, D. & Donovick, P. J. (1970) JCPP, 73, 150.
Fanselow, M. S. (1980) ABP, 6, 65.

412

Fanselow, M. S. (1984) B, 98, 269.

Fantino, E. (1977) In W. K. Hinig & J. F. R. Staddon (Eds.) Handbook of operant behavior. New York: Appleton-Century-Crofts.

Farel, P. B., et al. (1973) JN, 36, 1117.

Farris, H. F. (1967) JEAB, 10, 213.

Feldman, J. M. (1971) JEP, 91, 318.

Feldon, J. & Gray, J. A. (1979) QJEP, 31, 675.

Ferster, L. B. & Skinner, B. F. (1957) Schedules of reinforcement. N.Y.: Appleton-Century-Crofts.

Finch, D. M., et al. (1978) EXN, 61, 318.

Findley, J. D. (1962) JEAB, 5, 113.

Fischoff, B. (1975) HPP, 1, 288.

Fisher, C. B. (1979) CD, 50, 1088.

Fisher, R. P. (1979) MC, 7, 224.

Fisher, R. P. (1981) JEP, 7, 306.

Fitzgerald, P. G. & Picton, T. W. (1981) CJP, 35, 188.

Fitzsimmons, J. T. (1972) Physiol. Rev., 52, 468.

Flaherty, C. F. & Checke, S. (1982) ALB, 10, 177.

Fleischer, S. & Slotnick, B. M. (1978) PHB, 21, 189.

Fleming, D. E. & Bigler, E. V. (1974) PHB, 13, 757.

Flexser, A. J. & Tulving, E. (1978) PR, 85, 153.

Flory, R. K. (1971) LM, 2, 215.

Fontenot, D. J. & Benton, A. L. (1972) N, 10, 447.

Ford, J. M. & Hillyard, S. A. (1981) P, 18, 322.

Fowler, H., et al. (1977) LM, 8, 507.

Frederickson, C. J., et al. (1980) BNB, 28, 383.

Fredrickson, M., et al. (1984) P, 21, 219.

Freeman, R. N. & Thibo, L. N. (1973) S, 180, 876.

Frey, P. W. & Sears, R. J. (1978) PR, 85, 321.

Fried, P. A. (1972) PBUL, 78, 292.

Friederici, A. D. & Schoenle, P. N. (1980) N, 18, 11.

Fuld, P. A. & Buschke, H. (1976) JVLVB, 15, 401.

Fuster, J. M. (1973) JN, 36, 61.

Gabriel, M., et al. (1980) JCPP, 94, 1087.

Gabrieli, J. D. E., et al. (1983) Soc. Neuro. Ab., 9, 28.

Gaffan, D. (1979) LM, 10, 419.

Gaffan, E. A. & Hart, M. M. (1981) QJEP, 33, 77.

Galbraith, R. C. (1975) HLM, 1, 23.

Galef, B. G. & Clark, M. (1972) JCPP, 78, 213.

Gallistel, C. R. (1980) The organization of action. Hillsdale, NJ: Lawrence Erlbaum Associates.

Garcia, J., et al. (1972) In A. H. Black & W. F. Prokasy (Eds.) Classical conditioning II. New York: Appleton-Century-Crofts.

Gardiner, J. M., et al. (1974) JEP, 103, 71.

Garner, W. R. (1974) The processing of information and structure. Hillsdale, NJ: Lawrence Erlbaum Associates

Garrod, S. & Sanford, S. (1977) JVLVB, 16, 77.

413

Gates, A. & Bradshaw, J. L.  (1977) BL, 4, 403.
Gazzaniga, M.  (1975) In M. Gazzaniga & C. Blakemore (Eds.)
  Handbook of psychobiology. New York: Academic Press.
Gerard, H. B.  (1976) JPER, 35, 91.
Gerard, H. B. et al.  (1974) In L. Berkowitz (Ed.) Advances in
  experimental social psychology. New York: Academic Press.
Geschwind, N.  (1980) In D. Caplan (Ed.) Biological studies of
  mental processes. Cambridge, MA: MIT.
Gibbon, J. (1977) PR, 84, 279.
Gibbon, J. et al. (1980) ALB, 8, 45.
Gibbons, J. L. & McHugh, P. R.  (1962) J. Psychiatr. Rsch., 1, 162.
Gibbs, C. M., et al.  (1978) ALB, 6, 209.
Gibson, E. J.  (1969)  Principles of perceptual learning and
  development.  New York:  Appleton-Century-Crofts.
Gick, M. L. & Holyoak, K. J.  (1983) COG, 15, 1.
Gilani, Z. H. & Ceraso, J.  (1982) JVLVB, 21, 437.
Gillund, G. & Shiffrin, R. M.  (1981) JVLVB, 20, 575.
Ginsberg, S. & Furedy, J. J.  (1974) P, 11, 35.
Girdner, J. B.  (1953) AP, 8, 345.
Girgis, M. K.  (1972) In B. Eleftheriou (Ed.)  The neurobiology of
  the amygdala. New York:  Plenum.
Gittelson, P. J., et al.  (1969) PS, 17, 242.
Glanzer, M. A. & Cunitz, A. R.  (1966) JVLVB, 5, 351.
Glass, A. L. & Holyoak, K. J.  (1976) C, 3, 313.
Glass, D. C.  (1964) JPER, 32, 395.
Glassman, R. B., et al.  (1981) PHB, 26, 107.
Glazer, H. I.  (1974a) JCPP, 86, 267.
Glazer, H. I.  (1974b) JCPP, 86, 1156.
Glenberg, A. M.  (1976) JVLVB, 15, 1.
Glenberg, A. M.  (1984) LMC, 10, 16.
Glenberg, A. M. & Adams, F.  (1978) JVLVB, 17, 455.
Glenberg, A. M., et al.  (1977) JVLVB, 16, 339.
Glenberg, A. M. et al.  (1983) LMC, 9, 231.
Glendenning, K. K., et al.  (1975) JCN, 161, 419.
Glickman, S. E. & Sroges, R. W.  (1966) B, 26, 151.
Glidden, L. M., et al.  (1977) AJMD, 82, 84.
Gloning, K.  (1977) N, 15, 355.
Gloor, P.  (1972) In B. Eleftheriou (Ed.) The neurobiology of the
  amygdala. New York: Plenum.
Goddard, G. V.  (1964) PBUL, 62, 89.
Goethals, G. R. et al.  (1979) JPSP, 37, 1179.
Gold, P. E. & King, R. D.  (1974) PR, 81, 465.
Goldberg, E., et al.  (1978) BL, 5, 249.
Goldberg, M. E. & Bushnell, M. C.  (1981) JN, 46, 773.
Goldman-Rakic, P. S. & Schwartz, M. L.  (1982) S, 216, 755.
Goldstein, A. G. & Chance, J.  (1971) PP, 9, 237.

Gollub, L. (1977) In W. K. Honig & J. E. R. Staddon (Eds.) Handbook of operant behavior. New York: Appleton-Century-Crofts.

Goodenough, C., et al. (1977) Lang & Speech, 20, 11.

Goodglass, H. & Stuss, D. T. (1979) COR, 15, 199.

Goodglass, H., et al. (1970) J. Spch. Hear. Resch., 13, 595.

Goodman, D. A. & Weinberger, N. M. (1973) In H. V. Peeke & M. J. Herz (Eds.) Habituation V. 1. New York: Academic Press.

Goodman, J. H. & Fowler, H. (1983) ALB, 11, 75.

Goomas, D. T. (1980) PHY, 8, 97.

Gordon, D. A. & Baumeister, A. A. (1971) JECP, 12, 95.

Gordon, H. W. (1980) N, 18, 645.

Gordon, S. K. & Clark, W. C. (1974) JGER, 29, 654.

Gottlieb, G. (1979) JCPP, 43, 831.

Gotz, A. & Jacoby, L. J. (1974) JEP, 102, 291.

Graham, F. K. (1973) In H. V. Peeke & M. J. Herz (Eds.) Habituation V. 1. New York: Academic Press.

Graham, F. K. (1979) In H. D. Kimmel et al. (Eds.) The orienting reflex in humans. Hillsdale, NJ: Lawrence Erlbaum Associates.

Grant, D. A., et al. (1983) ABP, 9, 63.

Grauer, E. & Thomas, E. (1982) JCPP, 96, 61.

Gray, J. A. (1970) PR, 77, 465.

Gray, J. A. (1982) The neuropsychology of anxiety. Oxford: Oxford U.

Green, J. D. & Machne, X. (1955) Am. J. Phys., 181, 219.

Greenbaum, C. W. et al. (1965) JPER, 33, 46.

Greenspoon, J. & Ranyard, R. (1957) JEP, 53, 55.

Grice, G. R. (1948) JEP, 38, 1.

Griffith, R. R. & Thompson, T. (1973) PREC, 23, 229.

Grings, W. W., et al. (1961) JCPP, 54, 143.

Grings, W. W., et al. (1962) PM, 72, 588.

Grings, W. W., et al. (1979) JEP, 108, 281.

Gross, N. M. (1972) PP, 12, 357.

Grossman, S. P. (1964) JCPP, 57, 29.

Grossman, S. P. (1972) In B. Eleftheriou (Ed.) The neurobiology of the amygdala. New York: Plenum.

Groves, P. M. & Thompson, R. F. (1970) PR, 77, 419.

Groves, P. M., et al. (1970) BRES, 18, 388.

Guilford, J. D. (1967) The nature of human intelligence. New York: McGraw-Hill.

Gustaffson, J. W., et al. (1975) JCPP, 85, 1136.

Guth, S., et al. (1971) HB, 2, 127.

Haberlandt, K. & Bingham, G. (1978) JVLVB, 17, 419.

Haggard, M. P. & Parkinson, A. M. (1971) QJEP, 23, 168.

Hale, G. A. & Morgan, J. G. (1973) JECP, 15, 302.

Halgren, C. R. (1974) JCPP, 86, 74.

Halgren, E., et al. (1978) ECN, 45, 585.

Halgren, E., et al. (1983) In W. Seifert (Ed.) Neurobiology of the hippocampus. New York: Academic Press.
Hall, G. & Pearce, J. M. (1979) ABP, 5, 31.
Halperin, Y., et al. (1973) J. Acoust. Soc. Amer., 50, 46.
Hamilton, L. W., et al. (1970) JCPP, 70, 79.
Hamner, W. C. & Foster, L. W. (1975) Org. Beh. Hum. Perf., 14, 398.
Handel, S., et al. (1980) PP, 28, 205.
Hanson, J. D., et al. (1976) BBIO, 16, 333.
Harkins, S. W., et al. (1979) JGER, 34, 66.
Harris, E. W., et al. (1978) BRES, 151, 623.
Hartlage, L. C. (1970) PMS, 31, 610.
Harvey, L. O. & Gervais, M. T. (1981) HPP, 7, 741.
Harzem, P., et al. (1975) JEAB, 24, 33.
Hasher, L. & Chromiak, W. (1977) JVLVB, 16, 173.
Hasher, L. & Clifton, D. (1974) JECP, 17, 232.
Hasher, L. & Griffin, M. (1978) HLM, 4, 318.
Hasher, L. & Johnson, M. K. (1975) HLM, 1, 567.
Haskett, J. & Hollar, W. D. (1978) AJMD, 83, 60.
Hayes-Roth, F. (1979) PR, 86, 376.
Hayes-Roth, B. & Hayes-Roth, F. (1977) JVLVB, 16, 321.
Hearst, E. (1975) In G. H. Bower (Ed.) The psychology of learning and motivation V. 9. New York: Academic Press.
Hearst, E. (1978) In S. H. Hulse, et al. (Eds.) Cognitive processes in animal behavior. Hillsdale, NJ: Lawrence Erlbaum Associates.
Hearst, E. & Franklin, G. (1977) ABP, 3, 37.
Hebb, D. O. (1949) The organization of behavior. New York: Wiley.
Hecaen, H. & Albert, M. L. (1978) Human neuropsychology. New York: Wiley.
Henderson, L. & Henderson, S. E. (1975) MC, 3, 97.
Henke, P. G. (1973) JCPP, 84, 187.
Henke, P. G. (1975) PHB, 15, 537.
Henke, P. G. (1980) JCPP, 94, 313.
Hennesy, M. B. & Levine, S. (1977) PHB, 18, 799.
Hennesy, J. W. & Levine, S. (1979) In J. M. Sprague & A. N. Epstein (Eds.) Progress in psychobiology and physiological psychology V. 8. New York: Plenum.
Hennesy, J. W., et al. (1977a) JCPP, 91, 1447.
Hennesy, J. W., et al. (1977b) JCPP, 91, 770.
Herman, L. M. (1975) ALB, 3, 43.
Hermann, T., et al. (1980) PHY, 8, 29.
Hermelin, B. & O'Connor, N. (1967) COR, 3, 163.
Hertel, P. T. & Ellis, H. C. (1979) HLM, 5, 386.
Hess, W. R. (1957) The functional organization of the diencephalon. New York: Grune & Stratton.
Hickis, C. F., et al. (1977) ALB, 5, 161.
Higgins, E. T., et al. (1979) JESP, 15, 16.

Hill, A. J. (1978) EXN, 62, 282.
Hillyard, S. A. (1971) ECN, 31, 302.
Hilton, A. (1969) JCPP, 69, 253.
Hilton, M. & Zbrozyna, A. (1963) JP, 165, 160.
Hinde, R. A. (1970) Animal behavior. New York: McGraw-Hill.
Hinderliter, L. F., et al. (1975) ALB, 3, 257.
Hintzman, D. L. (1976) In G. H. Bower (Ed.) The psychology of
  learning and motivation V. 10. New York: Academic Press.
Hintzman, D. L., et al. (1972) JVLVB, 11, 741.
Hintzman, D. L., et al. (1973) JVLVB, 12, 229.
Hintzman, D. L., et al. (1975) HLM, 1, 31.
Hirsch, H. V. B. & Spinelli, D. N. (1970) S, 168, 869.
Hirsh, R. (1973) BRES, 58, 234.
Hirsh, R. (1974) BBIO, 12, 421.
Hirshkowitz, M., et al. (1978) N, 16, 125.
Hockey, R. (1979) In V. Hamilton & D. M. Warburton (Eds.) Human
  stress and cognition. New York: Wiley.
Hoehler, F. K. & Thompson, R. F. (1979) PHY, 7, 345.
Hoehler, F. K. & Thompson, R. F. (1980) JCPP, 94, 201.
Hogan, J. A. (1973) JCPP, 83, 355.
Hogan, J. A. (1977) JCPP, 91, 839.
Holden, E. A. & Winters, E. A. (1977) AJMD, 81, 578.
Holland, P. C. (1977) ABP, 3, 77.
Holland, P. C. (1981) LM, 12, 1.
Holland, P. C. & Forbes, D. T. (1982) ALB, 10, 249.
Holland, P. C. & Rescorla, R. A. (1975) ABP, 1, 355.
Holloway, F. A. & Wansley, R. A. (1973) S, 80, 208.
Holman, E. W. (1975) LM, 6, 358.
Holman, E. W. & Mackintosh, N. J. (1981) QJEP, 33, 21.
Holmes, D. R. & McKeever, W. F. (1979) COR, 15, 51.
Holmes, J. E. & Egan, K. (1973) PHB, 10, 803.
Holmes, P. W. (1972) JEAP, 18, 129.
Holyoak, K. J. (1977) COG, 9, 31.
Homa, D. (1978) HLM, 4, 407.
Homa, D. & Chambliss, D. (1975) HLM, 1, 351.
Homa, D., et al. (1973) JEP, 101, 116.
Honig, W. K. (1974) LM, 5, 1.
Hornstein, H. A. & Mosley, J. L. (1979) AJMD, 84, 40.
Horowitz, L. M. & Prytulak, L. S. (1969) PR, 79, 519.
Hovland, C. I. (1937) JEP, 21, 261.
Howard, D. V. & Goldin, S. E. (1979) JECP, 27, 87.
Hoyer, W. J., et al. (1979) JGER, 34, 553.
Hudson, R. L. & Austin, J. B. (1970) JEP, 86, 43.
Hughes, H. C., et al. (1984) PP, 35, 361.
Hughes, R. J. & Andy, O. J. (1979) ECN, 46, 444.
Hull, C. L. (1943) Principles of behavior. New York: Appleton-
  Century-Crofts.

417

Hull, C. L. (1952) A behavior system. New Haven, CT: Yale U.

Hulse, S. H., et al. (Eds.) (1978) Cognitive processes in animal behavior. Hillsdale, NJ: Lawrence Erlbaum Associates:

Humphrey, N. K. (1970) BBE, 3, 324.

Hunt, E., et al. (1975) COG, 7, 194.

Hunt, G. L. & Smith, W. S. (1967) JCPP, 64, 230.

Huppert, F. A. & Piercy, M. (1976) COR, 12, 3.

Huppert, F. A. & Piercy, M. (1978) QJEP, 30, 347.

Huppert, F. A. & Piercy, M. (1982) In L. S. Cermak (Ed.) Human memory and amnesia. Hillsdale, NJ: Lawrence Erlbaum Associates.

Hurvich, L. M. & Jameson, D. (1974) AD, 29, 88.

Hutchinson, R., et al. (1968) JEAB, 11, 489.

Imig, T. J., et al. (1977) JCN, 171, 111.

Innis, N. K. & Honig, W. K. (1979) ALB, 7, 203.

Isaacson, R. L. (1974) The limbic system. New York: Plenum.

Isaacson, R. L. & Kimble, D. P. (1972) BBIO, 7, 767.

Isaacson, R. L. & McClearn, G. E. (1978) BRES, 150, 559.

Isaacson, R. L. & Pribram, K. H. (Eds.) (1975) The hippocampus V. 2. New York: Plenum.

Iuvone, P. M. & van Hartesveldt, C. (1977) BBIO, 19, 228.

Iversen, S. D. & Mishkin, M. (1970) EBR, 11, 376.

Izawa, L. (1970) JEP, 83, 340.

Jacobs, B. L. & McGinty, D. J. (1972) BRES, 36, 431.

Jacobsen, S., et al. (1978) BRES, 159, 279.

Jacoby, L. L. (1974) JVLVB, 13, 483.

Jacoby, L. L. & Craik, F. I. M. (1979) In L. S. Cermak & F. I. M. Craik (Eds.) Levels of processing in human memory. Hillsdale, NJ: Lawrence Erlbaum Associates.

Jacoby, L. L. & Hendricks, R. L. (1973) JEP, 100, 73.

Jahnke, J. C. & Duncan, C. P. (1956) JEP, 52, 273.

James, W. (1890) Principles of psychology. New York: Holt.

James, W. & Rotter, J. B. (1958) JEP, 55, 197.

Jarman, R. F. (1978) AJMD, 82, 344.

Jarrard, L. E. (1973) PBUL, 79, 1.

Jarrard, L. E. & Elmes, D. G. (1982) JCPP, 96, 699.

Jeffrey, W. E. & Cohen, C. B. (1965) JECP, 2, 248.

Jenkins, H. M. (1977) In H. Davis & H. M. B. Hurwitz (Eds.) Operant-Pavlovian interactions. Hillsdale, NJ: Lawrence Erlbaum Associates.

Jenkins, H. M. & Moore, B. M. (1973) JEAB, 20, 163.

Jenkins, H. M. & Ward, W. C. (1965) PM, 79, #594.

Jenkins, H. M. & Sainsbury, R. S. (1970) In D. Mostofsky (Ed.) Attention. New York: Appleton-Century-Crofts.

Jensen, R. A. & Riccio, D. C. (1970) PHB, 5, 1291

John, E. R. (1967) In G. C. Quarton, et al. (Eds.) The neurosciences. New York: Rockefeller U. Press.

John, E. R., et al. (1973) JN, 36, 893.

Johnson, E. & Donchin, E. (1982) P, 19, 183.
Johnson, M. K., et al. (1979) HLM, 5, 229.
Johnson, P. R. (1977) COR, 13, 385.
Johnson, R. C., et al. (1977) COR, 13, 295.
Johnson, W. & Kieras, D. (1983) MC, 11, 456.
Johnston, W. A. & Uhl, L. N. (1976) HLM, 2, 153.
Jones, B. & Mishkin, M. (1972) EXN, 36, 362.
Jorgenson, D. O. & Papciak, A. S. (1981) JESP, 17, 373.
Joseph, J. A. & Engel, B. T. (1981), PHB, 26, 865.
Joseph, J. A., et al. (1982) PHB, 28, 653.
Julesz, B. (1967) In W. Wathen-Dunn (Ed.) Models for the percep-
tion of speech and form. Cambridge, MA: MIT.
Jwaideh, A. R. (1973) JEAB, 19, 259.
Kaada, B. R. (1972) In B. Eleftheriou (Ed.) The neurobiology of
the amygdala. New York: Plenum.
Kaada, B. R., et al. (1971) PHB, 7, 225.
Kamberi, I. A. (1973) Prog. Brain. Rsch., 39, 201.
Kamin, L. J. (1968) In M. R. Jones (Ed.) Miami symposium on the
prediction of behavior. Miami: U. of Miami.
Kamin, L. J. (1969) In B. A. Campbell & R. M. Church (Eds.)
Punishment and aversive behavior. New York: Appleton-Century-
Crofts.
Kapp, B. S., et al. (1978) BBIO, 24, 1.
Karpicke, J. & Hearst, E. (1975) JEAB, 23, 76.
Kasper-Pandi, P., et al. (1969) PHB, 4, 815.
Kaufman, A. & Baron, A. (1969) Gen. Psychol. Mono., 80, 151.
Kaufman, F., et al. (1982) N, 20, 439.
Kausler, D. H. & Kleim, D. M. (1978) JGER, 37, 87.
Kaye, H. & Pearce, J. M. (1984) ABP, 10, 90.
Kazdin, A.E. (1973) Beh. Thera., 4, 73.
Kean, M., et al. (1980) In D. Caplan (Ed.) The biological study of
mental processes. Cambridge, MA: MIT.
Kellas, G. et al. (1975) HLM, 1, 84.
Kellicut, M. H. & Schwartzbaum, J. S. (1963) PREP, 12, 351.
Kemler, D. G. & Smith, L. B. (1979) JEPG, 108, 133.
Kemler-Nelson, D. G. (1984) JVLVB, 23, 734.
Kendall, S. B. (1967) JEAB, 10, 311.
Kendall, S. B. (1972) JEAB, 17, 161.
Kendler, H. H. & Kendler, T. S. (1968) In K. W. Spence & J. T.
Spence (Eds.) The psychology of learning and motivation V. 2.
New York: Academic Press.
Keppel, G. (1971) In C. P. Duncan, et al. (Eds.) Human memory.
New York: Appleton-Century-Crofts.
Kertesz, A. & McCabe, P. (1975) BL, 4, 387.
Keryen, G. & Baggen, S. (1981) PP, 29, 234.
Kesner, R. P. & Andrus, R. G. (1982) PHY, 10, 55.
Kesner, R. P. & Connor, H. S. (1972) S, 176, 432.

Kesner, R. P. & Cook, D. G. (1983) B, 97, 4.
Kesner, R. P., et al. (1970) EXP, 27, 527.
Kessen, W., et al. (1972) JECP, 13, 9.
Key, B. J. & Bradley, P. B. (1959) ECN, 11, 841.
Kihlstrom, J. F. & Evans, F. J. (Eds.) (1979) Functional disorders of memory. Hillsdale, NJ: Lawrence Erlbaum Associates.
Killeen, P. (1975) PR, 82, 89.
Kimble, D. P. (1968) PBUL, 70, 285.
Kimble, D. P. & Ray, R. S. (1965) AB, 13, 530.
Kimble, D. P. & Bre-Miller, R. (1981) PHB, 26, 1055.
Kimble, G. A. (1961) Hilgard & Marquis' Conditioning and Learning. New York: Century.
Kimble, G. A., et al. (1955) JEP, 49, 407.
Kimmel, H. D. & Goldstein, A. J. (1967) JEP, 73, 401.
Kimmel, H. D., et al. (1967) Cond. Reflex., 2, 227.
Kimmel, H. D., et al. (1979) PHY, 7, 283.
Kimura, D. & Vanderwolf, C. H. (1970) BR, 93, 769.
King, W. M., et al. (1980) JN, 43, 912.
Kinsbourne, M. & Winocur, G. (1980) N, 18, 541.
Kinsbourne, M. & Wood, F. (1975) In D. Deutsch & J. A. Deutsch (Eds.) Short term memory. New York: Academic Press.
Kintsch, W. (1974) The representation of meaning in memory. Hillsdale, NJ: Lawrence Erlbaum Associates, 1974.
Kintsch, W. & Bates, E. (1977) HLM, 3, 150.
Kirby, J. R. & Das, J. P. (1977) JED, 69, 564.
Kirk, M. D. & Wine, J. J. (1984) S, 225, 854.
Kish, G. B. (1955) JCPP, 48, 261.
Klatzky, R. L., et al. (1982) MC, 10, 195.
Klee, H. & Gardiner, J. M. (1976) JVLVB, 15, 471.
Klein, K. & Saltz, E. (1976) HLM, 2, 671.
Kleinsmith, L. J. & Kaplan, S. (1963) JEP, 65, 190.
Kling, A. (1972) In B. Eleftheriou (Ed.) The neurobiology of the amygdala. New York: Plenum.
Kling, A., et al. (1970) J. Psychiat Rsch., 7, 191.
Klinger, J. & Gloor, P. (1960) JCN, 115, 333.
Klopfer, P. H. (1973) In G. Bermant (Ed.) Perspectives on animal behavior. Glenview, IL: Scott Foresman.
Knight, R. T., et al. (1981) ECN, 52, 571.
Knutson, J. F. & Kleinknecht, R. A. (1970) PS, 19, 289.
Koepke, J. E. & Pribram, K. H. (1967) JCPP, 64, 502.
Koestler, A. (1964) The act of creation. New York: Macmillan.
Kohler, C. (1976a) BBIO, 18, 89.
Kohler, C. (1976b) BBIO, 16, 63.
Kohn, B. & Dennis, M. (1974) N, 12, 505.
Kohn, S. E. et al. (1984) BL, 22, 160.
Kolers, P. A. & Ostry, D. J. (1974) JVLVB, 13, 599.

Komisaruk, B. R. (1977) In J. M. Sprague & A. N. Epstein (Eds.) Progress in psychobiology and physiological psychology V. 7. New York: Academic Press.

Komisaruk, B. R. & Beyer, C. (1972) BRES, 36, 153.

Koolhaas, J. M., et al. (1977) PHB, 18, 329.

Kopp, R., et al. (1966) S, 153, 1547.

Koranyi, L., et al. (1967) PHB, 2, 439.

Kosslyn, S. M. (1980) Image and mind. Cambridge, MA: Harvard.

Kovach, J. K. (1983) COMP, 97, 240.

Kremer, E. F. (1978) ABP, 4, 22.

Krettek, J. E. & Price, J. L. (1977) JCN, 172, 687.

Krieckhaus, E. E. & Wolf, G. (1968) JCPP, 65, 197.

Kristofferson, M. W. (1972) CJP, 26, 54.

Kruglanski, A. W., et al. (1971) JPER, 39, 606.

Kruk, Z. L. & Pycock, C. J. (1983) Neurotransmitters and drugs. Baltimore: University Park Press.

Kubie, J. L. & Ranck, J. B. (1983) In W. Seifert (Ed.) Neurobiology of the hippocampus. New York: Academic Press.

Kubota, K., et al. (1980) BRES, 183, 29.

Kusyszyn, I. & Paivio, A. (1966) JEP, 71, 800.

LaBarbera, J. D. & Caul, W. F. (1976) ALB, 4, 389.

LaBarbera, J. D. & Church, R. M. (1974) ALB, 2, 199.

Lachman, R. & Mistler, J. L. (1970) JEP, 85, 374.

Lachman, R. et al. (1977) Cognitive psychology and information processing. Hillsdale, NJ: Lawrence Erlbaum Associates.

Lair, C. V., et al. (1969) DEV, 1, 548.

Lake, D. A. & Bryden, M. P. (1976) BL, 3, 266.

Landau, B. L. & Hagen, J. W. (1974) CD, 45, 643.

Landfield, P. W. (1977) PHB, 18, 439.

Landfield, P. W. & Lynch, G. (1977) JGER, 32, 525.

Lantz, A. (1973) ALB, 4, 273.

Lanzetta, J. T. (1963) In A. J. Harvey (Ed.) Motivation and social interaction. New York: Ronald Press.

Lanzetta, J. T. & Driscoll, J. M. (1968) JPSP, 10, 479.

Lash, L. (1964) JCPP, 57, 251.

Lashley, K. S. (1950) Symp. Soc. Exp. Biol., 4, 454.

Lashley, R. L. & Rossellini, R. A. (1980) PHB, 24, 411.

Lavin, M. S. (1976) LM, 7, 1973.

Lawless, H. & Engen, T. (1977) HLM, 3, 52.

Lawrence, M. W. (1967) PS, 9, 209.

Layden, T. A. & Birch, H. (1969) PHB, 4, 1015.

Leander, J. D., et al. (1968) PS, 18, 469.

Leaton, R. N. (1976) ABP, 2, 248.

Lee, K., et al. (1980) JN, 44, 247.

Leiber, L. (1977) N, 15, 217.

Lenneberg, E. H. (1973) Daedalus, 102, 115.

Lepper, M. R. & Greene, D. (1975) JPSP, 31, 479.

421

Lepper, M. R., et al. (1973) JPSP, 28, 129.
Lettvin, J. Y., et al. (1959) Proc. Inst. Radio Engr., 47, 1940.
Leung, P. M. B. & Rogers, Q. R. (1973) PHB, 10, 221.
Leventhal, A. G. & Hirsch, H. V. B. (1975) S, 190, 902.
Levine, M. et al. (1959) JCON, 21, 41.
Levine, M. D., et al. (1970) PHB, 5, 919.
Lewin, K. (1938) The conceptual representation and the measurement of psychological forces. Durham, NC: Duke U.
Lewis, D. & Lowe, W. F. (1956) Proc. Iowa Acad. Sci., 63, 591.
Lewis, M. (1976) Origins of intelligence. New York: Plenum.
Leyland, C. M. & Mackintosh, N. J. (1978) ALB, 6, 391.
Lhermitte, F. & Signoret, J. L. (1976) In M. R. Rosenzweig & E. L. Bennett (Eds.) Neural mechanisms of learning and memory. Cambridge, MA: MIT
Libby, M. E. & Church, R. M. (1974) JEAB, 22, 513.
Liberman, A. M. (1982) AP, 37, 148.
Light, L. L. & Schurr, S. C. (1973) JEP, 100, 135.
Lippman, G. & Meyer, M. E. (1967) PS, 8, 135.
Livesey, P. J. (1975) In R. L. Isaacson & K. H. Pribram (Eds.) The hippocampus V. 2. New York: Plenum.
Locke, S., et al. (1973) A study in neurolinguistics. Springfield, IL: Charles C. Thomas.
Lockhart, R. S., et al. (1976) In J. Brown (Ed.) Recall and recognition. New York: Wiley.
Loftus, E. F. & Loftus, G. R. (1980) AP, 5, 409.
Logan, C. A. & Beck, H. P. (1978) JCPP, 92, 928.
Logan, G. D. & Zbrodoff, N. J. (1982) HPP, 8, 502.
Lorch, R. F. (1982) JVLVB, 21, 468.
Lovelace, E. A. & Southall, S. D. (1983) MC, 11, 429.
Lovely, R. H., et al. (1971) JCPP, 77, 345.
Lovibond, S. H. (1969) P, 5, 435.
Lowe, C. F. (1979) In M. D. Zeiler & P. Harzem (Eds.) Reinforcement and the organization of behavior. New York: Wiley.
Lubar, J. F., et al. (1970) PHB, 5, 459.
Lubow, R. E. (1973) PBUL, 79, 398.
Lubow, R. E., et al. (1975) ABP, 1, 1978.
Luria, A. R. (1980) Higher cortical functions in man. New York: Basic Books.
Lynch, G. S., et al. (1978) In K. Elliott & J. Whelan (Eds.) Functions of the septo-hippocampal system. Amsterdam: Elsevier.
Lyon, D. O. & Millar, R. D. (1969) PS, 17, 31.
Mackintosh, N. J. (1978) In S. H. Hulse, et al. (Eds.) Cognitive processes in animal behavior. Hillsdale, NJ: Lawrence Erlbaum Associates.
Mackintosh, N. J. (1983) Conditioning and associative learning. Oxford: Oxford U.
Mackworth, N. H. & Bruner, J. S. (1970) HD, 13, 149.

Maclean, P. D. (1970) In F. O. Schmitt, et al. (Eds.) The neuro-sciences: second study program. New York: Rockefeller U.

Madigan, S. A. (1969) JVLVB, 8, 828.

Magliero, A., et al. (1984) P, 21, 171.

Mah, C. J., et al. (1972) PHB, 8, 283.

Maier, N. R. F., et al. (1963) Personnel Psychol., 16, 1.

Maier, S. F., et al. (1983) ABP, 9, 80.

Maisiak, R. & Frey, P. W. (1977) ALB, 5, 309.

Maki, W. S., et al. (1977) ABP, 3, 156.

Malamud, N. (1972) In C. M. Gaitz (Ed.) Aging and the brain. New York: Plenum.

Maltzman, I., et al. (1977) JEPG, 106, 141.

Maltzman, I., et al. (1978) JEPG, 107, 309.

Maltzman, I., et al. (1979) PHY, 7, 193.

Mandler, G. (1967) In K. W. Spence & J. T. Spence (Eds.) The psychology of learning and motivation V. 1. New York: Academic Press.

Mandler, G. (1980) PR, 87, 252.

Mandler, G. & Pearlstone, Z. (1966) JVLVB, 5, 126.

Marchant, H. G. & Moore, J. W. (1974) JEP, 102, 350.

Marcucella, H. (1981) JEAB, 36, 51.

Margules, D. L. & Olds, J. (1962) S, 135, 374.

Mark, V. H., et al. (1972) In B. Eleftheriou (Ed.) The neuro-biology of the amygdala. New York: Plenum.

Markowitsch, H. J. & Pritzel, M. (1977) PBUL, 84, 817.

Markus, H. (1978) JESP, 14, 389.

Marlin, N. A. (1982) LM, 13, 526.

Marlin, N. A. & Miller, R. R. (1981) ABP, 7, 313.

Marr, M. J. (1969) In D. P. Hendry (Ed.) Conditioned reinforcement. Homewood, IL: Dorsey.

Marsden, H. M. & Slotnick, B. M. (1972) Am. Zool., 12, 360.

Martin, E. (1972) In A. W. Melton & E. Martin (Eds.) Coding processes in human memory. Washington, DC: Winston.

Martini, L., et al. (1970) The hypothalamus. New York: Academic Press.

Marx, M. H., et al. (1955) JCPP, 48, 73.

Mason, J. M. (1978) AJMD, 82, 467.

Mattes, J. A. (1980) CPSI, 21, 358.

Mathews, N. N., et al. (1980) JVLVB, 19, 531.

Matthews, W. A. (1966) QJEP, 17, 31.

May, R. B. & Tryk, H. E. (1970) CJP, 24, 299.

Mayer, A. D. & Rosenblatt, J. S. (1980) JCPP, 94, 1040.

McAdam, D. W. & Whitaker, H. A. (1971) S, 172, 499.

McAllister, W., et al. (1971) JCPP, 74, 426.

McAllister, W. R. & McAllister, D. E. (1967) AJP, 80, 377.

McCall, R. B. (1977) S, 197, 482.

McCallum, W. C., et al. (1983) P, 20, 1.

McCarthy, G. & Donchin, E. (1976) P, 13, 581.

McCleary, R. A. (1966) In E. Steller & J. Sprague (Eds.) Progress in physiological psychology V. 1. New York: Academic Press.

McClelland, J. L. (1978) HPP, 4, 210.

McCrystal, T. J. (1970) JEP, 83, 220.

McDonough, J. H. & Manning, F. J. (1979) PHY, 7, 167.

McDonald, K. (1983) COMP, 97, 99.

McDonnell, M. F. & Flynn, J. P. (1966) S, 152, 1406.

McEwen, B. S. & Pfaff, D. W. (1970) BRES, 21, 1.

McFarland, C. E. & Kellas, G. (1974) JEP, 103, 343.

McGaugh, J. L. & Gold, P. E. (1974) In G. H. Bower (Ed.) The psychology of learning and motivation V. 8. New York: Academic Press.

McGaugh, J. L. & Herz, M. J. (1972)(Eds.) Memory consolidation San Francisco: Albion.

McGaugh, J. L., et al. (1984) In G. Lynch, et al. (Eds.) Neurobiology of learning and memory. New York: Guilford.

McGeoch, J. A. (1942) The psychology of human learning. New York: Longmans Green.

McGinnis, M., et al. (1978) PHB, 20, 435.

McGlone, J. (1977) BR, 100, 775.

McGowan, B. K., et al. (1972) BBIO, 7, 841.

McGraw, K. O. (1978) In M. R. Lepper & D. Greene (Eds.) The hidden costs of reward. Hillsdale, NJ: Lawrence Erlbaum Associates.

McGraw, K. O. & McCullers, J. C. (1974) JECP, 18, 149.

McGraw, K. O. & McCullers, J. C. (1979) JESP, 15, 285.

McIntyre, C., et al. (1970) PP, 7, 328.

McKeever, W. F. & Vandeventer, A. D. (1977) COR, 13, 225.

McLean, J. (1978) AJMD, 83, 80.

McNaughton, N. & Miller, J. J. (1979) Neurosci. Lett. Suppl., 3, 572.

Medin, D. L. (1977) In A. M. Schrier (Ed.) Behavioral primatology. Hillsdale, NJ: Lawrence Erlbaum Associates.

Medin, D. L., et al. (1984) LMC, 10, 333.

Meehl, P. E. (1950) PBUL, 47, 52.

Megela, A. L. & Teyler, T. J. (1979) JCPP, 93, 1154.

Meisel, C. J. (1981) AJMD, 86, 317.

Melikian, L. (1959) JSOC, 50, 81.

Melkman, R. & Deutsch, C. (1977) JECP, 23, 84.

Melton, A. W. (1970) JVLVB, 9, 596.

Melzack, R. & Scott, T. H. (1957) JCPP, 50, 155.

Mendelson, J., et al. (1972) JCPP, 80, 30.

Mendoza, M. E. & Adams, H. E. (1969) PHB, 4, 307.

Mervis, C. B. & Rosch, E. (1981) In Ann. Rev. Psychol. V. 2., Palo Alto: Ann. Reviews.

Merzenich, M. M. & Brugge, J. (1973) BRES, 50, 275.

Merzenich, M. M. & Kaas, J. H. (1980) In J. M. Sprague & A. N. Epstein (Eds.) Progress in psychobiology and physiological psychology. New York: Academic Press.
Merzenich, M. M., et al. (1976) JLN, 166, 387.
Meudell, P., et al. (1978) N, 16, 507.
Meyer, D. E. & Schvaneveldt, R. W. (1971) JEP, 90, 227.
Meyer, D. E., et al. (1974) MC, 2, 309.
Meyer, V. & Knobil, E. (1967) ENDO, 80, 163.
Micco, D. J., et al. (1979) JCPP, 93, 323.
Mikami, A., et al. (1982) BHVB, 5, 219.
Miles, R. C. (1956) JCPP, 49, 126.
Millenson, J. R. & deVilliers, P. A. (1972) In R. M. Gilbert & J. R. Millenson (Eds.) Reinforcement. New York: Academic Press.
Millenson, J. R., et al. (1977) LM, 8, 351.
Miller, D. B. (1980) JCPP, 94, 606.
Miller, G. A. (1956) PR, 63, 81.
Miller, J. W. & Groves, P. M. (1977) PHB, 18, 141.
Miller, N. E. (1951) In S. S. Stevens (Ed.) Handbook of experimental psychology. New York: Wiley.
Miller, R. R. & Marlin, N. A. (1984) In H. Weingartner & E. S. Parker (Eds.) Memory consolidation. Hillsdale, NJ: Lawrence Erlbaum Associates.
Milner, B. (1968) N, 6, 191.
Milner, B. (1969) N, 6, 175.
Milner, B., et al. (1968) N, 6, 215.
Mischel, W. G. & Metzner, R. (1962) ABN, 64, 425.
Mischel, W. et al. (1969) JPSP, 11, 363.
Mishkin, M. & Delacour, J. (1975) ABP, 1, 326.
Mishkin, M. & Manning, F. J. (1978) BRES, 143, 313.
Mishkin, M. & Petri, H. L. (1984) In N. Butters & L. R. Squire (Eds.) Neuropsychology of memory. New York: Guilford Press.
Mishkin, M. & Pribram, K. H. (1956) JCPP, 49, 36.
Mishkin, M., et al. (1982) In S. Corkin, et al. (Eds.) Alzheimers Disease. New York: Raven Press.
Mogenson, G. J. & Phillips, A. G. (1976) In J. N. Sprague & A. N. Epstein (Eds.) Progress in psychobiology and physiological psychology V. 6. New York: Academic Press.
Moore, J. W. (1979) In A. Dickinson & R. H. Boakes (Eds.) Mechanisms of learning and motivation. Hillsdale, NJ: Lawrence Erlbaum Associates.
Morgan, M. J. (1974) ANB, 22, 449.
Morgan, M. J. & Firsoff, G. I. (1970) LM, 1, 248.
Morris, D. (1977) Manwatching. New York: Abrams.
Morris, M. D. & Capaldi, E. J. (1979) ALB, 7, 509.
Morris, R. G. M. (1983) In W. Seifert (Ed.) Neurobiology of the hippocampus. New York: Academic Press.
Moscovitch, M. & Craik, F. I. M. (1976) JVLVB, 15, 447.

Moscovitch, M., et al. (1976) HPP, 2, 401.
Mosley, J. L. & Bakal, D. A. (1976) AJMD, 81, 41.
Mowrer, O. H. (1960) Learning theory and behavior. New York:
  Wiley.
Munoz, C. & Grossman, S. P. (1980) PHB, 24, 179.
Murdock, B. B. (1962) JEP, 64, 482.
Murphy, J. T., et al. (1968) BRES, 8, 153.
Muter, P. (1978) MC, 6, 9.
Naatanen, R. (1979) In H. D. Kimmel et al. (Eds.) The orienting
  reflex in humans. Hillsdale, NJ: Lawrence Erlbaum Associates.
Naatanen, R., et al. (1982) BP, 14, 53.
Nachson, I. & Carmon, A. (1975) COR, 11, 123.
Nadel, L. (1968) PHB, 3, 891.
Nadel, L. & O'Keefe, J. (1974) In R. Bellairs & E. G. Gray (Eds.)
  Essays on the nervous system. Oxford: Clarendon Press.
Nagy, Z. M. (1976) Dev. Psychobiol., 9, 389.
Nairne, J. S. (1983) LMC, 9, 3.
Nairne, J. S. & Rescorla, R. A. (1981) LM, 12, 65.
Narabayashi, H. (1972) In B. Eleftheriou (Ed.) The neurobiology
  of the amygdala. New York: Plenum.
Nauta, W. J. H. (1972) ANE, 32, 125.
Neely, J. H. & Wagner, A. R. (1974) JEP, 102, 751.
Neely, J. H. et al. (1983) LMC, 9, 196.
Neisser, U. (1967) Cognitive psychology. New York: Appleton-
  Century-Crofts.
Neisser, U. & Lazar, R. (1964) PMS, 17, 955.
Nelson, D. L. (1979) In L. S. Cermak & F. I. M. Craik (Eds.)
  Levels of processing in human memory. Hillsdale, NJ: Lawrence
  Erlbaum Associates.
Nelson, D. L. & Brooks, D. H. (1973) JEP, 98, 44.
Nelson, D. L., et al. (1971) JEP, 87, 361.
Nelson, D. L., et al. (1973) JEP, 101, 242.
Nelson, D. L., et al. (1975) HLM, 1, 711.
Nelson, D. L., et al. (1976) HLM, 2, 95.
Nelson, M. N. & Ross, L. E. (1974) JEP, 102, 1.
Nelson, T. O. & Vining, S. K. (1978) HLM, 4, 198.
Nevin, J. (1973) The study of behavior. Glenview, IL: Scott
  Foresman.
Nevin, J. A. (1974) JEAB, 21, 389.
Nevin, J. (1979) In M. D. Zeiler & P. Harzem (Eds.) Reinforcement
  and the organization of behavior. New York: Wiley.
Nickerson, R. S. (1972) PM, 4, 275.
Nickerson, R. S. (1978) In J. Requin (Ed.) Attention and perform-
  ance VII. Hillsdale, NJ: Lawrence Erlbaum Associates.
Nickerson, R. S. & Pew, R. W. (1973) JEP, 98, 36.
Niki, H. & Watanabe, M. (1979) BRES, 105, 79.
Nonneman, A. J. & Kolb, B. E. (1974) BBIO, 12, 41.

Norman, D. A. (1968) PR, 75, 522.
Norman, D. A. & Bobrow, D. G. (1975) COG, 7, 44.
Norton, P. R. E. (1970) BRES, 24, 134.
Numan, R. (1978) PHY, 6, 445.
Nunnally, J. C. (1978) Psychometric theory. New York: McGraw-Hill.
O'Connor, N. (Ed.) (1966) Present day Russian psychology. London: Pergamon Press.
O'Gorman, J. G. & Jamieson, R. D. (1975) PHYS, 3, 385.
O'Gorman, J. G., et al. (1970) P, 6, 716.
Ohman, A. (1971) P, 8, 7.
Ohman, A. (1974) BIP, 1, 189.
Ohman, A. (1979) In H. D. Kimmel, et al. (Eds.) The orienting reflex in humans. Hillsdale, NJ: Lawrence Erlbraum Associates.
Okada, Y. C., et al. (1983) ECN, 55, 417.
O'Keefe, J. & Bouma, H. (1969) EXN, 23, 384.
O'Keefe, J. & Dostrovsky, J. (1971) BRES, 34, 171.
O'Keefe, J. & Nadel, L. (1978) The hippocampus as a cognitive map. Oxford: Oxford U.
Olds, J. (1956) JCPP, 49, 281.
Oliver, D. L. & Hall, W. C. (1978) JCN, 182, 459.
Olton, D. S. & Pappas, B. C. (1979) N, 17, 669.
Olton, D. S., et al. (1979) BBS, 2, 313.
Oscar-Berman, M. (1973) N, 11, 191.
Owen, F. W., et al. (1971) Mono. Soc. Rsch. Child. Dev., 36, 4.
Owens, G. & Williams, M. (1980) N, 18, 85.
Pagano, R. R. & Goult, F. P. (1964) ECN, 17, 255.
Paivio, A. (1963) CJP, 17, 370.
Paivio, A. (1971) Imagery and verbal processes. New York: Holt, Rinehart, & Winston.
Paivio, A. (1978) HPP, 4, 61.
Paivio, A. & Csapo, K. (1973) COG, 5, 176.
Papez, J. W. (1937) AMA Arch. Neurol. Psychiat., 38, 725.
Paramonova, N. P. (1965) In L. G. Voronin et al. (Eds.) Orienting reflex and exploratory behavior. Washington, DC: Am. Inst. of Biol. Sci.
Paris, S. G. & Lindauer, B. K. (1976) COG, 8, 217.
Parmeggiani, P. L. & Rapisardi, C. (1969) BRES, 14, 387.
Parsons, P. J. & Spear, N. E. (1972) JCPP, 80, 297.
Pasley, J. N., et al. (1978) NENDO, 25, 77.
Passingham, R. (1978) BRES, 152, 313.
Pate, J. L. & Bell, G. L. (1971) PS, 23, 431.
Pavlov, I. P. (1927) Conditioned reflexes. London: Oxford.
Pavlov, I. P. (1941) Conditioned reflexes and psychiatry. Gantt (trans.) New York: International Pub.
Pearce, J. M. & Kaye, H. (1984) ABP, 10, 90.
Pease, D. M. & Goodglass, H. (1978) COR, 14, 178.
Peeke, H. & Veno, A. (1973) BBIO, 8, 427.

Pendery, M. & Maltzman, I.  (1977) JEPG, 106, 120.
Penfield, W. & Perot, P.  (1963) BR, 86, 595.
Penney, J. & Schull, J.  (1977) ALB, 5, 272.
Peretz, I. & Marais, J.  (1980) N, 18, 477.
Perfetto, G. A., et al.  (1983) MC, 11, 24.
Perlmutter, M. & Mitchell, D. B.  (1982) In F. I. M. Craik & S. Trehub (Eds.) Aging and cognitive processes. New York:  Plenum.
Perlmutter, M. & Ricks, M.  (1979) JECP, 15, 73.
Peterson, G. B., et al.  (1972) S, 177, 1009.
Peterson, L. R.  (1963) In C. N. Cofer & B. S. Musgrave (Eds.) Verbal behavior and learning. New York:  McGraw-Hill.
Petrich, J. A.  (1975) MC, 3, 63.
Pettigrew, J. D. & Freeman, R. D.  (1973) S, 182, 599.
Pettit, T. C.  (1982) In F. I. M. Craik & S. Trehub (Eds.) Aging and cognitive processes. New York:  Plenum.
Pfaff, D., et al.  (1973) In E. Stellar & J. M. Sprague (Eds.) Progress in physiological psychology V. 5.  New York:  Academic Press.
Pfautz, P. L. & Wagner, A. R.  (1976) ALB, 4, 107.
Picton, T. W., et al.  (1978) In J. Requin (Ed.) Attention and performance VII.  Hillsdale, NJ:  Lawrence Erlbaum Associates.
Plunkett, R. D. & Foulds, B. D.  (1979) PHY, 7, 49.
Polich, J. M.  (1980) COR, 16, 39.
Popik, R. S., et al.  (1979) ALB, 7, 355.
Poplawsky, A. & Hoffman, S. L.  (1979) PHB, 22, 679.
Poplawsky, A. & Isaacson, R. L.  (1983) BNB, 38, 61.
Popp, R. & Voss, J. F.  (1965) JED, 70, 304.
Porjesz, B. & Begleiter, H.  (1975) P, 12, 152.
Porrino, L. J., et al.  (1981) JCN, 198, 121.
Posner, M. I.  (1969) In G. Bower & J. T. Spence (Eds.) Psychology of learning and motivation V. 3.  New York:  Academic Press.
Posner, M. I.  (1979) Chronometric explorations of mind.  Hillsdale, NJ:  Lawrence Erlbaum Associates.
Posner, M. I. & Keele, S. W.  (1967) S, 158, 137.
Posner, M. I. & Keele, S. W.  (1968) JEP, 77, 353.
Postman, L.  (1971) PR, 78, 290.
Postman, L.  (1976) In J. W. Brown (Ed.) Recall and recognition. New York:  Wiley.
Postman, L. & Burns, S.  (1973) MC, 1, 503.
Postman, L. & Parker, J. F.  (1970) AJP, 83, 171.
Postman, L. & Stark, K.  (1969) JEP, 79, 168.
Postman, L. & Underwood, B. J.  (1973) MC, 1, 19.
Postman, L., et al.  (1974) AJP, 87, 33.
Postman, L., et al.  (1978) JVLVB, 17, 681.
Poulos, C. X. & Hinson, R. E.  (1984) ABP, 10, 75.
Powell, D. A. & Buchanan, S.  (1980) PHYS, 8, 455.

Premack, D. (1971) In R. Glaser (Ed.) On the nature of reinforcement. New York: Academic Press.
Pressley, M., et al. (1980) HLM, 6, 163.
Pribram, K. H. (1960) In J. Field, et al. (Eds.) Handbook of physiology Sect 1, V. 2. Washington, DC: Am. Physiol. Soc.
Pribram, K. H. & McGuinness, D. (1975) PR, 82, 116.
Pritchard, R. M., et al. (1960) CJP, 14, 67.
Prokasy, W. F. (1965) Classical conditioning. New York: Appleton-Century-Crofts.
Prokasy, W. F. & Ebel, H. C. (1967) JEP, 73, 247.
Prokasy, W. F. & Gormezano, I. (1979) ALB, 7, 80.
Proudfoot, R. E. (1982) BC, 2, 25.
Puff, C. R. (Ed.) (1979) Memory organization and structure. New York: Academic Press.
Pylyshyn, Z. W. (1973) PBUL, 80, 1.
Pylyshyn, Z. W. (1979) PR, 86, 383.
Raaijmakers, J. G. W. & Shiffrin, R. M. (1981) PR, 88, 93.
Rabinowitz, J.C., et al. (1979) JVLVB, 18, 57.
Rachlin, H. (1976) Behavior and learning. San Francisco: Freeman.
Raisman, G. (1966) BR, 86, 317.
Ranck, J. B. (1973) EXN, 41, 461.
Ranck, J. B. (1975) In R. L. Isaacson & K. H. Pribram (Eds.) The hippocampus V. 2. New York: Plenum.
Randlich, A. & Lolordo, V. M. (1979) PBUL, 86, 523.
Randolph, M. & Semmes, T. (1974) BRES, 70, 55.
Rankin, J. L. & Kausler, D. H. (1979) JGER, 34, 58.
Rao, K. V. & Proctor, R. W. (1984) LMC, 10, 386.
Raphaelson, A. C., et al. (1965) PS, 3, 483.
Rashotte, M. E., et al. (1977) ALB, 5, 25.
Rawlins, J. N. P., et al. (1979) EBR, 37, 49.
Ray, W. J., et al. (1976) N, 14, 391.
Razran, G. (1965) In W. F. Prokasy (Ed.) Classical conditioning. New York: Appleton-Century-Crofts.
Razran, G. (1971) Mind in evolution. Boston: Houghton-Mifflin.
Redgate, E. S. (1970) ENDO, 86, 806.
Reed, S. K. (1972) COG, 3, 282.
Reed, S. K. & Johnson, J. A. (1975) MC, 3, 569.
Reinis, S. & Goldman, J. M. (1982) The chemistry of behavior. New York: Plenum.
Reis, D. J. (1974) In R. D. Myers & R. R. Drucker-Colin (Eds.) Neurohumoral coding of brain function. New York: Plenum.
Reiss, S. & Wagner, A. R. (1972) LM, 3, 237.
Rescorla, R. A. (1967) PR, 74, 71.
Rescorla, R. A. (1971) JCPP, 75, 77.
Rescorla, R. A. (1972) In G. H Bower (Ed.) The psychology of learning and motivation V. 6. New York: Academic Press.
Rescorla, R. A. (1973a) JCPP, 82, 137.

Rescorla, R. A. (1973b) In F. J. McGuigan & D. B. Lumsden (Eds.) Contemporary approaches to conditioning and learning. Washington, DC: Winston.

Rescorla, R. A. (1975) In W. K. Estes (Ed.) Handbook of learning and cognitive processes V. 2. Hillsdale, NJ: Lawrence Erlbaum Associates.

Rescorla, R. A. (1979) ABP, 5, 79.

Rescorla, R. A. (1980) Pavlovian second order conditioning. Hillsdale, NJ: Lawrence Erlbaum Associates.

Rescorla, R. A. (1982) ABP, 8, 23.

Rescorla, R. A. & Cunningham, C. L. (1979) ABP, 5, 152.

Rescorla R. A. & Heth, C. D. (1975) ABP, 1, 88.

Rescorla, R. A. & Solomon, R. S. (1967) PR, 74, 151.

Rescorla, R. A. & Wagner, A. R. (1972) In A. Black & W. F. Prokasy (Eds.) Classical conditioning II. New York: Appleton-Century-Crofts.

Revusky, S. H. & Garcia, J. (1970) In G. H. Bower (Ed.) The psychology of learning and motivation V. 4. New York: Academic Press.

Reynolds, B. S., et al. (1974) J. App. Child. Psychol., 2, 253.

Reynolds, G. S. (1968) A primer of operant conditioning. Glenview, IL: Scott Foresman.

Reynolds, J. H. (1977) HLM, 3, 68.

Riccio, D. C. & Stiles, E. R. (1969) PHB, 4, 649.

Richards, R. W. & Rilling, M. (1972) JEAB, 17, 405.

Richardson, J. T. E. (1978) J. Ment. Imag., 2, 101.

Richardson, J. T. E. (1980) Mental imagery and human memory. New York: St. Martins.

Richardson, W. K. & Clark, D. B. (1976) JEAB, 26, 237.

Richman, C. L., et al. (1978) AJMD, 83, 262.

Rider, D. P. (1980) JEAB, 33, 243.

Riesen, A. H. (1961) In D. W. Fiske & S. R. Madd (Eds.) Functions of varied experience. Homewood, Ill.: Dorsey.

Riley, D. A. & Roitblat, H. L. (1978) In S. H. Hulse, et al. (Eds.) Cognitive processes in animal behavior. Hillsdale, NJ: Lawerence Erlbaum Associates.

Rilling, M., et al. (1969) JEAB, 12, 917.

Rilling, M., et al. (1973) LM, 4, 1.

Rips, L. J., et al. (1973) JVLVB, 12, 1.

Ritter, W., et al. (1974) JEP, 102, 726.

Rizley, R. C. & Rescorla, R. A. (1972) JCPP, 81, 1.

Roaden, S. K., et al. (1980) AJMD, 84, 518.

Roberts, W. A. & Grant, D. S. (1974) LM, 5, 393.

Roberts, W. A. & Smythe, W. E. (1979) LM, 10, 313.

Roberts, W. W. & Bergquist, E. H. (1968) JCPP, 66, 596.

Roberts, W. W. & Kiess, H. O. (1964) JCPP, 58, 187.
Robinson, T. E. & Vanderwolf, C. H. (1978) EXN, 61, 485.
Roediger, H. L. (1973) JVLVB, 12, 644.
Roediger, H. L. (1974) MC, 2, 261.
Roediger, H. L. (1978) MC, 6, 54.
Rolls, E. T. (1972) BRES, 45, 365.
Rolls, E. T., et al. (1976) BRES, 111, 53.
Rolls, E. T. & Rolls, B. J. (1973) JCPP, 83, 248.
Roper, T. J. (1978) JEAB, 30, 83.
Rosch, E. (1973) In T. E. Moore (Ed.) Cognitive development and the acquisition of language. New York: Academic Press.
Rose, D. (1980) In D. Caplan (Ed.) Biological studies of mental processes. Cambridge, MA: MIT.
Rose, J. E., et al. (1963) JN, 26, 294.
Rosenkilde, C. E. (1979) BNB, 25, 301.
Rosenkilde, C. E. (1983) APS, Suppl. 514.
Rosenkilde, C. E., et al. (1981) BRSC, 209, 375.
Ross, B. H. & Landauer, T. K. (1978) JVLVB, 17, 669.
Ross, L. E., et al. (1964) PS, 1, 253.
Ross, L. E., et al. (1974) JEP, 103, 603.
Ross, M. (1975) JPSP, 32, 245.
Ross, M. (1976) In J. H. Harvey, et al. (Eds.) New directions in attribution research. Hillsdale, NJ: Lawrence Erlbaum Associates.
Ross, M. et al. (1976) JPSP, 33, 442.
Ross, R. T. & Randich, A. (1984) ABP, 10, 127.
Ross, R. T., et al. (1984) BN, 98, 211.
Rossellini, R. A. & Burdette, D. R. (1980) ALB, 8, 647.
Rourke, B. P. (1976) In R. M. Knights & D. J. Bakker (Eds.) The neuropsychology of learning disorders. Baltimore: University Park Press.
Routtenberg, A. & Kay, K. E. (1965) JCPP, 59, 285.
Rozin, P. (1976) In J. M. Sprague & A. N. Epstein (Eds.) Progress in psychobiology and physiological psychology. New York: Academic Press.
Rubin, R. T., et al. (1966) S, 153, 767.
Ruchkin, D. S., et al. (1975) P, 12, 591.
Rudel, R. G., et al. (1974) NEUR, 24, 733.
Rudel, R. G. et al. (1976) COR, 12, 61.
Rudy, J. W. & Cheatle, M. D. (1979) In N. E. Spear & B. A. Campbell (Eds.) Ontogeny of learning and memory. Hillsdale, NJ: Lawrence Erlbaum Associates.
Rundus, D. (1971) JEP, 89, 63.
Rundus, D. (1973) JVLVB, 12, 43.
Runquist, N. N. & Runquist, W. A. (1978) HLM, 4, 370.
Sabelli, H. C., et al. (1974) In R. D. Myers & R. R. Drucker-Colin (Eds.) Neurohumoral coding of brain function. New York: Plenum.

Sakai, M. (1978) BRES, 147, 377.
Sakitt, B. (1975) S, 190, 1318.
Salafia, W. R. & Allan, A. M. (1982) PHB, 29, 1125.
Salafia, W. R., et al. (1977) PHB, 18, 207.
Salmaso, D. & Denes, G. (1982) PMS, 54, 1147.
Salthouse, T. A. (1977) HLM, 3, 18.
Saltzman, I. J. (1949) JCPP, 42, 161.
Sanghera, M. K., et al. (1979) EXN, 63, 610.
Schandry, R. & Hoefling, S. (1979) In H. D. Kimmel, et al. (Eds.) The orienting reflex in humans. Hillsdale, NJ: Lawrence Erlbaum Associates.
Scheibel, M. E. & Scheibel, A. B. (1977) In K. Nandy & I. Sherman (Eds.) The aging brain and senile dementia. New York: Plenum.
Schmaltz, L. W. & Theios, J. (1972) JCPP, 79, 328.
Schneider, J. W. (1972) JEAB, 18, 45.
Schneider, W. & Fisk, A. D. (1982) PD, 31, 160.
Schneider, W. & Shiffrin, R. M. (1977) PR, 84, 1.
Schonfield, D. & Robertson, B. (1966) CJP, 20, 228.
Schonfield, D. & Stones, M. J. (1979) In J. F. Kihlstrom & F. J. Evans (Eds.) Functional disorders of memory. Hillsdale, NJ: Lawrence Erlbaum Associates.
Schreiner, L. & Kling, A. (1953) JN, 16, 643.
Schrier, A. M. & Povar, M. L. (1979) ALB, 7, 239.
Schull, J. (1979) In G. H. Bower (Ed.) The psychology of learning and motivation V. 13. New York: Academic Press.
Schwartz, B. (1980) JEAB, 33, 153.
Schwartz, B. (1982) PBUL, 111, 23.
Schwartz, B. & Gamzu, E. (1977) In W. K. Honig & J. E. R. Staddon (Eds.) Handbook of operant behavior. New York: Appleton-Century-Crofts.
Schwartz, M. (1976) P, 13, 546.
Schwartzbaum, J. S. (1961) AJP, 74, 252.
Schwartzbaum, J. S. & Donovick, D. J. (1968) JCPP, 65, 83.
Schwartzbaum, J. S. & Gay, M. (1966) JCPP, 71, 59.
Schwartzbaum, J. S. & Spieth, T. M. (1964), PS, 1, 145.
Scott, C. A. & Yalch, R. F. (1978) JESP, 14, 180.
Scott, J. P., et al. (1974) Dev. Psychobiol., 7, 489.
Scott, M. S. & House, B. J. (1978) JECP, 25, 58.
Scoville, W. B., et al. (1953) Proc. Assoc. Rsch. Nerv. Ment. Dis. 31, 347.
Searleman, A. (1977) PBUL, 84, 503.
Segal, M. (1973) BRES, 64, 281.
Segal, M. (1979) BRES, 162, 137.
Segal, S. J. & Fusella, V. J. (1970) JEP, 83, 458.
Segal, M. & Olds, J. (1972) JN, 35, 680.
Seligman, M. E. P. & Hager, J. L. (1972) Biological boundaries of learning. New York: Appleton-Century-Crofts.

Semba, K. & Iwahoras, E. (1974) BRES, 66, 309.
Semba, K. & Komisaruk, B. R. (1978) ECN, 44, 61.
Seymour, P. H. K. (1979) Human visual cognition. New York: St. Martins.
Shallice, T. & Evans, M. E. (1978) COR, 14, 294.
Shallice, T. & Warrington, E. K. (1977) N, 15, 31.
Shepard, R. N. & Chipman, S. (1970) COG, 1, 1.
Shepard, R. N. & Podgory, P. (1978) In W. K. Estes (Eds.) Handbook of learning and cognitive processes V. 5. Hillsdale, NJ: Lawrence Erlbaum Associates.
Sherman, J. E. (1979) LM, 10, 383.
Shettleworth, S. J. (1972) Adv. Study Beh., 4, 1.
Shettleworth, S. J. (1975) ABP, 1, 56.
Shettleworth, S. J. (1978) ABP, 4, 152.
Shiffrin, R. (1973) S, 180, 980.
Shipley, J. E. & Kolb, B. (1977) JCPP, 91, 1056.
Shoben, E. J., et al. (1978) HLM, 4, 304.
Shull, R. L. (1979) In M. D. Zeiler & P. Harzem (Eds.) Reinforcement and the organization of behavior. New York: Wiley.
Shurtleff, D., et al. (1983) ALB, 11, 247.
Siddle, D. A. T. (1971) AJP, 23, 261.
Siddle, D. A. T., et al. (1979) P, 16, 34.
Siddle, D. A. T., et al. (1983) P, 20, 136.
Siddle, D., et al. (1983) In D. Siddle (Ed.) Orienting and habituation. New York: Wiley.
Siegel, S. (1977) ABP, 3, 1.
Silverman, A. J., et al. (1966) J. Psychosom. Rsch., 10, 151.
Simpson, A. A., et al. (1973) JEND, 58, 576.
Simson, R., et al. (1976) ECN, 40, 33.
Sinclair, B. R., et al. (1982) JN, 48, 1214.
Sinnamon, H. M., et al. (1978) JCPP, 92, 142.
Skinner, B. F. (1938) The behavior of organisms. New York: Appleton-Century-Crofts.
Skinner, B. F. (1950) PR, 51, 193.
Slamecka, N. J. (1968) JEP, 76, 504.
Slamecka, N. J. (1969) JEP, 81, 557.
Slamecka, N. J. (1975) JVLVB, 14, 630.
Slotnick, B. M. (1973) PHB, 11, 717.
Smith, A. & Sugar, O. (1975) NEUR, 25, 813.
Smith, A. D. (1975) Int. J. Aging Hum. Dev., 6, 359.
Smith, E. E., et al. (1971) JVLVB, 10, 597.
Smith, E. E. et al. (1974) PR, 81, 214.
Smith, G. P. (1973) In E. Stellar & J. M. Sprague (Eds.) Progress in physiological psychology. New York: Academic Press.
Smotherman, W. P., et al. (1976) BBIO, 16, 401.
Smotherman, W. P., et al. (1977) Hormones, 8, 242.
Sodetz, F. J. (1970) PHB, 5, 773.

Sokolov, E. N. (1963) Perception and the conditioned reflex. Oxford: Pergamon Press.

Sokolov, E. N. (1969) In M. Cole & I. Maltzman (Eds.) A handbook of contemporary Soviet psychology. New York: Basic Books.

Sokolov, E. N. (1975) In E. N. Sokolov & O. S. Vinogradova (Eds.) Neuronal mechanisms of the orienting reflex. Hillsdale, NJ: Lawrence Erlbaum Associates

Solheim, G. S., et al. (1980) BNB, 30, 250.

Solomon, P. R. (1977) JCPP, 91, 405.

Solomon, P. R. & Gottfried, K. E. (1981) JCPP, 95, 323.

Solomon, P. R. & Moore, J. (1975) JCPP, 89, 1192.

Solomon, R. L. (1980) AP, 35, 691.

Solomon, R. L. & Corbit, J. D. (1974) PR, 81, 119.

Spear, N. E. (1978) Retention and forgetting. Hillsdale, NJ: Lawrence Erlbaum Associates.

Spear, N. (1979) In Kihlstrom, J. F. & Evans, F. J. Functional disorders of memory. Hillsdale, NJ: Lawrence Erlbaum Associates.

Spearman, C. (1923) The abilities of man. London: Macmillan.

Spearman, C. (1946) BJP, 36, 117.

Spellacy, F. & Blumstein, S. (1970) COR, 6, 430.

Spence, J. T. (1963) JVLVB, 2, 329.

Sperber, R. D., et al. (1976) AJMD, 81, 227.

Sperling, G. A. (1963) HF, 5, 19.

Spevack, A. A. & Pribram, K. H. (1973) JCPP, 82, 211.

Spevack, A. A., et al. (1975) PHB, 15, 199.

Spigel, I. M. (1964) JCPP, 57, 108.

Spinelli, D. N. & Pribram, K. H. (1966) ECN, 20, 44.

Spitz, H. H. & Nadler, B. T. (1974) DEV, 10, 404.

Spitz, H. H. & Semchuk, M. T. (1979) AJMD, 83, 556.

Spitz, R. & Cobliner, W. (1965) The first year of life. New York: Intl. U. Press.

Spooner, A. & Kellogg, W. N. (1947) JEP, 60, 321.

Sprague, J. M., et al. (1977) JCN, 172, 441.

Springer, A. D. (1975) JCPP, 88, 890.

Squire, L. R. (1974) BBIO, 12, 119.

Squire, L. R. & Cohen, N. J. (1984) In J. L. McGaugh, et al. (Eds.) The neurobiology of learning and memory. New York: Guilford Press.

Squire, L. R. & Slater, P. C. (1978) N, 16, 313.

Staddon, J. E. R. (1972) JEAB, 18, 223.

Staddon, J. E. R. (1975) In J. E. R. Staddon & W. K. Honig (Eds.) Handbook of operant behavior. New York: Appleton-Century-Crofts.

Staddon, J. E. R. & Ayres, S. L. (1975) B, 54, 26.

Staddon, J. E. R. & Innis, N. K. (1969) JEAB, 12, 689.

Staddon, J. E. R. & Simmelhag, V. L. (1971) PR, 78, 3.

Starr, B. J. & Katkin, E. S. (1969) J. Ab. Psychol., 74, 670.

Starr, M. D. (1978) ABP, 4, 338.

Starr, M. D. & Mineka, S.  (1977) LM, 8, 332.

Stein, B. S. et al.  (1978) JVLVB, 17, 165.

Steiner, J. E.  (1979) In H. W. Reese & L. P. Lipsitt (Eds.) Advances in child development and behavior V. 13.  New York: Academic Press.

Sternberg, R. J.  (1977) Intelligence, information processing and analogical reasoning.  Hillsdale, NJ: Lawrence Erlbaum Associates.

Sternberg, S.  (1966) S, 153, 652.

Sternberg, S.  (1969) ACP, 30, 276.

Sterritt, G. M. & Rudnick, M.  (1966) PMS, 22, 859.

Stevens, J. R., et al.  (1969) ARCH, 21, 157.

Stoloff, M. L., et al.  (1980) JCPP, 94, 847.

Storandt, M.  (1977) JGER, 32, 175.

Stubbs, A.  (1968) JEAB, 11, 223.

Stubbs, D. A.  (1976) JEAB, 26, 15.

Stubbs, D. A. & Cohen, S. L.  (1972) JEAB, 18, 403.

Stumpf, L.  (1965) Int. Rev. Neurobiol., 8, 77.

Stumpf, W. E. & Sar, M.  (1971) Proc. Soc. Exp. Biol. Med., 136, 102.

Suess, W. M. & Berlyne, D. E.  (1978) BBIO, 23, 487,

Sumby, W. H.  (1963) JVLVB, 1, 443.

Swann, W. B. & Pittman, J. S.  (1977) CD, 48, 1128.

Swanson, L. W. & Cowan, W. M.  (1977) JCN, 179, 1153.

Swanson, L. W. & Cowan, W. M.  (1979) JCN, 186, 621.

Swisher, L. & Hirsh, I. J.  (1972) N, 10, 137.

Switzky, A. N., et al.  (1979) AJMD, 83, 637.

Szlep, R.  (1964) B, 23, 203.

Talland, G. A.  (1965) Deranged memory.  New York:  Academic Press.

Tarr, R. S.  (1977) PHB, 19, 1153.

Taylor, D. A.  (1976) HPP, 2, 417.

Teichner, W. H. & Krebs, M. J.  (1974) PR, 81, 15.

Teitelbaum, P.  (1977) In W. K. Honig & J. E. R. Staddon (Eds.) Handbook of operant behavior.  New York:  Appleton-Century-Crofts.

Teresawa, E. & Timiras, P. S.  (1968) ENDO, 83, 207.

Terrace, H. S.  (1971) LM, 2, 148.

Terren, S. S. & Miller, N. E.  (1964) JCPP, 58, 55.

Terry, W. S. & McSwain, B. J.  (1984) JEAB, 12, 62.

Thatcher, R. W. & John, E. R.  (1977) Foundations of cognitive processes.  Hillsdale, NJ:  Lawrence Erlbaum Associates.

Thatcher, R. W. & Purpura, D. P.  (1973) BRES, 60, 21.

Thios, S. J.  (1972) JVLVB, 11, 789.

Thios, S. J. & D'Agostino, P. R.  (1976) JVLVB, 15, 529.

Thomas, E. & Evans, G. J.  (1983) PHB, 31, 673.

Thomas, E. & Wagner, A. R.  (1964) JCPP, 58, 157.

Thomas, E. A. C.  (1974) PR, 81, 442.

Thomas, J. R.  (1967) PREP, 20, 471.

Thomas, R. K.  (1980) BBE, 17, 454.

Thompson, C. I., et al.  (1977) JCPP, 91, 533.

Thompson, L. W., et al. (1978) In K. Nandy (Ed.) Senile dementia. Amsterdam: Elsevier.

Thompson, R. F. (1967) Foundations of physiological psychology. New York: Harper & Row.

Thompson, R. F., et al. (1979) In H. D. Kimmel, et al. (Eds.) The orienting reflex in humans. Hillsdale, NJ: Lawrence Erlbaum Associates.

Thomson, D. M. & Tulving, E. (1970) JEP, 86, 255.

Thorndyke, P. (1977) COG, 9, 77.

Tiffany, S. T., et al. (1983) BN, 97, 335.

Timberlake, W., et al. (1982) ABP, 2, 62.

Tinklepaugh, D. L. (1928) COMP, 8, 197.

Tomlinson-Keasey, C. & Kelley, R. R. (1979) COR, 15, 97.

Transberg, D. K. & Rilling, M. (1980) ABP, 33, 39.

Trapold, M. A. (1962) JCPP, 55, 1034.

Trapold, M. A. & Overmier, J. B. (1972) In A. H. Black & W. F. Prokasy (Eds.) Classical conditioning II. New York: Appleton.

Tulving, E. (1968) PS, 10, 53.

Tulving, E. (1972) In E. Tulving & W. Donaldson (Eds.) Organization of memory. New York: Academic Press.

Tulving, E. (1974) JEP, 102, 778.

Tulving, E., (1976) In J. Brown (Ed.) Recall and recognition. New York: Wiley.

Tulving, E. (1979) In L. S. Cermak & F. I. M. Craik (Eds.) Levels of processing in human memory. Hillsdale, NJ: Lawrence Erlbaum Associates.

Tulving, E. & Patkau, J. E. (1962) CJP, 16, 83.

Tulving, E. & Patterson, R. D. (1968) JEP, 77, 239.

Tulving, E. & Pearlstone, Z. (1966) JVLVB, 5, 381.

Turvey, M. T. (1973) PR, 80, 1.

Tversky, A. (1977) PR, 84, 327.

Tversky, B. G. (1969) PP, 6, 225.

Tzeng, O. J. C. (1976) AJP, 89, 577.

Uhlir, I., et al. (1974) NENDO, 14, 351.

Umilta, C., et al. (1979) COR, 15, 597.

Underwood, B. J. (1945) PM, 59, #273.

Underwood, B. J. (1964) JVLVB, 3, 112.

Underwood, B. J. (1972) In A. W. Melton & E. Martin (Eds.) Coding processes in human memory. Washington, DC: Winston.

Underwood, B. J. (1983) Attributes of memory. Glenview, IL: Scott Foresman.

Underwood, B. J. & Ekstrand, B. R. (1966) PR, 73, 540.

Underwood, B. J. & Ekstrand, B. R. (1967) JED, 74, 574.

Underwood, B. J. & Lund, A. M. (1981) AMJP, 94, 195.

Underwood, B. J. & Malmi, R. (1978) JVLVB, 17, 279.

Underwood, B. J. & Postman, L. (1960) PR, 67, 73.

Underwood, B. J. & Schulz, R. W. (1960) Meaningfulness and verbal learning. Philadelphia: Lippincott.
Underwood, B. J., et al. (1975) HLM, 1, 160.
Underwood, B. J., et al. (1976) MC, 4, 391.
Unger, J. M. (1964) JEP, 67, 11.
Urith, J. L., et al. (1978) PHB, 20, 43.
Ursin, H. & Divac, I. (1975) JCPP, 88, 36.
Ursin, H. & Kaada, B. R. (1960) EXN, 2, 109.
Ursin, H., et al. (1967) ECN, 23, 41.
Ursin, H., et al. (1969) PHB, 4, 609.
Usher, D. R., et al. (1974) NENDO, 16, 156.
Valenstein, E. (1973) Brain control. New York: Wiley.
Vandermeer, N. & Amsel, A. (1952) JEP, 43, 261.
Vanderwolf, C. H. (1971) PR, 78, 83.
Vanderwolf, C. H. & Leung, L. W. S. (1983) In W. Seifert (Ed.) Neurobiology of the hippocampus. New York: Academic Press.
Vanderwolf, C. H. & Vanderwart, M. L. (1970) CJP, 24, 434.
Vanderwolf, C. H., et al. (1975) In R. L. Isaacson & K. H. Pribram (Eds.) The hippocampus V. 2. New York: Plenum.
Van Hartesveldt, C. (1975) In R. L. Isaacson & K. H. Pribram (Eds.) The hippocampus V. 1. New York: Plenum.
Van Olst, E. H. (1971) The orienting reflex. The Hague: Mouton.
Vaughan, W. & Greene, S. L. (1984) ABP, 10, 256.
Velden, M. (1978) P, 15, 181.
Vellutino, F. R., et al. (1975) N, 13, 75.
Vernon, P. E. (1979) Intelligence San Francisco: Freeman.
Veroff, A. (1978) BL, 5, 139.
Vinogradova, O. S. (1975) In E. N. Sokolov & D. S. Vinogradova (Eds.) Neuronal mechanisms of the orienting reflex. Hillsdale, NJ: Lawrence Erlbaum Associates.
Vinogradova, O. S. & Brazhnik, P. L. (1978) In K. Elliott & J. Whelan (Eds.) Functions of the septo-hippocampal system. Amsterdam: Elsevier.
Von Saal, F. S., et al. (1975) PHB, 14, 697.
Von Wright, J. M. (1972) SJP, 13, 159.
Voronin, L. & Sokolov, E. (1960) ECN, 12, 335.
Vurpillot, E. (1968) JECP, 6, 622.
Waber, D. P. (1976) S, 192, 572.
Wagner, A. R. (1961) JEP, 62, 234.
Wagner, A. R. (1976) In T. J. Tighe & R. N. Leaton (Eds.) Habituation. Hillsdale, NJ: Lawrence Erlbaum Associates.
Wagner, A. R. (1978) In S. H. Hulse, et al. (Eds.) Cognitive processes in animal behavior. Hillsdale, NJ: Lawrence Erlbaum Associates.
Walker, H. J., et al. (1975) AJMD, 79, 545.
Wallace, J. E., et al. (1980) JGER, 35, 355.
Walley, R. E. & Weiden, T. D. (1973) PR, 80, 284.

437

Wantanabe, M. (1981) BRES, 225, 51.

Wapner, W. & Gardner, H. (1979) BL, 7, 363.

Warburton, D. M. (1975) Brain, behavior and drugs. New York: Wiley.

Warr, P. B. (1964) BJP, 55, 19.

Warrington, E. K. & Weiskrantz, L. (1968) N, 6, 283.

Warrington, E. K. & Weiskrantz, L. (1978) N, 16, 169.

Warrington, E. K. & Weiskrantz, L. (1982) N, 20, 233.

Wasserman, E. A., et al. (1975) ABP, 1, 158.

Waters, W. F., et al. (1977) P, 14, 228.

Watkins, O. C. & Watkins, M. J. (1975) HLM, 104, 442.

Watkins, M. J. (1975) JVLVB, 14, 294.

Watkins, M. J. (1979) In C. R. Puff (Ed.) Memory organization and structure. New York: Academic Press.

Watkins, M. J., et al. (1976) JVLVB, 15, 505.

Waugh, N. C. & Norman, D. A. (1965) PR, 72, 89.

Weiner, B. (1972) Theories of motivation: Chicago: Rand-McNally.

Weiner, H. (1969) PREC, 20, 445.

Weiner, R. I. & Ganong, W. F. (1978) Physiol. Rev., 58, 1905.

Weiskrantz, L. & Warrington, E. K. (1970) PS, 20, 210.

Weisler, A. & McCall, R. B. (1976) AP, 31, 492.

Weisman, R. G., et al. (1980) ABP, 6, 312.

Werka, T., et al. (1978) JCPP, 92, 672.

Wetzel, L. D. (1979) HLM, 1, 556.

Wetzel, W., et al. (1977a) BBIO, 19, 534.

Wetzel, W., et al. (1977b) BBIO, 21, 32.

Whishaw, I. W. & Vanderwolf, C. H. (1970) Proc. Can. Fed. Biol. Soc., 13, 48.

White, M. & White, K. (1975) N, 13, 377.

White, N. M. & Fisher, A. E. (1969) PHB, 4, 199.

White, S. H. (1966) In O. J. Harvey (Ed.) Experience, structure, and adaptability. New York: Springer.

White, S. H. (1970) Bull. Orton Society, 20, 41.

White, W. F., et al. (1979) BRES, 178, 41.

Whitlow, J. W. (1975) ABP, 1, 189.

Whitlow, J. W. (1984) LMC, 10, 733.

Whitten, W. B. & Leonard, J. M. (1980) HLM, 6, 127.

Wickelgren, W. A. (1967) QJEP, 19, 97.

Wickelgren, W. A. (1975) DEV, 11, 165.

Wickelgren, W. A., et al. (1980) JVLVB, 19, 387.

Wickelgren, W. A. & Isaacson, R. L. (1963) NAT, 200, 48.

Wickens, D. C. (1970) PR, 77, 1.

Wickens, D. D. (1972) In A. W. Melton & E. Martin (Eds.) Coding processes in human memory. Washington, DC: Winston.

Wickens, D. D., et al. (1970) JEP, 84, 462.

Wickens, D. D., et al. (1977) JEPG, 106, 47.

Wickens, D. D., et al. (1981) JEPG, 110, 1.

Wilcott, R. C. (1977) N, 15, 115.
Wilhelm, H. & Lovaas, O. I. (1976) AJMD, 81, 26.
Williams, A. & Weisstein, N. (1978) MC, 6, 85.
Williams, B. A. & Heyneman, N. (1982) ALB, 10, 72.
Williams, B. W. (1980) JPSP, 39, 599.
Williams, D. R. (1965) In W. F. Prokasy (Ed.) Classical condition-
ing. NY: Appleton-Century-Crofts.
Williams, D. R. & Williams, H. (1969) JEAB, 12, 511.
Willoughby, R. H. (1969) JECP, 7, 299.
Wilson, C. L., et al. (1981) ABP, 7, 165.
Wilson, M. & Critchlow, V. (1973) NENDO, 13, 29.
Winocur, G. (1979) PHB, 22, 339.
Winocur, G. & Bindra, D. (1976) PHB, 17, 915.
Winocur, G. & Black, A. H. (1978) PHB, 21, 39.
Winocur, G. & Breckinridge, C. B. (1973) JCPP, 82, 512.
Winocur, G. & Kinsbourne, M. (1978) N, 16, 671.
Winograd, E. (1968) JEP, 76, Part II.
Winograd, E. (1981) HLM, 7, 181.
Winson, J. (1972) BBIO, 7, 479.
Wise, R. A. & Albin, J. (1973) BBIO, 9, 289.
Wiseman, S. & Tulving, E. (1976) HLM, 2, 349.
Wishart, T. & Mogenson, G. (1970) PHB, 5, 31.
Witelson, S. F. (1976) In R. M. Knights & D. J. Bakker (Eds.) The
neuropsychology of learning disorders. Baltimore: University
Park Press.
Wong, P. T. (1977) ALB, 5, 5.
Wood, G. (1967) JED, 58, (6, Part 2)
Wood, G. (1971) JVLVB, 10, 52.
Woodward, A. E., et al. (1973) JVLVB, 12, 608.
Yaremko, R. M., et al. (1970) PS, 21, 115.
Yekovich, F. R., et al. (1979) JVLVB, 18, 535.
Yoshii, N., et al. (1957) ECN, 22, 143.
Yuille, J. C., et al. (1969) CJP, 23, 459.
Zaidel, E. (1976) COR, 12, 191.
Zaidel, E. & Sperry, R. W. (1973) COR, 9, 34.
Zaidel, E., et al. (1981) COR, 17, 167.
Zajano, M. J., et al. (1974) JEP, 103, 1147.
Zajonc, R. B. (1965) S, 149, 269.
Zajonc, R. B., et al. (1969) JPSP, 13, 83.
Zanna, M. P. & Cooper, J. (1974) JPSP, 29, 703.
Zeaman, D. (1949) JEP, 39, 466.
Zeaman, D. & House, B. J. (1963) In N. R. Ellis (Ed.) Handbook of
mental deficiency. New York: McGraw-Hill.
Zeiler, M. D. (1972) JEAB, 17, 177.
Zeiler, M. (1977) In W. K. Honig & J. E. R. Staddon (Eds.) Hand-
book of operant behavior. New York: Appleton-Century-Crofts.

Zeiler, M. D. (1979) In M. D. Zeiler & P. Harzem (Eds.) Reinforcement and the organization of behavior. New York: Wiley.

Zeiler, M. D. & Kelley, L. A. (1969) JECP, 8, 306.

Zentall, T. R. & Hogan, D. E. (1977) LM, 8, 367.

Zimbardo, P. G. et al. (1969) In P. G. Zimbardo (Ed.) The cognitive control of motivation. Glenview, IL: Scott Foresman.

Zimmer-Hart, C. C. & Rescorla, R. A. (1974) JCPP, 86, 837.

Zimmerman, D. W. (1959) JCPP, 52, 353.

Zimmerman, J. J. (1975) AJP, 88, 277.

Zola-Morgan, S. & Squire, L. R. (1982) Soc. Neurosc. Ab., 8, 24.

Zolovick, A. J. (1972) In B. Eleftheriou (Ed.) The neurobiology of the amygdala. New York: Plenum.

Zuccolotti, P. & Oltman, P. K. (1978) COR, 14, 155.

Zurif, E. B., et al. (1972) N, 10, 405.

Zurif, E. B., et al. (1976) COR, 12, 183.

Zuromski, E. S., et al. (1972) JCPP, 78, 83.

# Author Index

441

# Subject Index

## A

Abstraction, 275-78, 303-08, 367-70
Adjunctive behaviors, 177-81
Amnesia: amnestic agents, 281-83
  anterograde, 343, 347
  infantile, 335-36
  Korsakoffs, 339-44
  medial temporal, 344-48
Amygdala:
  electrical activity, 210, 345-47
  functions, 205-06, 398
  mood state formation, 212-17
  primary cue formation, 217-20
  septal connections, 239-41, 244, 247-48
  stimulus processing, 206-07, 210-11
Analogical encoding, 15-16, 33-34, 260-63, 291-93, 395
  and aphasias, 376-78
  neurological evidence, 34-36, 258-60
  vs. propositional codes, 31-33, 36-39
  and verbal-spatial aptitude, 379-85
Aphasias, 374
  Broca, 375-78
  Wernicke, 376-78
Associations, 266-67, 395-96
  conceptual peg, 292
  contiguity, 270-72
  and distinctiveness, 243-98
  featural, 269-70, 322-24
  interference, 314-21
  semantic, 322-27
  Type II rehearsal, 286-87 290-91
Asymptote of conditioning,
  match-mismatch theory, 169-73
  problems, 162-63
  in R-W model, 157-60
Attributions, 202

## B

Automatization of encoding, 260-62, 320-21, 325, 347, 395

Behavioral Analysis Division, 12, 18-22, 79-80, 396-400
  and response control, 96
  and Sensory-Perceptual Division, 80, 83
Blocking, 157-60, 166-67, 169-74, 225, 232

## C

Chain Schedules, 146-52
Choice Behavior, 201-02
Classical conditioning, 86-87, 133-35, 155-64
  in humans, 165, 197-99
  and instrumental learning, 48, 96, 169-74
  neurological substrates, 210-18
  and the OR, 164-69
  responses, 97
  second order, 141-46
Cognitive development, 330-39
  in children, 331-33
  in the elderly, 337-39
Cognitive dissonance, 199-200
Comparator theories of habituation
  Sokolov's, 24-25, 120-124
  Wagner's, 121-22
Compound cues, 368
  correlational studies, 157-60, 166-72
  second order, 143-44
Concept learning, 105,06, 306-08, 331-33, 337-39, 348-49, 367-70
Concrete-abstract words, 291-93, 305-06

457